SECRETS OF THE SAMURAI

The Martial Arts of Feudal Japan

SECRETS OF THE SAMURAI

The Martial Arts of Feudal Japan

OSCAR RATTI and ADELE WESTBROOK

TUTTLE Publishing

Tokyo | Rutland, Vermont | Singapore

Please note that the publisher and author(s) of this instructional book are NOT RESPONSIBLE in any manner whatsoever for any injury that may result from practicing the techniques and/or following the instructions given within. Martial arts training can be dangerous—both to you and to others—if not practiced safely. If you're in doubt as to how to proceed or whether your practice is safe, consult with a trained martial arts teacher before beginning. Since the physical activities described herein may be too strenuous in nature for some readers, it is also essential that a physician be consulted prior to training.

Published by Tuttle Publishing, an imprint of Periplus Editions (HK) Ltd.

Library of Congress Cataloging-in-Publication Data

Ratti, Oscar.
Secrets of the samurai : the martial arts of feudal Japan / by Oscar Ratti and Adele Westbrook.
399 p. : ill. ; 27 cm.
Includes bibliographical references and index.
ISBN 978-4-8053-0960-5 (hardcover)
1. Martial arts--Japan. I. Westbrook, Adele. II. Title.
GV1100.77.A2.R37 2009
796.815--dc22
2009014305

ISBN 978-4-8053-1405-0

20 19 18 17 16 5 4 3 2 1 1604MP
Printed in Singapore

ABOUT TUTTLE

"Books to Span the East and West"

Our core mission at Tuttle Publishing is to create books which bring people together one page at a time. Tuttle was founded in 1832 in the small New England town of Rutland, Vermont (USA). Our fundamental values remain as strong today as they were then—to publish best-in-class books informing the English-speaking world about the countries and peoples of Asia. The world has become a smaller place today and Asia's economic, cultural and political influence has expanded, yet the need for meaningful dialogue and information about this diverse region has never been greater. Since 1948, Tuttle has been a leader in publishing books on the cultures, arts, cuisines, languages and literatures of Asia. Our authors and photographers have won numerous awards and Tuttle has published thousands of books on subjects ranging from martial arts to paper crafts. We welcome you to explore the wealth of information available on Asia at **www.tuttlepublishing.com**.

Distributed by

North America, Latin America & Europe
Tuttle Publishing
364 Innovation Drive
North Clarendon, VT 05759-9436 U.S.A.
Tel: 1 (802) 773-8930
Fax: 1 (802) 773-6993
info@tuttlepublishing.com
www.tuttlepublishing.com

Japan
Tuttle Publishing
Yaekari Building, 3rd Floor
5-4-12 Osaki, Shinagawa-ku
Tokyo 141 0032
Tel: (81) 3 5437-0171
Fax: (81) 3 5437-0755
sales@tuttle.co.jp
www.tuttle.co.jp

Asia Pacific
Berkeley Books Pte. Ltd.
61 Tai Seng Avenue, #02-12
Singapore 534167
Tel: (65) 6280-1330
Fax: (65) 6280-6290
inquiries@periplus.com.sg
www.periplus.com

TO THOSE RARE MASTERS OF BUJUTSU

who revered the arts of the warrior—

but who revered human life even more;

and

TO THOSE SCHOLARS

without whose reflections

and painstaking recollections

this book would not have been possible

If we open ourselves up to the divine Life Force in its physical and spiritual manifestations we are all right, as individuals and as societies of individuals. If, on the contrary, we turn our backs on the God-made universe and insist on living in the home-made, verbal universe of fancies and ideals, imagining that we can improve on nature and make God in our own image, then we ruin our private lives, physically and spiritually, and create societies such as we live in today. Our habit of doing most of our living in a home-made world of words, fancies, and illusions is so deeply ingrained that it requires hard work with special techniques to "get back to where we have always been"—that is to say, to the given reality of Nature and Grace, to things as they really are, in themselves, and *quoad nos*, in relation to our egos.

Aldous Huxley
The Selected Letters of Aldous Huxley
James Sexton, editor
Ivan R. Dee. 2008

TABLE OF CONTENTS

4. Armed Bujutsu

5. Unarmed Bujutsu

PART III INNER FACTORS OF BUJUTSU

6. Control and Power

CHARTS

FOREWORD

Secrets of the Samurai is the end result of a man and a woman's passionate commitment to the literary and artistic possibilities inherent in the combination and integration of word and image, whatever the subject, and—more particularly—to Oscar Ratti's unique ability to bring life to every page with drawings infused with the vitality and humanity of the individual and of the collective spirit. We are all part of something larger than ourselves, and yet we are all individual entities with almost unimaginable potential for enhancing and contributing in a positive way to the ongoing, turbulent stream of life; to learn—sometimes through very painful experiences—how to expand our horizons and those of others.

Down through the ages, philosophers, writers, artists, and all reflective individuals, have grappled with the quandary Shakespeare had Hamlet consider: "To Be, or Not To Be, that is the question..." Whether to grasp the nettle of existence firmly and fight the good fight—in whatever form an individual's strengths may render that the most positive—or to shrug, throw up one's hands, and withdraw, prematurely, into the shadows. (Or, which is even worse, because it causes pain beyond the personal dimension—thrash about violently, doing damage and harming instead of helping.) Of course, there is always the Law of Unintended Consequences lurking in the background or the "Black Swans"—unforseen events, but the only way to deal with those realistically, is by continual reference to Trial and Error: How do certain actions and behaviors stand up to an objective analysis of their results? Might certain course corrections be worth consideration?

Recent scientific discoveries may provide some guidance here, and some encouragement. Research into the neuroplasticity of the brain has shown that what we think and what we do can have a powerful effect on who we are and who we can become, and that this potential is present for as long as we live and can be actuated by our conscious focused thoughts and actions.

In addition, the latest scientific findings indicate that we all share ninety-nine percent of our DNA, but the one percent that differentiates each one of us is so complex that the variety of formations in individuals is yet to be completely understood or appreciated. Moreover, life experiences will contribute to expressing or repressing certain genes, so that each one of us is a combination of genetic inheritance and multiform environmental exposures. Of course, the genetic package and certain life experiences may be beyond our control, but that which is within our sphere of influence—our conscious, determined patterns of thought and action intended to positively develop our physical, spiritual, intellectual, and emotional powers not only for our personal fulfillment, but to contribute to the wider world and extend a life-enhancing influence far beyond the boundaries of our individual existence—all of that summons us with a clarion call to enter the fray.

Perhaps we could think of life as a giant Tapestry full of bright colors and dark accents. Each one of us is a thread that can be altered within the pattern by the action of weaving and the combination of colors. If anyone of us fails to fill his or her proper place within the Tapestry, the whole will be less and that space can never be filled. Other threads will continue the interweaving but the Tapestry as a whole will always be less than it could be, and the lack of even one strong, luminous thread will always be felt, even if not always clearly evident.

Whatever our particular circumstances, and despite setbacks—as well as the inevitable pain and loss that we will all have to face in our own lives—as long as we live we have the potential and the ability to envision positive actions within our individual spheres and the personal power to take the steps that will bring those visions to life. We can all reach out—sometimes at pivotal moments—to help others achieve their potential and overcome obstacles that might be impeding their development. We are all part of the larger mosaic of existence, but each tesserae or tiny patch of color contributes to and enriches the reflection of life as both an art and a craft.

On the aesthetic level, almost any human activity can be raised to the level of art—but it is not easy. It requires not only talent, but also dedication and endurance. It calls for a willingness to withstand the strain of tedium and periods when even one's best efforts seem woefully inadequate. Above all, there must be an overwhelming desire to produce something of transcendent value.

Is it worth it? Is it worth the inevitable sacrifices and disappointments? Each person must pose that question to himself or herself. Others may inspire, support, encourage, but the ultimate answer can only come from the depths of an individual's heart and soul.

I would like to take this opportunity to thank the members of our extended families and our friends worldwide for all the loving and unstinting support they have provided, in innumerable ways, since Oscar departed this dimension of our shared existence in August 2005. They are all living examples of the inestimable value of that interconnected web which integrates our fragile, often challenging lifespans.

And, to all those who are struggling, or who will struggle, with the aftereffects of a painful loss, I say, as my Celtic, Anglo-Saxon, and French ancestors would: Courage! And, as Oscar's Italian ancestors would echo: Corragio!

Adele Westbrook
New York City, 2008

PORTFOLIO OF DRAWINGS

Since there are times and places where an image may indeed be worth a thousand words, here are several thousand words worth of classical images by Oscar Ratti that show how line and tone can be infused with the vibrant, enduring spirit of their creator.

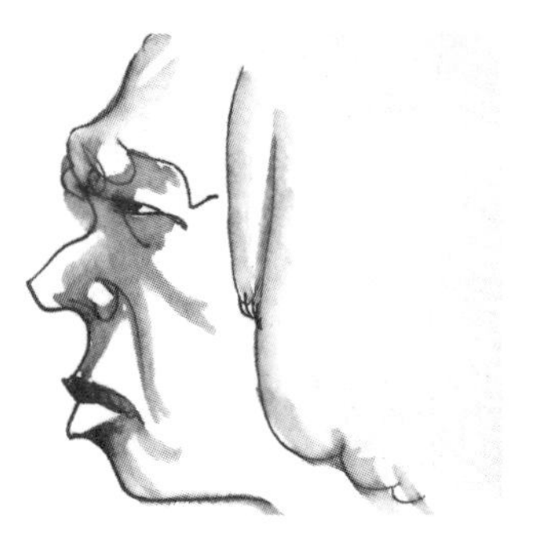

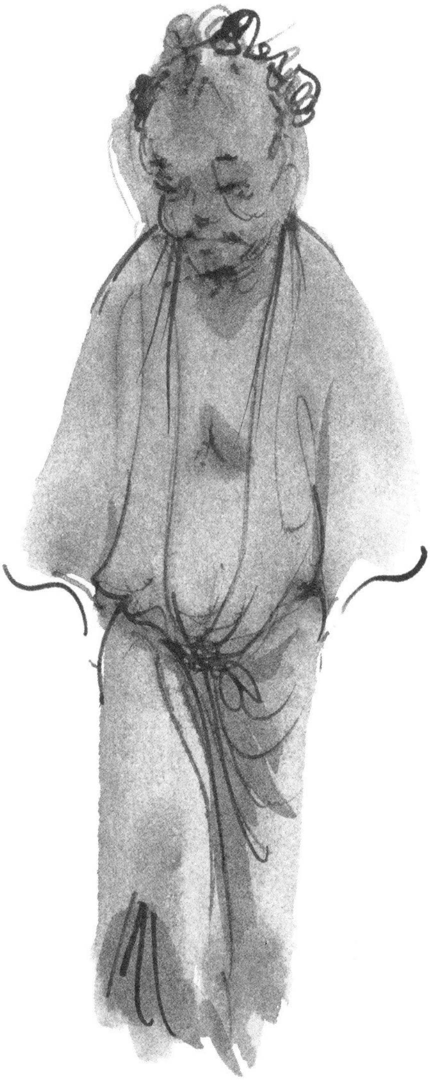

ACKNOWLEDGMENTS

IN RESEARCHING, selecting, and organizing the material for the original manuscript of *Secrets of the Samurai,* the authors have availed themselves of, and wish to express their indebtedness to, the works of all those scholars and authors whose painstaking research over the past one hundred years has produced the rich body of information which has made this study possible. The names of these men will appear again and again within the text of the book; they are also listed alphabetically in the Bibliography, together with the titles of those works considered by the authors to be indispensable to any study of *bujutsu.*

In particular, the authors would like to express special thanks to Sophia University in Tokyo (since 1938 sponsor of the periodical *Monumenta Nipponica)* and to the Japan Society of London (since 1892 the publisher of *Transactions and Proceedings of the Japan Society).* These institutions were particularly gracious in granting permission to use freely and liberally much of the material relevant to bujutsu contained in their collections of essays. Material from back numbers of the *Transactions of the Asiatic Society of Japan* also proved to be quite valuable. Unfortunately, the authors have not been able to locate any offices or officers of this society, which appears to have become inactive during recent years. In any case, the authors wish to acknowledge their indebtedness to the work of this society. Readers who live in or near New York City may avail themselves of the collections of these three major sources of information (and countless others) at the New York Public Library's Fifth Avenue main branch in room 219 of the Oriental division. We extend our sincere thanks to the staff of this division—Dr. John L. Mish and the indefatigable Mr. Francis W. Paar and Miss H.K. Kim—who guided us through many research reefs and shoals with unflappable good humor and enthusiastic professionalism.

Publishing houses which gave us their permission to quote freely from their editorial material on bujutsu include Brussel & Brussel, publisher of the monumental *A Glossary of the Construction, Decoration and Use of Arms and Armor* by George Cameron Stone, and W. Foulsham & Company, publishers of E. J. Harrison's invaluable book *The Fighting Spirit of Japan,* a pioneer work on bujutsu which can be obtained in the United States from Sterling Publishing Company, 419 Park Avenue South, New York, N.Y., 10016. Our special thanks go to Mr. H. Russell Robinson, assistant to the master of the armories in Her Majesty's Tower of London, for his generous permission to quote from *The Armour Book in Honcho Gunkiko,* published by the Charles E. Tuttle Company.

Our analysis of the great variety of Japanese weapons used throughout the feudal age of Japan was greatly facilitated by the opportunity to observe at close range the collections in the Metropolitan Museum of New York and the Museo Orientale of Venice, as well as in the British Museum and the Victoria and Albert Museum in London. By far the most extensive and diversified of these collections is contained within the Museo Orientale, presently housed in the Palazzo Pesaro, where it occupies a substantial portion of the third floor in this ancient Venetian palace. We were graciously given permission to examine the exhibits there closely and to use them as the basis for many sketches, ranging from those of intricate suits of armor to an entire spectrum of bows and arrows, spears, swords, daggers, and even the elaborate standards used by different clans and families of feudal Japan. Acquired in 1888 (twenty years after the Restoration) by Enrico di Borbone, Count of Bardi, during his extensive travels in Japan, the collection was sold in 1906 to a Viennese art dealer, who, in turn, sold many valuable pieces to foreign museums and private collectors. The objects which were presented to the Italian government after World War I still constitute a substantial and detailed representation of arms, armors, and accoutrements which any serious student of bujutsu might profitably explore. Photographs of many of these pieces, in fact, comprise the major portion of H. R. Robinson's book *Japanese Arms and Armour*, listed in the Bibliography.

We are also obliged to Routledge & Kegan Paul of London and Princeton University Press for permission to use material from Daisetsu T. Suzuki's *Zen and Japanese Culture;* to Random House and Alfred A. Knopf for their permission to use direct quotations from Edwin O. Reischauer's *Japan: Past and Present;* to Jay Gluck for the use of direct references drawn from his *Zen Combat.*

The authors wish to warmly thank all those students and instructors of bujutsu in the Eastern and Western hemispheres who so generously illustrated and explained, either in person or in lengthy correspondence, techniques and strategies of bujutsu which have contributed to the substance of many illustrated sequences in this book. Illustrations can often provide a more dynamic and vivid idea of the practical aspects of the many specializations of bujutsu than lengthy, abstruse descriptions, and we have relied heavily upon such illustrated material.

A special thank-you is extended to Mrs. Anneliese Aspell for her assistance in the translation of difficult German passages illustrating the educational system developed for the warriors of the Tokugawa period.

Finally, we feel ourselves at a loss in attempting to express our thanks to our friend and mentor Edvi Illes Gedeon, who, acting as a veritable one-man foundation, tracked down and provided many valuable texts on bujutsu. Last but not least on our list are the editors of the Charles E. Tuttle Company for their active interest in this as well as other works by the same authors, and for their efforts in handling a difficut editorial format in a manner always consistent with the traditions of their house.

PREFACE

THE JAPANESE experience in, and contribution to, the theory and practice of individual combat, armed and unarmed, is certainly among the most ancient, sophisticated, and enduring ever recorded. One need only consider the present worldwide popularity of jujutsu, judo, karate, aikido, kendo, kyudo, and so forth, which are essentially modern adaptations or derivations, to appreciate the continuing influence of ancient Japanese methods of combat. The ancient martial arts were developed and refined during an extended period of direct experimentation on the battlefields of pre-Tokugawa Japan; later, during the centuries of absolute isolation which generated the proper conditions, they were thoroughly revised and ultimately ritualized into transmissible patterns of exercise and technique. The effectiveness of the modern adaptations is attested to by the fact that they have deeply influenced and, in many instances, almost completely replaced other national methods of combat practiced for sporting purposes and as part of the utilitarian and practical training programs of military and police forces.

The present work is a survey of the major specializations of the martial experience, known in feudal Japan as martial arts, or *bujutsu*. These arts are presented in terms of the persons directly or indirectly involved with, or subjected to, this systematic violence (part 1); the particular weapons and techniques which assigned to each martial art its position and relative importance within the body of bujutsu teachings, here termed the doctrine of bujutsu (part 2); the factors of inner control and power as well as strategies and motivations, which, when compared to the above-mentioned elements, were considered by the ancients as being of equal (if not greater) significance, due to their importance in implementing the various combat methods (part 3).

Any inquiry into the history, instruments, and strategic functionality of the martial arts of feudal Japan is bound to encounter serious and often seemingly insurmountable obstacles in the selection of basic reference material as well as in the interpretation of the terms employed therein. In this work, terminology should present no difficulties, for in the Index the terms most frequently used in the martial arts to define and illustrate their functional characteristics are listed along with the number of the page on which each term appears for the first time in the main text and where its meaning is briefly explained and/or illustrated. Decidedly more difficult to resolve are doctrinal problems— that is, problems arising from conflicting references (direct and indirect, ancient and modern, in both the original language and in translation) to the specializations of the Japanese experience in the ancient art of combat.

Among the direct sources of information used in the compilation of this book are translations of records contained in scrolls *(makimono)* and manuscripts belonging to masters and representatives of particular schools of the martial arts, whose founders were courageous enough to defy the age-old Japanese custom of secrecy and exclusiveness in order to add the results of their experience, as Yamashita phrased it, to "the common stock of knowledge" of the entire human race. Direct information of particular value to any study of armed bujutsu is also provided by a review of the huge collections of weapons and armor available in the major museums and art galleries of the world, as well as items of interest held by private collectors. Indirect sources of information on bujutsu in general would include the Japanese classics, religious and philosophical texts and treatises, and poems and chronicles of the nation—primarily works which concern themselves with aspects of the national culture other than the military but contain oblique and often highly illuminating references to the specializations of bujutsu.

All these sources are equally vital because they integrate, confirm, or modify one another, thus helping the student of bujutsu to determine their respective degrees of reliability, historical authenticity, and, consequently, their usefulness to any program of research and interpretation. In carrying out such research, it becomes evident that the doctrine of the Japanese martial arts is heir to that failing common to every doctrine devised by man; that is, the further back one's historical research is carried, the harder it becomes to distinguish fact from fiction. The Japanese chronicles of antiquity are particularly susceptible to animistic and mystical interpretations of events, and this tendency—still very much in evidence in the records of disciplines of combat which have emerged during the last century—is further compounded by the highly individualistic approach of each master to the theory and practice of armed and unarmed combat. This approach is clearly exclusivistic and unilateral, being centered primarily upon the merits and virtues of this or that representative or founder of a particular school, with only a few obscure references to those techniques or methods of combat which made them famous.

When confronted with the wealth of available written records concerning the schools of unarmed combat (presumably issued in the seventeenth and eighteenth centuries), each extolling a particular school of bujutsu or a particular master, the modern observer is often forced to ask himself a question similar to that posed by a famous translator of Lao-tzu's *Tao Te Ching,* in relation to the various philosophical schools active during a particular period of Chinese history: "May it not be the case that some of these schools were very much alike but each had to put up a different 'slogan' in order to be an independent school, since in the Warring States period, so much was to be gained by this claim?" (Lau, 50). This particular approach to the problems of combat (adopted by many ancient and modern teachers of bujutsu, and so reflected in chronicles of the martial arts) is historically misleading because it presupposes an initial originality at the root of each school, as well as a widespread and individualistic type of excellence which is very rare in any culture and must have been particularly unusual in the highly conformistic and restrictive world of feudal Japan. Numerous warriors, after all, had trained in many different schools of bujutsu, and almost all the masters of those schools had done exactly the same thing before opening their own centers of instruction—which would implicitly negate a basic prerequisite of strict originality: isolation. Such an approach, moreover, makes any attempt to produce a syncretic and anthological study of the martial arts extremely difficult, because it presents a kaleidoscopic collection of arts, each pulling centrifugally away from any concept of basic unity.

The aim of the present study, therefore, is to establish a platform of observation from which the martial arts of feudal Japan may be analyzed as expressions of a strongly unified and conformistic culture and, consequently, as methods of combat which, notwithstanding obvious differences in their choice of weapons, produced great similarities in their bodies of techniques and, above all, an almost identical conception of those inner factors and activating motivations which made those techniques relevant and effective in combat. This global and syncretic approach to the study of bujutsu is necessitated by the current abundance of specialized presentations of the individual martial arts and, in particular, of those derived from ancient bujutsu, which, as indicated earlier, have made such names as jujutsu, judo, karate, aikido, and kendo famous the world over. The authors' aim has been primarily that of restoring a certain balance between the specialized knowledge of each martial art and the comprehensive knowledge of them all, even if only from a historical standpoint. The twin dangers which we have recognized and sought to avoid were those of overspecialization (an exaggerated emphasis upon only one expression of the Japanese experience in the art of combat) and superficial eclecticism (a dispersive and necessarily diluted exposition of them all). It is our hope that a general knowledge of all the martial arts will help to deepen and expand the reader's understanding of each—the way a detail, for example, becomes even more significant when observed within that larger, richer, and more harmonious context of which it is but a part.

Those of us interested in the evolution of that experience in the art of individual confrontation throughout its many forms and specialized manifestations must inevitably seek to relate the parts to the whole. Thus a syncretic approach to bujutsu, intended to provide a general framework within which to comprehend clearly its various components, underlies and motivates the present study in its entirety.

In synthesis, for those readers particularly interested in bujutsu, it is to be hoped that this introductory study will satisfy an immediate need and constitute a broad foundation for further studies of the ancient Japanese martial arts, or at least provide a panoramic background for those already in existence.

It is also intended to provide the basis for another type of research, linked to the problem of human violence as systematically exercised in those practices man has found difficult to discard along the path of his evolutionary history. This type of research enters the domain of ethics, of those moral justifications which supposedly influence man's actions and (within the context of bujutsu) will determine his behavior in combat against his fellowman. Unfortunately, considerations and analyses of the *morality* of the martial arts (viewed as being of primary significance by those masters who have provided interesting and varied solutions to the moral dilemma a man had to confront and resolve in combat) will, of necessity, be somewhat limited in this work, since its central subject is their historical background, their weapons and techniques, their strategies and phases of application—those factors and elements which made them extremely effective within the immediate and utilitarian reality of combat. The observations on the ethical implications of bujutsu which the authors have included in the text form the foundation for an ensuing volume (tentatively entitled *Budo: The Way of the Warrior)* which will deal almost exclusively with the motivations, ethics, and metaphysics of those arts which, throughout their long and bloody history, have seemed truly noble and worthy in a universal or comprehensive sense in only a comparatively few, exceptional instances.

As will become apparent from a cursory glance at the Table of Contents, this study embraces a variety of martial arts and covers an extensive period of Japanese history. Consequently, it revolves around and upon an immense amount of material which had to be considered, interpreted, and presented systematically if a more illuminating doctrine than the one available today were to be developed. It is not the authors' intention to provide a definitive answer to all the problems of doctrinary interpretation found in the vast amount of literature on bujutsu, or to engage in a doctrinary monologue of their own which, however expressive or novel, would still, by its very nature, be unrelated to and radically different from that dialogue in which the "common stock of knowledge," mentioned by Yamashita in his analysis of the secretive approach to bujutsu, is enriched through the active contributions of many individuals. In fact, the studies and opinions of many authors who have written about bujutsu, both ancient and modern, have provided the initial basis for this syncretic approach to the martial arts (as clearly evidenced by the extensive use of direct quotations, often from works presently relegated to undeserved oblivion, notwithstanding their value as pioneer attempts in the exploration of this particular aspect of an alien culture).

In this context it will doubtless be useful for the reader, wishing to retrace our steps through the ofttimes confusing maze of the doctrine of bujutsu and personally refer to the sources of information we have used in preparing this work, to understand the "key" to the system of quotation and referral we have adopted. This system is, first of all, generic and comprehensive, as expressed through the lists of books collected in the Bibliography of this study and arranged in alphabetical order according to the names of those authors whose works have been invaluable in providing a first, panoramic view of bujutsu. But this system is also specific and specialized, as expressed through the many direct quotations which appear throughout the text, extracted selectively from the works of those authors whom we consider invaluable sources of information concerning particular aspects of bujutsu. The reader who wishes to explore any of these particular aspects will find, at the end of each quotation, in parenthesis, the name of the author and the number of the page in his book or article which contains the passage quoted. The reader may then turn to the Bibliography for details concerning the edition to which we are referring. For example, the first quotation in the section entitled "The Military Tradition in the History of Japan" is followed by parentheses which contain the name "Hearn" and the number "259." The reader who refers to the Bibliography under the alphabetical listing of "Hearn, Lafcadio" will find the title of the book from which the quotation was extracted: "*Japan: An Interpretation,*" plus details of publication, "Tokyo: Charles E. Tuttle Co., 1962." There are, however, a number of authors who have written more than one pertinent book on the subject of bujutsu. In those cases where more than one book is listed, each work has been assigned a number, and this number appears in the Bibliography within brackets and as a superior number after the author's name within the parentheses which follow the pertinent quotation in the body of the book. Quotations from the three studies on bujutsu by Edward Gilbertson, for example, are identified by the name of the author with in parentheses at the end of each quotation in the text, then by a superior number 1, 2, or 3 after the name (depending upon which study is being referred to), and finally by the page number within that particular study. This will provide the reader with the necessary "key" to the bibliographical listings of Gilbertson's works.

Throughout the book Japanese names are given in the order customary in Japan, family name followed by personal name.

It would be highly gratifying if, spurred by the present study, other students of bujutsu were encouraged to overcome any narrow or sectarian barriers of doctrinal, scholastic, or organizational isolation and exclusiveness which might be separating them from one another, and plunge courageously into the study and analysis of records, manuscripts, and current practices relative to the Japanese arts of combat. The resulting dialogue or debate would enable them to share their experiences and findings with others, thus furthering the development of a more comprehensive perspective. But a dialogue, as Socrates pointed out, can only begin to stimulate the interest by starting at a certain point and at a certain moment—which is exactly what the present study, in its own way, from its own platform of observation, and with its own method, has set out to do.

Finally, it is the authors' fond hope that this book may prove as stimulating to the reader as its production was to them, especially when they surveyed the multiform landscape of an ancient culture and the often tragic but brave attempts of its subjects to cope, in their own way, with the demands of a harsh reality. Confronted as we are today with social and political turbulence, living under the moment-to-moment threat of nuclear catastrophe, all studies of man's experience in the art of violent confrontation have acquired a particular relevancy. Almost everyone seems to agree that we must attempt to determine whether man will be forever trapped by his apparently constitutional inclination to employ any method, however lethal, to ensure his dominance over his fellowmen, or whether he may—in time—be capable of ritualizing and then, ultimately, transforming that pattern. In this endeavor, thoughtful studies of man's past, with all its pitfalls and bloody errors, may prove to be a necessary and valuable factor in the final equation.

—The Authors

New York

INTRODUCTION
The Martial Ethos

Definition of Bujutsu and Its Specializations

The long history and complex tradition of the Japanese art of combat is embodied in a variety of forms, methods, and weapons, each of which constitutes a particular specialization of that art. Each specialization, in turn, is known as a *jutsu,* a word which may be translated as "method," "art," or "technique" and is indicative of the particular way or ways in which certain actions are performed. Historically, each art or method has developed certain procedures or patterns which set it apart from the procedures and patterns of other arts. In the context of the Japanese art of combat, therefore, a specialization consists of a particular, systematic method of using a specific weapon.

Very often, a specialization of combat was identified by the name of the weapon used by its practitioners. An example of this system of identification would be kenjutsu— that is, the art *(jutsu)* of the sword *(ken).* However, a combat method could also be identified by the particular, functional way of using a weapon in order to achieve an opponent's subjugation. Among the specializations of the art of unarmed combat, for example, jujutsu identifies the art *(jutsu)* of suppleness *(ju)*—that is, the art of using suppleness in a certain technical way in order to defeat an opponent. Frequently, a main specialization of combat would produce subspecializations, many of which, through constant refinement, effectively improved upon the original method to the extent of substituting for it entirely, thus becoming independent specializations of combat in and of themselves. In such a case, the subspecialization would generally be identified by the name of its main feature. Kenjutsu, the art of the sword, for example, was further refined into a deadly specialization known as iaijutsu—the art *(jutsu)* of drawing *(iai)* and simultaneously cutting with the sword; it was also the matrix for nito-kenjutsu, the art *(jutsu)* of fencing with two *(nito)* swords *(ken).* Finally, a specialization could be identified by the name of the master who had devised his own particular style of fighting or by the name of the school where this particular style was taught.

The specializations of the Japanese art of combat which are of particular relevance to this study are those which were developed and brought to the highest degree of systematic perfection during the feudal period of Japanese history. This period embraces a span of approximately nine centuries, from the late ninth and early tenth centuries to the nineteenth century—more precisely to the year of the Meiji Restoration (1868), when, in a manner characteristically Japanese, the feudal era was declared formally closed. During the centuries of dominance by the Tokugawa (1600 to 1867), the specializations of the art of combat inherited from the previous ages of turmoil were thoroughly polished and perfected by a system of study surprisingly modern in its methods of experimentation and observation; at the same time, new specializations were devised and applied to help resolve the eternally precarious problems of combat. The era of comparative peace forcefully imposed by the Tokugawa, in fact, actually made it possible for many masters of the art of combat to delve quite deeply into the mysteries and techniques of violent confrontation and to test their findings within the repressed, hence extremely virulent and explosive, reality of individual combat (large-scale battles being few and far between).

CHART 1

BUJUTSU IN FEUDAL JAPAN

Japanese nomenclature in italics

ARMED			UNARMED
Major	Minor	Collateral	
Archery— *kyujutsu* *kyudo* *shagei* Spearmanship— *sojutsu* *yarijutsu* *naginatajutsu (naginata)* *sodegaramijutsu* *sasumatajutsu* Swordsmanship— *tojutsu* *kenjutsu* *kendo* *iaijutsu* *iaido* *tantojutsu* Horsemanship— *bajutsu* *jobajutsu* *suibajutsu* Swimming— *suieijutsu* *oyogijutsu* *katchu gozen oyogi*	Art of the war fan— *tessenjutsu (tessen)* Art of the staff— *jojutsu (bo)* *jodo* *tetsubojutsu* Art of the jitte— *juttejutsu (jitte)*	Art of the chain & other implements— *kusarijutsu* *kusarigamajutsu* *manrikikusari* *chigirighutsu* *gegikanjutsu* Occult arts— *ninjutsu* *toiri-no-jutsu* *shinobijutsu* *chikairi-no-jutsu* *shurikenjutsu* *yubijutsu* *koppo* *fukihari* *suijohokojutsu*	*aikudo* *aikijustu* *chikarakurabe* *chogusoku* *genkotsu* *gusoku* *hakushi* *judo* *jujustu* *karate* *kempo* *kiaijutsu* *kogusoku* *kosht-no-mawari* *Kosni-no-wakari* *kumiuchi* *roikumiuchi* *shikaku* *shinobi* *shubaku* *sumai* *sumo* *taido* *taidojutsu* *torite* *wajutsu* *yawara*

In the doctrine of the Japanese martial arts we find long lists of combat specializations. They are usually divided systematically according to the particular views of the author discussing them. Certain authors, for example, make a clear distinction between those specializations formally practiced by the Japanese warrior *(bushi)* and those which he despised because they were practiced by the members of other, "inferior" classes within the rigidly stratified hierarchy of the Japanese nation. Other authors divide them into armed and unarmed categories according to the predominance of mechanical or anatomical weapons as the primary instruments of combat.

In order to give the reader a panoramic view of the warrior's specializations in the art of individual combat, we have endeavored to list in chart 1 as many as possible of the various *jutsu* we have discovered in the doctrine. The only attempt we have made to classify them at this time is by dividing them into two major groups—armed and unarmed—subdividing the former into three categories according to the importance and prestige traditionally assigned them within the culture of feudal Japan. We have not attempted to provide a specific translation of each name used in the Japanese doctrine to identify a particular specialization of bujutsu or one of its possible subspecial izations, since many different names may be used to identify the same basic method of combat. We have therefore deemed it advisable to leave the task of proper identification to those sections in part 2 wherein they will be examined individually. It is obvious that the Japanese nomenclature presents an initial set of problems in identifying these *jutsu,* since so many of the names imply or refer to concepts and functions of a rather complex and esoteric nature—to the extent of defying attempts to establish a clear identification in English without preliminary examinations of these concepts and functions.

The entire body of these specializations, the generic art of combat, is most often termed *bujutsu.* This word is the phonetic rendering of two Chinese ideograms, 武 *(bu)* and 術 *(jutsu).* Even in the earliest records of the Japanese nation, *bu* was employed to denote the military dimension of its national culture, as differentiated from, for example, the public dimension *(ko)* or the civil dimension *(bun),* both of which were related primarily to the functions of the imperial court. *Bu* thus appears in the composites *buke* and *bumon* to identify "military families," as differentiated from the *huge* and *kugyo (ku* being a phonetic variation of *ko)* which referred to "public nobles." *Bu* also appears in *bushi,* "military nobles," and in *buke seiji,* "military rule," both being neatly differentiated from *bunji* and *bunji seiji,* "nobles" and "civil government." Even after the military class, upon accession to national power, had become mired in its own bureaucracy, the original semantic associations with *bu* remained to a considerable degree. As one scholar points out:

> In contemporary parlance, the Tokugawa shogunate was a particular instance *of buke seiji* or *bumon seiji,* that is, "military government." In general, that expression meant government by soldiers, or at least by officials whose titles implied military command. It suggested the philosophic sense of a government which relied for its control on force or the threat of force. (Webb, 5)

Combined with *justu,* which, as indicated above, may be literally translated as "technique," "art," or "method," *bu* is used to represent the idea of military technique or techniques (the plural being implied by the context in which it is used), military arts, or military methods. Since the military aspect of Japanese culture was almost entirely dominated by the figure of the Japanese feudal warrior (the prototype of the fighting man, known as a *bushi* or *samurai),* the term bujutsu was, and to a great extent still is, employed to denote the techniques, arts, and methods of combat developed and practiced primarily (if not exclusively) by the members of the military class. By semantic implication, then, the term bujutsu identifies the martial arts of Japan.

There were, of course, other terms employed by the doctrine of these arts in an attempt to express as clearly and as specifically as possible their nature and purposes. The word *bugei,* for example, is one of these—formed by the combination of the ideogram 武 (*bu:* military, martial) and the ideogram 芸 (*gei:* method, accomplishment). Bujutsu, however, seems more particularly related to the technical nature and strategic functionality of these arts, to the instrumental "how," or way, in which these techniques of combat achieved their purposes, while *bugei* appears to be a more generic and comprehensive term, including and implying technically quite specialized forms of bujutsu as well as various subspecializations.

The word bujutsu, then, is used in the Japanese doctrine of the art of combat to represent all those specializations of the general art of combat practiced by the Japanese fighting man, or professional warrior of Japan, as well as by various members of other social classes who practiced any of the individual combat arts. Bujutsu, we wish to emphasize, is particularly related to the practical, technical, and strategic aspects of these arts, as indicated by the use of the ideogram for technique. When these specializations are intended as disciplines with an end or purpose of a more educational or ethical nature, "technique" becomes "way" *(do),* meaning the "path" toward a spiritual rather than purely practical achievement.

The criteria used by the authors in deciding whether a specialization should be included in this study were as follows: it must have occupied a position of traditional importance in Japanese feudal culture; it must have been strategically relevant in and to individual combat; and, finally, it must have been widely known and practiced. The specializations fulfilling all three of these requirements are examined in part 2 after a preliminary study of the armor which influenced so many of the weapons and techniques used in the various arts. The order followed in presenting the various martial arts assigns a position of priority to archery, spearmanship, swordsmanship, horsemanship, and swimming in armor, since the main protagonist of Japanese history, the warrior or *bushi*, practiced these arts on a professional basis. The discussion of these specializations, which are termed "major martial arts," will then be followed by an examination of other arts, termed "minor martial arts," such as the art of the war fan and that of the staff, which were also considered traditional as well as strategically important and were quite popular with the members of various other classes of Japanese society. Finally, we will examine several specializations of the art of combat which do not fulfill all three of the criteria listed above and, therefore, are termed "collateral arts of combat." The science of firearms *(hojutsu)*, that of fortification *(chikujojutsu)*, and that of field deployment *(senjojutsu)* are excluded from this study because they are related more specifically to the art of war—to the art of collective rather than individual combat.

All these major, minor, and collateral specializations of bujutsu are classified as armed because they were based predominantly upon the use of mechanical weapons or assortments of weapons, which distinguished them from those specializations of the art of combat in which the primary weapon was a part or parts of the human body. The unarmed specializations will be examined in part 2.

In addition to an analysis of the historical background, the discussion of each art includes a study of its characteristic factors, such as the weapons employed, the particular techniques or ways of employing them, the mental attitude adopted in order to face combat with confidence, and the type of power or energy needed to use those weapons properly—all the factors that blend in forming the art and guarantee its strategic efficiency in combat as well as its significance as a contribution to the theory of combat.

The authors have divided the above-mentioned factors into two categories: the first includes factors such as the weapons and the techniques of each specialization, which may be qualified as *outer* or *external* because they are easily perceivable; the second embraces factors such as mental control and power, which may not be as visually (or immediately) impressive as the factors in the first category but which determine, from within, the degree of efficiency of both the weapons and the techniques. This second category of factors, therefore, contains the *inner* or *interior* factors of bujutsu. In the study which follows, the outer factors are examined in part 2 and the inner factors in part 3. The main reason for treating these factors separately is that while the weapons and techniques of bujutsu differed to a certain extent in structure and functionality from one specialization to another, the mental attitude and the power needed to control them from within appear to have been substantially identical. Hence, it was decided to illustrate these inner factors separately and as a systematic whole, avoiding a repetition of concepts and ideas which are basically uniform throughout the various specializations. Even so, particular references are made to the ways in which these inner factors were interpreted and applied in the most important specializations.

In part 3, our aim is to present a unified and systematic view of certain theories propounded by a number of ancient masters of bujutsu—theories which, by and large, appear only in a fragmented fashion in the doctrine and are generally interpreted in an exclusivistic sense by the adepts of each specialization. The theories of the major strategies of combat and the principles of their application are also illustrated so as to unify them within a systematic whole and avoid having the particular character of one confuse or blur a panoramic view of all.

The Qualification "Martial" (Bu) and the Exponents of Bujutsu

The extensive and general use of the qualification "martial" by Western authors when discussing the art of combat (although admittedly based upon Japanese records) can be misleading. We may be easily led to falsely assume, for example, that the warrior *(bushi)* of feudal Japan, the prototype of the martial man, was the sole originator of these arts or that he alone practiced them. "Martial" is, of course, etymologically related to Mars, the Roman god of war, and consequently to war, warriors, military pursuits, and soldiers. By implication, this assumption could also lead us to qualify the specializations of the art of combat as arts of war, thus relating them more to the battlefield and to mass involvements of men and materiel than to individual confrontations. Neither of these assumptions, however, would be quite correct. To begin with, the Japanese warrior of the feudal era was not the sole practitioner of bujutsu, nor was he, by any means, the sole originator of its specializations. His predominant identification as the Japanese fighting man par excellence may be traced back, with a certain degree of accuracy, to 1600, when the military clan of the Tokugawa rose to power and, by forcefully organizing all the other major clans into a separate class with separate duties, rights, and privileges, extolled and elevated its members, de jure et de facto, above the members of all the other social classes. Before 1600, however, Japanese history provides abundant evidence that, during the ages of the original clans *(uji)* and the court nobles or aristocrats *(kuge)* in Nara and Kyoto, the distinction between such as the clansman-farmer, artisan, and merchant (including the clansman-priest) and the clansman-fighter was apparently not as clearly delineated as it was to become during the feudal era.

In the ages preceding the consolidation of the country into the rigidly stratified society of the Tokugawa—which made the passage from one class to another among commoners *(heimin)* extremely difficult and the admission of a member of another class to the military class *(buke)* almost impossible—the demarcation lines between classes were not strict. Until the very end of the fifteenth century, as Cole points out in his study of Kyoto during the Momoyama period, "almost any man of ability could carve a career by himself" (Cole, 58).

The decree disarming all commoners and the militant clergy, issued in the seventh month, eighth day of Tensho (1588) by Nobunaga's successor, Hideyoshi, provides the clearest and most telling proof that many commoners had not only possessed weapons such as bows and arrow, spears and swords, but had evidently been quite well versed in their use. "The possession of...implements of war," the decree candidly admitted, "makes difficult the collection of taxes and dues and tends to foment uprisings." Thus did Hideyoshi move to deprive all other classes of those martial options his own class had found so effective. Throughout the centuries which led to the absolute predominance of the military class, in fact, its right to rule was often hotly contested, particularly by the militant orders of Buddhist priests and monks, who finally had to be slaughtered en masse during the Ashikaga (Muromachi) and Momoyama periods before they could be discounted as effective opponents.

The assumption that the members of the military class were the sole practitioners and interpreters of bujutsu is even less valid in relation to those minor methods of combat which involved the use of wooden instruments such as the staff (or even the human body itself) as primary weapons of combat. Numerous methods of using these weapons flourished during Japan's feudal era, particularly after the establishment of the Tokugawa military dictatorship. Schools of martial arts frequented by the samurai often included a number of these arts in their training programs, but there is also ample evidence in the doctrine of bujutsu that they were practiced with equal fervor and dedication by members of other classes as well. Even a poet, the famous Basho, is said to have been skilled in the handling of the staff *(bo)*, and countless hermits, abbots, and philosophers, as well as commoners of every class, could use their fans or pipes with flair and deadly accuracy—even against swords. In certain cases, these people were recognized as being the originators of particular specializations of the art of combat which even the warrior found impressive enough to include in his own program of military preparation. The skill of certain religious sects in the use of fists and feet is amply recorded not only in Chinese chronicles but also in manuscripts written by Japanese masters who claimed to have studied their methods of unarmed combat in China.

Actually, even in relation to those martial arts which, by law, warriors alone could practice—such as swordsmanship (kenjutsu) and spearfighting (yarijutsu)—we find evidence that members of other classes practiced and applied them against the warrior himself, although he alone had a legal right to possess and use such weapons. Many of these illegal users were obviously outcasts from the military class. But many were not, and these often formed the backbone of such groups as the famous bands of professional fighters hired by merchants to protect shipments in transit from attack by bandits or to guard warehouses, or the groups of professional bodyguards hired by patrons who needed and could afford the cost of protection, or the leagues of guardians hired by farmers to safeguard crops at harvest time. These fighters were not recruited only from among the rejects of the military class (although, quite naturally, these men were a primary source of material for mercenary fighting). During the decline of the Tokugawa, for example, "The Tokaido's Number-One Boss," Jirocho of Shimizu (1820-93), who controlled the gambling underworld there, belonged to the merchant class. The origins of the jovial Ishimatsu, however, one of his lieutenants, whose violent death at the hands of assassins after a prolonged sword fight in the forest cost the latter dearly, were so obscure that they were not even recorded. Going back even further in time to the more rigidly controlled period of the early Tokugawa era, the famous Chobei of Banzuiin, chief of the Otokodate in Edo, was a *chonin* (townsman), not a military retainer.

The Qualification "Martial" (Bu) and the Art of War

As indicated in the previous paragraphs, the adjective "martial" is semantically linked to military endeavors and, therefore, to the primary function of the military as a class: the waging of war. In this sense, could we say that all the specializations of the art of combat qualified is arts of war? It is obvious, from even a cursory glance at the various specializations and subspecializations listed in our introductory chart, that not all of these methods could be used effectively on the battlefield; consequently, the all-inclusive qualification "martial" is either inaccurate or else rests upon foundations not directly related to practical effectiveness solely within the broad dimensions of general warfare. Early chroniclers of bujutsu, after all, had made a distinction of sorts when they listed the following specializations of the art of combat as the exclusive arts of the warrior, hence as arts of war: archery, spearmanship, swordsmanship, horsemanship, fortifications, and use of firearms and military seamanship (which included swimming). Among the methods of unarmed combat used by the warrior in a subsidiary manner, the same chroniclers mention the art of suppleness, or jujutsu. A substantial number of specializations are omitted from these military records—a fact that should not surprise us, since from the standpoint of a warrior, the art of the war fan could hardly be compared to archery, nor the art of the wooden staff to the science of firearms. Why, then, this determination so apparent in the general doctrine of bujutsu, and so widely displayed by almost all masters of arts and disciplines of combat, to use the adjective "martial" (*bu*) to qualify all these methods?

At least a partial answer, we feel, may be provided by an examination of the importance assigned by the Japanese to the military tradition in the history of their country. Before we proceed to discuss these traditions in the following paragraphs, however, we must briefly reiterate that the art of war as strategies involving large numbers of men in massive confrontations on the battlefield is not a part of this study. Our primary concern here is individual combat—the art of direct and personal confrontation between two (or a few) men and the weapons, the techniques, and the attitudes used therein. We shall not plunge into the doctrinary debates concerning the degree of sophistication of the Japanese art of war, which, in the opinion of certain authors, was rather rudimentary. Brinkley, for example, while describing the individual warriors of Japan as composing "the best fighting unit in the Orient, probably one of the best fighting units the world ever produced," added in the same paragraph that "it was, perhaps, because of that excellence that his captains remained mediocre tacticians" (Brinkley[1], 172). Repeated references may be found in ancient treatises on warfare to the high level of development of the art of war in China and to its major theorists, such as General Sun-tzu, who repeatedly emphasized the social, massive character of combat in war and the absolute predominance of masses and logistics in defeating an enemy. But in the centuries preceding the Momoyama period (1568-1600), Japanese armies were still "made up of small, independent bands of soldiers who fought more as individuals than as units of a tactical formation" (Wittfogel, 199). This was the way the Japanese warrior of one clan fought against the warriors of another clan; this was the way he fought against the Koreans during the first, legendary invasion of the Asiatic mainland; and this was the way he faced the invading Mongolian hordes in 1274 and 1281. The individual character of the art of war was still very much in evidence in the colossal confrontations at Sekigahara, witnessed by William Adams (1564-1620), and at Osaka Castle in 1615. "Feudal Japan," Wittfogel concludes, perhaps a trifle sweepingly, "like feudal Europe, failed to develop the art of war" (Wittfogel, 199).

The individual character of the art of war in feudal Japan, so romantically emphasized in national sagas and by chroniclers of the age, actually facilitates our study of the particular specializations of bujutsu, for it allows us to adopt the *individuality* of direct, personal confrontation as our primary term of reference. In turn, the matrix of our study of all the possible applications of bujutsu will be the man-to-man encounter— whether on the battlefield or in the streets of a teeming city, whether on a lonely mountain road or in a temple, or even within the confines of a man's home. And this will also facilitate our inclusion of all the weapons, techniques, and attitudes devised to resolve the problems of individual confrontation.

The Military Tradition in the History of Japan

The extensive use of the qualification "martial" in the doctrine is explained by the extraordinary, some authors would say excessive, importance assigned by the Japanese even today to their military tradition, to the function of the military class in shaping the destiny of the nation, and to the ethics adopted by this class to justify its existence and policies. This importance is based upon the fact that, when we refer generically to the martial experience of Japan, we refer to one of the longest and most ancient involvements of a nation in such a dimension. As Lafcadio Hearn aptly pointed out, "About the whole of authentic Japanese history is comprised in one vast episode: the rise and fall of the military power" (Hearn, 259).

A panoramic survey of the events through which that power expressed itself with varying degrees of subtlety for almost nine centuries is found in chart 2 (p. 33) and in greater detail in Part 1. Down through the centuries, then, the innermost fiber of the Japanese nation was imbued with the warrior's particular ideas, ethics, and sense of mission. These elements, which spurred the *bushi* to act on the stage of history, were rooted in a firm belief in Japan's divine origins, in the determination to confirm that belief by force of arms, even if it meant death, and in that code of behavior which demanded unquestioning obedience to the commands of one's immediate superior, who constituted the link with the divine past and thus would know the ways in which to successfully fulfill the mission implicit in those distant origins. For centuries these truths, as well as the way of life they represented, were inculcated into the Japanese character, seeping down to all levels of society and coloring every stage of the national development. It was a process of relentless indoctrination from above, both conscious and unconscious, which began in earnest at the end of the Nara period, with the emergence of the warrior clans whose services proved invaluable (although ultimately costly) to the feuding clans of the court nobles *(huge)* and the emperor *(tenno)* during their bitter power struggles. The *bushi* brought with them their simple ideas of excellence, translated concretely into personal loyalty to one's immediate superior, and a readiness to fight and die without the slightest hesitation. These ideas, according to generally accepted historical records, contrasted vividly with the highly sophisticated and introspective patterns of the culture of Nara.

The contrast and resulting friction was ultimately resolved through force of arms. Many aristocratic clans were totally destroyed, and the few nobles who survived were deprived of any effective influence, being restricted to the representational precincts of the imperial court, together with the emperor. Also destroyed were the huge monasteries and libraries which contained the essence, the distillation of Heian culture: its scriptures, its records, and its works of art. By 1600, the slate had been almost wiped clean. From that point on, the Way of the Warrior flowed both brutally and subtly into the consciousness of the entire population: the farmer, a large portion of whose rice crop would be appropriated by the retainers of the local *daimyo,* or provincial lord, looking up from his hoeing to gaze at a group of samurai, their weapons glinting in the sun as they ran rhythmically alongside a palanquin bound for Edo; the chance traveler who paused by the side of the road, a silent witness to a duel, often to the death, between two swordsmen; the surging, excited populace at the festivals held at various times during the year, staring wide-eyed at the martial arts demonstrations which were often a focal point of such festivals. In thousands of incidents, both minor and of great social significance, the drama of a potentially lethal confrontation between one man and another was restaged again and again, until this particular form of human experience was burned almost indelibly into the Japanese soul.

Actually, during the Tokugawa period, the traditions of the military class, under the guise of a continuation of ancient culture, so thoroughly conditioned the national character that Western observers of the age were led to describe the Japanese people as being "naturally addicted to wars." The intensity of warfare and civil strife in Japan astounded even those observers who, it must be remembered, came from a Europe which was not at that time (nor had ever been) a haven of peace. Griffis, in a paper presented to the Asiatic Society of Japan in 1874, noted how endemic warfare had been in Japan, indicating that war was considered "normal" and peace the "exceptional condition of its inhabitants" (Griffis, 21). The same author also emphasized the contrast between the delight the Japanese took in calling their country the Land of Great Peace and, for example, the names of streets in Edo—names such as "Armor," "Helmet," "Arrow," "Bow," and "Quiver," all related to implements of war. In his analysis of the Japanese character, Brinkley wrote as follows:

> Hidden beneath a passion for everything graceful and refined, there is a strong yearning for the pageant of war and for the dash of deadly onset; and just as the shogun sought to display before the eyes of the citizens of his capital a charming picture of a gentle peace, though its setting was a framework of vast military preparation, so the Japanese of every era has loved to turn from the fencing-school to the arbor, from the field of battle to the society of rockery and the cascade, delighting in the perils and struggles of the one as much as he admires the grace and repose of the other. (Brinkley[2], 11)

Did the military class succeed in completely saturating the national psyche with its particular interpretation of the national spirit *(Yamato-damashii),* in imposing its values upon the rest of the country, in freezing history at that stage of national development which historians identify as feudal? The answer to these questions can be provided only by a study of the post-Meiji history of Japan, beginning in 1868. This study should reveal whether the military tradition and the influence of the warrior class had been terminated or only curtailed with the restoration of power to the emperor. In this context, there seems to be general agreement among Japanese and Western historians that no nation could be expected to emerge unscathed from centuries of the relentless conditioning undergone by Japan during her feudal era. No one has expressed this point better than Reischauer.

> The two centuries of strictly enforced peace under the watchful eye and firm hand of the Edo government have left an indelible mark upon the people. The bellicose, adventurous Japanese of the sixteenth century became by the nineteenth century a docile people looking meekly to their rulers for all leadership and following without question all orders from above. (Reischauer[1], 93-94)

The people had become thoroughly conditioned to look "instinctively" to the military leaders of the land for guidance and to assume that, because of their position, these leaders "were always honest and sincere." The same author concluded as follows: "Seven centuries of domination by the feudal military class has left patterns of thought and behavior which have not been easy to discard in recent times and which will not be easily erased even today" (Reischauer[1], 55).

The protagonist of that which Hearn considered "the whole of authentic Japanese history," the warrior of feudal Japan, had achieved a position of such importance, therefore, that his influence was not (probably could not be) eliminated, even after the military dictatorship of the powerful feudal barons was officially abolished in 1868 and society had been given a wider and firmer base through a massive educational effort intended to provide the foundations for the expertise necessary in an industrialized and highly competitive era. However, in the uncanny way in which a firmly entrenched traditional power structure often manages to survive the dawn of a new day by assuming various disguises or, more frequently, by broadening its base of support among all classes of people so that more citizens begin to identify with it, so did the military class manage to survive in Japan. The power of the Tokugawa clan and their allies was severely curtailed by the efforts of other powerful clans of warriors, including the Choshu and Satsuma clans, which were to provide the "new" Japan with the nucleus of an Imperial Army and Navy destined for greater glories and greater disasters in the decades to follow. The Restoration was, in effect, a ritualistic "changing of the guard," with waves of new warriors from the provinces advancing upon the capital where they jostled and finally dislodged the older, privileged class of warriors from their entrenched positions. Significantly, we are told by Yazaki (300) that the *Kyakkan Rireki Mokuroku,* or directory of government officials for the Council of State *(Dajokan)* held in 1867-68, listed the following percentages by lineage in its composition: 78.9% belonging to the warrior class, 18.1% to the higher class of daimyo, 1.8% to the ancient imperial court recently restored (along with the emperor) to power, and 0.7% to the commoners.

It was this "new" leadership, then, which was to guide the nation in the liberated times of the modern age. In order to accomplish their task with the utmost efficiency, they embarked upon a fantastically intense effort to expand the traditional loyalty concept from the narrow confines of the clan to the wider horizon of the entire nation, enlarging the focus of unquestioning obedience to one's immediate superior and feudal lord to include blind and absolute fealty to the emperor. Kurzman noted that "if a man would willingly die for his lord, a person of mortal heritage, they reasoned, then his loyalty to the Sovereign, descendant of the Sun Goddess, could be nurtured to similar extremes" (Kurzman, 41). Accordingly, after the Meiji Restoration:

> In classrooms and army barracks, the young Japanese was taught to glory in Japan's military traditions. He came to believe that death on the battlefield for the emperor was the most glorious fate of man and to believe in the unique virtues of a vaguely defined "national structure" and an even more vague "Japanese spirit." Together the government and army succeeded in a few decades in creating in the average Japanese the fanatical nationalism already characteristic of the upper classes, and an even more fanatical devotion to the emperor, which had been cultivated by historians and Shinto propagandists and fostered by oligarchs around the throne. (Reischauer[1], 129-30)

This was possible, according to Mendel, because of the vagueness of the Meiji Constitution concerning "the location of political power"—a vagueness which the military, who had direct access to the throne, promptly exploited. They assumed "special privileges" and largely ignored the newly created civilian cabinet which was modeled upon Western systems of government. This independence of action in matters of governing was promptly dubbed "dual diplomacy," and its effects were to haunt the members of the civilian cabinet, who were ultimately unable to steer into more peaceful channels of national development the singular dedication of the military to ideals of racially exclusive predominance. Members of the military class continued to hold fast to the pursuit of a goal whose attainment they believed their destiny and, by implication, the destiny of their country since time immemorial. Eventually, members of every class in Japan began to feel fully justified in calling that destiny their own. By the early part of the twentieth century, this process of military identification on a nationwide scale had grown to such an extent that the authorities had "even succeeded in convincing these descendants of peasants, who for almost three centuries had been denied the right to possess swords, that they were not a downtrodden class but members of a warrior race. Japanese political and military indoctrination was indeed thorough and spectacularly successful" (Reischauer[1], 130).

It had also been successful during the Tokugawa period, when the military tradition inculcated from above had elicited the desired responses from below. Repeated attempts by innumerable commoners *(heimin)* throughout the entire feudal era to rise to the privileged level of the warrior were noted in many records. Although such ambitions were officially discouraged, the possibility of adoption into a military clan did exist—many wealthy merchants being willing to part with subtantial sums in exchange for the right to have the insignia of a warrior clan embroidered on their sleeves.

When the desired status itself was not accessible, anything resembling it, however remotely, would serve to fulfill most aspirations. All associations of commoners, whether farmers, merchants, or artisans (even the clergy), were organized according to the vertical pattern of the military class, a pattern which linked the ancient clan structure to the contemporary period, thus imparting to it an aura of antiquity which, in Japan (as in many other countries), made it divine.

Even before the Meiji Restoration, the military tradition had permeated the whole of Japanese life to the extent of having lost its primary identification with a single class. That it had become the sole tradition of every Japanese subject was proven by the fact that when the military class tried once again to seize power from the emperor, the armies of "sword-wielding samurai" were crushed on the battlefields by an imperial army whose ranks were filled with conscripts from every class, including many farmers. The crushing of one of these rebellions, after 1868, wrote Browne,

> signified much more than the collapse of feudal opposition to the government and the new order. In the conflict the regular soldiers like Hidenori Tojo and the conscripts who had fought along with them had shown that the valor and martial skill which had made the samurai elite such formidable fighters could be found in all the levels of the nation. (Browne, 17)

Thereafter, bowing to expediency, the leaders of the military class gradually acknowledged that every Japanese subject was heir to the tradition they had considered their own for so many centuries, and began to exhort their fellow countrymen to think of Japan as a nation of warriors. At the same time, they discovered new and effective ways of translating that tradition into political patterns of conduct, which the nation adopted and applied with irresistible zeal in such countries as Manchuria, China, Malaysia, and the Philippines. These patterns endured without serious challenge until the surrender of Japan on September 2, 1945, when it became apparent that the defeat of the Japanese military effort had precipitated the collapse not only of a firm belief in a particular government policy, but actually of the entire moral universe of the Japanese nation. The identification between government policy, subject to the vagaries of political and military convenience, and the morality of the nation, which is of a more stable nature and has deeply rooted collective interests to promote and defend, had become so absolute in Japan that defeat on the battlefield left most Japanese "entirely disoriented" (Dore[1], 162). It seemed incredible to them that such a fate could have befallen the heirs of a divine past, a nation tracing its origins back to the dawn of human history, or that the "way" *(michi)* of the race had not triumphed over all others, which, being foreign, had automatically been considered imperfect.

Today, surveys of many kinds—anthropological, sociological, political, and religious—have documented (and are continuing to follow) the astounding recovery of Japan from the disastrous effects of World War II. The positive side of their tradition helped the Japanese to "endure the unendurable" and to bravely face and survive the occupation, to close their depleted ranks and rebuild an industry in shambles, and to speedily reassume a position of prominence in the modern world. The military virtues of the past were applied to reconstruction with the intensity that had made the Japanese fearsome foes on the battlefield, making them, in turn, skillful and tireless competitors in world markets.

But the spirit of the *bushi* flickers restlessly in the dark recesses of the Japanese soul. Dore, in his study of city life in Japan, has noted in detail the tremendous difficulty encountered by the Japanese in attempting to shift their concept of morality and traditional values from the social ethic of the country, rooted in the feudal interpretation of reality as proposed and enforced by the *bushi,* to an individual morality based upon a personal interpretation of reality and a man's individual responsibility within it. Even today, the life of a Japanese subject is dominated by society the way an enlisted man's life is dominated by the army. Perhaps more than anywhere else in the world, the compactness of Japanese society, like the protective but monolithic embrace of a modern army (or of a military clan in days gone by), dictates from above and from without that which is to be believed, the ways in which relationships are to be structured, how individuals must behave in order to fulfill their obligations. Duties continue to be emphasized, while rights are muted and still seek concrete expression in new laws or customs and, above all, in a new spiritual conviction of the individual's value and independence within the group, originating from deep within that individual's being—a conviction which will sustain him when his group and its leaders, in their historical evolution, pass through the tragic crises which afflict all national groups. That spiritual certainty does not necessarily have to agree with the external dictates of the group, expressed in laws or customs, and may even be in opposition to pronouncements made in the name of the group by the individuals in power. In Japan, perhaps to a degree rarely encountered in other sophisticated cultures of the past or present, "morality is not summoned up from the depths of the individual" (Maruyama, 9), but is still to be sought elsewhere in society—thus being easily identified with and supplanted by external power. It must be added, in this context, however, that Japanese society is not (and has never been) alone in confronting this problem.

Classic tradition, hence the military tradition of the country, confronts the Japanese today. The artistic expressions of that tradition are quite revealing. The fearless retainer of a feudal lord, the much-heralded samurai, or the independent masterless warrior, the *ronin,* still cut their way through a maze of evil with slashing swords in kabuki and in countless adventure movies *(chambara).* Dore tells us that even today, in neighborhoods such as Shitayama-cho, salesmen appear in samurai garb and shout the virtue of their wares using the sharp jargon of the Tokugawa warriors. The martial pattern of the feudal tradition can still be detected by Western observers of the Japanese business world today in that particular relationship between the employer on one side, with his paternalistic but authoritarian attitude, and the employees in their orderly but feverishly dedicated ranks on the other. It is reflected in the formation of colossal industrial complexes which have elicited "both apprehension and envy" abroad, their combined power bearing a striking resemblance to the prewar cartels *(zaibatsu).* In this context, most analysts of Japanese industry, in fact, have come to realize that the element which worked exceedingly well for the Japanese was their time-honored "traditional approach" applied to industrial productivity. We are told by De Mente, on page 51 of the March-April 1970 issue of *Worldwide Projects and Industry Planning,* that surveys carried out by the *Oriental Economist* in 1968 and 1969 revealed that the largest corporations in Japan had never relinquished the traditional management system, "but had actually strengthened it over the past 10 years." This system remains, in essence, that which it has been for centuries: a vertical clan system under the guidance of the patriarchal leader, geared to operate smoothly and efficiently for the welfare of the "clan." This ever-present awareness of the past in all forms of Japanese life, according to Dore, "is not surprising in view of the recency of the feudal past contrasting so clearly with the whole tenor of modern urban life" (Dore[1], 245).

This awareness cannot be expected to fade away or be replaced by a less rigidly organized conception of man's loneliness in the heart of creation, by an increased awareness of the self as a responsible agent capable of individual decisions which might clash against the dicta of the clan, the house, the family, or, finally, society, until that feudal tradition has been reevaluated and redefined. "Real tradition," wrote Yves Montcheuil, "is constitutive, not constituted" (Brown, 60). It grows as men evolve individually, as well as collectively. It adapts to new circumstances of time, place, and culture, and it stimulates new responses which themselves become a part of that tradition. It does not force the present into the rigid mold of the past, nor does it apply unyieldingly to the present values developed during an era which contituted only a phase of the national development. A constantly enriched and enriching tradition would not, in brief, impose a system of ethics developed and accepted by the military clans of feudal Japan upon the whole country and, progressively, upon the rest of the world under professed principles of brotherhood and universal harmony within the human family *(hakko-ichiu)*. That system of ethics, that martial code, represented only one particular interpretation of reality and of man's role in it. Even a cursory glance at Japanese history, after all, provides ample evidence that other interpretations predated and then coexisted with those of the military class—interpretations which were less successful perhaps in teaching a man how to use a sword, but no less admirable and often more useful in helping him to comprehend the true dilemma of his existence.

Considering the great significance assigned by the Japanese people to their military tradition, then, the qualification of "martial" *(bu)* so freely attributed to almost all the specializations of the art of combat in the doctrine of bujutsu finds its own semantic justification. It was much more selectively applied during the feudal era, when the warrior generally used it in reference to those arts which were his professional prerogative or when he extended it to include other arts still rather strictly correlated to the former. Its use increased with the progressive expansion of the military tradition among all classes of Japanese subjects and their striving toward total identification with it.

It is undeniable that the feudal warrior played the major role upon Japan's national stage. It was, after all, the warrior who used those methods of combat, often with consummate skill, as he strove to rise to power in the face of an armed and equally determined opposition. It is also true that, consequently, he was the indirect activator of an intense interest in bujutsu on the part of members of other classes of Japanese society, who were forced to learn his methods or invent new ones if they wished to compete with him for even a semblance of political influence, to challenge his position of exclusive privilege or merely to defend themselves against his excesses or his inability to protect them from lawlessness. For not always, nor in every part of the country, was the warrior capable of totally imposing his interpretation of law and order. In such instances, citizens were forced to rely heavily upon themselves and their civil organizations in an effort to safeguard their lives and property.

The *bushi*, however, remained the main practitioner of bujutsu, since whenever he was exposed to new methods of combat intended to minimize or reduce his own military power, he was forced to learn them in the interests of self-preservation. The most notorious example of this necessity was provided by his involvement with the population of the Ryukyu Islands. It was in these islands—according to a predominant theory in the doctrine—that he learned how inadequate his armor and his array of traditional weapons (which had hitherto won the respect of enemy warriors in Korea) could prove to be, when pitted against the bare hands and feet of a peasant sufficiently desperate and properly trained in the ancient Chinese techniques of striking. These methods, said to have originated in the distant reaches of Asia (India, China, Tibet), helped men to develop their capacities for hitting or striking with hands, feet, and other parts of the body. The *bushi* was, therefore, caught in an uncontrollable spiral of escalation. He had to practice traditional methods of combat and continue to learn new ones—in a manner similar to the modern military establishment, which keeps devising new methods of destruction, even though these soon become obsolete, which, in turn, necessitates the development of even more destructive methods, ad infinitum. In any case, as noted earlier, after the sixteenth century the *bushi* alone had the legal right and enough time to practice and perfect various forms of bujutsu. The main schools of the martial arts were usually directed, in fact, by masters of arms attached to a clan, or by unattached warriors who had been granted permission to teach (for a fee) by the lord of the district. These schools kept records of their students and methods, thus providing a continuity in the process of expansion and development of certain arts which other schools, more removed from the military dimension, did not possess—such a lack often resulting in the disappearance of certain schools and methods, which have left us only fragmented references to indicate that they ever existed.

Finally, modern disciplines of unarmed combat, which have become famous under their Japanese names the world over, were developed by masters who acknowledged their indebtedness to the bujutsu of the ancient military class of Japan. Actually, and with only a few exceptions, these masters seem to take great pride in linking themselves and their innovations in the art of combat to a tradition that has an indefinable and irresistible charisma derived from its very antiquity. Even in those few cases where modern masters point out the differences between their methods and others (both ancient and modern), differences which make their methods unique and therefore a contribution to bujutsu rather than merely repetitions of its ancient theories and practices, their position within a well-defined, traditional stream of evolution is, by implication, unmistakably clear. The only and, indeed, rare cases of a clear break with this tradition occur when the basic premises of bujutsu as arts of combat, as arts of war and violent subjugation, are denied and their techniques transformed into arts of pacification and harmless neutralization. This subject, however, requires a further, detailed exploration, which the authors hope to undertake in a subsequent volume.

Origins of Bujutsu

The authors of books and treatises dealing with the Japanese martial arts, as well as almost every important master of the ancient and modern disciplines and methods of combat derived from them, have all presented their views on the subject of the primary sources, the first systematic presentation of techniques, and so forth in an effort to provide a satisfactory answer to the question: How, when, and where did bujutsu begin? The history of Japan in general and the doctrine of the martial arts in particular do not provide us with definite or precise answers to this question. Both the historical records of the Japanese nation (employing the Chinese system of calligraphy) and the more specialized manuscripts of the various schools of bujutsu refer to a variety of practices and methods which were ancient and codified long before any actual records were kept. Chinese writing is said by most historians to have been introduced into Japan in the sixth century, probably together with the first Buddhist texts. By that time, Japan had already evolved through the pre- and protohistorical periods, such as the Jomon, Yayoi, and Asuka, which culminated in the formation of a political organization revolving around the Heijo capital, Nara (710-84), with its resplendent imperial court. These periods of development, which preceded the Heian period (794-1185), were to see the emergence and eventual consolidation of one of the most ancient social units in the history of mankind: the clan. In many history books, in fact, these periods are referred to as the age of the original clans *(uji)* and of hereditary titles (*kabane,* or *set).* These units emerged from a nebulous "age of the gods" (*kami-no-yo)* and from an imperfectly known blending of tribes, some of which had apparently emigrated from the Asiatic mainland or from islands of the south, while others are considered to have been the original inhabitants of the islands of the Japanese archipelago. Indirect references in Japanese records would seem to indicate the existence of two major tribes: the first included the clans of the emperor and the nobles *(kobetsu),* known as the Imperial Branch, while the second included the Divine Branch, or clans of other, less specified subjects *(shimbetsu).* Both groups of clans claimed the same divine origins, tracing these back to two divinities, Izanagi and Izanami, but the *kobetsu* tribes reportedly coalesced "when the sun came into being," while the *shimbetsu* tribes took shape "when the lower forces of nature were evolved" (Brinkley[2], 5). According to a prevalent school of thought, it seems that "the invaders of Japan, in the sixth century before the Christian era, found the islands already inhabited by men of such fine fighting qualities that mutual respect grew out of the struggle between the two, and the vanquished received in the new hierarchy a position little inferior to that assumed by the victor" (Brinkley[2], 182-83). Below these two major groups of noble tribes was the "mass of the people" forming the Foreign Branch *(bambetsu)*. Every claun belonging to a particular tribe seemed to embrace both direct and indirect (lateral and collateral) descendants from the same ancestors, and their original bond was, accordingly, one of blood. Like the ancient Chinese clan *(tsu)*, the Japanese *uji* developed its kinship ties into territorial bonds which were primarily related to the countryside and villages in a certain vicinity. Although the clan had a strict relationship to (almost an identification with) rural groups of people descended from common ancestors, its basic pattern of structure and functionality was quite smoothly and effectively adapted to town and city life, where it blended with, and reinforced, other forms of organizations, such as professional guilds and corporations. Kinship and territoriality, whatever their basis, seem also to have found their primary spiritual expression in a religicous cult centered upon a clan's ancestors and upon the latter's origins. Each clan, therefore, worshiped its own deities *(uji-kami)* and strove to impose them upon others, as appears evident from the progressive encroachment and eventual primacy of the solar cult of the Yamato clan.

In structure, each clan consisted of a central, dominating house or family, which gave the clan its name, and various affiliated units known as *tomo* or *be*. Other categories of subjects also appear, confusedly, in the records, between those two classes of clansmen and the serfs or slaves known as *yakko* at the very bottom of the ladder (who bore no family name). All were subject to the power of a headman *(uji-no-osa)*, who was the absolute and undisputed leader and master of the clan. This interesting figure seems to have played a predominant role in determining the direction and function of clan life. Originally a military leader, as indicated by the references to an invasion from continental Asia, he seems to have subsequently evolved into a hierarchical representative of, and link to, the divinity. As military skill, following the natural process of specialization of functions and roles in an age of settlement, was increasingly delegated to sub-leaders, the particular capacity to contact the gods, reveal mysteries, and appease the forces of heaven through invocations *(norito)* and an intricate liturgy *(matsuri)* became the primary role and function of the highest clan leaders and, to a supreme degree, of the emperor. This religious character, it should be noted at this point, eventually became one of the most salient expressions of power and privilege. Every clan which was later allowed to develop, regardless of its particular raison d'être, found its highest justification and strength in the mystical powers of its leaders. A pattern of vertical, mystical supremacy was also apparent in those groups of people with special professional skills, such as earthenware-makers *(suebe)*, carpenters *(takumibe)*, and masons *(ishizukuri-be)*, whether they endeavored to function alone or, as was more frequently the case, attached themselves to the major clans of the nobles. In the first case, the members of these professional guilds looked upon their own leaders as the repositories of an awesome professional knowledge, divinely inspired, which the leaders generally monopolized. In the second case, they and their professional leaders looked upon the clan headman, *uji-no-osa*, as the exclusive repository of an even more comprehensive type of knowledge, whose overtones of divine inspiration made it doubly potent politically. The most noted examples of the persistence to the present day of this mystic concentration of power are swordsmiths and masters of martial arts who refer, in their practices and teachings, to secret rituals and forms directly or indirectly related to the metaphysical dimensions of man's existence. This element will appear over and over again as an important factor in the evolution of bujutsu.

The clan, as a primary social unit, had achieved self-sufficiency through the cultivation of its own rice paddies and the production of its own artifacts, textiles, agricultural instruments, and, naturally, weapons. From the very beginning, the history of these clans was not one of peaceful coexistence. The archaic weapons found in the mounds and dolmens of the period from 250 B.C. to A.D. 560 indicate that, as was true during every other national age of formation, warfare was the predominant condition. By 600, these weapons were quite highly developed. Chinese records, compiled at the court of the Sui dynasty on the basis of testimonials given by Japanese envoys a century before the first written classic of the Japanese nation came into existence, related that "bows, arrows barbed with iron or bone, swords, crossbows, long and short spears, and armor made of lacquered hide constituted their warlike equipment" (Brinkley[2], 105).

Historians are still searching for other, more illuminating references to the five original *kobetsu* clans: the Otomo, the Kumebe, the Nakatomi, the Imibe, and the Mono-nobe, which are mentioned in the early records of the nation together with the clan of Emperor Jimmu, the Yamato. Eventually, this clan gained supreme but by no means unchallenged ascendancy over all the others. From its central hierarchy and from its descendants came the emperors who were to be titular heads of the nation, while its cult of the sun goddess, Amaterasu, overcame and absorbed all the other cults in the hitherto simple polytheistic worship of the age which is the root of Shinto, the indigenous religion of Japan. Every major clan had its own cohorts of warriors, but three clans in particular seem to have been concerned with the art of combat and, therefore, with its traditional specializations. The Otomo, for example, were referred to as Great Escorts, the Kumebe as Military Corporations, and the Mononobe as Corporations of Arms, while the Nakatomi and the Imibe were linked to more specifically religious and political functions. It is not clear whether these military clans and their affiliated "corporations" *(be)* were independent units (as the feudal clans emerging from the provinces centuries later proved to be) or simply branches of the imperial clan through which it carried out its policies of expansion and centralization of power. Given the gradual but relentless consolidation of power by the Yamato clan, the second thesis seems more plausible. The very existence and specific compactness of these early military clans, however, clearly implies the existence of strong opposition and competition among various militant forces, in addition to the resistance provided by the alien Ainu at the ever receding frontiers.

The clan, then, was the sum of the Japanese soul. Seligman, in fact, qualified the Japanese subject as being, throughout his long history, "essentially a clansman, with all the group feelings which a clan organization implies" (Seligman, 129). In such "group feelings" many historians find the first roots of a human commitment to force as the primary instrument for imposing a new social entity, as well as for preserving the primacy of that social form. This commitment to the use of arms in developing the earliest structures of Japanese society seems to have been particularly intense—to the extent of actually relegating all the other features of their national psyche to a subordinate position even when the necessity for fighting in defense of clan interests ceased to be an overriding one. In his observations concerning the Japanese character, Seligman wrote that "fighting came to him so naturally that when, as was generally the case, there was no outside enemy, clan fought against clan and district against district, so that the greater part of Japanese history, at least up to the Tokugawa times, is a series of civil wars" (Seligman, 129). The facility with which the Japanese resorted to armed and unarmed violence became identified, in the eyes of Western observers as well as in the eyes of the Japanese themselves, with his nature, with his interpretation of man's role in reality, with his tradition. St. Francis Xavier (1506-52) was among the first Westerners to define them as "very warlike," and centuries later, even such an aesthete as Okakura Kakuzo (1862-1913) still referred to them as "fierce warriors."

After the seventh century, with the adoption of the Chinese system of political centralization and recognition of the imperial court as the nucleus of an expanding and homogeneous nation, all clans provided soldiers for a unified army through a system of general conscription which, although widely despised, was the only possible answer to constant engagements at the frontiers with tribes of aborigines who were retreating reluctantly before the steady advance of the new empire throughout the archipelago. Conscription on a massive basis could hardly have been a permanent system at this time, however, since the clan subjects who were asked to fight were also (for the most part) the clan farmers who produced the only means of subsistence the new nation possessed. Sustenance through conquest, after all, had been possible only where the conquered peoples had riches to surrender or advanced systems of production that could be made to operate for the conqueror. There is little evidence to prove that, in archaic Japan, the local aborigines were such a people. The Japanese clansmen were confronted, generally, with nomadic tribes whose agriculture was quite primitive and who relied heavily upon their rude farming and hunting methods for fulfillment of their daily needs—as did most nomadic tribes of northern Asia. The only riches available, then, must have been the land itself. Thus, it seems, the massive military organizations which emerged from the records of this age were intrinsic parts of a massive colonizing effort which maintained a strong identification between the Japanese soldier and the Japanese farmer—both often being (as was true of the Roman legionnaires) one and the same. If such an assumption appears reasonable enough in relation to large numbers of clansmen bearing arms, it also appears reasonable to infer from the records the existence of a smaller but more stable line of military succession based on heredity. At the frontiers, for example, a military organization of officers and veterans was maintained to insure the conditions essential to expansion in a militarily administered territory: continuity and professionalism. The origins of the feudal warriors who imploded from the provinces back into the center of political power in the sixteenth century are considered by most historians to have been in these military organizations. Tightly knit groups, they were led by officers whose entire lives were devoted to arms and arts of combat such as kyujutsu, yarijutsu, kenjutsu (using the long *tachi)*, and jobajutsu—arts which were ancient even in the tenth century, when the rise of the military class clearly began.

It would appear, then, that bujutsu actually began to take shape with the early Japanese clansman and has followed him in one form or another ever since. Any attempt to further probe the origins of bujutsu would encounter the infinitely more difficult question of the origins of that fighting biped—man himself. That which appears incontrovertible, even in times as ancient as those of the original *uji,* is the clannish nature of bujutsu—the feeling of total commitment to the theories and practices of combat adopted by a specific social unit, to the exclusion (often violently expressed) of those adopted by other social units. This was a pronounced characteristic during the feudal ages of Japan, not only within the military class, which, after all, was intrinsically clannish, but also in all those other classes whose members organized themselves in guilds or corporations according to the vertical hierarchy and structure of the archaic clan. Even religious orders in Japan, although supposedly removed from the harsh competition and the exclusivism of mundane affairs and inspired by the universal simplicity of Buddhist brotherhood, generally repeated the clan pattern in their religious or para-religious organizations. This pattern is still very much in evidence in almost all modern clubs and organizations where ancient as well as modern forms of bujutsu are practiced in Japan. And, perhaps due to Japanese domination of these arts (at least at the highest levels), this clannish tendency is often found even in Western clubs where these arts are taught.

If we are to arrive at a correct and comprehensive understanding of all the major and minor specializations of the martial arts, we must examine in somewhat greater detail the nature, history, and role of the various classes of subjects who appear inextricably linked to bujutsu after its emergence during the age of the clans, and who contributed to its development and evolution throughout the ages that ensued. Such a study follows in Part 1.

CHART 2

CHRONOLOGY OF JAPANESE HISTORY

ERAS, AGES, AND PERIODS WITH their chronology		MAJOR CHARACTERISTICS AND EVENTS considered as relevant in bujutsu
Prehistoric Age *(Jomon)*		Paleolithic and mesolithic periods of a nomadic culture based on hunting, followed by the neolithic (use of pottery).
Protohistoric Age		Age of the ancient clans *(uji)* and of the hereditary titles based on rice cultivation and the use of bronze utensils.
		Rise of the first social classes on the tribal level of culture.
	A.D. 57	First envoy of Japanese islanders of Nu to the Han Court in China.
		Invasion of Western Japan by the Yamato tribes.
		Military victories of Takeru-no-Mikoto and development of the clan into a kingdom.
		Appearance of iron weapons in dolmens.
	c. 360	Tradition refers to an invasion of Korea by Japanese warriors led by Empress Jingo.
The Beginning of Recorded History	*c.* 405	Introduction of writing from Korea.
		Revolt in Kyushu against the dispatching of Japanese warriors to protect Japanese interests in Korea.
	552	Introduction of Buddhism under the sponsorship of the Soga clan against the opposition of the Mononobe and the Nakatomi.
		Elimination of Japanese power in Korea by the rise and expansion of the kingdom of Silla.
	587	The Soga clan imparts a mortal blow to the Mononobe.
	594	Buddhism is proclaimed the religion of state.
	604	The Chinese calendar is adopted.
	607	First embassy is sent to China.
	645	The Soga clan is eliminated by Naka-no-Oe and Nakatomi Kamatari.
	663	The Taika Reform is promulgated.
		Defeat of Japanese warriors in Korea and destruction of their ally Paekche by Silla supported by the T'ang dynasty.
	672	Emperor Temmu usurps the throne.
	702	Promulgation of the Taiho Code.
Nara Period (710-784)	710	Bureaucracy patterned on the Chinese model and establishment of the first permanent capital in Nara.
	712-20	Compilation of official records *(Kojiki)*, gazettes *(Fudoki)*, and chronicles *(Nihongi)*.
	740	Revolt of Fujiwara Hirotsugu against the influence at court of the monk Gembo.
		Flourishing of Buddhist sects in Nara.
	764	Defeat of Fujiwara Nakamaro and reestablishment of power in the hands of Empress Koken (Shotoku), who appoints abbot Dokyo as Prime Minister.
	784	The capital is moved to Nagaoka.
Heian Period (794-1156) or the Age of the Court Nobles *(kuge)* Sometimes divided into the Fujiwara Period (866-1160) and the beginning of the Taira Period (1156).	794	Heian-kyo (Kyoto) is founded.
	801	Defeat of the Ainu tribes in the north by Tamuramaro Sakanoue.
		Decline of imperial power as the leaders of the Fujiwara clan emerge as regents *(sessho)* and civil dictators *(kampaku)*.
	833-967	Period of intrigues, struggles, and revolts involving the emperors, the regents, and the directors.
	939-40	Revolt and execution of Taira Masakado.
		Establishment of the "cloistered governments" as retired sovereigns *(joko)* or sovereigns joining monastic orders *(ho)* influence public affairs from secluded sites.
	1051-62	Earlier Nine Years' War: the Minamoto warriors eliminate the Abe clan in northern Honshu.
	1083-87	Later Three Years' War: Minamoto Yoshiie eliminates the opposition of the Kiyowara clan in northern Honshu.
	1095	First descent of marauding monks from Mount Hiei into Kyoto.
	1156	Taira Kiyomori, of the military aristocracy in the provinces, takes control of the civil government in the capital.

Eras, Ages, and Periods with their chronology		Major Characteristics and Events considered as relevant in bujutsu
The Age of Feudal Barons and Military Nobles *(buke)* (1156-1868)	1156-85	*Rokuhara Period,* characterized throughout by the active role of the Taira clan
	1156-58	Hogen War and destruction of most Minamoto leaders by Taira Kiyomori.
	1159-60	Heiji War, further expansion of Taira power.
	1180-85	Gempei War leads to the destruction of the Taira clan.
	1185-1333	*Kamakura Period.*
	1192	Minamoto Yontomo founds the Kamakura shogunate.
		The Hojo clan ascends to power (1205).
	1232	Publication of the *Jon Shikimoku* as the basic law of the land.
	1274	First Mongol invasion.
	1281	Second Mongol invasion.
	1331-36	Genko War.
		Inauguration of Emperor Go-Daigo's direct rule and end of the Hojo regency.
	1336-1568	*Ashikaga Period,* which includes and leads into the *Muromachi Period* (1392-1573)
		Emperor Go-Daigo is forced to flee to Yoshino and a rival emperor occupies his throne in Kyoto under the protection of Ashikaga Takauji.
	1336-92	Period of great wars between the Northern Court in Kyoto and the Southern Court in Yoshino (also known as the *Nambokucho Period*).
		Takauji becomes shogun (1338).
	1339	Publication of the *Jinno Shoto-ki* (Records of Legitimate Succession of Divine Sovereigns).
	1365-72	Battles on Kyushu between warrior clans led by Prince Kanenaga and those led by Imagawa Sadayo. Reunification of the two courts in 1392.
	1467-77	Wars of Onin and endemic strife throughout the land. Peasant uprising in Yamashino province (1485).
	1543	Introduction of firearms into Japan.
	1568-1600	*Momoyama Period,* also referred to as the Period of the Country at War *(sengoku jidai)* which overlaps and links the Ashikaga and Tokugawa periods.
	1534-1600	Oda Nobunaga occupies Kyoto (1568) and razes major Buddhist temples to the ground, eliminating opposing clans and their conditions.
	1587-88	Nobunaga, murdered in 1582, is avenged by Hideyoshi, who disarms Japan.
	1592	Hideyoshi unifies the country and invades Korea twice, in 1592 and 1597, before dying in 1598.
	1600	Tokugawa Ieyasu overcomes the opposition of other military clans at Sekigahara and conclusively destroys Hideyori's Osaka stronghold in 1615.
	1600-1867	*Tokugawa Period,* also known as the *Edo Period.*
		Ieyasu establishes the Tokugawa shogunate in Edo (Tokyo) in 1603 and issues the *Buke-Shohatto* (Laws of the Military Houses) in 1615.
	1624	The Spaniards are expelled.
	1637-38	The Shimabara Rebellion.
		Expulsion of the Portuguese in 1639 and all other foreigners in 1640, with the exception of a small Dutch company.
		Compilation of national chronicles *(Dainihon-shi)* in 1657 and of the *Honcho Tsugan* (General History of Our State) in 1670.
	1685	Formulation in writing of *bushido* by Yamaga Soko.
	1701-3	Incident of the forty-seven *ronin.*
		Great famines and disorders from 1732 to 1786.
	1791	The Edo shogunate tries various fiscal and social reforms (1787) while suppressing heterodox learning in 1790.
	1867	American and Russian warships appear.
		Internal disorders and rice riots (1837).
		Increased weakness of the shogunate prompts the last shogun, Tokugawa Yoshinobu, to resign in 1867, thus restoring the supreme administrative power to the emperor (1868).

PART I

EXPONENTS OF BUJUTSU
The Bujin

1
THE BUSHI

The Rise of the Military Class

The military class (*buke*) began to play a determinant role in the history of Japan during the tenth and eleventh centuries (the late Heian period) as the power of the emperor, the nominal head of the Yamato clan, slowly but irresistibly began to disintegrate in the wake of the nobility's constant internecine struggles. During this period, the aristocratic clans (*kuge*) battled one another unendingly—when, that is, they were not warring against the powerful organizations of militant priests and monks near Nara. This phenomenon can be seen as early as the middle of the sixth century, when a comparatively new clan, the Soga, challenged the power of the five original clans: the Otomo, Kume (Kumebe), Imibe, Mononobe, and Nakatomi. The members of the dynamic and extremely capable Soga family, in fact, eventually managed to insinuate themselves into the imperial line of inheritance, using every conceivable means to attain their ends. Two imperial princes were murdered as a result of their "intrigues, which culminated in the assassination of the Emperor Sosun (591 A.D.)—the only crime of its kind openly admitted by Japanese historians" (Brinkley[2], 42-43).

At the time, the country was also in the throes of a spiritual upheaval precipitated by the clash between monotheistic Buddhism and the pantheistic animism of the indigenous religion (Shinto). The spreading of the former doctrine and its mystical polarization of images further emphasized the supreme authority of the emperor-priest, thus making him an even more particular target of those powerful and ambitious noblemen who were determined to wield that power themselves. The clan struggles were not always expressed in terms of bloodshed, however. The members of the Soga clan also became famous in Japanese history for their skill as diplomats—managing the kingdom either directly, as regents (*sessho*) and civil dictators (*kampaku*), or indirectly, as befitted an emperor's maternal or paternal relatives and mentors. Their hold was finally broken by Kamatari, head of the ancient Nakatomi clan. As a consequence of his efforts, "the Soga family became extinct—a euphemism signifying that every male bearing the name of Soga, greybeard, youth, or child, was put to the sword. That was the method of dealing with such cases in ancient times, and it continued to be the method throughout medieval and even up to comparatively modern times" (Brinkley[2], 43).

In accordance with what had, by that time, become the political custom of the land, Kamatari restored power nominally to the emperor, but reserved those offices through which that power was exercised for himself and the members of his clan (upon which the emperor bestowed the name "wisteria plain," or Fujiwara). In time, this clan became supreme among all those descended from the ancient *kuge.*

As a result of the decimation which characterized the Heian period beneath its exterior splendor, a power vacuum was created in the political center of the nation, and a new class of men was drawn into that vortex by the irresistible forces of history. These men formed a military aristocracy of sorts which, at least initially, seemed to have been excluded from the political process of decision making. The function

Court nobles

of this class was primarily that of enlarging and protecting the boundaries of the nation. Thus its members inherited the ancient martial tradition which had once been the prerogative of the ancient and expanding noble clans before they had become centralized—first in Nara and then in the permanent capital of Kyoto. Slowly but surely, this centralization had separated the *kuge* from the real basis of power at that time: land ownership. As Grinnan pointed out, "the history of the land tenure of a country is always closely connected with its political development. This is especially true of ancient times, for then land was the sole or principal source of wealth and power" (Grinnan, 228).

The almost complete concentration of the ancient clans in the capitals and their continual absenteeism from even their nearest estates had considerably weakened their capacity to develop their lands, supervise the management of their properties, and collect the taxes due them. Within the boundaries of both nearby estates and others in provinces far from the capitals, new and vigorous clans began to coalesce.

Provincial territories had customarily been assigned by imperial decree to large landowners who acted, in Nitobe's estimation, as had the Latin *tenantes pro capite* or as representatives of the emperor. In addition, other territories, reclaimed from wilderness or taken from enemies, were transformed into productive provinces whose occupants, along with their cohorts, were eventually confirmed in their positions as landowners by imperial decree. These landowners were called *daimyo* ("great names") and they also used to sublet their fiefs to particularly favored retainers or vassals *(kerai).*

> These provincial magnates gradually developed into great military chiefs, with large forces of well armed and carefully disciplined retainers under their command. They were called *bu-ke,* or military houses, to distinguish them from the *ku-ge,* or Court-houses, whose heads lived in Kyoto, monopolizing the administrative positions, but seeing their emoluments and their influence steadily circumscribed as the provinces passed beyond their sway. (Brinkley[2], 47)

The daimyo gradually became more independent and removed from the sway of the emperor, who, as Nitobe expressed it, "lived in the invisible seclusion at the capital, Kyoto." The contrast between the life of the retainers of the court nobles in Kyoto and that of the provincial lords had always been quite marked. As early as the eighth century, when conscripts "selected by lot" were sent either to serve in the distant provinces or to serve in the "six corps of guards" at the capital, "the provincial troops, constantly exercised in the use of the sword, the spear, and equestrian archery, attained and maintained a high degree of efficiency" (Brinkley[2], 50). On the other hand, "the metropolitan guards soon yielded to the enervating

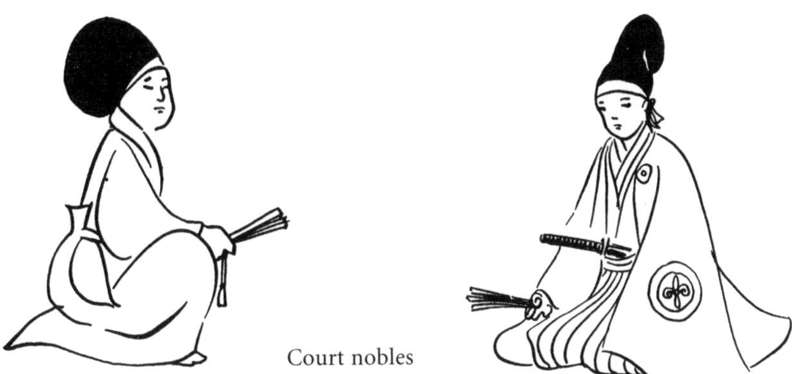
Court nobles

influences that surrounded them, and ceased to be useful except as factors in the pageant of pomp and parade affected by the great nobles, or as instruments in furthering their intrigues" (Brinkley[2], 50).

To be sure, there was at least an indirect relationship between the feudal barons of the provinces and the court with its nobles, that is, between the *buke* and the *kuge*. Often this relationship was closer than that presupposed by legalistic and traditional bonds of loyalty based on the formal appointment of a feudal baron to rule a province or a district; it was also one of blood ties or affiliation through marriage or adoption.

The most important families among the feudal barons, who were instrumental in raising their class to a position of prominence and in establishing a successful dictatorship, were the Minamoto (Genji) and the Taira (Heike). Both claimed direct or indirect descent from members of the imperial family who, in accordance with ancient custom, had been sent to the provinces when there had been "no place for them at court." Usually, such exiled royal subjects changed their names after six generations. The fourteen families of the Minamoto clan traced their origins to the emperors Saga (786-842) and Seiwa (850-80), while the four families comprising the Taira clan claimed Emperor Kammu (737-806) as their ancestor. These claims, however, must be studied critically in view of the fact that any new center of power usually tries to link itself to the tradition of the older, supplanted power in order to justify, reinforce, and consolidate its position. The strong reaction of the court to the new leaders, who were often spitefully referred to in imperial decrees as being "people of all ranks," indicates that in most cases we can presume the claimed relationship to have been nonexistent. This historical probability is further confirmed by the emergence of leaders from the lower social strata in later times—men such as the warlords Nobunaga and Hideyoshi, among others, who prepared the way for the Tokugawa dictatorship, which was to emerge in the seventeenth century. Furthermore, even when extant, such a relationship did not prevent the independent formation of these new and formidable clans, which were led by strong, ambitious men of arms and organized militarily within their own provincial areas.

Their independence during the early part of the Heian period had become so absolute that, according to Sansom, numerous imperial decrees (largely ignored) were issued from 889 to 897, referring to the fact that "people of all ranks" in the provinces were oppressing farmers, defying the officers of the imperial court, and generally running things to suit themselves. The same scholar also states that by the middle of the Heian period the court could no longer keep peace among the provincial clans and that twice it was even threatened directly by their rebellious policies. In 939-40, Taira Masakado, who had been sent as an officer of the crown to supervise the eastern provinces, found them so well organized and militarily prepared that he decided to place himself at their head and turn against the central government. In a short time, he and his forces occupied most of the Kanto plain. He was killed in a battle against hostile clans before an imperial general (hurriedly appointed to quell the revolt) could even arrive on the scene. Then Fujiwara Sumitomo, appointed by the crown to deal with piracy and sedition in the provinces and along the coastline, led local pirate bands against government forces and seized control of large areas along the Inland Sea.

In both cases it was clearly shown that provincial forces could challenge the central government and that such challenges could not be met successfully by an imperial response, but only by relying upon similar groups of armed men led by their own local leaders. In this way, ironically enough, the emperor himself, as well as the rest of the nobility and the ancient families of regents, eventually came to rely upon the forces of these feudal barons for their very survival during the dramatically intense struggles which followed. Unfortunately, like the unleashing of ills from Pandora's box, the military forces released from and within the provinces proved to be largely uncontrollable in spite of various attempts in this direction on the part of the imperial court and other exalted patrons. Moreover, these forces were seemingly not able to come to terms even among themselves, but turned against one another, each usually fighting not for the emperor or an aristocratic family, but for itself alone.

By the early part of the twelfth century, clashes were occurring regularly between the largest and most powerful associations of feudal barons—one led by the Taira and the the other by the Minamoto. The Hogen War of 1156 was still fought in the name of the imperial heirs, Goshirakawa and Konoe (sons of the retired emperor Toba), who were competing for the throne. But the Gempei War of 1180-85 was clearly a direct confrontation in which the forces of the Minamoto were dealt a crushing defeat. The head of the Taira clan, Kiyomori (1118-81), consolidated his power at court through a series of skillful manipulations and marriages which finally put one of his nephews, Antoku, on the throne at the age of two. This feudal baron, who had at last reached the apex of power through force of arms, defended his position ruthlessly

against any threat, from any source. One of the major obstacles he encountered was the resistance offered by certain religious communities who had armed forces of their own, which they used to control the vast and productive territories assigned to them over a period of centuries by many different emperors. Without the slightest hesitation, Kiyomori moved against them, putting to the sword the priests and monks of Todai-ji and Kofuku-ji before sacking their monasteries in Nara.

The age of supremacy of the Taira clan is known as the Rokuhara period (1156-85). It came to an end when Minamoto Yoritomo (1148-99), whose life had been spared after the defeat of his clan in 1160, succeeded in rallying and uniting the clans hostile to the Taira. Under his leadership, these forces defeated the Taira at Ichinotani (1184), Yashima (1185), and Dannoura (1185). This interesting military leader, who had been raised in Izu by vassals of the Taira clan (the clever Hojo family), usually employed skilled generals to great advantage on the battlefield—men such as his younger half-brother Yoshitsune and his cousin Yoshinaka. Both of these men and their families, however, were promptly dispatched (either forced to commit suicide or killed outright) after they had won great victories for him. Yoritomo then assumed the title of *Seii Tai-shogun.* This title appears to have evolved from the ancient imperial commission *Seii-shi* ("sent against the barbarians") and the title *taisho,* denoting the general-in-chief of an army. The latter title appears in the records of the ninth century in relation to the commanders of the imperial guards. It had been assigned by imperial decree to earlier leaders of renown, such as Sakanoue Tamuramaro, who, after scoring impressive victories at the end of the eighth century, promptly returned the title to the emperor. With Yoritomo, however, it became a hereditary right of his house, and it was assumed and retained by a long line of military dictators who ruled Japan in the name of the emperor until the late nineteenth century. In its abbreviated form, such rulers were generally known throughout the land as *shogun.*

Yoritomo established the center of his military command, characteristically known as camp office or tent headquarters *(bakufu),* in Kamakura. From his stronghold there, once he had expropriated the Taira's estates (as well as those of the feudal barons who had unwisely allied themselves with that doomed clan), he placed constables or guards *(shugo)* in each province and district headmen *(jito)* in every taxable area, thus establishing the financial basis which made it possible for his clan and the clans of his allies to maintain military forces in a permanent condition of professional readiness. The period during which his

clan ruled the country (through a succession of military leaders) is known as the Kamakura period and lasted from 1185 to 1333. The ancient system of landownership, characterized by the *myoden* and the *shoen* and based upon a chain of owner-manager-tenant-laborer, became more military in structure and function. The members of the new territorial units controlled by each clan were expected to be familiar with and practice the use of traditional weapons of combat. The leaders of the clans, naturally, either maintained or assumed for themselves a position of privilege, and this, in time, became despotically absolute and practically unassailable.

When Yoritomo died in 1199, the power held by the Minamoto clan was wielded by the Hojo family, whose members, once vassals of the Taira, had sheltered him in Izu. Rewarded munificently by him, they proved to be exceptional statesmen during the troubled Kamakura period, maneuvering skillfully to crush a revolt of the nobility in 1221, reorganizing the selection of emperors and the election of domestic court officials, redistributing confiscated lands to loyal barons, issuing one of the first feudal codes of law (the *Joei Shikimoku*), reorganizing the administrative and fiscal machinery of the state, rallying the clans against the Mongols in 1274 and 1281, developing the arts and literature (mostly epic and martial), and promoting the Zen school of Buddhism, whose austere simplicity of thought and action was to prove so congenial to the pragmatic soul of the warrior.

The efforts against the Mongols, however, badly depleted the financial resources of the feudal barons, and a new era of rearrangement of existing landownership began: merchants were forbidden to press for repayment of loans made to warriors; new and old lands were forcefully appropriated by state officials who appointed themselves owners of the territories formerly in their charge; and strong military landowners expanded and aggrandized their estates at the expense of their weaker neighbors. In this age of disorder, Emperor Godaigo tried to rally dissatisfied barons against the military government of Kamakura. After several attempts and with the help of Takauji of the Ashikaga clan (orginally sent *against* him by the Kamakura authorities), Godaigo was successful to a degree in restoring imperial power in 1334.

The following year, however, Takauji drove him out of Kyoto, set on the throne a member of a rival branch of the family, and established his own military dictatorship during an era referred to as the Ashikaga period (1336-1568). Throughout this age, internecine warfare was again rampant, clans fighting among themselves, torn between the Southern Court of Godaigo in the region of Yoshino and the Northern Court of Takauji's puppet emperors. New centers of provincial power began to emerge as the long-established feudal barons (repeating the historical mistake which had cost the emperor and the nobility their territoral empires long before) lost contact with their fiefs while maneuvering for power in the capital. In this age, the cherished ethos of clan loyalty to the immediate superior, which was to be so emphatically reasserted in later centuries, was only a pale shadow of what it claimed to be. The opposing principle of inferiors striking superiors *(gekokujo)* became the inspiration behind many political and military commitments. The farmers' revolt near Kyoto in 1485, another revolt by farmers led by militant priests from Hongan-ji Temple in Osaka during the same period, and the Onin War (1467-77) finally threw the country into complete chaos, disrupting any attempts at centralized administration and substantially altering the system of land ownership so laboriously constructed during the previous age. Many Western observers in Japan during this period have left vivid descriptions of Japanese behavior as the vertical system of direct loyalty which had held the clan together began to crumble. In his letters, Alessandro Valignano, S.J., (1539-1606) was appalled at the facility with which Japanese vassals began to turn against their lords, or returned to serve former masters only to betray them once again. Joao Rodriguez (1561-1643) also noted the general proclivity to plunder, betray, blackmail, and exterminate ruthlessly, saying that he understood why the average Japanese of the time was eminently distrustful and "always kept his weapons at hand" (Cooper, 31).

At the height of this national chaos, during an age marked by the arrival of the first Europeans (1543) and the consequent introduction of firearms *(tanegashima teppo,* or iron rods of Tanegashima), there emerged three men of infinitely broader political vision and determination than their compatriots: Oda Nobunaga, Toyotomi Hideyoshi, and Tokugawa Ieyasu.

Oda Nobunaga was the son of an estate manager for the Shiba family—a clan fulfilling the function of provincial constables in Owari province. From this territory, he launched a series of progressive attacks upon all those provincial barons who were feuding among themselves. Already divided, they did not prove difficult to conquer. He eventually reached Kyoto, where, after a brief encounter with the exhausted leaders of the once powerful Ashikaga clan, he closed the period which had borne their name for almost 170 years (1568). His rise to absolute power was interrupted, however, by the application of a stratagem quite popular at the time: treason. He was surrounded unexpectedly by the troops of his vassal Akechi Mitsuhide, who was supposed to be leading those troops to the front. Father Luis Frois, S. J., (1532-97) relates that Nobunaga, although wounded by an arrow as he was washing his hands, seized a *naginata* and fought mightily against his many attackers until he was totally exhausted. He then "retreated into his chambers and shut the doors" (Cooper, 103). He was either burned alive or forced to commit formal suicide at his Honno-ji headquarters.

One of his most successful generals, Toyotomi Hideyoshi, was of peasant ancestry. He immediately avenged the death of Nobunaga by defeating Akechi's forces at Yamazaki. Fleeing, Akechi fell into the hands of looting peasants, who promptly murdered him. Hideyoshi then proceeded to conquer the rest of the country, launching swift campaigns in Shikoku (1585), Kyushu (1587), and Odawara (1590). It was Hideyoshi who, in the seventh month, eighth day of Tensho (1588), instigated what the country

derisively called the Taiko's Sword Hunt when he issued the famous decree which disarmed the nation. This decree stated that "the people of the various provinces are strictly forbidden to have in their possession any swords, short swords, bows, spears, firearms or other types of arms" (Tsunoda et al., 329). Hideyoshi admitted quite frankly that widespread possession of weapons made it extremely difficult to collect taxes and tended to "foment uprisings."

He was on his way to Korea when he died, and the powerful Tokugawa clan (allies of his and of Nobunaga before him) immediately moved to assume the title and power of the regency. The leader of this clan, the astute Ieyasu, eliminated any possible contenders—including Hideyoshi's son, Hideyori, whom he had formally promised to protect. With the successful outcome of a series of battles culminating in the Sekigahara slaughter in 1600 and the Osaka siege in 1615, Ieyasu became the *Seii Taishogun* of Japan. His clan and its military dictatorship were to determine the course of Japanese history for 267 years, until political power was nominally restored to the emperor in 1868 and Japan began its rapid but painful transition from a feudal to a modern state.

At the end of the Momoyama period (1600), however, Ieyasu had inherited an exhausted but still heavily fortified Japan. The landscape was dotted with castles and fortifications of every possible size and style, which the provincial warlords had erected wherever it was feasible to station garrisons of warriors. Every strategic site which afforded a superior defense against armed attack and an optimum position for controlling the movements of people and goods had been well fortified. Castles were erected at the top of a small mountain *(yamajiro, sanjo)*, or on the hill between a mountain and a plain *(hirayamajiro, hirasanjo)*, as well as on the plain itself *(hirajiro, hirajo)*. Military clans had constructed castles and established garrisons in major towns, near important temples and shrines *(monzen-machi)*, at highway intersections *(shukuba-machi)* and markets *(ichiba-machi)*, near ports and sea inlets *(minato-machi)*, etc., thus forming that typical balance between military protection and exploitation on one side and commercial productivity on the other, which was also the salient characteristic of those medieval Japanese castle-towns *(jokamachi)* which had actually sprung up around a feudal lord's manor.

In structure, the castle of feudal times had evolved into a sophisticated and, eventually, practically impregnable fortress. It was generally designed as a series of "concentric compounds isolated from each other by ramparts, moats, or walls" (Kirby, 12), and comprised such an intricate network of courts and passages that if one compound were lost to an invader, it could be recaptured from either side or totally cut off without substantially weakening the defensive strength of the other compounds. The approaches to its fortified perimeter were protected by excavations filled with water, by ditches, by swamps, or by a combination of all three. Water-filled moats *(hori)*, as Kirby relates, were considered "the best guarantee against penetration." Earthen walls *(doi)* or stone walls *(ishigaki)* rose massively from that first defensive line, offering only two major openings—the heavily fortified main gate *(otemon)* and the equally strong but smaller rear gate *(karamete)*, both usually constructed of large timbers, plated with copper or iron, and densely studded with large nails. The passages within, linking one courtyard to another and each compound to the next, were usually designed in such fashion as to lead through cleverly arranged double gates *(masugata)* in which one gate was set at right angles to the second, allowing room enough between them to contain (and control from the sides and from above) only a certain number of people—which Hideyoshi had decided should never exceed a maximum of 240 warriors or forty cavalrymen.

The castle compounds *(kuruwa)* were generally composed of three units: the main section in the center *(hommaru)*, surrounded by the second section *(ninomaru)*, and then the third section *(sannomaru)* of fortifications, containing respectively the main tower and residences of the warlords, the storerooms, and the living quarters of the garrison. All of these were elongated structures integrated into massive walls, with doors and passageways on the inner side and openings on the outer. The openings *(sama)* were of different sizes and angles according to the weapons employed to repel an invader at that point. Rectangular openings for arrows *(yasama)*, circular, triangular, or square for guns *(tepposama)*, and, later, large

The impregnable fortress

Approach to the castle

oval openings for cannons *(taihosama)* were widely distributed among other chute-like ducts *(ishiotoshi)*, trapdoors which opened wide to send huge stones crashing down upon the heads of foes beneath.

Towers *(yagura)* rose from these compounds. They consisted of structures containing three or more levels, heavily fortified, with the uppermost functioning primarily as an observation post or, in times of peace, as a spot for contemplating the moon or performing ritual suicide, depending upon the circumstances. These towers were located at the most strategic points: on the outer compounds, toward the northern *(kitanomaru)* and the western *(nishinomaru)* sides of the horizon; at the corners of the compounds *(sumiyagura)*; in the center, where they were given the poetic name of "guardian of the sky" *(tenshu-kaku)* or, more prosaically, the "keep" *(tsunemaru)*, because this point represented the final defensive position against invading forces (Yazaki, 105).

Yazaki also tells us that a vast network of supporting fortresses, auxiliary castles *(shijo, edashiro)*, and smaller outposts *(hajiro)* were constructed to form a wide, defensive line that encircled and protected the boundary line of a provincial domain and its base castle *(honjo, nejiro)*. Military outposts of smaller size and abbreviated function confronted one at the most unexpected places and were generally identified by their primary purpose, such as boundary surveillance *(sakameshiro)*, watchpost *(banteshiro)*, communication *(tsutaenoshiro)*, and attack *(mukaishiro)*. It is recorded that the Lord of Obi, head of the Ito clan, had forty-eight forts grouped around his castle in Hyuga province—but the Uesugi clan topped even this with 120 forts surrounding their three major castles.

Encased in this vast network of fortifications, lorded over by fiercely independent clans of warriors, the larger masses of commoners were, for all intents and purposes, imprisoned. By the time Ieyasu consolidated his power over the country, the warriors had assumed those professional characteristics which he was to acknowledge formally and embody in the law of the land. Their ranks were arranged vertically in strata descending, by order of importance and wealth, from the daimyo, who was often the heir of a former provincial protector or caretaker, to the upper ranks of his warriors *(kyunin)*, who possessed their own estates, to the middle ranks of warriors *(gokenin,jikan)*, subordinated to the *kyunin*, and then to the lower ranks of foot soldiers *(ashigaru)*, with their cohorts *(chugen)* and servants. Beneath all of these, in the provincial territories, labored the large masses of farmers, bound to the land and carefully watched. In the larger towns, the civilian population had developed several professional classes which seemed to consist primarily of a number of ruling landlords, wealthy wholesalers, and moneylenders, who lorded it over the various guilds and corporations of merchants, craftsmen, and farmers tied to the productive land around the towns. Below these were apprentices, tenant-farmers, and servants in near-slavery. At the bottom of this social stratification were entertainers, porters, foreigners, the destitute, and, below even these groups and outside society, the unmentionable outcasts *(eta)*. All these classes, with all their categories and ranks, which were to play a part in the evolution of bujutsu, confronted the first shogun of the Tokugawa clan.

The Military Structure of Tokugawa Society: The Shogun

Ieyasu established his central government in Edo, a small hamlet transformed into a prosperous town in 1456 by a son of the provincial governor of Tamba, Ota Dokan (1432-86), and destined one day to become Tokyo, the "Eastern Capital" of the nation. With the first leader of the Tokugawa clan "an age of disorderly splendor and democratic promise" ended (Cole, 46), and the nation saw the major social divisions of the Ashikaga (Muromachi) and Momoyama periods congeal into a rigid system of class separation clearly defined by the new laws of the land and strictly enforced by the new aristocrats on horseback.

In all their laws and regulations, Ieyasu and his direct descendants sought to establish guidelines for the creation and preservation of a stable national structure. These guidelines defined the primary morality of public and private subjects, established the agencies that fostered that morality throughout the entire national body, and punished transgressors. This primary morality was clearly based upon public rapport

Shogun in court attire

Moat guard

Follower of Fuke sect of Buddhism, KOMUSO

between master and subordinate, which was then reflected in the private rapport between father and son. The former determined the shape and functionality of the major social organizations of Tokugawa society: the various classes and the clans within each class, in a descending order of hierarchical subordination. The latter determined the composition and function of the basic unit of any society: the family. This morality, inherited from China and reinforced by her scholars throughout the ages, had evolved in Japan into an essential motivation of national purpose and function—nay, of national existence and, in times of crisis, of actual survival. In feudal Japan, there was no more despicable crime than that of rebellion against a master (or father); and no series of punishments, inflicted cumulatively according to the dictates of the penal code *(Kujikata Osadamegaki),* was considered harsh enough to erase the deed or even atone for it. As Yazaki tells us, "The heaviest penalties were given those who violated the master-subordinate relationship, so essential to maintaining the feudal system." In the fifty-third section of his *Legacy,* Ieyasu proclaims:

> The guilt of a vassal murdering his suzerain is in principle the same as that of an arch-traitor to the Emperor. His immediate companions, his relations—all even to his most distant connections—shall be cut off, hewn to atoms, root and fibre. The guilt of a vassal only lifting his hand against his master, even though he does not assassinate him, is the same. (Hearn, 347-48)

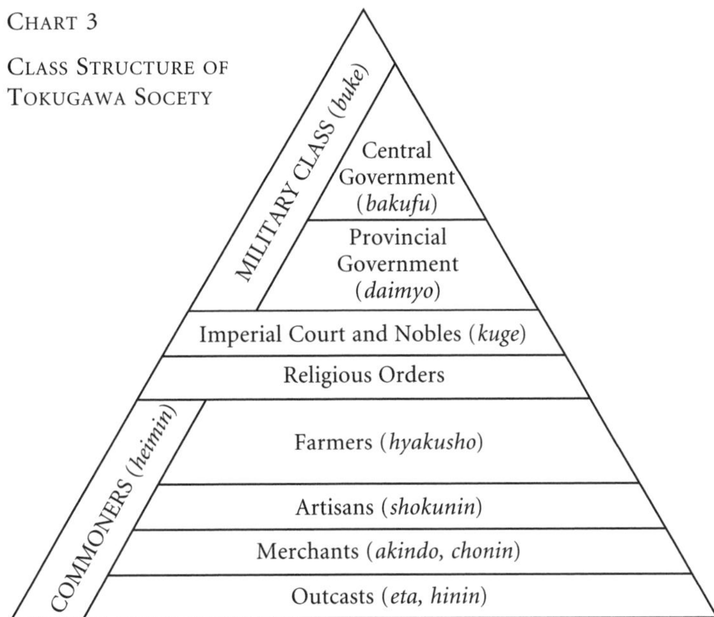

Upon this base the Tokugawa elevated that social structure which sealed the subjects of the nation into classes according to a vertical order of pragmatic importance, drawing heavily upon the military character and strength of the warriors to whom all other subjects were subordinated.

The previous ages had witnessed the beginning of that process of social selection and specialization which the Tokugawa practically confirmed, once they had positioned their class above all others and their clan at the summit of the social pyramid. A body of laws and regulations emanated from the new government from time to time, defining and clarifying divisions of class, function, and rapport within the national body politic. From 1615 onward, laws specifically determining the legal positions and functions of the imperial court and its aristocratic families *(Kuge Sho-hatto)*, of the military class *(Buke Sho-hatto)*, of the religious orders *(Jin-hatto)*, of the farmers *(Goson-hatio)*, of commoners in Edo and, by analogy, in every other town *(Edo-machiju-sadame)* were issued by the military government of the Tokugawa shogun. Guidelines covering police administration, the penal codes, and the judicial procedures were published in a series *(Kujikata Osadamegaki)*, and agencies were created to insure that these laws and regulations would be observed—any infractions being swiftly and mercilessly dealt with.

The society which emerged during the Tokugawa period as a result of the reorganization effected by the Edo government was structurally arranged as illustrated in chart 3. There were a series of classes, which, in the order of their importance, included the military class at the apex *(buke)*, with its professional warriors and their families *(shi, bushi)*; followed by the agricultural class (*no*), with its peasants or farmers *(hyakusho)*; the industrial class *(ko)*, which consisted mainly of artisans *(shokunin)*; and the commercial class *(sko)*, represented by merchants *(akindo, chonin)*.

It is interesting to note the continuation of a fundamental attachment to this feudal division even after the power to rule had been nominally restored to the emperor in 1868 and Japan had officially become a "modern" state. The laws issued in 1869, for example, replaced the feudal system of the *buke* with a "new" order listing court nobility and feudal barons (daimyo) as aristocrats *(kazoku)*, the warriors or former samurai as gentry *(shizoku)*, and lumping all the other subjects of the nation (such as farmers, artisans, merchants, and even outcast groups) under the single qualification of commoners *(heimin)*.

Under the Tokugawa, the titular emperor and his court nobles were forced to live in virtual seclusion in Kyoto. There they were kept under continual, direct surveillance by appointed officials of the Edo government, and their financial affairs were strictly regulated in such a fashion as to deprive them of the necessary means of rallying dissenting clans to their banner or of subsidizing independent forces of their own. Their political relevance thus became almost nil, although their excellence in the cultural achievements of the age continued to be encouraged and widely admired. As related by Webb, the main outline of Tokugawa policy in regard to the emperor was that of, on the one hand, rescuing him from the depths of utter destitution into which he had fallen during the previous age of continuous warfare, while, on the other hand, simultaneously isolating him to insure his continuing political irrelevance. As this author so aptly expressed it: "Though Ieyasu may be said to have constructed a prison and housed emperors there, it was a prison that had all the dignity and splendor of a cathedral" (Webb, 58).

Kept under equally strict surveillance after their ranks had been decimated during the Ashikaga (Muromachi) and Momoyama periods, forbidden to gather together ever again to form those large communities which had proved so uncontrollable in the past, the priests and monks of the various religious sects of feudal Japan formed another class, relegated almost exclusively to spiritual and educational dimensions.

As for the commoners *(heimin)* who formed by far the largest and the most productive segments of the nation,

> however rich they were or however wise and intelligent they were, whether they wished or not, [they] had almost no political right whatsoever. Their condition is summed up by Mr. Dickins in his "Life of Sir Henry Parkes," in the following words: "The people were scarcely items, politically speaking, in old Japan. Their business was to grow, make, carry, multiply and—above all—pay taxes." (Hayashi, 70)

During the reign of the Tokugawa clan, the military class formed "an immense standing army" numbering "over 400,000 families." In Brinkley's words: "It was an exceptionally costly army, for the families of the samurai had to be maintained as well as the samurai themselves; and the officers, that is to say, the feudal nobles and their chief vassals, enjoyed revenues far in excess of any emoluments ever accounted elsewhere on account of military service" (Brinkley[1], 116). The country was divided officially into provinces and districts, over which the Tokugawa exercised the powers of military government and fiscal control, either directly through special agencies or indirectly through the provincial lords (daimyo) of certain powerful military clans who had been appointed or reconfirmed as regional governors by the Tokugawa after 1600. These provinces irradiated like spokes from the political center of the nation, Edo, where the shogun resided with his government and the cohorts of warriors under his direct command. The size and location of each province depended upon the political importance of the governor appointed by the Tokugawa to rule there: governors belonging to clans unswervingly loyal to the Tokugawa were positioned closer to the center, while those considered less trustworthy were relegated to provinces further away, at the periphery of the kingdom.

> The central part of Japan, including the Kanto Plain on the East and the old capital in the West, was held directly by the Tokugawa themselves, by various branches of the family, and by the feudal lords and warriors who had backed Ieyasu in the great battle for supremacy in 1600. This central area was strategically the heart of the country. It contained most of the larger plains and most of the best agricultural land of Japan, and also a large proportion of the commercial towns and cities. (Reischauer[1], 81)

The shogun ruled supreme from Edo over all these territories. His government, in accordance with the military traditions of the class he represented, was called *bakufu*—a denomination which, as previously noted, was the ancient name for the generalissimo's headquarters or tent on the battlefield during the

Kamakura period. This term was used until the Restoration to designate the headquarters of successive dynasties of Tokugawa leaders.

The shogun resided in a mighty castle in Edo—a vivid contrast to the dwelling place of the emperor in Kyoto. As described by Brinkley, the shogun's immense fortress was surrounded by a triple barrier of huge moats, "the outermost measuring nine and a half miles in length, the innermost one and a half, their scarps built up with colossal blocks of granite" (Brinkley[2], 10).

Even the gardens inside these walls, with their sophisticated grace intended to be reminiscent of Heian culture, could not conceal the military nature of the roads and paths leading to the central buildings. They constituted a veritable labyrinth whose pattern was a heavily guarded secret, and they passed beneath bridges or were lined with bastions in such a way as to expose any unwelcome guests, regardless of their number, to a concentrated attack with bows and arrows, cross-bows, or firearms. Rodrigo de Vivero y Velasco (1564-1636), who visited this castle in 1609, remarked upon its huge moats with their openings for guns, its massive drawbridge and ramparts. At the first gate he passed through two thousand warriors armed with harquebuses (guns with hooks) and muskets, divided into two ranks. At the second gate stood four hundred warriors armed with pikes and lances; three hundred more, armed with the curved spear *(naginata)*, stood at the third gate. The same author relates that the armories of this enormous military compound contained enough armors, spears, swords, and muskets "to equip one hundred thousand men" (Cooper, 141).

According to Yazaki, the construction of this elaborate stronghold began before 1607 and was completed in 1639 under Iemitsu, third shogun of the Tokugawa clan. Lavishly furnished, its central sector covered 181.4 acres. Moreover, it could easily accommodate, in the splendor to which they had become accustomed, "over 260 daimyo, together with 50,000 standard-bearers if necessary" (Yazaki, 177).

Oda Nobunaga had realized that the numerous fortifications scattered all over Japan represented a basic challenge to the attempt of any lord or clan to attain national supremacy. Each castle, in fact, formed a base of operations not only for defensive purposes but, more importantly, for launching invasions or revolts. Nobunaga, therefore, issued directives *(ikkoku-ichijorei)* ordering all provincial lords who had sworn allegiance to him to see to it that there should be "but one central castle in each province" (Yazaki, 129); all other fortresses and outposts were to be dismantled promptly. Ieyasu implemented the edict during the Genna era (1615-24) with a thoroughness that left most provincial lords without any defensive castle *(shiro-kengo)*, leaving them only "provincial strongholds" *(tokoro-kengo)*. In relation to himself and his most loyal warlords, however, as the records would seem to indicate, the edict was not applicable.

Of all the warriors concentrated in Edo, almost one-half were kept in a state of constant readiness under the direct command of the shogun. They were called "direct retainers" of the *bakufu (bakushin)* and were divided into two major categories: *the hatamoto* and the *gokenin*. The other half *(baishiri)* included warriors from all the provincial clans who served their lords in the capital, or waited upon the shogun after having been delegated to him by their lords for specific duties or a certain period of time.

The title of *hatamoto* is generally translated as "banner knight" or "standard-bearer," and it was traditionally assigned to personal bodyguards of the military commander who rode with him and protected him in battle. The Tokugawa assigned this title to retainers *(okunishu)* who had served Ieyasu when he was still Lord of Mikawa, as well as to retainers who had pledged their loyalty to him after he had left that province *(kingokushu)* or after he had settled in Edo *(kantoshu)*. It was also bestowed by the Tokugawa upon descendants of families of illustrious lineage or "men of exceptional learning and skill" (Yazaki, 202). These *hatamoto* constituted a "petty nobility" of a sort, whose members served as officials *(yakukata)* in the deliberative and executive agencies of government or as castle guards *(bankata)*.

In the former capacity, they occupied such important positions as commissioners of finance *(kanjo-bugyo)*, town magistrates *(machi-bugyo)*, grand censors *(o-metsuke)* in charge of surveillance of the various daimyo, censors *(metsuke)* supervising their own ranks, and officers *(hyojosho-tomariyaku)* carrying out the decisions of higher commissioners of the *bakufu.* They had the privilege of maintaining watch over the grounds and gates of the shogun's castle, which they patrolled regularly in five groups *of hatamoto* and subalterns *(banshi).* Organized into professional groups *(yoriai-gumi),* they lived in or around the central Edo compound, supporting themselves on incomes geared to the rank each occupied within the category—ranging from five hundred to ten thousand *koku* yearly, paid to them directly from the shogun's warehouses. In 1722, according to Tsukahira, they numbered 5,205. Regardless of the difference in their ranks and functions, they soon became an elite devoted ferociously to the shogun, extremely jealous of their prerogatives and enormously powerful.

The title *gokenin* is variously translated as "honorable member of the household," "inferior vassal," or "household member." In the Kamakura period, it was assigned to warrior leaders who had pledged their loyalty to a warlord. The title was used in Muromachi times to identify vassals of warrior leaders of *kyunin* rank and, finally, was applied to Tokugawa retainers who were granted fiefs of less than a hundred *koku.* Unlike the *hatamoto,* the *gokenin* did not enjoy the privilege of direct audience with the shogun but could be promoted, for excellent service and exceptional merit, to *hatamoto.* They also resided in and around the Edo castle and constituted another, larger category of armed men ready to be moved into battle at any time. In 1722, there were over seventeen thousand registered *gokenin.*

The medieval chronicles of Japan are filled with the exploits of these special "guards," who came to consider themselves the new military aristocracy of Edo. They were envied by all the warriors affiliated with provincial clans, and their privileged position as retainers linked to the most powerful clan in feudal Japan (which gave them easier access to offices of control throughout the land) made them generally insufferable. In particular, their familiarity with the offices of censorship and positions as secret inspectors *(metsuke)* caused them to be feared by all. Proud and always suspicious of people's motives, they were quick to take offense; the chronicles relate many cases of armed clashes in Edo between the *hatamoto* and the warriors of provincial clans, between the latter and the *gokenin,* and even between the *hatamoto* and the *gokenin.*

It is interesting to note that, when the restoration of power to the emperor in Kyoto was formally declared by edict in 1867, cohorts of "banner knights," large numbers of "house vassals," and warriors of clans loyal to the Tokugawa began immediately to move from Osaka toward Kyoto with the intention of suppressing that which, to their eyes, was a treacherous revolt against the shogunate, which had ruled the land and guaranteed their exalted titles for over two hundred years. They were crushed in battle at Toba and Fushimi by the imperial forces, formally declared enemies of the emperor, and forced to retreat to Edo. Finally, in 1868, by order of the shogun himself (who had fled the besieged city), they surrendered. Eventually, most of these once proud representatives of martial prowess and power had to abandon their mansions in Edo, release their own retainers, and either return to their regional country fiefs (if these had not been confiscated) or engage in commercial enterprises.

In Tokugawa times, at the height of their privileged careers, both the *hatamoto* and the *gokenin* lived in mansions to the west and north of the shogun's castle in Edo. This castle, with all its magnificent splendor, was actually a huge military enclave whose inner moats surrounded the mansions of the more powerful warlords of those clans faithful to the shogun. Chieftains of lower category and rank had establishments closer to the periphery of this enormous site, but still within an area protected by the outer moats. Those direct vassals who had been allowed or ordered to establish residences and observation posts outside Edo were generally within a day's traveling distance from the castle and thus able to answer promptly any summons from the shogun, whatever the time or season.

The deliberative structure of the Tokugawa government, as illustrated in Chart 4, consisted of the following major agencies: often presided over by a Grand Elder *(tairo),* a council of four or five Elders *(roju),* who were selected from among the most powerful daimyo of the *fudai* category who owned their own castles; a council of Younger Elders *(waka-doshiyori),* also selected from the *fudai* daimyo, but who did not possess castles of their own; the commissioners of temples and shrines *(jisha-bugyo)*; the commis-

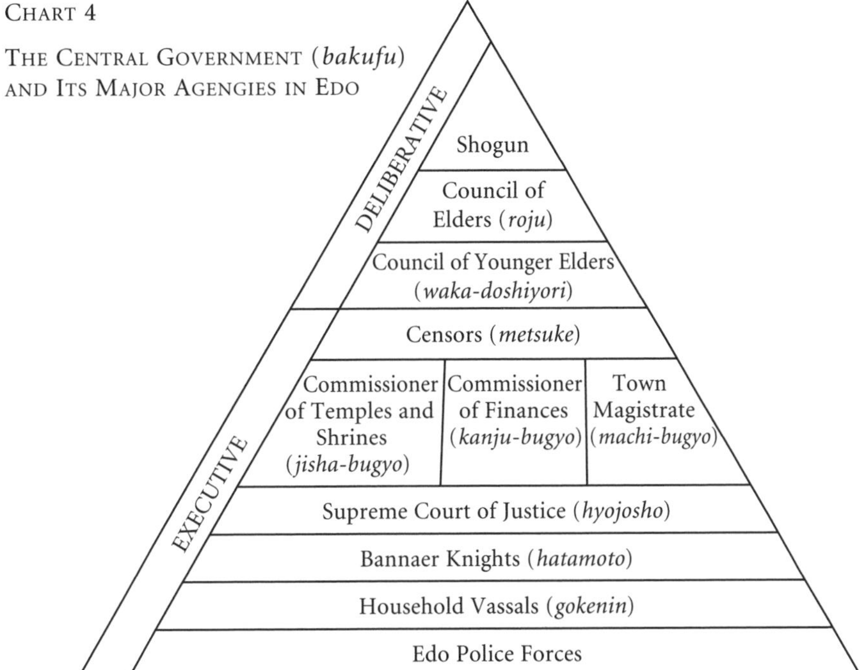

sioners of finances *(kanjo-bugyo)*; the town magistrates *(machi-bugyo)*, who formed the supreme court of justice *(hyojosho)*; and the powerful censors *(metsuke)*, presided over by the Grand Censor *(o-metsuke)*. Under these agencies were positioned a vast and differentiated body of executives embracing the previously mentioned *hatamoto* and *gokenin*, the tax collectors *(daikan)*, and the police forces. The latter were in charge of the Edo districts and consisted of guards *(yoriki)*, policemen *(doshin)*, patrollers *(okappiki)*, and official supervisors who controlled points of major and minor passage within the city. Supervisors of military residences *(tsujiban)* were further divided according to their area of surveillance: supervisors of *hatamoto* districts *(kumiai-tsujiban)*, supervisors of daimyo districts *(daimyo-tsujiban)*, and direct supervisors of the government *(kogi-tsujiban)*. The civilian districts had their own supervisors *(jishimban)* and gate-watchmen *(bantaro)* who closed the gates at the end of each street in the town at 10 P.M., after which no one was allowed to pass in or out without official permission.

In 1600, Ieyasu had begun to grant sites in and around Edo to his most trusted vassals and to the provincial governors, who consequently found themselves with two or more official residences. The size of these sites was determined on the basis of the *tsubo*, a measurement equivalent to approximately 36 square feet, and the sites could range from 90,000 square feet for lower-ranking feudal lords to 252,000 square feet for the highest ranking and most powerful among them.

Leaders of the loyal military cohorts of the shogun lived in splendid, fortified mansions within the city proper and scattered throughout the countryside surrounding it. All daimyo had to maintain mansions in Edo, where they were required to remain in residence in alternate years and where the members of their immediate families (wives, sons, etc.) had to remain whenever the governors visited their fiefs. These mansions *(yashiki)* were generally built in accordance with the ancient military design of the encampment—with the general's tent in the middle, surrounded by those of his officers and, at the outer limits, those of the warriors. The provincial castles of feudal Japan also followed this basic blueprint, with the stronghold in the middle and the warriors' barracks surrounding it placed near the outer walls.

In Edo, the private mansions consisted of a modified version of that design, with a long, uninterrupted building *(nagaya)* so constructed as to enclose the garden and the central palace of the feudal lord. That building, with strong walls on the side facing the street and rows of fortified windows, contained the retainers' barracks and their armories. Facing the main street was the central gate *(o-mon, omote-mon),* whose huge, armored portals opened wide only on great occasions. Normal traffic was handled through smaller side-doors (the front gate *[tsuyo-mon],* the back gate *[ura-mon],* and the smaller posterns called *hijo-mon, yojinguchi* and *kuguri),* all of which opened into a yard lined with guard-rooms, which were

> ornamented with bows and arrows, lances, firearms, and staves with iron-heads studded with spikes, serving as grappling irons wherewith to seize and disarm any unwelcome intruder. Whenever a retainer passed out, he hung up in the guard-room the wooden ticket, inscribed with his name, which he always carried at his girdle; on his return to the *yaskiki* this ticket was restored to him. By this means the porters could tell at a glance how many retainers were absent on leave at any time. (McClatchie[1], 171)

The *nagaya* surrounded the inner barracks *(naka-nagaya)* which sheltered other troops and included storehouses, as well as buildings assigned to those higher officials who managed the clan's affairs for their lord. These inner-houses, both in Edo and in the provinces, contained the

> residences for the councillors *(karo),* the commercial agent *(yonin),* the representative of the lord during his absence *(rusui),* the financial officer *(kanjo bugiyo),* the building officer *(sakuji bugiyo),* and the doctor *(isha).* In the great clans, the number of these officers was considerable, but in the *yashiki* of the lower daimyo and of the *hatamoto* there were frequently fewer officers. (McClatchie[1], 172)

A paved way led from the main gate to the entrance of the main building, the residence *(go-den)* of the lord, which selected retainers kept under strict surveillance day and night. These retainers "were the only vassals (with the exception of a few pages to attend on the lord) who were permitted to pass the night in the *go-den.* All others, including even the cooks and the scullions, had quarters allotted to them in the nagaya, and came over early in the morning to resume their duties" (McClatchie[1], 173).

At the beginning of the Tokugawa period, a site for a single mansion in Edo was granted to each daimyo, in addition to the one he had in the provinces. With the passing of time, however, as ostentatious display and parasitic inactivity began to erode the stern military virtues of the past, many lords began to acquire three or more "chief mansions" *(kami-yashiki),* in addition to their urban and suburban middle *(naka-yashiki)* and lower *(shimo-yashiki)* mansions, and a variety of summer residences both large *(besso)* and small *(kakae-yashiki).*

Until 1868, according to Brinkley, so many of these "ominous" *yashiki,* with their extensive *nagaya,* lined the streets of Edo and

> such a multitude of their inmates were to be met striding along, a pair of razor-edged swords in their

> girdles and the pride of arms in their mien, that for all the pretty parks and dainty mansions of the nobles, for all the disguise of soft sward and tender-sprayed pines that overlay the grimness of the central castle's battlements, Edo could never be mistaken for [other than] what it was, the citadel of a military system embracing all the warlike resources of a battle-loving nation. (Brinkley[2], 13)

The basic problem confronting the Tokugawa rulers of feudal Japan was that of controlling the whole in order to control its parts, and vice-versa. As early as 1636, Japanese subjects were expressly forbidden by law to leave the country or, once having left, ever to return to its shores—the penalty being death in either case. Having thus effectively sealed off Japan from the international community, its rulers enforced a system of rigid separation of each province from all the others, insisting that even within the individual provinces the movement of various subjects in and around their villages and towns be severely limited or, if necessary and authorized, strictly controlled. The main land routes, known as the "Five Roads" *(gokaido)*, and the roads linking the provinces were kept under constant surveillance. Garrisons with special inspectors were placed at barriers *(sekisho)* strategically located along these routes. At each barrier, every traveler was required to present a pass *(sekisho-fuda)*, issued by his or her territorial superiors, before being allowed to continue his or her journey. This pass was known as the *sekisho-tegata* for men and the *onna-tegata* for women. At these barriers, women were subject to particular scrutiny, as Statler points out in his *Japanese Inn*. Their value to the shogun as hostages was incalculable, and each woman's *onna-tegata* minutely specified her position in society (widow, wife, prostitute, etc.) and her physical appearance so as to prevent misrepresentation through disguise, of which the Japanese of the period were masters. Each woman was given a physical examination by officials of her own sex, and the results were closely compared to the description inscribed on her *onna-tegata*. If any discrepancy was noted, she might be detained for days until the case could be decided in Edo.

The history of Japan contains descriptions of several famous incidents that took place at the Hakone barrier on the Eastern Sea Route (Tokaido) between Kyoto and Edo, as well as at the Fukushima barrier on the Middle Route (Nakasendo). The essential objective of this system was obviously to control the daimyo, their women, and their weapons, since both "outgoing women and incoming guns" *(de-onna ni iri-deppo)*, as we read in Tsukahira, "were seen as the necessary first steps in any attack upon the shogunate" (51). The daimyo were, in fact, subject to the most stringent system of control imaginable. It was, moreover, so effective a system that the decentralizing and separatistic tendencies of certain daimyo (especially those ruling clans positioned far from Edo) were repressed for over two hundred years and had to wait for a fortuitous convergence of favorable circumstances—the "coming of the barbarians" in 1853 and the weakening of the Tokugawa government from within—before they could reassert themselves.

The methods devised to achieve full control over these important upper echelons of the *buke* are illustrated in the following section. The shogun exercised the full power of a military dictator over the masses inhabiting the provinces under his direct supervision and also, through the daimyo, over the masses in the other provinces of the country. Farmers were registered in their villages and forbidden to leave their assigned places. Merchants and artisans in the towns and large provincial centers had to be duly registered with appropriate guilds or corporations *(za)*, whose officials had the duty and the responsibility of maintaining tight control over their members and keeping the higher authorities informed concerning any developments of an "uncommon" nature among their membership. The warriors themselves were tightly supervised through a chain of direct superiors linked to one another vertically by the legal institution of vassalage established through an oath of allegiance and loyalty to a clan, house, or individual, and duly registered by the official keepers of records. As in Edo, control over the movement of commoners in metropolitan centers all over Japan was maintained through the installation of special gates across the intersections of every two streets. These gates were supervised by special officers of the daimyo who checked the passes of anyone trying to move from one ward to another at night when the gates were closed, or during the day,

for that matter, if the individual in question was not known to the ward officials.

The penalties for unauthorized movement and other crimes were exceptionally harsh and (much to the surprise of Western observers, but quite in keeping with the principle of collective responsibility typical of the clan culture) involved not only the guilty party but his entire family.

Penalties were of two types: the heavier penalties ranged from public admonition to confinement, public flogging, expatriation, and execution; the lighter ones included penalties such as public exposure, tattooing, confiscation of property, and reduction in class or rank. In accordance with the primary division in classes, punishment was inflicted with differing rituals and in varying measures according to the rank of the criminal, with the warriors bearing the heaviest brunt of the penal code for any infractions, which were seen as a direct insult to the system they represented and were expected to uphold.

In examining the primary morality of feudal Japan, we saw that the rapport upon which the whole conception of the state rested was that of master-subordinate. The particular interpretation of Confucianism which the Tokugawa government adopted as its inspirational theory of state was that of Chu Hsi (in Japanese, Shu Ki, 1130-1200), who had stressed the unquestioning and loyal attitude of inferior toward superior. His presentation of Confucian ideas *(shushi-gaku* or *sogaku)* became "the theoretical foundation for feudal society" (Goedertier, 273), to the point of forcing the exclusion, by edict *(kansei igaku no kin)*, of heterodox learning from the state schools.

Shushi-gaku emphasized the concepts of vertical hierarchy and stern pragmatism in discharging the duties assigned by one's superior within the hierarchy. There was no mention of social preeminence based upon personal merit rather than heredity, nor was the conception of social justice impartially and broadly applied (to everyone, including the emperor and shogun) a part of this interpretation. This version of Confucian theory concerning government and society was to spark a revival of interest in Chinese studies and give birth to a school of thought which was not necessarily favorable to the military dictators. In the main, however, and for quite an extended period of time, this interpretation confirmed the shoguns' position and justified their consolidation of power. It also provided material for the clearer formulation of the warrior's "creed" *(bukyo)* and the samurai's "way" *(shido)*—both of which were to blend harmoniously in that particular code of honor known as "The Way of the Warrior" *(bushido)*.

All these legalistic, philosophical, military, and social devices made it extremely unlikely that anything "unexpected" could happen within the country, in practice as well as in theory, without the Tokugawa being immediately informed. They are said to have acquired "the dubious distinction of being one of the first governments in the world to develop an extensive and efficient secret police system and to make of it an important organ of state. With the centuries of experience in such practices, it is not surprising that the secret police should have loomed so large in the political make-up of Japan in recent years" (Reischauer[1], 83-84).

In such a martial culture, there was no place for new ideas or even for ancient but contradictory theories that might have forced a man to confront the problem of personal responsibility, of individual values different from, if not actually contrary to, those of his society. As in every military dictatorship the world has ever known, knowledge was considered a dangerous commodity and its wide dissemination

strictly forbidden. Although limited "Dutch studies" *(rangaku)* were allowed under close official supervision, any breach of the regulations was punishable by death. Not only the members of other classes, but "intrepid samurai, such as Sakuma Shozan, Watanabe Kazan, and Yoshida Shoin, paid with their lives for their desire for wider horizons in knowledge" (Blacker, 305). And even during the declining years of the Tokugawa rule, when the country and its entire social structure groaned and shuddered within the confines of its military bonds, and afterward, when the restoration of political power to the emperor had activated an intense process of adaptation to a frighteningly new international reality, "almost any conceivable obstacle was placed in the way of the aspiring student of Western learning. There were no grammars and few dictionaries; the weight of feudal and Confucian disapproval and even the assassin's sword was directed against him" (Blacker, 305).

The Daimyo

Immediately beneath the Tokugawa clan in order of importance were the clans headed by the daimyo—"the territorial rulers of self-contained political units called *han* which were at once minor states and fiefs" (Tsukahira, 18). The word *daimyo* may be translated as "great names" and seems to have been derived from a combination of *dai* (great) with *myo* or *myoden* (used to identify a rice-producing fief). Notoriously belligerent and generally rapacious, the lords of such estates capable of sustaining them and their military retainers had fought ceaselessly among themselves throughout the early and middle periods of Japan's feudal era. Only leaders such as Nobunaga, Hideyoshi, and, ultimately, Ieyasu had been able to coerce them into a sort of uneasy alliance wherein their individualistic and expansionistic tendencies were controlled by a severely repressive system of checks and balances. Ieyasu and his descendants were (and remained throughout the succession of Tokugawa dynasties) aware that the downfall of the emperor and his court nobles had, to a large extent, been due to lack of control over the provincial centers of military power, which, however necessary for peacekeeping purposes throughout the realm (as well as that of maintaining the other classes of the nation in a state of subjugation), had become increasingly self-sufficient and, in the end, alienated from the emperor and his nobles.

Due to this lack of centralized control, the feudal "barons" had been able to apply and tighten their stranglehold upon the crown and upon all the other classes of Japanese subjects who stood in their way, thus effectively displacing them all. Eventually, the only obstacle revealed itself to be themselves and their individual ambitions. For the Tokugawa, the feudal governors (from whose ranks they had emerged) were, and always remained, the chief source of trouble since they owned and ruled over independent fiefs, maintained their own cohorts of warriors, and had the necessary wealth to finance armed adventures. It was not only conceivable but, in an age of still rampant political instability and military turbulence, a relevant possibility that these daimyo might, if left to their own devices, increase and organize their own military forces beyond the limits considered advisable by the central government in Edo. Those forces, in turn, might be used to unseat the Tokugawa in accordance with the ancient and famous principle of displacing the superior in order to make room for the inferior *(gekokujo)*—a principle of political gamesmanship which had become almost commonplace during pre-Tokugawa times and which the Tokugawa themselves had successfully applied on several occasions.

Accordingly, if on one side these daimyo were not only the powerful leaders of military clans, but also the main instruments of indirect control over the country at large, on the other side, as Tsukahira wrote, "it became the chief preoccupation of the early Tokugawa to weaken and divide" them in order to maintain that control. The measures adopted by the Edo *bakufu* for this purpose were many and thorough. Differences in fief size, income, and rank at the court of the shogun in Edo were established to create artificial barriers among the daimyo, and, naturally, "mutual jealousies and rivalries were kept alive and fostered" (Tsukahira, 27). Continuous and intense surveillance by the shogun's sinister censors *(metsuke)* of the various daimyo (when in Edo in periodical attendance, at home in their own territories, or even in transit from one to the other) insured that their activities would be properly assessed by the shogun on a regular and continuing basis. Finally, their obligatory attendance at the shogun's court every other year, with the concomitant obligation to leave their wives and children in Edo when they returned home, reduced their freedom of action substantially.

The number of daimyo during the Tokugawa period seems to have been about 260. Their status was qualified according to several interconnecting criteria. The first criterion was based upon and determined by the feudal relationship between a daimyo and the shogun himself. Daimyo who were collateral members of the Tokugawa house, for example, were qualified as "related feudatories" *(shimpan)* or "family daimyo" *(kamon)*. They included the "three exalted families" *(sanke)*, occupied provinces closer to Edo, and held important offices in the central government.

The *shimpan* daimyo were followed by the "hereditary daimyo" *(fudai)*, who had been vassals of the Tokugawa since before the great and decisive battle of Sekigahara. They also occupied important positions in the *bakufu*, and their fiefs protectively surrounded the central contiguous territories which were under direct Tokugawa supervision.

The "outside" daimyo *(tozama)* were those important clan leaders, once peers of Ieyasu, who had acknowledged his title of shogun after the battle of Sekigahara. Their fiefs were generally located beyond those of the *fudai*.

These major categories were further classified according to other criteria based on the type of territory assigned to each daimyo, his holdings, and the productivity at his disposal. Lords of a province *(kunimochi* or *kokushu)*, for example, ranked above other lords of less definite territorial stature *(jun-kokushu* or *kunimochi-nami)*, who were followed, in their turn, by the lords of a castle *(josku)*, by those whose titles were equivalent to that of a lord of a castle *(joshu-nami)*, those without castles *(mujo)*, and the possessors of residences *(jinya-mochi, ryoshu)*. Finally, daimyo were classified according to the seats they were authorized to occupy in an audience with the shogun. These seats, the assembly halls containing them, and the seating arrangement for each category of daimyo are illustrated in Chart 5.

When being invested with the title of daimyo, a subject of this, the highest rank in the *buke* class under the shogun, had to submit written oaths and swear personal fealty to the shogun. This ritual, and the registration of the oath in the records of the *bakufu* in Edo, was repeated by each daimyo every time a new

Chart 5

Classification of Daimyo Ranks
according to the Audience Room at the Shogun's Court in Edo

Rank	Audience Room	Category of Daimyo
1st	Grand Corridor *(o-roka-zume)*	Members of the three exalted families *(sanke)*
2nd	Lounge *(tamarima-zume)*	Members of the Matsudaira families *(gokamon)* and of the hereditary daimyo *(fudai)*
3rd	Main Hall *(o-hiroma-zume)*	Members of the Matsudaira family *(gokamon)*, of the hereditary daimyo *(fudai)*, and of the "outside" daimyo *(tozama)* with over 100,000 *koku* in yearly income
4th	Reception Hall *(teikannoma-zume)*	Members of daimyo families of the third rank with less than 100,000 *koku* in yearly income
5th	Willow Room *(yanaginoma-zume)*	"Outside" daimyo *(tozama)* with less than 50,000 *koku* in yearly income
6th	Wild Goose Room *(karinoma-zume)*	Hereditary daimyo *(fudai)* with less than 50,000 *koku* yearly income
7th	Chrysanthemum Room *(kikunoma-zume)*	Daimyo without castle *(mujo daimyo)* with a yearly income between 10,000 and 20,000 *koku*
8th	Other less-celebrated halls	Other lords

Tokugawa leader assumed the title of shogun. With this oath, the daimyo obligated himself to perform a series of duties. Primary among these were his military obligations, such as maintaining his quota of warriors in active service and ready to move into battle at the shogun's command, whenever needed; he also had to provide troops for guard duty at any station specified by Edo, such as the thirty-six gates of the shogun's castle, the imperial court at Kyoto, various coastal sites, the barriers and checking points along the highways, and as shogun's envoys on official missions. Duties of a more administrative nature were those of keeping peace within the territories under their direct control and providing funds, materials, and workers for public projects devised and assigned by the shogun *(tetsudai)*.

In relation to their fiefs, each of these feudal lords "was a paternalistic but absolute monarch. . . . Aiding him in his rule over the soldiers, peasants, and merchants of the principality was a class of officials and military officers, who formed the little court at the central castle of the daimyo and lived on the hereditary salaries he assigned them and their families" (Reischauer[1], 77).

He exercised judicial and administrative control over his subjects and supervised them through the use of cohorts of warriors that, while belonging to one or more military clans, were pledged to him as the *uji-no-osa* and as the rightful representative of the shogun. Very seldom, however, was a military governor sent to rule over military clans not related to him, either directly or indirectly, by ties of blood, territory, or sworn oath.

The warriors who served under the daimyo in his fief were also organized into a vertical system of categories and ranks which varied from clan to clan, from region to region. Some of his retainers, called *tachikaeri*, followed him anywhere he went or resided, whether in his fief or in Edo; others *(jofu)* remained permanently in Edo with their lord's and their own families, as guards of his mansion in the capital; and still others *(kimmuban)* were rotated periodically to fill the various clan offices in the provinces and in Edo.

One example of a large and complex clan ruling in the provinces after the Tokugawa's rise to power is provided by the clan of Yamanouchi Kazutoyo, who was sent by Ieyasu to rule as daimyo over Tosa in the Shikoku Islands. This province had formerly belonged to the Chosokabe clan, whose members (unfortunately for them) had opposed the Tokugawa and had subsequently been dispossessed of the estates

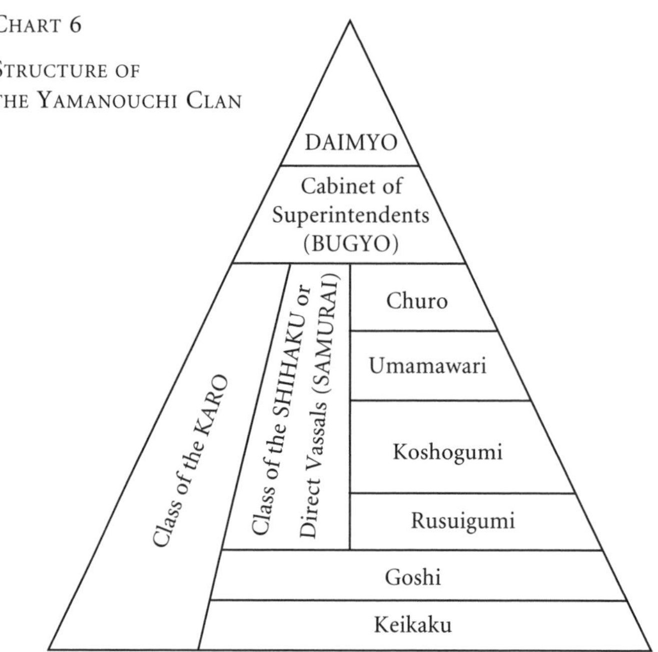

they had taken from the Ichijo clan. Following the classic pattern of vertical hierarchy, the Yamanouchi clan was structured like a pyramid (see Chart 6). At the top was the daimyo, with his advisory and administrative cabinet of superintendents *(bugyo).* He owned the best and most productive land *(kura)* in the province. This land was divided into large classes of territories such as *honden,* prime, original land which had been cultivated for ages, and *shinden,* land cleared for cultivation after his appointment as governor of the province. He also supervised and granted tenure to new but secondary lands, such as the *yaguchi,* cleared by retainers of samurai rank, and the *ryochi,* cleared by retainers of *goshi* rank. All these lands were variously classified as central lands of the clan or "house-lands" *(yashiki);* as rice-fields *(ta)*; as up-lands *(hata),* usually reserved for the cultivation of wheat, barley, vegetables, etc.; as pasture or grass-lands *(hara)*; as virgin-lands, forests, woods; and so on.

Under the provincial governor of Tosa were two classes of retainers. The first was the class of the *karo* or Elder Councillors. These retainers were semi-independent, owned their own lands, ruled over their own villages and farmers who paid taxes directly to them, and commanded their own warriors. The *karo,* whom Grinnan rightly qualified as "under-lords," were very powerful and usually paid no taxes to the daimyo. Although they were required to provide the governor with troops when he needed them, this was done only after they had cleared the daimyo's request with the central government *(bakufu)* in Edo. Naturally, they were "the subject of jealous concern to the daimyo," but their effectiveness in checking his political ambition and power within the boundaries of his assigned province proved itself again and again during the Tokugawa period.

The second class of retainers consisted of warriors who owed allegiance directly to the provincial governor. They were called *shihaku* or samurai, and their cohorts were also divided into several ranks, each with its own prerogatives, privileges, duties, and income. In the first category of direct retainers were the *churo,* who had the right to wear the two swords *(daisho)* and to ride on horseback "in time of peace and of war." They were not paid in rice but in prime land from the *honden* or *shinden* of the daimyo—land which was capable of producing the quantity of rice their position entitled them to. These lands, known as *chigyo,* gave to their owners the title of *jikata-tori.* In the second category of direct retainers were the *uma-mawari* warriors, some of whom were paid in land and some in rice, while in the third and largest

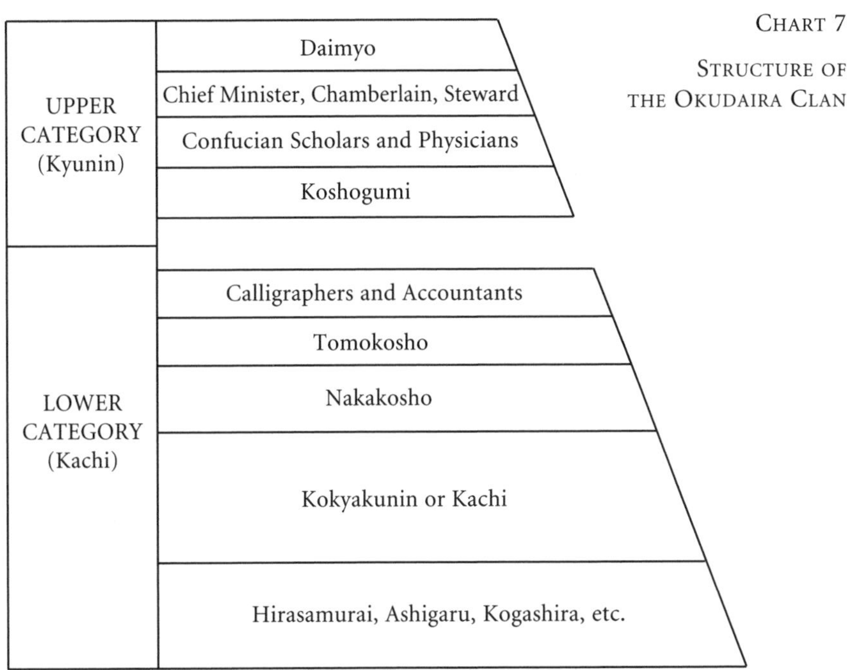

CHART 7

STRUCTURE OF THE OKUDAIRA CLAN

category we find the *koshogumi,* who were paid in rice produced on the daimyo's *kura,* according to the rice system of income *(kokuso).* All these warriors had the right to wear the two swords, but only some of them were permitted to ride horses. In the third category were also those retainers who were paid in rice but not according to the rice system of income; their emoluments were usually referred to as *fuchi-kippu.*

The provincial governor of Tosa also commanded the loyalty of two other classes of warriors, known as *goshi* and *keikaku.* The *goshi,* or "country-warriors," were ancient retainers *(kerai)* of the defeated Chosokabe clan who were left "in undisputed possession of the lands they had received from their former masters" because they had submitted "gracefully" to the new masters appointed by the Tokugawa. Grinnan qualified the position of these *goshi* as being "unique in the annals of Japanese feudalism," and their number, naturally, was quite limited. They also owned lands and horses (which they had the right to ride), wore the *daisho,* or two swords, fought in wars, could dispose of their own property—although if they sold all their lands they lost their titles, and in any case could transmit their titles only to a firstborn heir. It is interesting to note that after the Meiji Restoration, while most of the daimyo appointed by the Tokugawa had to return their estates to the new central government of the emperor, the *goshi* were allowed to retain their holdings because their titles had not been granted them by the Tokugawa. Below these country warriors, finally, was a class of retainers known as *keikaku,* or "country gentry," who were paid in rice, wore two swords but possessed no horses, and generally lived far from the provincial castle at the outskirts of cities or country towns, "within a day's call" of the daimyo's main residence.

Describing the Okudaira clan of Nakatsu, Fukuzawa gives us an idea of stratification of functions and denominations in an average-size clan (see Chart 7). The Okudaira clan, in fact, consisted of about 1,500 men entitled to wear the *daisho,* or two swords. They were divided into two categories, upper and lower—the former being "about one third the size of the latter." In the upper category of warriors *(kyunin)* were included the chief minister, chamberlain, steward, Confucian scholars, physicians, and retainers of first rank *(koshogumi),* as well as "a body of attendants on the daimyo consisting especially of boys who had not yet come of age." The lower category of warriors *(kachi)* included the calligraphers and accountants who discharged the duties of administrators and bookkeepers for the clan; the daimyo's attendants who always escorted him, bearing his swords *(tomokosho)*; and others such as the armorers, stable boys, grooms *(nakakosho)*, the large cohorts of palace guards *(koyakunin)*, and the foot soldiers *(ashigaru)*. Beneath these we find lightly armed troops, such as the *kogashira*, led by *chugen*.

Finally, the daimyo owed the shogun the service of attendance, which was officially described as "the duty of attendance upon the shogun by turns," or "reporting for attendance alternately"—the institution of *sankin-kotai*, which obliged each daimyo to leave his province every other year and spend several months in Edo at the shogun's court. When the daimyo returned to his fief, he was required to leave his wife and children in Edo as "guests of state"—actually as hostages. This practice was strictly enforced and minutely regulated, as was the restriction on the number of warriors the daimyo could take with him from his fief, since the natural tendency (often more for reasons of prestige and appearance than for fomenting a revolt) was to travel with as imposing a contingent of warriors as a daimyo's wealth would permit. Frequent congestion in Edo and upon the highways was a common occurrence, as were the incidents caused by concern for precedence at crossings or barriers. In 1721, new regulations from Edo established that the rulers of fiefs yielding 200,000 *koku* of rice or more were not to travel with or station in Edo more than 20 cavalrymen *(bajo)*, 130 foot soldiers *(ashigaru)*, and 300 petty attendants *(chugen, ninsoku)*. And yet, it was not uncommon for powerful daimyo to disregard these injunctions. As Tsukahira notes, the lord of Mori in Choshu kept over two thousand warriors in his mansion in Edo. It is not difficult to imagine the effect produced by this and other bands of mounted knights, warriors of high rank, foot soldiers, and assorted troops as a long procession, containing the palanquin of the lord and those of his most important vassals in the middle of the column, moved at a majestic pace through towns and along the roads of the nation, their standards floating high and their weapons glinting in the sun. These periodical journeys became one of the most salient events of the Tokugawa period and its most stirring form of military pageantry. Only time and the progressive impoverishment of the *buke* gradually reduced these processions in size and pomp. After 1747, "the average size of a daimyo's procession ranged between 150 and 300 persons" (Tsukahira, 80).

The daimyo, as the highest representative of the military class after the shogun, had to adhere strictly to the Thirteen Laws of the Military Houses *(Buke Sho-hatto)* promulgated by Ieyasu. These laws imposed upon each daimyo, among other obligations, that of capturing and surrendering immediately to the shogun's representatives any rebels who were to be found within the boundaries of his domain, since anyone acting against the state acted against the law and social order (Articles 3 and 4). It is interesting to note that the authorities recognized a distinction between that morality which was based upon reason and that which was accepted a priori as the basis of social law. In these articles, for example, it is actually specified that since the law is the essence of social order, reason could be violated in favor of the law, but the law must *never* be violated in favor of reason. Each daimyo had to prevent unauthorized outsiders from entering or remaining in his fief (Article 5). He could not even make any substantial repairs to his castle nor to those of his vassals without the shogun's express authorization, and he was absolutely forbidden to build a new castle or fortifications of any kind (Article 6). He had to send a report to Edo concerning conspiracies being hatched in neighboring domains (Article 7), and he could not enter into any alliance by marriage without the shogun's permission (Article 8)—such an unauthorized act being considered the "root of treason." He could not surround himself with large numbers of retainers when traveling to Edo, unless such an escort was composed of the shogun's own troops. If he were a daimyo of high rank, he might be permitted an escort of about twenty horsemen (Article 9). As an honorary consideration, all daimyo were entitled to wear special types and qualities of official attire (which insured that they would be readily identifiable) and ride in special palanquins (Article 11).

Daimyo retainers in SANKIN-KOTAI procession

The Military Retainer: The Samurai

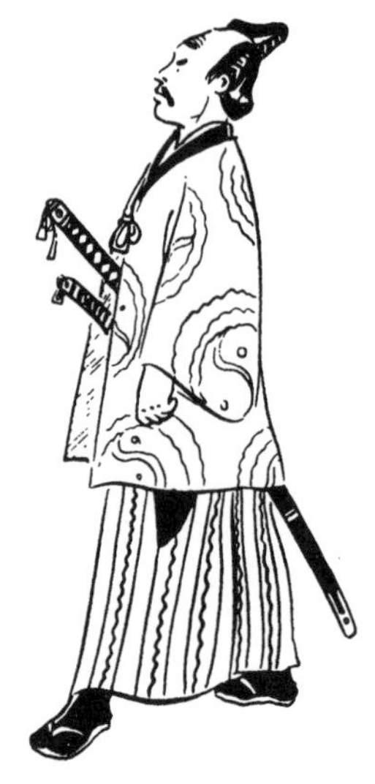

All these retainers in the service of the shogun, or stationed in the provinces under the command of the various daimyo, formed an "immense standing army" (Brinkley[1], 116). From the humblest foot soldier entitled to wear the *daisho* to the highest among the warriors of the upper ranks who were permitted to ride horses, they all belonged to the same warrior class, the *buke,* and were known as men of war *(bushi)* or, more commonly, as retainers *(mononofu, wasarau).* After 1869, they were qualified as former military subjects *(shizoku),* but the world at large continued to refer to them by that Chinese name which has become famous in many languages and is generally translated as "vassal" *(samurahi, samurai).* In its ancient form, the title of "samurai" had once been assigned (according to Frederic) to the leaders of armed clans in the North and, in a slightly modified form *(goshozamurai),* to warriors of aristocratic clans attached to the imperial court during the Muromachi period. Contracted phonetically into "samurai," the term was extended to denote all warriors who were permitted to wear the long and short swords *(daisho)* in the service of a lord, and was more specifically and correctly translated as "one who serves."

Emerging from the mists of the eleventh century, these samurai had witnessed (and often helped to bring about) many portentous changes in the social climate and structure of their land. As we have noted in surveying the major wielders of power in ancient Japan and the instruments through which that power was effectively exercised, the warriors organized under the feudal lords were, by the time Ieyasu elevated them to a position of primary prestige, structured and positioned within categories and ranks whose number and importance varied according to their master's position in the central or provincial hierarchy of the *buke,* the size and wealth of the clan to which they belonged, and the function they were called upon to perform within their clan. The complexity of their professional composition during the Tokugawa period reflected the enormous increase in their number and the enlarged range of their professional sophistication, which had spilled over from the guard-posts and the battlefields into the administrative precincts of the social and political life of Japan. That complexity bore only a faint resemblance to the original simplicity of those military clans which had once been so closely related to, and dependent upon, the productive land of the *myo* as to have been barely distinguishable from the clans of farmers. The prototypes of that early composition were, admittedly, still a factor in the social mix, although submerged beneath the accretions of rank divisions and subdivisions, prestige, wealth, and so forth.

Warriors had once appeared in small, armed groups composed primarily of a leader, a number of mounted horsemen, and additional warriors on foot *(zusa).* The latter, in particular, had been the vital substratum of the class and had become increasingly numerous as the political unrest of the 1500s and 1600s began to offer many farmers and—although to a lesser degree—townsmen, a chance to move up socially and economically (as did Europe's soldiers of fortune) by gaining a position in a clearly ascending class, or by enriching themselves on the spoils of a troubled era. These warriors on foot became known as the fighters with "agile legs" *(ashigaru),* and this category of lower warriors, being directly exposed to the ethics of the upper warriors whom they faithfully obeyed in times of peace or whom they followed unhesitatingly into the thick of battle, gradually acquired the same attachment to and identification with the *buke* as their masters. From their ranks was to emerge Hideyoshi, one of Japan's greatest feudal leaders, who preceded Ieyasu as supreme military dictator *(kampaku)* over the entire country.

The *ashigaru* were followed, in turn, by numerous "small assistants" *(chugen, komono, arashiko)* who performed all the menial and undignified tasks which the categories of warriors above them refused to perform—with increasing regularity.

Chart 8

Major Divisions within the Warrior Army in Feudal Japan

- Leaders
  - General
  - Officer on horseback
- Troops
  - Foot Soldiers
    - Cavalrymen
    - Archers
    - Spearmen
  - Petty Attendants and Servants

General

Officer

Cavalryman

Archer

Spearman

Attendants

These cohorts of warriors and their leaders could all look back, then, upon those ancient days gone by when the appellations of "barbarians" and "rebels" had been hurled at them by an increasingly effete and impotent aristocracy in Kyoto. They had all been denounced at that time as "enemies of the state" who "made illegal use of power and authority; formed federations; practiced military skills daily; gathered and trained men and horses under pretext of hunting; threatened the governors of the districts; looted the population; violated young girls and brides; stole cattle and used them for their own purposes, thus disrupting work in the field" (Leonard, 55). As such, if captured alone or in "gangs armed with bows and arrows," the authorities at one time had even been instructed to "throw them in jail" like common "highway bandits."

By the Tokugawa period, however, these same samurai were said to have displayed all those features which were to make them, according to the observation point selected by a chronicler, either the object of undiluted admiration (often transformed into a formal cult) or the object of total contempt and hatred only mitigated in a few instances by pity for their condition. Between these two extreme approaches to an historical evaluation of their role—one of which saw them as brute instruments of power cleverly manipulated by ambitious masters, while the other praised them as the embodiment of all those virtues a man could ever hope to attain—it has been left for a few observers to view the samurai as the sadly uncomfortable example of that rigid conditioning to which historical circumstances can subject man if and when he slides into an unreserved commitment to any dogma or creed, especially one which future historians, with the broad irony of hindsight, will reveal to have been less noble than it had once appeared.

It is, in fact, the unreserved quality of the retainers' commitment which makes them appear as much the victims of history as its protagonists, since they usually honored their bond to the bitter end—even to the extent of laying down their lives whenever the occasion demanded. This observation seeks to embrace the positive and negative characteristics of the samurai equally, within a comparatively balanced vision of their position in history. It does not, however, absolve their leaders from a large measure of responsibility for the conditioning and use made of the samurai and his skills down through the centuries. These leaders must bear a greater part of the burden of responsibility for the excesses of the *buke,* because they were in positions of great power where the options for good or evil on a large scale were often substantial and because, in positions of eminence, there were more opportunities to study, to observe, and thus to draw conclusions whose ethical imperative must have been insistent—even if widely ignored.

As the specific translation of the term "samurai" clearly denotes, such warriors were men who served a master; therefore, the primary function they were professionally called upon to perform was that of carrying out any and all orders issued by those superiors to whom they had pledged their loyalty and that of their families. This obligation bound each retainer directly to the leader he had chosen or inherited as his lord and who had accepted his oath of loyalty and service. The relationship between the retainer and his lord in feudal times was so binding and exclusivistic that it actually proved a serious obstacle to the further development of the military class, for when the various leaders fought among themselves (as they did for centuries), their cohorts of warriors, for the most part, followed them unquestioningly into one decimating battle after another—until at last the Tokugawa, through cunning, astute alliances, and the effective application of military might, succeeded in uniting all the clans under their suzerainty. This tie between retainer and master also constituted a serious obstacle to national unity after the restoration in 1868, when it was necessary to transfer the bond of loyalty from the clan leader to the head of the Japanese national family, the emperor. Such a transferral of loyalty necessitated an intense phase of reeducation which was, understandably, a turbulent one marked by armed clashes between the conservative retainers of the traditional clans and those of the progressive forces of the emperor, who represented the "new" Japan.

The warrior of feudal times pledged his loyalty in a ceremony whose rites were drawn from the indigenous religion of Japan, Shinto, with its emphasis on the cult of ancestors. Gaspar Vilela, S.J., (1525-72) wrote that the pledge was inscribed on a scroll *(kishomon)* with a brush dipped in the warrior's own blood

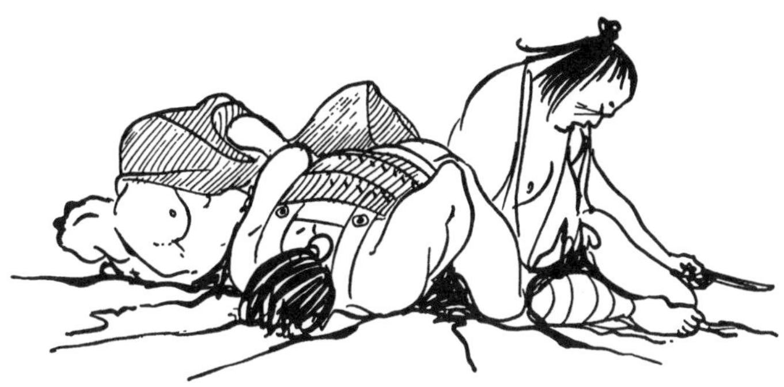

(keppan), then burned before the deities venerated by that particular clan, the ashes being dissolved in liquid and subsequently swallowed. The pledge, naturally, was duly inscribed in the clan's records, and the retainer, his family, and his dependents became totally identified with their master, whose desires and wishes became, from that moment on, their own. So all-encompassing was the bond thus established that when a master died (even of natural causes) many of his retainers took their own lives in order to follow him in death as they had followed him in life. This type of self-immolation was called *junshi,* and it often left a clan decimated by the loss of many of its most valiant vassals. In fact, this practice became so common that it had to be forbidden by law and the proscription enforced by the inflicting of harsh penalties upon the retainer's family if he defied the law. And many a master, in order to safeguard his own family, had to explicitly forbid his retainers to commit mass suicide if and when he should die.

This custom, although it became less common, never disappeared entirely, however. One of the most famous episodes in Japanese literature dealing with the feudal period is that of the mass suicide of the forty-seven *ronin* after they had avenged their lord. The most notable modern case may well be that of Count Maresuke Nogi (1849-1912), the great general who took Port Arthur from Russia in 1905, losing two sons unflinchingly in the Russo-Japanese War: he committed ritual suicide upon the death of Emperor Meiji, and his wife followed her lord as he had followed his.

In battle, the retainer fought under his direct superior's command, carried out his orders, and protected any attempted retreat; if his superior decided to escape capture by committing ritual suicide, the retainer acted as his second *(kaishaku),* who had the duty of shortening the agony of a self-inflicted, mortal wound by severing the dying man's head with a single sword cut. Usually the retainer would flee with his master's head to prevent enemies from making a war trophy of it, in accordance with the martial customs of the age. Often, however, a retainer would enable his master to escape capture by donning his lord's armor and riding off, drawing the enemy away from his master; or a retainer disguised as his master would allow his own head to be cut off and dragged away by another retainer whom the enemy was certain to pursue, while their master made good his escape.

If ordered to fight to the bitter end by his master, a retainer would do so; or, if permitted, he might choose to follow the ancient custom of those martial tribes whose members never willingly allowed themselves to be captured. Since time immemorial, Japanese warriors have always displayed a marked preference for death over capture. In his studies of Japanese culture, Joao Rodriguez, S. J., (1561-1634) noted how the warriors of a besieged lord, when they were on the verge of being overwhelmed by the enemy, would slay their women and children, set fire to their last stronghold, and then take their own lives. Exceptions to this practice were generally due to a special pledge to save the progeny of their doomed master for the purpose of future revenge. The custom has been explained by historians as being a direct result of the traditional concept of mass responsibility which exempted no one in the clan from the consequences of its leader's decisions or actions. It is conceivable that the widespread practice of exterminating not only individuals, but their entire clan as well, might have helped to stimulate the custom of anticipating such an end by taking one's own life, thus making it a privilege generally extended to every member of the

…to the bitter end

warrior class. It was common practice, for example, when a warrior on the battlefield realized the futility of his efforts, for him to retreat to a nearby grove or some other isolated spot and take his own life while his enemies stood by—often assisting in the ritual.

In feudal Europe, the problem of dealing with prisoners had evolved into an institution of the art of war which successive ages endeavored to refine even further under the civilizing influence of reciprocal laws and customs regulating armed conflict among nations. International law, for example, may be said to embody the highest expression of this interpretation of conflict which had been shared by the Greeks and the Romans during the classic ages of both Mediterranean cultures and which even Islam, centuries later, had come to accept. Provisions were eventually made, and recognized as binding, concerning the status and the treatment of prisoners of war, who were thus protected, to a certain extent, from the dangers intrinsic in the position of a military man whom the fortunes of war, and not necessarily cowardice, had placed at the mercy of his foes. According to certain scholars with whom the authors tend to agree, such a development in the art of war was possible in Europe because of the large-scale, mutual involvement which forced almost all nations to adopt supranational concepts of warfare.

Japan, on the other hand, with its persistent and prolonged isolation from the international community, had neither been exposed to such ideas nor developed them independently. Clannish feudal customs and notions about the collective responsibility of the social unit were thus retained in modern Japan to a far greater extent than in Europe or even in Asia. The preservation of military tradition was also responsible, in large measure, for the continuing aversion to capture and the concomitant contempt for prisoners which was such a notable factor in Japanese behavior during the nineteenth and twentieth centuries. It was also remarked that while the Japanese attitude toward alien prisoners of war was singularly contemptuous, their own reactions when captured ranged from extremes of sheer desperation (usually a prelude to self-immolation) to an eerie form of fatalistic relief often transformed into full cooperation with their captors, which, if not authorized by an immediate superior, was explained by scholars as being the result of resignation to disgrace and, therefore, to any degradation. Modern episodes drawn from the archives of World War II provide startling examples of the reactions of the Japanese military man (as well as those of great numbers of Japanese civilians) when faced with the possibility of capture. From the centuries-old performance of *hara-kiri* by numerous commanders who used their swords to make the traditional first cut before being shot in the head or beheaded by their lieutenants, to the less ritualized suicides of lower-ranking officers after they had beheaded their own soldiers; from the individual suicides of soldiers who pressed grenades against their bodies or balanced them on top of their heads, carefully replacing their caps before the explosion, to the mass suicides of Japanese soldiers and civilians—an orgy of self-destruction was the salient characteristic of Japanese behavior when confronted with defeat and the prospect of capture.

This orgy, sickening to Western troops, "who were powerless to halt it," reached tragic proportions at Marpi Point on Saipan, where it was said to have expressed "the horror of Bushido" (Leckie, 354), but it was in evidence everywhere, from the islands of the Pacific to China, Korea, and even the Japanese mainland itself, where it continued for months after the defeat of Japan had been formally acknowledged by the emperor. In contrast to Western directives concerning honorable surrender, Japanese "battle ethics" commanded every soldier to "never suffer the disgrace of being taken alive" (Leckie, 348). In fact, any surrender terms offered by an enemy, even though intended to prevent useless bloodshed, were considered by most Japanese commanders as an insult, when not simply a hilarious notion. "How could a samurai surrender? A samurai can only kill himself" was the usual answer (Leckie, 518).

The entire body of Japanese military ethics, in fact, had been inherited from feudal Japan, where the bond of service and loyalty between a retainer and his master was so absolute that any attack on the latter was, in effect, an attack on the former, who was honor-bound to redress the wrong. All clan cultures contain the concept of institutionalized revenge, the official vendetta which, in the military culture of the Tokugawa, became a ritual with minutely organized norms and procedures. The warrior whose master had been, or considered himself, the victim of any type of offense, ranging from a procedural slight to a verbal insult, from an attempted assassination to an actual murder, assumed the obligation of avenging his master even if this took years to accomplish. Such a duty was particularly binding when a retainer's master had either been killed or forced to take his own life. The ancient Confucian precept that no one should be willing to live under the same heaven with the slayer of his father was interpreted by Japanese law and custom in favor of one's master, who, as head of the clan, was the father of all. Failure in this context could mean utter disgrace, "for not only was the man who revenged himself regarded as a man of honor, but further, the man who was weak enough not to try to put to death the murderer of his father or his lord, was obliged to flee into hiding; from that day, he was despised by his own companions" (Dautremer, 83). Vengeance *(kataki-uchi)* was considered complete according to ritual when the head of the enemy was placed at the master's feet or, if he had died, upon his tomb.

As a man of war *(bushi)*, the retainer usually had to be prepared to serve his master primarily in his capacity as a warrior. This obligation could be discharged in an absolute manner only if he had no reservation whatsoever about confronting the dangers intrinsic in the professional use of arms. His entire philosophy, accordingly, revolved around the concept of complete disregard for his own safety, even his own life, which, by oath, he had placed unreservedly at his master's disposal.

His code of honor (Bushido) and all the classics related to it stressed the point of never pausing to ponder the nature, significance, and effects of a superior's command. The *Hagakure*, a record (written at the beginning of the eighteenth century) of the words of Yamamoto Tsunetomo, a military retainer of the Nabeshima clan, was very specific in this respect and warned the warrior to carry out every order immediately, lest reasoning about it should make a coward of him or inhibit action in any way. The commentaries attached to this military classic were also explicit concerning the elimination of thought and mental discrimination from the process of reacting to and obeying a command. When the third shogun of the Tokugawa clan, Iemitsu, consulted military retainers in charge of the warriors' formation in the Kii clan concerning the essence of successful strategy, their answer was one of pragmatic simplicity unsurpassed in any other military culture: "One should never ponder!" The decision, after all, had already been made elsewhere, by others. Their task was to obey. This reply, understandably, "pleased Iemitsu" (Norman, 111).

In order to enable the warrior to overcome any mental impasse precipitated by man's natural fear of death, he had to be trained to think of himself as a man whose life was not his own—a constant theme in Japanese lore and literature where the samurai is often portrayed as a tragic figure caught in the web of a blind cult of death to which he adheres faithfully, whatever the consequences. The *Hagakure* itself stated quite clearly that the code of the warrior, the famous Bushido, was indeed a code of death. Hence, the warrior had to be always prepared for a sudden and violent end. His whole life as a warrior in the service of a military leader, in fact, was a constant reminder of this. "There is no nation in the world," wrote Francesco Carletti in the sixteenth century, "which fears death less" (Cooper, 42). This conditioning, which made the Japanese warrior's contempt for death renowned the world over, began in infancy. The child of a military household was exposed to cold in winter and expected to endure the heat of summer without complaining; he was often sent on difficult errands which were purposely prolonged. His fear of death and of the supernatural (to which all classes in Japan were prone during the feudal era) was substantially reduced, Nitobe tells us, by sending him to such uncanny places as cemeteries and places of execution at night, even while quite young, in order to familiarize him with and, in time, inure him to that chilling sensation which the presence of death usually elicits. Physical pain had to be endured without betraying the slightest emotion, and the young warrior's conditioning reached its apotheosis in careful training intended to prepare him for the ceremony of self-destruction, that ritualistic form of suicide known generally as *hara-kiri* ("abdomen cutting") or *seppuku* (a more refined rendition of the Chinese character expressing the same idea).

Ritualistic suicide, considered the highest manifestation of command over one's own destiny and unflinching courage in the face of death, represented a privilege in the eyes of the Japanese warrior. It had begun as a simple act of lonely self-annihilation on the battlefield, performed to escape capture or destruction at the hands of the enemy. In time, it grew into a ceremony which could rightfully be performed only by members of the *buke* and in accordance with minutely described rules of etiquette, including the presence of an assistant and witnesses who evidenced the social rather than individual or private nature of the ceremony. The reasons for committing ritual suicide, once so directly related to the desire to maintain full command over one's own destiny to the very last or the desire to follow one's master in death, became somewhat diluted during the ages of comparative peace following the rise of the Tokugawa to power. Among the main voluntary forms of ritual suicide, for example, the military classics of that age mention those resulting from a feeling of guilt because of one's own inadequacy, from imprudent or reckless behavior, or from failing to fulfill one's duty to a superior. This form of suicide was known as *sokotsu-shi.* Another reason for committing suicide sprang from rage or enmity *(munen-bara, funshi)* which could not be discharged against its cause. The warrior could also choose to kill himself as a form of protest or outrage at a master's unfair treatment of him or to make his lord reconsider a certain decision. This was called *kanshi.* Among the main involuntary or imposed forms of ritual suicide, the same classics list those resulting from the commission of a crime for which the warrior could atone by taking an active part in his own punishment, in accordance with the laws regulating his special status in society. Also listed are forms which resulted from a master's command when a retainer's actions might have caused his lord embarrassment or when the master wished to absolve his retainer (or himself) from a certain responsibility.

In practice, ritual suicide in the military dimension was performed by using a special blade to cut into the part of the body which was considered the seat of a man's life and the source of his power: his lower abdomen *(hara).* Using his short sword *(wakizashi)* on the battlefield during earlier periods and then, in later centuries, a special knife whose size, shape, and decoration would vary according to procedural circumstances, he would draw a horizontal cut from the left to the right side of his abdomen and then, if his strength permitted, follow this with another cut upward, either prolonging the first cut or starting a new one from the middle of the first and driving it upward in the direction of his throat. Originally, the aim of the first horizontal cut with a long blade was to sever the spinal nerve centers. The second cut implemented the first, being directed toward the aorta.

Since it was not always possible to insure a quick death by such complicated cutting, the assistance of another party in this act became the custom. Such a man was generally either a comrade in arms, a friend of equal rank, or a retainer of a lower rank (when not a functionary appointed by the authorities). His duty, as explained previously, was to decapitate the would-be suicide once the latter had completed the

Ritualistic suicide, HARAKIRI or SEPPUKU

ritual cuts and offered his neck. As the ages of turmoil receded and the martial simplicity and primitive strength of ancient customs gave way to sterile sophistication and emphasis upon procedural appearances, the role of this assistant became increasingly pivotal, until he actually came to resemble a formal executioner—many times not even waiting for the voluntary first cut before cleaving the unfortunate man's head from his body.

Any man as thoroughly familiarized with and reconciled to the idea of his own destruction as was the *bushi* would obviously develop into an extremely dangerous fighter who often needed to be restrained lest he throw his life away heedlessly in combat. Upon the issuing of a command by his direct superior, any *bushi* worthy of the name would respond without a moment's hesitation. Since his absolute and concentrated commitment was usually matched by that of his opponent, combat encounters often resulted in mutual slaying. In large-scale battles, then, a master was often forced to rely heavily not so much upon the valor of his individual retainers as upon their number or, in exceptional cases, upon his own strategic acumen—an area in which, as we have seen earlier, few of these leaders are said to have excelled.

The eagerness with which the thoroughly conditioned warrior of the early feudal period engaged in combat was proverbial. In times of peace, and particularly during the long Tokugawa period, that eagerness betrayed itself in gratuitous, picayune manifestations of contempt and disdain for all other classes, as well as in an hysterical tendency to overreact to even imagined indications of "lack of respect"—if not to turn just plain murderous. These degenerative qualities were clearly linked to the futility and general pointlessness of a samurai's existence as it became increasingly parasitical during those periods of prolonged peace when he was resented and despised by the "downtrodden masses" (i.e., all other classes) behind their masks of forced servility. "Priests and warriors: dogs and animals!" *(shukke, samurai: inuchikusho),* as Norman tells us, was a "popular saying," applied quite often to "these idle and gluttonous fellows" during the Tokugawa period. A retainer's obsequiousness and servility toward his immediate superiors within the clan hierarchy was a vivid contrast to his arrogance and undisguised contempt for those commoners whom, according to Article 71 of the criminal code (*Osadamegaki*), he had the freedom and even the duty to cut down on the spot *(kirisutegomen)* should any unfortunate person, regardless of sex or age, behave toward him in a manner the samurai considered disrespectful or even "unexpected." His privileged status in society as a whole, however, could not completely disguise the fact that he too was trapped in a system which weighed almost as heavily upon him as it did upon others. For warriors "were subjected to an elaborate, unwritten code of ceremonies and therefore their freedom of thought and liberty of action were extremely limited. They were not allowed to think freely, nor to act according to their own will" (Hayashi, 70).

The status of a warrior within the clan of his birth or the clan to which he had been assigned by a lawful superior was generally immutable. Only exceptional circumstances might release him from the bond of loyalty and turn him into a masterless warrior *(ronin).* The ancient ordinances issued by Hideyoshi

Warrior in travel attire

Position of rest: arms folded inside kimono

restricting any changes in a retainer's status and residence were further reinforced by Ieyasu. Any warrior who severed ties with his clan without permission could not be accepted into the ranks of any other clan. Moreover, the leaders of all other clans were obliged by law to return such a retainer to his former master or answer to the military authorities for lack of compliance with the law. Should a retainer attempt to conceal himself among the peasants, the system of collective responsibility *(gonin-gumi)* would bring disaster upon the entire town or village if the subterfuge were to be discovered.

Thus, no matter where he turned, the retainer found the way barred against him, insuring that, for the most part, he would cling ferociously to the position assigned to him within the social order.

Education and Status of the Buke

The education and status of the *buke* may be viewed as developing different characteristics and institutions throughout three major phases of Japanese history: during the Heian period (794-1156), during the period preceding the rise of the Tokugawa (1157-1600), and finally, during the Tokugawa period (1600-1867). In each phase there was a clear distinction between the education and status of the *buke* leaders—that is, the upper category and ranks of the military class—and the education and status of their retainers and vassals, the samurai of the lower category and ranks. It appears obvious, in fact, that the second category did not enjoy the privileges and status considered an inherent right by the first category, and that even the privileged status of the second category (privileged, that is, in comparison to the subordinated remainder of the nation) was still markedly inferior to the status enjoyed by the military leaders of the nation. Furthermore, the concept of education discussed in these pages in relation to the *buke* was clearly limited and quite strictly defined.

Many definitions of the word "education" have been advanced by scholars, both past and present. All of these definitions may be reduced for easier exposition to two major types or, more correctly, attitudes. The first is active and embraces all those definitions which refer to the role of education as an intellectual search for and within new or expanding fields of knowledge. The second is passive and embraces all those definitions which consider education as training in the mastery of various skills. The former type of education (therefore, of knowledge) embraces the entire range or as many aspects as possible of man's reality, thus becoming an independent inquiry into the unanswered dilemma his reality proposes at almost every turn. The latter type of education concentrates mainly upon a few, supposedly "known" and established aspects of that existence which it reiterates and reconfirms. One reaches out into the unknown and in every possible direction, while the other revolves around the familiar and, therefore, moves in one direction alone. In this context, it will be seen that the military class, by its very nature and emphasis upon professional qualifications, tended to concentrate upon the second type of education, which it defined, quite conservatively, as the repetition of orderly and expected patterns of thought and behavior, according to a precise sequence leaving little or no room for improvisation.

Although the military class had many illustrious precedents to draw upon—expecially from the latter part of the Heian period—its undeniable admiration for that culture still could not induce the leaders of the *buke* to accept the best which the Heian experience had to offer. Instead, their selections were highly restricted, and this narrowness eventually wreaked havoc upon the military class itself, dooming to failure the repeated attempts made by its leaders to freeze time and custom forever at the high point of feudalism. In fact, the leaders of the warrior class were actually forced to swiftly retrench their position in the national system, in order to ride the political waves generated by the restoration of power to the emperor.

When the *bushi* began to develop their professional traits and coalesce as a class during the eleventh century, they were confronted by the highly sophisticated culture of the Heian court and its aristocracy. Members of this culture had reached pinnacles of scholarship in their studies of classic literature, were exploring the complexities of religious ideas imported from India and laden with Chinese accretions, had developed a theocratic theory of state and nationhood, and were beginning to reach out into unexplored dimensions of pure speculation. By the time the warriors had turned their sights from the provinces to the capital and ultimate power, Heian culture had left far behind the ancient emphasis placed by the original clans in the age of *kabane* upon arts *(waza)* considered generally as esoteric manifestations of the divine, upon invocations *(norito)* insuring their correct manifestations, and upon liturgy *(matsuri)*. Instead, the Heians had shifted to a thorough absorption of the complexities of Chinese culture and, with this, to a correlated emphasis upon quality, as well as an increase in the quantity of schools, libraries, and scholars. Steps had already been taken to institutionalize the function of scholars who had lectured or tutored in the mansions of aristocratic clan heads or at court, by forming a national school system tracing its legal roots to the eighth century, to the Taiho Code (A.D. 702). Centers of instruction had been established at the imperial court under a director of public education *(fumiya-zukasa-no-kami)*, and in each provincial area *(kokugaku)*. The imperial college *(daigaku)* and its college-house *(daigakuryo)* had mushroomed into a proper establishment in its own educational right, with a rector *(daigaku-no-kami)*, vice-rector *(suke)*, upper and lower heads *(tai-jo* and *sho-jo)*, as well as upper and lower subofficials *(tai-shakan* and *jo-shakan)*. Under these officials had operated many professors and assistants who provided introductory and advanced instruction in the following major subjects:

Chinese Classics *(myokyo)*
Law *(myoho)*
Calligraphy *(sho, shodo)*
Mathematics *(san)*
Composition and rhetoric *(monjo, mongaku)*
Chinese poetry *(shigaku)*
Japanese poetry *(kagaku)*
Planning and strategy *(shusai)*
Political theory *(shinshi)*
Divination *(in-yo)*
Calendar *(koyomi)*
Astrology *(temmon)*
Music *(gagaku)*
Medicine and pharmacy *(tenyaku)*

CHART 9

CHINESE CLASSICS *(myokyo)*

MAJOR COMBINATIONS	ENGLISH TITLES (with the Chinese and Japanese denominations)	MINOR Combinations
Thirteen Classics	1. *Books of Documents (Shu Ching* or *Shang Shü, Shokyo* or *Shosho)*	Small Classics *(shokyo)*
	2. *Book of Changes (I Ching* or *Choü i, Ekikyo* or *Shueki)*	
	3. *Spring and Autumn Annals (Ch'ün Ch'iü, Shunju)*	Great Classics *(daikyo)*
Five Classics *(gokyo)*	4. *Record of Rituals (Li Chi, Raiki)* (a) *Book of Great Learning (Ta Hsüeh, Daigaku)*	
	(b) *Doctrine of the Means (Chüng Yung, Chuyo)*	Middle Classics *(chukyo)*
	5. *Classics of Songs (Shing Ching* or *Mao Shih, Shikyo* or *Moshi)*	
	6. First section of the *Spring and Autumn Annals* (see above)	
	7. Second section of the *Spring and Autumn Annals* (see above)	
	8. *Ceremonies and Rituals (I Li, Girai)*	
	9. *Rituals of Chou (Chou Li, Shurai)*	
	10. *Analects (Lun Yu, Rongo)*	
	11. *Mencius (Meng Tze, Moshi)*	
	12. *Classic of Filial Piety (Hsiao Ching, Kokyo)*	
	13. *Etymological Dictionary (Erh Ya, Jiga)*	

Source: from Kaigo Tokiomi

Each of these major subjects or academic disciplines had become highly complex and, at its superior levels, often downright esoteric, merging as it customarily did with metaphysics and the intuitive. As illustrated in Chart 9, the Chinese Classics alone, for example, consisted of thirteen texts, each accompanied by its own specific commentaries and appendices drawn from Chinese and Japanese sources. And mastery of them all was expected by the examiners who tested the preparation of their aristocratic students. Scholars had had to specialize in the study of those texts either one by one or, as a requirement for higher office, in major groups of texts, e.g., the collections known as the Small Classics *(shokyo)*, the Great Classics *(daikyo)*, or the Middle Classics *(chukyo)*. Rare indeed, even then, was the man who could claim a thorough knowledge of them all.

The aim of education during the major part of the Heian era had thus obviously been less that of enlarging and deepening the realms of knowledge for the sake of understanding and appreciating the unfolding of life's innumerable possibilities, than that of forming proper functionaries of a state which had already chosen one of those possibilities (an imitation of a Chinese model) and strove continually to maintain and perfect its essentially theocratic and aristocratic structure. Appearance *(katachi)* had traditionally been one of the most important aims of education, since it visually represented prestige and power. Intellect (*zae)* had had to be more specialized, since the functions the nobles were called upon to perform in the service of the system were many and administratively varied. In fact, the nobles had concentrated mainly upon the study of imperial liturgies and court ceremonials *(yusoku kojitsu)*, the installation rituals *(jimoku)*, law and theories of government, and so forth. Provincial aristocrats had been directed more toward studies in law, mathematics, divination, astrology, planning, and strategy.

As a collateral extension of the interesting fervor surrounding education during the Heian period (as reported by Tokiomi), private schools had also been established for the education of "the greatest number of people." Schools such as the Nikyoin of Kibi-no-Makibi, the Untein of Iso-no-kami Yakatsugu, and the priest Kukai's own institute, the Shugeishoin, had been established and operated outside the national system of education, valiantly attempting to do for the other classes of the nation that which the system had done for the nobles. Their existence was often threatened, and eventually they all had to close. However, the attempt had demonstrated the centrifugal and expansionistic effects of a broad approach to education and constituted a precedent for intermittent attempts to establish centers of popular learning whenever and wherever possible. Deep within this culture and at its outer limits, therefore, there seethed an irresistible impulse to expand and experiment which defied constrictions and was, perhaps, at the root of that period of trouble and glory which followed hard upon the heels of the Heian period.

The warriors of the eleventh century had been dazzled by the cultural splendor of the late Heian period, and, even when its luster had dimmed considerably with the passing of time, the *buke* evidenced the lingering effect of this initial fascination either by scorning the trappings of that culture a trifle too heatedly, or by endeavoring to recreate its aura (although obviously on a different basis and with a different content) whenever and wherever they could. At the beginning of their history as a separate class in search of its own character and destiny, those clans drawn into the spinning center of the nation during the late Heian period had endeavored to send their leaders' children to aristocratic colleges and academies in order to prepare them for their new and expanded responsibilities. There, these "new" men, who—although of the *buke's* upper ranks—had been bred in provincial towns to bear arms and to live simply, almost rustically, stood out in uncomfortably sharp contrast to the "effete" offspring of the nobility who despised and instinctively feared them. The nobles, in fact, were obscurely aware that, although these rustic members of the "family of archery and horsemanship" were indispensable instruments of power, they were also potentially dangerous contenders for that power. The resentment of the upper categories of warriors who were only reluctantly admitted to aristocratic centers of learning is abundantly recorded, and it found concrete expression in many of their policies during the succeeding centuries, when they repaid the *kuge* in full (as well as the clergy, who had held a large number of the highest teaching positions) for every slight inflicted by the aristocrats and priests— insults which the *buke* bore with the cold determination of military men whose time was manifestly to come.

Pragmatists by nature and function, the military leaders of the emerging *buke* had had to decide early whether they would be absorbed by the Heian culture or would instead select and adapt from it those features which best served their distinct purposes without allowing their own sharply differentiated individuality to be diluted. The example of many military clans, whose members had been lured into accepting the Heian culture unreservedly and had subsequently been swallowed up by the general process of decadence, induced many leaders to strongly favor the second option. The general tendency of the *buke,* consequently, was that of continuing to emphasize, as the primary justification for their own existence, the military arts *(bu),* while at the same time mastering those administrative skills *(bun)* by which the nation was run. Their choice was further limited as to the subject and content of possible studies, since operative and functional knowledge was largely restricted to the upper category and ranks of the *buke.* In addition, their curriculum ignored large areas of knowledge whose speculative and expanding nature, capable of leading the mind of man into unknown and unexplored domains (as had been the case with so many scholars and priests of the Heian period), was a disturbing factor to warriors who based their very existence upon the regularity and rigid discipline of military life.

A definite cultural selection of subject matter was evident, therefore, as the upper *bushi* began to attend aristocratic academies during the late Heian period. Public administration, mathematics, law and the administration of justice (as well as military planning and strategy, of course) seem to have been the major subjects of academic interest for this "new" breed of men, backed by so many strong and brooding warrior clans. The executive positions of magistrates, court supervisors, and generals began to be filled, with increasing regularity, by members of the *buke* who submitted themselves to the system of career advancement run by the imperial court. From within and from without, those leaders pressed on and began to close in upon Kyoto. But while the upper category and ranks of warriors were thereby exposed to learning (although on an increasingly selective basis), the interest of their retainers seems to have been concentrated almost exclusively upon perfecting those military skills which had opened so many doors for the leaders of the *buke.* Expertise in handling the bow and arrow, the spear, and the sword was of paramount importance to the samurai then, and became even more so as the center of imperial power was slowly and irresistibly eroded. Those weapons became the ultimate instruments for devising and executing the policy of the *buke.* The lower samurai, therefore, was trained at home or in the clan centers of military instruction—his education in the literary sense being neglected to the point of almost completely eliminating its influence upon his life. The continuing condition of rampant illiteracy among the lower samurai is reported upon at length in many chronicles dealing not only with the late Heian period, but also with the advanced stages of the pre-Tokugawa period, deep into the Ashikaga (Muromachi) period.

With the establishment of the Kamakura shogunate (1192), the displacement of the *kuge* by the *buke* began in earnest. Large military clans established centers of superior education where their leaders concentrated upon the study of the disciplines and functions of government. The Hojo clan, which provided outstanding leadership throughout the dangerous Kamakura period (1185-1333), is reputed to have been the motivating force behind the Kanazawa Bunko, an institution of eclectic learning within the grounds of Shomyo-ji Temple, housing large libraries filled with Chinese and Japanese classics. The Ashikaga clan is also known to have established its own school during the age which followed (Muromachi, 1336-1568), although the cultural tradition of this particular family is said to have reached as far back as the eleventh century, when one of its leaders, Yoshikane (?—1199), founded a study-center *(gakumonjo)* in the family's Banna-ji Temple. The increased importance of expertise in administrative skills *(bun)* is evidenced by the repeated admonitions, directed to military leaders by their elders and advisors, "that there should be training in both cultural and military arts" (Kaigo, 20). These admonitions were clearly well received by the highest category and ranks of the *buke,* for there is ample historical evidence that the military leadership of the Rokuhara, Ashikaga (Muromachi), and Momoyama periods, from 1156 to 1600, became well versed in the finer points of power manipulation at which their aristocratic predecessors, the *kuge,* had excelled. The latter had slowly begun to lose ground as the military centers of power turned into semi-imperial courts, attracting scholars and artists of various denominations.

The same cannot be said for the lower category and rank of samurai, however. As indicated earlier, they seem to have been and to have remained, for the most part, functionally illiterate. Frederic relates that in the Kamakura period (1185-1333) the incidence of warriors unable to read Sino-Japanese written characters was not a rare one. Their constant involvement with warfare, as their leaders jostled for power and prestige, made even the lowest level of scholarship not only irrelevant to their condition but often downright detrimental, since it took time (of which they, as retainers in the service of a lord, had very little to call their own) and, furthermore, might have encouraged them to develop insights into other dimensions and possibilities which those same leaders had clearly marked as being above and beyond the status of the lower ranks. At this point, still very close to the emergence of the professional warrior, we see the development of an interesting phenomenon, often qualified by scholars of Japanese history as "anti-intellectualism," to identify a peculiarly Japanese aversion for uncontrolled knowledge—that is, knowledge left unfettered so that one might explore, in an active sense, the entire range and all the aspects of human existence. A note here is particularly intriguing: the Japanese language in feudal times contained no term which would be the equivalent of the English word "curiosity"—nor does it contain such a term today (Dore[2], 51).

With the singular intuition of military leaders the world over, the high-ranking members of the *buke* (that is, the lords and masters of the various military clans) had understood from the first that a wide range of knowledge was a prerequisite for successful choice, evaluation, and decision in any field of human endeavor. This, in turn, implied the admission of a certain individuality of opinion as the basis for independent action— even though the rigid stratification of clan culture was a direct practical as well as theoretical negation of any such freedom of thought or action. The comparatively equalitarian condition enjoyed by the court nobles *(kuge)* during the Heian period and, to a certain extent, by the leaders of the military knights *(buke)* during successive periods was not easier to assimilate in Japan than it had been in Greece during that country's classical age. The court nobles of Nara and Kyoto had been notoriously factious and belligerent in their dealings with one another, as were the feudal barons of the military clans in the provinces, who plunged the country into their own version of chaos before finally being forced to adhere to the uneasy truce inaugurated by Ieyasu in the seventeenth century (which they promptly abrogated after 1868, once the hold of the Tokugawa clan and their allies upon the nation had been broken).

Fully aware of the centrifugal effects of unrestricted knowledge, each lord and master usually endeavored to limit the intellectual development of his retainers to those levels which would insure the retainers' efficiency in carrying out the functions and duties assigned to them, but no others. The intellectual preparation of each clan's warriors, accordingly, was increasingly restricted as they descended in rank from the higher to the lower levels. Beyond that knowledge and skill in the use of specific weapons which the retainers of each clan were expected to pursue, they received specialized instruction in various administrative functions which, being largely hereditary, did not usually provide any scope for creative innovations. By the beginning of 1600, each provincial lord had conditioned his military retainers in such a specialized way that, in place of the ancient spontaneous and creative clansmen with their many skills, who had survived the "ages of troubles" (from the tenth to the sixteenth century), there emerged a compact mass of fighting "technicians," conditioned by and committed to a cult of absolute loyalty to their warlords and masters.

There were, of course, warriors of the lower category and ranks who did not agree wholeheartedly with such an extreme specialization of their existence. Whenever and wherever they could, such men would send their children to temples and monasteries, where they joined the "long-haired novices" *(chigo-suihatsu)*, learning to read and write. That education, in a few adventurous and often unfortunate cases, gave a number of lower samurai the basis for independent thinking, thereby leading to clashes against a system which was slowly congealing into a social rigidity to which Tokugawa Ieyasu was to give the final touches.

With the advent to power of the Tokugawa, in fact, the process of military specialization and conditioning reached its apotheosis. The leaders of this clan carried to their extreme and ultimate consequences the implications of their predecessors' restrictive policies concerning the education of both the upper and lower categories and ranks of the *buke*. They began with the leaders themselves, the provincial lords of the military clans—the daimyo. Centers of instruction for children of military lineage and especially for the offspring of provincial governors were opened in the provinces, thus removing the *buke* from the direct in-

fluence of those schools and universities in and around Kyoto where the intellectual and exclusivistic influence of the *kuge* still predominated. In these new, provincial centers, although the principle of absolute loyalty to one's direct superior (in the case of the provincial lords, to the shogun) was stressed in accordance with strict Confucian patterns governing social relationships, the scope of instruction was enlarged beyond the narrow confines of clan affairs to embrace provincial problems and those of the nation as a whole in order to prepare these lords to comprehend and carry out successfully the directives emanating from the *bakufu* in Edo. This preparation, however, was still carefully restricted in an effort to reduce the chances of producing an overlord who might develop an enlarged and potentially threatening vision of his own function; but it was clearly broader in scope than the narrow vision of life which the retainers of these lords were allowed to entertain.

Among the centers of instruction frequented by the *buke* were the renowned Yokendo in Sendai, the Kojokan in Yonezawa, the Kodokan in Mito, the Chidokan in Kago-shima, and the Meirinkan in Hagi, to mention only a few. The central institution which supervised them all, naturally, was the Seido located in the military capital, Edo. A scholar, Koike Kenji, has described the history, organization, and training program of one of these centers, the Nisshinkan in Wakamatsu, which was primarily concerned with the literary and physical education of the provincial lords, higher retainers, and leading administrators of the ancient Aizu clan. The training of high-ranking children of this clan began systematically and officially when they were eight or nine years old. Before that, as was customary, these children had already been prepared through preliminary indoctrination in martial etiquette, and at the age of five, boys had already received their first samurai costumes and swords (which they would never again be without).

After receiving his first swords, a boy would join other children in groups divided according to various sections of the town and follow one or more leaders who would be responsible for him to a teacher in a temple or at the institute. Under the strict surveillance of these teachers, the children memorized the literary texts of instruction (without explanation), beginning at about their tenth or eleventh years. From the ages of ten to fourteen, they were taught and expected to practice official etiquette. At thirteen they began to study archery, swordsmanship, and spearfighting, which they would henceforth practice regularly throughout their lives. At fifteen they approached the Chinese Classics, and individual inclinations in the various branches of military administration were encouraged and cultivated by a personal tutor. At sixteen, the group dissolved, and each youth was indoctrinated by a series of teachers in their specialties (listed in Chart 10). This program continued until the boy's twenty-second year. Then, if he had satisfactorily absorbed and completed the program, he could either stay on at the Nisshinkan Institute or further his education by visiting other institutions throughout the country. In general, he was encouraged to embark upon a specialized career, in accordance with the rank held by the head of his family, whom he was expected to succeed when the latter retired or passed away. Allowances were made for less talented students, who were given more time and extra care in order to help them catch up with the others. Failure, of course, meant utter disgrace, because it often entailed (in characteristically Japanese fashion) the demotion of the entire family to a lower rank in the military hierarchy, due to the son's inability to follow in his father's footsteps.

The Tsu clan boasted of four sheds for the study of jujutsu, three sheds for gunnery, one shed for archery, three sheds for riding, one shed for strategy, three sheds for spearmanship, three sheds for swordsmanship, and one shed for the halberd—all within the same compound, according to Dore. In most central

CHART 10
PROGRAM OF INSTRUCTION IN THE NISSHINKAN INSTITUTE

Japanese nomenclature in italics

Obligatory		Optional
Literary	Military	
Chinese Classics *(jugaku)*	Art of the bow & arrow *(kyujutsu)*	Tea ceremony *(sado)*
Indigenous religion and literature *(shinto oyobi kogaku)*	Various specializations of spearmanship *(yarijutsu, naginata, bojutsu,* etc.)	Poetry *(shisaku)*
Calligraphy *(shogaku, shuji)*	Various specializations of swordsmanship *(tojutsu, kenjutsu,* etc.)	Impromptu versification *(sokuseki)*
Etiquette *(reishiki)*	Art of unarmed combat with or without armor *(jujutsu)*	Hunting *(torioi)*
Classical music *(gagaku)*	Artillery and firearms *(hojutsu)*	
Mathematics *(sugaku)*	Art of fortifications *(chikujojutsu)*	
Medicine *(igaku)*	Art of horsemanship on land and in the water *(bajutsu, suibajutsu)*	
Astronomy *(temmon)*	Art of swimming in armor *(suiei)*	

and provincial schools, mornings were devoted to the literary disciplines and afternoons to the military skills, thus combining both *bun* and *bu*. The proportion of teachers assigned to different disciplines may be gathered by the list of salaries included in the budget of the Choshu school in 1797. As reported by Dore, this school availed itself of the services of five teachers of Chinese Classics, fifteen teachers of military arts, one teacher of calligraphy, one of mathematics, two tutors, two librarians, and one clerk, as well as two shrine attendants. Concerning the status of these teachers in particular, more is said later in this part.

The plan of the Nisshinkan Institute included here shows an almost inordinate amount of space allocated for the practice of the listed specializations of bujutsu. Most of the institutions (and sometimes even private houses of warriors of high rank) followed more or less the same design. In almost every one we find shooting ranges, indoor and outdoor, for archery and firearms; various ponds for swimming in

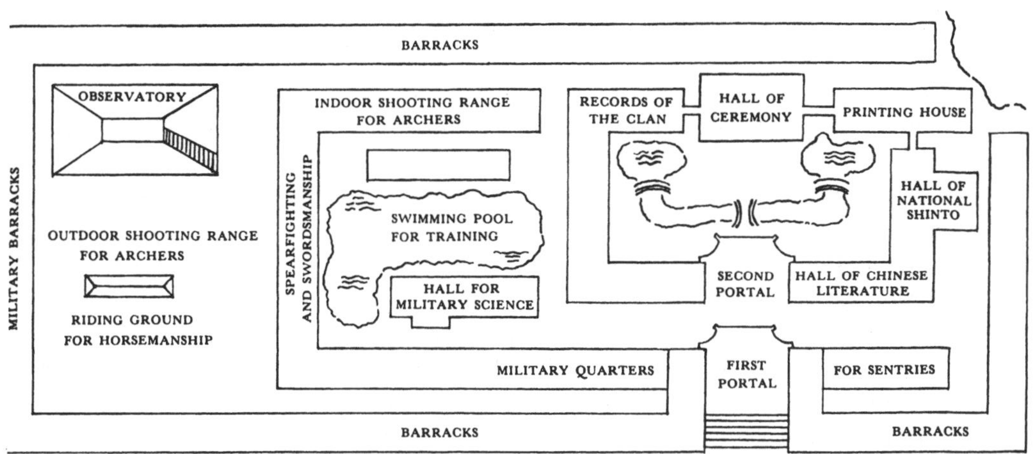

Plan of the Nisshinkan Institute

armor or without, or on horseback; open squares for horseback riding and all sorts of equestrian maneuvers; long halls for spear-fighting and fencing practice; and smaller halls for man-to-man combat, armed and unarmed, at close quarters.

The Tokugawa encouraged the establishment of schools for lower samurai, both in the provinces under their direct supervision and in the provinces under the supervision of military governors (the daimyo). These schools *(hangaku, hanko)* were generally established in castle-towns and were subsidized by the clans, usually through the appropriation of revenues from a certain tract of rice-producing land. The quality of instruction, however, seems not to have compared favorably with that available to the upper category and ranks of the *buke,* and its content was strictly defined and limited. In some clans, for example, the ranks at the bottom of the lower category of warriors were even excluded (Dore[2], 226). In general, this division between the upper and lower warrior was sharp and unbridgeable, although the lower samurai were clearly in the majority.

As Fukuzawa tells us, the warriors of the upper ranks of the Okudaira clan of Nakatsu, for example,

> were well-fed and clothed and thus had plenty of leisure time to devote to the arts, literary and military. They would read the Confucian classics and the Books of History, study military strategy, practice horsemanship, spearmanship, and swordsmanship, and generally indulge in all the branches of art and learning which were considered at the time to be cultured and noble. Thus their manners were naturally elegant and aristocratic and many of them could be considered most cultured and refined gentlemen. (Fukuzawa, 313)

By contrast, warriors of the lower ranks "practiced the military arts in such little time as they could spare from their sidework, but in literature they would get no further than the Four Books and the Five Classics and, at a little more advanced stage, one or two books of Meng Ch'Iu and the *Tso Chuang.* What they studied most was writing and arithmetic, and in this they were certainly far superior to the upper samurai" (Fukuzawa, 313). In fact, because of such recording and computing abilities, the calligrapher's rank was considered highest among the lower ranks, and the warriors who attained it were expected to carry out the fundamental duties of administering the clan's affairs, collecting taxes, and keeping the records of the clan current.

While, in theory, every *bushi,* regardless of rank, was expected to excel in the specializations of bujutsu, it soon became apparent that, during the long periods of enforced stagnation (otherwise known as periods of relative peace), a certain degenerative process was set in motion, as the effect of prolonged inactivity upon the martial skills of these lower-ranking retainers began to make itself felt. The time and attention devoted not only to their literary instruction but even to their military preparation, a prerogative of their class, was markedly less than during the martial, pre-Tokugawa era, when the retainers' very lives often depended upon their martial capacity on the battlefield—such a capacity depending, in turn, upon their skill with the spear and sword (the bow and arrow being considered more aristocratic and exclusive in nature). Before the Tokugawa period, when the feudal barons depended upon the martial skills of their retainers, inspired leaders understood the fundamental importance of foot soldiers in the winning of battles, and warriors of the lower ranks, such as the *nakakosho,* the *tomo-kosho,* and the *kachi* (that is, the huge mass of foot soldiers *[ashigaru]),* were properly trained and even encouraged to develop their abilities to the

point where they might even attain a position of supreme command as had Oda Nobunaga, Hideyoshi, and others equally famous. The age of heroes defeating armies singlehandedly had always been more myth than reality—history proving with depressing regularity that battles were usually worn by using masses of troops in the most advantageous manner.

Even great warriors, vastly skilled in the arts of archery and spearmanship, were, upon occasion, cut to pieces by veteran spearmen of *hirazamurai* rank or by their attendants *(chugen)* led by leaders of *kogashira* rank. Each group of spearmen composed of warriors of these ranks was a formidable unit of combat that could be neutralized, not by a lonely knight charging blindly and vaingloriously into their midst, but only by a similar body of trained archers or spearmen. Once the compact unity of the group had been shattered, the warriors of higher rank and their sword-wielding officers could finally engage in individual, close-range swordplay. And there is evidence to indicate that even then many of these officers and leaders fell beneath the skilled spear-thrust of an obscure veteran of the lower ranks.

During the Tokugawa period, the noticeably inferior quality of the education and preparation of low-ranking retainers, who represented the great majority of the *buke,* began to accelerate as the gap between these retainers and their higher-ranking leaders widened. By the latter part of the seventeenth century, the ancient position of clan leader, which could be held by one emerging from almost any rank of the warrior class, had become virtually impossible for a *bushi* of the lower ranks to attain. In this way, it began to mirror the position once held only by high-ranking members of the *kuge* at the imperial court of Nara and Kyoto. This division in the *buke* even began to assume that aura of interpretation of divine intent that had once been the prerogative of imperial circles. In time, the clans became so irrevocably divided that it seemed as if "there were two different races of people within the same clan" (Fukuzawa, 312). The distinctions between clansmen were based upon many virtually insurmountable differences of rights, kinship, income, education, household economy, manners, and customs. To begin with, "under no circumstances was marriage permitted between those of the rank of *kyunin* and those of the rank of *kachi.* Such alliances were forbidden both by clan law and by custom. Even in case of adultery, both parties nearly always came from the same [rank]" (Fukuzawa, 311). Not even merits or talents of an exceptional nature (although such qualities had raised peasants to the rank of military dictator in earlier periods) could bridge the gap between the upper and lower categories of warriors in Tokugawa times, when the stratification became so rigid that in the Okudaira clan, for example,

HIRAZAMURAI spearmen against armor-clad BUSHI

> a lower samurai, whatever his merits or talents, could never rise above an upper samurai. There were a few examples of men rising from the position of calligraphers (the highest rank in the lower category), for instance, to that of member of the *koshigumi* (the lowest rank in the upper category), but no more than four five during the whole period of 250 years. (Fukuzawa, 309)

Financially, the warrior of the lower category received a stipend of approximately fifteen *koku* of rice, or thirteen *koku* plus a ration for two persons, or ten *koku* plus rations for one person. A ration represented the unit value of what an average person needed each month, valued usually from one to five *sho.* This income "was not sufficient to cover even the necessities of life such as food and clothing. Hence, everyone in the family capable of work, both men and women alike, eked out a poor livelihood by odd jobs such as spinning and handicrafts" (Fukuzawa, 313).

Naturally, open as well as disguised forms of corruption were rampant among the warriors, a plague which edicts and official decrees of every sort were never able to eradicate (perhaps because they were concerned primarily with the effects of that corruption rather than with its cause). It assumed so many guises that "even a straight and upright official, trusted by the people because he refused absolutely to have anything to do with bribery or perquisites, could yet hardly help but slip unawares into the tempting trap of corruption" (Fukuzawa, 316). The practice became so widespread and generally accepted, in fact, that it even acquired its own particular name: *tashi-buchi,* or "eking out one's stipend."

Thus the larger masses of warriors in the lower categories began to assume characteristics formerly associated with commoners *(heimin)* in general and, in particular, with those highly dynamic and irrepressible merchants *(chonin),* whose counterparts in Europe had changed the course of that continent's history centuries earlier by moving against the feudal castles from their "burgs," with their guilds, corporations, associations, and banks all uniting firmly behind the new urban troops.

In Japan, the erosion of the feudal military power did not seem to come (as it had in Europe) from without, or as the result of a direct confrontation between those who lived in castles and the inhabitants of the towns. On the contrary, the erosion seemed to take place within the military class itself, as its lower-ranking members began to merge in ever-increasing numbers with members of other social classes. Intermarriage between the warriors of the lower categories and the *chonin,* for example, was more frequent "than intermarriage between the lower samurai and the upper samurai" (Blacker, 307); it proved to be a highly satisfactory arrangement for all parties concerned, because "samurai would be adopted into the families of wealthy *chonin* for the material comforts there to be found. *Chonin* could, through the prac-

tice of adoption, in effect, purchase the status of samurai" (Blacker, 307). This fusion, according to many historians, "provided one of the greatest motive forces behind the Restoration [in 1868]. It could well be said that the Restoration was accomplished by the initiative and enterprise of the lower samurai combined with the wealth of the *chonin*" (Blacker, 307).

In actuality, the situation created by the sharp division between those two broad categories of warriors had made conditions so bleak for those of the lower classes that many of the lower-ranking warriors became mutinous and "suddenly changed their whole attitude to military and literary pursuits. This was probably why some of them opened halls for teaching their children swordsmanship" (Fukuzawa, 321).

During the final phase of the Tokugawa period, in fact, many obscure warriors (affiliated with clans, but as samurai of lower rank) are mentioned in the chronicles of bujutsu, where they are described as excellent swordsmen who often gave higher-ranking warriors fierce opposition in swordplay. Many masters of the various arts of unarmed combat who were active during this final period of the Tokugawa's domination belonged to the lower ranks of the samurai class. And, even before this, warriors who had abrogated their pledges of affiliation to a lord or castle and become their own masters (re the masterless warrior, or *ronin)* had begun to reverse the process of deterioration activated within the *buke* by its own harsh, segregationist laws. These masterless warriors were usually known as fearsome fighters whom a wise samurai, regardless of rank, skill in the use of weapons, or reputation, would not needlessly confront.

As one might expect, this merging of the lower categories with members of the subordinate classes of farmers, artisans, and merchants involved the transmission of military ethics, spirit, and skills to the latter, who, thus prepared, flowed smoothly into the ranks of the new imperial army of 1873. Thus the conservative clans of traditional warriors found that the new soldier of Japan who confronted them on the battlefield was characterized by that discipline, dedication to military duties, and determination to fight to the bitter end which had once been considered the hallmark of the *bushi* alone. This new army of conscripts from all classes, imbued with the tradition of the feudal *bushi,* operated with remarkable efficiency whether in Japan or on the Asian continent. It proved to be the perfect instrument for carrying out policies devised by the leaders of those ancient clans, whose roots were so deeply feudal in nature that they probably could not have been eradicated without doing serious damage to the inner fiber of a nation which had undergone such a long period of martial nurturing.

At the dawn of the Tokugawa period, however, and throughout most of its evolution, the military class, despite its sharp division according to clan and rank, was the proud center of power in Japan. Pride in their status was a predominant characteristic of the warriors, and even the lowest among them felt and behaved like a monarch before commoners *(heimin),* whether farmers, artisans, or merchants. Failure to behave respectfully toward the *bushi* (i.e., as prescribed by custom and law) meant instantaneous death at his hands. As indicated earlier, Ieyasu's laws were most specific: no one was allowed to interfere with a samurai in the act of cutting down a commoner who had behaved toward him in a rude manner. This freedom of judgment and action under the law, limited only by possible fear of immediate reprisals, was the very root of that "practice-murder" in which a sword blade was tested upon a defenseless pilgrim, an isolated farmer, or a solitary commoner—the shout which accompanied the blow acting as a warning that sent everyone in the vicinity scuttling for shelter.

The pride of the samurai was such that, on a general scale, it was often indistinguishable from plain arrogance and brutality. In fact, the arrogance of these samurai, who, with "their supercilious manner and foppish mien" (Nishida, 32), constituted the "most overbearing class in Japan" (Mitford, 67), could be and often was deadly, whenever one of their number felt, rightly or wrongly, that he had been shown less than the proper, submissive respect due him. In time, the lower samurai might even be said to have melded with the other classes of the nation on a more democratic level in the nineteenth century, in response to the pressure of historical circumstances. But the higher-ranking samurai and their leaders in the various clans were, and generally remained, well insulated from the broader reality of the society they ruled (as was also true of those aristocracies which emerged in feudal Europe by the force of their own military power or, in more modern times, those leaders and their cohorts whose strength was drawn from the industrial and mercantile complexes). Naturally, most high-ranking samurai continued to oppose fiercely any course of national history or evolution except those strictly in accordance with the principles of clan supremacy and ancestral worship which formed the core of their traditions and constituted their ultimate raison d'être.

The Samurai Woman

A salient and thought-provoking characteristic of most ancient cultures is the predominant role played by women in the history and management of clan affairs. Historiography often seems to minimize the early, strongly matriarchal aspects of man's social units; the frequently myopic views of chroniclers of later ages and periods, bent upon reinforcing the preconceived notions of their patrons, tend largely to either denigrate woman's role in the military history of early civilizations or ignore it entirely. Ancient sagas, archaeological discoveries, and the painstaking work of anthropologists, however, indicate widespread participation by women in clan or tribal life in pre- and proto-historical times, from the icy lands of Nothern Europe to the tropical cultures of Egypt and Mesopotamia, in both ancient Sparta and the Celtic clans of Western Europe, as well as in nomad tribes roaming the steppes of Mongolia and, of course, in the many clan cultures of Southeast Asia and China.

In Japan, woman's originally predominant role finds its first expression in the mythological records of that land, which traditionally emphasize the supremacy of Amaterasu, the solar goddess, among all the deities in the Japanese pantheon, as well as equating the position of Izanagi, the female, with that of Izanami, the male, on the fighting level. The long shadow cast by ancient matriarchal influence is also apparent in the predominance of the solar cult, which was female in its original Japanese conception.

Even the first chronicles of Japanese history are filled with the exploits of warrior queens leading their troops against enemy strongholds in the land of Yamato or across the straits to Korea. In time, the growing influence of Confucian doctrine began to reduce her position of preeminence, hedging her about with restrictions of every sort, which, however, were not always accepted as meekly as later historians would have us believe. In the Heian period we find her not on the battlefield perhaps, but occupying a position of prominence in the cultural hierarchy of the age. Certain aristocratic ladies of *kuge* status emerged as literary figures of astounding insight and sophistication. Their literary production, although not expressed in the rigid and pedantic forms of classical Chinese writing generally preferred by the scholars of the time, provides one of the first manifestations of a truly indigenous form of expression, whose depth of perception, as well as complex content, help to explain why the various empresses and aristocratic dames of Nara and Kyoto wielded such power, whether governing directly or guiding more subtly (if just as effectively) the affairs of state from places of retirement or seclusion.

From the provinces, a new breed of women, the female members of the *buke*, joined their menfolk in the struggle for political and military predominance. These women did not lead troops as in archaic times, but, steeped in the same martial tradition and clinging to those warlike customs which characterized their men as a class, they were a stern reflection of their male counterparts. As such, they acted to consolidate and reinforce those qualities considered of fundamental importance to the emerging class of the *buke*. The product of a particular system, the samurai woman became its soundest basis and transmitter.

One such woman was Lady Masa (Masako), wife of the first Kamakura shogun, Minamoto Yoritomo. Mere quoted Brinkley in describing her as "astute, crafty, resourceful and heroic," adding:

> During her husband's lifetime she wielded immense influence and after his death she virtually ruled the empire. This seems to be the only recorded instance in the history of Japan when the supreme power was wielded by a woman who was neither Empress nor Empress-dowager. Nominally, of course, Lady Masa did not rule, but her power and influence were very real. (Mere, 16)

The samurai woman was trained to be as loyal and totally committed as her father, brothers, and husband to their immediate superior in the clan hierarchy and, like her male relatives, was expected to carry out every authorized assignment, including those which might involve force of arms. Thus it is not surprising to find in the literature of bujutsu the annotation that women of the *buke* were trained in the use of traditional weapons, which they were expected to use against a foe or, if necessary, to end their own lives. Moreover, many episodes concerning the rise of the warrior class mention women who played militarily determinant roles—even joining their menfolk on the battlefield upon occasion. Certain chronicles, for example, mention Tomoe, the wife of one of Yoshitomo's nephews, Yoshinaka. Authors who have discussed her exploits are almost unanimous "in praising her great strength and skill with weapons, her superb horsemanship and her fearless courage" (Mere, 15). She used to ride into battle with her husband, leading and encouraging his troops with her initiative and bearing. She even displayed that peculiar anger typical of the professional fighter when an opponent handles him cavalierly. It is related, in fact, that she killed several enemy retainers in single combat at the battle of Azazu-no-Hara: "when their leader, Uchida Iyeyoshi, attempted to capture her, she struck her horse and her sleeve, which he had seized, was rent and a part of it was left in his hand. Angered at this, she wheeled her charger and attacking him in her turn, cut off his head, which she forthwith presented to her husband" (Mere, 14-15).

Among the weapons the samurai woman handled with skill was the spear, both the straight *(yari)* and the curved *(naginata)*, which customarily hung over the doors of every military household and which she could use against charging foes or any unauthorized intruder found within the precincts of the clan's establishment. She was also equally well versed in handling the short dagger *(kaiken)*, which, like the male warrior's *wakizashi*, was always carried on her person (usually in her sleeve or sash) and which she could deftly employ against armed foes in close combat or throw with deadly accuracy. This same dagger was the one a samurai woman would use if she undertook to commit ceremonial suicide, not by piercing her lower abdomen as would her male counterpart, but rather by cutting her throat in accordance with the exact rules of ritual suicide, which also instructed her in the correct manner of tying her ankles together, in order to insure that her body would be found properly composed, whatever her death agonies. Under the name *jigai*, in fact, suicide was as familiar to her as it was to her menfolk.

She not only accepted death resignedly at the hands of her male relatives or superiors if capture by enemy forces was imminent, but even dispatched the men herself if, for any reason, they were unable or unwilling to perform the ritual act, sparing neither herself nor her children in such a situation. One of the

The women of the BUKE

most ancient episodes concerning the making and executing of this decision in accordance with martial tradition is to be found in the ancient sagas which describe the destruction of the Taira clan during the great sea battle at Dan-no-Ura, in the straits of Shimonoseki. Nii-no-Ama, grandmother of the infant Emperor Antoku (son of Kiyomori's daughter Tokuko or Kenrei-mon-in), when confronted with the alternative of surrendering to the warriors of the Minamoto clans, clasped the child tightly in her arms and plunged with him into the waves of the straits, followed by other court ladies and Tokuko as well. The emperor's mother was rescued by force, but the others succeeded in drowning themselves and the infant heir.

The samurai woman also used suicide as a form of protest against an injustice she felt had been perpetrated against her by a superior. One of the most striking examples of this is related by François Caron (1600-73). The powerful lord of Higo had engineered the murder of one of his most loyal vassals so that he might include the beautiful wife of the deceased among his concubines. The woman requested a certain period of time within which to mourn and bury her husband and then asked the lord to assemble the highest dignitaries of the clan and her husband's friends on the tower of his castle, ostensibly to celebrate the end of her mourning period. Since she might very well have stabbed herself with her *kaiken* if anyone had tried to force her to violate her mourning period, her requests were granted. On the appointed day, as the ceremony in honor of her slain husband drew to a close, she suddenly threw herself from the tower "and broke her neck" (Cooper, 83) before the very eyes of the lord of Higo, his vassals, and the dignitaries of the clan. This type of suicide, although not performed strictly in accordance with the rules of ritual suicide, was recognized as one of valid protest *(kan-shi)* against a master's injustice. It created a dilemma in military minds, however, since it was also a breach of the code of absolute loyalty which dictated that the lady's life was not hers to dispose of, especially not in such an independent manner.

Equally famous in Japanese literature and theater is the story of Kesa-gozen, the wife of an imperial guard in Kyoto during the twelfth century, when the *buke* was being drawn toward the imploding and collapsing center of the empire. This lady was the object of another warrior's passion and he was determined to have her. When her pursuer planned to murder her husband in his sleep, she substituted herself in her husband's bed and allowed herself to be decapitated in his stead, thus saving her honor and her husband's life at one and the same time.

As ferocious and determined as male members of the *buke*, the samurai woman also took upon herself, when necessary, the duty of revenge which the particularly Japanese interpretation of Confucian doctrine had rendered both an absolute and virtually automatic response to the death or dishonor of one's lord. "Not only did man consider it his duty to avenge his family or lord," wrote Dautremer, "but woman herself did not fail before the task. Of this, Japanese history gives us many instances" (Dautremer, 83). Even throughout the long and debilitating Tokugawa period, she remained generally attached (often even more strongly than her male counterpart) to the clan's rule of loyalty, that is, to the *uji-no-osa* and, by delegation, to her husband. In an era characterized by the degeneration of martial virtues, by effeminate behavior, profligacy, and dissipation within the "floating world" *(ukiyo)* of a new culture, she was noted for her chastity, fidelity, and self-control. For centuries, she remained a forbidding figure, clearly traditionalist and conservative in outlook and action, who clung tenaciously to the martial ethos of her clan not only in essence (which the Tokugawa period was diluting substantially), but also in form and paraphernalia.

As the nucleus of those households which even today maintain the ties linking them to the feudal past, many of these women continue to resist change and bring up their children beneath the aristocratic shadow of the family's *kami*—an ancient suit of armor before which sticks of incense burn night and day. Many of their sons enter the military academies of Japan, while their daughters face one another across the spacious *dojo* where the ancient art of naginatajutsu is taught to them, as well as to other girls of lesser military lineage but of equally intense attachment to the tradition which produced the samurai woman.

The Masterless Warrior: The Ronin

A position of particular importance in the development and evolution of bujutsu, especially within the rigid and stratified society of Tokugawa Japan, was occupied by "a sinister figure of dread in the land; a spectre that ever haunts the dreams of the officials, making the weaker-kneed among them sweat the cold sweat of terror" (Murdoch, vol. 3, 704).

This scholar was referring to the samurai without a master, the warrior who had been set adrift, like a wave, on the sea of life: the *ronin*. The literal translation of this name, in fact, according to Brinkley, "would be 'wave man' and it signified one who is tossed about aimlessly, hither and yon, as by the waves of the sea" (Brinkley[2], 56).

According to Yazaki, the dissolution of many fiefs by order of the Tokugawa left large numbers of samurai to fend for themselves. This author estimates that their number to have been some 400,000 and divides them into three major groups, with those wealthy retainers who had voluntarily resigned their positions listed first, followed by those who had been "fired" by their lords, "as a result of momentary discord" for which many would try to make amends in order to be allowed to "return to their posts" (Yazaki, 204). The third group, "at the bottom," included warriors dismissed "for personal errors or greed who could not reveal the names of their former masters" (Yazaki, 204-5). The reasons underlying a warrior's change in status from affiliated samurai to *ronin,* however, were numerous and varied. First of all, a man could be born a *ronin* if he were the son of a masterless samurai who had never renounced his status as a warrior. But an affiliated retainer of a military clan could also become a *ronin,* due to certain changes in his, his master's, or his clan's circumstances. He might be dismissed from service by his lord, for example, or he might request dismissal in order to be free to embark upon a particular adventure which could conceivably discredit or involve his former master if the retainer had not severed his clan ties. Most frequently, the *bushi* became masterless through a stroke of misfortune, as when, for example, the fortunes of war turned against his master, who would then usually be executed or exiled by his enemies, or when his master's clan was disbanded by order of the shogun or reduced in size for whatever reason.

The frequency of these social ruptures kept the roaming hordes of *ronin* replenished until the end of the Tokugawa shogunate in 1867. Of particular interest are the tales of military retainers who joined the ranks of the *ronin* willingly (as indicated above) in order to avenge themselves, or their masters, by a murderous deed which, had they remained affiliated with their original clan, might have implicated their own lord and fellow retainers as participants in the deed and, therefore, made them answerable to the

authorities. Such a device, quite obviously, exempted many masters from the consequences of their own hatred, consequences which were loyally borne by a retainer who assumed full responsibility for the act. Often warriors became *ronin* to relieve a tense situation in a clan, returning when things had returned to normal. After the opening of Japan to the Western powers, many retainers chose to become *ronin* in order to serve in the Western compounds and learn from the hairy barbarians (also known as round-eyed devils) before resuming their status in the clan where they could share their newly acquired knowledge with their masters and fellow clansmen. The *ronin* status, finally, could be acquired if a samurai were to join a ward *(za)* and become a tradesman.

Left to their own devices, and without visible means of support, many *ronin* taught bujutsu for a fee to anyone who could afford it. They often hired themselves out as bodyguards *(yojimbo)* to wealthy patrons of *heimin* status; many others supported themselves by pillage—that is, by joining or leading groups of bandits whose presence cast a brutal shadow over the countryside. The underworld in every town and city was populated by many of these, whom some authors qualified as "disreputable knights-errant," whose only profession was that of bearing arms and, therefore, of systematic violence.

As indicated above, the *ronin* formed an active and numerous class of warriors during the entire span of the Tokugawa dictatorship. The progressive elimination of those large and ancient clans which the Tokugawa considered unreliable resulted in a rapid increase in the number of *ronin.* Stalking the countryside and lurking in the cities, these bitter men, whose weapons were theirs by both law and custom, were forced by circumstances to develop a certain independence of mind if they were to survive. Interestingly enough, while they usually continued to despise commoners, most of them also assumed a defiant attitude toward their formerly affiliated peers, the samurai and their lords. Many *ronin,* however, sought a new master to serve—a desire which their very condition of disenfranchisement often thwarted, since accepting the service of such a retainer meant setting a precedent, an act generally frowned upon by most would-be masters.

In time, a number of these errant warriors took a definite liking to this more difficult but generally more exciting mode of existence, which taxed their wits and imagination to the fullest and forced them to mature further than was generally the norm at that time. Those *ronin* who kept their weapons and did not lose their identity by merging fully with the class of people among whom they lived, whether this was the clergy or one of the various classes of commoners, stood out rather starkly in the rigidly stratified society of feudal Japan. In the increasingly conformistic culture of the Tokugawa, many *ronin* sought

paramilitary positions as wardsmen in the cities or as leaders of groups set up for the protection of some particular social units (villages, cooperatives, warehouses, etc.). Upon occasion, their skills proved so valuable that a military baron would invite them to join his clan, thus enabling them to return with full honors to the ranks of the class from which they had become separated. Some of them became addicted to a life of comparative freedom, however—at least as much freedom as was conceivable in feudal Japan. These *ronin* traveled all over Japan, meeting and accepting challenges on the road and often actually going out of their way to seek them.

Bujutsu owes these warriors a great deal. Here was the ideal fighting man—ideal because self-reliant and self-disciplined, therefore unpredictable in combat and always in a state of readiness. As a class, their fighting potential was acknowledged repeatedly by the best military leaders in the land. Even the huge armies of Ieyasu could do very little against the groups *of ronin* "who had lost their property after the battle of Sekiga-hara" (Cole, 51) and had subsequently been hired by Hideyori to defend his Osaka castle. They proved to be indomitable foes, due to both their skill and their hatred of Ieyasu and his forces. Only devious negotiations and the unwise weakening of the fortifications finally made it possible for Ieyasu's forces to overwhelm the defenders of the castle. Even then, as Nishida relates, groups of *ronin,* led by the famous swordsman Sanada Yukimura, cut their way through the massed enemy lines, using their spears and swords with deadly effect, actually reaching Ieyasu's main headquarters, to the great consternation of his generals and retainers.

Before Hideyori and Ieyasu, Oda Nobunaga had realized early in his career as warlord the tremendous value of such men whom the fortunes of politics and/or war had made outcasts. Akechi, who ultimately killed Nobunaga, had been a *ronin,* one whose skill and personality were so impressive that Nobunaga had raised him to a position of equal standing with that other famous general, Hideyoshi.

During the Momoyama period, these roaming groups of *ronin* tended to gravitate toward the cities where earning one's livelihood, however meager and in whatever manner, often seemed preferable to life in the ravaged countryside. They often united for brief periods to lead their own or other people's revolts against the constituted authority of the times; even after Ieyasu's rise to power and throughout the Tokugawa period, they remained a troublesome lot whose riotings and brawls, although regularly suppressed by force of arms, continually erupted anew. Every shogun of the Tokugawa clan feared and distrusted the *ronin* intensely and had them kept under strict surveillance throughout the entire period of their dominance. These sulking warriors were a problem both in the mass and as individuals. In groups, they proved

what they could do against *bakufu* forces at Shimabara, when they rushed to join the peasants of Arima and Amakusa, who were revolting against their provincial governors. It took the *bakufu* months of intense warfare and a prolonged siege involving more than fifty thousand warriors, as well as the contribution of Dutch warships with their powerful guns, to crush the insurrection.

The rule of the Tokugawa was continually disturbed by the *ronin's* plots and the assassinations they attempted or engineered. The names of certain individuals, particularly troublesome *ronin,* fill the annals of the shogun's secret police. One such was Shosetsu, the errant *ronin* who traveled throughout Japan during the early part of the Tokugawa period, testing his swordsmanship against masters of bujutsu, while cementing friendships and arranging alliances with other warriors until he had surreptitiously amassed a force of over five thousand armed warriors, strategically placed in and around Edo (some of whom were even instructors of government officers). Although the police, alerted by a number of merchants and bankers who had unwittingly financed the plot, trapped Shosetsu and his chief aides the night before the plotters were to launch their revolt, they were unable to exhibit any prisoners to the shogun, only corpses with abdomens slashed according to the rules governing ritual suicide.

Ultimately, as a category, the *ronin* proved to be one of the most powerful forces among those in league against the Tokugawa system of direct affiliation to provincial lords, which they helped to overthrow in favor of a system of general affiliation with and loyalty to the emperor, within whose modern army they finally found their rightful place.

An individualist by necessity, the *ronin* had to rely almost entirely upon himself and upon his martial skill, whether with weapons (especially the sword or spear) or without, when challenged by any affiliated samurai (usually in the company of other samurai) who decided to be offended by the very existence of such a social freak. A *ronin,* after all, affronted all the laws and customs of clan affiliation just by being what he was. Furthermore, in slaying such a man, an affiliated samurai did not have to fear anyone's subsequent displeasure, nor did he run the risk of the slain warrior's lord or clan seeking vengeance—since a *ronin* had neither lord nor clan.

As late as the nineteenth century, the judo master Yokoyama reminisced about an encounter between one of these wandering warriors, "rather shabbily dressed and...evidently very poor," and three young samurai in the Kojimachi ward of Kudan. The younger men forced the *ronin* to accept their challenge to a duel because his scabbard had inadvertently touched the scabbard of one of the three.

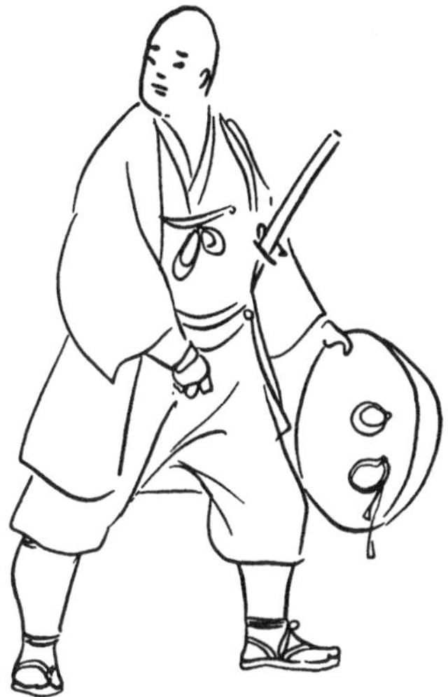

In accordance with custom, the combatants exchanged names and swords were unsheathed, the three samurai on one side facing the solitary opponent with whom the sympathies of the onlookers evidently lay. The keen blades of the duellists glittered in the sun. The *ronin,* as calm as though engaged merely in a friendly fencing bout, advanced steadily with the point of his weapon directed against the samurai in the centre of the trio, and apparently indifferent to an attack on either flank. The samurai in the middle gave ground inch by inch and the *ronin* as surely stepped forward. Then the right-hand samurai, who thought he saw an opening, rushed to the attack, but the *ronin,* who had clearly anticipated this move, parried and with lightning rapidity cut his enemy down with a mortal blow. The left-hand samurai came on in his turn but was treated in similar fashion, a single stroke felling him to the ground bathed in blood. All this took almost less time than it takes to tell. The samurai in the centre, seeing the fate of his comrades, thought better of his first intention and took to his heels. (Harrison, 71-72)

The *ronin* in question then "repaired to the neighbouring magistrate's office to report the occurrence, as the law required." This in the nineteenth century!

For centuries, then, these unaffiliated warriors could be found traveling across the length and breadth of Japan, often bearing deep in their hearts a mortal grudge against those whom they felt had injured them, that is, other, affiliated warriors as well as their lords and teachers. A number of the latter—especially teachers of bujutsu—met their match in the use of sword or spear when answering an open challenge from an obscure, itinerant *bushi,* clearly masterless. Affiliated samurai, on the other hand, who were traveling for instruction, very seldom engaged in mortal combat, since they were journeying at their masters' command and for a definite purpose: to learn. The *ronin,* with neither master nor purpose, had only his strange revolts and violent, individual explosions, which often made him a popular figure among commoners, who, through his efforts, might see another hated samurai cut down.

In the interests of survival, the range of the *ronin's* knowledge of bujutsu had to be as extensive as humanly possible. He had to be well acquainted not only with the traditional methods of combat practiced by the military class but also with those employed by the common people, among whom he spent much of his time, and with whom—owing to the pride intrinsic to his warrior heritage, however unaffiliated—he usually felt he had very little in common.

It has often been assumed that a *ronin,* freed of the traditional bond of allegiance to a lord and a clan, automatically became the enemy not only of individual lords and samurai but of the very system upon which Japanese feudal society was based, thus becoming the natural protector of commoners, who, after all, helped to keep him alive. In most cases, this assumption would not be correct. To be sure, a *ronin* was usually in revolt against his fate, but generally (with certain notable exceptions) not so much because he felt that the system itself was unjust and despotic, but rather because he by force of circumstances had been separated from the military establishment and, therefore, deprived of his rightful position of honor within the system. Being in bad odor with the military establishment, however, did not make him a member of any of the other social classes, which he (staunch warrior of the feudal age that he was) tended to despise quite heartily. If anything, his independent position usually made him even more arrogant and overbearing than the affiliated samurai, since control over him through pressure by other samurai or clan regulation was impossible. He made his own decisions according to the circumstances, and this freedom, when not accompanied by the moderating influence of a well-developed sense of personal responsibility, could produce an uncontrolled brute whom the police forces of many towns had great trouble in subduing. Indirect references in military chronicles to "tame *ronin,*" supported by farmers for the purpose of learning the military arts (Dore[2], 242), actually indicate that the general attitude toward life entertained by many such warriors was often decidedly untamed and quite ferocious. In general, he was and remained always a warrior, with a sustained belief in his continuing military status, despite the fact that he had become separated from the *buke's* military organization. In isolated cases, as indicated above, a particular warrior would take a truly independent stance, which, due to the massive force of the establishment he was battling on an individual level, often produced a fighter of truly heroic proportions whose exploits comprise some of the most fascinating episodes to be found in Japanese history and literature.

2
THE HEIMIN

The Farmers

The distinction between the warrior and the farmer, between the *bushi* and the *hyakusho (no),* became a formal principle of social stratification with the advent to power of Tokugawa Ieyasu.

The pragmatic step which made this principle enforceable had been taken by Hideyoshi years earlier (in 1588) when he instituted the famous "sword-hunt" *(katana-gari).* This widespread confiscation of weapons, as pointed out by Goedertier, was clearly intended to disarm the peasants as a class and thereby put an end to the "agrarian uprisings" (Goedertier, 128) which were a threat to the supremacy of the family of the bow and arrow. An equally important and highly respected principle, however, which had been considered valid during the previous ages and remained so to a certain extent until the Restoration (at least for the lower category and ranks of warriors), was the principle that the "samurai originated from the peasant class and should return to it" (Dore[2], 221). It was this principle which kept the warrior class in the provinces very close to the land—the source of wealth and power—and to those who cultivated it. The lower levels of the military pyramid merged with the upper levels of the peasant class, and the vicissitudes of either tended to affect the other vitally throughout the entire feudal period, until the industrial revolution shifted the focus of history from the countryside to the cities. This principle, in fact, found its primary expression in the position of the peasant class, which Ieyasu listed immediately after the warrior on the social scale, and in the prestige associated with the positions of district-headman *(ojiya)* and village-headman *(shoya),* who "were allowed to wear swords," could send their offspring to the fief schools, and who "enjoyed a status distinctly superior to that of an ordinary foot-soldier" (Dore[2], 221). This preferential treatment is understandable when one recalls that even after the formation of strong corporations or guilds *(za)* of artisans *(shokunin, ko)* and merchants *(akindo, sho)* in the feudal and castle towns, cities, and provincial centers, both during and after the Heian period (and deep into the Tokugawa period), the national economy rested essentially upon the production of rice. Rice was power, and he who controlled the growth and distribution of the former was able to wield the latter.

From the beginning of the *buke's* history, therefore, it had been almost impossible to make a clear distinction between those masses of low-ranking warriors who comprised the armed forces of provincial centers, castles, and districts, and the equally large masses of farmers, organized in tight clans and village groups, who produced rice and protected it within their own territories. By the late Heian period these armed forces (generally able-bodied men of peasant stock) had become more or less permanent standing armies—the first step toward that military specialization which was to form the root of a new and compact class. During this period, a distinct character and intrinsic exclusiveness, as well as a sense of mission, began to develop in these men. Before the Heian period, during the ancient periods of imperial supremacy and of intense struggle among the aristocratic families of the land, the imperial decree of general conscription had clearly identified the aristocratic leaders on one side and the great mass of conscripts furnished by the provincial centers on the other. The erosion of central, imperial, and aristocratic power, which we have described in previous sections, forced many aristocrats at the periphery of their class to join the rural masses, and thereby facilitated the emergence of new leaders whose power rested not upon imperial decree but upon the strength of cohorts of fighting farmers loyal to those leaders. But we must add that although there are indications in the records that many a leader of the new, emerging class of warriors in the tenth century was of aristocratic lineage, it appears equally true that the great majority of them were not. Even a carefully edited presentation of history in succeeding centuries could not conceal the resentment felt by the crown and the ancient aristocrats toward those "people of all ranks" who were making their power felt, often in direct opposition to the administration and its provincial tax collectors. And even the characteristically Japanese need to trace one's lineage back to a divinity or its direct representative on earth (that is, the emperor and his aristocratic entourage) could not erase the fact that as late as the Momoyama period, the leaders who shaped the military history of Japan for centuries to come (Nobunaga, Hideyoshi, Kato Kiyomasa) were originally of peasant stock.

For centuries, then, the great mass of farmers comprised, and remained, a potentially formidable mass of fighters. According to Seligman, their nature as clansmen (which they shared with all their countrymen, regardless of class) and their history worked to reinforce this potentiality. In addition to furnishing foot soldiers for the imperial and provincial armies that ravaged his lands and villages down through the centuries (from the first recorded period of Japanese history until Tokugawa times), the farmer had to defend himself, as best he could, from armed bands of brigands roaming the countryside, as well as from the government's rapacious tax collectors. In this context, we find in the annals of Japan numerous and lengthy reports concerning uprisings of the "soil people" *(domin)*, those explosive revolts *(ikki)* called *do-ikki* in the Muromachi period and *hyakusho-ikki* during the Tokugawa period, which became a deeply-rooted tradition to which peasants resorted when their conditions became intolerable. Every one of those revolts was a bloody affair which necessitated sending armed forces from the various government centers to quell it.

Interestingly enough, the outcome of a confrontation on the battlefield between trained soldiers, armed with the most sophisticated weapons of the period, and undisciplined groups of farmers armed with anything readily available, was not always favorable to the professional warriors. As early as the latter part of the Heian period, many imperial tax collectors found themselves unable to carry out their duties in certain provinces, notwithstanding the presence of armed escorts.

Resistance was offered not only by clans whose forces had been organized on a professionally military basis, but also by small villages whose inhabitants followed the lead of their elders. In 1428 and 1485, for example, village elders in the provinces of Omi and Yamashiro led a series of peasants' revolts against the Ashikaga representatives appointed by the government, who could not protect the farmers from the scourge of feudal armies laying waste the countryside. The farmers, in turn, foiled every attempt to overcome their resistance subsequently made by the government and neighboring military clans, for more than seven years. Another famous farmers' revolt occurred in the province of Echizen in the fourteenth century, when peasants rose up against the armies of Lord Asakura, which had been sent to force payment of taxes to the great metropolitan center in Kyoto. The farmers, led by their local priests and armed with crude weapons generally adapted from agricultural tools, proved more than a match for the professional swordsmen of the *buke*.

Even after the Tokugawa had established their military hold over the nation and an era of comparative peace was declared, the fighting capacity of the Japanese farmer was still often tested on the battlefield—this time against a more professionally organized military establishment than he had faced before (in the view of many scholars). Several hundred rebellions broke out during this era. It was during this time that the remnants of that social and territorial mobility which the emerging *buke* had progressively reduced in centuries of continuous warfare were almost totally erased. Farmers were restricted to their villages

(mura) and then further divided into groups of five families, in accordance with the system of collective responsibility known as *gonin-gumi,* which made these five families responsible jointly for any action considered unlawful by the military authorities of the district, whether that action was performed by all the members of the group or, even without their knowledge, by only one of them. Hideyoshi borrowed this system from China, "where it was known as Pao-Chia system" (Norman, 102), and introduced it into his military administration of Japan in 1597. Every group of five families had a formal headman *ikumigashira* or *kumicho),* and these group leaders, together with other village notables *(toshiyori),* were responsible to the village headman *(nanushi, shoya),* who, in turn, reported directly to the military representative of the territory, the *gundai* or *daikan.* The farmers "lived upon and tilled all the land of the province and paid a rent directly to the daimyo, *karo* or samurai" (Grinnan, 12). These rents were based upon immutable values; that is, they were not affected by the vagaries of nature, such as a bad season, floods, or other disasters, whether man-made or natural. In special cases, officials of the military administration might recognize a particularly distressing situation and reduce the rent for a limited period of time, but the sums due were never wholly remitted.

Restricted to their *mura* and their allotted fields, forbidden under threat of the most dire penalties (both individual and collective) to leave their homes or fields, subjected to continual pressure from "impoverished samurai and feudal lords" (Embree[2], 6), it is no wonder that even in the Tokugawa period "more than a thousand peasant rebellions took place" (Rudowski, 255). Yazaki gives a more specific number—1,240 revolts "during the 268 years from 1599 to the end of the Edo era in 1867" (Yazaki, 251). These revolts, as indicated earlier, were extremely violent and feared even by the *buke* because of the desperate commitment of the peasants themselves to the use of force, once they had been goaded into action. The scope of such revolts ranged from desertion of fields to destruction of property and armed clashes. They were usually put down quite harshly and the leaders (although they were sometimes able to obtain for their followers redress of the abuses which had triggered the revolt) promptly executed, often displaying that stoic indifference to pain and contempt for death which the *bushi* considered his exclusive and distinctive characteristic. This last practice seemed to have been generally accepted as unavoidable. Many peasant leaders, however, and their closest followers refused to submit to this custom. Instead, their revolts went underground, as they slipped away to the hills where bands of brigands and outlaws had always found a haven; or else they disappeared into the seamy underworld which existed in every heavily trafficked coastal town or metropolitan center.

One notable case which exemplified the remarkable martial potentialities of the peasant and, in this particular instance, the role played by European firearms in helping the *buke* to quell a revolt is related

straw coat, MINO

by Geerts in his papers on the Arima rebellion, which took place during the early part of the seventeenth century and resulted in the famous Shimabara massacre. The original lord of this domain had been transferred by the shogun to another fief. He left the majority of his old retainers behind in Arima, and when the new lord, Matsukura, arrived with all his cohorts and their families, he deprived the former lord's retainers of their income and dispersed them among the farmers of the territory. This new daimyo then inaugurated one of the most repressive and exploitative agrarian programs in the history of Arima, forcing the farmers "to raise such a quantity of rice as it was impossible for them to do." As a penalty for failure to meet the production quota he had set arbitrarily, without any concern for the productive capacity of the land, farmers were tied with rope and dressed "in a raw straw coat made of a kind of grass, with long and broad leaves and called *mino* by the Japanese, such as is used by boatmen and other peasantry as a raincoat" (Geerts, 57). These coats were then set on fire, and the unfortunate victims of what became known as the "*mino* dance" *(mino-odori)* died of their burns or killed themselves by "bumping their bodies violently against the ground or by drowning themselves" (Geerts, 57). Their womenfolk were not spared either. Hung naked by their ankles, they were "scoffed at in various other ways." The peasants, finally, took up arms and "set fire to all the habitations of the nobility and citizens, murdered some of the nobles, and [drove] the remaining gentlemen within the walls of the castle" (Geerts, 57).

The example they set and the contagion of their anger activated another revolt on the island of Amakusa. The farmers there also proceeded to murder their military regent and ultimately forced the provincial aristocracy to seal itself off in the central manor. Thirty-seven barges and cargo boats loaded with warriors were immediately dispatched to Amakusa by the magistrates of Karatsu (Hirado), but "only one single boat with two mortally wounded noblemen returned to Hirado on the 3rd of January" (Geerts, 59). The method then adopted by the central authorities in Edo to quell the rebellion provides a revealing insight into the psychology of the age. The shogun ordered the lords of Arima and Karatsu to engage the rebels with the remnants of their retainers in order to weaken the rebel forces—even if it meant their own destruction. The rationale behind the shogun's order was clearly that of punishing these lords for having caused the revolts in the first place. In the meantime, he ordered all the other lords of "the lower provinces" to journey to their respective castles and establish themselves there "in order to keep good order amongst the population." He then commanded the lords of Hizen, Chikugo, and Higo to move against the rebels from various positions, but not "before both the lords of Karatzu and Arima had been defeated." Even so, the peasants continued to resist, and the shogun finally had to resort to the tactic of mass starvation through prolonged siege. Repeated attacks launched by waves of warriors against the dilapidated defenses of these indomitable farmers (who had been joined by thousands of *ronin,* eager to take up arms against the Tokugawa) were repulsed again and again, many warriors losing their lives in these attempts. At one point, the military authorities requested that Dutch ships use their huge guns to bombard the rebels' positions and asked that the Dutch supply the armies of the *buke* with firearms, bullets, and gunpowder. The Dutch ships were eventually withdrawn from the vicinity by order of the Japanese military authorities, however, presumably because "it would not be furthering their own reputation, when foreigners were summoned for aid and assistance at the moment when there was already such a powerful army in arms" (Geerts, 95).

The influence and inclinations of the farmer as a fighter and, consequently, as a developer of weapons and arts of combat typically rural in derivation is evident in his vast arsenal of sickles, connected sticks and chains, rice grinders, slings, and so forth —in addition to any of the traditional weapons which he could obtain from the warriors in one way or another. His influence was limited in metropolitan centers where artisans and merchants formed the majority, although there are indications in the doctrine of bujutsu that the latter were susceptible to some of his ideas on tactics and weapons when forced to fight their common enemy. In the provinces, however, the farmer remained a potentially formidable opponent with whom most warriors preferred not to tangle, if at all possible. A traditionalist by nature, he also adopted the stern code of ethics which had inspired the *buke,* and, steeped as he was in the territorial tradition of the clan, he was particularly influenced by the Confucian ideals of loyalty to father and lord. Fearless peasants of both sexes often set out with impressive determination to avenge a mortal offense to their family or clan. Dautremer relates that one of the most popular tales "is the story of Miyagi and Shinobu, who in the 17th century (Gokomei, 1644-1654) avenge the murder of their peasant father, slain by a daimyo's *kerai*" (Dautremer, 83).

That many farmers also kept abreast of the latest developments in the traditional arts of bujutsu (which were considered the exclusive domain of the *buke)* is confirmed by the existence of several complaints lodged by military chroniclers concerning those comparatively well-to-do farmers who supported "a tame *ronin* in their household" for the purpose of learning "military arts unsuited to their station in life" (Dore[2], 242).

As indicated earlier, the farmer could face the prospect of execution and death with a stoicism equal to the warrior's, although tinged with that melancholy peculiar to a man whose entire struggle for his own and his clan's survival had been inspired primarily by the principle of life and growth. One such was Sakura Sogoro (1612-53), a headman of Kozu (governed by the daimyo Hotta Masanobu), who decided to try to avoid bloodshed when the peasants of the 386 villages in the district were preparing to revolt against excessive local taxation. He took it upon himself to bypass the provincial daimyo and appeal their case directly to the shogun in Edo, fully aware that such an act would mean certain death. He was, in fact, publicly beheaded, together with his wife and small children.

The samurai found the farmers confronting them again on the battlefield after the Meiji Restoration, and it was from the farms and rice fields of the nation that modern Japan obtained the bulk of its new imperial army and the dedicated, extremely clannish cadres of its lower officers, who were to play such an important role in the destiny of Japan and Asia in the twentieth century.

The Militant Clergy

A position of importance in the practice of bujutsu, considered by certain authorities comparable to that occupied by the *bushi,* was held by that interesting figure, the militant monk or priest, who played a relevant role in the history of Japan not only during the late Heian period but throughout those troubled centuries which culminated in the Tokugawa dictatorship. Almost every organized religion has assumed a military posture at some point in its development, especially during those early stages marked by the emergence of man from the shadows of prehistory. Those feelings of wonder and terror inspired by the unknown forces of existence which buffeted man about, reinforced by his survival instinct, all contributed to the

Buddhist high priests Shinto priest

highly mystical nature of most national beginnings. Actually, in most cultures, the early kings were also high priests who ruled theocracies wherein a faith in a particular divinity helped the nation to coalesce and establish its foundations, this faith being expressed through rites or through force of arms, or, more usually, through a combination of the two, in forms of combat considered divinely inspired.

During the early periods of Japanese history, as we have seen in our study of the clans *(uji)*, the religious factor was already predominant. As one scholar who had studied the early ages of that country put it, "Government and religion were then united by tight bonds" (Renondeau, 35). The ascendancy of the solar cult of the Yamato clan until it finally attained a position of supremacy over the cults of all other clans, as well as over the vague animism of the indigenous religion, Shinto, is inseparable from the political turmoil of the period. Political or military pragmatism and religion actually expressed and reinforced one another, maintaining an identity of interests which was to characterize the history of Japan well into the modern era.

This virtual identification of religion and politics (especially in their military expression) also characterized the history of Western culture, in both its classical and medieval stages. The militant theocracies of Egypt and Mesopotamia, the Greek and Roman consecrated wars, the popes who led armies and the kings who ruled by divine right, the holy wars in the Middle East and the conquests in the Americas made in the name of the faith are all expressions of that fundamental identity assigned by the ancient and medieval man to things divine or spiritual and things practical or concrete. A fracture between the two occurred in Western culture during the sixteenth and seventeenth centuries, when empirical knowledge and objective classification of phenomena on the basis of direct cause and effect assigned a position of importance in history to scientific, analytical modes of thought.

In Japan, this fracture did not take place until the nineteenth century, and even then the fact that it was imposed from without in the form of a forced cultural invasion (which also stimulated a frantic acceleration to match Western developments in military science in a matter of mere decades) did not permit a fracture of sufficient depth in their tradition to genuinely revolutionize the outlook of the Japanese people. Nor was it possible to establish the foundation for a truly indigenous scientific tradition, that is, one largely dissociated from, when not openly antagonistic to, the strongly fused and pantheistic view of the divine which embraced and colored everything and everyone in the Japanese conception of existence. There are indications, however, that the occupation of Japan at the end of World War II served to widen the rift in the national psyche and make it more difficult for the modern Japanese man or woman to fully and unquestioningly return to that ancient and undifferentiated blending of the divine with the concrete (so often violent) aspects of their reality which had characterized the beliefs of their forebears.

In ancient Japan, therefore, the divine predominated. The emperor was the high priest of that shamanistic animism which was at the root of Shinto and, later, of the hybrid and syncretic form of Buddhism adopted from Chinese sources by the imperial court at Nara. The clash between the former and the latter, according to some historians, was not exceedingly violent because, in Japan, neither remained pure and consequently intransigent. Buddhism (like Taoism, which also came to Japan from China) was Japanized and adapted to the national conception of the divinity and of existence in general. There is historical evidence, however, that the establishment of Buddhism in Japan (largely through the patronage of the Soga clan) was by no means entirely bloodless. In time, however, Buddhism developed into a series of strongly Japanized sects and schools whose adherents often organized themselves into units of a strongly military or paramilitary character. The chronicles of the Nara period mention the Six Nara Sects of Buddhism: Jojutsu, which was derived from the Hinayana (Sautantrica) doctrine and is said to have eventually merged with the Sanron sect; Kusha, introduced by two Japanese priests in 658 as a derivation of the Sarvastivada doctrine; Hosso, founded by the monk Dosho from the Middle Vehicle doctrine of salvation (Yogacara), with important, independent temples in Nara such as Kofuku-ji and Ganko-ji; Sanron, derived from the Madhyamika doctrine of salvation (Middle Path), founded in India by Nagarjuna and supposedly introduced into Japan by the Korean priest Eikan, with its headquarters in Horyu-ji Temple; Kegon, derived from the Avatamsaka (Greater Vehicle) doctrine and introduced into Japan by Ryoben in 736, with its center in Todai-ji Temple; and the Ritsu sect of the Vinaya doctrine, which reached Japan in 754.

During the late Heian period, when the Fujiwara occupied the central position in the capital of Kyoto, other Buddhist schools were established. Among these were the Jodo sect, founded by Honen Shonin (Genku), who had studied in Tendai schools; the various Amida sects which had sprung from the teachings of Genshin in the tenth century; the highly controversial and rebellious Nichiren sects; and the various Zen sects of the same periods (among which the Rinzai, the Soto, and the Obaku are still active today). Most of these sects became large landowners (as had been true of the Church in Europe during that continent's feudal period), and their leaders, appointed by the emperor and the aristocratic families in power, always took an active interest in politics, which, quite naturally, involved them in continual intrigues and territorial conflicts or holy wars carried out, ironically enough, in the name of Buddha. Special guard units *(ozonakama)*, formed of both priests and laymen, had always been assigned to stand watch over important temples in order to protect sacred property from sacrilege; their secularization, following the territorial aggrandizement policies of the temple authorities, necessitated the formation of ever larger units of armed men, usually recruited from the ranks of monks and priests *(tera-bushi)* or dispossessed peasants, mercenary soldiers, and so forth.

The great monastic orders living high in the mountains, however, with their warlike cohorts of "mountain warriors" known as *yamahoshia* and, later, as *yamabushi,* were among the great protagonists of Japanese history from the tenth to the sixteenth and seventeenth centuries. These orders appear to have evolved originally from clusters of hermits, ascetics, and other "holy men" who, following the path of solitude in the wilderness, endeavored to acquire supernatural powers. Their search *(shu)* for these powers *(ken)* gradually coalesced into various methodologies *(do)* which became known as the "way of supernatural powers" *(shugendo).* This *shugendo,* according to many scholars, "does not have a founder" (Renondeau, 26), but ancient chronicles insistently mention En-no-Ozuno (d. 701), better known as En-no-Ubasoku ("the practicing laic") or, generally, as En-no-Gyoja ("En, the practitioner"). The myths and legends surrounding this figure so obscure history that En bears a strong resemblance to Merlin, the wizard at King Arthur's Court, who was also said to have commanded people and elements from his mountain retreat, as well as to be able to walk over water and fly through the air (and, of course, appear simultaneously in many different places with unsurpassed ease). From the mass of references available, Renondeau deducted

Traveling monk   YAMAHOSHI   Itinerant YAMABUSHI

that En lived in the second half of the seventh century, that he was a Buddhist laic, and that he practiced magic. He left no school, but men of his ilk, that is, men of magic *(kenja, kenza,* or *shugenja)* who inhabited the mountains, were feared as much as respected for their knowledge and use of occult practices, for those capacities which made them closely akin to the ancient shamans of Asia, much of whose culture they seem to have assimilated. They were in great demand as healers or mediums *(miko)* who could forecast the future or reconstruct the past. Magistrates used them in investigations of the "other" world or to probe people's minds with their trancelike or hypnotic abilities. Male *(otoko-no-miko)* and female *(onna-no-miko)* healers appear again and again throughout the history of Japan, and traces of their presence can be detected in the countryside even today.

Organized groups of these "wild men" of the mountains are mentioned in records of the tenth century, together with "men of the plains" *(nanushi).* The chronicles describe these clusters as being attached predominantly to the temples of the Shingon and Tendai schools of Buddhism. The Shingon doctrine (Chen-yen in Chinese) was imported into Japan by Kukai (774–835), better known as Kobo Daishi, the posthumous title conferred upon him by Emperor Daigo. Kukai had studied the Buddhism of the Sanron sect, traveled to China, and then returned to Japan to found the Kongobu-ji Temple on Mount Koya, south of Kyoto. He ordained many abbots, among whom was Saicho (762-822), a monk who also went to China to deepen his knowledge of the Tendai doctrine (T'ien-t'ai in Chinese) before returning to Japan to found a monastic order on Mount Hiei, in the Enryaku-ji Temple. Both the Shingon and the Tendai doctrines were based upon the fundamental identity of the universe with the Buddha—a supreme being (Indian Vairocana, Japanese Birushana or Dainichi) according to the Shingon sect, or its historical incarnation in Sakyamuni for the Tendai sect—whose infinite powers man could tap if he acquired correct knowledge, thus overcoming the "ignorance which enfolds him." In both doctrines, the path toward enlightenment was to be found in solitude and in the practice of esoteric disciplines *(mikkyo),* which were lengthy and gradual in the practices of the Tendai sect. Those of the Shingon sect were shorter, and, if proper use was made of magic rituals, immediate enlightenment was even considered possible.

Both sects looked upon the mountains as the proper setting for any search for salvation, as well as for the practice of magic. Their temples, accordingly, provided perfect abodes for the *yamabushi,* who also seem to have brought with them their own experiences and varying methods of *shugendo,* many of which were to be added to the esoteric *mikkyo* which formed the foundation for both doctrines. In the major

temples high in the mountains, from those in the territory of Kimbusen to those in Kumano, from Omine to Yoshino, quarters *(seishin-ya)* for the *yamabushi* were erected, and the "king of mountain creeds," the *shugendo,* began to appear, together with exoteric *(kenshi)* as well as esoteric doctrines *(misshu),* explanations *(nosetsu),* eloquence *(seimei),* poetry *(wa-ka),* and—a very important factor in our study—military practice *(buyu),* in the program of instruction followed by most monastic orders. How the last specialty came to be included among the various ascetic disciplines studied by monks and priests remains somewhat of a mystery. We do know, however, that abbots who mastered all these disciplines were chosen to occupy high positions in the clerical hierarchy at court; that ministers, chiefs of state, and generals often retreated to monasteries either to study or to refresh themselves spiritually before returning to their positions of responsibility. (This practice is still generally followed by many leaders who withdraw to the Zen temples of modern Japan.) We also know that court notables, even emperors, upon retiring from public affairs, often selected certain Buddhist temples in the mountains or on the plains near the capital as their final residences. We must note here that such retired rulers often maintained a firm (even if indirect) hold upon the central power levers. Consequently, one begins to understand how and why these religious orders gradually became independent centers of power.

By the period of the Northern and Southern Courts *(nambokucho),* there were well-organized cohorts *(konsha)* of *yamabushi,* other warrior-monks *(sohei),* and "men of the temples" *(shinjin),* whose activities were directed by their major centers (the Shogo-in for the Tendai sect and the Sambo-in for the Shingon sect). From these centers, two major militant subsects emerged: the Honzan-ha and the Tozan-ha, both of whom participated actively "in the civil wars" (Renondeau, 68). The fugitive emperor Go-daigo, who had once placed two of his sons in the temple on Mount Hiei, was assisted by the *yamabushi,* who fought the Kamakura warriors from hill to hill, mountain to mountain, and temple to temple, with a savage display of valor which equaled—where it did not surpass—that of the professional warriors. Names of religious strategists who planned and directed their own campaigns, or counseled generals on how to conduct theirs, abound in the chronicles of the age. The abbot Soshin is particularly famous for the clever assistance he provided on the battlefield to the besieged Kusunoki Masashige, the "Great Nanko" (1294–1336), who was a loyal general of the banished emperor. Also frequently mentioned is Takeda Harunobu Shingen, the astute leader of the mountain warriors in Kai, who assisted Nobunaga in his fight against Uesugi Kenshin in 1568. Another great thinker and educator, the abbot Sessai Choro, rector of the Seiken-ji and Rinza-ji temples, was a tutor of Tokugawa Ieyasu and the planner of Imagawa Yoshimoto's war strategies. For ages,

these ecclesiastical figures (very much like the Vatican diplomats of the Middle Ages and those powerful cardinals in France and Italy whose political influence was often pivotal) appear broodingly in the shadows of those powerful men who left their imprint upon the history of Japan.

It took the *buke* more than four hundred years of continuous warfare, of repeatedly battling the militant clergy of the plains and of the mountains as well as the single-minded priests of the Ikko sect and others, before the *yamabushi* were finally eliminated as dangerous contenders in the struggle for absolute power, which, in the ninth century, had been wrested almost entirely from the hands of the emperor and his once-landed nobility. Reading of the riots and violent protests instigated by hordes of priests and monks in the capital, one can understand why Emperor Shirakawa (1073-86) complained that only three things disregarded his wishes: the rushing waters of the Kamo River, the unpredictable dice, and the mountain priests.

Indeed, it would seem that during the turbulent age which preceded the direct intervention of the warriors, when the countryside and the capitals (Nara and later Kyoto) were terrorized and ravaged by

the forces of the monasteries clashing with one another while imperial forces proved powerless to keep order, a theocracy more pronounced than the one envisioned by Shinto doctrine was on the verge of being established in Japan by followers of a Buddhist faith which, in both theory and practice, bore little if any relationship to the original doctrine of the compassionate Indian Gautama. Only the sectarian nature of the various schools of these thoroughly Japanized forms of Buddhism and the intrinsic exclusivity of the clan approach they adopted prevented them from attaining their goal by uniting against the only other potentially dangerous class, the military, as it began to implode dangerously from the periphery back toward the center of national life and power. Riddled with dissenting factions, each sect fought against all the others, wasting men and treasure in the process. As late as 1536, with the military class in the final stages of consolidation—the union and federation of its armed and disciplined clans making it an increasingly powerful force—the priests of the Hokke sect were still busy driving other priests (those of the Shingon sect) out of Kyoto. In turn, they were attacked by the Hiei-zan monks, and so it continued.

But even though the monks' efforts were seriously hampered by this intramural dissension (which often bordered on complete chaos), the warriors still found them serious competition in the struggle for control of the government. It is reported by some historians that only the introduction of modern methods of warfare, such as the use of firearms (muskets and heavy guns imported by the Portuguese, Dutch, and Spanish emissaries), made it possible for Nobunaga, in the sixteenth century, to effectively dislodge the militant clergy from their hitherto unassailable positions of power.

It was Oda Nobunaga, in fact, who dealt them a mortal blow during the Momoyama period, when he systematically razed their temples and exterminated their occupants. Historians still express shock at the treatment of the Shin temples in Mikawa (1564), of the great Hiei-zan (1571), of Nagashima (1574), of the Osaka Hongan-ji (1580). The details of the battles waged, of the prolonged resistance exemplified in sieges lasting as long as ten years, of the ultimate slaughter of monks and priests, fill many bloody pages in the chronicles of this period. The *Hoan Nobunaga-ki,* for example, describes the fall of the temples on Mount Hiei:

> Everything, everywhere, from the central cathedral to twenty-one shrines of the Mountain King, the bell tower and the library, were burned to the ground. Moreover, the holy scriptures—both esoteric and exoteric—and the records of the imperial capital under generations of emperors were destroyed at once. Great scholars, men of rare talents, aged priests and young boys—still with their innocent,

> delicate features—were either beheaded or taken captive. The roar of the huge burning monastery, magnified by the cries of countless numbers of the old and the young, sounded and resounded to the ends of heaven and earth. (Tsu-noda *et al.*, 316)

Nobunaga's successor, Hideyoshi, attacked and subdued the temples of Negoro-san, Saiga, Kumano, Kokawa-dera in Yoshino, as well as others, thus completing the neutralization of the militant clergy as a political and military factor in Japanese life. The Tokugawa sealed their fate during the following ages. During the period of Tokugawa dominance, in fact, they were kept under strict and continuing surveillance, troublesome monks or priests being immediately and mercilessly suppressed. The communities of monks were limited in number and the monks themselves dispersed among numerous, manageable centers, their prerogatives being severely limited or assumed by other officials. Of their once formidable reputation, only an echo remains in the lore and literature of Japan.

These militant priests and monks had usually been extremely skilled in the use of traditional weapons and methods of combat. Bows and arrows, swords, and—above all—spears were familiar weapons to them. The naginata described in Part 2, for example, is said to have actually been invented by them and later adopted by the *bushi* who had experienced the deadly efficiency of this weapon when it was used against him. Down through the ages, even after their crushing defeat at the hands of Nobunaga's warriors, these monks and priests still continued to participate actively in developing bujutsu, being considered experts in its theory, particularly in regard to those inner factors based upon mental control and coordinated power which are described in Part 3. Thus they provided the traditional specializations of bujutsu with practically the only theory its practitioners would ever have. The *bushi* themselves acknowledged this theoretical dependency upon their religious masters by flocking in large numbers to the temples or abodes of abbots or humble monks who had become famous as teachers of techniques and disciplines which strengthened the personality and developed the character of a man, thus enabling him to face, without flinching, the hostile and dangerous reality of combat. The names of these religious teachers are still cherished in the martial chronicles of Japan; an idea of the range and depth of their contribution to the *bushi's* methods of combat and, in general, to the Japanese art of combat, may be gauged by the survey in Part 3 of these teachers and the way in which they influenced the evolution of such arts as kenjutsu, jujutsu, and aikijutsu by applying to these disciplines the intuitive principles of Buddhism, especially those of the Zen sect.

Artisans and Merchants

Although usually relegated to a minor position by most chroniclers of bujutsu (when they are mentioned at all), the artisans *(shokunin, ko)* and the merchants *(akindo, sho)* who populated many of the rural and most of the metropolitan centers of Japan during the feudal era were also quite active in developing their own specializations of bujutsu. From the earliest periods of recorded history, every member of a clan was expected to be able to fight, whether as a conscript by imperial decree or in defense of his own territorial unit. Although the farmers were the main source of foot soldiers, all the members of a clan, whatever their profession—from the artisans who made swords, spears, and other weapons to the merchants who traded whatever the clan produced in order to pay military expenses—were expected to do their part when the clan was attacked or went to war. During the Heian period, the artisans and merchants were concentrated mainly in and around the capital and large towns, where they organized themselves into increasingly larger and ever more powerful corporations and guilds, patterned after the usual model of the patriarchal clan.

In time, and as the vagaries of fortune displaced this or that lord from his castle-town, many of these corporations and guilds became autonomous. Self-governing bodies arose during Japan's feudal era, well before the Tokugawa rise to power, especially in towns like the ancient capital Nara, in Kyoto, in the shrine town of Uji-yamada, in Sakai, Hichicho, and Amagasaki. Often, these local forms of self-government, strongly influenced by the merchants, assumed a violent aspect when they clashed with the expanding number and demands of the *buke* during the "fluid age of civil wars" (Yazaki, 158). Those merchants, in particular, who had acquired great wealth not only from normally shrewd business transactions, but also from dealings with sources of income represented by elements such as the pirates *(wako)* who were rampant in the East China Sea, did not hesitate to invest their wealth in procuring weapons, in hiring mercenaries, and in mobilizing their own cohorts in order to confront and repel the *buke.* Certain cities, such as Amagasaki, paid dearly for their resistance. Others fared somewhat better. But the *buke* never forgot nor forgave its former opponents. According to Yazaki, it was precisely because the merchants had been capable of standing up to the "unsettled feudal lords" that when "the most powerful of the feudal warlords succeeded in giving the nation its most thoroughgoing unification in the pre-modern history of Japan, these merchants were swiftly disarmed and swept to the bottom of a rigidly-controlled social scale" (Yazaki, 115). They thus found themselves below the farmers over whom they had held sway during the Muromachi period.

During the Tokugawa period, the *heimin* were encased even more firmly in the strictures of a class-conscious society, ranks being assigned to them in rural clans or in the towns, where they were restricted to particular sectors, areas, and streets which were easily identifiable and easy for the military authorities to control. Almost every Western visitor to Japan during the sixteenth century was immediately impressed by the stern surveillance to which the urban *heimin,* in particular, were subject. "Each street, or section of it," wrote Griffis in his paper on the streets and street names of Edo, "was under the supervision of a petty officer, or monitor, who lived in the street over which he exercised supervision. Over these monitors, a ward officer, with assistants, presided" (Griffis, 28).

A ward *(za)* was usually an area larger than two streets, supervised by local officials such as the secretary in charge of registers concerning such matters as family compositions, residences, and taxes; there were also a fire chief, with his teams of fire fighters, and gate keepers. "Every ward," in fact, "was surrounded either by canals, walls or fences; the entrances to which were closed by guard gates. In case of disturbances of any kind, it was comparatively easy to shut the gates, and confine the infection of disease, riot, etc., to a single ward" (Griffis, 28). At night these wards were tightly sealed off from one another, and anyone who, for any reason whatsoever, had to leave his or her own ward after dark was obliged to obtain the appropriate authorization, a pass that was carefully inspected before the gates were opened, announcing the passage of a visitor to the next ward "with a clatter of sounding boards" (Dore[1], 270). This clearly repressive system, which, according to François Caron (1600-73), was imposed "on all the towns of the country" (Cooper, 153), was further augmented by the extension of the *gonin-gumi* system of collective responsibility to include the urban population as well. "The house-holders" in each street, in fact, "were grouped together into fives, one of them being accountable for the others, and all acting as spies and checks upon each other. Under this system it was usually an easy matter to fix the responsibility of the origin of a conflagration, theft, riot, etc., upon the real offender" (Griffis, 28). Householders and ward officials were responsible to three town elders *(machi-doshiyori)* who did not belong to the *buke* but held the title permanently and could transmit it to their heirs. These town elders were directly answerable to two magistrates of the military class *(machi-bugyo).*

Nevertheless, although they were strictly regimented and their weapons confiscated whenever and wherever possible, these classes still managed to maintain their own traditions in matters of combat—traditions which, ironically, the "hated samurai, with their supercilious manner and foppish mien" (as Nishida described them) were instrumental in insuring they would strive to preserve. Indeed, even during the long period of Tokugawa military dictatorship (and evidently as a reaction to its intrinsic rigidity), popular movements of protest or of disguised and confined rebellion *(uchi-kowashi)* often shattered the peace of a neighborhood or a city district. Moreover, these movements, although confined and promptly suppressed, were not lacking in the fire and bitterness of so many other political and social resistance movements, even if in Japan they never seemed to have been inspired by a truly revolutionary motivation, in the sense of suggesting a radically new political doctrine.

Scholars have repeatedly expressed their amazement at the depth of this resistance to established power—a resistance manifesting itself primarily, however, in reactions and revolts against excesses of a particular regime or class, rather than against the class idea itself. The records of the Tokugawa period could not avoid making at least passing reference to certain groups of men living in the towns and cities whom Bush characterized as "rebellious." These men did not belong to the military class but called themselves the "host of heroism" *(kyokaku)*. They were not bound by the specific code of the *bushi* but, like their military counterparts and perhaps as an unavoidable reaction to the overbearing exclusiveness of the samurai, developed their own code of conduct, known as *kikotsu,* to which they were fiercely loyal. Repeating an observation which is often found in studies of the Japanese feudal period, Bush states that "the majority of writers on Japan have completely ignored" this interesting development in that country's culture, thus further confirming the strong suspicions voiced by many scholars concerning the reliability of so much "official" and "authorized" historiography, which seems to have recorded for posterity an idealized version of an otherwise more painful reality. Yet, this commoners' code "has been responsible for inspiring [the Japanese] with the habit of defiance and rebellion against anything unjust and unreasonable, as also with compassion for the sufferings of fellow-men" (Bush, 132). It is certainly to be hoped that further research on this and similar aspects of the national ethos of feudal Japan will help to throw a more illuminating light upon the *kyokaku* and those concrete aspects of bujutsu (the weapons, techniques and methods of combat) which helped the adherents of *kikotsu* to resist so valiantly the "overbearing" samurai.

Greatly renowned, as well, were those societies of fighters known as *otokodate.* The name means, literally, plucky or manly fellow, and the societies of these men were "bound together by an obligation to stand by one another in weal or in woe, regardless of their own lives, and without enquiring into one another's antecedents" (Mitford, 68). These societies are said to have been formed as a necessary response to the common brutality of many warriors—especially those belonging to the shogun's elite corps in the cities, some of whose members had organized themselves into special fighting units *(hatamoto-yakko)* and went out of their way to make life miserable for the merchants and artisans. The latter, in turn, formed their own fighting groups based on territorial units of block communities, covertly financed by the guilds and corporations *(za),* for the purpose of governing and defending themselves. In such cases, these *otokodate* had more specific names, such as *machi-yakko* or *machi-gumi,* and their paramilitary societies, according to custom, were organized vertically with a headman called "father." In many districts and wards this headman wielded more power over the people than the military authority nominally in charge of the area. It is narrated, for example, that the power of these societies had grown so impressively during the late Tokugawa period that when one of the last military dictators of this family, Tokugawa Iemochi, had to leave his stronghold in Edo to travel to Kyoto, he had to be protected not only by his cohorts of *hatamoto* but (and primarily) by the bands of Shimmon Tatsugoro, who was "father" of the *otokodate* controlling the provinces Iemochi had to traverse with his caravan of retainers. Although of commoner status *(heimin),* Shimmon Tatsugoro was later "raised to the dignity *of hatamoto*" for his "many faithful services" (Mitford, 69).

It has been observed by some authors that many of the *machi-yakko,* as well as most of their leaders, had formerly belonged to the military class before becoming, for one reason or another, masterless men who roamed the country like waves *(ronin)* until they finally joined one or another of these local organizations. The paramilitary structure of these civilian organizations and the strong esprit de corps which bound their members to one another gives a certain substance to this hypothesis. However, many great leaders of the *machi-yakko,* whose names are still preserved in the doctrine of bujutsu, clearly traced their lineage back to the artisan or merchant class. If we consider, then, that the inhabitant of Edo—the common Edokko—

OTOKODATE   Pipe-bearer

"was a forthright character [who] detested moodiness and vacillation in any form . . . [and] was quick to take offense, quick to forget, and not averse to jumping into a good fight" (Nishida, 36), it appears quite reasonable to accept the historical hypothesis that commoners formed the bulk of these organizations.

The *machi-yakko* were able fighters. Indeed, they had to be extremely resourceful in combat since, by law, they were denied the right to wear the traditional weapons of Japan. As excellent streetfighters, they developed certain methods of combat (especially unarmed) to the highest degree, since their primary targets were sword-wielding warriors. There are indications in the records that they used, with consummate skill, the dirk or short dagger, which could be easily concealed beneath street clothes. Even more impressive are reports of their command of tessenjutsu, the technique of using the iron fan against an armed or unarmed foe. As Casal tells us (Part 2), these iron fans became so thoroughly identified in the eyes of the authorities with weaponry that official decrees forbidding their use were issued. The civilians then turned to rods and other types of staves, often reinforced by the addition of iron rings and caps which helped to nullify any advantage their armed opponents might have been supposed to possess because of their swords. The contribution of the *machi-yakko* to the development of the art of the staff, described in Part 2, therefore, must be considered substantial. As traders and manufacturers whose professions often brought them into various and ofttimes dangerous localities (as was also true of many itinerant priests), they had found an ideal weapon in the homely staff which helped them to overcome the fatigue of long journeys on foot. Unpatrolled roads were often traveled (or barricaded) by groups of cutthroats, bandits, aggressive beggars—and always by obnoxious warriors who were likely to take offense at a supposedly disrespectful attitude and use this "insult" as a pretext for testing a new blade. The staff, maneuvered by deft hands according to precise techniques and patterns of attack and counterattack, became one of the chief weapons used on Japanese highways during the feudal era, and (as in England during the twelfth and thirteenth centuries) the sight of pilgrims battling in groups or in couples in the open fields, in ditches, near inns, or even on the main roads was not an uncommon one.

A peculiar item which became a redoubtable weapon in the hands of the *machi-yakko* was the long smoking pipe used in the fifteenth century. These pipes (illustrated in Part 2), in addition to being very long, had handles protected by veritable guards *(tsuba)* and they were "stuck in sashes like a sword, or carried behind by a retainer" (Satow[2], 71). Satow also relates that in 1609 many leaders of rival factions in Kyoto were jailed and executed for their role in street riots in which these pipes, together with swords, were used to such an extent (and so effectively) that they were finally forbidden by direct decree.

It is interesting to note at this point that as the power to control local affairs was concentrated more and more in the hands of the professional guilds and corporations of merchants and artisans (while the power of the military dictators of the late Tokugawa period declined apace), an unmistakably degenerative process began to affect these guilds and corporations, both in spirit and in function. The ancient challenge of an oppressive regime, which had often forced the *machi-yakko* to the wall and caused them to stand together as "men among men," had been substantially diluted by the weakening of the government during the late Tokugawa period. The vitality of the government itself, of course, had been sapped by more than two centuries of feudal stagnation and progressive impoverishment, which had reduced an army with no major battles to fight to the debasing role of a state police force, concerned mainly with the problems of maintaining the status quo, while the other classes evolved through successive stages of enrichment and consequent awareness of their disenfranchisement.

The merchants and artisans were the ones who, eventually, came to possess, direct, and control the use of the financial means responsible for the growth of the national economy. They kept the nation functioning and alive, while the military clans continued to cling to their territorial empires—even as these became increasingly obsolete. The civilian organizations of the late Tokugawa period, ascending toward the seat of central power as the military establishment descended, tended to assimilate the ethos of exclusive predominance typical of the warrior class. This assimilation, naturally, tended to take place at the upper levels of the classes concerned—rich merchants, for example, courting the favors of the military authorities and often buying them outright, as the latter came to rely more and more heavily upon the financial and organizational abilities of the young, dynamic men of the *za*.

Eventually, it came to pass that, although born as a reaction to the military establishment and its domination, the majority of these civilian organizations began to do for the *bushi* what the warriors could no longer do for themselves. "Fathers" of the once rebellious *machi-yakko*, as we have seen, became members of the *hatamoto* and kept order in their wards. The degenerative effects of the long feudal era were finally taking their toll; in place of the once proud, independent city dweller, who had been so actively involved in unfolding and shaping the reality of his culture during the fifteenth and sixteenth centuries, there was only a docile and highly malleable instrument who could (and usually did) operate smoothly on command, carrying out the decisions of his old masters, assisted by their new vassals, in accordance with that military tradition which he had finally come to consider his own.

The Police Forces and the Underworld

We have come, finally, to a category of important subjects whose total involvement with force in upholding or in violating the laws of the land constitutes one of the major motivations underlying the development, application, and transmission of methods and techniques of individual combat. They are represented, in feudal Japan, by the various police forces and by their direct counterparts in the underworld. In a separate group, more akin to the latter in their notorious disregard for the law and social conventions, we must include the famous pirates of Yamato.

From the earliest recorded periods, each military clan in the provinces had its own police corps whose main function was to maintain law and order within the boundaries of the clan's territories. This function applied not only to control over the common people, the farmers, the artisans, and the merchants affiliated to the clan, as well as to any travelers or strangers, but also to the clan's warriors. These local authorities functioned, in short, as a sort of military police, and, in times of peace, they exercised control and endeavored to prevent or neutralize any form of criminal behavior which might disrupt the organization and functionality of the provincial unit. All villages, districts, and towns either were under the jurisdiction of organized police forces and their military supervisors or developed their own law-enforcement agencies which, in any case, were directly responsible to castle and clan representatives. Order in the ancient capital of Kyoto, for example, was maintained by local agencies in each district of the city, all of whom were responsible to the city magistrates and, ultimately, to the imperial court.

The use of military contingents from the provinces became increasingly necessary, however, during the decline of the Heian culture and, with it, the emergence of a state seeking a new balance among its belligerent components. The device of allowing the various emerging classes of citizens to police their own area by forming law-enforcement groups of citizens, under the leadership of one or more officials, soon became a tradition never entirely abandoned, since its effectiveness in controlling disorders or crimes was determined by the principle of collective responsibility wherein everyone was required to pay for the fault of even one individual.

The Tokugawa, however, have the "dubious distinction," as Reischauer qualified it, of having systematized and elevated the function of the police to previously unattained levels of efficiency and pervasiveness. As we have seen in the section on the structure of Tokugawa society, a vast and intricate network of police controls slowly materialized throughout Japan, beginning in Edo, the military capital of the land, where the cohorts *of hatamoto* and *gokenin,* the garrisons of provincial warriors held ready to do the shogun's bidding, and a series of local agencies of the most diversified nature reinforced one another in maintaining law and order with functions of preventive surveillance or prompt reaction to that which was defined at the time as "criminal behavior."

It is very difficult, in examining a system of military dictatorship such as the one established by the Tokugawa, to make a clear distinction between military law and civil law, between the institutional means of enforcing the former and those specifically concerned with enforcing the latter. Such a distinction is almost impossible and, in most cases, irrelevant when discussing despotic societies wherein the possessive totality of command displayed by a central authority over the entire nation makes every crime, even the most individual and limited, a direct challenge, not to a local statute or custom alone, but to that central command which embraces and determines every aspect of national life. One must remember that the law of the Tokugawa, the most powerful of the military clans, was "a martial law" (Embree[1], 18). As such, it "was largely repressive in nature," since it carried to their extreme conclusions the dictates of any law concerned with the preservation of certain legal and social forms at a given time and place in history. The elasticity of the law in transitional phases of development, and its broad interpretation as a society evolves, is intrinsically abhorrent to the martial tradition, which is, by definition, rigid and specific. The latter, it should be added, was on the one hand a reaction to the fluidity and the horrors of the age of civil wars (1336-1600) which had exhausted the nation. On the other hand, it seemed particularly congenial to, and an expression of, that conception of human behavior which had been inherited from China but adapted specifically to Japan in its most extreme form. This interpretation visualized a morality that was essentially social in nature, not individual and private. Therefore, anything a citizen did was the concern of society, hence of the state and, if the state had become a militarily controlled entity, of its military representatives.

Edo was awash with cohorts of warriors and civil appointees, all with police duties to perform. Garrisons *(kumiai-tsujiban)* of direct vassals of the shogun, the *hatamoto,* were strategically located in and around Kyoto. Yazaki reports that there were 669 *hatamoto* watchpoints which were flanked by others set up by the *bakufu* and by the provincial governors who had duties and mansions in Edo. They controlled one another to a certain extent, and, when considered together, they controlled over a thousand watchpoints set up among the commoners' districts *(jishinban).* These guard-posts were manned by civil officials appointed by the corporations and guilds in each ward. Such officials were divided into three major categories according to social status, income, and duties. Guards *(yoriki),* policemen *(doshin),* and patrolmen *(okappiki)* had groups of armed men at every district entrance and, under military supervision, at every town-gate. They were usually divided into five companies of men, according to tradition, with spheres of influence which became increasingly clear and predetermined as the system took hold. Under these companies we find hired assistants *(tesaki)* and helpers drawn chiefly from another group of social

outcasts, the *eta*. Given the Buddhist abhorrence for any soiling contact with blood (somewhat paradoxical within the context of a culture which had made a cult of the sword), it fell to these *eta*, in return for a virtual and highly lucrative monopoly right, to slaughter animals, tan their hides, and produce leather goods such as armors, and also to serve "as prison guards, guards for persons paraded publicly as punishment, and as executioners" (Yazaki, 218).

Groups of these *eta*, with their assistants *(tedai)*, were often charged with the arrest or elimination of determined criminals. More difficult tasks, involving criminals of higher status or those who possessed greater skills, were carried out by them under the supervision of, and working together with, groups of *yoriki, doshin,* and *okappiki.*

It is no wonder that this pervasive and cumbersome police apparatus degenerated into excesses of almost every kind. The accusation of bossism, for example, was commonly hurled at the *doshin*, the *okappiki*, and their underlings, the *tesaki*. Arrests of innocent citizens on "false charges to collect fines as supplementary incomes" were reported (Yazaki, 225). In some cases, the townsmen's reaction, especially when combined with overtaxation or food scarcities, could provide the spark needed to generate an open revolt. However, the armies of warriors looming behind these police officials and surrounding Edo on every side insured that any such reactions, if they occurred at all, remained of a limited and localized nature.

Openly supervising the police apparatus in times of peace, through a series of civil and military officials, was the town-commissioner *(machi-bugyo)*. More covertly, all police were under the supervision of the censors *(metsuke)*, who controlled military and civilian subjects alike through their "extensive, elaborate, and extremely efficient intelligence organization, the spiritual forebear of the secret police of modern times" (Kennedy, 125). Their preferred instruments were the professional "magic men" *(ninja)* examined in Part 2.

There is ample evidence that the feudal police officers and their assistants devoted much time and effort to the development of weapons and techniques directly related to law enforcement against violators who, for the most part, were armed and (given the nature of feudal punishment for any violations) usually desperate. In addition to the need to defend themselves against the ofttimes deadly reaction of an armed criminal seeking to evade capture, police officials frequently had the unpleasant task of trying to arrest citizens of superior rank without hurting them if at all possible. In certain cases, capturing a man alive was of the utmost importance because of his value as a source of information to the censors *(metsuke)* concerning potential revolts, conspiracies, and so forth. Accordingly, it is in connection with the police forces of feudal Japan that we encounter the forked dirk *(jutte, jitte)* and its specialization *(jittejutsu)* wherein the

slash of a razor-sharp sword could be neutralized; the spiked pole *(sode-garanu)* and its techniques, which closely resembled those of the staff *(jojutsu)* but were aimed more particularly at impeding movement by hooking an armed man's sleeves or trousers; the spike and chain *(manriki-gusari),* reputedly devised by Dannoshin Toshimitsu, head guard at the gate of Edo castle; and the other chained instruments used in the manner of lassoed bolas, primarily to paralyze and subdue, only secondarily to kill. Police officers are also mentioned in connection with the development and application of techniques of unarmed combat. Famous in the chronicles of Japan during the Tokugawa period, for example, is Yamamoto Tamizaemon, a police officer in Osaka, who was reputedly the founder of the Shin-no-Shindo school of jujutsu. The art of individual combat owes to these men—and to pariahs such as the *eta*—a great debt as the modifiers of many old, and the creators of certain new, specializations *(jutsu)* in armed and unarmed confrontation. And this is true even though the official chroniclers of the *buke* often include them grudgingly, only indirectly giving them their rightful due as contributors to the art of handling a spear, a sword, a forked baton, or a fan.

Confronting the police forces of feudal Japan, at the outer limits of legality and well beyond, we find the gambler, the outlaw, or the bandit—all those who constituted the underworld of the town or the scourge of the countryside. In organization, these groups also followed the hierarchical pattern adopted by the military masters of the country and their warlords: they were organized vertically, with a "father" at the head and many lieutenants who carried out his orders. These bands had their own territorial limits which they defended ferociously against intrusions of any kind, thus posing a great and ofttimes insoluble problem for the authorities throughout the entire Tokugawa period.

During earlier periods of Japan's feudal history, the countryside had been fertile ground for the formation of large bands of outlaws and brigands who terrorized and taxed neighboring villages until the military leaders finally moved to clear the outlaws from their estates, thereby reducing them greatly in number. The decline of brigandage (which had been rampant from the eleventh to the seventeenth century) corresponded with the rise of the town criminal in the Tokugawa period, as the artisan and merchant classes began to expand during the final phase of feudalism. In fact, the criminal, the gambler, and the fugitive from the law were often hired as bodyguards by the *za* wardsmen because of their skill and determination

Testing a KATANA

as streetfighters. Jirocho, the Number One Boss of the Tokaido Highway during the late Tokugawa period, began as a gambler and developed his remarkable qualities of leadership while evading the innumerable traps set for him by the police and by rival gangs, until opposition to him ceased almost entirely and he even achieved a quasi-official position in the territorial chain of command within his province. Like many other leaders of confraternities, corporations, and guilds, he also found himself doing for the *bushi,* who were nominally in power, that which they were increasingly unable to do for themselves—that is, maintain and protect a crumbling society against the onslaughts of new customs and aspirations which heralded the dawn of another era in the history of Japan.

The rebellious spirit of such outlaws was notorious. Not only did they refuse to surrender their freedom or lives without a costly fight (which amply justified the stipends earned by police officers), but they often displayed a particular form of contempt for the police and their functions, even in the face of impending death. It was the practice in feudal Japan to test the sharpness and resistance of new swords owned by warriors of the upper category and ranks upon the bodies of executed criminals. In certain instances, usually for influential personages who could afford it, the test was carried out upon live bodies. It is recorded that a thief who had been sentenced to decapitation, noticing the presence of an official sword-tester and his witnesses among the police officers, asked him: "Are you going to test that blade on me?" "Yes," was the reply. "I am going to try for a diagonal cut from the shoulder down *[kesa]."* "Pity I wasn't told," remarked the condemned man with wry humor. "Otherwise I would have swallowed a couple of large stones and thus ruined your precious blade."

Finally, this survey of the importance of all classes and types of people in the development of weapons and techniques of individual combat cannot be satisfactorily concluded without a reference to the pirates who infested the waters around and terrorized coastal towns of Korea and China from the earliest periods of Japanese history. References to these audacious sea rovers are found not only in Japanese records but also in Chinese chronicles of the utmost antiquity. They were known as "children (sons) of Japan" *(wako; wa* being the ancient Chinese name for Japan), and they came mostly from the western provinces

Japanese buccaneers fighting English sea dogs

of Honshu, Kyushu, and Shikoku, where, "as in Elizabethan England, the Japanese buccaneers were often financed by the leading families of the land, who were by no means averse to taking their share of the proceeds" (Kennedy, 75).

These pirates pushed their vessels all the way to the Philippines, Thailand, Java, and even India, where, according to Williams, "they were not suffered to land in any port . . . with weapons, being accounted a people so desperate and daring that they are feared in all places where they come" (Williams, 30).

Colonies of these *wako* were even found inland, in Nanking, and their virulent raids defied centuries of efforts by the Chinese and Japanese fleets to curb them (such as the Taira expedition in 1129). Particularly active during the fourteenth, fifteenth, and sixteenth centuries, they were practically eliminated by Hideyoshi and the Tokugawa dictators, who had issued a ban on any contact with the outside world. Enforcement of the ban, which forbade any Japanese either to leave the country or, once having left, to return to Japan (under threat of immediate execution), literally destroyed the bases of operation from which the *wako* had moved in their search for riches and to which they had returned with their spoils. However, before their centuries of activity had come to an end, they had become famous all over Asia for their "fine fighting qualities and their utter disregard of death" (Kennedy, 101)—qualities which the European powers, as they transferred their predatory quarrels to the Asiatic theater, cleverly exploited by hiring and using these pirates as mercenaries and soldiers of fortune. It is probably to the medieval *wako* that bujutsu owes the acquisition of alien methods of individual combat and their dissemination throughout pre-Tokugawa Japan. There is no doubt, in any case, that they fought extremely well even against overwhelming odds, regardless of the numbers of men or quality of weapons arrayed against them. There is also no doubt that, notwithstanding their origins, they shared with the majority of their countrymen that martial characterististic of the Japanese clansman: the resignation to and expectation of death in the event of defeat.

In 1604, two English ships, flying the Cross of St. George, met "a junk manned by Japanese and sailing under the flag of Hachiman...the God of War" (Williams, 29). The encounter between the "sea dogs of England and the Japanese pirates" off the coast of Bintang, near Singapore, developed into a "most bloody" battle, with the short and thick-set *wako* trying to capture the English vessels, the *Tiger* and the *Tiger's Whelp,* but succeeding only in killing the captain of the former before being overwhelmed by the superior numbers and firepower of the British buccaneers. Badly mauled by grapeshot fired point blank into their midst by the British ship's guns, and with the bulkhead of their main cabin shattered, the Japanese pirates continued to fight to the very end, and only one of them was eventually captured alive as he jumped overboard. Held prisoner for the night, he was dragged out in the morning to be hanged. In the words of a witness, "this Japonian...broke the Rope and fell into the Sea. I cannot tell whether he swamme to the land or not" (Williams, 30).

3
THE CENTERS OF MARTIAL INSTRUCTION

The Ryu

The existence of specific weapons of combat, as well as direct and indirect references to particular ways, styles, and techniques of using them in combat, all presuppose the existence of centers of systematic instruction (from the most rudimentary to the more sophisticated), where practitioners of bujutsu were able to familiarize themselves with the theory and practice of individual combat. In these centers, practitioners learned to cope with the innumerable and unpredictable circumstances they might expect to encounter in a combat situation. Records compiled by scribes of the military clans from the eleventh century onward, especially the chronicles of the Edo period, generally refer to these centers as "schools of martial skills" *(bujutsu-ryu)*. This definition, naturally, applies primarily to the centers of martial instruction attended by the professional fighting man of feudal Japan, the warrior *(bushi)*, since he dominates the historiography of the period.

Thus, by definition, a *ryu* represented a school wherein a publicly acknowledged expert taught a number of students the strategic use of a particular weapon, in a particular style and according to particular concepts. The primary purpose of the martial *ryu*, therefore, was educational in the sense that it involved the transmission of systematic knowledge in the specializations of bujutsu through the use of teaching specialists who were considered capable of producing fighting specialists. As illustrated in Chart 11, each school was generally identified by the family name of the founder or inventor of a particular style of fighting taught at that school, or by the name of the clan under whose aegis the *ryu* was officially allowed to function, or by highly imaginative names assigned to the strategies and techniques typical of the school, or by a certain "esoteric" principle of combat reputedly considered the didactic milestone or salient characteristic of its teaching.

The martial culture of ancient and feudal Japan made ample allowance for the proliferation of the greatest variety of these martial *ryu*. The ages of turmoil from the ninth to the seventeenth century provided fertile ground for devising, testing, and refining weapons, styles, strategies, and practices of combat—and for teaching them systematically. Six basic types of *ryu*, however, seem to predominate in the doctrine. These six types often overlap and merge, following the vagaries of time, place, and circumstances.

The first type of martial school may be qualified as *original;* that is, it was administered by the founder himself or by his immediate successors under his personal supervision. The second type was the *derivative* school, which was supervised by instructors and teachers who had studied under other experts of the specialization and style they taught before opening their own centers of instruction. There are no firm criteria which can be used to determine the degree of originality of a particular school, since they all shared a similar tradition, and, according to the biographies of many outstanding teachers, they all

Chart 11

Major Schools of Bujutsu in Feudal Japan

School *(ryu)*	Specialty
Aisu-Kuge	swordsmanship
Araki	chained weapons
Daito	close combat
Hakutsu	close combat
Hasegawa	swordsmanship
Hioki	archery
Hoki	swordsmanship
Hozo-in	spearmanship
Isshin	chained weapons
Itto	swordsmanship
Jukishin	close combat
Juki	close combat
Kajima	archery
Katori-Shinto	swordsmanship
Kito	close combat
Kyushin	close combat
Kobo	swimming
Koto-Eiri	swordsmanship
Kukishin	staff
Kankai	swimming
Masaki	chained weapons
Miura	close combat
Mukai	swimming
Muso-Jukiden-Eishin	swordsmanship
Muso-Shinden	swordsmanship
Nen	swordsmanship
Nichioku	archery
Nihon	archery
Nito	swordsmanship
Omori	swordsmanship
Sasanuma	swimming
Sekiguchi	close combat
Shibukawa	close combat
Shinden	swimming
Shindo-Muso	staff
Shinkage	sword and spear
Shin-no-Shindo	close combat
Shinto	swordsmanship
Soken	archery
Sosuishitsu	close combat
Suifu	swimming
Takeda	swimming
Takenouchi	close combat
Tendo	spearmanship
Tamiya	swordsmanship
Tenjin-Shinyo	close combat
Tenshin-Shoden-Katori-Shinto	sword and spear
Toda	chained weapons
Yagyu	swordsmanship
Yagyu-Shingan	close combat
Yamanouchi	swimming
Yoshin	close combat

Each school also practiced other specialties. The one indicated here appears with greater frequency in the doctrine of bujutsu as the specialty for which the school was particularly noted.

may safely be said to have developed individual styles, strategies, techniques, and so forth (often new weapons of combat, as well) after having studied under the best experts in the various martial skills of the period. Obviously, these men were anxious to tap the widest range of experience in bujutsu before settling down to teach their own strategic interpretations and specialized knowledge.

The third type of martial art school is represented by the *hereditary ryu,* a school which operated under the direction of a specific family of teachers who transmitted their systematic experience in bujutsu from father to son, for generations. When it was impossible to transmit the techniques of a certain hereditary *ryu* by blood line, either because a master had no son or because the one he had was incapacitated or inadequate, adoption of a willing and able student was an accepted practice. To this adopted heir were entrusted the school's records and didactic tradition, as well as the teacher's name.

In direct contrast to this type of martial art school was the *nonhereditary ryu,* often referred to in the doctrine of bujutsu as *ryu-ha* (Draeger, 84). It appears, however, to have been a less common type—perhaps because the records of the nonhereditary school lacked the duration of, and were generally not preserved as carefully as, those of the hereditary (hence more permanent) type of school.

A fifth type was represented by the *public* school, which had been officially allowed by the authorities of the period to operate in a specific location and had been granted an income either in the form of productive land or, more commonly, in rice stipend. The sixth type was represented by the *private* school, which operated without official permission and was tolerated on fief land but without a stipend, or else ignored, when not actually forbidden.

The total number of these centers of martial instruction reported in the chronicles of ancient and feudal Japan has varied from period to period, and often the figures given must be considered with a certain degree of skepticism, since a carefully tabulated census of the various martial *ryu* in pre-Tokugawa times was an impossibility. Even later, when, for reasons of political expediency and self-preservation, the Edo *bakufu* compiled its own records of the martial *ryu,* they concerned themselves primarily with the schools selectively approved by the central authorities, which were generally schools of the first and fourth types. The lists do not include, therefore, those minor schools merely tolerated in some distant fiefs nor, obviously, the clandestine schools of martial skills operating outside the law at many levels of society in feudal Japan.

In 1843, for example, the classic *Bujutsu Ryuso-roku,* quoted by Dore, lists 159 major martial arts schools, further subdivided by order of "their relative importance" into eight major specializations of bujutsu: sixty-one concerning themselves with swordsmanship, with five more specializing in iaijutsu (the techniques of swift, coordinated drawing of the sword); twenty-nine of spearmanship, probably yarijutsu, since the same author quotes two additional schools specializing in the use of the halberd (naginata); nineteen schools of musketry; twenty schools of unarmed combat, probably jujutsu, the feudal predecessor of judo; fourteen schools of archery and nine of horsemanship. Minor schools also included in the list were concerned with swimming and water horsemanship and with drumming and the blowing of the shell-horn, both used as "means of giving battle signals" (Dore[2], 149).

Other schools are also listed in a subsidiary manner, evidently in response to the exigencies of the

Tokugawa period, such as those concerned with the capture of criminals alive, wherein the duties of the warrior class of yore became increasingly those of police forces.

As to location, the *ryu* were to be found everywhere. Each military clan in ancient and feudal Japan included centers of specialized martial instruction within the territory under its jurisdiction. From the smallest clan with only one main residence to the largest ones with several, they all included within their precincts sufficient space for ranges and training halls where weapons could be used and the techniques of combat employing them practiced under expert guidance, until a sufficient degree of skill had been attained and the student was judged ready to face a foe on the battlefield (or anywhere else). The mansions of clans belonging to the *buke* (and, even earlier, to the *kuge* of the artistocratic Heian period) seem to have always included large areas specifically assigned to the teaching and practice of the various specializations of bujutsu such as archery, horsemanship, spearmanship, and swordsmanship. In these areas, the leaders and higher-ranking members of each clan quite naturally received special attention, while the more numerous retainers of the lower ranks were instructed and trained to an extent and in a style considered commensurate with their station.

In the nineteenth century, as indicated by Dore, every military clan employed the services of a teacher in each military skill, who was permitted to teach in his own training hall or shared it with the teacher of another martial skill "on alternate days" (Dore [2], 149). More prosperous clans could afford to have "several teachers of each skill, all belonging to different *ryu*," who taught either in their own houses or went to teach in the houses of warriors of the upper categories and ranks. Private schools abounded where a single specialist of a weapon or a style taught selected pupils, to such an extent that some authors have advanced the theory that all martial schools in the various fiefs were in origin simply private schools—a theory also supported by the fact that most warriors trained their own children personally, at least in the most traditional arts of combat. If private, in this context, means other than public, in the sense of schools that did not belong to a uniform, national system, the theory holds true. However, since the fief-school was generally established by the authorities of the clan for the benefit of its own warriors, the qualification "private school" assumes a more general and comprehensive significance than that of a school wherein a single teacher taught individual, selected students. In our estimation, "private school" is more correctly used in reference to this last type of school.

As described earlier, the militant orders of priests and monks had their own, often intensely active centers of martial indoctrination in buildings adjacent to the major temples and shrines or in isolated mountain areas, during the late Heian period as well as throughout those periods which preceded the Tokugawa rise to power. A number of them were attended not only by monks with a military bent, but also by members of the other classes, not infrequently by the warriors themselves. Most of these centers were ruthlessly suppressed by the *buke* during the "ages of trouble" (actually from the end of the Heian period until the rise to supreme power of the Tokugawa) and never regained their ascendancy as training grounds for the recruitment and preparation of armies of skilled combat professionals in religious garb. Nevertheless, those that did survive, although kept under close surveillance, continued to be regarded as valuable centers of theoretical indoctrination by warriors with inquisitive minds, even after the establishment of the Tokugawa shogunate.

Farmers, in pre-Tokugawa times, were trained in the arts and techniques of bujutsu by their immediate superiors—either the warrior family to which they were affiliated or the head of the village to which they belonged (both types of leaders generally belonging to the lower ranks of the *buke).* Once having been disarmed by Hideyoshi and restricted to their villages and rice-paddies by Ieyasu for more than two centuries, however, they seem to have had little time and even less opportunity for systematic training in those arts of combat which, by then, the *bushi* considered his own exclusive province. And yet we read in the chronicles of the Edo period of children belonging to farmers of high reputation and prestige who were allowed to attend the fief school for warriors and even to carry swords, and of farmers who managed to indulge in the practice of martial arts under the guidance of a warrior on a pilgrimage or, more commonly, a *ronin* who would repay hospitality by offering lessons in spearmanship or swordsmanship.

If the farmers' proficiency in traditional bujutsu, which had been notable in pre-Tokugawa times, ceased to be of much consequence on a large scale after the sixteenth century, they still continued to excel in less traditional or orthodox forms of combat which were not any the less lethal, as the *bushi* who were exposed to a farmers' revolt often learned (even if too late). And, needless to say, the peasants were generally proficient in the type of guerrilla warfare adopted by farmers the world over whenever necessary: that is, those methods of combat based on the use of agricultural tools such as the staff, the scythe, the sling, and various combinations of ropes and lassoes (these forms having always represented the type of combat heritage to which they were most naturally adapted, the use of such tools being an everyday part of their lives). The system of teaching the combat uses of these tools was generally the responsibility of the head of the family or his counterpart in the village hierarchy. More often than not, such arts were taught by a village expert whose family had always maintained a certain traditional skill in a particular method of combat, or by one who had acquired his proficiency at the hands of a traveling fighter.

In the cities and towns, the *heimin* and their corporations, guilds, and unions had also established centers of martial instruction, reflecting a more local approach to the problem of social violence and disorder. These centers, naturally, increased in importance during the ages of social upheaval and persistent disorder, such as those which were common during the decline of the Heian culture and the period preceding the rise of the Tokugawa, when the cities and towns of feudal Japan were exposed to the ravages of war as well as to the attacks of roaming bands of warriors, monks, and assorted groups of outlaws and bandits. Organized primarily for the purpose of producing fighters who could defend the neighborhood in times of trouble, in many cases they enlarged their scope to the point of preparing actual armies of fighting men who attempted to carry out the expansionistic policies of wealthy merchants and craftsmen. The wrath of the *buke* descended upon them as well, and they were either crushed completely or allowed to continue only within the limits of local and individual self-protection. During the Tokugawa period in particular, extensive stables and ranges for the training of large numbers of commoners *(heimin)* in the traditional arts of archery and horsemanship were unthinkable. The controls of the age and its vast network of spies made any such attempt not only vain but extremely dangerous. However, the mansions of certain merchants who had martial (hence, political) ambitions did provide ample room in their architectural designs for possible adaptation to and often illegal use of space for training in martial arts, such as spearmanship and swordsmanship, under the guidance of a private teacher belonging to an acknowledged *ryu* of bujutsu. Centers of instruction in methods of unarmed combat seem to have been particularly active in towns, cities, and various boroughs, in cooperative concerns as well as in private houses—the main reason being that commoners were forbidden to carry weapons by law and were thus continually subject to the temperamental vagaries of the armed men in their midst. Those commoners who had inherited any knowledge of combat methods from ancestors who had fought on the battlefield during the so-called "ages of trouble" seem to have kept that knowledge alive in many cases, or else to have acquired it for a fee from any master willing and able to teach them, whether an affiliated warrior or a masterless samurai *(ronin)*. The police forces in towns and cities, furthermore, had their own centers of instruction in methods of unarmed combat, to which commoners were directly exposed and which they often learned for their own self-defense. That there were transmissible styles of combat which varied from place to place is clearly indicated in references to styles of fighting that differentiated a fighter of Osaka, for example, from a Kyoto fighter.

In structure, each school was based upon two major categories of practitioners, with the teacher and his assistants on one side and the students on the other. Like all the other social units of ancient and feudal Japan, from the family to the clan, from the social class to the nation, the structure of the *ryu* was vertical and reflected in its microcosm all the essential features of the primordial, patriarchal clan: a tight organization hierarchically arranged under a head who occupied the highest position of control, a direct subordination of each member of the school to his immediate superior on the social scale, an intense feeling of commitment and obedience to the organization (to which corresponded, in the best schools, an equally intense feeling of responsibility for those entrusted, as inferiors and dependents, to one's care within the hierarchy), and, finally, a bond of secrecy and mutual assistance intended to protect and preserve the practice, ideas, and members of the *ryu* against all outsiders. This tight correspondence of internal rapports, which created a dynamic tension within each school and, at the same time, made it stand as a unified entity among all the other social units of feudal Japan, was present in the schools of martial skills attended by all the practitioners of bujutsu, from the largest and richest to the smallest and poorest.

Students were accepted by an individual school almost always upon the recommendation of people considered reputable by the teacher, if the school was of the nonaffiliated type. Affiliated schools were generally assigned their students by authorities of the clan that supported the school. The students were generally divided into two large groups, the first encompassing those who were seriously determined not only to excel in a certain martial discipline, but actually to become professional teachers themselves. They were allowed to "board with the teacher—just as an apprentice might board with a craftsman" (Dore[2], 72) and lived, therefore, within the compound of the school itself, wherein they trained constantly and which they helped to maintain as did the monks in their monasteries, whose life-style and dedication the martial arts students often endeavored to imitate. The close and continuing relationship between the dramatic, violent aspects of the Japanese culture of feudal times and the religious elements, which were used to substantiate and justify its martial features, is reflected in the name assigned to the training hall of the martial *ryu*. This hall was generally referred to as a *dojo*—the name being borrowed from the Buddhist nomenclature for the halls set aside for meditation and other spiritual exercises in virtually every monastery and convent. Following the practices of the commercial class during the Edo period, the resident students of this group were generally known as apprentices *(uchi-deshi)*.

Students of the second group simply attended classes and then returned to their homes, but all would-be practitioners of bujutsu trained until their skill in a chosen martial specialization was qualified as being satisfactory by their teacher, who would then issue a graduated but limited series of certificates of proficiency *(menkyo)*, marked with the seal of the school. In exceptional cases of outstanding and dedicated students, some teachers were known to have issued a "full license" *(mokuroku)* indicating that "the teacher had taught his pupil all he knew" (Dore[2], 152).

In this context, it is interesting to compare such scholastic qualifications in the ancient and feudal *ryu* of bujutsu with the practices adopted by most modern schools of the martial arts, which, although generally founded in the nineteenth century, claim as their heritage the martial tradition of bujutsu, often linking themselves to martial *ryu* of ancient or extinct lineage. In modern schools of judo, karate, aikido, kendo, kyudo, and so forth, the students are assigned, on the basis of their experience and proficiency, to the categories and ranks illustrated in Chart 12, each generally being indicated by the color of the belt *(obi)* worn by the student over his training outfit *(gi)*. The colors most commonly used are white, yellow, green, brown, black, red, and purple.

According to some authors, this modern system, referred to as the *dan* system (the name assigned to the graduate who has attained the rank of black belt), represents not only a modification of the ancient system (referred to as the *menkyo* system), developed in response to changed circumstances of time and culture, but also a degenerative dilution of the ancient martial simplicity and unity of qualification into an inferior complexity of ranks and categories associated more with institutional formalism and organizational requirements of the martial arts than with the thorough knowledge of their essence: the techniques. While it seems true that an excessive concern with promotional procedures and ranks may often suggest a correlative diminution of the purpose for which those ranks were established initially, there are indications that some of the feudal *ryu* of bujutsu also divided their students into "as many as nine grades of achievement" (Dore[2], 90) and that the device of using colors to identify ranks, after all, traces its roots as far back as the bureaucratic system of the Heian culture, which, "in imitation of the contemporary Sui dynasty of China," presented a kaleidoscopic picture at court. "Purple was for officials of the fifth rank and upward. *Nin* was green, *rei* red, *shin* yellow, *gi* white, and *chi* black. Princes and chief ministers wore the cap of the highest rank, viz. *toku*" (Tsunoda et al., 46).

As to the content of martial instruction, each *ryu* generally had adopted from its inception a program embracing not only the practical side of a particular martial specialization, such as the postures and displacements which prepared the ground for effective and conclusive techniques of combat, according to specific patterns of strategies in attack, counterattack, and defense against one or more opponents. The program also included specialized training for the development of factors such as mental control, will power, determination, and the utmost concentration of specific strategies and goals at the precise moment of confrontation. This kind of comprehensive program of martial instruction seems to have been preferred by the *ryu* which were active during the "times of trouble" in pre-Tokugawa Japan, when the ideal of a fighting man, regardless of the class to which he belonged, was that of a man able to hold his own in combat with any weapon available (from his own bow and arrow, spear, or sword, to his opponent's, if necessary) and able to face, with equanimity, whatever problem the dramatic and violent reality of the times might present. The approach to teaching in the ancient martial *ryu*, therefore, was clearly wider in scope and depth than that prevalent in later periods, and attempted to include as many of those combat possibilities which a fully developed personality could be expected to handle efficiently and with style.

It seems, however, that this comprehensive approach to the knowledge of bujutsu slowly began to erode during the Tokugawa period, until it was almost completely superseded by another, more limited but definitely more specialized approach, which was intended to develop perhaps fewer fighting capacities in the students, but to develop them to exceptional levels of efficiency and strategic keenness. The *ryu* which operated primarily to prepare warriors, in fact, seemed to have accepted the principle of man's limitations in learning and in performing to the best of his capacity on a *wide* martial level, and to have accordingly shifted their theoretical and practical concern to a super-specialized development of knowledge and performance in each branch and discipline of bujutsu. This tendency, which was embryonic during previous periods (since even then, although the fighting man needed to be more eclectic, he also tended to prefer those specific weapons and techniques best suited to his temperament), became the norm in Tokugawa times, when the *ryu* of the *bushi,* in particular, began to produce superb specialists of the spear who were ill at ease with the sword, and vice versa. The super-specialized approach also affected the various possible styles, techniques, and strategies within each martial art. As indicated earlier, the *ryu* which used the spear as their main weapon were quite numerous, and they differed (often radically) from one another in the

CHART 12

RANKING SYSTEM IN MODERN DERIVATIONS OF FEUDAL BUJUTSU

CATEGORY	RANKS (B/B Stands For "Black Belt")	
DAN (*dan* means "step" and is generally identified by the black belt)	B/B 10th degree (*judan*)	teacher (*hanshi*)
	B/B 9th degree (*kudan*)	
	B/B 8th degree (*hachidan*)	instructor (*kyoshi*)
	B/B 7th degree (*shichidan*)	
	B/B 6th degree (*rokudan*)	assistant instructor (*renshi*)
	B/B 5th degree (*godan*)	
	B/B 4th degree (*yodan*)	
	B/B 3rd degree (*sandan*)	
	B/B 2nd degree (*nidan*)	
	B/B 1st degree (*shodan*)	
KYU (*kyu* means "class" and is identified by variously colored belts)	Student of 1st class (*ikkyu*)	
	Student of 2nd class (*nikyu*)	
	Student of 3rd class (*sankyu*)	
	Student of 4th class (*yonkyu*)	
	Student of 5th class (*gokyu*)	
	Student of 6th class (*rokkyu*)	

The progression in the ranking system of modern bujutsu begins with the 6th rank in the kyu category and proceeds upward.

tactical ways of using that weapon. The *ryu* of swordsmanship were even more extreme in their particular approaches to the postures, techniques, and strategies based upon the use of the sword in combat. Finally, this emphasis on specialization tended to affect the basic program of instruction to such an extent that violent criticism was often hurled at *ryu* accused of favoring only the outer technical aspects of a martial art (posture, displacement, technique, strategies, etc.), while neglecting the interior factors which made the practice effective (development of mental control, will power, concentration, determination, etc.). Naturally, certain *ryu* were accused of exactly the opposite tendency.

The problem of martial specialization which afflicted the *ryu* of the Tokugawa period in particular is considered by some authors to have been the primary source of that scholastic rivalry which expressed itself not in harmless doctrinary debates, but in violent confrontations (armed and unarmed) anywhere students of different schools chanced to meet. Feuds that often lasted for years originated in pre-Tokugawa times when life was held cheap and a challenge to duel to the death was common. These bloody encounters merged with and were largely indistinguishable from the innumerable clashes which rocked Japanese society in the so-called "age of troubles." The Tokugawa dictators, however, were not inclined to tolerate disorders of any kind, especially if they might spark an even greater eruption. During the Edo period, therefore, "attempts were made to discourage such a spirit of rivalry" (Dore[2], 151), to isolate each *ryu* within its own compound where it could be kept under close surveillance and where even the practice of once deadly arts of combat could be progressively modified in the direction of increased safety for the adherents of each school. Those fighters who had reputations to establish or preserve by a deadly commitment to their art either had to face the consequences of their disregard of those laws and edicts banning duels, or engage in such encounters as far from Edo's jurisdiction as possible. A famous confrontation between two sword masters of the period, Miyamoto Musashi and Sasaki Kojiro, who advocated different styles of swordsmanship, had to take place on a remote islet in the Kammon Straits, although the confrontation was covertly sponsored by provincial governors and other powerful bettors of the age.

A feature of instruction in the martial *ryu* of ancient (prefeudal) Japan which has greatly intrigued scholars of bujutsu is the secrecy which was a dominant characteristic in almost every school. A pledge of secrecy was the prerequisite for admission to a school, as clearly specified in the oath which a pupil took as he submitted himself to the master for consideration as a pupil. This bond of absolute secrecy, formally requested and willingly given, represented an inhibiting device which was not restricted to martial skills only, nor to the paramilitary schools of combat rooted in Japanese culture. "In Japan," writes Yamashita, "one continually hears about *hiden* ('secret traditions'), the *hijutsu* ('secret arts'), the *okugi* ('inner mysteries') of nearly every undertaking" (Yamashita, 265).

The use of this device was, in fact, extremely widespread—each organized branch within that culture, regardless of its nature and function, seeming to follow its own clannish and exclusivistic pattern of self-aggrandizement. In committing to writing, for example, the folk-plays *(kyogen)* inherited from his father (plays which had been "handed down from generation to generation by oral tradition"), Toraki excused himself at great length for divulging trade secrets which each performing troupe or family was supposed to transmit only to its own sworn members, never to outsiders. Even mathematics (considered a "rare and somewhat esoteric skill") was taught in special *ryu,* each of which had a particular method of teaching the subject as well as particular "terminologies and notations" and, naturally, "its own 'mysteries' which were not printed in their books but reserved for oral communication to advanced pupils" (Dore[2], 147).

These "secret" teachings of the various *ryu,* which Yamashita considered "on close examination" to have "absolutely nothing mysterious or supernatural about them" (Yamashita, 265), seem to have consisted primarily of particular ways or methods of doing something, ways developed in a manner differing somewhat from the usual, and so "unexpected." Seami, the scholarly actor and playwright of the fourteenth century, expressed this fundamental idea most clearly when, in discussing the main element of a play (the flower or climactic stage of the presentation), he said that it consisted in forcing upon the audience an emotion which they did not expect. According to Yamashita, the esoteric aura of mystery and of occult power typical of any primitive, animistic culture would usually fare badly under close, analytical scrutiny. "Some of the *hiden* of flower arrangement merely explain the particular way in which certain flowers should be treated in order to keep them fresh for a long time. *Hiden* in fencing is often nothing more than a certain dexterous manipulation of the sword that experience has proved to be the best method" (Yamashita, 265). Although the existence of so many secrets in Japanese culture has been explained by many Japanese authors as being largely due to the fact that "the lack of printing presses necessitated individual teaching, and that the professors derived no little pecuniary benefit from imparting the secrets to their pupils" (Yamashita, 265), still it must be added, in all fairness, that these strategic *hiden* were of great practical importance—especially in bujutsu, since the very life of the fighting man of feudal Japan often depended upon them. Once they had been divulged, the secret ways of using this or that weapon in any of the specializations of the art of combat tended to become "expected" and thus lose a great measure of their surprise effect. This, in turn, would place additional strain upon the fighter's skill, when and if he had to cope with an opponent who also knew those secrets and had been well trained in their practical use in combat.

Here too, however, there existed a sharp distinction between the trickster, who (like the *ninja)* was forever inventing new tactics and subterfuges, and the expert, who could display exceptional skill, style, and efficiency even within the most commonly accepted and strictest rules of his martial specialization. For the latter, it was not so much a question of tricking an opponent with an unknown strategy, that is, taking advantage of his ignorance and, therefore, of his intrinsic weakness (although in many minds foul play was often equated with good strategy). Rather, the expert desired to be genuinely superior to an opponent in those arts in which both were expected to excel. Naturally, those who espoused this mode of behavior were clearly in the minority—as indicated by the abundance of so-called secret ways used to surprise and defeat the unwary. This was not only because truly loyal and honest men (in the Western sense of loyalty to a personal idea or ethic, which differs radically from that of blind loyalty to a superior) have always been rare, but also because it might take a man a lifetime to become well versed in various esoteric and exoteric methods of combat, while, on the other hand, a challenge to fight for one's life might be issued unexpectedly, at any moment.

Of the ancient pattern of instruction and its salient characteristics, that which is still prevalent in most schools where ancient and modern derivations of bujutsu are being taught and practiced seems to be the vertical type of absolute predominance of the chief instructor or master over his students and over all other instructors in the school. Bowing to the times, and in accordance with more democratic ideas assimilated from Western culture, particularly in relation to teaching methods, large institutions such as the Kodokan in Tokyo and the Budokway in London have attempted to provide a more collegial and horizontal contribution of the best and most imaginative judo instructors, who, ideally, would participate cooperatively (not in exclusivistic competition) in promoting the development of their martial discipline. The times, and the increasing sophistication of the means of communication, from printing to traveling, have also contributed to the substantial alteration of the secret character of many specializations of bujutsu, making those who still cling to absolute exclusiveness seem sadly anachronistic. As Yamashita observed, the ancient "exclusivistic" idea of a clannish and primitive age whose subjects seemed split and sealed within their own secretive groups of suspicious initiates, narrowly self-centered, was to give way to an enlarged awareness of the "human culture" and experience whose innumerable patterns and ways "with the present-day facilities for printing and the ever-increasing number of books on technical subjects . . . are being exposed to the light of the day, and added to the common stock of knowledge" (Yamashita, 265).

The quality of instruction provided in the martial *ryu,* as indicated by the survey of its contents, varied with the times, the men, and, of course, circumstances. If any general trend in the evolutionary pattern of bujutsu can be gleaned from the records presently available, we may say that two major qualitative phases appear to have characterized and affected the teachings of bujutsu in the major centers of martial instruction: the first, positive and real, when bujutsu was a vital necessity to men who were forced to cope with the dramatic reality of their existence through the constant and extensive application of its specializations; the second, negative and formalistic, when the immediacy of bujutsu as a means of survival or development receded in time and application until it became primarily a romantic tradition, expressed in ritualistic displays. This cycle is evident even within the scope of Heian culture, when the military virtues and skills of the aristocratic clans' attempts during the archaic ages to establish a balance in the Kingdom of Wa (indicated by official ranks and insignia) became largely empty qualifications which many nobles scornfully shunned. "To be given a post in the Ministry of War," writes one scholar in his study of court life in ancient Japan, "was regarded as a most unfortunate development in one's career" (Morris, 97). Even the regimental guards in Nara, Nagaoka, and finally Kyoto had become "by Murasaki's time . . . entirely ceremonial."

This cycle was also evident in the martial culture of feudal Japan, wherein the practice of bujutsu (and, therefore, the schools which taught all its forms and specialized style) had attained great heights of excellence during the long "age of troubles," as well as in the early Tokugawa period, before starting to decline during the middle and late phases of the Tokugawa rule. During this extended period of time, when the nation held its peace and pace under the watchful eyes of the shogun's cohorts in Edo (as well as in the provinces), when open duels or competitions among students of different *ryu* were banned and each *ryu* remained isolated within its own compound, a noticeable decline in standards of excellence and a passive, almost bored attitude toward teaching the martial arts began to spread throughout the once vital, fermenting world of bujutsu. Combat with real weapons or substitutes "was less and less practical," and exercises with the sword and the spear became, in Dore's words, "increasingly a matter of formal gymnastics and disciplined choreography—nothing more than a game for children, as Fujita Toko said" (Dore[2], 151).

Teaching, correlatively, was qualified in the records of bujutsu critics as "quite plainly dull and in addition almost meaningless" (Dore[2], 152). The situation had degenerated so badly that the Edo *bakufu*, concerned about the threat posed by the Western nations and their military envoys who were besieging Japan in the nineteenth century, belatedly reversed its previous course in an attempt to halt, if at all possible, the advanced state of decline in the quality of bujutsu instruction available to the warriors of the new industrial and expansionistic times. Provincial governors "began to encourage duels as a form of training" (Dore[2], 173), and the first feature of bujutsu teaching to come under immediate attack was precisely the "secretive exclusiveness of the various *ryu*"—now indicted as being "an abuse and a hindrance to the development of useful skills." The martial arts schools were urged "to train together," and some military clans carried their attempts to revive a martial vitality strongly diluted by controls and empty formalism to rather extreme lengths. Any unknown expert in spearmanship and swordsmanship who applied for the position of teacher in the *ryu* of a fief had to demonstrate his capacity in a practical manner, "by winning at least six out of ten duels with would-be teachers of other *ryu*" (Dore[2], 173), and any school which failed to produce an expert capable of winning six duels "was to become extinct."

By the nineteenth century, however, the qualitative phase of the decline had become too steep, and even the frantic attempts of the military authorities to rectify a situation they had helped to create were to prove fruitless. That healthy competition and, with it, the process of selection among vital centers of martial instruction that had been common in pre-Tokugawa Japan's admittedly turbulent but comparatively freer society could not be artificially reproduced in a brief span of time after such prolonged exposure to paralyzing feudal controls. By the late Tokugawa period, traditional bujutsu, as well as the martial centers of instruction, had become largely obsolete and had receded into the realms of practices and customs which a nation preserves as a reminder of past glories. Simultaneously, Japanese society began to develop new practices and customs, to institute new centers of orientation and new schools capable of fulfilling the requirements of an era within which the historical context would require an almost total transformation of an already heavily diluted martial tradition. The use of terms such as "martial ways" or "martial ethics" *(budo)* rather than "martial skills" *(bujutsu)* was indeed ancient, for it is found in chronicles of the early Edo period. But it became almost absolute during the late Tokugawa period and afterward, when almost all the schools involved with the systematic teaching of specializations derived from feudal bujutsu referred to them primarily as *budo* specializations, that is, educational ways of achieving purposes other than those sought by the ancient *ryu* of bujutsu.

The Sensei

At the heart of the *ryu* we find that often mysterious figure upon whom the very existence of bujutsu, as well as the preservation and development of its theory and practice, depended : the master of arms, the teacher, the martial arts instructor—the *sensei.* At this point, the topic of martial education moves from the collective dimension of the *ryu* to the individual dimension of the dispenser of martial knowledge. Therefore, in this section we will consider the role of the *sensei* as an important subject of bujutsu and his relevance to the establishment, preservation, and transmission of martial theories and practices in a systematic fashion.

Whether destined to be used on the battlefield or in individual confrontations, the forms of bujutsu and the history of the martial arts as a whole have always been deeply indebted to the *setisei*—that individual who, whether following a natural and spontaneous inclination toward combat or adapting knowledge gained in other fields of human activity to the resolution of the problems of armed and unarmed confrontations, spent the major part of his life immersed in the forms of bujutsu. He experimented with its weapons, tested the techniques and strategies of the various specializations in real combat, and devised new styles or ways of coping effectively with the greatest number of possibilities presented by that dramatic event within which a man could easily lose his life. Above all, he taught his methods to others. Such teachers occupy a position of some prominence in the doctrine of bujutsu, according to ancient canons of historiography, which tend to place events in a perspective strongly determined by the role of heroes and leaders. Without minimizing the role undoubtedly played in the history of bujutsu by countless masses of unknown and unsung fighters of every class and rank, who often prepared the way and provided a favorable climate for the emergence of various remarkable *sensei,* it is the latter who made an effort to establish clearly defined systems, to create schools, to organize students, and to transmit records of their own experience in such a manner as to insure the preservation of their ideas and practices throughout the ages which were to follow.

Very little is known about the criteria adopted to evaluate a candidate for assignment as a master of arms. It must be assumed that (initially, at least) the most naturally inclined and talented men of arms from among the members of the clan were so appointed. In Chinese culture, this appointment had come to depend primarily upon individual merit, as ascertained through a series of public examinations, and upon constant supervision of a candidate's performance during his official career. In Japan, however, it became largely hereditary in nature and, consequently, was rigidly transmitted from the original teacher to his natural or adopted son. Thus, while the records of masters of arms in China abound with names of individual fighters known for their prowess in various specializations of the art of combat, in Japan we read primarily of "schools" and of "families" of bujutsu experts who took great pride in recalling a long line of professional ancestors who had preceded them and whose written or oral instructions they tended to follow quite closely.

The period of political instablity which followed the collapse of the Heian culture and was associated with the beginning of the military age quite naturally disrupted the traditional ties with the past. During this era, new men, increasingly qualified as professional fighters, began to emerge from the clans, particularly during the social turmoil of the Rokuhara era and the Kamakura, Ashikaga, and Momoyama periods. It was during these ages that the traditional arts of combat seem to have reached their highest levels of

sophistication. Characteristically, these new men, in turn, became the founders of new families of instructors who presented their traditional credentials to this or that lord, head of a clan, in order to become that clan's officially appointed teacher of bujutsu. By the time the Tokugawa rulers had consolidated their power, the ancient pattern of hereditary affiliation to a clan had been firmly reestablished and reinforced by an even more pronounced military character.

The prospective teacher usually began as a student of a particular specialization of bujutsu, either by joining a *ryu* and training under the generally severe and decisive guidance of its *sensei,* or by being born into a family of bujutsu instructors. He then progressed through those stages of development deemed appropriate by his teacher or himself. Finally, he would commit himself to that specialization until he either became a *sensei* in his teacher's school or was permitted to open his own *dojo* in another location. Often he completed the training programs of several *ryu,* in which various specializations of bujutsu were taught and practiced, before he developed his own syncretic method and opened his own independent school.

In approaching this pivotal practitioner of bujutsu, a sharp distinction must be made between the teachers of the military class and those belonging to other classes. The *sensei* of the first category naturally were in the majority—as one might expect in a culture so thoroughly rooted in the martial ethos. This category included (in order of importance) *sensei* who had specialized in the martial arts of archery, spearmanship, swordsmanship, general strategy, and in several subordinated styles of unarmed combat, such as jujutsu and aikijutsu, which were to be used in combination with the traditional armed specializations of the military class. Among these, the teachers of equestrian archery, which had been practiced by the ancient nobles *(kuge)* whom the *buke* had formally replaced in 1600, occupied a place of honor linking them to the earliest periods of Japanese history. They were followed in order of prestige by the teachers of swordsmanship, who became increasingly important during the Tokugawa period, when warfare on a general scale became rare while clashes between the military retainers of different clans, or between the samurai and the *heimin,* became increasingly commonplace. The latter, with the clergy and the farmers, had their own teachers, whom they obtained either from the ranks of those *bushi* who had changed their positions or from among the number of qualified men who emerged from the ranks of their own classes. This last group was a minority, being men who usually specialized in arts of combat which could be practiced without arousing the attention and concern of the military authorities. Among these teachers, we find *sensei* of methods of unarmed combat or of methods based upon the use of special instruments employed by the members of various classes, such as the staff, for example, or the fan, iron pipes, and

various chained blades. As might be inferred from the tenor of the entire martial culture, these instructors increased in social relevance as the prolonged period of enforced peace during the reign of the Tokugawa tended to reduce somewhat the role of traditional weapons as determinant factors in resolving conflicts of interest; but they can hardly be said to have attained the level of prestige enjoyed in feudal Japan by the *sensei* who taught traditional forms of bujutsu. It is interesting to note that even today, among the originators of methods of combat based upon Japanese bujutsu, those who have acquired a certain degree of fame in the Eastern and Western hemispheres have usually studied the traditional specializations of combat, such as spearfighting or swordsmanship, at some point in their careers, thus infusing their methodologies with the aura of traditional significance which Japan has always assigned, and still accords today, to those specializations or arts developed centuries ago. This degree of social significance was reflected in the rank and position assigned to each *sensei* within a clan's hierarchy. They were generally rewarded quite handsomely, both before and during the early Tokugawa period—especially when their students were clan leaders, who, quite naturally, would receive special attention. As noted earlier, many wealthy clans had a *sensei* for every specialization of bujutsu recognized as martial by the *buke;* some clans even had more than one *sensei* for the same specialization. In such cases, the proliferation of instructors was not only due to the fact that different ranks of retainers had to be trained, but also to the understandable desire on the part of the clan's warriors (especially the higher-ranking ones) to avail themselves of the widest range of knowledge and skill in the fighting arts.

The second distinction to be made, in considering the teachers of a single specialization of bujutsu, is based upon the role they played in creating new styles of combat or in merely transmitting these styles from one generation to the next. In this context, we distinguish *sensei* who developed and taught their own styles of bujutsu, thus founding their own schools *(ryu)*, from *sensei* who joined or inherited a school founded by another master, in which they taught the style of bujutsu transmitted to them from the founder of that school. The instructors of the second category were by far the majority in feudal Japan, their ranks being constantly replenished, generation after generation, by the successors, descendants, and students of *sensei* of the first type, who, whether as creators or innovators of weapons, techniques, strategies, or styles of bujutsu, are and have always been comparatively few. This type *of sensei,* in fact, was an individual who had acquired a reputation not only as an inventor of new weapons or as a teacher who had improved upon traditional ones, but as a master who had devised new methods for using those weapons effectively on the battlefield, in duels to the death, or in public demonstrations and competition. As we have said earlier, however, he was often known primarily for his skill in explaining the intricacies of his method to others and for his ability to train other people systematically in such a fashion as to produce individuals or teams of students equally prepared to confront and to successfully cope with the dramatic reality of combat. His skill in handling the weapons of the armed specialization of bujutsu which he preferred, or in using his body in the unarmed methods of combat, was stylistically his own and differed unmistakably from that of other fighters or other *sensei* who were experts in the same or similar specializations. But that which made him a *sensei* in the truest sense of the word was, naturally, his particular capacity to communicate to others the essence of his particular style, his ability to transmit it widely and thereby insure that it would not be lost to succeeding generations. This capacity distinguished him from those bujutsu experts who could fight with unsurpassed efficiency and style but who could not or would not explain their particular methods to others, preferring to take their secrets with them to the grave, leaving no disciples and no school to mark their passing. The special character of a *sensei's* style and teaching was the basis of his reputation as a teacher, and of his school as a vital center of martial instruction. With the increase in number of students attending his particular school and the passing of time, such a reputation tended to acquire the sacred nature of a tradition, which, as we have observed previously, added its own weight and emphasis to the already relevant and practical appeal of his teaching.

The *sensei* of the second category were the inheritors, the successors, the administrators, who consolidated the fame of an original founder of a *ryu* and preserved its existence and function as a center of martial instruction beyond his lifetime. This kind of *sensei* was, and of necessity had to be, a different type of man, since his primary function was that of preserving a particular method and of transmitting its essence as closely in line as possible with the founder's original conception and intentions. As such, they were not as creatively inclined as the men from whom they received their instruction and validation as teachers. Also, one may assume that, logically, an innovator would select for his successor an individual who gave the best assurance of strict adherence to the canons which the founder had established as the basis for his own school or method. Notwithstanding their general lack of originality, it is to the second type *of sensei* that bujutsu owes the preservation and transmission of certain original messages which otherwise would have been lost to us. And, despite man's natural tendency to elaborate upon an inherited method, to adapt its techniques and strategies to varying circumstances of time, place, and culture, as well as to improve upon and thereby change that method, many *sensei* of the second type remained faithful to a certain style, even as it progressively lost its youthful flavor and its relevance to a changing world. By transmitting various methods to others or by recording their technical connotations in scrolls and manuscripts, these *sensei* helped bujutsu to mark its own historical progression and to determine the value of each method as a contribution to the theory and practice of the martial arts.

The *sensei* of the first category emerged from all classes and ranks during the period of unrest from the tenth to the sixteenth century, moving much more easily than in the ancient Heian period or in the Tokugawa period through the barriers set up to seal each Japanese subject within the social cell assigned to him by the authorities of the age. That turbulent era in Japanese history, in fact, produced individuals of outstanding ability who are mentioned in the doctrine of bujutsu as the originators of martial specializations or as the innovators of new styles and methods for using both new and traditional weapons with exceptional skill. Even during the rigidly stratified times of Heian and Tokugawa domination, however, individual talent continued to display its disregard for social conventions, political rigidity, and hereditary barriers. There are examples in both ages of notable fighters and outstanding teachers emerging from the countryside or from among the *heimin,* whom the aristocrats of the ancient *kuge* in Kyoto and later the barons of the *buke* in Edo tried to repress, suppress, or, in a more subtle if no less painful maneuver, absorb into their own clans, often by raising them to the status of retainers. These exceptional men, however, were a distinct minority, since both the Heian and Tokugawa cultures were based primarily upon the constitutional concepts of hereditary rights officially established in the clan records and transmitted solely from father to son, from ancestors to descendants, in a vertical line which insured that both would remain firmly rooted in the rank and position assigned to them by the accident of birth and/or the wishes of their superiors.

A third distinction, therefore, must be made: between the *sensei* affiliated with a clan and the *sensei* who was not, that is, who managed his *ryu* on an independent or semi-independent basis. Again, in a culture closely patterned upon the vertical model of the clan, teachers of the first category constituted the majority. They might belong to this basic social unit either by birth or by affiliation—the latter could be voluntary, as in the case of a masterless *sensei* applying for the position of instructor in a lord's clan, or imperative, as when an affiliated *sensei* was requested by his own lord and master to pledge himself to another. Once having given their oath, they were permitted to operate schools in the territory of the clan in whose records their names had been inscribed. They were assigned a predetermined income whose value depended upon their reputation and position within the clan hierarchy. They had their own training halls and living quarters, either in the immediate proximity of the lord's mansion or in his castle when they instructed the lord himself and retainers of high rank, or in a location easily accessible to the warriors of the clan whom they were called upon to instruct. As members of a clan, the exclusivistic and highly segregated nature of their styles and methods of combat would become even further accentuated. It must be remembered that each clan was a self-centered unit, territorially independent and intrinsically jealous of its own prerogatives, traditions, and power, which it preserved and enforced through and by the use of bujutsu. Its very existence and individuality among so many other clans depended upon its exclusivistic sense of mission and its exaggerated sense of importance in the national scheme of things. The *sensei* of a clan, therefore, endeavored to keep that clan's methods of bujutsu secret and available only to the rightful members of the clan or to those duly authorized to attend their classes by the lord of the clan.

As indicated earlier, affiliated *sensei* could be the founders of a particular style of bujutsu, who had been born into and raised in a clan or who had been accepted by the clan authorities as rightful members of the unit and placed at a certain level within its hierarchy. Once having firmly established themselves, these teachers naturally bequeathed the secrets of their fighting style to their natural heirs—the position of teacher, like all other positions and ranks in Japanese feudal society, tending to be almost exclusively hereditary and transmissible in a direct, vertical line. When the relativity of life asserted itself by depriving a *sensei* of a natural-born heir, he would often adopt one chosen from among the best (and usually the most orthodox) students in his *dojo,* thus insuring that his method, together with his name and school, would be preserved within the clan. These *sensei*-in-residence, accordingly, founded dynasties of instructors, most of whom remained attached to a clan and the family of its leaders for ages.

Some *sensei,* however, such as the roaming "wave men" *(ronin),* were not bound by clan affiliations. They would simply obtain permission from clan authorities to reside in a specified territory and then teach bujutsu to the warriors of that clan or to anyone else who wished to learn and could afford the fee. Such men were naturally a minority, as were the itinerant *sensei* who visited the stronghold of one clan after another, accompanied by students, giving demonstrations of their prowess, and spending limited periods of time instructing the warriors of those clans whose leaders formally requested their services. A famous teacher of kenjutsu, for example, Tsukuhara Bokuden, used to journey through the land followed by more than a hundred students who were eager to learn from him.

Following an entirely independent pattern, finally, was the roaming expert whose extraordinary skill in combat was not the basis of any *ryu* but whose personal reputation was the activating force behind a persistent desire to test his skill again and again, by issuing or responding to challenges (particularly those involving other specialists of bujutsu, including accredited *sensei).*

Within his own *dojo,* a *sensei* was in a position comparable in mystique to that of the emperor in Kyoto and, in effective power, to that of the shogun in Edo or the daimyo in his fief—a position, that is, of supreme authority and unchallenged prestige. Each *sensei* represented the center of that social microcosm, the *ryu,* which was patterned upon the clan (as were all other social units in feudal Japan). In this context, much has been written concerning the autocratic nature of a Japanese leader who is placed by his culture in a position of absolute control over and, correlatively, total responsibility for other individuals. This type of leadership, which required unconditional loyalty and subservience from a teacher's disciples, represented, at its highest levels, a courageous attempt on the part of the *sensei* to assume the burden of caring and providing for his followers in a suitable manner. It could be, and often was, perverted into strange forms of irresponsible despotism on the one hand, corresponding to general inertia and passivity on the other. The major drawback in this particular relationship (which generally served to encourage conformity and sterile imitation) was that it acted as a barrier to the development of self-reliance and the assumption of personal responsibility by a *sensei's* followers. Japanese historians themselves have noted this characteristic of their culture during the feudal period and recognize that its traditional weight seems to strongly influence Japanese culture even today. Western historians, moving from a different cultural perspective, reached substantially the same conclusion. During World War II, for example, one of the tactical principles employed by the Allied forces in the Pacific theater against the imperial forces of Japan was that of eliminating Japanese officers and then proceeding to neutralize the thus-disoriented troops. It might be said that, in any military organization, the elimination of the officer as the activating director and coordinator of the military mass is a tactical principle widely applied. It is significant, however, that it was so extensively and systematically employed against the Japanese leadership elite, and with such notable success.

The supremacy of the bujutsu teacher in his *dojo*, therefore, was a cultural trait he inherited as a Japanese feudal subject, and he was conditioned by it with every breath he took. As an intrinsic part of a social system which demanded that he accept his role fully and unconditionally, only rarely did he become aware of the dangers inherent in such an unqualified acceptance. This conditioning began, one must remember, at the very moment of his birth and was strongly reinforced when he began to study bujutsu under the supervision of his first *sensei*.

Fujioka Sakutaro underscored the major effects of such a system upon the teacher-pupil relationship:

> A pupil was taught to walk "seven feet in the rear of his instructor, lest he should tread on the latter's shadow." The teacher showed the way and the pupil had only to follow it. Hence the pupil was not allowed to depart a step from the teacher's instructions: he was permitted to reproduce but forbidden to improve. It is not surprising, therefore, that the teacher should have become more sparing of his teaching as the pupil advanced, or that he should have tried to sanctify his art by surrounding it with all manner of mythical traditions. If the pupil happened to be of a free and ungovernable turn of mind, and attempted to add his own devices to what was imparted to him, he was certain to provoke his instructor's wrath, and even became liable to be "excommunicated." (Okuma, 449)

In his valuable study on education in Tokugawa Japan, Dore noted the striking difference between the degree of respect accorded the Japanese *sensei* and that extended to his counterpart in Chinese society. Dealing in particular with the teacher of literature, he advances the explanation that, while the extreme deference extended to the Japanese teacher may be due in large part, as indicated by Yoshikawa Kojiro, to Japanese "disciplinarianism," it might also be due to the position "of power, prestige, and of relative affluence" enjoyed by the Chinese literati, whereas the Japanese scholar of the Edo period "rarely exercised power and he was usually poor. Deference was all he could claim, and it is not surprising that he was jealous of this, his sole form of privilege" (Dore[2], 183).

A concomitant feature of the relationship which bound the bujutsu student to his *sensei* was its personal nature. A student registered in a particular *ryu* was primarily a pupil of the teacher who accepted him as a disciple. "Personal discipleship, rather than institutional membership" (Dore[2], 73), based on a direct contract between the student and the teacher of a martial *ryu* who received his oath, was the primary link

between them, and it often extended well beyond the limits of the usual instructional rapport. In many cases, it closely resembled the link between a stern father and a submissive son, in accordance with the patriarchal conception of the Oriental family, wherein the son is fully subject to his father's authority. It has been observed that even today one seldom witnesses a more pronounced form of respect, often virtually indistinguishable from actual subservience, than that accorded to a Japanese master of any art or discipline by his Japanese students. Archaic and amorphous but strongly determinant feelings, stemming from ancestor worship and veneration of a traditional past which the teacher is felt to represent and embody, are clearly at work in this context and constitute the motivation behind a cultural characteristic which has defied numerous attempts at rational or analytical explanation. Interestingly enough, there have been many attempts to export and transplant the type of relationship common in Japan between instructor and student to the West (in certain judo, karate, aikido, kendo schools, etc.). More often than not, the result of such an attempt has been frustrating and disappointing to both the Japanese instructor and his Western students, since the necessary cultural premises for such a transplant are almost entirely lacking in the West. For example, it is rare to find such a total personal commitment of one man to another man outside the Orient, even when the latter is invested with superior powers by his society. Also lacking in the West are the conditions which would enable a Japanese teacher to fulfill his traditional obligation toward a student, that is, a responsibility which would encompass a disciple's entire personal welfare and which, in the East, far exceeds in both depth and content that of the Western teacher toward his pupil.

The vertical and rigidly hierarchical system generally adopted in the public, affiliated *ryu* was also adopted and applied in the nonaffiliated schools of bujutsu where an instructor without a master (that is, a descendant of a warrior family or a master who had renounced his military heritage) would teach his method of combat to students for a fee—prospective students usually requesting such instruction through friends or other acquaintances of the instructor. There were many of these private schools, especially during the early stages of the Tokugawa period, when thousands of dispossessed warriors, whose clans had been destroyed or disbanded, roamed the land and lived as best they could. In most cases, these schools were opened by individuals of extraordinary skill in the art of armed and unarmed combat, who had to prove themselves to any challenger, since they were not protected by clan regulations concerning affiliation and collective force. In such schools, the absolute predominance of the master, who was considered (and considered himself to be) the sole source of authority and knowledge, was an accepted fact. Within the framework of a clan, on the other hand, an instructor's authority, although substantial, was always counterbalanced by the authority of the organization to which he had pledged his loyalty, to whose regulations he was subject, and to whose leaders he was bound to answer for any action that might affect the life and welfare of those students entrusted to his care.

There is hardly a significant example in the records of bujutsu (which span several centuries) of a less vertical type of instruction in feudal Japan—that is, of a more horizontal and collective system which would allow a student to profit simultaneously from the experience of many instructors, all skilled and working together to improve upon their respective specializations of bujutsu and not, as was commonly the case, proceeding along separate, diverging, or conflicting patterns of instruction. The attempts of the military authorities in the late Edo period to correct this situation, as indicated earlier, were ultimately to prove too little and much too late. During the major part of the Tokugawa period, the student determined to acquire skill and knowledge in the field of the martial arts was forced to subject himself to the rigid discipline of the martial *ryu* and its master, the *sensei.* He might thus spend a number of years in each one, and it was not unusual for him to spend an entire lifetime passing through the hands of several instructors in the art of swordsmanship alone—to mention only the most popular specialization of traditional bujutsu during the Tokugawa period.

As indicated previously, large clans could afford to provide their higher-ranking warriors with several instructors under the same roof and, often, with more than one in the same specialization of bujutsu. This last arrangement, however, was not as satisfactory as one might suppose, for a position as instructor in a Japanese clan of that period could be secured not by merit alone, but by custom and hereditary necessity or by ancient pledges which clan officials were generally reluctant to abrogate in favor of the dreaded "unexpected." Consequently, a student of bujutsu (affiliated with a clan) who became dissatisfied with the quality, range, and depth of instruction offered by the clan's official instructor might eventually ask his immediate superior (who had to make the necessary recommendations to the clan authorities) to allow him to engage in the pilgrimage called training in warriorship *(musha-shugyo).* If the desired permission was forthcoming, the student would begin his travels across the length and breadth of Japan, passing from school to school and from instructor to instructor, carrying with him a letter of introduction which would open some, if not all, doors to him.

One of the great activating forces of bujutsu in feudal Japan, a force which insured its development and refinement, was embodied in these traveling warriors. To a great extent, it was the itinerant *bushi,* and not the established instructor secure within the clan precincts or secluded in his private school, who furthered the progress of the martial arts in Japan by keeping the channels of communication and experimentation open among those subjects interested in the warrior arts. The official instructors usually acted to close such channels by withdrawing from active competition, often inferring that the degree of proficiency they had attained in their martial specializations was the highest possible. The real expert, then as now, continued to learn and to grow through direct involvement and experimentation—even challenging those who presumed that they had learned all there was to learn. More than one famous instructor, consequently, was publicly disgraced (when not killed outright) by an itinerant and unknown *bushi* who emerged one day from nowhere to challenge him (even within the precincts of the instructor's own school), before disappearing again into the mists from which he had emerged.

The great merit of an established instructor, naturally (whether affiliated or not), was that of insuring the organized and systematic transmission of ancient martial practices from one generation to another, whether through oral and direct communication or through manuscripts, records, scrolls, and other manuals of instruction. Such men rescued bujutsu from possible oblivion or kept it alive so that it was not necessary to begin anew each time. Today, many Japanese families descended from ancient military clans still cherish and guard such records (often written in archaic and esoteric language) transmitted by a long line of martial experts.

The militant clergy of pre-Tokugawa times had usually obtained instruction in bujutsu from retired warriors who, like the famous Shingen, seemed to find nothing inappropriate in fulfilling their violent ambitions even after having donned priestly robes. It seemed that the isolation and the comparative quiet of the monasteries (which encouraged the samurai to *think* more, in comparison to their previous occupation, which had forced them to *act* more) often provided these warriors with particular insights into the technical strategic possibilities of bujutsu which they could test and perfect at their leisure. Even after the rise of the Tokugawa to power in Japan, the fame of certain instructors who had isolated themselves in the wilderness brought many warriors to their monasteries, temples, or mountain refuges. Certain samurai would actually spend years learning the strangely esoteric methods such instructors had developed, while at the same time profiting from the regime of austerity such isolated situations naturally afforded, removed as they were from the many distractions of castle or town life. As a direct consequence of the example set by this more interiorized form of training (that is, as provided by ancient ascetic masters), the idea of training upon wooded slopes, in forests, or high in the mountains has retained its fascination for many adepts of those forms of modern bujutsu which have their roots in Japan's feudal past.

PART II

OUTER FACTORS OF BUJUTSU

Weapons and Techniques

In the Introduction we indicated that the Japanese art of combat and its specializations could be approached on two levels: the first, centered upon such factors as the weapons and techniques used by the various specializations of bujutsu, may be qualified as *outer;* while the second, centered upon the factors of mental control and energy, may be more precisely qualified as *inner.*

In Part 2, we will begin with a review of the outer factors of bujutsu, that is, with the weapons and techniques used in the specializations of bujutsu generally viewed as traditional martial arts, strategically important in individual combat encounters and commonly practiced by the Japanese fighting man of the feudal age. These factors not only provided each specialization with its own character and systematic individuality, but were often directly responsible for the particular name bestowed upon each art. Furthermore, the instrumental and functional characteristics of one specialization usually influenced and, in some cases, even determined those of another.

The art of spear fighting, for example, was influenced by the art of archery in relation to such basic concepts as those of trajectory and aim. In turn, the art of spear fighting influenced the art of swordsmanship with its concepts of various guards, movements, and techniques of rotation and penetration in combat. It also, by extension, influenced the art of the staff, the art of the fan, and even the arts of unarmed combat, which, in their ancient and in their derivative (modern) styles, employed the human body as a weapon with which to subdue an opponent in innumerable ways. However, from the standpoint of the instruments particularly employed by each bujutsu specialization, as well as the correlative methods or techniques devised for their use, each method requires a particular section within which to survey its individual characteristics.

4
ARMED BUJUTSU

<THE ARMOR>

Evolution of Japanese Armor

The armor worn by the *bushi* on the battlefield during the most ancient period of Japan's history, as well as the various other kinds of protective equipment he used during the latter part of the feudal era, are of particular interest to us, for this protective equipment was both a reflection of, and a determining factor in, the evolution and strategic use of those weapons employed against him in combat.

It is usually agreed, in fact, that the greater specializations of the bow and arrow, of the spear, of the sword, and so forth, all flourished during the so-called "ages of trouble" which preceded the Tokugawa era—a time of continual warfare among the various military clans, as each strove to attain a position of superiority over all the other clans. Warfare then (as in the Middle Ages in Europe) was waged on the battlefields of Japan by knights and their cohorts, all outfitted in protective armor. This, in turn, implicitly required the development of highly sophisticated methods of using various weapons in order to reach and penetrate a well-protected target, while conversely employing ever more sophisticated types of armor to protect oneself against attacks and counterattacks launched by the enemy.

In less warlike times, such as those following the unification of Japan under the Tokugawa, internecine strife moved from the battlefield to the streets, mansions, and castles, finding particular expression in a series of intrigues, assassinations, half-aborted revolts, and numerous instances of petty lawlessness. This type of strife, in turn, reduced the use of armor to a minimum or caused its elimination altogether. At the same time, the importance of the bow and arrow or of the spear in combat was lessened, while the instrumental and functional importance of the sword was greatly enhanced. In a subordinate manner, the human body itself began to figure more prominently as a weapon of unarmed combat which could be used against both armed and unarmed foes.

Even when the armor of yore had become mainly ornamental and ceremonial, while actual protective covering had been reduced to a light coat of mail or had been eliminated entirely, the ancient techniques of the spear and the sword, as well as the use of the war fan as a projectile (all originally intended for use against an opponent in armor), still influenced combat practices and strategies, including unarmed methods of combat. And these techniques continued to represent the fundamental nucleus of the major martial art specializations of Japan's late feudal era, as well as most modern versions of these specializations. Much of the technical repertoire of aikido, for example, is clearly based upon the ancient techniques of jojutsu and kendo, both being derived in turn from such arts as kenjutsu, yarijutsu, and naginatajutsu, originally methods of combat directed against a foe often in armor. And, at its highest levels, judo still contains formal exercises *oikata,* such as the ancient forms of judo *(koshiki-no-kata),* clearly derived from combat encounters between armored opponents and stylized for the purpose of developing that strategic coordina-

Clan armorers, 14th c.

tion which would permit a warrior to project a heavily armored opponent onto the ground. There are also ancient exercises of coordination performed in karate which, though obviously influenced by Chinese styles of boxing emphasizing the strategic predominance of the empty hand, still appear to follow those patterns of attack, counterattack, and defense which were once followed by a man wielding a sword, a dagger, or a spear. Both the Chinese and the Japanese were exceptionally skilled in the use of the spear, even when a wooden staff was subsituted for the traditional naked blade. The armor worn by the *bushi,* then, was an integral part of bujutsu because it influenced either directly (through weapons and techniques) or indirectly (through their modification or evolved adaptation) the development and application of the majority of the ancient and modern specializations of the warrior arts. The *bushi* of the Tokugawa period inherited a rich tradition in the protohistoric art of making and wearing armor. The members of every clan could easily follow the evolution of this art by examining the ancient and contemporary specimens which were part of every clan's heritage and combat equipment. A suit of armor often occupied a place of honor in the clan residence or in a nearby temple, in accordance with the custom of dedicating objects of worth or renown to a divinity. These sets of armor were once kept in special armories "built in the waste lands by imperial decree, and in each province arms, i.e., swords, bows and arrows, armours, were collected and stored" (Arai, 14). This custom seems to have been in force even during the time of Emperor Kotoku and, specifically, in the first year of Taika (645). During this period, no one, not even the professional soldier, was allowed to keep armor or weaponry of any sort in a private home. It is not clear when both armor and weapons began to be generally kept at home, but many authors look upon this practice as being the basis for the formation of a professional class of fighters, who eventually worked their way back from the periphery of the political body of Japan to the center of power. "This practice," wrote Arai Haku-seki, "gradually led to the break-up of the strict regulation of earlier days against the private possession of arms. It must have been a more reasonable arrangement for those who devoted themselves to military service" (Arai, 15). It was certainly considered a reasonable arrangement by the *bushi* and by other classes of Japanese subjects, such as those mountain priests *(yama-bushi)* and temple monks *(tera-hoshi),* mentioned by the same author, who battled the professional warriors of Japan down through the centuries.

Each clan, each military house, each family of samurai status had its own armor makers *(gusoku-shi),* the most renowned of whom also served other military groups on commission. Each clan also had its own theory and practice of armor wearing, which, in a sense, explains the richness and variety of Japanese military armor in feudal times. Naturally, each group kept its type and method of armor wearing a secret, the particulars of which were contained within the body of tradition available to the members of

Field commander in full armor, 14th c.

that group—and to no one else. These secret traditions were so well preserved that, eventually, the art of armor making, the style of the various elements, and even their particular use, became unintelligible during the ages of peace. Arai Hakuseki, the great Confucian scholar who served at the court of the shogun Ienobu (1662-1712), wrote a comprehensive treatise on armors *(Honeho Gunkiko),* in which he observed that "centuries have passed since the ancient style of armour was replaced by the *gusoku* of today, and it is already a century since arms were put away (i.e., there ceased to be any warfare), so that even among the armourers who made their living by their skills, there are few who know the old style of armour" (Arai, 30).

In the main, Japanese armor making seems to have concentrated upon a basic model which remained substantially the same in structure and components throughout the ages. This model, however, evolved from the military simplicity and high degree of functionality associated with the so-called "ages of trouble," to the lavishly decorated and cumbersome examples typical of the Tokugawa period, when armor and weapons were not viewed primarily as instruments of combat, but rather as symbols of power and hierarchical status—that is, of rank.

The basic model mentioned above consisted (as in Europe) of protective equipment for the head, the neck, the shoulders and the arms, the chest, the lower abdomen, and the legs and feet. It was usually a complete outfit for the *bushi* of higher rank who rode into battle; retainers who fought on foot were not equipped with all the items worn by the *bushi* on horseback. In general, the materials employed in the manufacture of armor reflected the characteristic preoccupation of Japanese armorers with speed and functionality, especially when compared with the massive suits of armor worn by European feudal knights and lords. In fact, most scholars of Japanese history seem to agree that, before and after the reign of Emperor Tenji (661-71), "armour seems to have been ordinarily made of leather" (Gilbertson and Kowaki, 115). Stone mentions, for example, the word *kawara (kawa* meaning leather), which identified a characteristic "armor made of leather scales sewed on cloth. It was used in very early times and only a few fragments of such armor are now in existence" (Stone, 346). Hakuseki, too, after studying the old manuscript *Sandai Jitsuroku,* mentions "ancient sheep-skin armours and cow-hide armours worn by the warriors of Ono-no-Ason-Uyu during the Konin era and given to his two sons, Mutsu-no-Kami-Harueda and Tsushimano-no-Kami-Harukaze, who fought in the Jogen era (976-97)" (Arai, 17). Leather always remained a great favorite of Japanese armorers, not only as the connective link which held the various pieces of armor together but also as the basic material for the armor itself—the plate of leather being reinforced by iron or steel plates, or mail, or else lacquered until an embossed and sturdy rigidity was attained.

Helmets and chest protectors made entirely of iron have also been found in dolmens dating back to 400 B.C. and even earlier (Stone, 60), providing evidence that iron armor of this type had been accepted, at least initially, by Japanese armorers quite early in their history. The specimens preserved, however, seem to be of iron skillfully worked in order to reduce its natural weight, by thinning it where it was used in one piece (helmets) or by riveting bands of iron together—small ones for helmets, large ones for chest protectors. Hakuseki wrote that "during the reign of Kwammu Tenno (782-806) the Ezo (Ainu) of Michinoku rose in revolt against the throne and were very strong; whereupon in March of the 9th year of Enryaku (790), the Emperor ordered the Dazaifu to prepare more than two thousand iron armours. Probably this is the first official record of armours being made of iron" (Arai, 14) .The expertise shown in handling iron in such

Samurai in corselet, 13th c.

a sophisticated manner was the obvious prelude to the development of that highly refined art of cutting, shaping, entwining, and lacing iron and steel plates of all dimensions together (with leather cords or links of iron mail) which made Japanese armorers, from the Heian period onward, famous the world over. The first specimens of armor of this protohistoric period (fifth to the seventh centuries) seem to have been called *tanko* (plate armor) and were the immediate predecessors of the armor made of a composition of leather and iron, called *kogane-majiri-no-yoroi* (in the ninth century) and *kawa-tsutsumi,* "in which the bands forming the cuirass were encased in leather" (Dean, 27).

During the late Heian period and afterward, armor seems finally to have developed into that masterpiece of composition made "of plates of iron sewn to each other by silk or leather cords, the cords forming a pattern by which the style of the armour was indicated, the mode of sewing together being called *odoshi*" (Gilbertson and Kowaki, 116). The plates of iron and steel, whether encased in leather or not, were adapted in size and shape to the protective purpose for which they were intended. Large plates could be used to protect the shoulders in the *sode* or the chest in the *do,* to cover the loins in the *waidate,* and so forth. They were held together by iron or leather laces. Small scales of metal *(kozane),* laced together with silk cords, were used in almost every part of the suit of armor, around and within the supporting framework provided by the large plates. An interesting method of selecting these scales is described by Hakuseki in his *Honcho Gunkiko:*

> There were also what is called *tameshi-zane* (tested scales). Kikuchi Higo-no-Kami-Takemitsu, while preparing to rise in arms during the Enbun era (1356-1360) had a strong warrior *(sannin-bari,* a man strong enough to draw a bow of *sannin-bari,* the string of which is put on by one man while two others bend it), shoot at each *kusazuri,* then, picking out the *sane* that were not pierced, mixed them with others in *ichi-mai-maze* (one iron *sane* between two of leather) and had his armour made from them. (Arai, 74)

Finally, chain construction and links of mail, of all sizes and every pattern, were woven with the large and small plates into a highly mobile and comparatively light garment lined with padded cloth, silk, or leather.

Comparative studies of the materials employed by European and Japanese armor makers during the Middle Ages, and of the ways devised to forge and adapt them to protect the warrior, have shown that

Spearman, 14th c. High officer, 17th c.

Europeans tended to put more emphasis upon size and weight, while the Japanese concentrated on mobility and lightness. In tactics, in fact, the European knight used both his own and his horse's heavy armor to strike the enemy, employing their full weight and momentum for this purpose. His lances were frequently broken upon contact, forcing him to resort to axes, maces, or cumbersome swords when battling an armored foe or those cohorts of lightly armed serfs employed as infantry during the early feudal era in Europe. In the East:

> All of the weapons used were much lighter and more manageable; the *lances* were shorter, lighter and better balanced, the swords were of better quality and better adapted for use at close quarters. Both swords and spears were meant for cutting and piercing and the smashing weapons, maces and axes, were much lighter and not as much used. (Stone, 430)

This writer also mentions the climate as being an important factor in determining the differences between Western and Eastern armor in the Middle Ages.

In general, the Japanese seem to have always considered excessive protection the antithesis of high strategic functionality, and to have recognized, with good reason, that a direct hit, whether with an arrow or (after the sixteenth century) with a bullet, could pierce any type of armor a man could reasonably be expected to wear. This widespread fatalism, in fact, is reflected in the following lines from the *Honcho Gunkiko:*

> Those *sane* (metal scales) which are not penetrated by arrows cannot resist musket balls, and those that withstand musket balls are pierced by *arrows.* The soft and the hard each has its own strong points, but it is difficult for anything to be complete with the strong points of both. Thus it seems almost futile to arm oneself. Does, or can, a warrior fighting at the front, amidst the missiles, choose between arrows and musket balls? Even if sheets of iron were worn ten-fold or even twenty-fold thick, there would have to be spaces between the sheets; otherwise the wearer of the armour would not be able to move his body. But if there are gaps, these are exactly where the enemy will seek to hit. It is not only these missiles that will pierce the armour; *tachi* (sword), *toshi* (dagger),*yari* (spear), and *naginata* (a glaive or spear with a sword-like blade) are also employed. It is also to be regretted that some warriors, too anxious for fame, and ignorant of the fate that awaits them, wear *yoroi* (armour) too heavy for them and thus meet their untimely death. (Arai, 75-76)

Field commander, 17th c.

Warrior leader, 16th c.

In time, a compromise was reached by cleverly entwining a combination of materials which, by deflecting blade, arrow, or musket ball, offered maximum protection against penetration while simultaneously being comparatively light and easy to wear. In this way, the need for protection was balanced by emphasis upon that other factor so relevant to combat: mobility (and its concomitant, elusiveness). Consequently, when European armor was introduced into Japan in the sixteenth century, only selected pieces, such as the corselet and chest protector, were tentatively accepted, and even these never became very popular.

What, then, of the fantastically elaborate suits of armor we admire in modern museums? The answer to this question is to be found in Japanese classics such as the *Honcho Gunkiko:* "it is not without purpose that great generals *(taisho)* have a number of such imposing armours made and ride into battle in them in order to raise the morale of their men" (Arai, 76). But, as Hakuseki goes on to specify, "this is not the same as in the case of self-preservation."

The system of lacing *(odoshi)* the large and small plates together, of lining them with mail, padded cloth, silk, leather, and so forth, became an art in its own right *(odoshi-gei).* Through the selection of colors or by the patterns of lacing employed, the *bushi* could distinguish one style of armor from another, and even identify the members of various clans by the particular colors used in the lacing and decorating of their armor. Empress Jingo's armor, for example, was "sewn with deep crimson cords" and was called, appropriately enough, "Red Lacing" *(hi-odoshi).* Gilbertson and Kowaki link the beginning of this custom of adopting color as a means of identification to the reign of Emperor Seiwa (858-76), when "the great families adopted special colours for the *odoshi,* the Taira selecting purple, the Fujiwara light green, the Tachibana yellow, etc." (Gilbertson and Kowaki, 116). Various shades of the same color were given different names, such as *hanairo-odoshi* for light blue lacing and *kon-odoshi* for navy blue lacing. Lacings of several different colors were quite common, and these were generally known as *iroiro-odoshi.* White, the color of mourning in Japan, was often used significantly, to indicate that the wearer of a suit of armor laced with cords of that color was engaged in a battle from which he did not expect to emerge alive.

The material used in the lacings was also a means of identifying styles of armor— leather cords characterizing the *kawa-odoshi* and Chinese silk damask the *kara-ya-odoshi,* for example. Naturally, the lacing itself—that is, the way of entwining the cords with one another and with the iron plates (a minor art known as *kebiki)*—was used as a means of indicating rank and position. Tight, elaborate lacing, for example, was used in the armor of *bushi* belonging to the higher ranks of the clan. Wide lacing *(o-arame, sugake),* according to Hakuseki, was used for the infantry troops of the fourteenth and fifteenth centuries and, later,

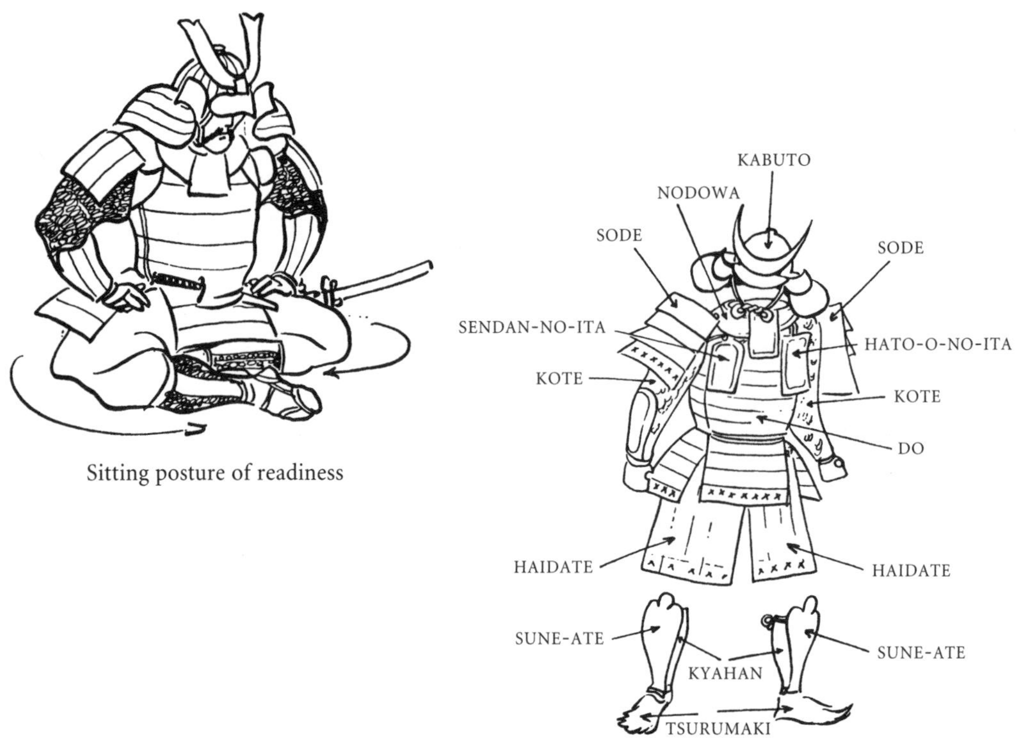

Sitting posture of readiness

Major components of the Japanese suit of armor

for "all classes of warriors, rank being denoted by the number of pairs of laces in the neck-guards" (Arai, 114). Widely spaced lacings, such as the *kebiki-do-maru* and the *sugake-do-maru,* became very popular because the armor thus laced "was very elastic and was said to be cooler in hot weather and warmer in cold than that made of plates" (Conder, 164).

Styles of lacing often involved the most diversified and imaginative patterns, which, in time, became identified with and gave a name to the armor in which they were used. The *omodaka,* for example, was a type of armor laced and embroidered according to the triangular design of the aquatic plant of the same name, and the *ko-zakura odoshi* featured lacing of light blue leather stamped with white cherry blossoms *(sakura).*

Strong criticism of laced armor was voiced by several Japanese authorities. In the *Tanki Yoriaku,* published in the eighteenth century, we find that Sakakibara Kozan was opposed to most types of tight lacing in armor because once water-soaked, whether from rain or immersion in a river or stream, such lacings became very heavy and could not be dried quickly. In this state, "the weight is oppressive and in winter the whole may freeze. Moreover, no amount of washing will completely free the lacing from any mud which may have penetrated it, so that on long and distant campaigns, it becomes evil-smelling and over-run by ants and lice, with consequent ill effects upon the health of wearer" (Garbutt[2], 143). More to the point, perhaps, are Kozan's observations concerning the strategic disadvantages of laced armor in combat, since the laces could hold the point of a spear or an arrow, instead of letting it slide by harmlessly. Kozan definitely qualified laced armor as belonging to later ages of comparative peace and as "mere toys meant to tickle the fancy of art-connoisseurs! The soldiers of fighting times...would have none of them!!" (Garbutt[2], 143).

Hakuseki divided Japanese armor into two general classes: "old" armor, made before the sixteenth century, known *asyoroi, katchu, haramaki, do-maru,* and so forth, and "new" armor, made after this period. This later type of armor was generally known as *gusoku*. Both types seemed to have referred to a classic model, all of whose components were included in the term *hei(tsuwamono)-no-rokugu,* or simply *rokugu.* These components, more precisely, were "six articles of arms": the chest protector *(yoroi),* the helmet *(kabuto),* the mask *(ho-ate),* the armored sleeves *(kote),* the shin guards *(sune-ate),* and the loin guards *(koshi-ate).* In later periods, however, the term *gusoku* came to represent "a complete suit of armor" (Stone, 271), although it was also used in combination with other names to indicate particular military equipment, such as the archer's outfitting *(ite-gusoku),* the bow and related equipment *(yutni-gusoku),* and the saddle and its fittings *(kura-gusoku).*

In summary, the high-ranking *bushi* on horseback leading his troops into battle generally wore a full suit of armor consisting of a heavily ornamented helmet with a metal mask for the face, large plates protecting his arms and hands, a strong corselet with an armored apron hanging beneath it, shin guards, and fur boots. His lieutenants, who followed on foot, wore substantially the same armor, although of lighter construction and simpler materials. Samurai of the lower ranks usually wore the helmet, the armored sleeves, the cuirass with short tassels, and shin guards—all of still lighter material (generally leather with iron heads, etc.). The history of Japanese armor, however, revolves almost entirely around the model worn by the *bushi* of the upper ranks (the general or feudal lord). Its name, *yoroi,* which originally referred to the central piece of any suit of armor (i.e., the corselet or cuirass protecting the warrior's chest and abdomen), was eventually used to identify the entire suit of armor, from the helmet to the fur boots. The *yoroi,* in short, included all the basic elements employed at one time or another, alone or in various combinations, by all classes of warriors.

Entire outfits of armor, made famous by the clan leaders who had worn them, survived through the centuries, religiously preserved (as noted earlier) in temples or in the place of honor in a *bushi's* house. Some of these celebrated suits of armor (in accordance with the markedly pan-animistic tendencies of Japanese culture) were further identified by specific names (a custom prevalent in Europe as well, during that continent's Middle Ages, although more particularly related to specific weapons than to suits of armor). As related in Arai Hakuseki's chronicle, the names bestowed upon these suits of armor were often derived from their decorations or from significant deeds wrought by he men who had worn them. For example, the armor worn by Genzammi Yorimasa (1106-80), called *genda-ga-ubuginu* or *shichi-ryu,* was famous, as were the suits of armor originally belonging to Kiso Yoshinaka (1154-84) and Minamoto (Nitta) Yoshisada Ason (1301-38), called *usugane,* as well as the *karakawa* or "Chinese leather armor" of Taira Sadamori (mid-tenth century).

A detailed tradition connected with the wearing and use of armor once it was in place was inherited by the *bushi* from his ancestors. Ingenious ways of putting it on without the aid of a retainer were minutely described in classic manuals on the subject. Some methods were based upon the use of ropes by which the central piece of the armor, the corselet or *do,* was hung from the ceiling so that the *bushi* might slide inside it from underneath. Sometimes the armor case itself was used, so that he might work his way inside the armor from the back (if the corselet were of the *haramaki-do* style) or from the side (if it were of the *do-maru* style). Instructions were provided concerning the proper way to sit down when clad in armor, and various ways of getting up were devised. Elements of the suit of armor could be removed in accordance with the circumstances of combat. For example, when climbing or scaling fortifications, the iron mask was removed and the sword set vertically, either at the side or on the back. Fighting in the water and hard fighting required the elimination of all unimportant items of equipment, which usually reduced the suit of armor to a corselet and helmet. It could be reduced even further, for "when anyone is wounded or not strong enough to wear armour," the martial classic translated by Garbutt instructed him to "go without it," adding: "we then call him *suhada-mono,* 'an unarmed one.' In such a case, the head will be covered by a turban and the legs by *kakama* [trousers] and *sune-ate* [shin-guards] and the body with the *kigomi-baori* [war coat]." It was specified in such a case, however, that "the badges such as *sode-jirushi* and

Warrior in DO-MARU, 13th c.

High officer in O-YOROI, 14th c.

Spearman in HARAMAKI-DO, 13th c.

Spearman in HARA-ATE, 13th c.

Spearman in lightly armored body protector

kasa-jirushi must be always carried, so that it may not be said merely from the absence of armour that one is not a fighting man" (Garbutt[2], 178).

With the Tokugawa at the helm of the Japanese nation, however, the age of large-scale and oft-repeated clashes on the battlefield came to an end. With it, the tactical importance of traditional suits of armor also declined, but their value as symbols of power, of class and rank distinction, actually increased. The result was a series of grand armors *(o-yoroi)* which were worn by the daimyo during the ceremonies held at the court of the military commander and regent for the crown, otherwise known as the shogun. In this age of consolidation and of firm commitment to an ancient military tradition, Japanese scholars such as Arai Hakuseki, Sakakibara Kozan, and others collected a great deal of information concerning the *yoroi,* its manufacture, composition, evolution, and even the traditional ways of wearing it *(netori)* by different clans at different periods in their history. In this connection, it is interesting to compare the instructions contained in the manuscripts of different clans, the various elements which were considered to be integral parts of a suit of armor, the order followed in donning them, and the nomenclature used to identify them.

In *Honcho Gunkiko,* Hakuseki described the traditional procedure followed by the warriors of the Toyohara clan when donning their armor. The same order, in somewhat greater detail, was also outlined in the *Tanki Yoriaku* (subtitled *Hi-Ko Ben* [An Explanation of Armour Wearing]) published in 1735. The minor differences to be found in these texts seem the result of varying interpretations of customs and old manuscripts belonging to clans whose traditions of armor wearing were so ancient that they had become confused and unintelligible even before the Tokugawa period. During the more than two hundred years of the Tokugawa period, however, the need for protecting the body in combat was never completely eliminated. The struggle for power which the great houses had undertaken on the battlefield gave way (under the enforced pacification of the Tokugawa) to all manner of civil strife, political intrigues, duels (both individual and collective), assassinations, and limited revolts, which, in turn, spawned a rich assortment of light armor, such as the undergarment of fine mail *(kusari katabira)* and other secret protective equipment, worn under ordinary clothing by the affiliated warrior, the samurai, or the *ronin.* Armored sleeves derived from the traditional *kote* could be concealed under an overcoat, as could a light, tight-fitting corselet *(do)* to protect the chest and back, and an armored collar *(nodo-wa)* which covered the shoulders. Thus, even in times of comparative peace, the use of armor continued to influence the various specializations of bujutsu and, in its new dimension, gave a great impetus to the development of methods of close-range combat, such as kenjutsu and jujutsu, which had evolved from ancient methods of long-range combat, such as kyujutsu and yarijutsu, wherein the full suit of armor or *yoroi* had played such a significant role.

Elements of Japanese Armor

From Japanese texts on the subject of armor and armor wearing we gather that a *bushi* who donned his armor unaided began with a loincloth *(tazuna, fundoshi),* preferably of white linen or cotton, lined or unlined according to the season. Over this he put a shirt *(shitagi)* resembling the everyday kimono, secured at the waist by the inner belt *(obi)* which was wound twice around his body and usually tied in front, although some preferred to tie it in the back. This last method was not recommended by most veterans,

Steps in the donning of armor
(*continued on next page*)

11) Kote

12) Wakibiki

13) Do

14) Uwa-Obi

15) Sode

16) Daisho

17) Nodowa and Hachimaki

18) Mempo, Kabuto

however, since it was difficult to retie the belt under the armor if, by accident, it loosened on the battlefield. *Bushi* of the upper ranks, naturally, wore sumptuous robes over their loincloths, such as the various *yoroi hitatare.* Most of the lower-ranking *bushi,* however, restricted themselves to a short and highly functional shirt called a *hadagi.* Over this, the *bushi* with the rank of marshal's attendant *(kyushu, kosho)* used to wear that characteristic type of ceremonial trousers or divided skirt with a stiff back *(koshi-ita)* and openings at the sides, called a *hakama.* The average *bushi* wore a similar pair of trousers, but somewhat shorter and narrower, called *kobakama.* The warriors of the lower ranks wore an even shorter version of these trousers *(matabiki),* generally tucked under the shirt.

The *bushi* then put on a special pair of socks *(tabi)* with a division for the big toe. These were made either of tanned leather *(kawa-tabi)* or of cotton *(mobien-tabi).* Over these he put gaiters or leggings of a type called *kyahan* or *habaki,* which were made of linen or cotton, lined or unlined, again according to the season. They were usually tied on the inner side of the shin in order to avoid friction against the stiffer shin guards worn over them. On his feet, the *bushi* of higher rank wore the characteristic fur boots *(kegetsu, kutsu, tsuranuki)* lined with silk or brocade, which had soles of stiff leather and an upper side of bearskin. These boots came in various styles which, although not clearly specified in the records, seemed to have been related to rank and position. Classics such as the *Gempei Seisui-ki,* for example, tell us that "when Kuro Yoshitsune, during the war against Kiso Yoshinaka, went to the Ho-O Palace, he wore *kuma-no-kawa-no-tsuranuki* (bearskin boots) and his followers wore boots made of *ushi-no-kawa* (cow-hide)" (Arai, 95).

In later periods, warriors of lower rank wore sandals *(waraji)* of various materials, such as hemp, stalks of *myoga,* palm fibers, and cotton threads. They usually carried an extra pair of these hanging at the waist. Their officers often wore sandals made of small iron or leather plates connected by links of mail, or made of mail alone. The legs, from knee to ankle, were encased in shin guards *(sune-ate, shino-zutsu),* usually made of molded metal or lacquered leather in front, laced or sewn to padded cloth in the back. Some specimens were of metal only, and, in ancient times, knights on horseback used to wear shin guards with a broad plate on the outer side, jutting upward to protect the rider's thighs from spear and sword attacks. Most shin guards, however, were made of several longitudinal plates hinged together, sewn to padded leggings, with the central plates covering the knee (as in the *bishamon sune-ate)* when a knee cup was not worn. All usually included a leather guard *(abumi-zure)* on the inner side of the shin, which was thus protected from friction against the stirrup or saddle.

The knee was usually protected by a metal cup *(hiza-yoroikakuzuri),* which was sometimes an integral part of the shin guard or, less frequently, could be a separate plate. Stone mentions two main varieties of these knee cups: the *yama-gata* and the *juwa-gashira.*

The upper part of the thigh was usually protected by a peculiar loin guard called *haidate,* which resembled an apron, the lower rim being covered with the usual small plates *(kozane)* of iron, leather, or, in some instances, whalebone. This apron, split in the middle, was fastened with cords *(tsubo-no-o)* which wound around the waist and tied in front. Ancient manuals on warfare often recommended that, in order to be able to remove this apron when crossing a river or swamp, it was advisable to tie the cords outside the corselet *(do)* worn over it. Other types of loin protectors followed the outlines of the warrior's thighs, as did the European cuisse, and were sometimes made of metal plates laced with leather cords and secured to a heavy lining of silk or leather *(ita-haidate).* Others, constructed of lighter and smaller metal plates sewn to silk or cloth *(igo-haidate)* were preferred by the *bushi* on horseback because they were "more flexible than the usual form" (Stone, 304). A particular type of armored legging used by infantrymen in times of war, or by the *bushi* under their trousers in times of peace, was the mail or chain legging called *kusari-kyahan* (or *kyahan-suneate),* which, with its length of padded mail, covered the entire leg.

The warrior then pulled on gloves *(yugake)* of tanned skin, preferably unlined and often with a small hole in the center of the palm. Over these, in order to protect his arms from hand to shoulder, he put on "close-fitting sleeve[s] of padded cloth, silk or leather, widening at the mouth where [they] fit over

KUSARI-GOTE

Armored Sleeves, TETSU-GOTE style

the shoulder, covered in part by mail and additonal metal plates, and terminat[ing] in a hand-guard or semi-gauntlet" (Stone, 377). This armored sleeve *(kote tegai)* was mainly protected on the outside by a series of metal defenses which began with a plate *(kamuri-ita)* covering the shoulder beneath the other shoulder guard *(sode)* examined above. Two heavy cords tied this upper plate to the chest and a third to the other armored sleeve. The upper arm was protected by another large metal plate or plates fastened by mail *(gaku-no-ita),* while the elbow was covered with a circular and concave plate *(hijigane).* The forearm was also protected from elbow to wrist by a long plate *(ikada)* or by a series of longitudinal metal strips. Sometimes it was encased in a one-piece item of embossed and pierced metal to which was fastened at the wrist a rounded plate *(tetsu-gai)* covering the back of the hand only, from wrist to knuckles. This plate was lined with leather and had loops for the *bushi's* fingers. In ancient suits of armor, finger pieces of mail and rings were fastened to the gauntlet by chains, but, later on, heavy leather gloves were worn.

The inside of the arm, which required less protection than the outside, was covered with padded cloth or leather, laced throughout with silk or leather cords. Its defense was based more on the warrior's skill, however, than upon such pieces of armor, since this area was particularly vulnerable when he raised his arms for the common downward sword cut or whirled a spear to deliver a circular blow. The straight thrust of the spear toward the armpit or the upward, inside cut of the sword were famous techniques of yarijutsu and kenjutsu which could be used to paralyze an arm or sever it completely from the body. Some of these armored sleeves were connected to one another by cloth, leather, or light mail *(ai-gote),* or by a collar of leather and brocade *(tomi-nagakote),* which formed a sort of high, short corselet for the shoulders. Most of them, however, were separate pieces connected to one another and to the upper chest and shoulders by cords.

There was a fantastic variety of sizes, types, shapes, and materials which the *bushi* could select for this important garment. He could use the armored sleeve covered with or made of mail *(kusari-gote),* the upper and lower arm being further protected by plates or splints *(tetsu-gote).* There was a type of sleeve which protected the upper arm by covering it with a large plate (like an additional *sode)* fastened to the shoulder *(tsugi-gote).* There were sleeves whose upper parts were strengthened by a collection of scales *(gaku-no-ita)* on the biceps; sleeves with alternated bands of mail and splints *(oshi-no-gote)*; sleeves entirely covered with mail to which were fastened strong plates, regularly spaced and tied or strapped to the shoulders and chest in one of several styles *(shino-gote, etchu-gote, awase-gote).* He could also use a short armored sleeve for the forearm alone, covered with splints and mail and lined with padded cloth *(hansho-gote).* These armored sleeves, finally, could be even further specialized, in accordance with the particular martial pur-

O-YOROI worn in European fashion, 17th c.

pose for which they were intended. For example, there were special sleeves *(yu-gote)* usually devoid of any heavy protective covering and made of silk and brocade, which were worn in pairs hanging from the shoulders. These were particularly favored by archers, whose effectiveness in combat depended upon the ease with they could handle their bows and arrows. Upon occasion, archers would wear just one such sleeve, to protect "the right arm, shoulder and a good part of the chest and back. They [were] tied around the body" (Stone, 682). There were also armored sleeves made of mail tightly woven and covering the whole upper part of the body *(kogusoku-kote)* or ending in a shirt *(jiban-gote)* which covered the wearer's body to the knees *(kote haramaki)*. This flexible, lighter type of sleeve became especially popular after the fifteenth century, when the heavy suits of armor used in the ages of trouble became largely ornamental and were superseded by the lighter suit of armor called *gusoku*. A pair of military sleeves with an inflated shape *(fukuro-gote)* made of "silk and damask" was "worn as light armor or under ceremonial dress" (Stone, 240). Many of these armored sleeves were commonly used in times of peace, being worn under the kimono and overcoat, when the *bushi* expected or merely wished to be prepared for trouble in the streets.

The armpits, which were left unprotected due to the gap between the armored sleeves *(kote)* and the lateral plates *(watagami)* of the corselet *(do)*, were covered with special pads of mail, reinforced with plates or scales, called *waki-biki*. They were worn under the corselet, either separately or connected to one another by a mail band *(kusari waki-biki)*. They could be fastened with buttons *(botan-gake)*, hooks *(kohaze-gake)*, or cords *(himo-tsuki)*. A special type of equipment *(manju-nowa)* combined these *waki-biki* with a collar and shoulder pads.

The central element of a suit of armor in any country (together with the helmet, of course) has always been the chest protector *(do)*. In Japan, the style of these two elements represented and identified the armor of several periods in that country's history—the protohistoric *(tanko, katchu, kisenaga)*, the ancient *(yoroi)*, and the modern *(gusoku)*. The major portion of the *bushi's* body was usually encased in a corselet or cuirass made of large plates of metal which resembled the ancient corselets of riveted scales, *kaki yoroi* or *keiko*, worn in the fourth century B.C. There were also corselets of lacquered leather, however, padded on the inside and covered on the outside with strips of scales laced tightly together with silk or leather cords; or of scales of leather or metal set in an overlapping pattern upon mail, or riveted together *(okegawa-do)*. As noted earlier, leather was a great favorite with Japanese armorers, and the various kinds of leather used, as well as the various ways of treating it, gave rise to a series of corselets *(kawa tsutsumi)*, such as those of Chinese leather *(kara-kawa tsutsumi)*, red leather *(aka-kawa tsutsumi)*, and flowered leather *(hana-gawa tsutsumi)*. Many of the later corselets worn by the lower classes of retainers were made of black lacquered leather *(sewari gusoku)*. The plates of the corselet, however, were also sometimes covered with such material as sharkskin *(same tsutsumi)*, tortoise shell *(moji tsutsumi)*, and laced whalebone, which created beautiful patterns and lent exceptional strength to the garment.

There was an apparently endless variety of corselets and cuirasses in use in Japan at various times, and the doctrine has divided them into two main categories: first (and the most common), those made of several large pieces or plates laced together with strong cords *(do* proper); and second, those made of a single piece. The latter, called pigeon breast plate *(hatomune-do)* or saint's breast plate *(hotoke-do)* because they simulated the curve of the human body, were very rare. Covering the body from the neck to below the waist, they were said to have been worn in Japan during the seventeenth and the eighteenth centuries.

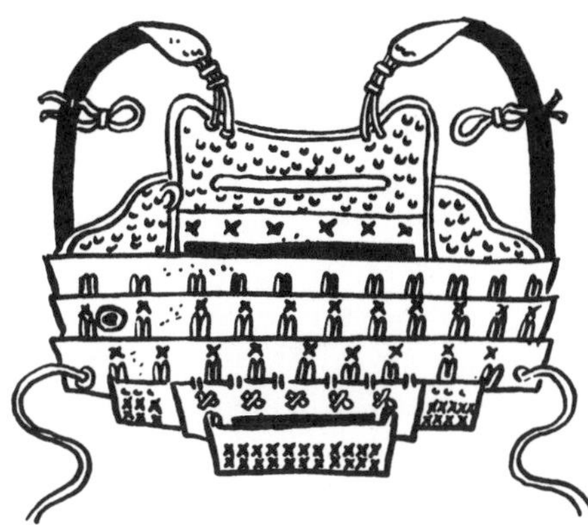
HARA-ATE, 12th c.

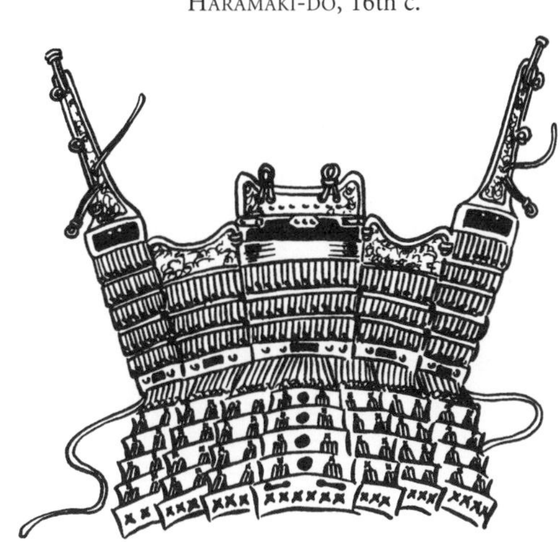
HARAMAKI-DO, 16th c.

They were "apparently copied from the European forms and often [of] European make" (Stone, 145). The first category included many corselets and cuirasses made of several large plates, further divided into two large classes: one which included all those having openings at the back *(haramaki-do),* and the other all those with openings at the side *(do-maru).* A few corselets (such as the *maewari gusoku* of later times) opened in front, with the right side crossing over the left (Garbutt[2], 161), but these were not common.

The first class seems to have been the earliest. The cuirass opening in the back, for example, is said to have been derived from a model devised for the empress Jingo who "was pregnant when she invaded Korea and therefore had to have a flexible and adjustable corselet" (Stone, 283). This model gave rise to a number of impressive, often lavishly laced corselets. In its more simplified forms, this model was also adopted by the lower-ranking samurai and their attendants, who had to be properly outfitted to overcome a foe on the battlefield or risk being slaughtered themselves. Among the various derivations of this model are such as the ancient *haraate-gawa,* which had laced leather scales covering "the front of the body, from the neck to the knees" (Stone, 281); the *sewari gusoku,* which closed in the back through the use of clasps and cords; and the *uchiawase gusoku,* made of two pieces, front and back, with hanging leather taces. The second class included those corselets and cuirasses which opened at the side *(do-maru).*

Both models were usually made of large plates riveted or laced together to cover the four sides of the body. They hung from padded straps *(kata-ate)* which rested on the shoulders, and they consisted of the following elements. First, a breastplate, such as the old *tate-nashi-do,* which was "believed to give sufficient protection to make shields unnecessary" (Conder, 264). This was generally ornamented and covered with a leather guard, the path for the bowstring *(tsuruberi),* which presented the archer with a smooth surface against which to draw back his bow. Then, a left-side plate *(waki-ita* or *imuke)* was usually fastened to the breastplate and backplate with hinges and cords. There was also a right-side plate *(waki-date* or *tsubo-ita)* which "was often a separate piece...tied around the body by cords before the other parts were put on" (Conder, 266). Finally, there was a backplate, such as the *oshi-tsuke,* strengthened on top with a separate plate *(moko-ita).* The second plate *(sata-ita)* was usually formed of one or more rows of laced scales in a crossed stitch pattern *(hishinui).* At the center of this plate hung that large, characteristic ring with its ornamental silk cord and tassels *(age-maki)* which also held the shoulder guards *(sode)* in place when the *bushi* was actually fighting. On this plate were two sockets to hold the shaft which supported the light banner of the Japanese cavalryman *(sashimono, shirushi),* with his crest emblazoned in the center. When

Do-maru, 12th c.

Haramaki-do, 14th c.

Haramaki-do with sode, 15th c.

Do-maru, 18th c.

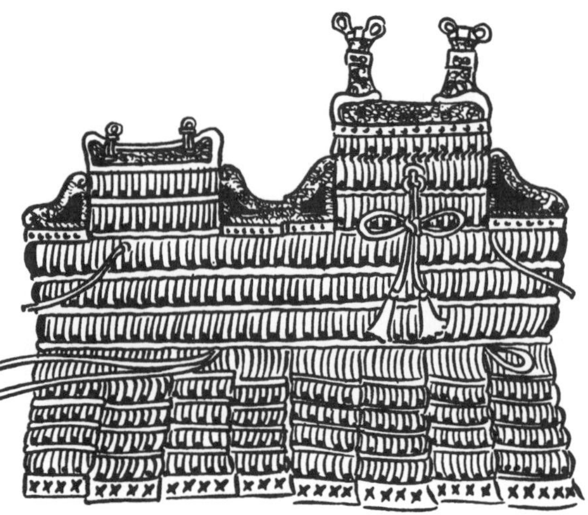

Do-maru, 14th c.

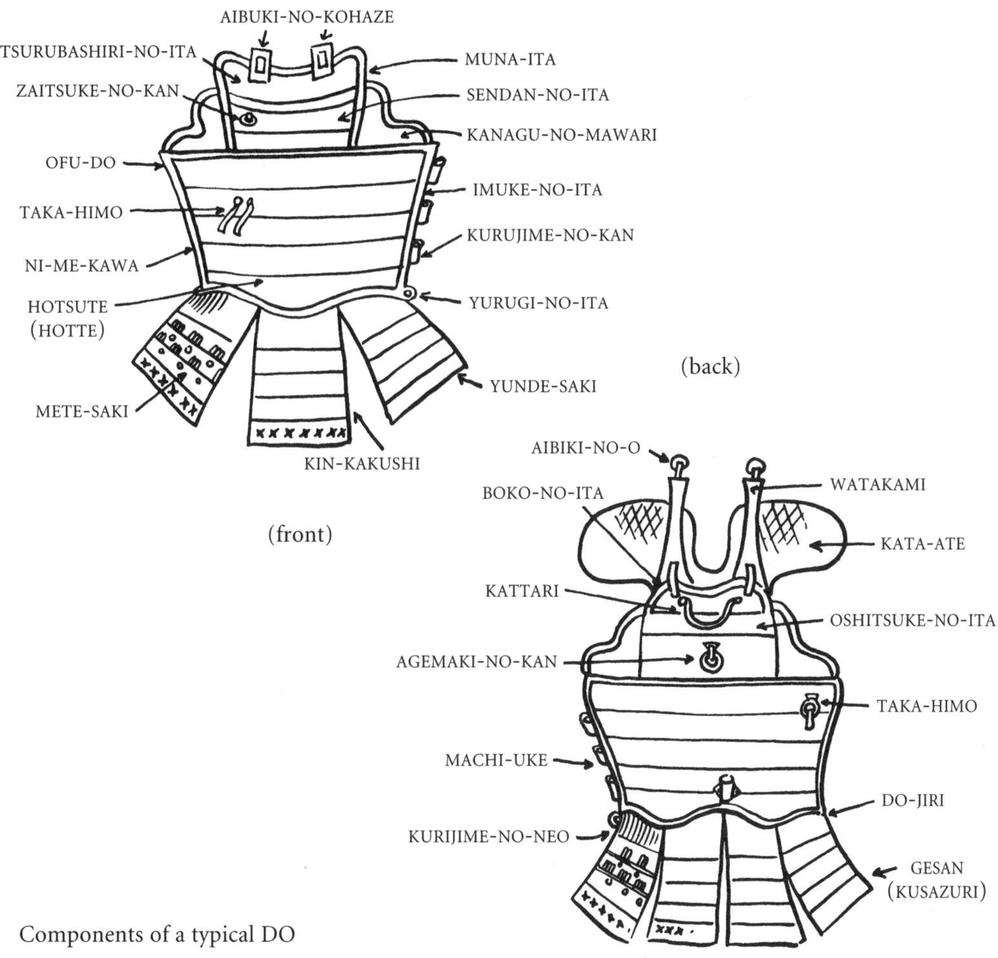

Components of a typical DO

this banner was not carried, streamers or a badge of leather or stiff paper *(koshi sashi)* with the crest in the middle were often substituted. Of the sockets on the backplate, the one on top, near the shoulder *(sashimono-gane),* lifted the shaft away from the large brim of the neck protector in the back *(shikoro)* while the lower *(uke-zutsu)* kept it in line near the waist. This characteristic symbol of rank and leadership is reported to have been in common use after 1573.

Additional plates were worn by the *bushi* of the upper ranks, under or in place of the above and tied to the others. Among these was the important *se-ita* (or *se-ita-no-yoroi)* which secured "the better specimens of Japanese armor that opened down the back" (Conder, 268). Two smaller plates were also worn in front, hanging from the shoulders, to protect the left armpit *(hato-o-no-ita)* and the right armpit *(sendan-no-ita).* The former was usually smaller, made of metal or thick, lacquered leather, highly decorated and with a metal border. The latter was generally made of three thick plates or rows of scales, heavily lined with leather. In later corselets, samurai of the lower ranks, who were not allowed to wear those two plates, wore smaller, leaf-shaped armpit guards *(giyo-jio-ita).* From these plates (i.e., from the waist down) hung a series of small, overlapping plates, or a laminated skirt *(kusazuri),* laced together and to the corselet with silk cords *(yurigi-ito).* The plates of the *do,* finally, hung from the shoulders on large, heavily padded straps of ornamented steel or leather *(kata-ate),* hinged to the backplate and fastened to the breastplate with various hooks, loops, buckles, and cords which rested upon the *eri-mawari,* a padded garment of leather or cloth, often reinforced around the neck by metal plates or sharkskin.

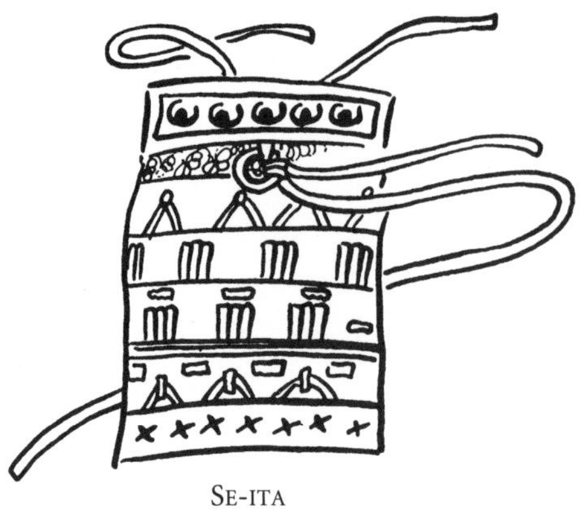

Se-ita

Plates of high-ranking bushi

Sendan-no-ita

Hato-o-no-ita

Waki-date

Warrior with tachi

Warrior with nodachi

Around the waist, the *bushi* wore a belt *(uma-obi)* made of linen or cloth, with tassels and bow in front. When he cut off the ends of this belt and threw away the scabbard of his sword, which he usually carried thrust through that belt (originally, hanging from it), his intention of dying on the battlefield was clearly manifested to his foes and the desperate nature of his fight emphasized.

The shoulders of the *bushi* of the upper ranks were protected at the sides by two large, characteristic guards *(sode),* each made of small scales arranged in several strips, laced tightly together with silk cords, upon a background of metal or lacquered leather. The top strip in both was always of solid metal, embossed and richly decorated *(kamuri-ita),* while the lower strip *(hishinui-ita)* was usually padded inside and fastened with the characteristic crossed stitches. They were often cast from a single slate of steel or iron, or else made of strips of metal hinged together in such a way as to form a flexible but strong unit. Samurai of the lower ranks wore simpler shoulder guards made of lacquered leather or of padded cloth covered with mail or chain *(kusari-sode),* hanging from a large metal plate. They also used large metal plates hanging from a broad top plate and fastened with strong leather cords *(kawara-sode).* The shape of these shoulder guards was usually rectangular or square, and the size varied from large *(o-sode)* to medium *(chu-sode)* and small *(ko-sode),* with many variations in between. Important officers, naturally, wore shoulder guards of the first two types. One popular model resembled a votive temple tablet *(namban-sode, gaku-sode),* the central part being of decorated metal and the border framing it of bright silver or some other ornamental metal. Another popular shape was the single oval plate *(maru-sode),* usually decorated with symbols, crests, or other evocative patterns and shapes. These shoulder guards were tied together over the chest and back of the wearer and also under his arms. In the back they were also fastened to the heavy silk cords with tassels *(age-maki)* in the middle of his cuirass or corselet, thus preventing them from swinging forward when the *bushi* stooped over or was engaged in combat.

The warrior then put on the left side of his corselet whichever type of sword hanger *(koshiate)* he preferred, to hold his two swords *(daisho),* both the short sword *(wakizashi)* and the long sword *(tachi).* In more ancient times, he also used to carry an extra sword called *nodachi,* which was quite heavy and generally longer than the normal *katana.* The *nodachi* was usually strapped to his back. Its use, once almost universal on the battlefield, became increasingly rare during the Tokugawa period.

The neck of the *bushi* of the higher ranks was protected in front by a gorget, or throat ring *(nodowa),* made of scales or small plates laced tightly together on a plate shaped like a U. This garment seems to have been developed in the sixteenth century from an armored collar formerly worn under the *do* and attached to a padded support called *eri-mawari.* In the Tokugawa period, however, it was worn over the armor in a variety of styles, among which collars fastened at the back of the neck by cords *(nodowa* proper), by hooks *(meguriwa),* or by buckles *(eriwa)* apparently predominated. This collar could be fastened to the *bushi's* mask and to the upper part of the cuirass, in a style *(manjuwa)* the *bushi* seemed to find less than satisfactory for actual fighting because it greatly reduced the mobility of his head and shoulders. The freer style *(tetsuki)* of the independent collar seems to have become the more popular style.

One episode connected with this particular piece of Japanese armor illustrates not only the peculiar attitude the *bushi* often displayed in combat but also the tremendous protection afforded by this piece of equipment:

> In 1564 (Yeroku V), on the 7th day of the first month, two battles took place at Konodai in Shimoza, between Hojo Ujiyasu and Satomi Yoshihiro, assisted by Ota Sukemasa Nudo Sanrakusai, in which the Hojo forces were victorious. Ota fought desperately and had received two wounds, when Shimazu Taroza Yemon, a man noted for his strength, threw down the now-weary Ota and tried in vain to cut off his head. At this Ota cried out: "Are you flurried, Sir? My neck is protected by a *nodowa.* Remove it and cut off my head!" Shimazu replied with a bow: "How kind of you to tell me! You die a noble death! You have my admiration!" But just then, as he was about to remove the *nodowa,* two

Major components of the medieval Japanese helmet

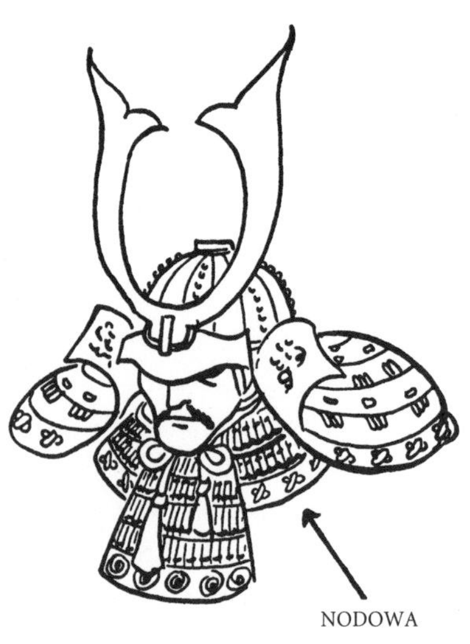

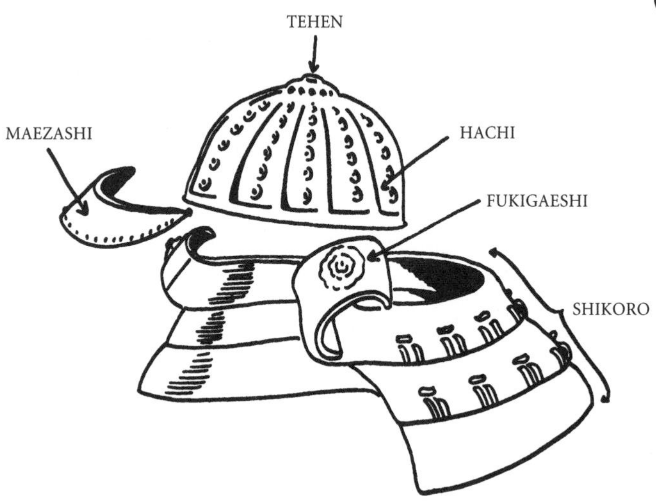

HACHI by Yoshitada Myochin

HACHI by Yoshinaga Myochin

HACHI by Munesuke Myochin

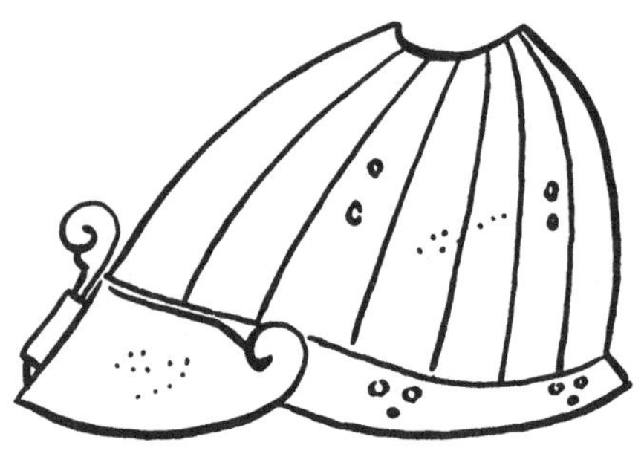

HACHI by Muneshige Myochin

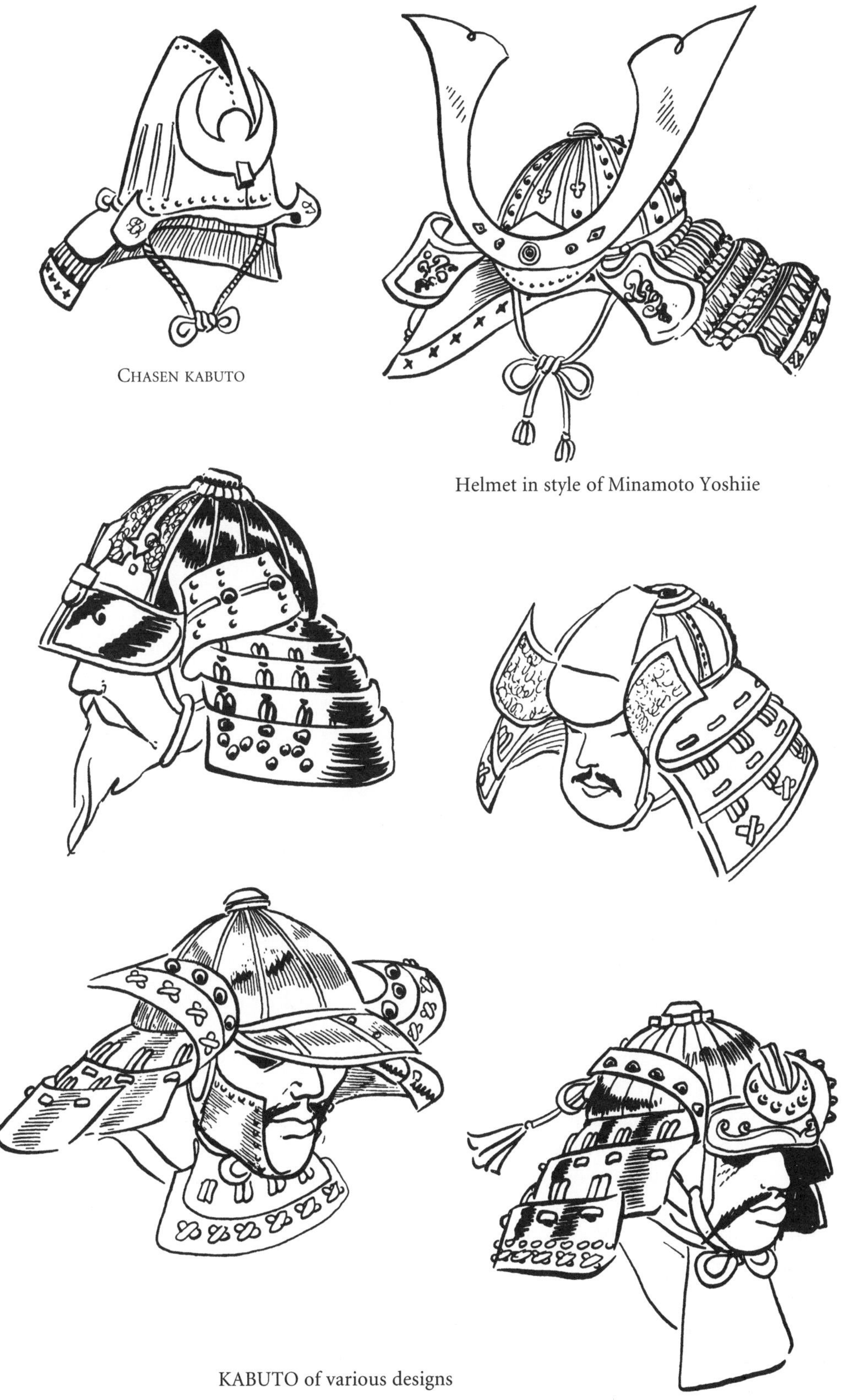

CHASEN KABUTO

Helmet in style of Minamoto Yoshiie

KABUTO of various designs

> young squires of Ota's rushed up, and throwing down Shimazu, enabled their master to decapitate him!" (Garbutt[2], 146)

The head of the *bushi* of the upper ranks was well protected by a series of armored elements which fit snugly together and covered his head, face, and neck. The central element, the helmet proper, was a metal dome *(hachi)* which followed the basic outline of a man's head and seems to have evolved from earlier models "of padded cloth or silk; but even as early as the reign of Emperor Kammu (782-805), iron ones must have been common, for he gave an order for 2,900, and it may be assumed that their usual form was that of the *kabuto* or pot helmet" (Gilbertson and Kowaki, 115). From these old models and from others even more ancient, such as the *maro-hachi* worn between A.D. 300 and 400, the helmet developed into the domed pot made of a number of iron strips riveted together vertically (from the top to the base) or horizontally to form a series of concentric rings pressed one within the other. It could also be cast in one piece. In any case, this dome was reinforced with ridges, rivets *(hoshi),* and ornamental bands parallel to the brim *(hoshi kumo),* which often projected out from the *hachi (hoshi kabuto)* and were intended not only as decoration, but, even more importantly, "to offer a powerful resistance to a sword cut, while keeping the general body of the helmet thin and light" (Gilbertson and Kowaki, 115).

By elaborating upon this basic metal dome, the Japanese iron artists of the various clans produced countless numbers of helmets in almost every shape imaginable. During the Momoyama and Tokugawa periods, as Hakuseki tells us, these shapes and styles were legion, and they included helmets resembling a demon's head *(kimen),* a great-domed mountain *(daienzan),* a flat-topped mountain *(heichozan),* a peach *(momonari),* a cone flattened to a blade shape at the top *(toppai),* a ceremonial hat *(to-kamuri),* or heads of lions, birds *(tori-kabuto),* and dragons. A helmet particularly favored by traveling *bushi* was the *tatami-kabuto:* "a folding helmet made of horizontal rings laced together so that it could be shut down almost flat" (Stone, 327). In almost every shape, however, the *hachi* retained a characteristic opening in the crown, at the top. This was called *hachiman-za, tehen,* or *tenku,* and it was generally surrounded by an ornamental socket *(hizuka),* usually in the shape of a chrysanthemum. According to some writers, this opening was said to have been left so that heavenly influences might reach the wearer's mind, thus explaining why it was commonly referred to as "the seat of Hachi-man Bosatsu," the god of war. Other writers, however, relate it to the short pigtail *(motodori)* worn upright in ancient times by warriors. Hakuseki believed it served the purpose of ventilation, associating the *tehen* with the opening called *iki-dashi-no-ana* ("hole for breathing") used in the helmets of his time (Arai, 38). This opening had a certain relevance in bujutsu as indicated by the fact that Ashikaga Matataro Tada-tsuna, at the battle of Uji, advised his men "not to lean backwards too far [lest] the inside of their helmets *(uchi-kabuto)* [be] hit by arrows, nor to bend so far forward as to be shot through the *tehen*" (Arai, 38). This opening was protected

> by a piece of silk tied over the top of the helmet by strings attached to form knobs of metal called *shi-ten-bio* or "the Four Deva Knobs," which were named after the four Deva Kings, Bishamon Ten, Jikoku Ten, Komoku Ten, Zocho Ten. Through two holes called *shida-no-hana,* a leather cord was passed which was fastened inside to the skull, preventing the helmet from pressing on the top of the head, and the ends were tied in a bow outside. (Gilbertson and Kowaki, 115)

At the front base of the *hachi,* there was a small peak *(maezashi)* heavily decorated on top and "frequently lacquered red to give a more terrible effect upon the countenance by reflection upon it, or upon the iron mask which served as a visor" (Gilbertson and Kowaki, 115-16). Above the peak, the helmet of a higher-ranking *bushi* had a special socket *(haraidate)* where the crest *(maedate)* and other ornaments were attached. These crests were usually decorated with mythical symbols adopted by the wearer to indicate special qualities: bravery, cunning, and so forth. They could also be worn near or above the opening on top

(kashiradate), at the back of the helmet *(ushirodate),* or on the sides—in which case there would be two crests *(wakidate).* Upon occasion, a *bushi* might even have three different crests affixed to his *kabuto.*

In this context, it should be noted that the Japanese had developed a complex system of heraldry based on the use of badges *(mon)* as a means of identification. Clans had one or more badges which had been inherited by their founders or adopted in commemoration of a significant event in the founder's or the clan's history. The Niwa clan, for example, had two broad crossed lines emblazoned on its standards, its portals, even the "curtains usually fastened to the upright posts so as to form an enclosure around a military encampment" (McClatchie[2], 7), as well as upon the small flags *(sashimono)* worn on the backs of the clan's cavalrymen and on the suits of armor worn by its warriors. These two crossed lines, according to the traditions of the Niwa clan, represented the bloodstains which had remained on an ancestor's *hakama* after he had wiped his swords across the left knee of his trousers. The Narita clan, on the other hand, used two parallel lines drawn across a circle, representing chopsticks on the rim of a bowl of rice that one of their ancestors, exhausted by a battle, had found in a mountain shrine. He had eaten the rice and then, feeling refreshed, had plunged back into the thick of combat, eventually carrying the day. McClatchie, in his notes on Japanese heraldry, relates that "most of the great nobles, as may be seen by a glance at any Japanese list of daimyo, possessed three badges, whilst those of lower rank had two, and ordinary samurai but one, except in rare instances. Of these, one was always termed *jo-mon* or 'fixed badge' of the family, the other being styled *kae-mon* or badges worn instead of the chief one" (McClatchie[2], 6).

According to some writers, the custom of registering the clan's badges with the *bakufu* began in the sixteenth century. The insignia thus officially registered *(jo-mon)* could not be used by anyone else without formal permission from the rightful title holder. A clan, naturally, could authorize a retainer or an independent individual, who had served the clan in an exceptional way, to wear the clan's badge on his clothing either temporarily or permanently, as a hereditary right. This system of heraldry produced a particular art of social recognition and a related class of experts, whose duty it was to know all the existing badges and crests which had been registered, so as to be able to recognize immediately the rank and the social position of their wearers. In Lee's words; "To ascertain the exact rank of a person whose retinue was seen to be approaching became almost a matter of life or death, and this most necessary knowledge was disseminated by the use of easily recognized emblems, by which rank and station could at once be determined" (Lee, 279). An elaborate system of etiquette, for example, regulated even the casual meetings of corteges and caravans from different clans. Special heralds with keen eyesight and even keener memories usually traveled at the head of each caravan; their primary task was that of identifying—even from a distance— the crest, rank, and position of the opposite party. This, in turn, assured that the appropriate ritual of respect and precedence would be followed. In times of peace, these identifying emblems were "generally worn in five places on the upper garment, namely at the back of the neck, on each sleeve, and on each breast. In some instances, however, the number was increased to seven by the addition of two upon the collar or margin of the garment, just over the chest, and in line with those on the breast" (McClatchie[2], 7). In time of war, the necessity of distinguishing friend from foe in the melee of battle made the use of these crests or badges even more imperative, and the helmet, naturally, bore the greatest number.

Concerning their predominantly circular shape, Haite links the Japanese preference for the circle to the sun worship underlying their culture: "The Japanese name for Japan—Nippon—means 'the land of the rising sun' and the mighty source of light and heat could be easily and readily symbolized by a disk or circle." He then went on to point out that "some of the crests, or badges, of the old families were suns pure and simple. It is easy to see how the simple disk went through the inevitable transition and became ornament" (Haite, 46).

The ornaments most frequently found surrounding the *mon* were those which represented the leaves of the water plant Sagittaria, extending in large arches to the sides and upward *(kuwagata)* from specially ornamented sockets *(tsunomoto)*. Other ornaments in various winged shapes were often attached to the sides of the helmet or the back— where there was also a ring *(kasa-jirushi-no-kan)* from which was suspended a special piece of cloth or ornamented knot with an insignia or other symbol *(kasa-jirushi)* which, in the case "of a commander, was usually of brocade with the device in gold or silver thread; those carried by the common soldiers were of silk or cloth with the device in black" (Conder, 278). This special ornament was also carried in front of the helmet, often affixed to a metal rod with three prongs, thus resembling a small flag *(chu-kasajirushi)*, which, according to some authors, was intended for bad weather (Stone, 179). Old helmets also had a second ring or hook higher up in the back, which was often used to hold the *bushi's* characteristic cape, the *horo*, in protective extension behind him.

Following the outline of the lower brim of the helmet, a special projection was cast to which "was fastened the *shikoro* or neck protector, composed of from 3 to 7 rows of metal plates sewn to each other by silk cords" (Gilbertson and Kowaki, 116). These strips, reinforced by stiff leather, often contained from 100 to 138 small plates or scales *(kozane)*, and the number and size of the strips could also be used to identify the helmet itself. For example, the *sammai-kabuto* had three strips, the *gomai-kabuto*, five strips; the *o-manju* was characterized by large strips and the *ko-manju* by small ones. According to Robinson's notes on Hakuseki's *Honcho Gunkiko*, the *sammai-kabuto* became popular during the second half of the fourteenth century, while the *gomai-kabuto* would seem to have been in use since the ninth century. The *shikoro* (of which there were many varieties, such as the *hineno)* had its top riveted to the helmet. Its lowest plate, called *hishitoji* or *hishinui-no-ita* because the cords in it were fastened in a characteristic star shape also found in other parts of the suit of armor, was generally lined with leather to prevent any "clattering against the armor" (Stone, 327-31) and fell upon the wearer's shoulders and back. The whole inner side of the neck guard was generally lacquered bright red, as was the lower part of the peak, in order to project an image of fiery fierceness.

KABUTO of various designs

Types of MEMPO

At each side of the helmet there was usually a characteristic ear guard *(Jukigaeshi)*, often formed by rolling back either the lower plates of the helmet or one or more of the strips on top of the neck guard. Both were heavily ornamented with embossed leather, silver, or gold. In old helmets, especially, the guard on the right might even be turned back on a special hinge to allow ample room for drawing back the right forearm when shooting with bow and arrow while in armor, whether on horseback or on foot.

The helmets of the Kamakura and Tokugawa periods were usually lined with cloth reinforced by the addition of crossed straps to create an inner cap *(uchi-bari)*, which separated the inner surface of the *kabuto* from the wearer's head. The straps *(chikara-gawa)* were fastened to the lower edge of the helmet and kept it tightly but elastically suspended "so that the metal did not press directly" upon the warrior's head (Conder, 262). In more ancient times, the *bushi* reportedly wore a special cap, the famous *eboshi*, which had a characteristically vertical shape to allow room for the queue of hair *(motodori)*, which was worn standing straight up by the members of most classes of Japanese society since time immemorial. According to old treatises on military costume, a stiff form of *eboshi* with a lacquered edge *(heitai)* was adopted at the court of Emperor Toba (1107–23), while the *eboshi* of the warriors (usually called *nashi-uchi-eboshi)* was a soft type, the upper extension folding neatly to the side when the helmet was donned over it. Nasu-no-Yoichi, a famous archer, was called upon to hit, while standing on shore, a war fan secured to the top mast of a distant Taira ship at Yashima. As he prepared to shoot his arrow according to the proper rules of kyujutsu, he "took off his helmet. . . and then pulled up his *momi-eboshi*" (Arai, 96), circling it with a band of cloth called *usu-kobai*.

When the historical evolution of customs and costumes made the *eboshi* obsolete (in the second quarter of the fourteenth century), an inner cap of leather *(ara-gawa)*, which fitted flush with the inner side of the helmet, represented the element of transition from the *eboshi* of yore to the cap of hemp cloth. This cap, usually lined with silk stitched in concentric circles, became known as *uke-bari, uke-ura*, or, as mentioned earlier, as *uchi-bari*. Under both helmet and inner cap, finally, the *bushi* wore a band of cloth around his head, tied either at the back under the *shikoro* or in front. This headband was called *hachi-maki*, and it was usually white in color, in deference to the ever-present possibility of death. Headbands in red *(aka)* were also used. These *hachi-maki* became extremely popular among Japanese fighters of all ages, classes, and periods. During World War II, white *hachi-maki* were employed as the insignia of the suicide pilots, the *kamikaze*, who hurled themselves and their planes loaded with explosives against enemy vessels in a desperate attempt to reverse the tide of war. These headbands are still used today in many Japanese clubs where arts of combat and other competitive sports are taught and practiced.

The *uchi-bari* was held securely in place by cords *(shinobi-no-o)* of soft cotton cloth or silk crepe folded tightly and fastened first around the wearer's head, then under his chin, and finally to rings *(ogatame-no-kane)* inside the helmet, through pairs of holes *(shida-no-ana)* around its lower edge. Thus, an intricate and cleverly arranged pattern of cords held the helmet securely but comfortably to an inner cap which distributed the weight evenly upon and around the wearer's head.

In order to protect his face, the *bushi* of the upper ranks usually wore a mask of iron, steel, or lacquered leather which covered the entire face from forehead to chin, or at least particular portions of it. Warriors of lower rank and foot soldiers generally wore masks of the second type. These masks could be made from a single, rigid piece of metal or leather, or from several plates hinged together to make them more flexible. According to Stone, there were five basic types. The first covered the entire face *(mempo, membo, so-mempo)* with removable pieces. The second covered the face below the eyes *(hoate)*. The third covered the cheeks and chin, leaving the nose and mouth exposed—thus resembling a monkey's face *(saru-bo)*. The fourth covered the lower part of the face (often the chin only) and was referred to as swallow-face *(tsubame-bo, tsubame-gata)*. The fifth covered the forehead and cheeks only. The masks which covered the chin had a hole *(asa-nagashi-no-ana)* or a short pipe *(tsuyo-otoshi-no-kubo)* to allow the perspiration to escape. They were fastened underneath to a neck guard of plates, mail, or scales *(yodare-kake)* which either hung independently over the larger neck guard *(nodowa)* or blended with it in front. (A handkerchief, or *fakusa,* was worn between the mask and the chin.)

These face masks—especially the first and second types—were patterned to represent "faces of men, demons or animals, and were cleverly made, old men selecting a youthful mask and vice-versa" (Gilbertson and Kowaki, 116). Especially famous were the Korean face *(korai-bo),* the ghost *(moriyo),* the evil demon *(akuryo),* the Southern barbarian face *(namban-bo),* the long-nosed sylvan demon *(tori-tengu),* and, of course, the old man's face *(okina-men),* the youth's face *(wara-wazura),* and even the woman's face *(onna-men).* All these masks were intended primarily to protect the face from spear and sword blows. Arrows were parried or repelled by the projecting flanges *(yadome)* of metal which extended from the mask. But these also served another important purpose—that of balancing and distributing more evenly the weight of the helmet across and upon the wearer's head. Stone observed that "a Japanese helmet is not only heavy, but top-heavy and the brim must be tipped back to allow the wearer to see effectively. The neck-guard is very wide and deep and a blow on the side would knock the helmet entirely out of place if it were not well-secured." Consequently, the rings and loops along the lower edge of the helmet and the hooks, pins, and rings on the metal mask were tied quite firmly together. "The middle of a soft, heavy cord was fastened to the ring at the back of the helmet and the cord was laced up and down from the rings in the helmet to the fastenings on the *mempo* (mask) and finally tied under the chin of the wearer" (Stone, 447).

The composition of both helmet and mask (with their inner surfaces cushioned, or smoothed down by lacquering to prevent chafing) insured maximum protection and, by distributing the pressure more evenly, also provided a certain degree of comfort, though "the wearer could not open his mouth" (Stone, 445-47). Ancient manuals concerned with military matters usually included instructions concerning methods of coping with various needs. If thirsty, for example, the bushi was advised to drink warm water by using the bamboo stem of an arrow as a tube (Garbutt[2], 180).

As was true of almost all the *bushi's* activities, that of wearing a helmet was raised to the level of an art with its own theory and practice—both dialectically related to the strategic necessities of combat and, ultimately, of bujutsu. Many styles were invented and subsequently became popular. The one which called for wearing a helmet with the peak tilted upward, thus enlarging the spread of the neck guard around and behind the wearer's shoulders, for example, was known as the style of the wild boar neck *(ikubi).* It was considered an excellent style for use when fighting with sword or spear, but it was also recommended for aesthetic reasons (Stone, 331).

The helmet was carried in the special case used for the armor *(gusoku-bitsu)* when going into battle or kept in a place of honor at home with the *bushi's* other major weapons. In fact, a complete system of etiquette was followed when the helmet was displayed or shown to guests, who, for example, would perhaps admire its exterior, decoration, design, but would not turn it upside down to look inside because such an act was considered very rude.

Lower-ranking samurai such as the *ashigaru* generally wore a conical or almost flat type of helmet *(jingasa),* which had a very large brim, often curved up in front for better visibility. These were usually cast from one piece of steel, copper, iron, or from as many as twenty strips of those metals riveted together in an overlapping pattern which served to reinforce the whole construction. They were also decorated or embossed, with two circular pads within the crown, through which cords were passed and tied under the chin. *Jingasa* made of finely lacquered leather or wood were used in ceremonies, parades, and other public events, as well as in battle. Certain mail helmets *(kusari-zukin)*—iron or steel caps of various shapes with a flexible net of mail hanging from the brim and covering the wearer's shoulders and back—were also used by retainers and foot soldiers, as were those peculiar copper helmets *(akane-gasa)* which the foot soldiers found useful as cooking pots. A special variety of the latter "worn in the Eastern provinces . . . had a loose piece on the crown that revolved when struck by a weapon or missile" (Conder, 280). Lower-ranking retainers sometimes wore leather helmets *(kawa-gasa),* usually made of a special kind of leather

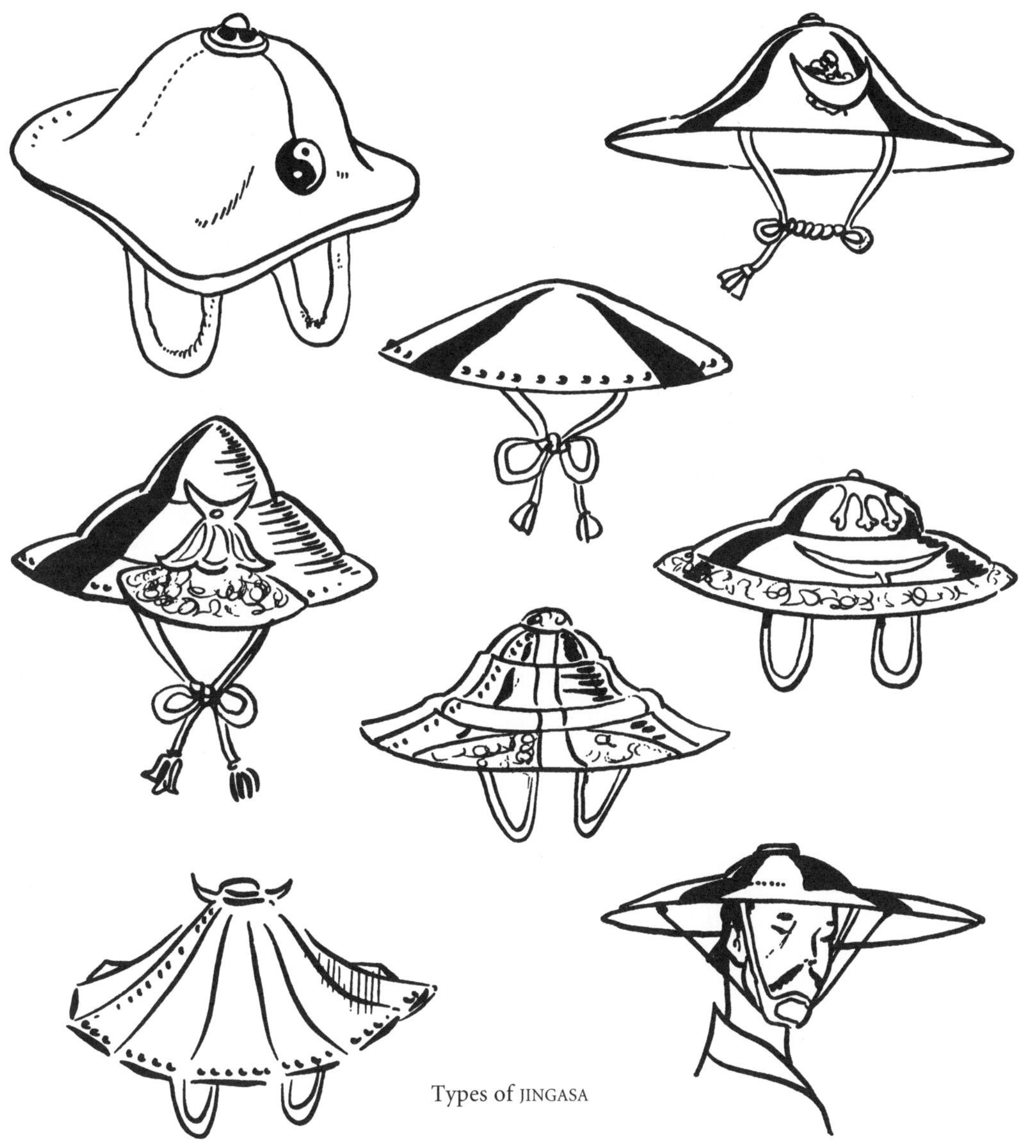

Types of JINGASA

(neri-gawa), which was heavily lacquered and embossed and had a pointed crown, a broad brim colored black, and the clan crest in front. Because of the excellent craftsmanship displayed by the armorers who specialized in making these helmets, some of them were even considered "superior to the mail helmets" (Stone, 346), both in style and in the degree of protection that their lighter weight and more extended brims usually afforded. A rich variety of iron or lacquered leather half-helmets *(hamburi, hachi-gane)* were also used by the *bushi* of the lower ranks and their cohorts. Some of these half-helmets were cut according to a pattern which provided protection for the crown of the head; certain types favored the forehead and temples, others the forehead and cheeks, while a number covered the head and chin. They were very light and particularly useful in duels involving swords, spears, and daggers.

A special type of surcoat worn over the armor by the *bushi* of the higher ranks was called *dijimbaori.* It was said to have been used in the military encampment before or after battle to give its wearer a more impressive appearance or "when beginning a march, retreating to rest, at inspections, when triumphantly returning, when calling upon anyone of higher rank, at the assembly of officers, when sent out as am-

High officers wearing JIMBAGRI

bassador, etc." (Garbutt[2], 153). In ancient scrolls, however, we also see it depicted as being worn in the thick of battle.

Finally, a special type of protective equipment worn with armor by the *bushi* on horseback is mentioned in old manuscripts of bujutsu. This consisted of "a cloth loosely fastened to the back of a mounted warrior so as to fill with wind and project from his back" (Stone, 299). This cloth was generally six feet long and, as described by Conder, composed of five strips of strong material reinforced with plaits. Crests were prominently displayed at the top, middle, and bottom. When worn loose, this cape was fastened on top to the *bushi's* helmet, and the lower end was tied with cords around the waist at the back. Hakuseki writes that the origin of this cape *(koro)* is uncertain but that it was a very ancient practice to wear it over the armor. Its main purpose seems to have been defensive, especially as a protection against arrows shot from behind, since in ancient times the warrior's back was not properly protected by the old-style corselet *(haramaki-do)*. In fact, some authors wrote that the *horo* was often stuffed with light material, specifically in order to repel arrows. The *horo* could be kept distended by light frames *(oikago)* made of whalebone ribs arranged in various fashions around a central staff that was fastened to the backplate of the *bushi's* corselet. These frames were said to have been invented by Hate Kayama Masanaga during the Onin War (1467-77). One type of *horo* illustrated in ancient scrolls was even draped in front like a tent, covering the head of the horse and the body of its rider, most probably during the gallop toward the enemy lines which often necessitated passing through a shower of arrows. It is logical to assume that many a *bushi* whose mount had been struck down from under him also used the cloth of the *horo* much like a whirling net or wrapped it around his free arm to parry spear and sword thrusts at close range, in the manner of the ancient *tertiarii* of Rome or the Gatalonian horsemen in Europe during the Middle Ages.

Worn by warriors according to their clans' traditional customs of dressing for battle, the *horo* was said to have had many other uses in addition to defense against arrows. Shrouded in the mystical aura which surrounded his military tradition, the *bushi* also wore the *horo* in order to drive away evil forces which might have conspired against him or his mission. In addition, he used the *horo* of his fallen foe as a receptacle for the defeated man's severed head, which was thus identified by the crest embroidered on the cape. Ancient military traditions, in fact, recommended the wearing of the *horo* on the battlefield because, if a *bushi* is killed, "the enemy will understand, as they recognize the *horo*, that the dead [warrior] was not a common person, and so your corpse will be well-treated" (Garbutt[2], 175). The same tradition indicated that the *horo* was used as a means of communication, often of resignation to a deadly fate on the

Warriors wearing JIMBAORI

battlefield. "When anyone is exhausted and decides to die in the field," a military manual advised such a warrior to fasten the cord of his helmet to the *haigashira,* then cut it off to show that it will never be put on again. Also, he must fasten the cord of the *horo,* called *hino,* to the *horo*-fastening ring on the helmet, and fasten the cord called *nami-tatsu-no-o* to the hole in the stirrup. This also means that it will fight no more. (Garbutt[2], 175).

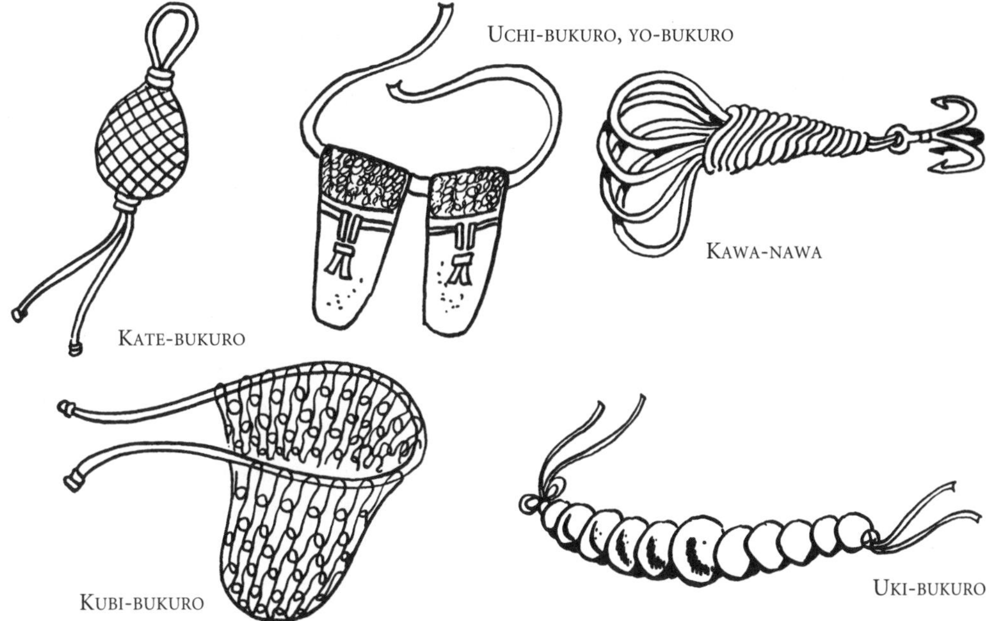

The entire suit of armor belonging to the *bushi* of the upper ranks in active service was carried in the *gusoku-bitsu (kara-bitsu),* which was a box "made of wood or papier mache."

> If the suit was a light one, the box had loops on the front through which the arms were passed and the box was carried on the back. If it was heavy, the box had iron handles on the ends with supplementary

Warrior in HARAMAKI-DO using KAWA-NAWA

Prisoners bound with TORINAWA

KAWA-NAWA in combat

loops on them which stood up above the box when the handles were turned up. When traveling, two men carried the box by a pole passed through the loops. (Stone, 271)

Many manuscripts concerned with bujutsu also mention a series of accoutrements that the *bushi* wore or carried on the battlefield along with his armor. These articles can be divided into three categories: the first includes bags and towels, the second ropes and belts, and the third insignia of various kinds.

Among the bags and towels which were part of his equipment for war, the records mention the ancient head bag *(kubi-bukuro)* made of net and used to carry the severed head of a worthy foe (if the *horo* was not handy, presumably). This bag was carried hanging from the *bushi's* waist when on foot and from the saddle when on horseback. The provision bag *(kate-bukuro)* was also a very important item and was carried at the right side of the waist. The type recommended for ordinary officers was the *koshizuto,* made of light, twisted paper string *(kan-yori).* A smaller ricebag *(uchi-gae)* with raw or baked rice inside, according to the weather, was also carried. Special purses for money *(uchi-bukuro),* handkerchiefs *(yo-bukuro),* and medical aids *(inro, kinchaku)* were carried in several ways under or over the corselet *(do),* as were the various towels and strips of cotton called *tenugui* and *nagatenugui.*

Among the ropes and belts carried when in armor, the texts mention the important *koshi-nawa* of the Chinese type *(kara-uchi-no-himo),* which the *bushi* fastened to his belt. It was used for various purposes,

Warrior with SASHIMONO

Warrior with KASA-JIRUSHI and SASHIMONO

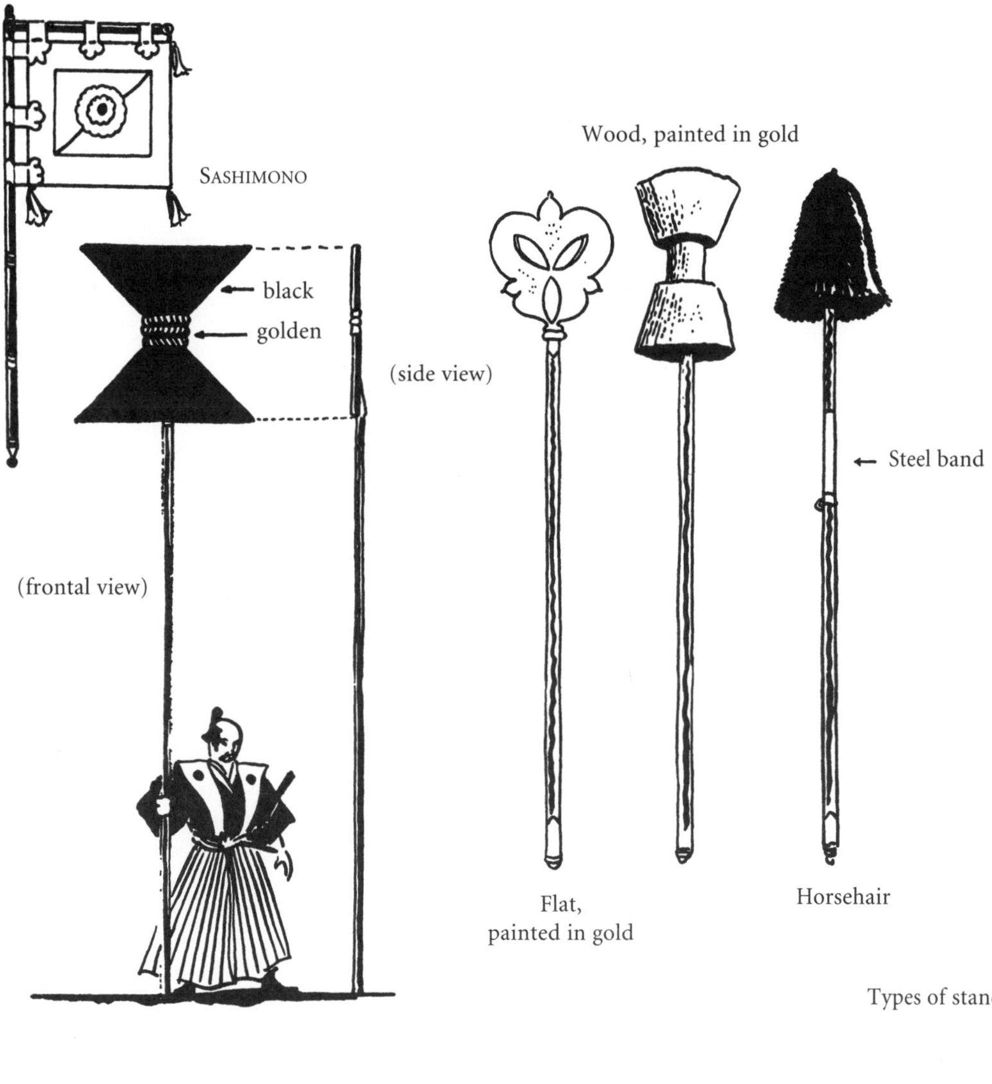

SASHIMONO

black

golden

(side view)

(frontal view)

Wood, painted in gold

Steel band

Flat, painted in gold

Horsehair

Types of standard

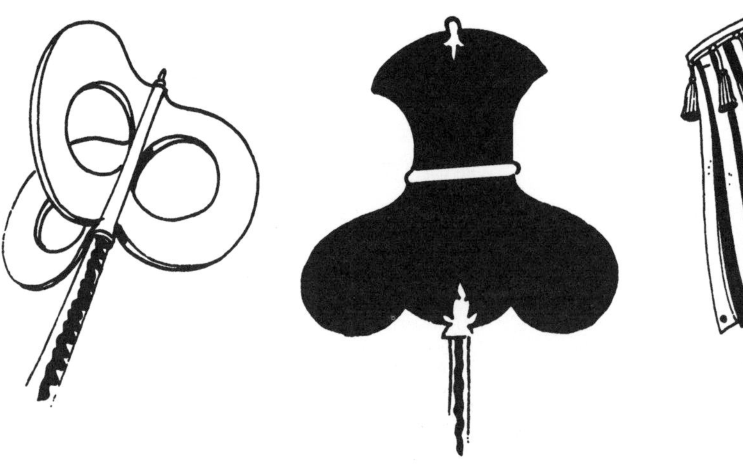

Three-faced standard, painted in gold

Flat standard, painted in black with golden band and decorations

Round standard with red tassels and stripes

such as securing a saddle *(kuragatame)*, tethering a horse *(shiba-tsunagi)*, and binding a prisoner *(tori-nawa)*. Warriors of the lower ranks and their officers carried another type of rope *(kagi-nawa, kawa-nawa)*, about ten feet long, with a "multi-pointed hook on the end. It was ...used in climbing walls, securing boats, hanging up armor and other purposes" (Garbutt[2], 153). An interesting article which the *bushi* in armor carried on the battlefield was a special lifebelt *(uki-bukuro)*, which consisted of some kind of inflatable material shaped like peaches side by side, and which he used when crossing rivers and lakes. It was said to have balanced the weight of the immersed armor and was tied around the waist or chest. When not using it, the *bushi* carried it, strapped to his saddle or on the horse's crupper *(shiode)*.

The insignia adopted by the *bushi* to identify himself and his rank and to communicate his intentions or orders in the melee of battle were many. The cavalryman, for example, used that typical little banner *(sashimono)* previously mentioned. It was generally made of silk, with the corners stiffened by the addition of strips of leather which kept it flat and made a characteristic snapping sound when the wind caught it. It was fastened to a stick held vertical by a socket on the lower part of the corselet's plate and by a ring higher up on the same plate, at the height of the *bushi's* shoulder blades. A smaller badge *(koshi-sashi)*, made of thick paper and attached to a short stick, was carried stuck in the rear of the belt. Other decorations worn in place of this little banner "in night attacks, ambushes, sea fights and on stormy days" were the badges called *kasa-jirushi*, which hung from the ring *(kasa-jirushi-no-wa)* at the back of the helmet, and the badge called *sode-jirushi*, which the *bushi* wore on the right shoulder plate. Foot soldiers used them as regimental badges. Decorative tassels *(agemaki)* of several designs, lengths, and colors were worn over the armor. The most important of these was the set that hung at the back plate of the corselet.

In addition to flags, the military clans also employed a number of standards to identify their houses. These were used extensively even in times of peace and were particularly visible on the highways, as each clan's lords and selected cohorts traveled to and from Edo periodically. Such standards were constructed mainly of wood, often reinforced with iron bands and covered with lacquer or horsehair. Tasseled and striped standards were also very common. Different colors were used by each clan, but black, gold, and red predominated.

The most representative among the symbols of rank and command adopted by the *bushi* in armor was the baton *(sai-hai, sai)*, followed by the rigid war fan*(gumbai)* and the folding iron fan *(tessen)*—all of which are examined in greater detail in the section "The Art of the War Fan." These fans (together with a seemingly endless variety of swords, spears, bows and arrows, etc.) introduce us to the formidable array of weapons used by the Japanese warrior, as well as to their respective arts.

<THE MAJOR MARTIAL ARTS>

The Art of Archery

For centuries, the bow and arrow was "the chief weapon of the fighting man in Japan" (Brinkley[1],128). Even after the introduction of firearms and the extended period of enforced peace under the Tokugawa had greatly reduced its strategic relevance, archery was still considered a noble art. Known generally as *shagei* (accomplishment in archery) or, more specifically, as kyujutsu (the art, or technique, of the bow), it was a fully developed art with a complex system of practices and techniques, an initially wide variety of styles which slowly merged into a few major ones, and a deep theory linking the art to the very birth of the Japanese nation. Inspired as it was by the mystical, esoteric dimension of that culture, it is not surprising to learn that, in the twelfth century, as Lidstone observes in his *Kendo,* "people in high positions were delighted when their ability as archers was acclaimed but made every endeavor to have their prowess with the sword hushed up" (Lidstone, 8). By the time the Tokugawa had unified the nation under the sway of their centralized, military dictatorship, kyujutsu had evolved into a discipline of mental and spiritual coordination, known and practiced far from the battlefield, under the austere guidance of teachers who acted more in the capacity of spiritual counselors than masters of arms. The name given to this discipline of spiritual development was kyudo—the way of the bow and arrow. As such, Japanese archery is still practiced today, although in a somewhat modified form. In feudal Japan, indoor and outdoor archery ranges *(matoba, iba, yaba)* for target practice *(kaka-uchi)* were to be found in the central houses of every major military clan. Archery equipment, that is, the bow and arrow *(kyusen)* and the characteristic bundle of straw in a barrel which was used as an elevated target *(makiwara),* were common sights on the grounds of most military mansions, as were the cylindrical stands *(yadate)* which held the arrows ready for target practice. Arrow cases *(ya-bako)* and bow stands *(chado-kake)* were also prominently featured in the houses of high-ranking *bushi.*

In tracing the origins of this art, it seems to have emerged with the appearance of the Japanese knight on horseback—the military nobleman. The archer *(ite),* also called the holder of the bow *(yumi-tori),* was, in fact, "a warrior of rank in old Japan. The bow and long sword were the weapons of the noble; the common soldiers used the spear and short sword" (Stone, 682). Kyujutsu was actually considered "an essential branch of the education of nobles and the habit of shooting from horseback while in swift motion,

Nara archers

so as to deliver an arrow accurately in any direction, was diligently cultivated" (Gilbertson[1], 112). The word "nobles" in this context, however, does not refer only to the military aristocrats, that is, the *buke* who emerged during and after the ninth and tenth centuries, but also to those even more ancient nobles, the *kuge,* who traced their lineage back to the earliest clan leaders. Archery contests are said to have been held as early as the fourth century A.D., in commemoration of the nation's founding.

Archery contests on horseback were especially admired by "effete" court nobles throughout the Heian period. It was during this period that the basic system of training in archery was developed and refined. Inevitably, this method was widely adopted by the ambitious warriors of the following age, their offspring often being presented with bamboo-grass horses and a bow in childhood (Kaigo, 21). The training program for archers was based upon repeated attempts to hit both fixed and mobile targets while on foot as well as on horseback. The major fixed targets were the large target *(o-mato),* the deer target *(kusajishi),* and the round target *(marumono).* The first, according to Kaigo, was set thirty-three bow-lengths and measured about sixty-two inches in diameter. The second consisted of a deer's silhouette covered with deer skin and marked to indicate the vital spots to be hit; and the third consisted of a round board, stuffed and then covered with strong hide. There are indications that these targets were often hung from poles and set in motion in order to develop skill in hitting targets whose movement would render them more elusive and difficult to pierce from a distance.

Training on horseback, naturally, was obviously more aristocratic, in both nature and tradition, than training on foot. It demanded great coordination in controlling a galloping horse, while simultaneously releasing arrow after arrow against a series of different targets which might be either fixed or in motion. Among the popular forms of archery were: three-target shooting *(yabusame),* bamboo-hat target shooting *(kasagake),* dog shooting *(inuoumono),* dog hunt *(inuoi),* bird hunt *(oitorigari),* and the grand hunt for deer, bear, and so forth *(makigari).*

Three-target shooting *(yabusame)* involved launching the horse at a full gallop in a pre-set direction, while releasing arrows directed against three targets, each constructed of a three-inch square board set on a pole along the horse's path. Bamboo-hat target shooting *(kasagake)* was performed within the confines of a course known as the arrow way *(yado),* properly fenced and with a shelf set at its end from which bamboo hats were hung. The rider was required to launch his steed at full gallop and begin to hit those hats, first from a distance *(tokasagake)* and then from close range *(kokasagake).* Dog-shooting *(inuou-*

mono) consisted of releasing a certain number of dogs into a closed arena and then chasing them around, while shooting at them from horseback. This particular training system developed into a ritualized contest in which thirty-six mounted archers were divided into three groups of twelve riders each. In turn, each group was allowed to enter the round, bamboo-fenced arena, seventy-two bow-lengths across, into which were then released fifty dogs for each group (Kaigo, 22). Revulsion at the sight of this pointless slaughter, prompted and deepened by the spreading of Buddhism's civilizing influence throughout Japanese society, resulted in edicts which commanded that the archers use non-lethal arrows with large round arrowheads in these dog-shoots, while the dogs were to be outfitted with special, padded corselets. With only a few lapses, this modified form of training and competing lasted for centuries.

Finally, hunts of almost every kind imaginable were used to augment the warrior's training. These hunts became very popular with the *bushi* toward the end of the Heian period, and remained so in the centuries which followed. The practice of setting up encampments in the countryside, on a hill, or in the mountains during times of peace and then searching for small and large game to bring down with arrows is reported in glowing terms in ancient chronicles. "The warriors who took deer and wild boar," writes Kaigo, "attained honour just as if they had killed an enemy general." Yoritomo is said to have been delighted when his son shot a deer in one of these hunts on Mount Fuji, going so far as to express his pride in a letter to his wife, Masako, in Kamakura. Even when warfare evolved from clashes between clans into full-scale battles between major armies, foot soldiers still were called upon to release the concentrated power of their volleys of arrows against opposing forces. Moreover, because of the excellence of their art, archers were assigned a position of privilege among the combined troops, a position which they retained long after the fifteenth century, when the strategic importance of the bow and arrow on the battlefield had declined substantially. Even as recently as the eighteenth century, "etiquette ordered that the archers should be placed at the left, the musketeers at the right, and the battle was formally opened by a shower of arrows" (Scidmore, 360). Gilbertson thought that this art, like so many others, probably came to Japan from China:

> We frequently find archers represented on metal works, especially in Chinese costume, the subjects being derived from Chinese history. One of the most common of these is connected with the famous Chinese archer Yoyuki, whom [the Japanese] called the Shogun of Divine Archery. He is reported to have brought down a goose that was flying above a cloud, and therefore invisible, his aim being directed solely by the cry of the bird. (Gilbertson[1], 112)

Another theory in the doctrine of bujutsu links the beginning of this art to hunting (and, therefore, to the nomad tribes who inhabited the northern regions of Asia), and eventually to the Ainu, those white aborigines who were slowly pushed back into the Northern lands of Hokkaido (where they dwell even today) by the expanding Japanese culture of the south. The Ainu were recognized in early records of Japanese history as being skillful archers, both in hunting and warfare. Their bows, made of that particular wood *(ouruma)* which resembles yew (Greey, 109), their arrows, with characteristic feathers *(otsuba),* and their flat quivers *(ika)* of well-carved willow are still precious specimens of a disappearing but once highly developed craft.

Skilled makers of bows had placed an impressive variety of the basic design at the *bushi's* disposal. The bow came in all sizes and shapes and could be used for a variety of purposes related to warfare, hunting, ritual, or sport. The Japanese had even developed and perfected the crossbow, some of which "used in the old fortresses had bows 12 feet long and a foot in circumference. They also used smaller ones shot from the shoulder" (Stone, 195). Specimens of the first type were called *o-yumi,* and bows of the second type, often found in museum collections, were known as *teppo-yumi.* In the latter category, the bow was about as long as the stock, which was made of bone or whalebone, often lavishly decorated. More difficult to locate are samples of the repeating crossbow *(dokyu),* which some authors link to Chinese models such as the *chu-ko-no* (Stone, 211). A short bow was also available, in styles ranging from the highly maneuverable *hankyu,* which was used in battle, to the equally accurate *yokyu* used for amusement or the bow used for hunting, the *suzume-yumi.* The short bow *(azusa-yumi)* was also used by sorcerers in their incantations (Stone, 84). A martial classic, the *Buki Niyaku,* describes and illustrates "five kinds of bows: the *maru-ki,* or roundwood bow; the *shige-no-yumi,* or bow wound round with rattan; the *bankyu* and *hankyu,* similar bows but of smaller size; and the *hoko-yumi,* the Tartar-shaped bow" (Gilbertson[1], 113). It was the *bushi's* proficiency in the use of one certain bow, however, that caused Chinese historians to call the Japanese "the people of the longbow." This was the war bow par excellence, the *daikyu,* used by warriors on horseback *(uma-yumi)* or on foot. It had a length ranging anywhere from seven feet four inches to eight feet; in ancient times, there were some that were nine feet long. In size, this particular bow seems to have been adopted on a wide scale by only one other people—the Soriono Indians of eastern Bolivia, studied by Holmberg, who has called them "the nomads of the long bow." The power *(go)* required even to bend such a bow must have been considerable. As Harrison indicated in his reminiscences, certain specimens of these bows that belonged to a member of the old, pre-Meiji *buke* "were so strong that I could hardly bend them at all, not to speak of using them with any hope of making a bull's eye, albeit the proprietor could handle them with comparative ease" (Harrison, 25). These bows were made of several lengths of wood (usually selected qualities of bamboo) glued together, with a characteristic bend near the end, called the shoulder *(kata),* which the bowstring *(tsuru, tsura, tsurao)* touched for a little distance. Interestingly enough, "this portion was faced with metal, and called the *otokane;* the bowstring striking against it when shooting produced a sound, often used for signalling. When the Mikado required water for washing in the morning, three of his attendants made a signal to that effect by twanging their bows" (Gilbertson[1], 113). The bowstrings were made by skilled specialists *(tsura-sashi)* from long fibers of hemp, sinews, or silk (silk being used generally for ceremonial bows). The strings came in many qualities, ranging from the hard, strong bowstrings of war bows to the soft and elastic bowstrings *(kusune)* used for hunting and sports as well as war. Spare bowstrings were always carried in the quiver or in a special reed or leather basket *(tsuru-maki),* often lavishly decorated. There were, as Gilbertson tells us, "many kinds of quivers *(yebira)*: some for war, others for the chase, besides more ornamented ones such as those worn by the *zuijin* or palace guards, in which the arrows were spread out behind their backs (somewhat like the tail of a peacock). These decorated quivers were called *heikoroku*" (Gilbertson[1], 113).

Beginning with ancient models, such as the *kachi-yuki,* Stone divides all Japanese quivers into two broad categories. The first includes open quivers which kept the arrows apart, thus protecting their feathers and making them easily available to the archer. Fifty arrows could be covered in these open quivers, but they were eventually replaced by lighter, covered containers *(yazutsu* or *yatsubo)* in which fewer arrows were carried. These closed quivers, shaped like boxes, kept the arrows well protected from the vagaries of weather, but were rather inconvenient when it was essential to launch the arrows in rapid succession. Nonetheless, although the feathers might have become somewhat ruffled if the arrows were not securely fastened inside, the closed quivers were still considered more convenient by mounted archers because, according to Jonas, the arrows themselves were better protected during hectic rides (often over rough and hazardous terrain) and in all weather, however inclement.

The archer in battle

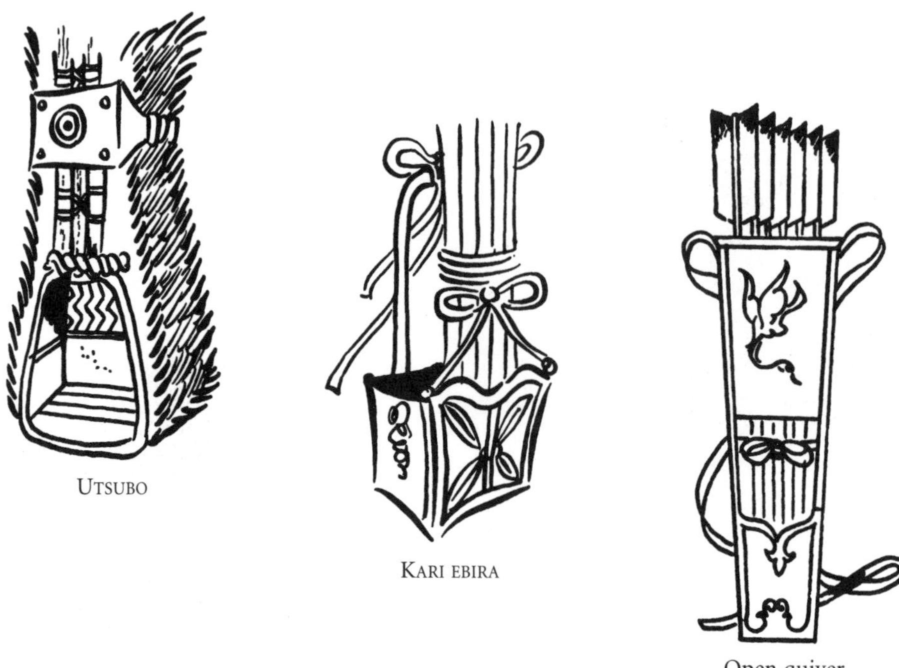

Utsubo

Kari ebira

Open quiver

Among the quivers of the second category, the doctrine of archery mentions the large and ancient *dohyo-yari;* the characteristic *utsubo,* usually covered with fur; and the strangely shaped *tsubo-yamagui.* Among the ceremonial quivers, the

> most common among those found in temples is something like an armchair with a very high back and short leg, to which the arrows were secured by thongs as in the *kari-yebira* (hunting quiver). These quivers held from two to three dozen arrows and appear to have stood on the ground; and other quivers worn at the back were conical or quadrangular, often lacquered and decorated. (Gilbertson[1], 117)

The quivers of the first category, or open type, such as the common *kari-ebira,* were "little more than a framework of bamboo, very light, to which the arrows were secured by thongs twisted around them" (Gilbertson[1], 117). These were the quivers used in both hunting and war by *bushi* on foot, while it is presumed the heavier types were either carried by a higher-ranking *bushi* on horseback or carried by his attendants.

The fletcher or arrow maker *(ya-haki)* also offered the *bushi* a wide assortment of arrows *(ja)* whose shafts of reed *(yagara)* came in varying lengths, with heads *(yajiri)* of every possible shape and material, in accordance with their particular purposes. For example, in target practice, the *bushi* used blunt arrows *(mato-ya)* with pear-shaped wooden heads *(ki-hoko),* which were also used in the celebrated dog hunts *(inuoi)* and dog shooting *(inuoumono)* reportedly begun by Emperor Toba in the twelfth century.

Other interesting arrow heads were those supposedly derived from the Chinese whistling arrows *(hao-shi, ming-ti)* described by Laufer. They had perforated heads shaped like turnips *(kabura-ya, hiniki-ya)* "through which the air rushes with a whistling sound. Sometimes it is mounted with a steel head projecting from the end" (Stone, 327). The sound *(hyago)* that was produced by these whistling arrows *(hikime, meiteki)* was particularly shrill and clear, making them very useful for signaling. With certain modifications they could also be used as rockets or fire arrows *(hi-ya)* against enemy fortifications.

Steel, of the highest temper, was the chief material used for both hunting and war arrow heads, but no one has, as yet, classified them all because of the variety of shapes and sizes devised by generations of

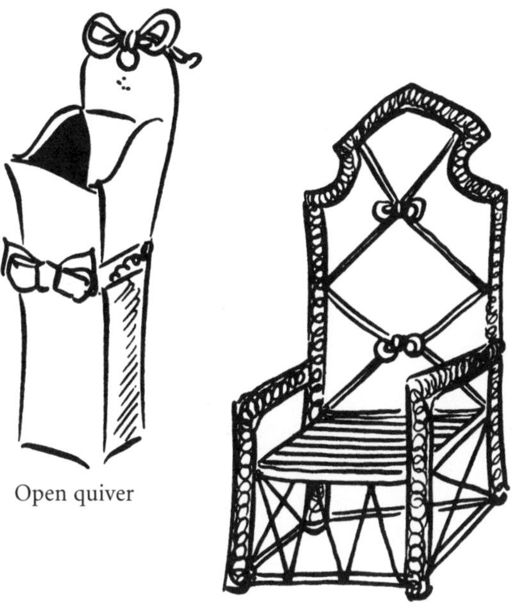

Open quiver

Standing quiver

Bow-stand with band holding set together

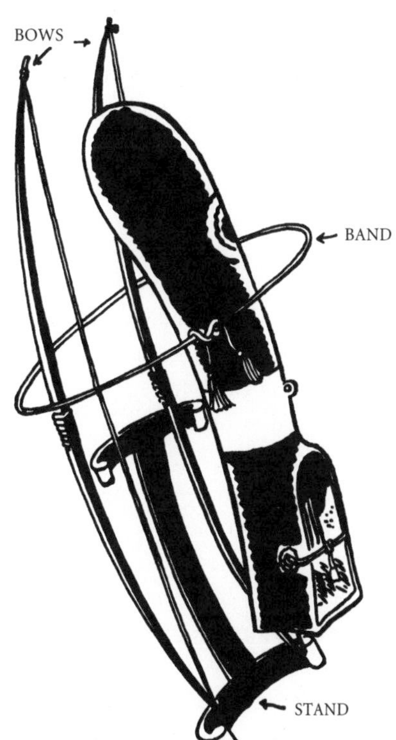

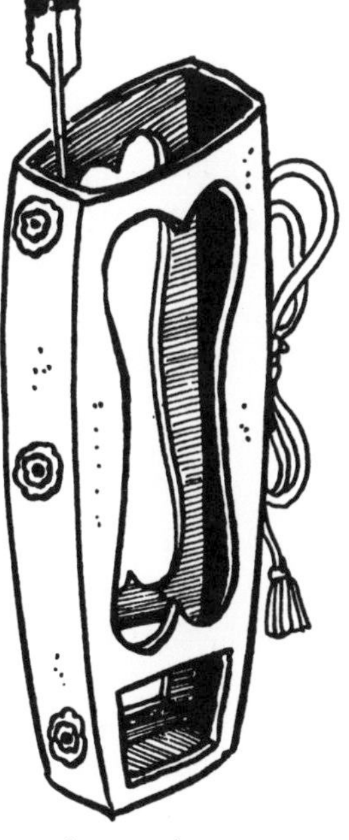

Open quiver

Closed Quiver

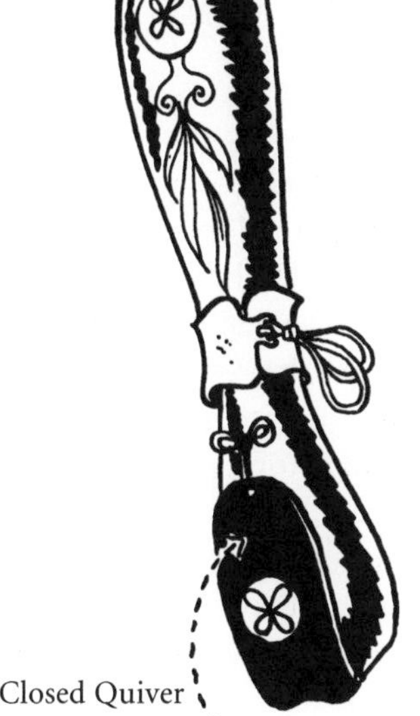

Closed Quiver

ya-haki. Their main divisions, as Gilbertson pointed out, seem to have been "the *yanagi-ba* or willow-leaf arrows; the *togari-ya* or pointed arrows; the *karimata,* bifurcated or two-pointed arrows; and the *watakushi,* flesh-tearer or barbed arrows. These were, however, subdivided into numerous forms" (Gilbertson[1], 118-19). Photographs or drawings of these arrowheads available in public and private collections today give only a general idea of the tremendous variety of these arrowheads—each of which, in the highly specialized world of feudal Japan, had a specific purpose. The fact that pointed arrowheads that were skillfully designed could pierce even iron and steel plates was demonstrated, on the one hand, by the comparative ease with which an imperial archer once skewered a Korean shield sent as a gift to the emperor, and on the other hand by the composition and structure of the armor worn by the *bushi,* who had a healthy respect for the deadliness of his foe's arrows.

Japanese archery, as a science and as an art, was used in war, in ritualistic ceremonies, for sport, and (at its highest level) as a discipline of coordinated integration. In the first dimension, for the *bushi,* "'war' and 'bow and arrow' *(yund-ya)* [were] synonyms. Men spoke of Hachiman, the God of Battles, *asyumi-ya no hachiman;* the left hand received the name of *yunde (yumi-no te* or bow-hand), by which it is still commonly designated and the general term for 'soldier' was 'bow-holder'" (Brinkley[1],128). On the battlefield, archery was employed primarily from horseback or on foot, when rows of archers would be used. As noted earlier, the former was generally considered the more ancient method, belonging to the epic days of those heroes who, according to Japanese legends, shaped the early history of the country. It was also considered to be intrinsically more aristocratic and individualistic in nature; in fact, if the arrows of the knight on horseback only wounded an enemy, such a warrior would not usually bother to administer the coup de grace himself (unless his foe was of equally high rank). In most cases, his foot soldiers would attend to such details.

Individuals of great renown had established their reputations as peerless archers since the earliest recorded periods in Japanese history, displaying skillful techniques and methods of handling the weapons of the age in accordance with the systematic principles of tactical application, all of which indicate proper training, instruction, or schooling at the hands of expert teachers. When the Mononobe clan was eventually destroyed by the Soga clan, Yorozu, a vassal of Mononobe-no-Moriya, refused to surrender and left his guard post at Naniwa for the hills. Hunted down by the archers of the Soga clan, he hid in a bamboo grove and kept his pursuers at bay with a series of strategems, such as tying bamboo stalks with strings in order to create movements and false impressions, thereby drawing his enemies' arrows in the wrong direction, while his own continued to disseminate death and panic. Finally wounded in the knee, he made for high ground and kept launching his arrows to the last, before casting his sword into the river and piercing his own throat with a dagger (Tsunoda et al., 42-43).

In the thirteenth century, equestrian archery played an important role in repelling the attempted invasion of Japan by Kublai Khan's Mongol hordes, who were also famous for their accurate and ferocious use of the crossbow. This mobile and highly individual form of archery was also a prominent factor in the struggles for political predominance which involved the major clans of Japan (the Taira and the Minamoto) from 1180 to 1185. Epic literature mentions Nasu-no-Yoichi, a warrior belonging to the Minamoto faction, who, when challenged, launched an arrow from the shore at Yashima and succeeded in hitting a distant fan bearing the royal crest which was atop the mast of a fleeing ship. Other famous names of exceptional archers are recorded in the manuscripts and chronicles of this venerable art. Yoshiie, of the Minamoto clan (ancestor of Yoritomo, the founder of the Kamakura system of military feudalism), was officially acclaimed as Hachiman Taro ("eldest son of Hachiman, the God of War") because of his exploits in clashes with the aborigines of the north. In time he took his place at court, where his bow guaranteed that the emperor's slumber would be untroubled. It has also been said that Tametomo, another uncle of Yoritomo, used a bow so powerful that he could kill two men with one arrow, as he did in the Hogen war (1156-58). He is also said to have hit, without causing injury, the helmet his brother Yoshitomo was

Kompaku-gata, by Kompaku Hidetsuge

Sampaku, maku-nuki (curtain-piercer)

Tsubeki-ne (chisel shape)

Tsurugi-jiri (sword point)

Tobu, tobi-naoshi (flying kite)

Hoso-yanagiba (narrow willow-leaf)

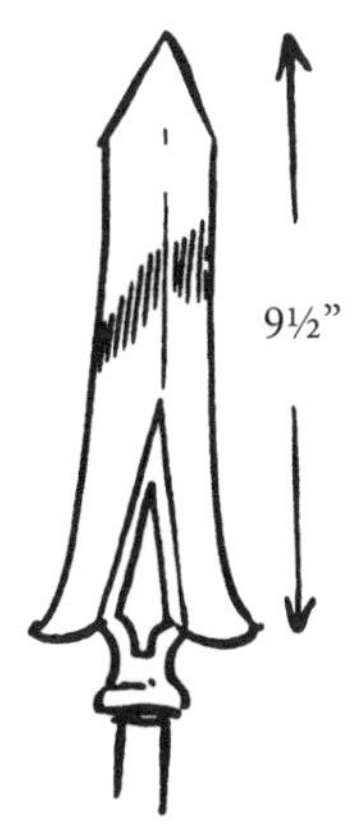

Watakushi of the Satake Clan

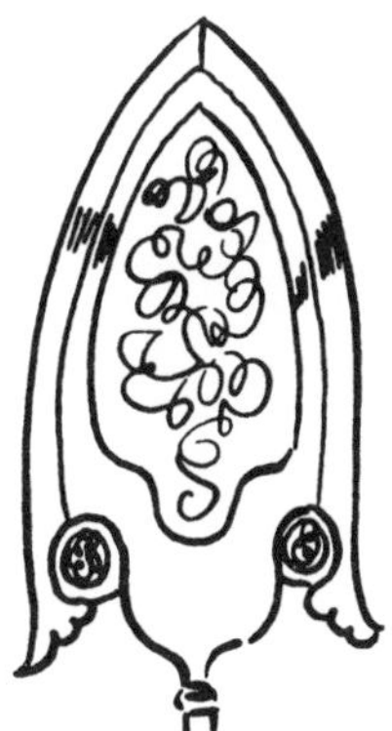
Watakushi (flesh-tearer)

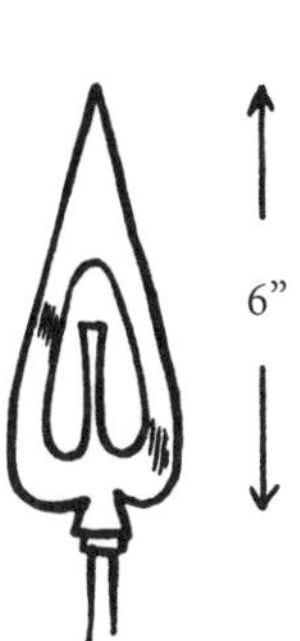

Yanagi-ba (willow leaf)

Togari-ya (pointed)

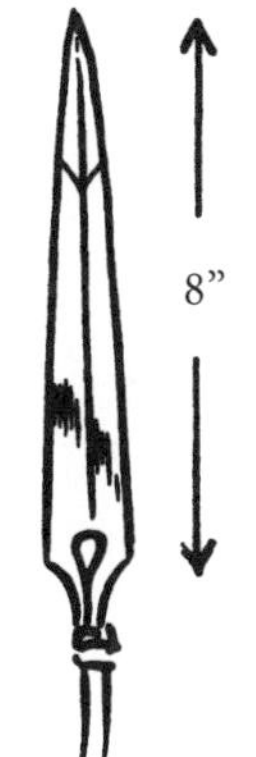

Togari-ya

Kira-ha-hirane

Sankaku (triangle)

Rinzetsu (dragon's tongue)

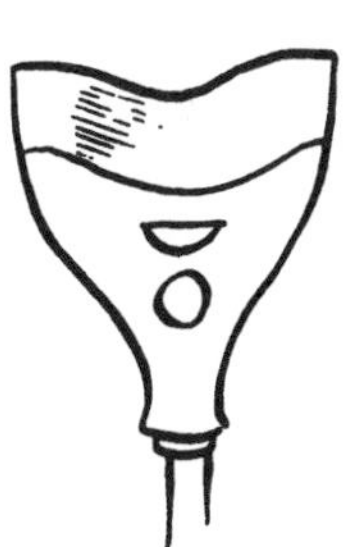
Ryokai

Types of arrowhead

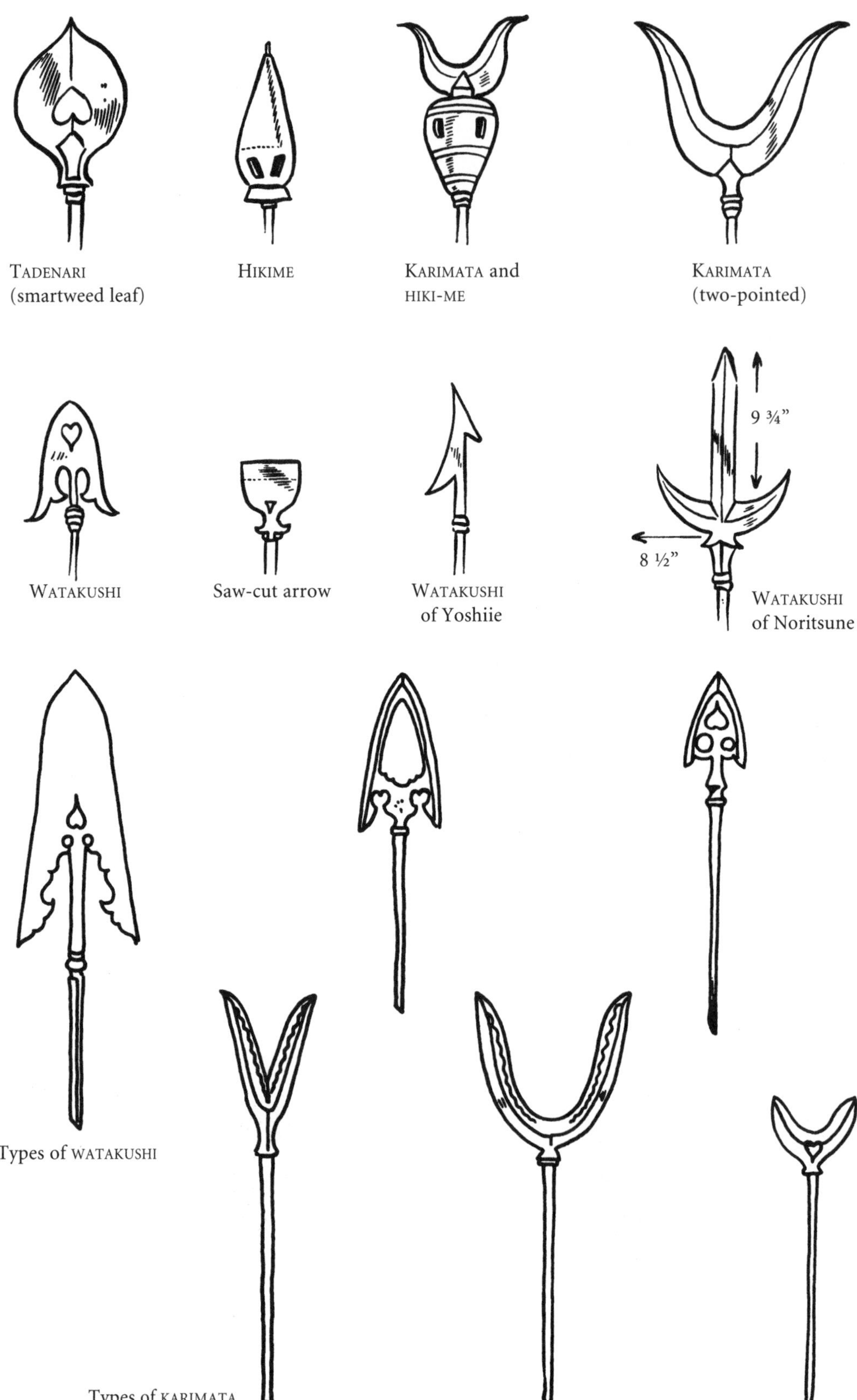

TADENARI (smartweed leaf)

HIKIME

KARIMATA and HIKI-ME

KARIMATA (two-pointed)

WATAKUSHI

Saw-cut arrow

WATAKUSHI of Yoshiie

WATAKUSHI of Noritsune

Types of WATAKUSHI

Types of KARIMATA

wearing, pinning it to the enemy's gate as a warning. When this indomitable warrior was captured, a sinew was extracted from his right arm and he was sent into exile to the island of Oshima. Tradition has it that, although he had been maimed in order to make it impossible for him to draw a bow, he subsequently developed a new and equally lethal method of releasing his arrows.

Tatebito is remembered in official records as the archer who shot an arrow through the first iron shield presented to Emperor Nintoku (313-99) by a Korean envoy. He was given the name Ikuba (target) after accomplishing this feat (Brinkley[1], 130-31). Asamura, a bowman in the service of Yoritsune in the thirteenth century, recaptured a precious pet bird with an arrow without killing it; and Mutsuru, a royal archer at the court of Emperor Toba (1108-23), used a forked arrow to cut off the feet of an osprey holding a fish just captured from the royal pond, thus saving the fish without violating the Buddhist precept against taking life within the confines of imperial grounds (Brinkley[1], 131). Shigeuji, one of the captains who followed Nitta Yoshisada against the army of Ashikaga Takauji at Hyogo, also shot an osprey soaring over enemy forces. When asked for his name by the admiring foe, Shigeuji sent it on an arrow with which he hit an enemy tower (and the sentry in it) at a distance of 360 paces.

Brinkley refers to certain "reliable" records concerning the accuracy of Japanese archery, and lists the names of Wada Daihachi and Tsuruta Masatoki. In Kyoto, the former sent 8,133 arrows from one end of the Sanjusangen-do (the Hall of the Thirty-three Pillar-spans) to the other in 1686. The distance between his bow and the target was approximately 128 yards, and the feat involved releasing an average of five shafts per minute, from sunset to sunset, during twenty-four consecutive hours. Masatoki, an archer in the service of the feudal chief of Sakai, discharged 10,050 arrows (5,383 hitting the center of the target) on May 19, 1852, in the Sanjusangen-do of Edo, during twenty hours of uninterrupted shooting, at an average of nine shafts per minute (Brinkley[1], 132-33).

The fifteenth and sixteenth centuries saw the employment of archers on a larger, more democratic scale, that is, as compact units composed of archers who maintained a steady stream of arrows by shooting alternately, row upon row, while advancing relentlessly toward the enemy. Many a hero had, in fact, fallen under just such a cloud of arrows when he had outdistanced his troops while launching himself against the Mongol hordes. The wiser *bushi* moved in to challenge his peers on the opposite side only *after* his archers had weakened the strong line of enemy archers, thus increasing his chances of presenting his challenge at a reasonable distance. As indicated earlier, the advent of firearms and their employment on a general scale greatly reduced the strategic relevance of the bow and arrow on the battlefield, but left intact (often even magnified) their significance as national heirlooms.

Ceremonial archery had developed almost simultaneously with the military use of the bow and arrow. It was, consequently, steeped in the same tradition. The sacred ceremonies commemorating the founding of the Japanese nation (mentioned in the early records of the reign of Emperor Seinei in A.D. 483) included aristocratic contests of skill in the art of archery, held within the sacred precincts of Shinto shrines. These contests, whose tradition is preserved even today in the colorful Yabusame performed annually in mid-September in Kamakura and Tokyo, significantly link the bow and arrow to the beginning of the Yamato race. Other ceremonial uses of the bow and arrow are to be found in the celebration of the New Year *(harai)*. These ceremonial displays of prowess in archery are said to have originated with the imperial family in the fifth century and to have been performed annually during the Nara and the Heian periods. Equally famous is the ritualistic plucking of the bowstring *(nuigen)*, whose vibrations are considered auspicious

for the royal newborn. Other widely known ceremonies include the *hikime,* in which the perforated arrow which produces a whistling sound in flight is shot to welcome a newborn *(tanjo-hikinu)* or to dispel evil spirits or disease *(yagoshi-hikime).* Finally, the bow made an appearance and lent its archaic significance to the blood-curdling *seppuku* ceremony in pre-Meiji Restoration times. As described in Satow's *Diplomat in Japan,* once the ritual cut had been completed and the body of the warrior lay still in death, the dirk would be removed and then an officer would come forward, carrying a bow, to receive the statements of the official witnesses (Maloney, 29). The bow is still used symbolically today, to close *sumo* tournaments, for example. This ceremony, which originated during the Edo period, marked the conclusion of the tournament then, as now. A precious bow was awarded to the victorious wrestler (represented today by a lower-ranked wrestler), who whirled the bow skillfully in a ceremony called *yumitori-shiki.*

But over and beyond the use of the bow and arrow as an instrument of combat or as an integral part of ritualistic performances, its use as an instrument of integration and coordination which involved the performer's personality on the widest scale (physical, mental, and, eventually, spiritual) was its most complex evolutionary step. Known as *kyudo,* this discipline is based upon the philosophical principles of Buddhism and Taoism, interpreted in a specific way and adapted to the Japanese mentality by the various esoteric schools of Zen, which the military class found so congenial and accepted so unreservedly. Zen, as we shall see in dealing with the inner factors of kyudo in Part 3, provided this discipline of integration with special techniques and exercises of inner, abdominal centralization intended to stabilize the mind and insure its positive control over every action. It also offered exercises and techniques of deep, abdominal breathing that could be used to further the development of the power necessary to draw, shoot, and follow the arrow through to its target. Finally, it provided kyudo devotees with certain levels of motivation, with certain purposes whose variety and complexity depended upon the degree of integration sought by the student. Accordingly, kyudo could be used as an exercise of physical coordination, a discipline of mental control, or a philosophy of balance—or as a synthesis of all these approaches.

The practice of kyudo, performed even today in traditional costume, is based upon the employment of the longbow against various targets of three basic types: a fourteen-inch target, a thirty-two-inch target *(hammato),* or a sixty-four-inch target *(o-mato).* The distance may range from 85 feet in the close style of shooting *(chikamato)* to 180 feet or more in the distant style of shooting *(enteki)* and the flight style of shooting *(inagashi),* in which the target is removed. Sophisticated targets (small candles, narrow strips of paper, emblems, etc.) are also used by skilled masters of the bow, following the ancient tradition of archers who were able to hit such targets under the most exacting conditions —even in semi or total darkness, or when blindfolded.

In ancient times, it was the clarity of execution, the poise, and the control over the bow (as evidenced by the archer's entire performance) which represented the main, the essential scope of kyudo—that is, its functional way of achieving the desired coordination. Training with the weapon was minutely specified and ritualistically embodied in sequences of fluid movement and action, each complete and well defined in and of itself and yet gracefully flowing into the motion which followed. The basic movements still preserved by the major schools of kyudo are the stance *(ashibumi)* in full balance; abdominal centralization and breathing *(dozukuri)*; the notching of the arrow *(yugame);* the raising of the bow with the drawing of the arrow *(uchiokoshi)*; the descent of the bow with the drawing of the arrow *(hikiwake)*; the completion of extension, with the arrow parallel to the line of the mouth and the sighting *(kai)*; the release *(hanare);* and the final pause *(zanshin)* which follows the arrow's flight, arms extended in opposite directions. The complete exercise constitutes a formal sequence *(kata)* which is repeated in full coordination, time and again, for its own sake. Calmness, mental stability, full extension of energy were its major objectives. Hitting the target, although important, was not the main purpose of this art, as many ancient instructors emphasized. They felt that marksmanship would result inevitably from coordinated control and approached the art accordingly.

Traditional kyudo is practiced extensively today in Japan and abroad, according to the styles of archery adopted by such schools as the Takeda, the Shigo, the Ogasa-wara, the Hioki, and the Nichioku, which are descendants of the even more ancient Nihon, Kajima, and Soken schools, among others. But there are indications that the discipline itself is being increasingly influenced by Western styles of archery which place greater emphasis upon marksmanship per se. Kyudo consequently is becoming more competitive, as might be expected in the broad sport dimension. This results in the subjective coordination of the individual (interior standards of excellence) being pitted against and compared to the style and coordination of another man or other men, thus involving certain objective standards of judgment and qualification which shift the emphasis from the inner factors of the art (control, spiritual balance, etc.) to outer factors, such as technique and accuracy.

The Art of Spear Fighting

In ancient mythology, Japan was known as "the country of one thousand fine halberds" (Nakamura, 490), and very seldom did an illustration of the ancient *bushi* outfitted for war fail to show him holding his spear—a weapon second in traditional significance only to the bow and arrow. The first samples of this weapon seem to have been drawn from Chinese models with their large blades and long, thick poles. One source mentions the *hoko* (halberd) as being the oldest recorded form of spear to evolve from continental models, and schools of bujutsu which specialized in the use of this type of weapon abounded in Japan (Gluck, 107). In certain manuscripts inherited by modern martial art schools, in fact, the references to ancient masters who traveled to China and studied the various methods of handling the *hoko* are numerous and explicit.

In both design and structure, the true Japanese spear (known generally as the *yari)* was similar to all Japanese blades in the high quality of its tempering, its lightness, and the ease with which it could be maneuvered. The great artists of steel forged these spears for the *bushi* with the same care and imagination they lavished on his swords. The spear blades were carefully protected by sheaths (a requirement included among military laws of the clans). The shafts *(nakae)* of these spears came in almost every weight and length imaginable. They were made of excellent wood, carefully seasoned and treated, usually reinforced by and decorated with strips or rings of metal *(sujigau)* at the points that would be under pressure when leverage was applied or a blow parried. These shafts were an impressive sight when arranged in the modest spear rack *(yari-kake)* of a *bushi's* home or lining one of the walls of the armory in a daimyo's mansion.

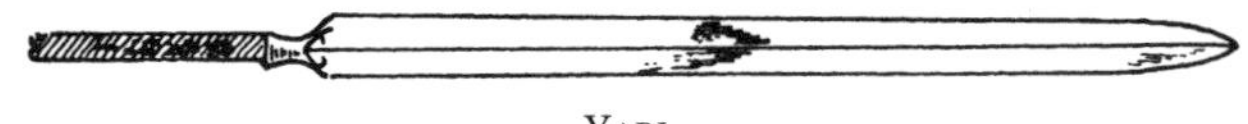

Yari

Naginata

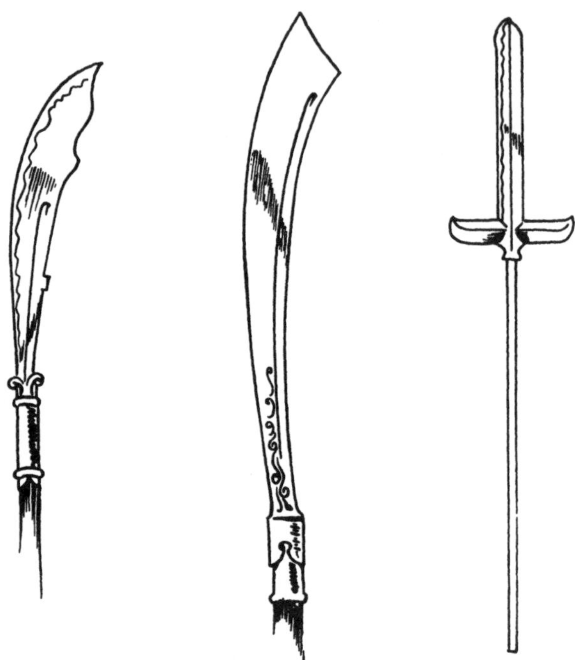

Types of naginata and yari

Curved spear, naginata

Straight spear, yari

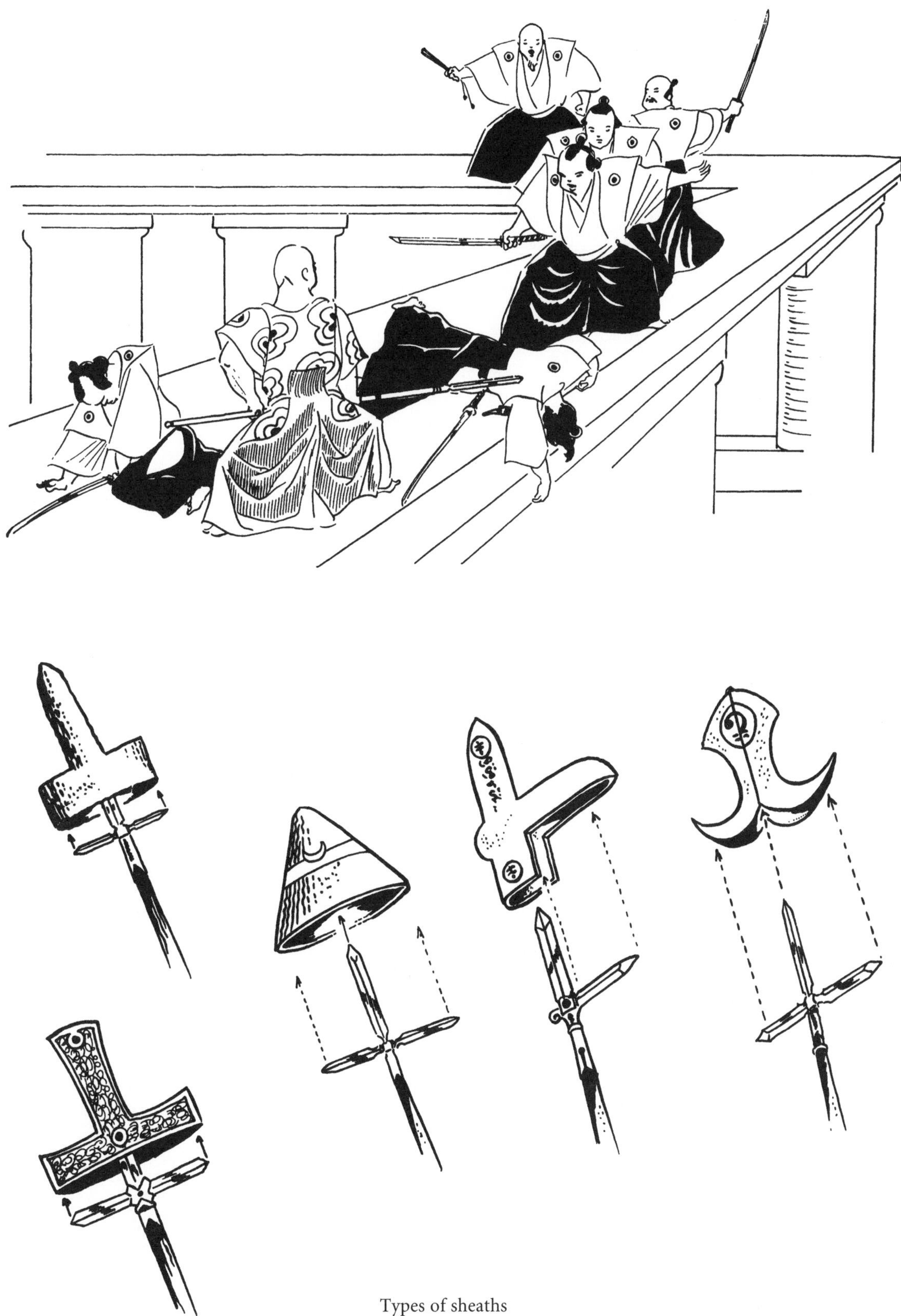

Types of sheaths

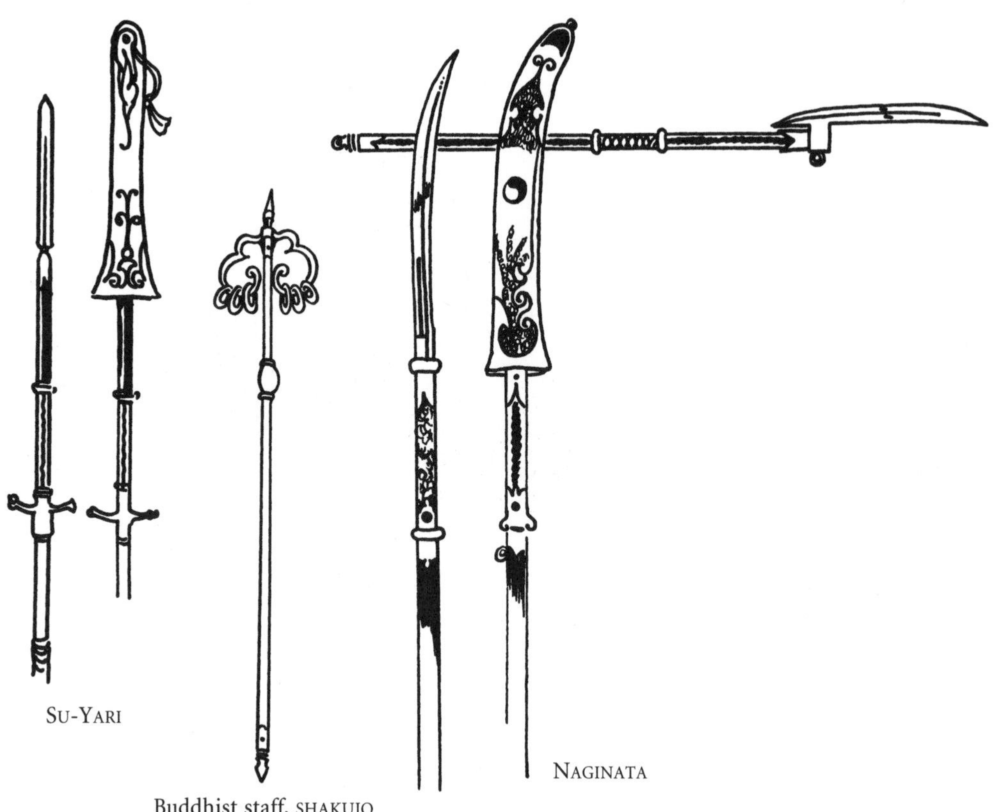

SU-YARI

Buddhist staff, SHAKUJO

NAGINATA

Spearheads (like the arrowheads examined in the preceding section) were cast of the same high quality steel used for swords and came in many lengths and shapes. They can be divided, however, into three major groups: straight spearheads, curved spearheads, and variously shaped spearheads. The straight spearhead was the most common. It was double-edged, almost like an abbreviated version of the archaic Japanese sword *(ken).* Its length and decoration, design of point *(jari-saki),* type of casting, and the quality of steel employed gave rise to several specific types, such as the *su-yari* and the *omi-yari. A* large and very ancient type of bronze spearhead was the *tsukushi-boko,* used predominantly by the warriors of Tsushima. Another straight type of spearhead was the "devious" *shakujo-yari,* embedded in an apparently innocuous pilgrim staff, "carried by samurai when they were on a secret mission and did not want to be noticed" (Stone, 550). A large variety of javelins was also available. Famous among these was the *uchi-ne,* characteristically equipped with feathers; the longer, stronger *nage-yari;* the *naguya;* the *te-yari,* or *te-boko;* and the long *makura-yari.* These javelins were kept handy on the battlefield or at home, near the pillow, and they were used by men and women alike either as deadly missiles or as a normal *yari,* for thrusting and parrying in close combat.

> At a point of transition between the straight spearhead and the curved spearhead is the blade of the *nakamaki,* which resembles that famous spear which gained great popularity among the *bushi:* the *naginata,* often erroneously referred to in English as a halberd. This term, however, as Brinkley observed, is a defective translation, for the Japanese *naginata* (literally, long sword) was not a pole terminating in a battle-axe and spear-head as the English name implies. It was a scimeter-like blade, some three feet in length, fixed to a slightly longer shaft. Originally, the warlike monks alone employed this weapon, but from the XIth century, when the Minamoto and the Taira clans began their long struggle, the *naginata* found much favor among the military men, its combined powers of cutting and thrusting being fully recognized. (Brinkley[1], 156)

The yari and the naginata in action

The blade of the *naginata,* in fact, was like that of a sword, curved near the point, where its shape became even more pronounced. Stone writes that there were three varieties: the first appears to have been the ancient *tsukushi-naginata,* the shaft of which was inserted into a metal loop on the back of the blade; the second and most common had the tang or base secured to the shaft; and the third and rarest had a socket at the base into which the shaft was inserted *(ta-no-saki).* They were all carried appropriately sheathed and their shafts, as might be expected, were heavily lacquered and decorated with metal mountings. The *naginata* became famous not only because of its tremendous versatility in combat but also because of the many individual schools which developed intricate styles and remarkable proficiency in its use. Certain authors, in fact, even believe that the introduction of protective armor for the legs and the lower part of the body was in answer to the development and lethal use of the *naginata.* This weapon was also called the "woman's spear" (Stone, 463), because women of the *buke* were expected to have mastered the use of the *naginata* by the age of eighteen. Mitford wrote that "the halberd is the special arm of the Japanese woman of gentle blood. That which was used by Kesa Gozen, one of the ladies of Yoshitsune, the hero of the XII century, is still preserved in Asakusa. In old-fashioned families, young ladies are regularly instructed in fencing with the halberd" (Mitford, 81). The wife or daughter of a *bushi,* in ancient times, "was always expected to prove her courage and martial capacity at any crisis in the career of her husband or father. In her hands the *naginata* often accomplished signal deeds, and even in the present days there are few more graceful or interesting spectacles to be seen in Japan than the manipulation of this formidable weapon by a highly trained female fencer" (Brinkley[1], 157).

The third group of spearheads includes a confusing variety of shapes, usually highly specialized. The *sasu-mata,* for example, was a spear with a forked head and hooks or spikes at its base that could be used to cut and pierce a target not only in front but also returning behind it. This weapon was said to have been widely employed by feudal police and firemen (Stone, 543). The *futamata-yari* was also a spear with a forked head, and the *magari-yari* was a beautiful trident, with the side-blades set at right angles to the central blade, their points turning slightly inward. The *kagi-yari* was also a hooked spear, while the sleeve tangler *(sode-garami)* was a lengthy pole with barbed hooks at its end that were used to entangle the sleeves of a swordsman or spearman, in an effort to paralyze him. The *tsuku-bo* presented a cross-shaped head "with teeth in it" and was usually kept "in a rack at the guardhouse of a castle" (Stone, 639), together with the rake or grappling hooks with many curved prongs and/or blades *(kumade)* used for climbing walls or hooking enemy armor from above or for dragging it down from below. A similar type of rake was the *uchi-kagi,* a grappling iron with two hooks used by ancient *bushi* to hold two ships together while a battle was in progress.

The *bushi* of higher rank carried his spear, when on horseback, fastened to his leg or stirrup in *iheyari-ate (yari-hasami* or *yari-sashi),* the spear rest, "made of iron or copper. The best type...has a hinge in its center so as to let it move freely" (Stone, 674). Foot soldiers *(ashigaru)* carried their spears, and often those of their officers, on their shoulders.

Naturally, there were many *ryu* and many *sensei* of bujutsu who specialized, often exclusively, in the use of the spear in combat. Famous among the former was the ancient Hozo-in *ryu,* named after the Hozo

monastery where spear fighting was widely practiced. The Shinkage *ryu,* famed for its skillful swordsmen, also included spear fighting in its program of instruction. According to the literature of bujutsu, an expert spearman trained in any of these schools was studiously avoided not only by single warriors armed with the formidable *katana* but even by groups of warriors whom he could scatter with an intricate, yet impenetrable and deadly circular dance—his long weapon cutting, thrusting, slashing, and parrying as it cut through the air around him in a series of murderous whorls. Competition among spearmen of these schools (as also among swordsmen) was fierce and inexorable. They often traveled in groups or singly the length and breadth of Japan, training with different masters, learning different styles of spear fighting, accepting challenges on the road—welcoming them, in fact, as a chance to test their skill and establish their reputations. These bouts, some of which are discussed in great detail in the martial arts chronicles, were originally fought with real spears, as on the battlefield. The result was often death for the loser, either at the hands of his opponent or, if merely incapacitated in the fight, self-inflicted to atone for his defeat. During the Tokugawa era, legislation proscribing duels not directly motivated by the officially sanctioned right to revenge or self-defense against an unjustified attack tended to reduce somewhat the socially disruptive effects of armed encounters to the death. Many contests of skill, whether officially supervised by competent clan authorities or not, began to substitute the use of bamboo spears *(take-yari)* or spears with padded heads *(tampo)* for those with live blades.

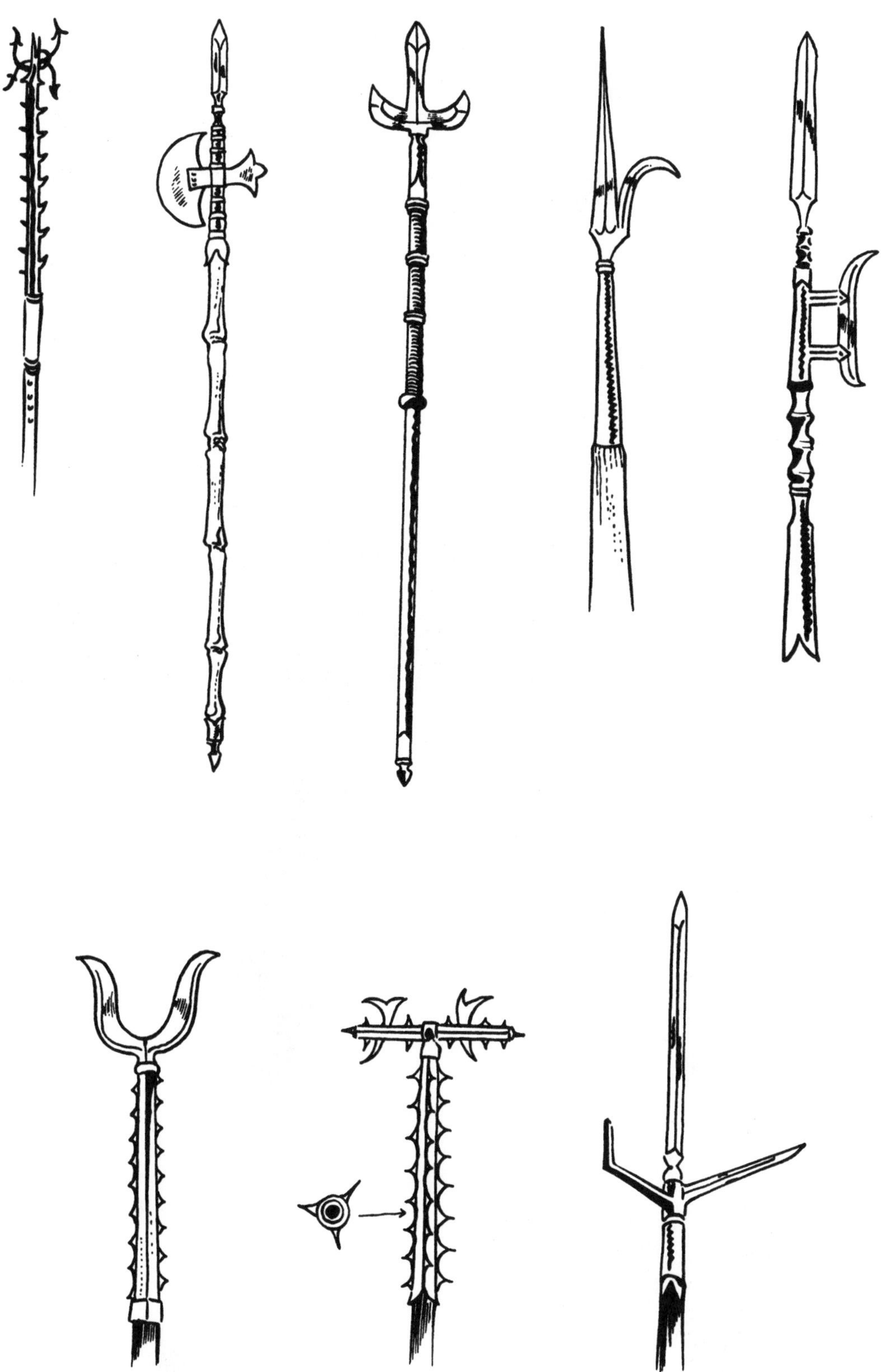

Types of SODE-GARAMI and YARI

The YARI in combat

The NAGINATA and the YARI in combat

According to the major types of spears, there were two major arts or methods of using them: yarijutsu, the art of the straight spear, and naginatajutsu (or simply naginata), the art of the curved spear. Each art was practiced in accordance with innumerable styles, and there were subspecializations centered upon the use of all the various types of long and short spears and javelins. All shared a substantial number of basic techniques, such as the thrusts *(tsuki),* strikes *(kiri),* and parries which, in common with all cutting weapons, were also found in swordsmanship. Postures of readiness, introductory movements, styles of moving in toward an opponent or of sliding out of range of his blade, manners of reaching a target or of evading an attack, varied from school to school and even, within each, from expert to expert. That which has been transmitted to us of feudal yarijutsu is to be found in the strongly modified techniques of jojutsu, the art of the staff, practiced in several modern schools of jodo (the way of the staff) and also as a supplementary exercise in certain schools of aikido. We do know, however, that in feudal times every part of the *yari* was used, including the bottom, which was usually capped with a pointed metal head; and that the position of readiness with the spear kept close to the side (in one of the predominant styles) was known as *kai-kumi.* We also know that several schools taught intricate patterns, high and low *(jumonji-yari),* in order to be able to strike not only from the front but also with characteristic sweeps directed at the opponent's rear, while other schools specialized in parrying, hooking, and deflecting techniques known as *kagi-yari.* Naginata-jutsu added to the techniques of the *yari* those circular cuts particularly appropriate to the curved shape of the naginata.

Even with the increase in popularity of the sword during the middle of the Japanese feudal era and the period that preceded the Meiji Restoration, spears were still displayed in official ceremonies, as well as carried by warriors who escorted provincial lords on their travels (the weapons themselves being kept in perfect condition in the clans' armories). Spearmanship continued to be professionally taught and practiced in the training halls of bujutsu schools for some time, but the sight of isolated spearmen, once familiar everywhere in Japan, became gradually less and less common until such warriors seem to have disappeared almost entirely. Of the innumerable schools of bujutsu that once taught the techniques of naginatajutsu, only a few (such as the Tendo and the Shinkage) are reported to be still active today. Their students wear protective equipment (as do students of Japanese fencing, or kendo) whose main elements have been drawn from the ancient suit of armor: a head protector *(men),* a breastplate *(do),* arm guards *(kote),* a padded apron *(aidats),* and shin guards *(sune-ate).* The razor-sharp naginata of yore has also been replaced by a staff of oak, six and one-half feet long with a bamboo blade twenty-one inches long, covered at the tip by a leather cap. This instrument, and longer ones, may be used against a partner in competition or training, or alone in formal exercises *(kata)* or against life-sized dummies *(uchi-komo-dai).* Techniques of attack, counterattack, and defense stem from fundamental postures of readiness and from basic displacements which, flowing smoothly from one into the other, make the resulting discipline (naginata-do) one of the most suitable methods of coordination among those which have evolved from the once-deadly art of naginatajutsu. Today, in fact, those schools (frequented for the most part by women) use the naginata not so much as a method of combat *(jutsu),* but rather as a discipline of mental and physical integration *(do),* with overtones linking the ultimate aim of these schools to the mysticism and esotericism that are intrinsic to the traditional culture of Japan.

The Art of Swordsmanship

"There is, perhaps, no country in the world," wrote McClatchie in 1873, "where the sword, that 'knightly weapon of all ages,' has in its time, received so much honour and renown as it has in Japan" (McClatchie[3], 55). Not even in England during the Middle Ages, when swords were given individual names and were considered to possess particular virtues, had there developed, as Harrison so aptly put it, such a veritable "cult of cold steel." The sword, wrote Brinkley, "has exercised a potent influence on the life of the Japanese nation."

> The distinction of wearing it, the rights that it conferred, the deeds wrought with it, the fame attached to special skill in its use, the superstitions connected with it, the incredible value set upon a fine blade, the honours bestowed on an expert swordsmith, the household traditions that have grown up about celebrated weapons, the profound study needed to be a competent judge of a sword's qualities—all these things conspired to give to the *katana* an importance beyond the limits of ordinary conception. (Brinkley[1], 142-43)

It seemed to have had a strange fascination for members of all classes, but to the *bushi* it signified the beginning of his life as a warrior, marked its progression, and was often the instrument of his untimely end. Legends surrounding the sword date back to periods and events already shrouded in the mists of time, when the military class began its drive toward the political center of Japan.

There were two major turning points in the life of a child born (or adopted) into the *buke.* The first was the introductory ceremony in which he was given his first sword, the *mamori-gatana,* "a charm sword with a hilt and scabbard covered with brocade, to which was attached a *kinchaku* (purse or wallet) ...worn

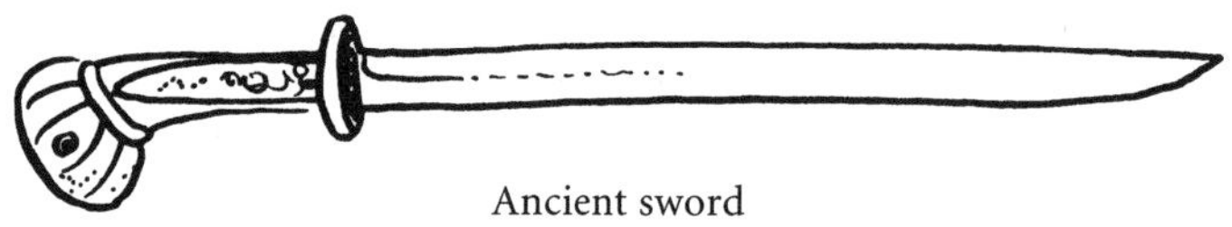

Ancient sword

by boys under 5 years of age" (Stone, 433). The second ceremony was the *gembuku,* which signified his acceptance as a man among men. At this time the child received his first real swords and armor and had his hair dressed in an adult coiffure. From this point in his life onward, he would be expected to specialize in the functions typical of his rank within the hierarchy of the clan, but without ever neglecting his training in the art of using the weapon that had been defined in the military code as the "living soul of the samurai."

All warriors, regardless of rank, were trained in swordsmanship. Those of the upper ranks, of course, had more time to devote to the pursuit of excellence in this art, and to the pursuit of superior instructors—which explains why a retainer of lower rank, notwithstanding his longer exposure to the hardships of military life, was usually no match for a higher-ranking *bushi* in a duel. This type of situation, clearly illustrated by Fukuzawa Yukichi in his *Kyuhanjo,* resembles that of Europe during the seventeenth and early eighteenth centuries, when hardened veterans of countless battles were still no match for a well-trained aristocrat with a sword—the noble's weapon which, with the rise of the bourgeoisie to power at the end of the eighteenth and early nineteenth centuries, became known as the gentleman's weapon. Holtom wrote that "like the ancient Greeks and Germans, as well as people elsewhere, the early Japanese 'deified' their swords and gave them *kami* names" (Holtom, 46). This author felt it was not difficult to understand "how a sword that has saved life, destroyed enemies, and performed other marvelous deeds, or one that is very old, tends to be regarded as a living being, full of strange, protective power, and therefore, *kami*" (Holtom, 46–47). *Kami* expressed in a single ideogram a variety of meanings related to tutelar beings or things divine. Thus it is not surprising to find that Japanese tradition animistically linked the sword to lightning—the *Nihongi* also mentioning the "short sword called *izushi,*" which was said to possess "the miraculous power of disappearing spontaneously" (Holtom, 45). Some authors feel that the religious significance assigned to this weapon is based upon its strategic importance in the ages of the coalescence of the Japanese nation, when the *bushi* moved relentlessly northward, pushing the warlike Ainu ahead of him. As indicated in Part 1, history and religion were very closely entwined during the earliest recorded periods of the Japanese nation, and it is understandable that the practical utility of this weapon on the battlefield became closely linked to the sense of purpose or destiny inherent in an emerging culture.

The bow and arrow and the spear played their part in combat at long and medium range; the sword was used to conclude encounters at close quarters. The mystique surrounding this weapon, in fact, is reflected and treasured in the chronicles of the mythological ages of Japan, in which chronicles, for example, reference is made to a sword that Prince Yamato (who united the Japanese nation) found in the tail of the dragon he slew. This sword, together with the sacred mirror and the sacred comma-shaped beads, form the three holy emblems and treasures of the Yamato race. The mystical significance attached to the sword and its ultranationalistic essence is also to be found in the historical records of many other countries during what is termed the middle or feudal age of their development. King Arthur's magic sword Excalibur in English chronicles, Roland's Durlindana in French literature, and Abn el Rashid's famed weapon in Arabian poetry were all mystical personifications of a national character, as well as the instrument of what was considered a divine mission. But in Europe, this significance declined at the end of the feudal era (sixteenth and seventeenth centuries) with the democratization of war, first in the bourgeois burg and town revolutions, and later in the proletarian revolutions of the industrial age. In Japan, such social upheavals did not take place until the nineteenth century; even then, when certain modifications of social standards were achieved with the promulgation of the Meiji Constitution (1888) and later under the statutes of the constitution adopted after World War II (1946), they were actually modifications imposed

The sword in combat

upon the Japanese people very late in their history, to which they submitted in the way a man submits to superior force or a calamity he is powerless to avoid. The nation itself had not evolved spontaneously from a feudal to an industrial society, and, consequently, even when the imposition seemed successful, it was a surface success (although spectacular indeed) that crowned the apparent sacrifice of older ways. Deeply buried in the hearts and minds of the Japanese people, however, the feudal tradition remained intact—as exemplified by the *bushi* of the twentieth century carrying his *katana* into battle during World War II, while an even more modern *bushi* used his short sword to cut down a political opponent in front of television cameras only a few years ago.

The shape of the weapon as we know it today, and as it was manufactured during the feudal era of Japan, evolved from extremely ancient models made of bronze (later of iron) either on the Asian continent or in Japan. Blades found in dolmens dating back to A.D. 700 were straight and single-edged, cast in a single piece from handle to point. Gowland, in fact, noted that these long iron swords "occupy a foremost position" in the dolmens. "It is important to note," he adds, "that they have only one cutting edge but especially that they possess one distinctive characteristic, i.e., they all have a perfectly straight back, and are thus distinguished from the swords of later times, all of which have a slight curvature" (Gowland, 151). They varied in size from quite long to very short—long swords measuring from two feet six inches to three feet from guard to point, and the short ones measuring from one foot eight inches to two feet. Other forms of straight, double-edged swords, heavily laden with ornaments, appeared almost simultaneously with the spreading of Buddhism in Japan during the Nara period, and they closely resembled the pre-Buddhist symbolic swords used in religious ceremonies in central Asia, particularly in the northern Indian territories of Nepal and Tibet, as well as in China.

As is true of almost every aspect of ancient Japanese culture, China casts its shadow over the Japanese sword. In fact, not only the shape, but the names of Japanese swords are related, directly or indirectly, to Chinese sources (as evidenced in both the written and spoken language of Japan). The ancient Chinese ideograms for *chien* (double-edged sword) and *tao* (single-edged sword or knife), for example, are held by Hawley and other scholars to be the semantic and phonic roots of both the Japanese renditions *ken* and *to,* which were to evolve into *katana*—the Japanese reading of *tao* which supplanted the more ancient rendition of *to.* Linked together, in reverse order, the Japanese *to-ken* was also used as a general term for all types of swords. This derivation is also apparent in other Japanese words for sword, such as *tsurugi* and *hojiu.* "Japanese authorities," wrote Gilbertson, generally agree "that the oldest form of their swords is the *tsurugi* or *ken, tsurugi* being the Japanese, *ken* the Chinese reading of the same [Chinese] character" (Gilbertson[2], 188). There seems to have been an interlude in the evolution of the ancient, straight-backed *ken* during which its single edge gave way to double-edged construction. In turn, this straight-backed, double-edged weapon with a heart-shaped point (made of bronze or iron) underwent a gradual change in shape and material during the mid-Heian period, until it became the curved, single-edged sword made of steel which we recognize today. According to legend, "Amakuni (who lived in the time of Emperor Mommu—A.D. 697-708) invented the *katana* or single-edged sword, by dividing the *ken* into two" (Gilbertson[2], 188). In any case, by the end of the eleventh century A.D., the sword had achieved its characteristically curved shape, although it is doubtful that the blade had yet acquired the astounding purity and cutting power which made *katana* famous the world over.

There were many types of *katana.* One of the most ancient curved derivations of the *ken* was the long, heavy *jin-tachi,* usually carried into battle by the *bushi's* attendant. From this weapon was derived the *tachi* (twenty-four to thirty inches long), a sword that hung edge downward from the ornate belt *(obi)* with which the warrior fastened his armor, before this style was finally discarded in favor of carrying the sword through the belt with the edge upward. Thus, regardless of its size, "a blade will be known as a *katana* when in a scabbard worn in the girdle, but the same blade becomes a *tachi* when the scabbard is suspended" (Gilbertson[2], 190).

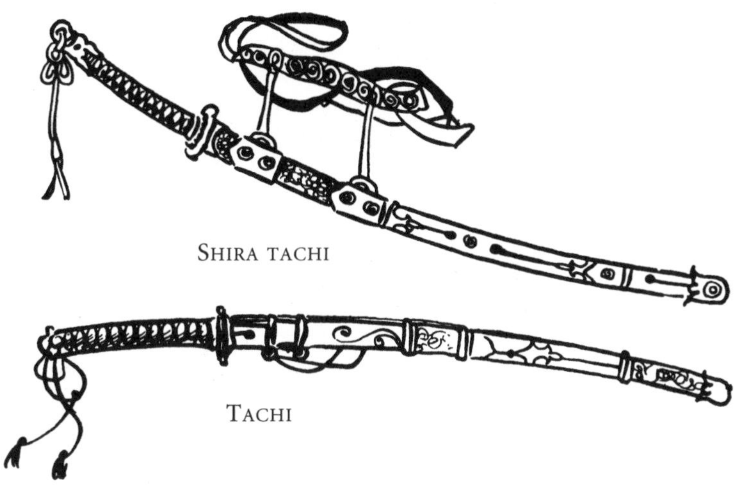

COMPARATIVE SIZES OF JAPANESE SWORDS	
DAITO	
TACHI KATANA	
WAKIZASHI	
TANTO	
AIKUCHI	

DAISHO
- O-KATANA
- WAKIZASHI

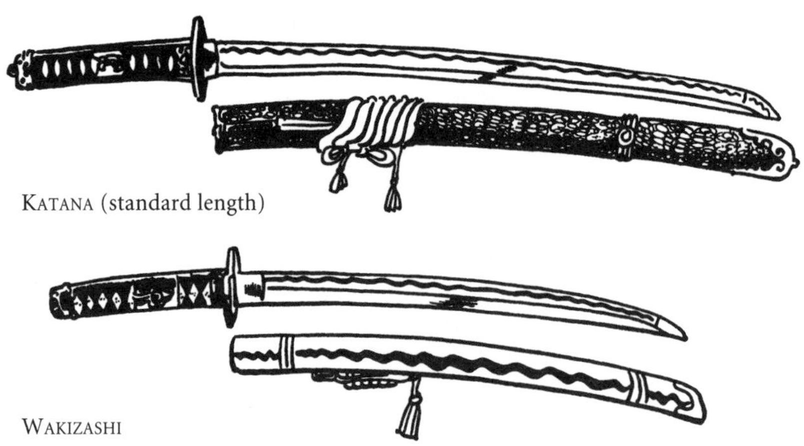

KATANA (standard length)

WAKIZASHI

The *bushi* usually carried two swords: the long sword *(katana* proper) and the short sword *(wakizashi).* These were the two blades *(daisho)* which he alone was privileged (by law) to wear and use—symbols of his position in Japanese society and the instruments for preserving that position. The long sword, ranging from very long (*nodachi* or *dai-katana)* to standard length *(katana),* measured twenty-four inches or more in length. This was the weapon used for combat at close quarters and employed to cut and thrust in various ways. The short sword or *wakizashi* measured from sixteen to twenty inches and could be used in combat as an auxiliary weapon as well as for a variety of other purposes, such as beheading an enemy or performing ritual suicide. Both were worn on the left side, secured at the waist in a particular style. In ancient periods, the long sword was carried hanging from the waist sash, fastened to it with a special cord. The styles used to secure both the long and the short sword have been painstakingly described in many manuals dealing with armor and armor wearing. In later periods, both blades were thrust through the waist sash, edge upward (the *katana* on the left side and the *wakizashi* across the stomach), their cords *(sage-o)* passing through the loops of the scabbards and securing both to the sash in various styles. When traveling, a *bushi* would use a special cover *(hikihada, shirazaya)* for the handles or entire scabbards of his *daisho,* while a *bushi* of higher rank had them carried in special cases *(katana-zutsu)* made of two pieces of lacquered wood, hinged and locked, usually ornamented with the owner's crest.

The short sword hardly ever left the *bushi's* belt for any reason, although the long sword could be removed when custom required: for example, when at home, or while visiting another *bushi's* home, or within the confines of the ruling lord's palace. At such times, the warrior was "permitted" (actually required) to leave the long sword in a safe place or in responsible hands, but this ruling and custom did not include the short sword. Often defined by its owner as "the guardian of his honour" (Stone, 658), the *wakizashi* was later replaced by a dirk for the grim purpose of ritual suicide.

Numerous variations on the early *katana* were developed: the *chisa-katana* (eighteen to twenty-four inches), halfway between the long and short swords of the *daisho,* and which, because of its lightness and intermediate length, was used by nobles at court; the *tanto* and the *hamadashi,* daggers with a large and small guard; the *aikuchi* (or *kusun-gobu),* daggers without guards; the *yoroi-toshi,* a kind of blade for cutting through armor; the series of *himogatana,* the onepiece stilettos made of fine steel; the innumerable *kozuka* knives, carried in the scabbard of the *wakizashi;* the *kogai,* or crested pin, which the *bushi* often left on the body of a slain foe for the purpose of identifying his kill—to mention a few.

The importance of the *katana* was based upon the position of the military class in the political power structure of feudal Japan, a power structure arranged vertically and inspired at every level by the mystical worship of ancestors which linked one generation to the next. A symbol of both the inner beliefs of the Japanese race and its laws, this sword represented simultaneously the past and the present, the center of

Sword-carrying case,
KATANA-ZUTSU

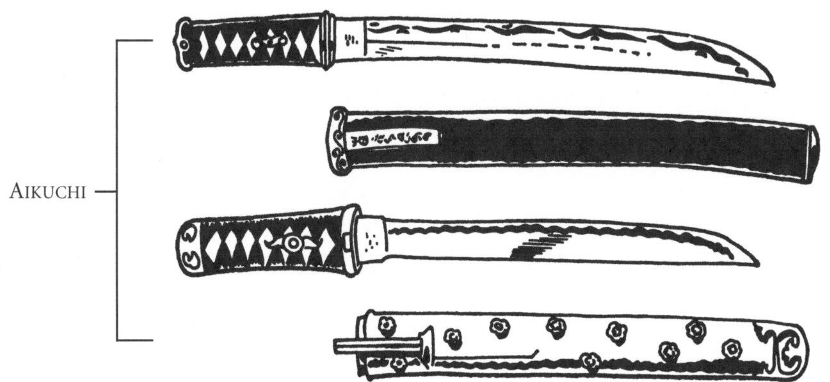

spiritual and political-military power and, of course, the personality of the man wielding it. This symbolism was reflected in every event related, whether directly or indirectly, to the *katana.* Harrison writes, for example, that "considering the exaggerated veneration in which the native *katana* has been held from the earliest times, it is not surprising that the occupation of a swordsmith should in feudal days have been regarded as an honourable profession, the members of which were men of gentle blood" (Harrison, 177). Such an occupation was considered "pleasing [to] the gods and...as a necessary preparation for success, the smith must lead a more or less religious life, abstaining from excesses of all kinds" (Gilbertson[2], 191). The casting of a sword was, therefore, a religious ceremony. For the occasion, the ancient smith (as well as those of later periods)

> clad himself in his ceremonial dress and wore the *jeboshi* or small lacquered hat, while a *shimenawa* or straw rope was stretched across the smithy, with *gohei* suspended from it, to scare away evil spirits and invite the presence of good ones. We are even informed that when Munechika was forging the *koritsure* sword, and his assistant failed him, the god Inarisama came and helped him at the critical moment" (Gilbertson[2], 191)

The swordsmith's skill was so highly regarded that even an emperor (Gotoba, 1184–98), taught by Ichimonji Norimune, forged sword blades. This emperor is credited with having given a great impetus to swordcasting by summoning twelve provincial smiths, selected for their exceptional skill, to Kyoto, where each worked for the emperor for one month of the year. There were other smiths held in reserve, should any one of the original twelve selected not be able to fulfill his duty at court, and another set of twenty-four smiths who also served, two in each month. Furthermore, a third group of six smiths from the province of Oki *(oki-no-bankaji)* also made swords for the emperor.

The twelfth and the thirteenth centuries are considered the great ages of Japanese smiths. Names such as the *sanhei,* the three smiths of Bizen: Kanehira, Sukehira, and Takahira; the *sanjo* smiths of Kyoto: Yoshiie, Arikuni, Kanenaga; the *san-saku,* or "three master-makers": Masamune, Yoshimitsu, and Yoshihiro; and countless others are engraved upon the best blades of the period. All these blades are defined in the history of sword casting as being old *(koto),* to differentiate them from those forged after 1596, which are qualified as new *(shinto).*

The forging of blades (a long and very complex process) was surrounded with ritual secrecy, and technical details were transmitted, in accordance with the Japanese cultural pattern of craftsmanship, from father to son, thus making many a family name famous for the excellence of its blades. Each smith had his own method of forging, his own technique for the blending of iron and steel, of testing the materials, and so forth. These professional or trade secrets he transmitted to his heirs, whether natural or adopted. These heirs, in turn, were required to swear a solemn oath never to divulge the method they were taught to anyone outside the family. In this connection, "there is a story that Masamune, when tempering a blade in the presence of another smith, saw him furtively put his hand into the water to ascertain its temperature, and struck it off with the sword" (Gilbertson[2], 196).

The personality, often very impressive, of the individual smith, was thought to be reflected or animistically embodied in the blades he forged. The records of sword making list prominently, for example, Senzo Muramasa, born in 1341 in the village of Senji, who was a pupil of the great Masamune. This compelling figure "was a most skillful smith but of a violent and ill-balanced mind verging on madness, that was supposed to have passed into his blades....They were popularly believed to hunger for blood and to impel their wearer to commit murder or suicide" (Gilbertson[2], 204). Such blades were considered unlucky for everyone, and especially for the Tokugawa family, "Iyeyasu having been twice accidentally wounded by them. At the battle of Sekigahara, Nagatake cut through the crest of the helmet of Toda Shigemasa, and Iyeyasu wished to see the weapon he had used. While examining it he cut himself and observed that it must

be a Muramasa blade, as it proved to be" (Gilbertson[2], 204). Consequently, notwithstanding their high quality of temper and manufacture, such blades were qualified as ignoble or bloodthirsty and unworthy by official experts such as Honami Kotobu, and were struck off the records of the experts' guild. The blades of Muramasa's master, Masamune, on the contrary, were considered not only blades of excellent quality and craftsmanship but also "morally worthy." This attitude toward blades was steeped in occultism: "There were unlucky ones; those bringing happiness and longevity; and *hin-ken,* swords giving wealth and power" (Gilbertson[2], 203).

Concerning the selection of the basic metals for casting and the methods of blending these metals, we have only fragmentary information. Gilbertson informs us that the main ingredients (iron and steel of "excellent quality") were derived from deposits of magnetic iron ore and ferruginous sand. One method of forging described by this author involved the welding of a strip of steel to a rod of iron (which acted as a handle) upon which other strips were welded into the required shape and length before the blade was split lengthwise, then folded and welded again innumerable times. He calculated that such a process, repeated many times, with alternate immersions in water and oil of graduated temperature, would result in a bar "composed of 4,194,304 layers of metal in its thickness" (Gilbertson[2], 191). The sword blade itself was usually composed of pure steel. A large number, however, were combinations of iron and steel. One of the most popular types "was the *sam-mai,* or 'three-plate' style in which a plate of steel was placed between two plates of iron, the steel of course forming the edge" (Gilbertson[2], 192). This type of blade is said to have been particularly favored by the smiths of Bizen, while Masamune preferred the *muku-gitai* or *tsukuri* method, which called for steel only.

The most important phase of the sword-casting process was usually considered to be the tempering of the blade, which resulted in "the production of the *yakiba* or tempered steel-edge of the blade, the clouded band, usually from ¼" to ½" broad, running along the edge of the sword, sometimes as a simple straight band, sometimes with very peculiar outlines" (Gilbertson[2], 195). For this purpose, the blade was encased in a protective mass of clay and the edge worked on between fire and warm water. This phase was so highly specialized "that we find it sometimes recorded on the tang that it was tempered by such a smith, the forging being done by another, and in one case it only mentions the name of the temperer" (Gilbertson[2], 197).

Once forged and tempered, the blade was scraped with a special knife *(sen)* and filed down before being ground on a special stone *(to-ishi)* for as many as fifty days, "the surface being gone over as many as 120 times" (Gilbertson[2], 198). This was followed by polishing on an oiled stone and a final rubbing with

composed flakes. The smith then placed his signature on the tang and completed any additional engraving or cutting of grooves on the blade. He then burnished it with a polishing needle, or *migari-hari;* this was generally done in winter because it was believed that newly polished swords were particularly susceptible to rust in summer.

It is not surprising, then, when one considers the importance of this weapon in the eyes of the samurai and the ritualistic regimentation of Japanese culture in the feudal era, that the capacity of "reading a blade, seeing and knowing the marks that indicate by whom and when it was made" became a highly sophisticated "art requiring not only special faculties and knowledge, but long experience" (Gilbertson[2], 194). For, as Gilbertson aptly pointed out, every warrior (from the highest-ranking daimyo to the humblest retainer) knew that "his hand had to keep his head" and that this was more easily accomplished with a trustworthy, and thus valuable, blade.

Because of the high monetary value assigned to quality blades, there were many skilled forgeries of the blades produced by master smiths and their best pupils. As a consequence, the authorities created a category of official experts *(mekiki)* "whose function it was to determine the origin and quality of a weapon, signed or unsigned, to estimate its pecuniary value, and to instruct samurai how to arrive at similar conclusions" (Gilbertson[2], 199). Certain experts were particularly honored for their learned opinions, their names being engraved in the annals of this art. The Honami family (active for more than twelve generations), for example, provided the experts entrusted with the imperial sword in the early part of the ninth century. From the twelfth century onward, such experts evaluated sword blades and signed a

> certificate or *ori kami* (folded paper)...written on a sheet of peculiar thick paper called *kaga bosho* made for the shogun in the province of Kaga, 100 sheets of which were delivered yearly. It stated the name and residence of the maker of the blade, its length and mentioned any peculiarity by which it could be recognized, adding an opinion as to its value in gold. This was signed by the *mekiki,* sometimes by more than one, and the seal or seals added on the other side of the paper. (Gilbertson[2], 200)

Thus this art, too, developed its own ritual, its own etiquette, and its own theory and practice of appreciation. A host considered it a great honor to be complimented by his guests on the beauty and quality of his swords, which were usually displayed. The procedure for examining blades was minutely regulated, as were the well-defined patterns of gestures and comments required of all who were involved in such a

ceremony. The blades were unsheathed gradually (but never completely), using clean tissue to touch the metal parts, inching them forward in various ways toward the light, "for it will be found it is only at a given angle of incidence that certain interesting details become visible" (Gilbertson[2], 199).

No mere symbol of power or object of admiration, however, the *katana* was a fearsome weapon in the hand of a man who depended so completely upon it and identified himself so closely with it. The study of the art of swordsmanship, known as kenjutsu, was considered one of primary importance. In fact:

> When in the West fencing is spoken of, men understand that they are referring to an art the principles of which have been reduced almost to an exact science....But it was never admitted in Japan that the possibility of *katana* fencing had been exhausted. In every age numbers of men devoted their whole lives to acquire novel skill in swordsmanship. Many of them invented systems of their own which received special names and differed from one another in some subtle details unknown to any save the master himself and his favorite pupils. (Brinkley[1], 137)

That the *bushi* was well versed in the use of this weapon has been attested to by sources that cannot be accused of being overly partial to the Japanese. For example, "a Chinese historian, referring to the Japanese invasion of Korea at the close of the XVIth century, says of the samurai in action that 'he brandished a 5-foot blade with such rapidity that nothing could be seen except a white sheen of metal, the soldier himself being invisible'" (Brinkley[1], 154). Every aspect of fencing was explored and highly sophisticated techniques were devised, tested, and applied in several styles (such as the *kumi-uchi, tachi-kaki,* and *tachi-uchi),* the majority of which could be employed both on the battlefield and in solitary encounters. The *ryu* of kenjutsu proliferated from the ninth century onward, and the names of many of these schools appear in the chronicles of bujutsu again and again. It has been said that at the end of the Tokugawa period, after the lengthy Tokugawa dictatorship, there were over two hundred active schools of kenjutsu. Among the oldest (that is, those which traced their beginnings all the way back to the fourteenth and fifteenth centuries), the chronicles list the Nen *ryu* of Yoshimoto Sanashiro; the Shinto *ryu* of Iishino Yamashiro-no-Kami Ienao, better known as Iishino Choisai; the Aisu-Kuge *ryu* of Aisu Iso (1452-1538), who taught kenjutsu to the warriors of the Yagyu clan; the schools of Chugo Nagahide, Fukida Bungu-ro, and In-ei, who was also known as a skillful master of spearmanship; the Itto *ryu;* and the esoteric Koto-eiri *ryu,* which taught effective techniques to be used against several swordsmen attacking at the same time.

Parry and double cut with body-leverage on katana

Evasive turn and double cut with katana

Notwithstanding the policy of strict secrecy adopted by various *sensei,* the methods and techniques practiced in each school of kenjutsu were usually influenced by (and influenced in turn) the methods and techniques practiced in other fencing schools. Kami-izumi Ise-no-Kami Hidetsuna, the founder of the Shinkage *ryu,* had studied and mastered the styles of the Aisaka *ryu* and the Shinto *ryu* before developing his own style, which combined elements of both. Referred to by a provincial lord as a man worth sixteen spearmen, this interesting kenjutsu master declined to join the powerful clan of Takeda Shingen after his own clan had been disbanded in 1563. Instead, he traveled across Japan (followed by his best students) teaching and giving fencing demonstrations. During the course of his travels he engaged in seventeen mortal duels, emerging from each without a scratch. By the time he finally settled at Fushimi, he had won a place in the imperial records as a teacher of the fourth rank. Moreover, the example he set was not unique. As Brinkley noted:

> Out of this perpetual effort on the part of hundreds of experts to discover and perfect novel developments in swordsmanship, there grew a habit which held its vogue down to modern times; namely,

> that when a man had mastered one style of sword-play in the school of a teacher, he set himself to study all others and for that purpose undertook a tour throughout the provinces, fencing whenever he found an expert and, in the event of defeat, constituting himself the victor's pupil. (Brinkley[1], 139)

Competition through direct confrontations and continual testing of abilities was merciless, since "defeat often meant ruin. A fencing master with a well-attended school, and a substantial income from the lord of a fief (whose warriors he trained in the Art) might find himself discredited for carrying on the former and deprived of the latter, in the sequel of an encounter with an itinerant expert" (Brinkley[1], 139-40). Victory, on the other hand, meant not only the attainment of a position of prestige within Japanese feudal society and thus the possibility of unlocking many doors; it also brought substantial material advantages, not the least of which was an assured income.

As indicated in Part 1, affiliated *sensei* who taught kenjutsu were accorded a high position in the clan hierarchy; they were relatively independent within their schools and often well paid. But even unaffiliated masters of the sword benefited from the age-old custom of indirect patronage which prompted the authorities to vie with one another in lavishing upon these champions and their teachers valuable gifts and impressive titles, even when the bond of direct clan affiliation was not established. In this context, there seems to have been a noticeable tendency on the part of established *sensei* to refrain, as far as possible, from direct confrontations with other fencing teachers or with any of the innumerable traveling champions who were always ready, and usually eager, to issue a challenge at the mere mention of a reputation. Advancing age, prudence, and, of course, fits of cowardice (all carefully concealed behind the protective screen of the clan organization) kept most affiliated kenjutsu instructors well insulated in their schools. There were always exceptional teachers to whom none of the above considerations applied, but they were in the minority then, as now. Many a student of the art of fencing, however, risked his life time and time again in an effort to establish that reputation which would enable him to become the head of his own school. Many of these young swordsmen practiced in one school after another, challenging other swordsmen (even those from distant provinces) and filling the world of bujutsu with lively expectation, as various experts and their masters debated styles and characteristics, in a fashion reminiscent of the intense betting fervor aroused among the patrician classes of imperial Rome by gladiatorial champions, or among the kings and barons of the Middle Ages in Europe, as they wagered fiercely on their favorite knights in each tournament. Particularly famous in Japanese chronicles of the age is the duel which took place on an island between Miyamoto Musashi, a stylist of the Nito *ryu,* and another swordsman, Sasaki Kojiro—the preparation for which extended over a span of years. Sasaki lost both the duel and his life.

Gradually, legislation was enacted in an effort to curb the shedding of blood in contests of fencing skill. Training with live blades in the *dojo* of pre-Tokugawa Japan had already been restricted in most cases to inanimate targets such as human-shaped *maki-wara* made of rice straw or, when against a live opponent, to that ritualistically controlled style known as *kata,* which is employed today in those schools where Japanese fencing with a live blade is still practiced. The use of an exercise sword made of wood *(bokuto),* which became widely known as the *bokken,* greatly increased the range of kenjutsu practice. But in time, the *bokken* itself grew to be a weapon with lethal possibilites in the hands of an expert who knew how to concentrate the full force of his blows upon vital parts of his opponent's anatomy. Contests of skill with wooden swords, which often resembled bloody duels with live blades, became increasingly frequent. And, since a student's natural tendency was to exercise less restraint and caution when using the *bokken* to deliver his blows, certain *sensei* adopted protective equipment in the post-Tokugawa schools of swordsmanship. Drawn from the basic elements of the warrior's suit of armor, the following were often used: a padded headgear *(men)* with an iron grid to protect the face; a chest protector *(do)* made from bamboo stalks; a thick apron with flaps; and, finally, wrist shields *(kote).* During the early part of the nineteenth century, these elements were adapted and combined to form the sturdy, highly polished uniform used in the practice of modern kendo.

Back counterattack with double turn.

Double cut with evasive turn on knee

Training with live blades

The main fencing art was, naturally, kenjutsu: the art of the *katana*, the regular sword. The ancient techniques developed for the sword seem to have been codified (but by no means exhausted) in 1350 by Choisai and Jion who, accordingly, are considered the originators of the major system of fencing used in individual confrontations in feudal Japan. Their system was one of the most rigorous and precise, being based upon the warrior's code of ethics and using its norms to regulate all the phases of sword-play: the initial preparation for combat; the posture and unsheathing of the weapon; the basic displacements and the strategies of attack, defense, and counterattack; the techniques applied; and, of course, the particular targets to be hit. Warriors who respected themselves, their opponents, and the rules of orthodox fencing were required to introduce themselves and state their reasons for engaging in combat. This requirement was even honored, when possible, in the heat of combat on the battlefield. After composing themselves, the duelists would unsheathe their weapons and advance slowly until they were the proper distance from each other. Each would then assume the posture appropriate to the strategy he intended to apply. From this point, the techniques would usually develop with blinding speed and total commitment. Certain techniques were clearly identified by number, name, or functionality. Brinkley wrote, for example, that

> 16 varieties of cut are delivered with the Japanese sword, and each has its own name, as the "four-sides cut," the "clearer," the "wheel stroke," the "peak blow," the "torso severer," the "pear splitter," the "thunder stroke," the "scarf sweep," and so on; appellations rather fanciful than descriptive, but of course, conveying an exact meaning to Japanese ears. (Brinkley[1], 142)

Particularly famous was the whiplike motion of the blade known as *kisagake,* which could be developed into any one of the techniques mentioned above.

The various techniques were generally divided into two main groups, the first comprising the techniques of cutting *(kiri)* and those of thrusting *(tsuki)* used in attack and counterattack, the second comprising the parries used in defense. Their targets were also clearly identified. According to orthodox canons of fencing, "no soldier was proud of having wounded an enemy in any other manner than the one established by strict samurai rule. The long sword had for its goal only four points: the top of the head, the wrist, the side, and the leg below the knee" (Sugimoto, 109). This author, in particular, seems to have been referring to the highly regulated canons of modern kendo, whose repertoire she interpreted as having been derived from the ancient norms of orthodox kenjutsu. The existence of innumerable secret styles of fencing, however, and the stern warnings left by many *sensei* concerning the degrading use of certain practices, would seem to indicate that observance of the code of orthodox fencing, whatever its content and significance for the

Various postures of readiness in one-or two-sword encounter

Iai draw and vertical cut in a formal exercise of iaido

members of the *buke* (or, for that matter, for the members of any other social class), was by no means a general phenomenon. Experts abounded who would study the techniques of orthodox fencing and then devise appropriate counter-measures—many of which were not in accordance with the standards of bushido. Unpredictable cuts, thrusts, and parries directed against any available target; various psychological devices intended to disturb an opponent's concentration; and continual reliance upon the element of tactical surprise were all said to have been so widely employed and to have characterized the styles of so many swordsmen that, for all intents and purposes, these "ignoble" techniques would appear to have been the norm rather than the exception. Almost every student of kenjutsu fancied himself the possessor of a secret, unique, and irresistible way of penetrating every other swordsman's defense with the razor-sharp edge of his *katana.* His teachers were forever busy devising new strategic ways of using this weapon, whether alone or in combination with other weapons (their individual interpretations often becoming skilled and self-sufficient subspecializations of kenjutsu).

The initial movement or drawing of the sword became a major art in its own right (iaijutsu). This art was based upon instantaneous, coordinated speed in unsheathing the sword and delivering a searing and often fatal blow as a continuation of the unsheathing motion. Particularly suited to an armed encoun-

ter in the course of daily life, as opposed to combat on the battlefield where weapons were already unsheathed, iaijutsu could be employed without warning against an unwary opponent or against one or more adversaries preparing to attack. One of the first Western observers of feudal Japan, Alessandro Valignano, S.J., (1539-1606) marveled at the speed with which a swordsman could kill his opponent with "the first or second blow" of his sword (Cooper, 45). The use of iaijutsu in this context against an opponent who had not yet drawn his own weapon from its scabbard often lent a certain air of disrepute to the art, however. The adjective "treacherous" crops up frequently in many records, and, in numerous instances where iaijutsu was used (or, rather, misused), this characterization would seem to have been justified. Many a warrior and scores of unsuspecting *heimin* (regardless of sex or age) fell beneath a sudden arc of steel slashing through the air either to take professional advantage of the possibility of tactical surprise when facing a potentially dangerous opponent—or merely to test the edge of a *katana* on a human body, in what became known as "crossroad cutting" (McClatchie[3], 62), "practice murder," "practice killings," or "sword-testing murders" (Butler, 131). There were a number of Japanese students of bujutsu who maintained that the use of this particular subspecialization of swordsmanship against a warrior who had not yet drawn his own weapon was still a legitimate application of kenjutsu, since a warrior was expected to be ready to confront danger at any moment, especially in a world dominated (as was feudal Japan) by the professional fighter. Such a justification loses its force, however, when the victims were commoners *(heimin)* who were not professional fighters and, moreover, were, actually forbidden by law to carry weapons. And it is admissible only with a certain reluctance, even in relation to the *bushi* themselves, when a warrior used the art to catch another unsuspecting warrior completely off-guard, since their professional code of ethics called for at least a minimum of openness and sincerity in indicating one's intentions.

Iaijutsu seems to have been a perfectly justifiable (and often imperative) mode of swordplay, however, when used in almost simultaneous counterattack against an opponent who was obviously about to, or actually in the act of, unsheathing his sword with deadly intent. The most reputable masters of kenjutsu, in fact, trained their students to respond immediately and effectively to this relevant possibility. A swordsman proficient in iaijutsu had to be able to discern instantaneously the technique his opponent was about to employ, so that he might direct his almost simultaneous counterattack in a direction his opponent's blade could not block while in flight. A vivid example of iaijutsu is offered in the final sequence of Kurosawa's film *Sanjuro,* where two swordsmen confront each other, swords in their scabbards. After an almost unbearable interval of dramatic tension, there is a sudden burst of action: one warrior unsheathes his sword, cutting down from above with the classic downward slash to the head, while, almost simultaneously, the other surges up from below, cutting across his opponent's chest with a sword held in the left hand. The second warrior's cut was the mortal blow. These romanticized versions of the art of instantaneous draw are, of course, hardly to be considered representative of reality. Many warriors were skilled in iaijutsu, and, usually, when two so evenly matched samurai challenged each other, both swordsmen would be either severely wounded or actually killed, which was known as mutual slaying.

In order to be instantaneous and effective, a response in iaijutsu had to be based upon the ability to act (or react) instinctively to a suddenly dangerous situation. As a principle, this condition of instinctive reactivity applied to all the specializations of bujutsu, but in iaijutsu in particular and in kenjutsu in general,

Iai draws and exercises

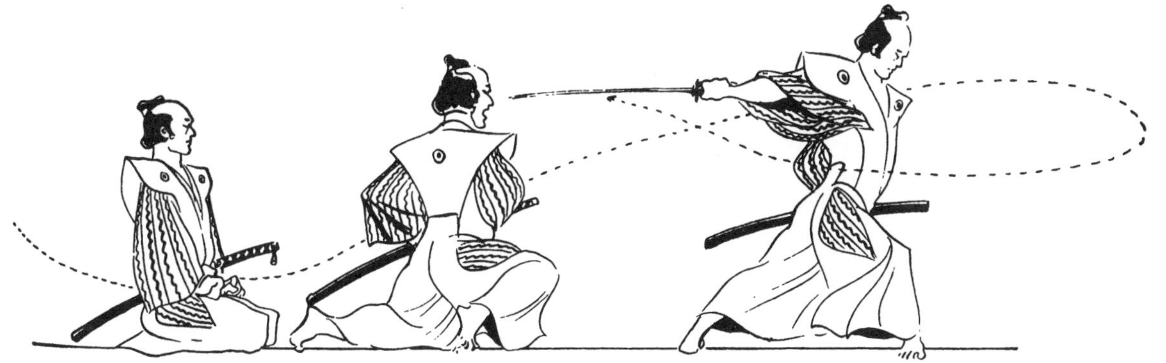

Iai draw as seen in Sanjuro

it was raised to unparalleled levels of coordinated response, dependent upon the development of the inner factors of bujutsu (Part 3). The techniques and basic training exercises of this art were represented by a progressively more difficult series of actions and reactions against both mobile and static targets, limited only by the imagination of the individual teacher. For example, at the sound of a sharp command, a warrior squatting in the middle of a mat (often blindfolded) would rise, his sword being instantly unsheathed in a single, fluid, and circular motion as he slashed at the four or more targets set on poles which had been placed at the borders of the mat. Without any interruption of the initial sweeping motion, he would return his sword to its scabbard and resume his squatting position. The time it took him to accomplish the entire sequence was duly computed and reduced to a flashing moment by rigorous, continuous training. In each kenjutsu school, accordingly, much time and effort was devoted to the techniques of iaijutsu and particular training programs were developed and transmitted in the utmost secrecy to those students who would remain linked to the school or who would swear never to reveal the method to anyone else if they left the school for any reason. Often practiced alone against fixed or mobile targets, the art of iaijutsu lent itself easily to systematic codification into formal exercises and sequences of prearranged movements *(kata).* As was true of kenjutsu, it also developed into a particular discipline of coordination based upon stern concentration and intense determination in the performance of a particular action, once decided upon. This discipline was expanded and refined until it entered the spiritual and religious dimensions of man's existence and, as such, became known as *iaido,* the way of iai, a name still used today in those schools wherein the ancient *kata* of iaijutsu (in somewhat modified form, of course) are practiced, that is, the Katori-Shinto, the Hasegawa, the renowned Yagyu, the Omori, the Mukai, and others.

The *bushi* also learned the techniques of other, minor subspecializations of kenjutsu. He could usually fence equally well with the short sword *(wakizashi)* or the intermediate sword *(chisa-katana),* using techniques substantially identical to those developed for the *katana,* although adapted to shorter distances. He also explored in detail the strategic efficiency of the *nodachi,* the long sword usually worn on the back with the handle jutting out behind the shoulder. The technical perfection of kenjutsu reached heights of unparalleled beauty and efficiency with the simultaneous use of two blades: the *katana* and the *wakizashi* or *chisa-katana,* in the so-called two-sword style of fencing *(nito)* made famous by Miyamoto Musashi in his school, the Nito *ryu.* Immensely complex and difficult, finally, were those techniques which called for the use of one or two swords against several opponents armed with swords or spears. These techniques were based upon displacements in which circular movements *(tai-sabaki)* in the form of gliding pivots and spins predominated. Performed either standing or sliding under the line of convergence being described by the encircling opponents, a warrior would deliver circular cuts in accordance with the zigzag style, the interlacing cross, the reversed dragonfly, the waterwheel, the eight-sides-at-once, and others—all of which were the specialties of particular fencing schools usually frequented by *bushi* of the higher ranks only.

The warrior was also expected to excel in the use of all the daggers, stilettos, and so forth that were usually carried with the regular brace of swords *(daisho),* often in the scabbard with the short sword. Diosy wrote that "the *ko-gatana,* a knife which fitted one side of the scabbard of the *wakizashi,* the short sword or dirk, was put to various uses. With it the 'coup de grace' was given to an enemy, the little knife being driven into his heart, and it was sometimes used as a missile, swordsmen being very skillful in throwing it" (Diosy[1], 100). Using or throwing a dagger or a knife, whether moving or standing still, and whatever the illumination (often in total darkness, or when blindfolded), developed into an art (tantojutsu) in which the women of the *buke* often became quite skilled. These women carried the dirk *(kaikeri)* on their persons at all times, this weapon being for them what the *katana* was for their male counterparts.

Even the *sage-o,* the strong silken cord (thought to have been derived from the cord slings which secured the ancient long sword or *tachi* to the warrior's belt and, later, fastened the *katana* to his girdle or *obi)* was employed in a particular way before a match, when the warrior was not in armor. This cord

Simultaneous draw

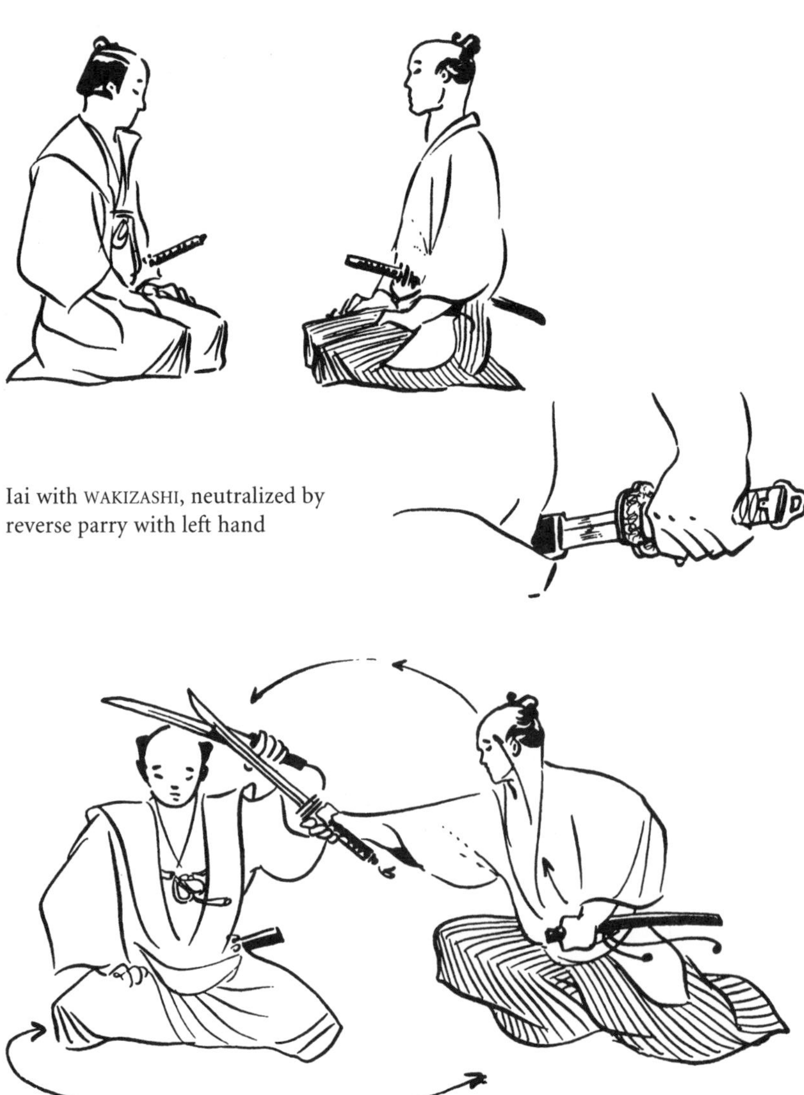

Iai with WAKIZASHI, neutralized by reverse parry with left hand

Iai from a sitting position

NODACHI in normal attire and in armor

> was drawn out of the *kurikata* (loop on the scabbard) when the swordsman prepared for action and [was] thrown, with wonderful rapidity, over the shoulders and tied behind the back, catching up the fullness of the wide sleeves and thus baring the forearms. This action of throwing and tying the *sage-o* was performed in an incredibly short space of time. (Diosy[1], 100)

This cord could also be used in other ways, such as securing a prisoner or climbing a wall, just like the ropes and cords found in the *bushi's* battlefield equipment.

Finally, there was that long pin *(kogai)* bearing the warrior's crest, which he carried in a special niche on the scabbard of his short sword or his shorter dagger. This "blunt, little *kogai* had many uses" (Sugimoto, 109). According to Stone, who quotes Sugimoto:

> "It was the key that locked the sword in the scabbard; when double it could be used as chopsticks *(hashi)* by the marching soldiers; and it has been used on the battlefield, or in retreat, mercifully to pierce the ankle of a suffering and dying comrade, and it had the unique use in a clan feud, when found sticking upright in the ankle of a dead foe, of bearing the silent challenge, 'I await thy return.' Its crest told to whom it belonged and, in time, it generally returned to its owner's ankle." (Stone, 370)

Usually, the warrior to whom the *kogai* belonged would also leave a full statement, signed and sealed, in which he took full responsibility for the deed and explained his reasons. This pin could also be used to avoid contamination on the battlefield:

> In the days of continual civil war in Japan, it was the custom to decapitate a fallen foe, if a warrior of any importance, and to present his head to the Chief or General, as a proof of prowess in battle. Now, a samurai could not touch a corpse without being defiled, but the *kogai,* stuck into the *mage,* or top-knot of hair, formed a handle by which the ghastly trophy could be carried without fear of contamination. (Diosy[1], 101)

The two-sword style of fighting

Two-sword fighting

The cult of the sword (even during the period of military supremacy when the Tokugawa ruled the land) had deeply rooted national connotations. If long blades were generally restricted to the warriors, there seemed to be a widespread use of shorter blades throughout the land by almost anyone who could afford them. As Jonas pointed out:

> The privilege of wearing swords was enjoyed only by the military class, but civilians when going on long journeys took the liberty of carrying a small dagger as a protection against robbers or to be used in case of necessity should unprovoked quarrels be thrust upon them on the way. This class of weapon was called *dochu wakizashi* ("traveling small sword") and *ayatate* carried by travellers and resembling such a sword in shape was known *asyatate wakizashi.* The part representing the sheath was so contrived as to hold the money required for traveling expenses instead of a blade, while the hilt contained the inkpot and brush. (Jonas, 121)

Today, of the ancient forms of kenjutsu and all its subspecializations, there are only a few, strongly modified forms extant in Japan, many of which are embodied in the highly ritualized exercises *(kata)* of *kumi-tachi* (live blades being used). Bouts with wooden swords *(bokken)* are also staged between students of these ancient disciplines of the sword. It is the art of kendo, however, which represents the most popular modern derivation of feudal fencing, whether practiced as a discipline of integration or adapted to the competitive dimension of modern sport. This discipline has its own particular weapons, techniques, ranks, and purposes, all of which are heavily impregnated with the tradition of the ancient art of Japanese swordsmanship. The sword used, for example, is a staff *(shinai;* ancient, *chikuto)* made of four sections of bamboo tightly fastened together in the shape of a straight sword, with a guard *(tsuba)* and long handle for double grasping. It is said to have been invented by Master Nakanishi Chuzo of Edo (in 1750) in order to minimize or eliminate the danger of injuries in the practice of swordsmanship, a danger ever present when real swords *(katana)* or even wooden ones *(bokken)* are used. The protective equipment worn by the kendo student is similar to that worn by students of the art of naginata and includes the head protector *(men),* the chest protector *(do)* with an apron *(tare),* hip pads *(koshi-ate),* the pleated, divided skirt *(hakama),* and finally the gauntlets *(kote).*

The basic kendo techniques are divided into three major groups: cuts *(kiri),* thrusts *(tsuki),* and parries *(katsugi).* Targets include the head, which must be hit frontally or at the sides, the throat, the sides of the

chest, and the hands or wrists. Each target is usually announced before striking, one blow being followed by another without any hesitation or pause. The techniques of kendo in the various stages of combat (attack, defense, and counterattack) are initiated from fundamental stances known as *kamae.* Balance in dynamic readiness is all-important in defense because of the comparative impregnability afforded by these stances, as well as the deadly counterattacks they make possible. From the basic stances, a variety of techniques can be developed in attack, defense, or counterattack (all, however, being characteristically linear or frontal in execution). The ranking system of kendo, like that of kyudo, is divided into two main categories: that of the *kyu,* or students below the black-belt level (usually subdivided into five or six ranks), and that of the *dan,* or practitioners above black-belt level (also subdivided into ten or eleven ranks, including trainers *[renshi],* instructors *[kyoshi],* and masters *[hanshi]).*

The purposes of kendo, as indicated, have progressed from strictly utilitarian, ritualistic, or ceremonial aims, associated with earlier forms of fencing, to those of integration for the development of the personality (typical of religions or philosophies at their highest levels). We should recall in this connection that, even in ancient times, many masters proclaimed that swordsmanship was intended to improve the character of the man wielding the sword—the improvement thus being not only functional in the sense of producing a more efficient fighter, but intrinsic in the sense of producing a better man. Traditionally, then, greater emphasis has been placed upon style, behavior, and character development in kendo than on mere effectiveness with the *shinai.* According to modern observers, however, there are indications that kendo (like kyudo) is beginning to respond to the pressure of competition for the sake of scoring, which is typical of utilitarian sports. Complaints have even been voiced that, with this increasing emphasis upon winning, the raison d'etre of kendo as a discipline of integration (that is, its form, style, training in concentration and mental extension), as well as the way in which a kendo man "won," may undergo a radical, even if gradual, transformation, with the consequent possibility that kendo may become a martial art method deprived of its traditional substance.

The Art of Military Horsemanship

The ancient *bushi* of the upper ranks was, by definition, the "knight on horseback," riding into battle at the head of his troops (both officers and foot soldiers). He had obviously mastered the art of horsemanship during the early centuries of the feudal era, as evidenced by the bronze and iron cheek-plates and muzzles found in Japanese dolmens.

Horsemanship had been considered an aristocratic art as early as the Heian period. It had, however, progressively lost much of its original appeal as the court nobles, modifying the ancient practices of their formerly warlike clans into the sophisticated forms of "civilized" methods of violence, eventually came to consider skill in the martial arts so vulgar that, in 1159, a captain of the guards of the Outer Palace could not even mount a horse properly, his awkward attempts arousing the jeers of provincial warriors standing nearby (Morris, 165).

Even during the earliest recorded periods, the *bushi's* house (i.e., the central residence of the clan to which he belonged) seems to have included a number of large stables as well as areas on the grounds where horses could be trained and kept, but there is no way of pinpointing exactly where and when the horse was introduced into Japan. According to certain scholars, this animal actually carried the immigrant waves of southern conquerors to Yamato. In any case, the horse used by the Japanese "knight on horseback" seems to have been the typical Asiatic pony, similar to the type used by the Chinese and Koreans, as well as by those Mongolian cavalrymen who actually were born among horses and spent their lives with and on them. The Japanese breed was probably crossed with various continental blood-lines, since these martial animals were often mentioned in the lists of royal gifts exchanged between the Chinese court and that of the Japanese emperor. In time, the breeding of horses became the specialty of certain clans, each having its own jealously guarded method. Horses bred by the Nambu clan, in particular, acquired great fame throughout Japan.

These animals were apparently smaller than the European or Arabian strains (in certain illustrations the horse appears dwarfed by the warrior and his voluminous armor), but extremely strong, surprisingly fast, and capable of executing highly sophisticated maneuvers. It was said to be "notoriously bad-tempered" (Stone, 461); an experienced hand was obviously required to control such a steed at any time, but particularly in the tumult of battle. The ancient *bushi,* like the formidable Mongol warrior, seems to have been highly skilled in handling this animal. He usually wore a special type of armor *(uma-yoroi)* when mounted. This armor was originally lighter and more functional than that developed in the seventeenth century when armor became predominantly decorative. It was basically the same armor he wore when on foot, with the addition of certain items, such as the peculiar cape *(horo),* the higher shin guards *(sune-ate),* and longer thigh protectors *(haidate)* to offset the disadvantage of being in an elevated position and thus an easy target for enemy spears and swords in the melee of battle.

Unlike the mounts of the European armored knights of the Middle Ages, the *buski's* horse was not itself burdened with heavy armor. Its head was usually protected by chamfrons of iron, steel, or lacquered leather which followed the contours of the animal's head or represented mythical monsters. Its body armor was composed of small scales of padded or lacquered leather sewn onto cloth. The flanchards on the sides (hanging from the saddle), were made of large pieces of the same material molded and gilded. The crupper was usually rectangular in shape and covered the beast's hindquarters. Various types of muzzles, bridle bits *(kutsuwa),* cheek plates *(kangama-ita),* nose straps *(hanagawa),* and reins *(kutsu-wazura)* helped the rider to control and manage his spirited mount. These reins, made of a cord of silk or of cotton, were often heavily ornamented and tasseled *(atsu-busa).* The saddle with all its trappings *(kura-no-baju),* the pad and the girth *(harubi)* beneath it, were of a high type with the front and the back rising at right angles from the seat *(kura-tsubo).* This model, again, seems to have been of Chinese derivation. From the saddle hung the stirrups *(abumi, batto),* which in "pre-Yamato" times "had hooded toes and quite long iron straps for the stirrup leather" (Stone, 1). Some of these ancient stirrups had openings in the foot plate so that the water collected when crossing a river or stream might drain out *(suiba-abumi).* Later versions had "no sides [and] a foot-plate large enough for the entire foot to rest on...made entirely of iron or iron-frames filled in with wood" (Stone, 1). A flexible stick or riding whip *(muchi)* completed the *bushi's* riding costume.

Volumes have been devoted to the art of military horsemanship, known as jobajutsu when referring to horsemanship on land and suieijutsu or suibajutsu when designating horsemanship in or crossing bodies of water. Among these is a famous treatise written by Hitomi Sensai Munetsugu in 1613. The techniques described in this and other works covered a wide range, from mass involvement of cavalrymen to individual displacements in relation to enemy lines. Techniques of the first group are usually considered part of the science (or art) of warfare on a large scale, which, as we have noted previously, cannot be covered adequately

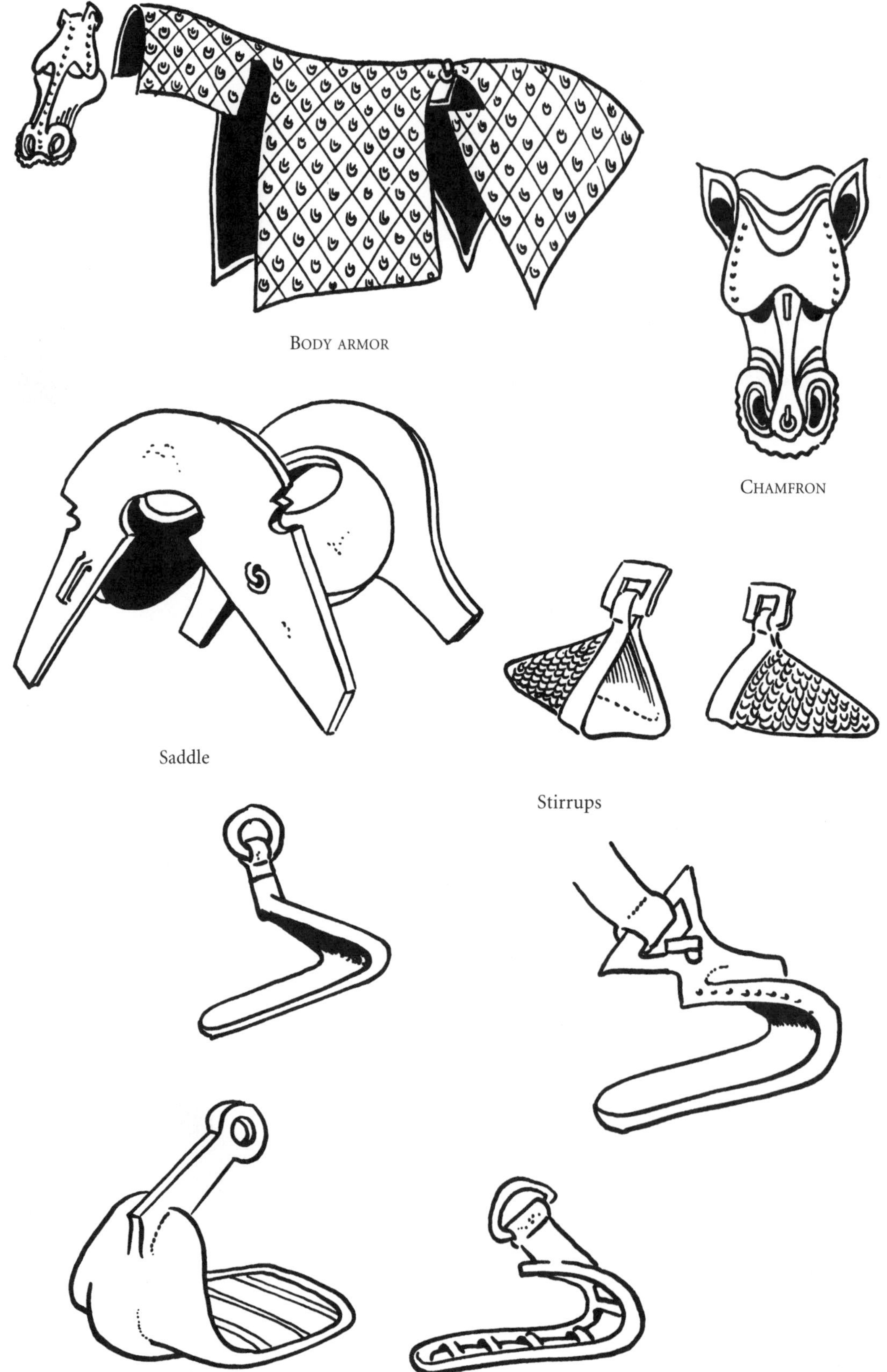

Body armor

Chamfron

Saddle

Stirrups

here. Those of the second group have not usually been dealt with in detail in most treatises on bujutsu, and the information we have been able to assemble is based mainly upon notes made by Westerners who had occasional opportunities to observe the Japanese cavalryman in action. Francesco Carletti, for example, wrote that the *bushi* used to mount the horse from the right side, throwing his weight onto the heel and not forward, as was the fashion in Europe (Cooper, 233). The warrior held the reins in both hands until ready to engage the enemy at close quarters, at which time he hooked them onto rings or hooks on his breastplate and controlled his steed with his knees (as well as by swaying his body in the desired direction).

The *bushi* on horseback would move toward the enemy lines, using an irregular pattern of convergence which made it extremely difficult for enemy archers to hit him, while he continually released his own arrows in their direction. Finally, at close quarters, his spear would be brought into play, or his long sword, as he wove in and out of enemy groups or engaged in single combat with another mounted warrior. In such an encounter, both horsemen would employ their mounts very much like two fighters on foot, in full mobility and perfect coordination of intention and execution. Under optimum conditions, the horse would be so in tune with his master's personality that he would seem to act instinctively, in full synchronization with his rider's movements, withdrawing (often whirling on his hindquarters) before a charge, rearing up to offer his rider the advantage of height for the delivery of a blow, or charging like a beast possessed into the thick of battle. Even at night, this animal could be used to stalk the enemy noiselessly, his bridle bound with a cloth and his mouth muffled in a special bag *(bat)*. These horses were also specially trained to ford the rivers, streams, and lakes which abound in Japan, techniques of horsemanship in the water being developed and practiced in those ponds usually found near the riding ranges which surrounded the houses of the major military clans.

Military horsemanship had a marked effect upon bujutsu, not only because it was a military specialization itself but because it involved all the other martial arts in a strategic rapport. Archery, spearmanship, swordsmanship, and techniques of unarmed combat were all directly affected, both from the standpoint of horsemen fighting one another and from the standpoint of horsemen battling warriors on foot. Horsemen, in fact, employed the methods of bujutsu in particular ways adapted to their elevated positions on moving steeds. Equestrian archery, as indicated earlier, was a highly developed subspecialization of kyujutsu. Special techniques of spearmanship were also developed to insure a better use of the spear from horseback, whether against another mounted warrior or one on foot, while hooked spears were used by foot soldiers in their attempts to unseat a mounted knight. Finally, there are many indications in the records and illustrated scrolls of the early feudal period that the *bushi's* horse was also mercilessly attacked with spears and arrows in an effort to bring his rider down. The long sword *(nodachi)*, like the heavy sword used by European armored knights, was also particularly adapted to equestrian swordsmanship and used according to precise techniques of kenjutsu against a peer on horseback or against the hordes of foot soldiers who would swarm around a mounted warrior. Even techniques of unarmed combat were sometimes used by a *bushi* against a mounted warrior, in (for example) the application of a hold based on the momentum of a *sutemi*—that is, a voluntary fall executed in such a way as to drag the warrior from his perch.

Horsemanship ceased to be a determinant factor on the battlefield much earlier in Japan than in Europe. As late as 1940, Polish cavalrymen were still hurling themselves against the armored divisions of the German Army. In Japan, on the other hand, the use of horses had been comparatively restricted, even among the *bushi* of the higher ranks during that country's feudal era, because of the prohibitive cost of breeding and keeping horses. In addition, the nature of Japanese terrain, with its islands, marshes, rice paddies, hills, and mountain ranges, was not particularly suited to the deployment of huge masses of cavalrymen which was common in Central Asia, in Central and Eastern Europe, even in North Africa and the Middle East. After 1600, moreover, the relative tranquility of the Tokugawa period and the absence of widespread warfare reduced horsemanship to a limited role, mainly in ceremonies intended to represent a function that had once been of major importance on the battlefield. It remained an exciting event in festivals such as the Yabusame, and there were always hunting expeditions, as well as pursuit of dogs within enclosed arenas. Then, too, horsemen usually accompanied the official corteges of provincial governors as they traveled to and from Edo, but the number of horses which the individual governors and chiefs of provinces could keep was carefully limited by the Tokugawa in the interest of maintaining effective military and political control. By the time Japan entered the modern era, the noble steed had disappeared for all intents and purposes into the history books.

The Art of Swimming in Armor

For an island people such as the Japanese, swimming has always been an almost natural accomplishment—almost as natural and necessary as breathing. Even today, Japanese fishermen and divers (especially the women who dive for pearls) are known the world over for their skill in the water; but this proficiency in swimming was not solely a natural technique developed in response to the Japanese environment. For the *bushi*, it was an art which could (and often had to be) used in combat. In Japan, battlefields always crisscrossed streams, rivers, and lakes, and many important battles took place on or near those expanses of water which separate one island from another or the various islands from the sea. Each of these particular types of water presented specific problems which the *bushi* had to face and for which, as a warrior, he had to be prepared. His problem was complicated by the fact that any swimming he might have to do would mean immersion while wearing a full suit of armor and carrying the full complement of weapons his station required.

Historically, the *buke* always paid great attention to maritime defense. The early Mongol invasions had taught the Japanese warrior not to rely solely upon coastal defense patterns of reflexive counterattack after the enemy had landed, but rather to actively seek to engage enemy forces while they were either poised for a landing or in the process of attempting to reach shore. According to the classic maritime text, the *Wakan Senyoshu,* as explained by Bonar in 1887, the Japanese had developed approximately forty-six types of vessels: twenty-one for fishing in coastal waters and twenty-five for navigation on the high seas. Among the vessels in the latter category were military vessels of smaller and more streamlined design than the commercial boats. They had specific functions and they carried contingents of warriors as military escorts. Among these we find the *o-mi-fune,* used by the emperor; the *suzu-fune,* used by the nobles of the ancient *kuge;* and the splendidly decorated vessels *(o-meshi-bune, goza-bune)* of the provincial governors. Warriors, however, employed certain types of boats which were extremely maneuverable combat units. One of the most widely used of these was the *kobaya,* a vessel without a deck or bridge, whose size ranged from those which could accommodate fifteen men (ten rowers, one helmsman, four warriors) to those large enough to hold twenty-seven (twenty rowers, one helmsman, six warriors), or even fifty-two (thirty-eight rowers, one helmsman, thirteen warriors).

Vessels with more than forty oarsmen were known as *seki-bune* and included a bridge and a deck. The contingent on these larger boats often rose to one hundred thirteen men (fifty-eight oarsmen, one helmsman, one captain, and fifty-three warriors), and, after the ascent to power of Hideyoshi, they were built to hold anywhere from one hundred eighty-one men (ninety oarsmen, three helmsmen, two captains, eighty-six warriors) to two hundred five men (one hundred rowers, two captains, three helmsmen, and one hundred warriors). The weapons carried on both types of ships were the traditional "lances, spears, bows and arrows" (Bonar, 115); after the sixteenth century, the *seki-bune* also carried one large gun and from twenty to twenty-two muskets. The difference between the *kobaya* and the *seki-bune* was based upon the tactical necessities of maritime warfare: speed, maneuverability, and concentrated power. The former two increased with the progressive diminution of the vessel, while the latter decreased proportionately. The early Japanese fleet employed the swift, elusive *kobaya* to infiltrate and disrupt the enemy fleet's united front—the *seki-bune* bearing down after them to engage the enemy in more direct and massive confrontations. For the *seki-bune,* therefore, which were notoriously "clumsy and difficult to propel . . . speed was never a consideration, and plenty of carrying capacity or fighting room was of more importance" (Bonar, 114). These ships, and the *kobaya* as well, were propelled by long oars *(ro)* in the frontal style preferred by eastern rowers,—the men faced the bow and pushed the oars ahead of them. In time of war, these oarsmen were often lightly armed and could thus engage the enemy in close combat once contact had been established. Both types of vessels used to bear down upon the enemy, while the *bushi* aboard ship released a steady stream of arrows with their long bows directed against selected and vital targets, such as the enemy helmsman, the captain, or the leaders of the military contingent (all of whom could usually be identified by their insignia or banners). As contact was actually established, spiked planks would be thrown across the water to link the ships, and the *bushi* would then rush aboard the enemy vessel, whirling their spears or long swords—oarsmen often taking their turn with bows and crossbows. On any solid surface, whether it rocked or not, the *bushi* in armor was in his element and could engage the enemy with the full concentration and professional skill he usually displayed on any battlefield. According to one author, swift carnage usually ensued. But the possibility of plunging into deep waters by accident, or the necessity of swimming through rough waters to rescue a leader or friend, was always present. A warrior could not always rely upon his oarsmen to rescue him if he should find himself struggling in the water and, consequently, had to be not only an able swimmer but, above all, one who could swim while wearing the panoply of armor which, even if not the cumbersome and highly ornamented type *(o-yoroi)* worn by his generals, was still quite heavy and compact.

Schools which specialized in and trained the warrior for this military form of swimming mushroomed in feudal Japan. They were usually attached to certain clans, though a few were comparatively independent. During the Tokugawa period, when training for combat was often a substitute for combat itself, they were particularly active. All these schools were concerned mainly with the techniques of swimming while outfitted in heavy armor *(katchu-gozen-oyogi)*. One school, the Kobo (Kobori) *ryu* of Kyushu, refined this specialization of bujutsu to an exceptional degree. Every school, however, concentrated upon the development of the *bushi's* capacity to employ his traditional weapons while fully immersed, and included techniques designed to enable a warrior to stay afloat for considerable lengths of time or swim long distances while wearing his armor. It should come as no surprise, then, to read of the *bushi's* often extraordinary skill in using the bow and arrow while in the water (remembering that the feathers of the arrows had to be kept dry if there was to be control over their trajectory). Swimming long distances was, as mentioned above, one of his proficiencies, often at night and even far from shore (a skill which made the Suifu *ryu* famous). The *bushi* also learned to use firearms while in the water, to carry the banner of his clan attached to a long pole, in the style made famous by the Yamanouchi *ryu*, and, of course, to fight in and under the water. The practice of swimming, therefore, was an integral part of military training, and very seldom, as we have indicated in the previous section, did the plan of a clan's central house fail to provide adequate room for a deep pond near the riding range or the martial arts practice halls where the techniques of swimming in armor could be assiduously practiced.

As late as the end of the nineteenth century, after the Meiji Restoration, the school programs of the new Japan still included special tests of skill in the water, with a type of competition whose military character was evident in its organization and execution, as well as in the weapons employed.

Matsudaira describes such a competition which took place in 1907:

> The whole number are divided into two parties, one wearing red caps and the other white caps, and each man wears also a small plate, *kawarake*, on his head, tied on with a string, and carries a straw-made stick held in his hand above water. Under the command of their respective leaders, both parties enter into combat, and at once the surface of the water becomes the center of mimic warfare. Fierce hand-to-hand fighting then takes place with the straw swords. Those who have their head-plates broken have to retire, and at last that party whose leader may have lost his plate is adjudged by our umpire to have been defeated. All these movements are carried out in sea or river where the water is very deep. (Matsudaira, 125)

Turning primarily to inland waters during both the early period of frequent civil wars and the long Tokugawa period which followed, many schools specialized in training warriors to handle themselves in the water according to the special nature, distance, depth, and force of the waters concerned. The Mukai *ryu* and the Shinden *ryu*, for example, accumulated a fund of knowledge concerning techniques which were useful in mastering the strong currents of rivers. Certain exercises *(sensu-morogaeshi)*, developed by the Mukai *ryu*, involved a paper fan which had to be kept above the rushing water (carefully held with fingers or toes) while the warrior was treading water, swimming, or floating. These forms are practiced even today by a small coterie of experts who consider this "standing swim" to be of "great importance." It is said to involve "keeping your body straight and unmoved, using your legs only, in which exercise both hands must be kept free, so as to write or paint with your right hand on a fan or sheet of paper held in the left hand" (Matsudaira, 125).

Lake swimming seemed to be the particular domain of the Sasanuma *ryu*, which (as was true of the above-mentioned Kobo *ryu* and the Takeda *ryu)* had been developed and perfected in the southern island of Kyushu. Swimming in the open sea, finally, made the Kankai *ryu* justly famous among the members of the *buke,* and the techniques developed by this school—which included swimming semierect via a typically circular and powerful movement of the legs *(maki-ashi)*—are mentioned in the epic literature of the martial arts. A particular place must also be assigned to the secret schools of swimming developed by those members of secret guilds or organizations, known as *ninja,* who will be discussed in detail in a separate section. As one might expect, competition was fierce among the various schools, and each specialized style of swimming was usually a closely guarded secret, in accordance with the traditional and exclusivistic ethos of the clan system.

Warriors who wished to become proficient in a number of styles would often be granted permission by their lords to travel the length and breadth of Japan, seeking instruction from the masters of major schools (ofttimes spending years training in each school). Occasionally, these different, specialized styles were compared on a grand scale in tournaments held before the shogun. The records of the martial arts mention a competition held before Tokugawa Iesada, in which twenty-five swimmers from each major school competed fiercely against one another for three days in their sophisticated specialties. Unfortunately, few of these specializations have survived, and the major part of their combined technical repertoire (so closely related to other ages, weapons, and modes of warfare) has either been superseded by modern means of amphibious warfare, or incorporated in a general way into the training methods of the modern art of swimming, at which Japanese athletes are so adept.

<THE MINOR MARTIAL ARTS>

The Art of the War Fan

At first, it may seem somewhat unusual to include the fan in a study of bujutsu. We know that, in Japan, fans of varying shapes and of almost every conceivable type of material were widely employed by individuals of every class for the most diversified purposes: to screen rice, wheat, and the like; as vital elements in theatrical representations, dance, poetry, sports (sumo refereeing); in social exchanges (greetings), business, and trade (advertising). It is, however, the fan as a potentially lethal weapon of combat which interests us here. One author writes that the use of the fan "as an article of military equipment is confined to Japan" (Stone, 160), and the doctrine of bujutsu contains many references to the various types of fans which were used as effective weapons, not only by the *bushi* but by members of every class of Japanese society.

Japanese fans, especially the large ones used in various ceremonies and for ornamentation or display, were not only widely employed throughout the country during the earliest recorded periods but were also highly valued on the mainland of Asia. The earliest mention of a ceremonial fan, the purple leaf-shaped *sashiba,* which was affixed to the top of a long pole, is contained in records of the reign of Emperor Yuryaku (A.D. 457-79). Ancient chronicles of the Sung dynasty in China also make repeated references to the importation of Japanese fans, which were considered remarkable specimens of craftsmanship, being elegantly ornamented and colored. These *sashiba* (as indicated by reconstruction based on the *haniwa* or clay grave figurines) "were rather large, round shields, woven of sedge, with a number of radiating struts, and with a longish handle-stick supporting the centre, like a prolonged radius...The handle was decorated with long scarves, to be held by assistant bearers" (Casal, 64).

SAIHAI

The exact origins of the fan, of course, are lost in the mists of legend. Many Japanese scholars have delved deeply into national customs, lore, and history (especially during the period of military predominance), but their records provide little verifiable information. In fact, "it was so long since things had happened and the investigators' attitude was so one-sidedly pro-Japanese or pro-Chinese, that we find the most conflicting statements. Japanese assertions are therefore to be taken cautiously. And others there are none" (Casal, 72). However, we do know from various sources that, from the very dawn of historical awareness in Asia, fans of every shape and size (the leaf motif predominating) were used for a variety of purposes. As indicated earlier, ceremonial and highly representational fans, consisting predominantly of a half-disc affixed to the top of a long pole (the fan itself being of feathers, silk, or rigid materials such as parchment or wood), were used at court and in religious festivals along the coast of continental, as well as insular, Asia. This usage was encouraged by the spreading of the colorful rites of Mahayana Buddhism in the fertile soil of that Oriental and animistic shamanism which, in Japan, was expressed in the ancestral pantheism of Shinto beliefs. The evolutionary descendants of these ceremonial fans were those huge silken fans, mounted on poles five feet long, called *uma-shirushi* (horse ensign), which the Tokugawa shoguns included among their "emblematic lances," "halberds," and other "processional paraphernalia." These giant fans were "decorated with enormous tufts of horse-hair or fibre" (Casal, 60) in obvious deference to the military tradition of this country, ruled by "aristocrats on horseback." Salvey writes that such fans

> were borne to the battle-field above the banners of the prince. The Tokugawa Shoguns used a fan as a military ensign, which was carried before them as a token of their presence. This fan standard was composed of twice 9 thicknesses of paper, glued together, covered with silk and then with pure gold leaf. It was attached to a pole 15 feet long and it was so contrived that it swung around with the wind. Princes and warriors bore fans of more ordinary dimensions above their standards. (Salvey, 35)

As many scholars have noted, however, ornaments and decorations made of organic materials such as feathers and skins were "never greatly developed in Japan." According to Casal, "it would not be surprising if this were partly due to its connection with the killing of birds. Not only was killing contrary to all Buddhist tenets, and at all times rigorously forbidden in whatever form, but anything dead was also taboo in Shinto" (Casal, 61).

This might explain why the small "fly-whisk," made of horsehair and used by Chinese generals as signs

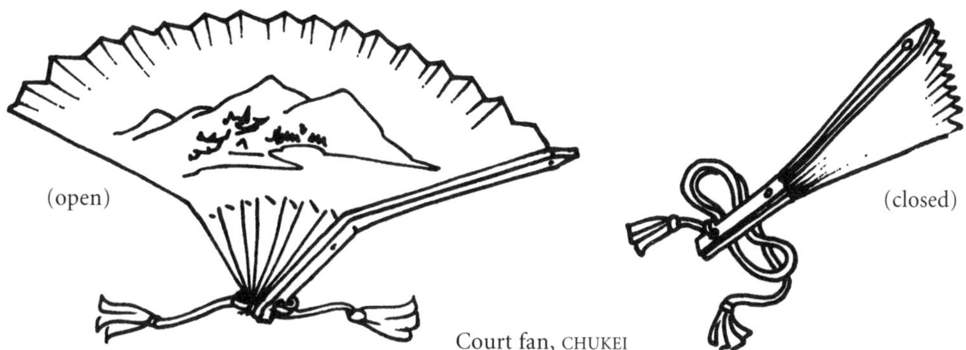

Court fan, CHUKEI

of rank, underwent a "drastic alteration" in Japan at an early date. In Japan, "feudal military leaders used a tassel of leather or tough paper strips, sometimes gilt or silvered, attached to a short handle. This was known as the *saihai* and acted as the 'baton' with which to emphasize command. We shall see that fans took over exactly the same function" (Casal, 57).

Small fans for personal use and as an integral part of one's attire have an equally ancient history whose beginnings are also lost in a maze of myths. Those which survived in distinct functional forms seem to have been of two basic types: "the stiff, usually roundish fan with prolonged stem, called *uchiwa* or *dansen* in Japanese, and the folding fan resembling the sector of a disk called *ogi* or *sensu*" (Casal, 65). The *uchiwa* is mentioned in the early chronicles of the Japanese nation. Casal, in particular, refers to the permission granted in A.D. 763 to a wise and infirm old man (Jozo) by Emperor Junnin (according to other authors by Empress Koken) to appear at court "carrying not only his staff but also his *uchiwa*. We can only deduct that by that time fans were commonly used at least by the learned, in imitation, probably, of the Chinese mode" (Casal, 65). At court, in fact, since time immemorial,

> in order to invest the courtiers and court ladies with a certain stateliness of deportment, it was customary to carry a small flat staff of wood or ivory, which was called a *shaku*. It was carried upright, placed against the lower part of the chest, at a slight angle, to give to the body a dignified bearing. Afterwards, a fan especially designed for court use was made obligatory and superseded the *shaku*. (Salvey, 36)

The folding fan is considered by many scholars to have been a genuine product of Japanese ingenuity, notwithstanding the obscurity surrounding its introduction into Japanese life. According to Casal, "later Confucianists of Japan, in their fervour for Chinese culture, did attribute it to China[, but] China had no folding fan of any kind until some Japanese specimens were presented to occasional ambassadors and visitors at a comparatively late date: early Sung (960-1279) chronicles refer to 'Japanese fans'" (Casal, 83). And for years, the chronicles of this dynasty continue to mention imports of folding fans from Japan. As to the origins of the *ogi*, we must call once again upon the rich but generally unsubstantiated store of Japanese legends, where we find, for example, the episode of the fan maker of Tamba, near Kyoto, during the Tenji era (661-671), who devised a folding fan which could be carried in one's sleeve after studying the wings of a bat that had fallen at his feet. This might explain the origin of a particular type of *ogi* adopted by the emperor of Japan and by the shogun, so constructed as to have "the appearance of being partially open when they were folded up. This effect was produced by a joint, or indentation in the outside frame" (Salvey, 37). We know that these fans became extremely popular at court, where they were used as part of one's personal insignia, denoting rank and position, and as symbols of ceremonial functions, very much in the manner of a king's scepter or a chamberlain's staff in the West. We deduce from the records that they were obviously sophisticated in structure, material, and ornamentation because "an entirely new departure was instituted when Minamoto No Yoritomo established his military government at Kamakura late in the XIIth century, and soldiers took over the functions of the *kuge.* The elegant *hi-ogi* of the nobles became martialized for the samurai by replacing the wooden *oya*-bone with iron ones, and strengthening the ribs through lacquering" (Casal, 80).

The military class of ancient Japan had already known and used a war fan, apparently of the stiff, roundish type *(uchiwa),* which became known as *gumbai.* "The date when the military commander's fly-whisk *saihai* became interchangeable with a stiff, solid *gumbai,* war fan," wrote Casal, "remains doubtful. 'Historically' it is said that it was adopted by the military during the Kamakura rule of the Minamoto-Hojo, between 1192 and 1333. It is known that Uesugi Kenshin wielded one at the battle of Kawanakajima in 1563, and the height of the *gumbai's* popularity appears to have been in the mid-XVIth century" (Casal, 72). The same author tells us that the *gumbai,* like the ancient *saihai,* "must have begun as the magical embodiment of power and might, of protection and right, which was the prerogative attribute of the tribal chief. The solid construction may be ascribed to its concurrent use as an occasional shield against a surprise attack. This will especially have been the case with those made of sheet iron or steel" (Casal, 70–71). Carried into battle by every group leader originally, the *gumbai* seems to have evolved into a special prerogative of the commanding generals only during the "highly conventional" Tokugawa period when war fans were used which were "most elaborate and the cords and heavy tassels of sundry colour combinations became significant for rank or clan of the owner" (Casal, 72). Such fans were originally decorated with representations of the major symbols of Chinese cosmogony: the sun and the moon as the equivalents of the active and passive principles of existence (the *yin* and *yang)* in the doctrine of alternates known as *ommyodo;* the Great Bear constellation as the center of the universe; dragons, destructive storms, and so forth. Later, the emblem of the clan or the family crest became the predominant motif. In many illustrated scrolls depicting battle scenes, "here and there in the melee...is seen an armoured hand, holding aloft a small fan of black paper with a red circular spot in the centre, or an iron fan of the *uchiwa* type, with which the general is signalling to his lieutenants the commands upon which may depend the fortunes of the day" (Salvey, 33).

The fan could also be used to offer a challenge:

> In pictures of the battle of Ichi-no-Tani (XII century), Kumagai-no-Jiro Nao-zane, one of the chiefs of the Minamoto party, is often represented beckoning with a fan to the youthful Taira No Atsumori (who is seeking to ride through the waves to a ship), to return and meet with him in mortal combat. In response to the challenge, Atsumori returned and met his death at the hands of his enemy. (Salvey, 33)

The *gumbai* is still very much in evidence today in the hands of the referee *(gyoji)* who oversees every sumo match. It has also been said that the champion of the first sumo bout held in Nara, Kiyobayashi, was awarded a battle fan and became, consequently, the first umpire by imperial decree. It is not clear whether such a battle fan was then adopted by military leaders or was drawn from preexisting military paraphernalia and awarded to the wrestling champion because of his martial prowess. We opt for the second possibility. In Japan, to "give the fan" became equivalent (as Casal points out) to our awarding the palm," both being symbolic gestures rooted in antiquity.

Less impressive than the *gumbai* perhaps, but markedly more lethal, was that folding fan which developed into the war fan *(gunsen)* carried by the *buski* in armor, and the iron fan *(tetsu-sen* or *lessen)* worn with everyday attire. These fans usually had eight or ten ribs and "were a handy weapon of attack or defence" (Casal, 81). Under the auspices of many clans, in fact, schools sprang up across the land where various styles of combat using the *gunsen* or the *lessen* were devised, tested, and continually improved upon (following for the most part a training program similar to that devised for the study of swordsmanship).

Types of GUMBAI-UCHIWA

As might be expected, legends abound about the beginnings of tessenjutsu, the method of combat which involved the use of an iron fan. Yoshitsune, the hero of so many Japanese sagas, for example, is said to have defeated the huge Benkei (who later became his devoted follower) by parrying the blows of the latter's spear with an iron fan. The secrets of this method of combat were supposedly taught to him by the sylvan deity *(tengu)* who also instructed him in his youth in the art of swordsmanship.

Also famous for their use of the iron fan were the swordsmen who were instructors to the Tokugawa shoguns and the stylists of tessenjutsu of the Yagyu *ryu.* In the literature of the martial arts "there are several instances of victories won with a 'war-fan' against a naked sword, and many examples of men killed by a blow from it" (Brinkley[1], 139). In fact, the art of tessenjutsu became so sophisticated (especially among the upper ranks of the *buke)* that "fencers who were convinced of their superiority did not deign to use a fencing sword but defended themselves with...such a fan" (Casal, 81). Using tessenjutsu, Ganryu, a famous swordsman of the late sixteenth century, emerged unscathed from a clash with several opponents whom he defeated with an iron fan. The art of using it in combat seemed to have also become popular among other classes in Japan during the feudal era, because we read of the famous *otokodate* of eighteenth-century Edo who, forbidden by law to carry swords, "armed themselves with iron-shod staffs and with large, heavy

GUNSEN

The GUNSEN in combat

iron fans. Their fans were so deadly that even they were afterward proscribed" (Casal, 82). The adaptability of such a fan is underscored in a famous episode, supposedly involving Araki Murashige, who is said to have been a prime mover in one of the many plots and counterplots so common in Japan during the late sixteenth century. Summoned to appear before Oda Nobunaga, Murashige knew that his life hung in the balance and that only his *tessen* stood between him and a most unpleasant demise (all swords being confiscated by the attendants who guarded the main entrance to every private mansion). "It must be explained that in those days foul play equaled strategy," writes Casal in his valuable paper, "The Lore of the Japanese Fan," and the method devised by Nobunaga's retainers to dispose of Murashige was that of snapping his neck between the heavy wooden door panels *(fusuma)* which separated the antechamber from the reception hall, when he performed the ritual bow of greeting across the threshold. When he bowed, however, Murashige instinctively placed his *tessen* in the groove along which the door panels slid, and "there was a terrific bang as the doors bounced against the steel rods—but no blood flowed. It is said that Araki acted as if nothing had happened, and so much sang-froid was immediately acknowledged by the hasty-tempered Nobunaga with a reconciliation and further favours" (Casal, 82).

There is no way of knowing whether this episode was the origin of the use of the iron fan, as some authors maintain. We think it more likely that Araki Murashige had merely applied a type of military wisdom based upon knowledge of previous encounters in which two or three brave soldiers had been similarly victimized. Other sources refer to an Araki Mataemon, "a renowned master of the art of fencing," as being the hero of this episode, while the lord who tried to trick him, because envious of his skill, remains anonymous. In this connection, many chroniclers "were chary of mentioning powerful lords by name when anything was to be recorded which did not redound to their credit. The old Japanese authors had reason for this reticence, as the equivalent for the law of libel was drastic in their times, its procedure being sharp and swift and generally applied with a long sword by a retainer of the offended lord" (Diosy[2], 56).

In synthesis, the *tessen* had innumerable functions directly related to the *bushi's* professional preoccupation, combat. The warrior could fence with it; fend off knives and poisoned darts thrown at him as illustrated in Hokusai's prints; hit a flying target with it as in the game called *ogi-otoshi,* which is still played today; use it to develop that type of general coordination applicable to any type of strategic circumstances; and use it in many other ways. As indicated in the preceding section, a fan was used as an integral part of certain formal swimming techniques taught in many bujutsu schools.

Today tessenjutsu is still practiced by a few experts in Japan, while the ancient, heavy *gumbai* appears occasionally with other specialized weapons of the feudal era in the training methods of several modern disciplines of coordination, such as karate, aikido, and kendo.

The Art of the Staff

As ancient as the art of the bow and arrow (perhaps even predating archery) was the art of the staff and those other blunt instruments related to it. This weapon, ranging in size and shape from the standard club to the elongated model of a spear-shaft, is almost as old as man himself, and there are many indications that the Japanese *bushi* knew it well and practiced with it assiduously. There are well-preserved examples of ancient stone clubs *(seki-bo)* used in pre-Yamato times. Iron clubs *(tetsu-bo),* which came in all sizes and shapes, were famous in both Japanese art and literature, especially that long iron club *(kanabo)* with which legendary heroes won their reputations on the battlefield. An entire arsenal of armed or spiked staves, shafts, and poles, generally of wood bound with iron, were developed concomitantly with the art of spearfighting, to the extent that the boundaries between the two arts became vague at best. The art of the staff as such is intended here as the art of using the wooden staff or stave (as well as similar weapons made of wood) as an instrument of combat. It was an ancient and noble art—the staff having even been accepted within imperial precincts in the form of a wooden club *(kirikobu)* carried by palace watchmen.

In a sense, the art of using the staff and similar wooden instruments as weapons represents the point of transition from armed to unarmed methods of combat. Wood, whether in its natural or polished state, and in every possible shape, has always provided man with a sturdy means of implementing his fighting capacities. It provided, if not the first, surely one of the earliest materials man used in manufacturing deadly weapons. In the Japanese dimension of the art of combat, however, wood was not (at least during the feudal era) the primary material used in the manufacture of weapons: iron and steel were. But it did constitute a fertile, although secondary, dimension whose strategic potentialities were duly explored, developed, and systematized until various methods began to take shape, each method complete and effective in and of itself. Because of the fact that they were comparatively less dangerous to practice with than a blade (whether spear, sword, or dagger), the staff and various other wooden weapons were often used in the training halls of bujutsu schools where the techniques of spear fighting and swordsmanship were taught. In time, this related use of wooden weapons became so well developed that real combat using the

Staff against the sword

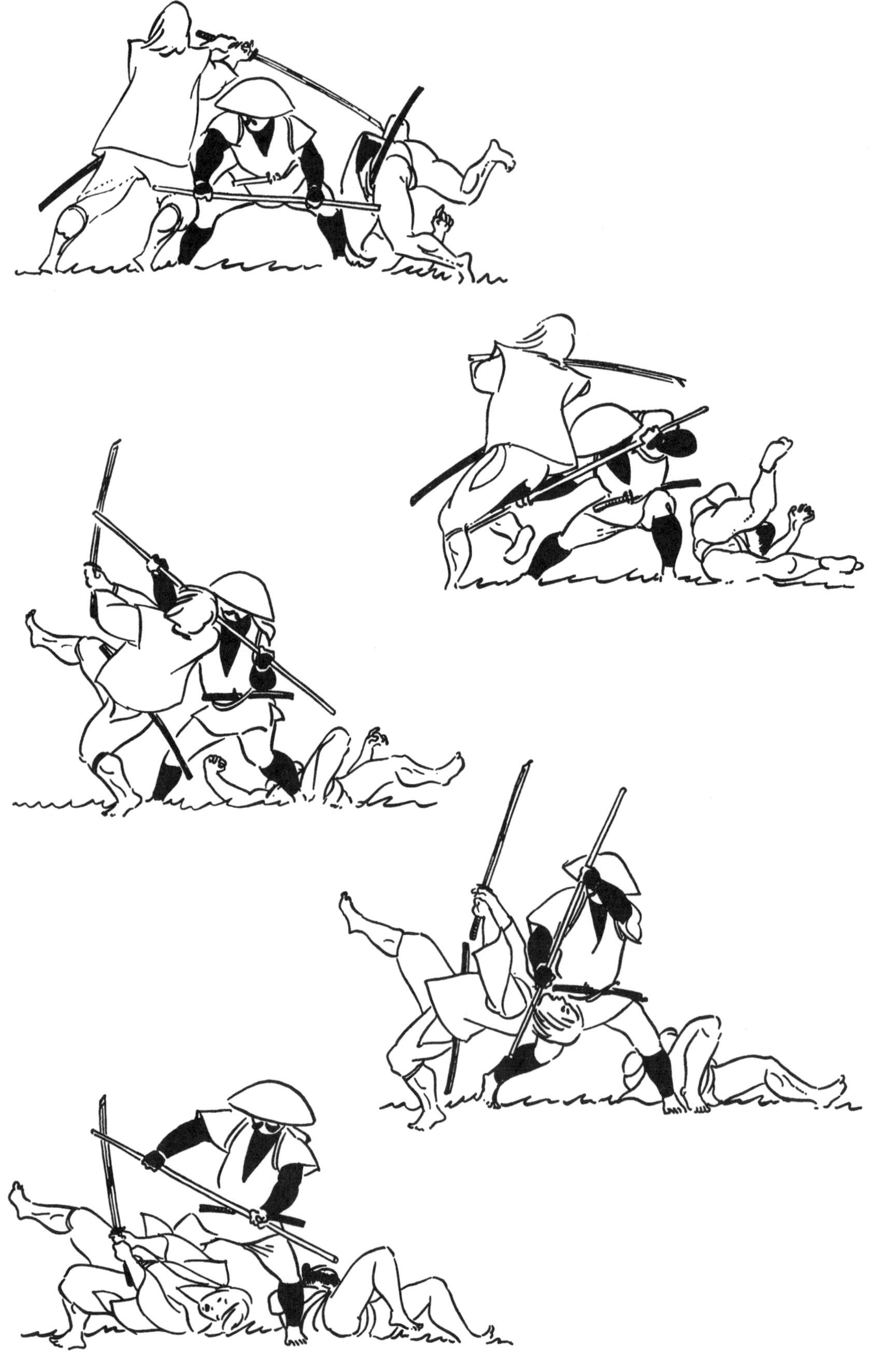

staff or a wooden sword could be engaged in by skilled warriors (even in self-defense against an unjust and potentially lethal attack, whether armed or unarmed). Thus, employing wooden replicas of iron or steel weapons, the possibility of undesirable lethal results could be minimized and, in cases of exceptional skill, eliminated almost entirely. This fact helps to explain the popularity of the staff among members of those social classes who abhorred the idea of shedding the blood of their fellowmen. Priests, monks, travelers, common folk (even poets) used the staff and other wooden instruments—many of which are still used today for various purposes. The warriors themselves often competed in tests of skill, using these weapons.

According to the dictionary, a staff is any one of a large variety of elongated items: pole, stick, bar, club, cudgel, and so forth. In the specifically military dimension of Japanese culture, however, the staff and similar wooden instruments were used primarily to train the *bushi* in techniques which, in real combat, would involve the use of a deadly steel blade. Thus we find as many specializations in the use of the staff as there were armed specializations, there being a wooden substitute for almost every weapon. And the relationship between the two (the staff and the weapon it represented) was such an intimate one that the techniques and strategies of one were virtually indistinguishable from those of the other. In fact, any discovery in the skilled employment of one was soon reflected in the use of the other, in an almost symbiotic exchange. A

A throw by means of the staff

Staff preventing an iai draw

Parry at wrist or guard

IRIMI hit from underneath

spearman could use the staff as efficiently as his spear, and a swordsman could employ the staff (properly shaped to follow the contours of a sword) with the precision of a live blade. The techniques *(jutsu)* devised for the effective employment of these wooden weapons, therefore, were substantially the same as those employed when using their steel or iron counterparts. Each, however, also developed independently of the discipline to which it was directly related—even producing its own lore and body of literature.

The first specialization, naturally, is represented by the art of the long staff, whose length was that of either the spear *(hassaku-bo)* or the halberd *(rokushaku-bo)*. The second specialization of the staff is represented by the art of the long stick, whose length was that of either the long sword *(jo* or *bo)* or the regular sword *(ham-bo)*. One of the particular methods of using the long stick is one that is practiced today not so much as an art of real combat (jojutsu), but rather as a discipline of integration known as jodo. It is practiced at Waseda University in Tokyo and in other, less well known *dojo* in Japan and abroad. This particular method is said to have been invented by the great swordsman Muso Gonnosuke approximately four hundred years ago, after a bout with wooden swords won by the famous Miyamoto Musashi, whose inimitable style of two-sword fencing was adopted by the Nito *ryu*. According to the same tradition, Gonnosuke then withdrew to a Shinto shrine and, after a lengthy period of purification, meditation, and practice with the staff, developed the art of the *jo* by blending the techniques of spearfighting and swordsmanship with those of other, minor methods of combat. He named his style Shindo-Muso *ryu* and promptly proceeded to challenge Musashi again. This time, Gonnosuke's method enabled him to mount an effective defense while skillfully penetrating Musashi's own two-sword defense *(juju-domai)*. Gonnosuke is reported to have practiced continually until he had developed the twelve basic blows and blocks (later combining them into more than seventy advanced techniques) which comprise the technical patrimony of modern jodo. These basic blows are usually practiced in the form of fluid, formal exercises *(kata)* performed by a student using a wooden sword *(bokken)* and his partner using the long stick *(jo)*. These *kata* include normal blows to the upper parts of the body, straight *(honto-uchi)* and reverse *(gyaku-uchi);* the response to a block *(hiki-otoshi);* the switch-hand *(kaeshi-tsuki)* and reverse-hand *(gyakute-tsuki)* thrusts; the straight *(tsuke-hazushi)* and the round, low parry *(maki-otoshi)*; the body pressure *(kure-tsuke)*; the body push *(kure-hanashi)*; and the body whirl *(tai-atari);* the middle body parry and counter *(do-harai-uchi)* and the spinning evasion and counter *(tai-hazushi-uchi)*. The study of *the jo* usually leads one to other arts and weapons, such as the art of the heavy club *(tanjo)*, of the chained sickle *(kusari-gama)*, of the fast draw *(iai)*, as well as to blows in karate and kempo or throws in judo and aikido.

The third specialization was the art of the wooden sword *(bokken)*, a staff carved and shaped in accordance with the contours of a real sword, often so skillfully that the result became a much appreciated object of aesthetic enjoyment and display. This art is not mentioned as frequently as one might expect, simply because it was linked so closely to kenjutsu that it was generally identified with or subordinated to the latter. Yet most duels among masters of different schools, all the tournaments among clansmen, all the examinations for rank, and so forth involved the use of the sturdy *bokken* which every *bushi* used as a part of his training equipment. In certain exceptional cases, it could even be substituted for the *katana:* for example, when skilled swordsmen became itinerant monks or men of peace and developed an aversion to the shedding of human blood, under any circumstances. In such cases, the *bokken* was used primarily as an instrument of pure defense.

The Art of the Jitte

It is still possible to observe in private collections of ancient Japanese weapons an interesting instrument of combat known, in the doctrine of bujutsu, as *jitte, jittei,* or *jutta.* This weapon usually consists of an iron or steel rod, a long hilt, and a characteristically square hook jutting out from the rod at the point where it meets the hilt. This instrument appears in many variations, from the simplest to the most elaborate. It was often implemented with a guard *(tsuba)* and a scabbard; in certain rare cases it was even mounted as a sword, with a blade. Some martial arts authors report that it was carried hanging from the belt or in a scabbard inserted in the waistband or sash *(obi)*, while others hold that it was usually carried hanging from the wearer's wrist by a cord tied to a ring on the weapon's hilt. In any case, there seems to be general agreement that it was a parrying weapon and was used by Japanese police officers in feudal times.

It is not clear exactly when and where this weapon first came into existence. Some chronicles claim it originated in the Ryukyu Islands, where it was known as a *sai.* Tradition has it that the natives of those islands, subjected to the brutal and exploitative rule of Japanese occupation forces during the last stages of feudalism, were rendered virtually helpless by the confiscation of their weapons. Using whatever implements they possessed or could devise, the natives began to develop defensive methods of combat directed primarily toward neutralizing the invader's primary weapon: his sword. The *sai* proved so effective in accomplishing this task that the Japanese warriors themselves imported it into Japan, according to this tradition. However, it might also be assumed that this weapon developed indigenously in the Japanese

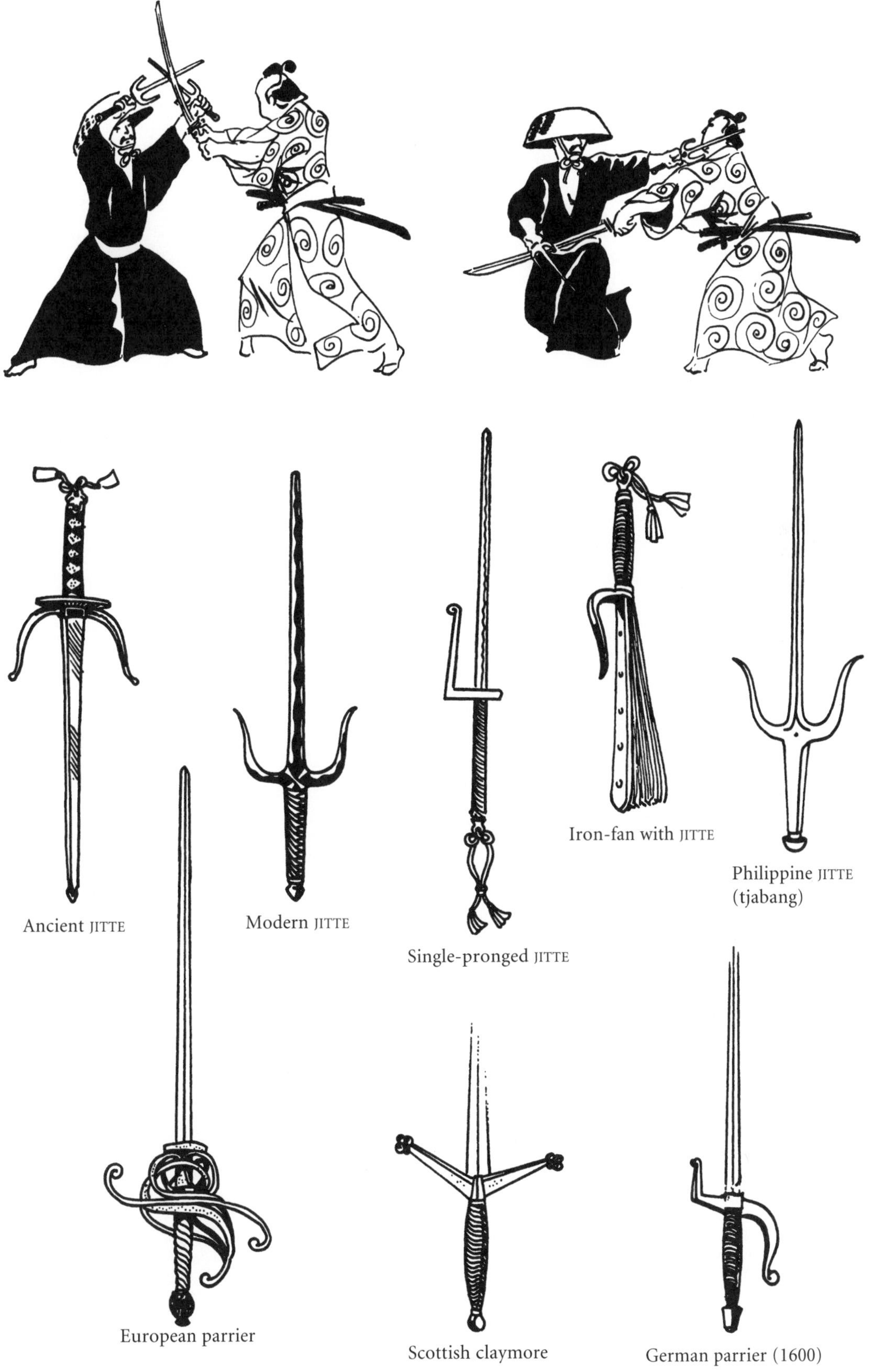

Ancient JITTE

Modern JITTE

Single-pronged JITTE

Iron-fan with JITTE

Philippine JITTE (tjabang)

European parrier

Scottish claymore

German parrier (1600)

Examples of the JITTE in use

culture concomitantly with the sword, to which it represented a logical antidote. A weapon of this basic design was commonly used either alone, as in Japan and the Philippines, or integrated with the blade, as in Europe, where some highly elaborate sword-guards are actually *jitte.*

Whatever its origins, this weapon gave rise to a sophisticated method of combat which became known in Japan as jittejutsu. Its techniques ranged from skillful parries against a sword attack to extremely effective blows directed against any exposed part of an opponent's body. The point of the *jitte* was used directly in thrusts to the eyes and throat, or the opponent's lower abdomen—parts of the body which became extremely vulnerable once a warrior's blade had been captured or diverted. The hilt of the *jitte* could also be used with devastating effect in delivering reverse blows that could maim or even kill an unwary opponent. Upon occasion, the *jitte* was also thrown.

Mastery of jittejutsu naturally depended upon consummate skill in that art of displacement *(tai-sabaki)* which made it possible for an expert to move with blinding speed from one position to another, sliding or whirling closer to or further away from an opponent, whose reach normally extended to the tip of his long sword. Evasion prepared the way for the parry, and the parry prepared the way for the counterattack which often concluded the encounter. Since the techniques of kenjutsu were virtually infinite, the techniques of jittejutsu, of necessity, had to be equally numerous and sufficiently conclusive to eliminate the possiblity of the opponent's being able to counterparry and attack again. This skill was invaluable to a police officer who was often "required to make arrests without injuring his prisoner, particularly if of much higher rank" (Stone, 326). The official use of the *jitte* was restricted to the police officers of the feudal era, who also used it as a symbol of their position. They became extremely skillful in its use, and the warriors were said to have dutifully acknowledged the efficiency of this instrument, which, in the hands of an expert, could snap a precious *katana* in two or send it whirling away, leaving the warrior disarmed and faced with a man holding a short, blunted rod against his throat. Other categories of Japanese subjects, however, managed to enjoy the advantages of jittejutsu in less obvious ways, by adding a hook to the iron ribs of their fans or to the stems of their pipes.

<THE COLLATERAL METHODS OF COMBAT>

The doctrine of feudal bujutsu makes indirect references to other weapons, methods, and styles of individual combat which do not actually qualify as either major or minor arts of armed combat nor, strictly speaking, as arts of unarmed combat familiar to the *bushi.* In nature and functionality, in fact, these particular weapons and their strategic functionalities were generally used by members of classes other than the warrior caste in feudal Japan—by people with whom the *bushi* (as had been true of the Heian aristocrats before them) did not generally associate on a level of social parity. Yet there are references which, however indirect they may be, do indicate that those weapons and methods did exert an influence upon the evolution of bujutsu because they added new dimensions to the range and nature of its specializations. Furthermore, they deserve a place (even if a collateral one) among the martial skills of the age because, according to the criteria adopted by the authors for the inclusion of an art of combat in this study, each of these weapons and its strategic methodology had its own tradition, was relevant in individual combat, and was commonly used by the members of various social classes in feudal Japan. Finally, these weapons and arts are related, even if indirectly, to the warrior because they were often used to curb his notorious belligerence. As for the qualification martial *(bu)* which these weapons and arts *(jutsu)* claim for themselves, we may simply observe that their relationship to the classic bujutsu of the warriors in feudal times was often one of real confrontation, which makes any academic qualification ultimately meaningless. We refer, of course, to a direct confrontation in armed combat. Finally, as mentioned in the Introduction, the qualification of "martial" in later periods descended on one side from the *bushi* who ruled the land and determined its primary sources of tradition, while on the other side it rose upon the wave of acceptance of that martial tradition by members of all the other classes of society in Japan.

We are referring, therefore, to an assortment of weapons such as the chained sickle, the rice-grinder, the rake, and so forth, used primarily by farmers to resolve conflicts among themselves or to defend themselves against the warriors, to axes of various types used by farmers and militant monks; to reinforced smoking pipes used by all classes in feudal Japan (including warriors) to fight efficiently against armed opponents, and to religious symbols which could be turned into vicious weapons when used by priests and monks expert in arts of mayhem.

We are also referring to a group of people, the *ninja*, whom the *bushi* employed to execute, with their particular weapons and supposedly occult methods, missions of dubious morality or of extreme difficulty, thus sparing the warrior the embarrassment of openly violating the norms of his own code of conduct (Bushido), which demanded that he behave as a soldier and gentleman, facing his enemies openly without resorting to dishonest ruses. The employment of such agents also saved him from the disgrace of being held directly reponsible for any of their possible failures.

As we indicated in the Introduction, firearms and their various methods of employment (with which the fighting man of feudal Japan had been familiar since 1543) are not examined in any great detail in the present study because they never became very popular as weapons of individual combat in feudal Japan. They were, of course, often used by the *ninja*, who were specialists in every form of assassination, as well as espionage. This fact also further repelled or prevented the members of the various classes from using them on a large scale. There are, indeed, samples of lavishly decorated hand-guns such as the *jitte-teppo*, with its particularly ingenious "swinging pan-cover" which kept the powder dry and allowed the bearer to carry it "primed, ready for instant use" (Stone, 326). They were, however, expensive to produce, and the smiths were generally kept under such constant police surveillance that only authorized overlords could commission them (or the members of the secret *ninja* guilds) and then only on a severely limited scale. Muskets, of course, had been imported by the Portuguese into Japan in 1542, and their production was so widespread that they belong to the study of war in general, rather than to this analysis of the weapons and methods of individual combat.

The Art of the Chain and Other Weapons

A particular group of weapons noted for their efficiency in neutralizing at close range that ubiquitous and terrifying weapon par excellence, the sword, or capable of reducing at a distance the strategic advantage of the spear, were those weapons based upon the use of metal chains.

The chain *(kusari)*, made of iron or steel, had made its appearance within the dimension of bujutsu with the construction of the first Japanese armor. Its application to combat, either alone (i.e., to parry and drag) or in combination with other weapons, seems to have been very ancient. It appears, in fact, to have been the link between weights of various sizes and poles of various lengths, such as the *nage-gama* (a javelin with a short sickle-like blade set in at right angles at one end, while a long chain was attached to the other end). Some authors believe that it was used mainly in the defense of castles and bastions, being thrown, for example, at besiegers and then immediately retrieved by a quick pull on its chain. Others visualize its use as a walking stick which could be instantly transformed, if necessary, into a deadly weapon. Militant monks and the dreaded *ninja* often favored the *nage-gama*, disguised in various ways, one of which consisted of a bamboo pole from whose hollow tip the *kusari* would snap out to disorient or entangle an opponent.

KUSARI-GAMA

The chain was also used in connection with sickles or picks *(kama)* of various lengths. Such a weapon

Chain-weapons in action

Manriki-Gusari

usually consisted of a shaft of iron, often with a protective shield for the hand, and a sickle set at right angles to it, while a chain hung from the back of the sickle. A weight was commonly attached to the chain. Weapons of this kind became known as *kusari-gama,* and their primary purpose was to paralyze an opponent's sword or spear with the whirling chain, while the sickle was left free to perform its deadly operations. Several schools, some of which traced their origins back to the twelfth century, were known to have produced fearsome fighters during the Tokugawa period—men who specialized in the use of the *kusari-gama.* One of these specialists was Yamada Shinryukan, who bested many a swordsman with his whirling chain and sickle before meeting death at the hands of Araki Mataemon, a skillful swordsman who cleverly trapped Shinryukan in a bamboo grove (Gluck, 111). Effective use of the *kusari-gama* obviously required sufficient space for the whirling of the weights and the ensnaring of the opponent's weapon before the sickle could be brought into play, either to attack the disarmed man frontally or to hook him from behind with its curved blade—both of which were obviously not possible in confined quarters, such as a bamboo grove.

The chain, finally, was often used alone as the primary weapon of combat. A particular method was devised, according to tradition, by a famous swordsman of the feudal era, Masaki Toshimitsu Dannoshin, who added two weights (one at either end) to a chain two feet long and devised a series of skillful ways of disarming and subduing an armed opponent. He named "his weapon *manriki-gusari (manriki* meaning '10,000 power' and *gusari* 'chain') because he felt it contained the power and the ingenuity of 10,000 persons" (Gruzanski, 28).

His school, the Masaki *ryu,* became widely known for the skill with which its students could fight against many armed or unarmed opponents simultaneously, the weights of their chains whirling ominously as they weaved in and out among their opponents, stunning them with accurate blows (even, by deft handling, using those weights to hit a man from behind while still facing him). The *manriki-gusari* could bring a man crashing to the ground when twirled around his ankles, or it could be used to choke him or to immobilize his forearms and wrists. Several techniques or methods of projecting an opponent down, often quite violently, were devised whereby the opponent (i.e., his weapon or clothing) would be hooked by the *manriki-gusari* while in motion, and he would then be sent spinning centrifugally away. Like the *jitte,* this weapon could also be used to parry and deflect a sword cut by stretching the chain taut before an oncoming blade, and then proceeding to hit the wielder of the sword with the weights of the chain itself. Many other schools evolved from the Masaki *ryu,* whose techniques, as well as the weapon employed, underwent several modifications, affecting mainly the length of the chain, its thickness, the shape and size of the weights, and, finally, the ways of using the weapon.

By itself, the sickle *(kama)* was an efficient weapon of combat which the farmers in particular seem to have employed extensively in a wide variety of forms—the variations being generally in the length of the handle. The *kama-yari,* for example, was a simple handle with a blade forged onto or set at right angles to its length. The blade could be folded up inside the handle, and a metal ring which slid along the handle was used to lock the blade firmly into an open or shut position. A larger version of the *kama-yari,* called *o-kama-yari,* is mentioned by Stone.

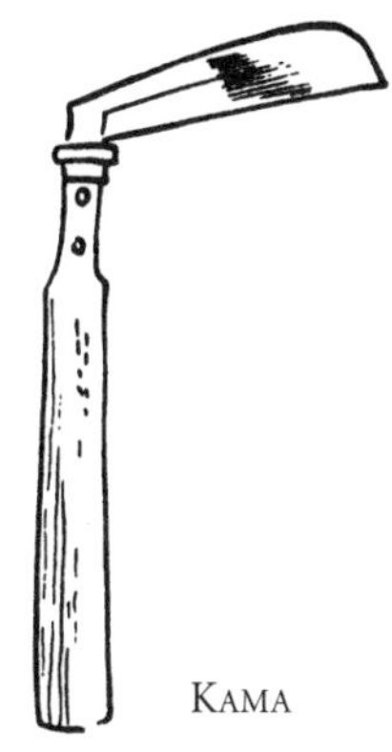
KAMA

Two particular weapons of combat at close range are also related to the fighting farmers of feudal Japan, because both are functionally connected with the cultivation, grinding, and polishing of rice. They are the *tonfa* and the *nunchaku,* instruments which modern schools of Japanese martial arts (especially those of karate) have recently brought back to popularity in their training methods. The former consists, as illustrated, of a rectangular piece of wood, with a handle protruding on one side, near one end. Whirled around with lightning speed, this apparently innocuous tool could be used to parry or deflect a blow, and then return it with a flourish. The latter consists of two blocks of wood connected by leather thongs, strands of horsehair, or even chains. Its snapping whirls could disrupt

The NUNCHAKU and TONFA in combat

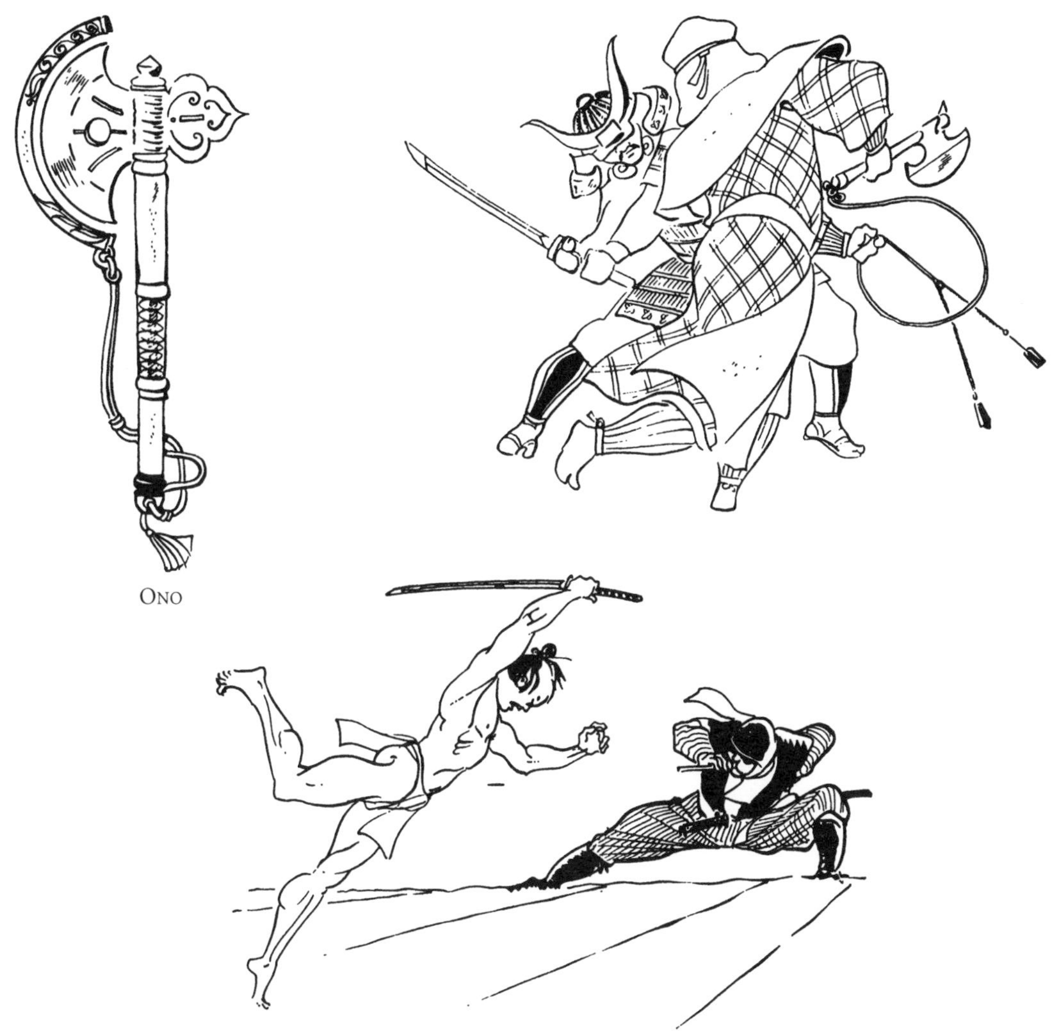
ONO

the deadly concentration of a swordsman; its pieces of wood could be used to hit and stun; its flexible connection could be employed to drag a man along or strangle him.

The axe and the mace were also known and used in combat during the earlier periods of Japanese history, although they were never very popular with the *bushi.* Stone axes *(raifu)* have been preserved in museums, and so have a variety of iron and steel axes such as the *fuetsu,* the battle-axe *(masa-kari),* and so forth—many being of excellent workmanship and fine temper. A particularly impressive specimen is the pole-axe *(ono),* featuring "a very large head with a very convex cutting edge and a large scroll-shaped peen opposite it. It has a sheath covering only the edge of the blade. The entire length is nearly six feet" (Stone, 475). Almost unanimously, these weapons are linked in the doctrine to the "warrior monks" *(yamabushi),* who, as noted in Part 1, occupy such an important position in any study of the evolution of bujutsu. These redoubtable fighters were indeed extremely skilled in the use of such weapons, as many an unwary *bushi* realized to his chagrin. The *yamabushi* used these pole-axes in the thick of battle, whirling them around at varying heights; or in individual encounters, using the pole in accordance with the technical rules applicable to naginatajutsu and jojutsu.

No collection of Japanese weapons would be complete without examples of those ancient weapons of ejection, the archaic forerunners of guns, which natives from South America to Borneo, Sumatra, Thai-

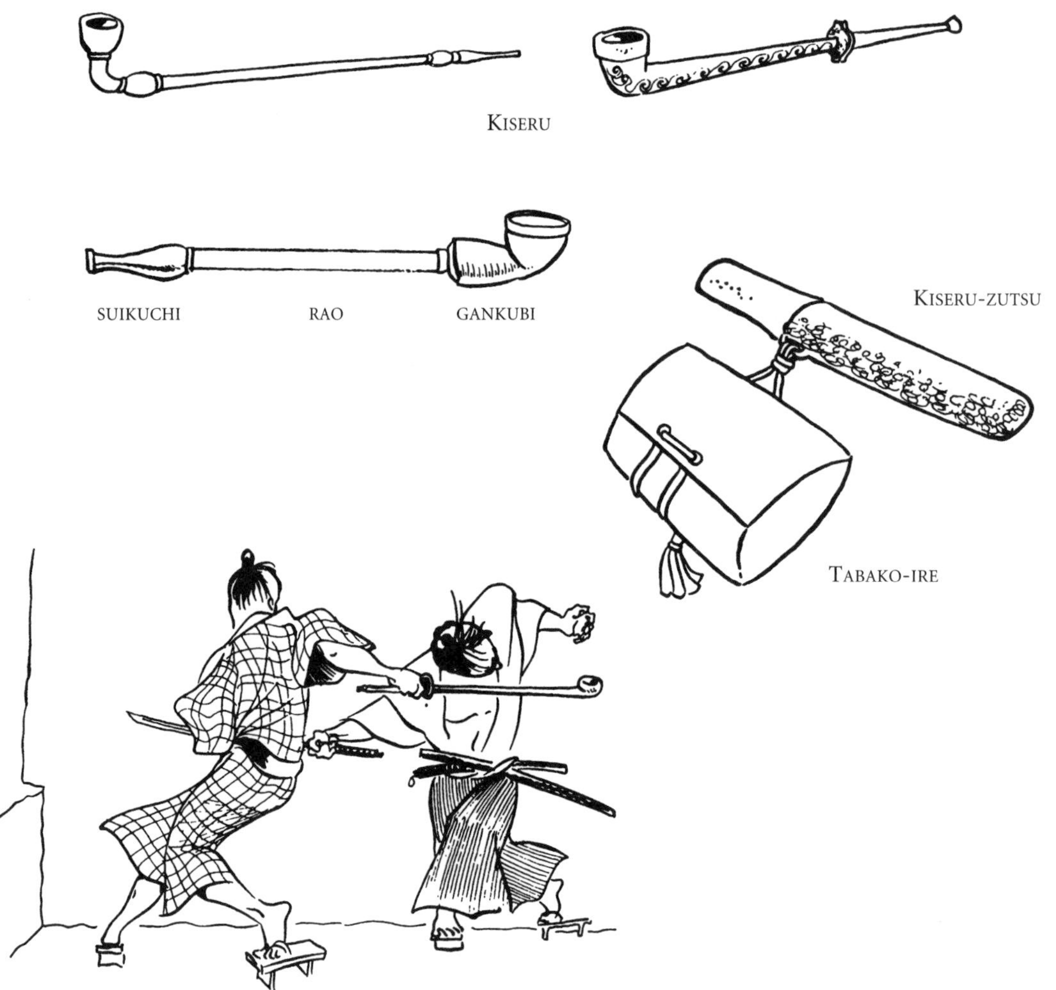

land, and elsewhere have used and perfected to a high degree of lethal efficiency. We find these weapons in various forms in feudal Japan too. The long blow-pipe, which could double as a staff, was quite common. Assassins also used short blow-pipes which could be easily concealed. Particular mention is also made of the *metsubushi* or *gantsubushi,* a peculiar pepper-blower "formerly carried by Japanese police for blowing pepper or dust in the eyes of a person they desired to capture....It is a lacquer, or brass box with a wide mouth-piece on one side and a hole, or pipe, on the other through which to blow the pepper" (Stone, 499). As mentioned in Part 1, smoking pipes of all kinds were used by all citizens as weapons. In feudal Japan, the typical pipe *(kiseru)* consisted of a bowl *(gankubi, gambuki),* a stem *(rao),* and a mouthpiece *(suikochi, suikuchi).* A pouch of leather or cloth *(tabako-ire)* or a box *(tonkotsu)* accompanied it, and a pipe sheath *(kiseru-zutsu),* often highly decorated, was used to protect it. A man's pipe was usually six or eight inches long, while a woman's might extend from one to two feet. In the sixteenth and seventeeth centuries, however, many pipes were made of metal and were often three or four feet long. Several edicts point to the fact that such pipes were used in brawls, probably in accordance with the technical rules governing kenjutsu and similar martial arts methods. Some pipes, in fact, were even fitted with regular guards *(tsuba),* just like swords.

Finally, among the most apparently innocuous articles of personal attire which (as was true of the fan used in feudal Japan) could double as a weapon of combat at close range in the hands of priests and

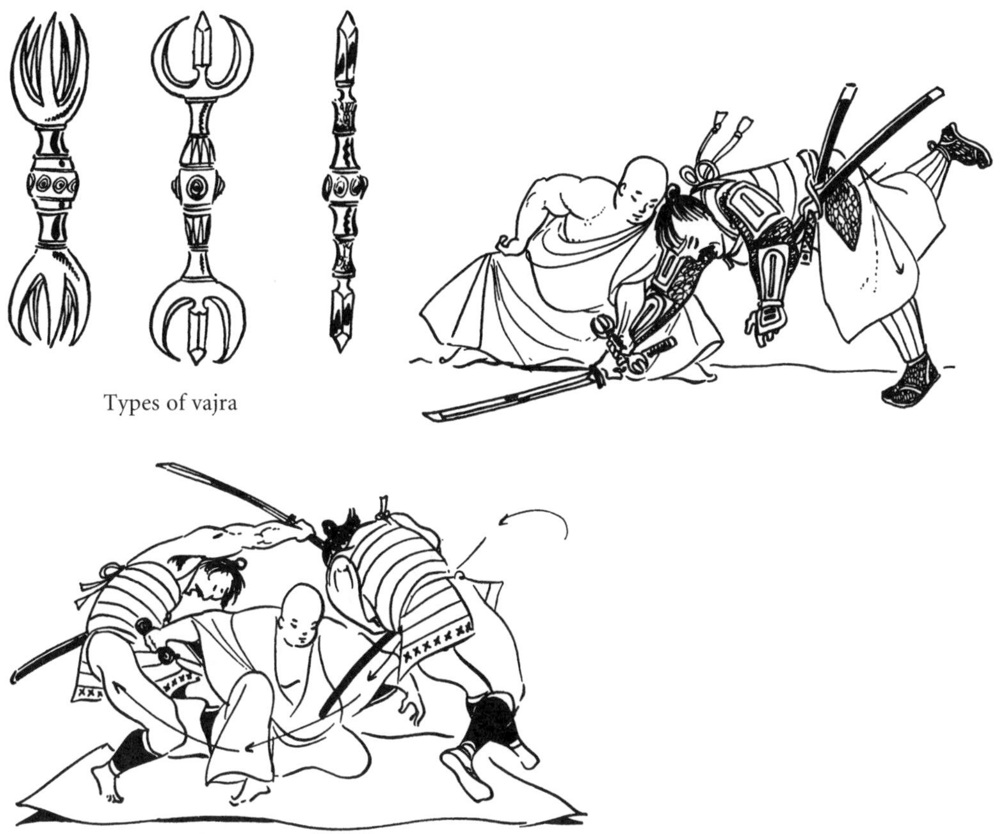
Types of vajra

monks, Gluck mentions the *vajra,* a Sanskrit symbol of Buddhist lore known in Tibetan as *dorge* and as *tokko* in Japanese, which was intended to express the idea of a thunderbolt (Stone, 652). It had prongs at both ends, and their number varied from one *(tokko, dakkosho)* to three *(sankosho, sanko)* or five *(gokosho, goko).* Often employed as a hilt in ceremonial swords, it became a representational element of Buddhist paraphernalia. Cast in bronze or iron, it could be used to block the deadly trajectory of a sharp blade, shatter it, or inflict paralyzing damage on an opponent's vital organs, in accordance with the techniques and strategic dictates of kenjutsu and tessenjutsu.

Ninjutsu

The origins of ninjutsu, placed approximately between 500 and 300 B.C., are commonly linked (as are most Oriental arts of combat) to Chinese sources. Mention is often made of the interesting section on methods of espionage which is embodied in the ancient treatise *The Art of War,* written by the legendary Chinese general Sun Tzu. There is no single English term that can be used to define with precision this art or science, nor to accurately describe its practitioners, the notorious *ninja.* One translation of ninjutsu might be "the art of stealth," which is a term commonly employed in the doctrine of bujutsu. This definition, however, identifies only one of the many characteristics and functions of ninjutsu—concealment, or the creating and perpetuating of an aura of mystery. The functions of the *ninja* may be represented in general as having been those of infiltration into hostile environments, performance of various acts of sabotage or assassination, and management of a successful escape once a mission had been accomplished. Infiltration of enemy centers and castles, in fact, gave rise to a particular subspecialization of ninjutsu which was known as toiri-no-jutsu, while slipping through enemy lines in time of open warfare or military alert be-

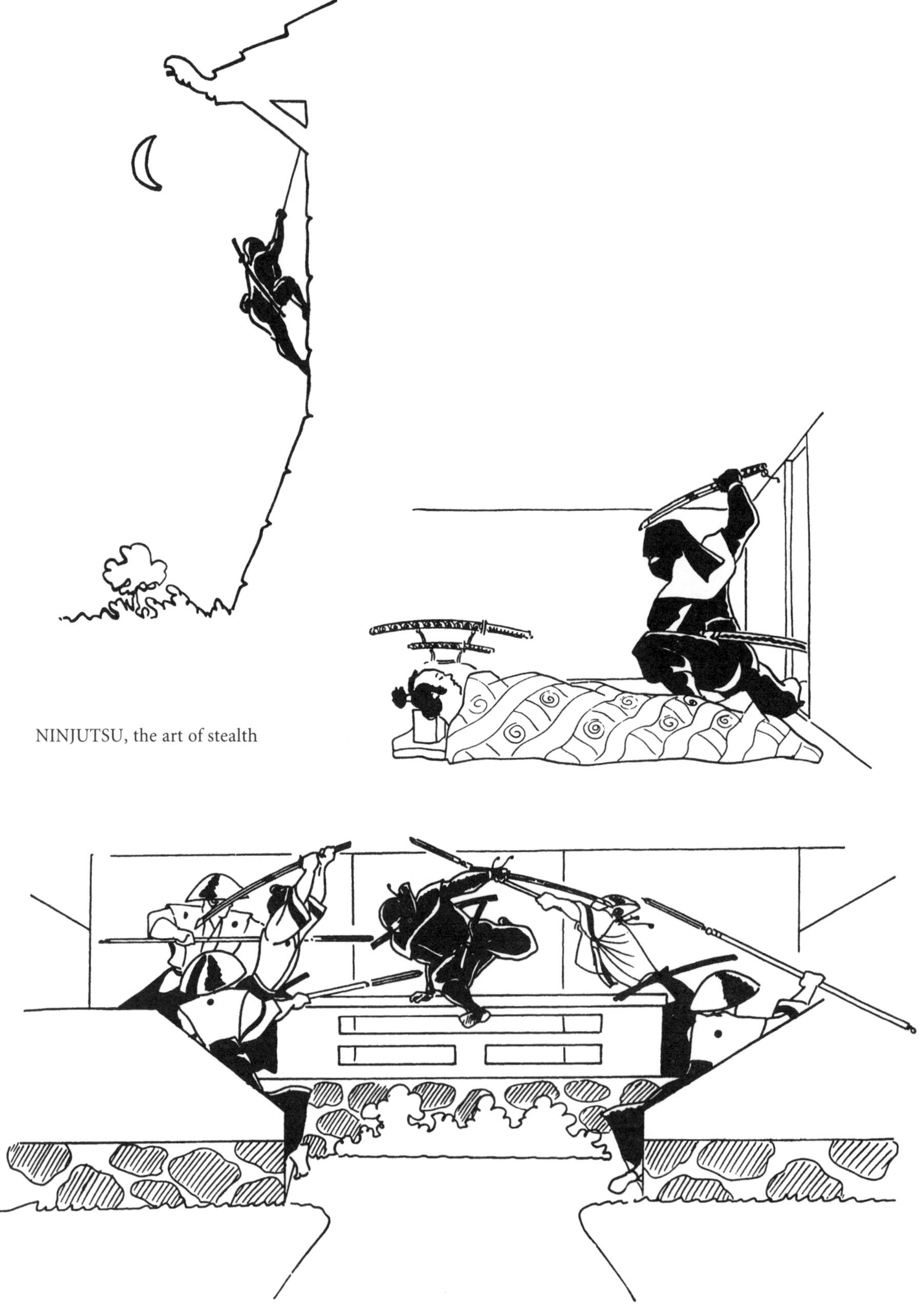

NINJUTSU, the art of stealth

came a specialty referred to as chikairi-no-jutsu. The various deeds to be performed once infiltration had been successfully accomplished were as varied as the military or strategic circumstances themselves. We can divide these deeds or acts into three main categories: first, the gathering of intelligence by espionage, and all of its correlated activities; second, assassination, subversion, destruction of enemy defenses; and third, action on the battlefield, including combat operations in almost every form, ranging from an open encounter to an ambush (whether against a defenseless victim or a heavily-protected lord).

Ninja, then, were often raiders who hired themselves out as spies, assassins, arsonists, terrorists, to the great and small lords of the Japanese feudal age. When certain "disreputable" tasks had to be undertaken, the honor-bound warrior (who was expected to fight openly against his foe in accordance with the rules of his profession) was not usually the one asked to perform them. Large organizations of *ninja* families, specializing in such tasks, were generally available to the highest bidder.

As spies, the *ninja* reportedly made their first notable appearance in the sixth century, with an employer of royal blood, Prince Regent Shotoku (A.D. 574–622). They were frequently hired by the fighting monks of the mountains, the redoubtable *yama-bushi,* who battled against both the imperial forces at the end of the Heian period and those of the rising military class *(buke).* Strong *ninja* guilds became firmly entrenched in Kyoto (which was virtually ruled by them at night), and their schools proliferated until there were at least twenty-five major centers during the Kamakura period. Most of these centers were located in the Iga and Koga provinces, and the concentration of these dangerous fighters had to be smashed time and time again by various leaders seeking to gain control of the central government. Oda Nobunaga is reported to have employed forty-six thousand troops against Sandayu at Ueno, destroying four thousand *ninja* in the process. The last impressive employment of these fighters on the battlefield seems to have been in the Shimabara war (1637), against forty thousand rebellious Christians on the island of Kyushu.

With the ascendancy of the Tokugawa and their heavily policed state, smaller groups *of ninja* were employed by practically every class against members of other classes, and even within a class by certain individuals against any clansmen who opposed them. *Ninja* were also used in the espionage network constructed by the shogun to control the imperial court and the powerful provincial lords. The *ninja* of Koga province, for example, were notorious throughout Japan as secret agents of the Tokugawa; and roaming bands of *ninja* are said to have engaged groups of warriors in local battles, either to suppress attempted sedition or to enlarge the *ninja's* own territorial control. Individual lords and powerful members of other classes such as the merchants, for example, also employed the *ninja,* who left behind them an unbroken record of more than five hundred years of intrigues, disruptions, assassinations, and other assorted forms of disorder.

The *ninja* families were tightly-knit microcosms well integrated into larger groups (in accordance with the ancient clan pattern). There were leaders *(jonin)* who formulated plans, negotiated alliances, stipulated contracts, and so forth, which subleaders *(chunin)* and agents *(genin)* then carried out faithfully. These groups formed larger guilds with individual territories and specialized duties—all jealously guarded. A man seldom joined a group in order to become a *ninja;* he usually had to be born into the profession. The arts, techniques, and weapons of each family, of each group, were kept strictly secret, being transmitted usually only from father to son and even then with the utmost circumspection. Disclosure of ninjutsu secrets to unauthorized persons meant death at the hands of other *ninja* of the same group. Death usually also followed capture, either at one's own hand or that of another *ninja,* who would leave behind only a corpse for the captor to question.

Books and documents *(torimaki)* related to the heritage, arts, and techniques of ninjutsu, therefore, were considered secret family treasures which it was the responsibility of each generation to preserve and transmit to the next. They contained instructions concerning those techniques of combat with which the *ninja* had to familiarize himself and which he had to master (including the traditional martial arts of the country: archery, spearmanship, and swordsmanship). In turn, the *ninja* cleverly adapted the use of these arts to suit his own devious purposes. He used an easily assembled short bow, for example, instead of the warrior's long bow, and he also devised methods of telescopically reducing a spear—with astonishing results when it suddenly sprang into full extension. Members of the Kyushin *ryu,* a school of ninjutsu, became noted for their unorthodox methods of using a spear *(bisento).* Swords and other assorted blades, finally,

SHAKEN

were also used on the ends of various collapsible poles to which chains were attached for quick retrieval; often blades were projected by hidden springs, or they were simply thrown by hand according to the techniques of shurikenjutsu. The *ninja* were also masters of the techniques of iaijutsu, which enabled them to draw swords or daggers with blinding speed. The Fudo *ryu,* another school of ninjutsu in feudal Japan, was considered vastly superior in the development of this particular kind of dexterity with blades.

The *ninja,* however, also had a full array of specialized weapons for his exclusive use, each with its particular and fully developed method of employment. Blow-guns, roped knives and hooks, garrotes, various spikes *(toniki),* brass knuckles *(shuko),* an extensive assortment of small blades *(shuriken),* including dirks, darts, star-shaped discs, and so forth, were all included in his arsenal. The *shuriken* or "needles" were usually kept in a band containing up to five deadly missiles, and they could be thrown in rapid succession from any position, in any light, and from varying distances. The ways of throwing the *shuriken* seem to have been grouped together, attaining the status of a full-fledged art (shurikenjutsu). Even members of the warrior class reportedly studied its techniques in order to be able to use their short swords *(wakizashi),* daggers *(tanto),* and knives (such as the *ko-gatana* and *kozuka)* with greater accuracy and effectiveness at long distances. *Shuriken* could also be forged into a star-shaped disc with many sharp points radiating from a solid center. Sometimes called *shaken,* these sharp stars were usually thrown with a whipping movement of the wrist which sent them spinning toward their target—often unnoticed until it was too late. Especially famous were the chains or cords with a whirling weight on one end and a double-edged blade on the other *(kyotetsu-shoge),* which the *ninja* knew how to use with merciless precision; there was also the innocent-looking bamboo staff carried by an apparently unarmed pilgrim—the staff concealing, however, a chain with a weight at one end and a lead block at the other.

The *ninja's* skill in penetrating enemy strongholds (houses, castles, military camps, individual rooms, etc.) was based upon his knowledge of practical psychology, as well as upon his mastery of a most impressive array of climbing devices (roped hooks, flexible ladders, special shoes, hand spikes, etc.), which he could also use as weapons. In addition, he usually carried breathing tubes and inflatable skins so that he could stay underwater for long periods of time or cross castle moats, lakes, or swamps with comparative ease. A skilled chemist *(yogen)* in his own right, the *ninja* often used poisoned darts, acid-spurting tubes, flash-

NINJA in action

powder grenades, smoke bombs, and so forth, cleverly adapting ancient Chinese discoveries in chemistry and inventions in explosives to his particular requirements. After the arrival of the Portuguese, he even used firearms. These weapons, in addition to the spiky caltrops which he dropped behind him as he made his escape, all contributed to his skill in evading capture by slowing down, blinding, killing, crippling, or merely surprising his pursuers.

Among the unarmed methods of combat which he mastered, jujutsu, in its most utilitarian and practical form, predominated. Schools of ninjutsu, however, also specialized in particular systems of violence seldom found elsewhere. The *ninja* of the Gyokku *ryu,* for example, were expert in the deadly use of the thumb and ringers against vital centers in the human body. This method became known as yubijutsu. The students of the Koto *ryu* were particularly proficient in breaking bones *(koppo).*

From the above, it appears obvious that a *ninja* was a truly dangerous foe, skilled and prepared to cope efficiently and ruthlessly with almost all the possible dimensions of armed and unarmed combat. His overall bodily control and range of muscular possibilities was often astounding. In addition to training in the various arts mentioned above, he is said to have been able to climb sheer walls and cliffs (with the help of certain equipment), control his breathing under water and his heartbeat under enemy scrutiny, leap from great heights (walls, etc.), disengage himself from knots and chains, walk or run for long distances, remain still for hours (even days, some authors claim), blend with shadows, trees, statues, and so forth, as well as impersonate people of every class, thus being able to move about freely even in areas which were under strict surveillance. In this context, his knowledge and command of practical psychology, as indicated earlier, appears to have been highly developed and is said to have included sleight of hand and hypnosis *(saiminjutsu)*—skills which may have formed the basis for a number of the *ninja's* more startling exploits.

5
UNARMED BUJUTSU

Specializations, Instruments, and Techniques

Direct references in the records of the major schools of bujutsu, and indirect references in the chronicles of Old Japan, indicate that many methods of unarmed combat were developed and applied by the Japanese during their "long feudal night," and a number of these methods are reported to have become important facets of the warrior's training.

By definition, a method of unarmed combat represents a systematic and ingenious way of employing the human body in combat in order to achieve the same strategic goals as those attainable through the use of weapons. The question concerning the chronological relationship between the armed and unarmed methods of combat—that is, which method did mankind adopt first in order to solve the problems of a violent confrontation—seems irrelevant at the present state of our knowledge about man's basic drives. Both methods seem to have coexisted almost from the very beginning of his recorded history, supplementing, integrating, or substituting for one another, in accordance with the demands of time, place, and circumstances. In fact, the observation that the human body could operate skillfully in combat as a primary weapon, and that mastery of its elements and functionality could enable a man to subjugate another man violently, while simultaneously insuring his own defense, must have been made whenever and wherever man began to analyze combat problems, since we find evidence of unarmed methods of combat in the earliest records of almost every nation.

In Japan, the methods of unarmed combat appear in the records under many names. A partial list of those encountered most frequently in the literature of feudal bujutsu is presented in alphabetical order in Chart 13. All of these methods shared certain instrumental and functional characteristics which are intrinsic to the concept of unarmed combat. All, for example, were based upon the use of the human body, properly trained, conditioned, and strengthened, as the primary instrument of combat. And they all required that the body be used in certain general, functional ways intended to achieve an opponent's subjugation or avoid being overcome forcefully oneself. These functional ways consisted of using the human body as a weapon for projecting an opponent down onto the ground, immobilizing or choking him, dislocating his joints or hitting him, as well as using that body defensively, in order to avoid becoming the target of another man's attack.

The masters of bujutsu whose methods of unarmed combat began to make a coherent appearance in the doctrine of the martial arts from the sixteenth century onward had inherited a body of actions or techniques *(waza)* from the past to which they added their own variations and innovations. All of these techniques were intended to achieve the opponent's subjugation in any of the various functional ways indicated above, as well as neutralize the opponent's own offensive attempts. One important group of techniques (known in sumo, jujutsu, judo, and so forth, as *nage-waza)* comprised a variety of ways in which particular parts of the human body could be used to remove an opponent from the ground before

CHART 13

Methods of Unarmed Combat

aikijutsu	kumiuchi (ryo-kumiuchi)
chikara-kurabe	shinhaku (shubaku)
gusoku (ko-gusoku, cho-gusoku)	shinobi
hakushi	sumo
jujutsu	taijutsu (taido)
kempo	torite
kiaijutsu	wajutsu
koshi-mawari	yawara
koshi-no-wakari	

projecting him down again—usually so that he landed flat on his back. Thus the category of *nage-waza* contained hip projections *(koski-waza)*—so called because the hip was the main fulcrum of removal, rotation, and projection used against an opponent. Also included under the heading of *nage-waza* were such techniques as the hand projections *(te-waza)*, the leg projections *(ashi-waza)*, and, finally, those powerful techniques known as self-sacrifices *(sutemi* in judo, *utchari* in sumo) in which a fighter, grasping an opponent firmly, would fall to the ground voluntarily— hurling his opponent into the air over his own falling body, in a spectacular projection.

In addition, almost all the major methods contained groups of techniques of immobilization, known as *osae-waza* or *tome*, which could be used effectively to paralyze an opponent, whether standing or lying down, and reduce his capacity to operate in combat without causing him to lose consciousness. These techniques were particularly useful in combat when an opponent had to be taken alive and were, therefore, favored by police forces in the towns and castle precincts of feudal Japan. The dangerous techniques of strangulation *(shime-waza)*, which provided innumerable ways of interrupting the flow of blood to an opponent's brain, or of air to his lungs, thus attacking the very roots of his capacity to perceive and react, were also a part of most programs. Techniques of dislocation *(kansetsu-waza)* were actions directed against an opponent's joints, especially those which could be quickly dislocated, thus rendering him incapable of pursuing an attack or defending himself effectively. And, of course, these methods usually contained techniques of percussion *(atemi-waza)* based on the delivery of blows and kicks directed against vital centers in the opponent's body. Finally, each method included in its repertoire a variety of defensive techniques particularly devised to neutralize an attempted projection, immobilization, or strangulation. These techniques of unarmed combat could be used either individually (as, for example, when a single, well-delivered blow directed at a vital spot in the opponent's anatomy put an end to the encounter right then and there) or in combination, that is, a projection followed immediately by a final strangulation or kick.

It is obvious that all these techniques could be deadly, and they usually were when applied in actual combat, whether on a crowded battlefield or in a confrontation between two men on a lonely road far from any spectators. A projection, directed in such a way as to force an opponent to fall awkwardly, twisting his spine for example, could result in a serious fracture. The same observation could be made concerning techniques of dislocation, while those of strangulation, if prolonged unduly beyond the stage of initial loss of consciousness, could cause death. Equally lethal were the techniques of percussion. However, whether for purposes of training or self-development through practice with a partner, in demonstrations or in open competition, ways were found to reduce the harmful effects of utilitarian combat so that these techniques could also be applied within the framework of safe, representational combat. An example of the latter application would be the famous method of unarmed wrestling known as sumo, while examples of unarmed combat methods used primarily for military training purposes (therefore, more strictly utilitarian in approach) would include the methods known as gusoku, kumi-uchi, jujutsu, yawara, and so forth, all

of which appear frequently in martial arts records. Both of these applications of combat strategy (that is, armed and unarmed) usually coexisted in relative harmony and influenced each other to a considerable extent, notwithstanding the barriers of secrecy which often divided their relevant schools. Discoveries in one category, whether resulting from intense study and experimentation in a quiet *dojo* or from direct experience in combat on the battlefield, were quickly assimilated (even if in a somewhat modified form) by the other.

A brief survey of those major methods of unarmed bujutsu and those schools which have carved a niche for themselves in the doctrine of the Japanese martial arts of the period will help to illustrate the fertility of ideas and the painstaking, systematic compilation of forms which accompanied and stimulated the development of so many theories and practices of unarmed combat based upon the use of the human body as a formidable weapon. With proper conditioning and training, a man could use that body to achieve the aims of combat smoothly and effectively, without the addition of mechanical weapons, whether he was battling for his life or merely performing for the emperor's edification at the Harvest Festival.

The Art of Wrestling

The art of wrestling in Japan appears to have evolved from a primitive and indiscriminate method of combat into a sacred ceremony and a form of military training—emerging finally as sumo, that form of wrestling still practiced in Japan today, where the various elements of its long tradition are highly regarded and have been faithfully preserved.

One important school of thought in the doctrine of bujutsu refers to the *Nihon Skoki* (a chronicle of the Japanese nation compiled by imperial decree in the year A.D. 720) as being the first source of information concerning Japanese wrestling. Public competitions of strength *(chikara-kurabe)* among the stalwart youths of that era, pitting a single man against another (both weaponless), seem to have taken place as early as 230 B.C., and were of sufficient social relevance to appear among court ceremonies. In particular relation to sumo, however, hardly a single reference work of any importance fails to mention the fierce bout which took place during the seventh year of the reign of Emperor Suinin (29 B.C.–A.D. 70) between the imperial guard Taema-no-Kuehaya, the Sharp-Footed, "a noble of great stature and strength" (Mitford, 141), and the equally famous Nomi-no-Sukune, of Izumo province. Various descriptions of this bout would seem to indicate that in these early competitions of strength or wrestling prowess, almost any and every imaginable technique could be used to eliminate or incapacitate an opponent. In this particular instance,

only one man emerged alive from the encounter, Nomi-no-Sukune, who broke Kuehaya's ribs and then smashed his loins for good measure.

The same Nomi-no-Sukune later became famous for his revolutionary suggestion that the retainers of a deceased lord not be buried alive in their master's tomb (as was the custom at that time) but that clay figures of horses, men, and so forth *(haniwa)* instead of living men be placed in the tomb. For this wise counsel (doubly wise since he was himself a retainer), he was elevated in rank. It is also claimed that he modified wrestling, producing a recognizable system which made it possible for young men to engage in tournaments with comparative confidence. This system became the foundation for the development and evolution of wrestling along lines still evident in sumo today. Interestingly enough, before these tournaments, the combatants "dedicated themselves to the divinity" in rites reminiscent of the prelude to the pancratium in the Olympic games of ancient Greece.

In its originally modified form, wrestling is mentioned as a sacred method of deciding questions of national leadership. Mitford relates that in 858, Emperor Montoku allowed his two sons, Korehito and Koretaka, to wrestle for the throne by proxy. Champion Yoshiro, wrestling for Korehito, won the crown for the latter by defeating Koretaka's champion, Natora. Korehito subsequently became Emperor Seiwa. In the era which followed, wrestling seems to have taken two main directions. First of all, it became a form of social representation whose value as entertainment or spectacle did not obscure its intrinsically sacred character. As such, it became an integral part of festivals and other public ceremonies. Empress Kogyoku (642-45), for example, is reported to have assembled the strongest men in the kingdom to wrestle before the Korean envoy. Emperor Shomu (724–40), a famous patron of Buddhism and the builder of many temples, is reported to have also included wrestling (called *sumo-no-sechie,* or Wrestler's Fete) among the traditional games and celebrations of the Harvest Thanksgiving Festival held in the month of August.

The second line of development was more pragmatic and militarily oriented. This was particularly evident in the advancement of that style of wrestling which we know as sumo, since throughout its early history the popularity of this art was closely linked to the position of the *bushi.* Clearly limited in appeal during the sophisticated Heian period, for example, it blossomed with the ascent to power of the new warrior class. According to Brinkley, "such a method suited the mood of the military epoch and was so zealously patronized by the great captains, Oda Nobunaga and Hideyoshi (the *taiko),* that the samurai of the XVIth century paid almost as much attention to wrestling as to archery or swordsmanship" (Brinkley[1], 86).

Professional wrestlers seem to have made their first appearance during the Sengoku era of civil wars. Available records indicate that in 1623, Akashi Shiganosuke requested and was granted permission from

the military powers to hold public wrestling matches in Edo with professional *sumotori.* His example was followed by the priests of Kofuku-ji in Yamashiro, who were authorized to hold wrestling bouts in order to raise funds for the construction of a temple. Such practices were encouraged by the military leaders of the period, who even employed teams of wrestlers in their own mansions. In time, sumo matches became full-fledged tournaments, and their number increased from one a year in Kyoto during the Kansei era (1789-1800) to two in Edo in 1869, then three and finally six a year.

Prior to the period between 1570 and 1600, wrestling appears to have been a relatively comprehensive form of combat which, although modified in regard to lethal blows and kicks (banned by imperial decree as "inelegant" during the reign of Emperor Shomu), did not seem to differ substantially from forms of Mongolian wrestling or even certain European styles. In 1570, however, the ring *(dohyo)* was introduced, and with it the fundamental rules establishing ranks, purposes, and basic techniques. The organization of sumo today still maintains the ancient division of its professional adherents into three groups: the wrestlers, the referees, and the judges. The wrestlers are unusually tall and powerful men selected for their size and then conditioned via appropriate training methods and diet until they reach gargantuan proportions. According to their wrestling experience and the number of their victories and defeats in tournaments, they are given titles ranging from novice to grand champion (see Chart 14, page 275).

A substantial body of lore, in the form of pomp as well as literature, surrounds the Japanese wrestler, especially the grand champion *(yokozuna).* Wrapped around their loins, for example, all *sumotori* wear the classic silken belt which tradition relates to the exploits of Hajikami or Omi, a wrestler of such strength and skill that in a tournament held in Osaka eleven hundred years ago the rules were as follows: any opponent who could merely grasp a rope *(shimenawa)* tied around Hajikami's waist would win. Needless to say, no one could do even that. Both before and after a bout, grand champions are allowed to wear the lavishly embroidered and decorated ceremonial girdle, the *kesho-mawashi,* which tradition again relates to a wrestler, the powerful Akashi, who in 1600 became embarrassed by his nudity in the presence of the emperor and wrapped himself in a huge standard affixed to a nearby pole, thereby unknowingly establishing a fashion which is still followed today. Grand champions are also privileged to arrange their hair in the elaborate style known as *ichomage,* which differs from the style *(chommage)* adopted by the lower ranks since the Edo period. Finally, these champions are escorted (as were feudal military leaders) by an attendant *(tsuyuharai)* and a sword bearer *(tachimochi).*

The referees *(gyoji)* also become an integral part of the generally restricted circles of sumo and of its traditions. With their appointment, they are assigned the names of those ancient families who were once officially recognized as being the highest authorities in the fine art of judging a sumo match. Two such

CHART 14

SUMO ORGANIZATION AND RANKING SYSTEM

<table>
<tr><td rowspan="5">First-rank division (maku-uchi)</td><td colspan="2">Grand champions (yokozuna)</td></tr>
<tr><td rowspan="3">Three orders of champions (sanyaku)</td><td>Champions (ozeki)</td></tr>
<tr><td>Junior champions (sekiwake)</td></tr>
<tr><td>Pre-champions (komusubi)</td></tr>
<tr><td colspan="2">Senior wrestlers (maegashira)</td></tr>
<tr><td colspan="3">Contenders for the first-rank division (juryo)</td></tr>
<tr><td colspan="3">Second-rank seniors (maku-shita)</td></tr>
<tr><td rowspan="3">Step division (dan)</td><td colspan="2">Third step (sandamme)</td></tr>
<tr><td colspan="2">Second step (jo-nidan)</td></tr>
<tr><td colspan="2">First step (jo-no-kuchi)</td></tr>
<tr><td rowspan="2">Apprentices</td><td colspan="2">Beginners (honchu)</td></tr>
<tr><td colspan="2">Recruits (Maezumo)</td></tr>
</table>

families were the Kimura and the Shikimori. Referees are divided into categories which reflect their experience and capacity to control bouts at the levels of the various ranks. They are dressed lavishly for the occasion in costumes which date back to the Ashikaga period, and the color of each referee's fan *(gumbai)* indicates his proficiency: blue and white for *the juryo* bouts, red and white for the *maegashim* bouts, white for the *sanyaku* bouts, and, finally, purple or purple and white for the *yokozuna* bouts. The power of the referee in the ring is evidenced by the respect shown him by the wrestlers, as well as by the other judges. This last category usually includes leaders of sumo societies, ex-champions, teachers, and so forth (dressed in formal attire, *montsuki,* and wearing the divided skirt, *hakama),* who flank the ring and assist the referee as consultants in judging a bout.

The ring itself *(dohyo)* is an elevated circular area, two feet high, once formed by linking sixteen rice bales to provide a diameter of fifteen feet. In this ring the ancient pageantry and combative spirit of Japanese wrestling unfolds in the centuries-old sumo style.

The tournament begins with an announcement of the program by a professional speaker *(yobidashi)* whose style of delivery resembles the type of narration used in religious events or theatrical representations (noh drama, kabuki, etc.). The tournament then proceeds with a series of ceremonies involving the public presentation of the wrestlers in the hall and preliminary matches, and then builds to an understandable peak of excitement as the grand champions perform the ancient rituals of purification and preparation before their match (the *shikiri-naoshi).*

The rules of the bout itself are simple enough: victory is achieved by either forcing the opponent out

of the ring or forcing him to touch the mat within the boundaries of the ring with any part of his body above the knee. This may be accomplished by the use of any one or a combination of approximately two hundred basic movements stemming from thirty-two "key techniques" based upon fundamental principles of application, such as pushing with the hands only *(tsuki)*, pushing with the whole body *(oshi)*, and clinching *(jiori)*. Sumo techniques, therefore, can be divided into two groups: those of limited body contact, such as slapping *(tsuppari)*, side-stepping *(hataki-komi)*, leg sweeps *(ketaguri)*, leg holds *(ashi-tori)*; and those of extended or full body contact. This last group includes an astonishingly high number of head throws, arm throws, hip throws, and thunderous projections performed by sacrificing one's own position in order to displace the opponent *(utchari)*. In accordance with the rules governing sumo bouts, however, if an *utchari* technique is to be successful, the wrestler attempting such a technique must not touch the mat with his body until after his opponent has already done so.

These techniques, based upon functional and dynamic principles of execution common to jujutsu, judo, aikido, and Western forms of wrestling (Greek-Roman, freestyle), as well as to sumo, are applied as follows. Starting from a squatting position, the *shikiri-no-kamae*, with toes on certain marks and bodies

resting on their heels, the wrestlers shift to the low position of readiness *(shikiri)* with feet and fists on the ground, and from this position attempt to launch various techniques, employing all the advantages of weight, strength, suppleness, and strategic intelligence which, throughout the dynamic variety of sumo attacks, counterattacks, and defenses, make this type of wrestling an unpredictable and ofttimes electrifying spectacle.

The military spirit of bygone eras is still vividly present in the costumes the main sumo protagonists wear, in the person of the sword bearer *(tachi-mochi)* who accompanies the grand champion, in the water ceremony *(mizu-sakazuki)* performed before the bout, and finally, in the bow ceremony *(yumitori-shiki)* which closes the tournament. As described by Brinkley in the early 1900s, the "water ceremony" was performed as follows:

> At the base of each pillar sits an expert whom age has compelled to retire from the arena, and who had acted as teacher to the men in the ring. Near him is placed a vessel of water with a wine-cup beside it and wrestlers, before a contest, take a draught of this water, in deference to the old custom of warriors on the eve of a perilous undertaking who exchanged "a water cup" *(mizu-sakazuki)* in token of farewell that might be forever. (Brinkley[1], 80-81)

Even with the changing of the physical setting of the bouts in modern sumo, as well as the changing times and mores, this ceremony has survived, though in a modified form. The bow ceremony is performed by a wrestler at the end of the tournament. He whirls a long weapon in a ceremony which tradition relates to the happiness of a winner long ago who had been awarded the precious longbow by military leaders during the Tensho era. The name of Oda Nobunaga, that great sumo patron, is mentioned again in this connection.

Wrestling was always thoroughly impregnated with the spirit and the forms of the ruling military class. It is not inconceivable that, with such an identification of ceremonial wrestling and war practices, of religious orientations as motivation and wrestling as execution, the *bushi* would incorporate the fundamental techniques of the former into his military training program, as the foundation for more specifically utilitarian purposes (if somewhat less spectacular or ethical in a broad sense). Whether the *chikara-kurabe* of those early days was actually assimilated into the utilitarian sphere of war practices and its associated methods of unarmed combat through sumo, or independently, is a problem of documentation for histo-

rians. There is sufficient evidence, however, to relate both in a very real sense to the martial tradition of the *bushi* and to his training program.

The Military Specializations of Unarmed Bujntsu

The sixteenth and the seventeenth centuries are generally considered to have been the golden ages of bujutsu. The records of most martial arts schools, in fact, link the origins of their schools to those troubled times of social struggle from which the Tokugawa emerged victorious. It is also generally conceded, however, that many of the techniques which became part of the various programs of instruction of these schools may have been much older—having emerged during the centuries of uninterrupted warfare which extended from the eleventh to the sixteenth centuries. By comparison, the Tokugawa period, with its tight controls and rigidly maintained order, would appear to have been a discouraging period for those interested in the development of unarmed bujutsu. However, it was an era particularly suited to the quiet, painstaking collection and systematization of all the unarmed practices of combat inherited from the past—practices which were then further refined, improved, or modified in the light of new circumstances and in accordance with the pressure of the times, customs, laws, and so forth.

It is true, of course, that even during the Tokugawa period there were combat encounters, but they seemed to be of a more limited and individuated nature. Gradually, certain new methods of unarmed combat (many of them actually modified forms of older methods, others created in direct response to a new reality) took their place in the doctrine of bujutsu. In examining these methods of unarmed combat, we have noted an obvious bias toward the actual use of the techniques in question for utilitarian purposes, overshadowing to a certain extent the more representational use of these techniques as ritualized expres-

ATEMI (percussion) technique applied with elbow in kenjutsu

sions of an encounter between two or more men. It would seem, therefore, that an initially strong bond existed between these unarmed methods and the armed methods of bujutsu previously examined.

Such a relationship appears immediately comprehensible from a historical point of view when one remembers that the military clans of the feudal era numbered among their many advantages the services of the best martial arts teachers, as well as that precious commodity necessary for the promotion and preservation of any art: time. To a certain extent, the same held true for monastic orders of a militant character whose records also contained many indirect references to secret methods of fighting effectively with or without weapons. Independent centers of instruction, those not affiliated with one or more clans, were almost nonexistent before the Tokugawa era. They began to appear with increasing frequency during the centuries of relative peace which followed the Tokugawa's ascent to power. In addition, the decline of many impoverished clans, the overabundance of masterless warriors *(ronin)*, as well as the development of large commercial centers which often needed and readily sought protection of their interests, all helped to encourage the establishment of private schools of armed and unarmed combat and the beginning of a recorded tradition which sought, in accordance with Japanese custom, to veil itself in the charismatic aura of the past and thus link itself to classic traditions. But, as we have indicated in Part 1, the tradition to which they referred was actually that of the military class which had emerged during the eleventh and twelfth centuries and, in the process of assuming control, almost totally obliterated the earlier heritage of the land of Yamato, except for those elements specifically retained because the *bushi* found them useful.

With the ancient names of gusoku (in its two variations of ko-gusoku and cho-gusoku), of kumiuchi (ryo-kumiuchi), yawara, wajutsu, jujutsu, aikijutsu, and so forth, we begin to approach methods of combat generally qualified as unarmed because they usually appear with, although differentiated from, the other traditional methods of unarmed combat said to have been practiced by the feudal warriors of Japan. But we have no way of knowing with any degree of certainty whether they were all really unarmed methods in a total sense, or whether they involved the subsidiary use of weapons in their strategies. We feel slightly more inclined toward the second possibility, because in feudal Japan weapons of any sort, whether legally carried and used by the warrior or camouflaged for use by members of other classes of Japanese society, were the norm rather than the exception; and because in those methods of unarmed combat which have survived—such as jujutsu, aikijutsu, kempo, as well as their modern derivatives, judo, aikido, karate—it is still possible to detect techniques clearly inspired by the use of swords, spears, sticks, parriers, and whirling blades of various kinds.

The relationship between weapons and various techniques of unarmed bujutsu appears undeniable, although somewhat confused, in studies of that ancient method of combat known as gusoku. A history of ancient bujutsu written in 1714 lists gusoku as an art which differed from the armed arts of archery, spearfighting, swordsmanship, and firearms. The same chronicle, however, contains indications that gusoku differed from the unarmed art of jujutsu as well (jujutsu being included in the warrior's training program in addition to horsemanship, maneuvering, and etiquette). Because of such an independent positioning, some authors are inclined to qualify gusoku as an "intermediate" method of combat performed in light armor, with or without a cutting weapon. Certain authors have translated the word gusoku as part of the clothing worn under the armor, while others have translated it as "short dagger" *(ko-gusoku)* or "long blade" *(cho-gusoku).* French sources of information mention the chronicle called the *Meitokuki,* in which ancient warriors were exhorted "to attack the soldiers with *cho-gusoku.*" But a master of modern jujutsu, Takeuchi Tojiro, of the Takeuchi school, claims that ko-gusoku does not refer to armor, "but the art of self-defense, capable of protecting man like an armor" *(Judo Kodokan,* VI, 4).

By the eighteenth century, the independent development of unarmed methods of bujutsu (sometimes even in opposition to armed methods of combat) seems to have become a generally well-established phenomenon. The long period of comparative peace and the many legislative and police controls strictly enforced by the central authorities in Edo had had a subtle weakening effect on the traditional armed specializations of bujutsu, which during that period could be used only in occasional individual and clandestine confrontations of an exceptional nature; meanwhile, unarmed bujutsu had begun to expand its sphere of application to fill the vacuum thus created. This expansion of unarmed methods of combat was also reflected in the increase in number, as well as in political and economic importance, of other classes of Japanese society who began to challenge the power of the warrior class—a power which had been gradually eroded by prolonged social pressure and military inactivity. Such a challenge, as noted in Part 1, was the result of opposition, not so much to a military, hierarchical state structure, as to an enlargement of that structure. The Establishment was reluctantly forced to accommodate other classes of Japanese subjects while maintaining (at least in theory) the original doctrines and traditions upon which it had based its original claims to legitimacy. Consequently, the martial spirit and traditional values of bujutsu were maintained by the schools of unarmed combat which had grown in popularity during the seventeenth century, as they concentrated ever more intensely upon the refinement of ancient methods of unarmed combat, as well as upon the development of new techniques.

From the seventeenth to the eighteenth centuries, therefore, a growing number of schools began to specialize in the methods of unarmed bujutsu. Considering the basic instrumental and functional possibilities of the human body in unarmed combat (upon which the instruction programs of all these schools were based), it might seem odd that there should have been so many different schools scattered throughout the length and breadth of Japan. Most of these, in fact, appear to have been offshoots or branches of certain central "mother schools." The latter, however, apparently differed among themselves in regard to the type and degree of emphasis placed upon the various functionalities of the human body in combat. For example, certain central schools, such as the Kito *ryu,* were famous for their techniques of projection; others, such as the Takenouchi *ryu,* were noted for the perfection of their techniques of immobilization;

still others, such as the Tenjin-Shinyo *ryu,* were famed for the power of their techniques of percussion. These central schools differed in relation to the predominance of certain strategic ideas concerning the value of attack, counterattack, or defense in unarmed combat. The schools of iaijutsu, for example, were inspired by the principle of sudden, total attack in swordplay. Many tactical ideas derived from and based upon this principle of initiative (therefore, of attack) filtered down to and influenced certain schools which specialized in unarmed martial-art methods. Others, including the great majority of jujutsu and aikijutsu schools, were seemingly inspired more by the principle of timely reaction to an opponent's attack and so geared their tactics and techniques to operate primarily as forms of counterattack. Still others explored the domain of pure neutralization in defense. In synthesis, then, it may be said that the types and number of schools of unarmed combat reflected the broad range of fighting possibilities inherent in the strategic use of the human body—possibilities which these schools explored and developed assiduously, often refining them to astounding degrees of strategic efficiency.

The problem of tracing the origins of each method and its related schools, of isolating the techniques of unarmed combat devised, taught, and practiced in those schools, as well as the particular principles of application they adopted, is an extremely perplexing one, given the records available. Every school, whether attached to a clan or independently maintained, claimed at one time or another (as many still do) a methodological originality and purity of origin, evolution, and character—although historically, it has been the interdependence of ideas and the interrelation of men's actions which have provided the basis for all notable human achievements. In any case, schools of unarmed bujutsu blossomed on the strength of principles and strategies which were quite obviously embodied in armed bujutsu. These principles merged or coexisted with other preexisting or coexisting principles of inspiration such as the principle of mental concentration *(haragei)* or of coordinated energy *(ki)* which were active in various methods of armed and unarmed combat.

The techniques of a school (therefore, its relative art and method) were often absorbed by and merged with those of other schools, thereby creating a strictly correlated whole, notwithstanding the veil of secrecy with which each school attempted to enshroud its method. It should not surprise us unduly, then, to learn that many of the specialized arts of the "empty hand" famous in Japan under the name of kempo and, more recently, of karate, although based almost entirely upon use of the body as a weapon for delivering blows and kicks, also employ that same anatomy, upon occasion, to hurl an opponent away. And we should be prepared to discover that particular specializations which call for the use of the anatomy mainly as a weapon of projection (jujutsu, judo, etc.) are sufficiently comprehensive to include (under the term *atemi)* an impressive repertoire of blows and kicks. Finally, all these arts, as we have indicated, show the pervasive influence of armed techniques, such as those used in spearfighting and swordsmanship, upon their own techniques of blocking, evasion, and counterattack.

Any logical examination of unarmed bujutsu, consequently, must consider certain broad principles of strategic application which (more than the particular techniques employed by any one school) will give us a panoramic view of the various trends followed by the specializations of the art of unarmed combat and its schools in feudal Japan (including the many ways in which these principles have affected and continue to influence modern martial arts methods).

The schools which played a determinant role in the history, theory, and practice of unarmed combat can be grouped into four major categories: the schools of jujutsu, the schools of aikijutsu, the schools of karate, and the schools of kiai. Their names, even if blurred by the mist of many legends, are still cherished in the doctrine of bujutsu, and their ancient methodologies still provide the foundation for the most famous modern methods of unarmed combat—those methods which Japan has exported with great success to the nations of the Western hemisphere.

The Schools of Jujutsu

The term jujutsu means, literally, technique or art *(jutsu)* of suppleness, flexibility, pliancy, gentleness (all varying renditions of the ideogram *ju*). All these terms, however, represent a single principle, a general way of applying a technique, of using the human body as a weapon in unarmed combat. Various techniques could be applied in accordance with this principle; and, in fact, each one of the many schools whose names are still familiar today interpreted the principle in a highly individual and technically differentiated way—a way which each endeavored to keep strictly secret and which became, in time, the salient characteristic of that particular school. According to certain authorities, the art itself appeared during the seventeenth century and is referred to in books dealing with the martial arts, such as the *Bugei Shogen* and *Kempo Hisho*. Master Kano Jigoro, founder of judo (a discipline also based primarily, if not entirely, upon this principle), traced the emergence of jujutsu to the period between 1600 and 1650. As applied to concrete combat strategies, the principle of *ju* consisted in adapting flexibly and intelligently to the strategic maneuvers of an opponent, in order to use his maneuvers and the force behind them to subjugate him or, at the very least, neutralize his attack. More will be said concerning the nature and significance of this principle in Part 3. Here, we merely wish to indicate how the technical perfection of each strategic interpretation of jujutsu was achieved. The vital question was always: "Does it work—is it effective in combat?" The answer was concretely provided by the results of individual duels and public competitions among the members of the various schools. The harshness of these encounters and their frequently lethal conclusions are vividly portrayed in Harrison's work, *The Fighting Spirit of Japan* (W. Foulsham & Co., Ltd., London):

> "In those days contests were extremely rough and not infrequently cost the participants their lives. Thus, whenever I sallied forth to take part in any of those affairs, I invariably bade farewell to my parents, since I had no assurance that I should ever return alive. Competitions were of such a drastic nature that few tricks were barred and we did not hesitate to have recourse to the most dangerous methods in order to overcome an opponent." (Harrison, 65)

Thus, in the Meiji period, reminisced the late Yokoyama Sakujiro, "perhaps the greatest practical exponent of Judo Japan had in my day produced" (Harrison, 65). In such turbulent encounters (as had historically been true of competitions among practitioners of spear fighting and fencing) it was often a case of "win all or lose all."

Such a process of qualification (one might say elimination) through practical testing, not only insured continuous striving to perfect both the weapons and the technical ways of employing them; it also estab-

lished the reputations of those schools where that strategic perfection was highly pronounced. There were innumerable schools which developed extremely effective methods of combat through the skilled adaptation of the principle of *ju* to their techniques. The following are mentioned prominently (among many others) in chronicles dealing with bujutsu as having been notable jujutsu schools: the Tenjin-Shinyo *ryu*, the Takenouchi *ryu*, the Sosuishitsu *ryu*, the Kito *ryu*, and the Sekiguchi *ryu*. Together with a number of others, these schools formed a modified synthesis in the school of judo founded by Master Kano Jigoro in the nineteenth century.

Particularly famous for its various techniques of percussion *(atemi-waza)*, of immobilization *(torae)*, and of strangulation *(shime)*, the Tenjin-Shinyo school of jujutsu is generally considered to have been the result of a fusion of two ancient schools, the Yoshin *ryu* and the Shin-no-Shindo. The origins of the Yoshin *ryu* are still the object of much debate in the doctrine. Many believe the founder of the art to have been a physician of Nagasaki, a certain Akiyama Shirobei Yoshitoki, who went to China in the seventeenth century to deepen his knowledge in the field of medicine. While studying various methods of resuscitation *(hassei-ko*, later to become the complex science of *kappo* or *katsu)*, he was exposed to Chinese martial arts and to their main principles of strategic application. In particular, he studied the techniques of percussion, which, even much later, appear to have been the main technical concern of this school. In Japan, he elaborated upon this technical nucleus in complete isolation (near a temple in the woods), his personal training program including both physical exercises and meditation. In time, he developed about three hundred techniques of combat based upon the principle of *ju* (suppleness), as indicated by the name he gave his method: *yo* meaning "willow," and *shin* meaning "spirit" or "heart." The image of the flexible, swaying willow which snaps back even after the fiercest hurricane, while the sturdy but rigid oak falls thunderously before the onslaught of the storm, was thus recorded in the chronicles of the martial arts—also serving to confirm, even if indirectly, Chinese influence upon that school of thought in Japan which held the principle of nonresistence to be superior to all others, not only in a moral sense but also (and to the warrior, above all) in the concrete and practical reality of combat.

The founder of the other school, the Shin-no-Shindo, is said to have been a certain Yamamoto Tamizaemon, of the Osaka police, who added other techniques (particularly those of immobilization) to the already impressive repertoire of the Yoshin *ryu*. Both schools were finally unified, becoming a systematic whole with a single name in the late seventeenth century, through the efforts of Master Yanagi Sekizai Minamoto Masa-tari (also known in his later years as Master Iso Mataemon), whose astonishing feats of prowess in the art of unarmed combat (particularly in the use of techniques of percussion, *atemi-waza)* fill many vivid pages in the literature of the martial arts. He is said to have been a remarkable jujutsu master, thoroughly versed in the practice and theory of unarmed combat. After having studied the techniques of the Yoshin *ryu* and Shin-no-Shindo under the guidance of Master Hitotsuyanagi and Master Homma, respectively, he traveled from school to school, challenging local champions. In the course of this pilgrimage (after which he opened a school in Edo, where his method was taught to retainers of the Tokugawa clan), he is said to have confronted a group of hired mercenaries who had come to extort an exorbitant sum of money from peasants who were sheltering Mataemon (or perhaps, as was customary under similar circumstances, had actually hired him). The records available describe the encounter as a "savage battle" in which the master and one of his best pupils demonstrated the devastating effects of well-applied *atemi-waza,* even when employed against professional, armed attackers who, upon this occasion, collected no booty but many bruises—much to the satisfaction of their intended victims. Mataemon was also a conscientious theorist who apparently leaned toward an ascetic view of the martial arts. His warnings to his disciples, concerning the inadvisability of partaking excessively of alcoholic beverages or of giving way to uncontrolled lust and venality, reflect a certain type of austere ethics rooted in a military past which, in his time, seemed to have gradually receded under the pressure of unrelenting mercantile opulence and general lassitude.

Of particular strategic importance to the development of the art were his ideas concerning the principle of *ju*—ideas still discernible today in various modern adaptations of unarmed bujutsu, such as Master Kano Jigoro's judo. Overdevelopment of the muscles and thus excessive reliance upon muscular force, according to Mataemon, entailed those qualities of rigidity and slowness usually associated with a suit of armor or, more pointedly, with encroaching old age and, eventually, death. Mataemon preferred to emphasize suppleness (like that of a child), which he felt was the most visible characteristic of life, of action. Accordingly, in combat, he recommended that his students apply the techniques of his school quickly, but without undue tension, and only when the opponent himself, by attacking, had weakened his own line of defense and provided the major part of that force necessary to subdue him.

The ancient and intriguing school known as Takenouchi *ryu* is reportedly still active today in Japan, having been guided by one successor after another for twelve generations. It is generally held to have been founded by a *bushi* of high rank, Hisamori (later and better known as Takeuchi Toichiro), during the dictatorship of Ashikaga Yoshiharu (1522-46), while Emperor Gonara occupied the throne (1526-57). Takeuchi is said to have systematized a substantial number of armed and unarmed bujutsu techniques both during and after a period of intense study and experimentation in the wilderness, where he practiced with a wooden sword *(bokken)* and stick *(jo)* against mobile targets. He emphasized the use of techniques of immobilization *(osae-waza),* which were organized systematically into five "keys" or groups (*go-kyu)* in accordance with certain principles of exposition still found in modern derivations of ancient bujutsu. Takeuchi taught these and other "keys," as well as techniques of combat based upon the use of daggers (all particularly effective at close range). This last feature of his methodology caused certain martial arts experts, such as Shidachi, to qualify his techniques as belonging to the art of ko-gusoku rather than to

the "pure art" of jujutsu (Smith[1], 52). In any case, the techniques of his school proved to be extremely effective, and countless warriors flocked to his *dojo.* According to the scrolls and manuscripts *(makimono)* which form the records of this school, Takeuchi's son was even requested to perform techniques from his father's program of instruction (which included more than six hundred techniques) before Emperor Gomizuno (1611-29). After the performance, the emperor bestowed upon the art the title of "supreme and unsurpassed art of combat" *(hi-no-shita toride-kaizan).* He also granted the disciples of this art his permission to use the imperial color, purple, for those cords employed in performing the school's special techniques (the immobilizations).

An interesting derivation of the Takenouchi *ryu* is the Sosuishitsu *ryu,* reputedly founded by a samurai of Bungo Takeda, Fugatami Hannosuke, in 1650. This *bushi* developed his own method of combat from those he had learned and, after a period of purification in the Yoshino mountains, named his method after "the pure flowing waters" of the Yoshino river. He then taught it to Shitama Mataichi—members of whose family, whether by direct lineage or by adoption, appear to have been masters of this art for centuries. Eventually, their school joined Master Kano Jigoro's successful synthesis of *ju* arts, known the world over as judo.

The Kito *ryu* merits a particular place in the doctrine of unarmed bujutsu because of the esoteric elements evident in its method—elements very similar, in fact, to those which characterize the schools of aikijutsu. Of particular interest in this regard are the formal exercises *(kata)* which have been preserved by the modern inheritors of the Kito *ryu.* Some of the available records relate the origin of this school to a Chinese method of combat based upon the principle of *ju,* as explained and illustrated by Ch-En Yuan-Pin (better known in Japanese records as Gempin) to selected warriors of the seventeenth century. A former dignitary of the Chinese court, Gempin had visited Japan in 1621, and then settled there permanently in 1638 in order to escape the rising power of the Manchu dynasty. A poet and scholar, he secured a position of rank with Japanese nobles of the period (the Owari family), producing a number of treatises on Chinese philosophers such as Lao-tzu and T'ung K'ao, and introducing the works of many Chinese poets into the mainstream of Japanese culture. He also collaborated with the learned Japanese priest Gensei in a number of literary endeavors. At one point Gempin is said to have instructed three masterless warriors *(ronin)* in a method of "seizing a man" which he had seen practiced in China. The names of the three *bushi* have been dutifully preserved: Fukuno Hichiroemon, Isogai Jirozaemon, and Miura Yojiemon. These men continued their studies of Gempin's method in the Kokusei monastery in Azabu and apparently grasped its central principles quite well, because they were said to have subsequently founded their own school—the Kito *ryu.*

Another interpretation of material available on this subject, however, indicates that the founder of this method was a certain Terada, a samurai in the service of Kyogoku, a daimyo closely associated with the Tokugawa. His method of combat, in turn, was inherited by two other great jujutsu experts, Yoshimura and Takenaka. These techniques, usually performed in full armor (or in formal robes reminiscent of armor) were centered mainly upon the projection of an opponent down onto the ground. In observing the sequences of a number of the formal exercises of this school *(koshiki-no-kata,* or "classic forms") practiced by high-ranking practitioners of Kodokan judo, one is immediately impressed by the smooth fluidity of the applied principle of *wa* (accord), seen not only as a "supple" *(ju)* blending of strategies, movements, and actions with those of an opponent, but as an even more comprehensive blending of the self with the whole environment, of which the opponent is only a part. As such, these techniques were considered extremely sophisticated and difficult to understand, even by bujutsu experts such as Master Kano and Master Uyeshiba, founder of modern aikido, both of whom had studied them at great length—Master Kano under Master Iikubo and Master Uyeshiba under Master Tozawa Tokusaburo—before incorporating many salient features of this interesting art into their own modern methodologies.

The powerful Sekiguchi *ryu* traced its roots back to the seventeenth century and the stern Sekiguchi Jushin, a teacher of warriors who is said to have excelled in the martial virtues of honesty and objectivity—

CHART 15

JUDO PROGRAM OF INSTRUCTION
(Kodokan style)

1. Techniques of projection *(nage-waza)*
   a) From a standing condition *(tachi-waza)*
      Hand-techniques *(te-waza)*
      Hip-techniques *(koshi-waza)*
      Foot-techniques *(ashi-waza)*
   b) From a falling condition *(sutemi-waza)*
      Dorsal falls *(masutemi-waza)*
      Lateral falls *(yokosutemi-waza)*
2. Techniques of immobilization *(osae-waza)*
3. Techniques of strangulation *(shime-waza)*
4. Techniques of dislocation *(kansetsu-waza)*
5. Techniques of percussion with the upper and lower extremities *(ate-waza)*
6. Formal exercises *(kata)*, nine series
7. Methods of resuscitation *(kappo)*

virtues he seemed to have successfully transmitted to his sons, together with the techniques of his School. The words of his eldest son, Rohaku, to a powerful baron in Edo in 1716 were recorded in the doctrine of bujutsu and indicate the son's contempt for those masters of bujutsu who "threw dust in people's eyes" by performing tricks to advertise their schools, thus debasing bujutsu as a whole and bringing dishonor upon the "real" masters.

Many other ancient and reputable schools, such as the Yagyu-Shingan *ryu* of the Date clan (which is said to have included over two thousand combat techniques in its program), and the Juki *ryu* of Sawa Dochi, as well as their various branches and affiliations, their steady progression of teachers and disciples, are listed in the doctrine of jujutsu as having been primarily inspired by the principle of *ju*, a principle interpreted with astounding efficiency by Count Kano Jigoro. This great educator and scholar emphasized certain educational purposes relating to the development of man's character and personality along ethical lines, modifying the medieval techniques of jujutsu and changing the name of this methodological synthesis to judo—the way *(do)* of suppleness or gentleness *(ju)*.

Notwithstanding this emphasis upon broader ethical considerations in combat, Master Kano's art, born into and eventually strongly influenced by a harshly competitive environment, established itself as the most sophisticated and yet practically effective method of combat inspired by this principle. The art spread throughout the world and, as a sport of competition, reached the heights of the Olympic games, thus fulfilling, even if posthumously, Master Kano's ultimate aspirations.

Judo offers a rich repertoire of techniques of combat, usually divided into five major categories (see Chart 15). These techniques involve the application of the principle of *ju* not only within the context of passive suppleness in a Buddhist sense but also as the active principle of counterattack which has made the art extremely effective whether used in real combat or in competition. Judo, as an art of combat, was thoroughly tested during a period which lasted from the late 1800s until the early 1900s. The recognition of its excellence in both theory and practice in the field of unarmed combat helped to rescue many other schools and methods from widespread neglect and eventual oblivion. In 1905, in fact, the majority of the old schools of jujutsu merged with Master Kano's school, and the fame of Kodokan judo began to spread throughout the world.

The schools of aikijutsu, however, did not join Master Kano's synthesis of *jutsu* arts. Today, as in the past, they remain independent in matters of organization and public affiliation, although exchanges of

instruction and instructors in this age of heightened and expanded communication are, of course, taking place with increasing frequency. Kodokan instructors, trained in the arts of ancient aikijutsu and those of its modern derivative, Master Uyeshiba's aikido, teach these techniques within the judo program of instruction, thus fulfilling a cherished dream of Master Kano, who had worked all his life to preserve the best arts and techniques which a long, ofttimes bloody tradition had produced. Whether he succeeded in truly injecting an element of morality *(do)* into the ancient military arts of bujutsu is a question that can be answered only by studying the techniques of judo as they are taught by the modern teachers of the Kodokan today, and observing the effects of their continual practice upon the personality and character of the judo student. This subject is too vast to be discussed here, but will be touched upon in Part 3 and analyzed in greater depth in another work concerning the moral aspects of the martial arts.

The Schools of Aikijutsu

This art may be described as the technique *(jutsu)* of coordinated, assembled, harmonized, or concentrated *(ai)* consciousness, spirit, or mind *(ki)*. Concerning the early history of this method, Harrison writes in *The Fighting Spirit of Japan* (W. Foulsham & Co., Ltd., London):

> It is recorded that more than 700 years ago there existed to the north of Mount Fuji a school of "Wo," the ancient martial arts. This school specialized in the teaching of so-called Aiki-Jutsu which was kept secret and disclosed to only a few disciples, for the most part nobles of ancient lineage. This art had originated from Ken-Jutsu or swordsmanship, and little by little it had become an art of combat superior to Ju-jutsu. (Harrison, 79)

The term *aiki* (like *ju)* also indicates a principle, a way of using the body as a weapon of combat, a way of performing a technique (almost any technique) successfully against an opponent. The central idea of *aiki,* as we shall see in Part 3, was that of using the coordinated power of *ki* (intrinsic or inner energy) in harmony *(ai)* with the various requirements and circumstances of combat, that is, with the opponent's strategy, his weapons, his personality, and so forth. By blending one's own strategy with the opponent's, it was possible to achieve full control over him and over the encounter, thus achieving the primary purpose of combat: the opponent's subjugation. Just how these results were achieved technically, in ancient times, however, is extremely difficult to say. Most of the schools of aikijutsu which had developed techniques and strategies for rendering the principle of *ai* concretely effective in actual combat have vanished.

Among these ancient schools, one of the most renowned was the Daito *ryu.* According to a modern bujutsu expert, Mr. Tomiki of the Kodokan, the manuscripts of instruction of certain secret martial arts *(den-sho),* compiled during the feudal era, refer to the aikijutsu practiced by this school as dating back to the Kamakura period. The school itself was reportedly founded by Minamoto Yoshimitsu (d. 1120), better known in various Japanese epics as Yoshitsune, and the art was practiced by the warriors of the Minamoto clan for several centuries before being inherited by the Takeda family (part of the military clan of Aizu). The legitimate teacher of the art derived from aikijutsu, according to the Japanese system of hierarchical transmission by blood, adoption, or affiliation, was Master Uyeshiba Morihei, the founder of aikido. The specific doctrine of aikido, however, links the beginning of this particular school of aikijutsu (that is, the Daito *ryu)* to the sixth son of Emperor Seiwa, Prince Sadasumi, who lived in the ninth century. In relation to the methodology of this school, Master Uyeshiba Kisshomaru writes, "Its theory is deep and the number of its techniques is great" (Uyeshiba, 150).

How the concept of *ai* was actually embodied in the ancient techniques of aikijutsu practiced by the Daito school, we have no way of knowing today. The fluid beauty and impressive efficiency of the method, however, are evident in the modern interpretation of techniques practiced in schools of aikido. If one watches these techniques being performed in combat against one or several opponents, with weapons or

Aikijutsu techniques

CHART 16

MAJOR OUTLINES OF AIKIDO PROGRAM OF INSTRUCTION

TECHNIQUES OF COMBAT (aikido *waza*)	FORMAL EXERCISES (aikido *kata*)
In defense: Techniques of evasion and centralization In counterattack: Techniques of projection Techniques of immobilization	

without, it is not difficult to understand why, in earlier times (as Harrison put it), aikijutsu "had become an art of combat superior to Jujutsu."

Master Uyeshiba Morihei was virtually the last representative of those schools of aikijutsu, which, through him, have filtered down from the feudal ages of Japan to the twentieth century—even if in a necessarily modified form. His aikido, like any other method of combat, contains an impressive number of techniques based upon the instrumental use of the human body as a weapon of combat. These techniques can be used to achieve, quickly and efficiently, the subjugation of a single opponent—or of several. They range from projections *(kokyu-nage)* to immobilizations and dislocations, to stylized blows. A systematic study of the first two categories is contained in the book *Aikido and the Dynamic Sphere,* by the authors of the present work. In this book, twenty-eight basic techniques and their possible combinations are analyzed. (These basic techniques can actually be developed into an almost limitless series of strategic possibilities, as practiced in the various schools which are linked to Master Uyeshiba's Aikikai So-Hombu (also known as Hombu Dojo) in Tokyo. Other schools which were influenced directly or indirectly by Master Uyeshiba's method include the Yoshinkan Institute of Master Shioda, the Yoseikan of Master Mochizuki, the Korindo of Master Hirai, and the Kodokan School of Judo where aikido is taught by Master Tomiki. Branches of the Daito *ryu* and Takeda *ryu* are also said to be still actively involved with the principle of *aiki.*

The techniques of aikido are all, in their strategic dimension, based upon the reflexive concept of *aiki,* that is, of total coordination of one's own reaction to an aggression with the aggressor's own power of attack. In Master Uyeshiba's method, however, coordination is not intended merely in a strategic sense—in other words, it is not viewed solely as a means of achieving the single or restricted purpose of counterattack through an intelligent employment of natural or anatomical laws, since this would restrict the value and significance of the principle and its techniques to the problem of combat alone. Such a limited purpose can, of course, be easily and efficiently achieved by the proper application of *aiki* techniques—actually, it can also be achieved by the use of *ju* techniques, *wa* techniques, or even the aggressive techniques of the ancient, unilateral methods of direct attack which did not usually concern themselves with an opponent's strategy *(go).* But coordination, in Master Uyeshiba's interpretation of *aiki,* had acquired a connotation infinitely more complex than that which generally characterizes combat and its correlative technical strategy *(jutsu).* It had been expanded to characterize the more comprehensive dimension of man's involvement with his total reality (spiritual and existential) from his first breath to his last.

Because of his desire to further the development of an integrated human personality, truly balanced in a continuing condition of harmony (that is, of the self within and the socionatural reality without), Master Uyeshiba adapted the ancient *aiki* techniques in a particular fashion, striving to devise flexible instruments which would make his goals realizable. The superior type of harmony he envisioned is obviously more difficult to attain—even to attempt. The *jutsu* techniques devised for combat purposes alone, although sophisticated, were intrinsically limited because of their very specialization. (Master Kano, too, had faced

this problem, which he resolved by modifying the techniques in question until he felt he had removed them from the jujutsu dimension to the dimension of judo). Master Uyeshiba, in accordance with a more complex design and interpretation of the principle of *aiki,* also modified the ancient *jutsu,* producing a new method which he called *aikido*—the "way of harmony" or "philosophy of coordination."

Whether he succeeded in moralizing the ancient methods and techniques of combat inherited from aikijutsu is a question whose answer depends in large measure upon how his art is taught and practiced, and thus upon the effects discernible in the character of advanced students and teachers. It is often the case, however, that individuals who are actually practicing a form of aikijutsu claim to be practitioners of aikido, thus mistaking the *technique* for the *way.*

The Arts of Striking

Various methods of efficiently striking an opponent in combat in order to achieve his subjugation without resorting to the use of mechanical weapons or techniques of combat other than blows or kicks, or both, were doubtless known and practiced by many *bushi* in Japan during the feudal era, as well as by the members of other classes of Japanese society at that time (and even earlier).

Striking (i.e., punching, kicking, etc.) has often been qualified as one of the most ancient and spontaneous of all the arts of combat. In Japan during the pre-Tokugawa period, however, the arts or methods of

striking do not appear to have been as specialized or as systematically grouped as certain ancient methods of boxing and kicking reportedly used on the Asian continent during the same period—methods which (according to the doctrine of bujutsu) strongly influenced many Japanese systems of combat based upon the predominant functionality of a man's arms and legs used as weapons of percussion. Moreover, in pre-Tokugawa Japan, these systems seem to have been an integral part of more comprehensive and diversified methods of bujutsu (both armed and unarmed), although apparently in a subordinate sense.

In this subordinate role, the art of striking appears in almost every major specialization of bujutsu. Many of the *kata,* or formal exercises, still practiced in the remaining schools of naginatajutsu, yarijutsu, and other arts provide examples even today of those skillful movements of blocking and extension which can be used to weaken or destroy an opponent's guard and thus prepare the way for delivery of unobstructed blows with the elbows or knees from inside or beneath that guard. In the light of available records, it is certainly not unreasonable to assume that these techniques were also used in combat to pave the way for the final blows delivered with spear or dagger. In kenjutsu, for example, a practitioner would use the blade of his sword to slash and thrust, but he would also use the butt of the guard (which was heavily ornamented) for reverse blows—blows which could be delivered with the edge of the hand or with the elbow. Many parries which engaged a warrior's hands in high extension left his abdomen temporarily unprotected and easy prey to murderous kicks, while his legs and trunk could be attacked with various unbalancing techniques to prepare the way for the inevitable and rarely delayed coup de grace.

The earlier records of Japanese wrestling (both the informal style which characterized the original contests of strength known as *chikara-kurabe* and the more sophisticated style of sumo) seem to indicate that originally wrestling included, when it did not consist entirely of, terrific blows delivered with every anatomical weapon available. This brings to mind the pancratium of ancient Greece which made many an athlete's "mailed fists" famous throughout the entire Hellenic world. Certain authors, in fact, when analyzing sumo techniques, link those based upon powerful slaps and heaving pushes, known as *tsuppari*—techniques which can send even the heaviest *sumotori* reeling helplessly out of the ring—to ancient techniques of percussion which were employed to dispatch opponents in the most ancient bouts.

These techniques of percussion, under the comprehensive name of *atemi-waza,* have continued to occupy a position of some importance in the major modern derivations of unarmed bujutsu: in jujutsu, in judo, and—although to a largely ritualized extent—in aikido. That position has become decidedly second-

ary, however, in the modified applications of these three disciplines—that is, as exercises of coordination, as forms of limited self-defense, and as regulated sports.

In actual, all-out combat, however, when proficiency in *atemi-waza* is added to a knowledge of techniques of projection, strangulation, or dislocation, an expert in any one of these arts becomes a most redoubtable fighter with a comprehensive range of strategic possibilities at his command. We can, therefore, perceive the position of importance the *atemi-waza* occupied in the ancient matrices from which the modern versions of those arts were derived: in the ancient forms of jujutsu practiced in feudal Japan and in the equally ancient aikijutsu practiced by professional fighters of all classes and, in particular, by the warriors of feudal Japan.

Today, the *atemi-waza* of unarmed bujutsu are seldom studied and practiced per se in jujutsu, judo, and so forth. Instead, they are usually part of a program of instruction which seems to place greater emphasis upon techniques of combat intended to project an opponent down onto the ground, or to immobilize him vertically or horizontally; or techniques of strangulation or anatomical dislocation (depending, of course, upon the particular art being employed), or both. As techniques which alone and by themselves can achieve the primary purpose of combat (the opponent's subjugation), *atemi-waza* forms are practiced most assiduously by the students of that art of combat known as karate.

The word *karate* is formed by combining two Chinese ideograms: *kara* meaning "empty" or "bare," and *te* meaning "hand(s)" or "fist(s)." The art of the "empty hand" as a complete method of combat, which could achieve an opponent's subjugation through the use of techniques of percussion alone, seems to have been a highly developed art centuries ago on the Asian continent. Almost every work on the subject of karate, in fact, seems to lead the student outside Japan proper and through the Ryukyu Islands (Okinawa) to Korea, China, Tibet, Siam, and so forth, where such methods of combat have always been very popular. Tales of extraordinary power displayed by Okinawans or Koreans using only their hands and feet as weapons were circulated among the *bushi* who, as members of the armies occupying these lands, had often been exposed to its devastating effects. In turn, many of those tales referred to even more esoteric schools of boxing in China—a reference which certain scholars feel is confirmed by the fact that the phonetic rendering of *kara* itself in Japanese may denote "empty" or "bare," but may also refer to China or anything originating in that land.

Various interpretations of the origins of this specialized art have produced a theory still prominent in the modern doctrine of bujutsu. It is commonly believed that the art of the fist might have developed as an overspecialization of ancient exercises performed in China and India as means of total integration (very much as yoga or tai-ch'i-chuan are practiced today) and usually based upon the doctrines of Centralization

and Intrinsic Energy described in Part 3. These ancient exercises were intended to further the development and maintenance of a condition of good health and supple functionality which would make it possible for a man to live fully and well. This had also been the goal of the ancient civilizations of Greece and Rome, as expressed in the axiom *nuns sana in corpore sano.*

Such a goal or purpose was clearly an ambitious one. In both China and India, each individual could perform these exercises in order to attain the level of integration which would be consonant with his or her degree of mental development and position in life. Thus a laborer could perform these exercises in order to maintain his health and improve his particular skills; a sick person to recover his health; a scholar to help deepen his insights and powers of analyzing experience; an emperor to insure a long and just reign; a general as an aid to the fulfillment of his duty with the utmost intelligence and determination; a soldier to develop his martial capacities.

Many names have been given to these exercises, which, according to certain scholars, were originally based upon stylized repetitions of movements derived from almost everything in creation: animals, human cycles of breathing, cosmic expansion and contraction in the seasonal progression of time, tides, and so forth. And the relationship between the concepts inspiring these exercises and a naturalistic, pantheistic vision of life is unmistakably clear and forceful even today. Taoism is considered a doctrine of direct inspiration for these exercises, and tai-ch'i is one of the names used most frequently to identify them. They also became known more specifically as tai-ch'i-chuan, kung-fu, pa-kua, and so forth, when they began to develop into that clearly more strategic dimension related to combat and to the use of the fist and foot as instruments for striking an opponent. Buddhism is also linked to the origins of certain specializations such as shaolin, to name only one. And it was in these specialized forms that (or so the generally accepted theory indicates) the art of striking came to Korea and the Ryukyu Islands, following the expansion of Indian and Chinese philosophy through the pilgrimages made by scholars and priests on the one hand, and through the activities of those pirates of mixed racial stock who dominated the South China Sea during the Ming dynasty (1368-1643) on the other.

A substantial number of students of Japanese bujutsu, obviously impressed by the strong influence exercised upon all the ancient martial arts by Buddhism in general and by the Zen sect in particular, trace the beginning of the art of striking to the founder of the Zen sect, Bodhidharma (P'u-Ti Ta-Mo in Chinese or Daruma in Japanese). This fierce first patriarch of Zen, who "did not suffer fools gladly," had originally emigrated from India to China. After meeting the emperor Wu, he spent a substantial period of time at the Shaolin (Ssiao or Hsiao or Hsiao-Lin) monastery at Sung-Shan, where he taught the doctrine of meditation *(ch'an, zen)* as a way of integration and ultimate salvation. During his stay in this monastery, he is said to have written certain pamphlets of instruction (such as *I-Chin-Ching)* as guides for his disciples to help them strengthen and unify their personalities in order that they might meditate well and thus achieve the ultimate goal of his doctrine. The results of his training methods are also said to have been systematically perfected and arranged until they grew into an art of percussion which became popular throughout China. No one, however, has ever been able to substantiate this theory of a religious origin of the art of striking in both its Chinese and Japanese dimensions. As a scholar of bujutsu, Mr. Hu, has aptly observed, Buddhism (and consequently its patriarchs, scholars, and monks) had generally embraced a nonviolent view of existence and of the means of understanding man's reality and living well within it. As such, that doctrine and its representatives were usually totally unconcerned with worldly attainment of any kind (including triumphs in violent encounters). The books or pamphlets the Bodhidharma was supposed to have written would seem to have been concerned in large measure with methods of deep breathing, meditation, and possibly calisthenics—but not with methods of using the fist or foot as instruments of percussion. Furthermore, as has been pointed out by a number of scholars, methods of combat using fists and feet (such as tai-ch'i-chuan, kung-fu, and kempo) seem to have been known and practiced in various forms even earlier than A.D. 520, when Bodhidharma is said to have reached China. Books of fist fighting, such as the *Shou-Pu,* were mentioned in lists of the ancient chronicles of the Han dynasty. Others, such as the *Han-Shu-I Wenchih,* had been compiled by Pan-Kun between 32 and 92—once again, centuries before Bodhidharma is said to have reached China (520–35).

Of course, there has always been a tendency on the part of some martial arts masters to relate their arts to motivations of a higher nature than those generally associated with the urge to fight. But, as will appear more clearly in Part 3, these masters turned to Taoism and Buddhism not only to justify their methods morally but also to provide themselves and their arts with a coherent theory and, above all, with certain techniques for the establishment of mental control. These techniques, which Taoism and Buddhism had developed for their own adherents, had been found by Chinese as well as Japanese masters of the various fighting arts to be effective means of developing reserves of power and courage in their students.

The Chinese art of striking, evolving from ancient forms of tai-ch'i, seems to have flourished (in various styles and schools) throughout the long history of that sprawling nation, especially during the turbulent era which preceded the fall of the Han dynasty in the third century A.D., when the "Yellow Turbans" fought ferociously, even unarmed, on the battlefield, thus setting an example which the protagonists of the Boxer Rebellion were to follow in 1900. In all of its many specializations, the art of boxing seems to have developed along lines which displayed the characteristics of either one or the other of its two primary styles: the "hard" *(wai-chia),* emphasizing muscular action and power in the execution of the techniques; and the "soft" *(nei-chia),* stressing the inner, intrinsic coordination of energy produced by the entire personality, unified and directed from within. Examples of the "hard" or "external" style of performance are reported to have included several methods of shaolin and kung-fu, while tai-ch'i-chuan, pa-kua, and hsing- i were cited as examples of the "soft" or "internal" style. This dualism, however, although still evident today in the doctrine of Oriental boxing, had no firmly fixed boundaries, since "hard" methods of boxing could become "soft" merely by shifting the emphasis in performance of techniques from pure muscular power to mental coordination, and vice-versa. It is evident that such a division affected the mechanism and the number of the techniques of percussion employed in the various forms only to a limited degree and was, therefore, related more to the development of the power with which they were delivered than to the techniques themselves.

Recent studies of the major Chinese specializations in the art of hitting have somewhat loosened the bond of secrecy which has long shielded these arts from the eyes of the curious Westerner. Thus we learn that tai-ch'i-chuan ("supreme ultimate fist"), for example, was reportedly founded in the fourteenth century A.D. by a Taoist philosopher, but that its roots extend all the way back to the fifteenth century B.C. and to Lao-tzu. If accurate, such a derivation would make tai-ch'i-chuan one of the oldest boxing arts practiced in the world. Its techniques developed in number through the combination of basic postures and actions in which all the parts of the body were used and from almost any position imaginable. In the doctrine of the art we find these techniques arranged in groupings which reflect the major symbols of Chinese cosmogony: fire, water, metal, wood, and earth, in accordance with the major directions in which they were applied—that is, forward, backward, to the right, to the left, and whirling in the center. Interestingly enough, they were all characteristically circular, the objection to straight movements being emphatically repeated in the majority of old texts. This characteristic, as we will see in Part 3, was predominant in methods of combat based upon the strategies of defense or counterattack. In such strategies, there is no direct, frontal clash with an opponent's attack; instead, the attack is influenced tangentially after it has been fully launched. From this basic nucleus, innumerable styles developed, from which, in turn, sprang an equally impressive number of schools where the ancient forms of tai-ch'i-chuan have been preserved for the most diversified purposes (eugenic, military, therapeutic) right down to the present day.

The Chinese method of combat known as pa-kua began to appear in the doctrine of individual combat in the nineteenth century, but many who have studied the history of this method trace its origins back to legendary times in China. Its theory appears thoroughly imbued with the naturalistic philosophy of the *Book of Changes,* the *I-Ching,* and, like tai-ch'i-chuan, it is perfectly in accord with the Taoistic vision of life. Its techniques, also largely circular in essence, were arranged according to the patterns of the "Eight Diagrams," which gave the art its name, and whose lines (whether solid or broken) express the primary characteristics of life as interpreted by the Chinese, such as power, receptivity, tumultuousness, and restfulness. The combination of these diagrams within the larger circle of creation was said to express and explain the ever-changing ebb and flow of existence (according to some, the very evolution of existence itself). The techniques of pa-kua were devised to cope with this multiform reality through circular actions of deflection and return which, as in tai-ch'i-chuan, dissipated the force of an attack and left an opponent vulnerable to a counterattack. This action was usually performed by the practitioner's using the palms of his hands in a seemingly endless series of varied movements—a characteristic which gave the art another name by which it was commonly identified: pa-kua-chang, the "palm method of the eight diagrams." According to some experts, the ancient purity of pa-kua was soon altered by the introduction of fist and foot techniques of percussion as the method began to expand and evolve, eventually merging with tai-ch'i-chuan and other popular methods. Most teachers of this art, however, have generally endeavored to preserve the internal or "soft" character of the art by avoiding excessive dependence upon tension and power generated by the muscular system alone, while at the same time emphasizing in the theory and practice of pa-kua, the role of total, coordinated energy, as well as coherent, mental control over the manifestations of that energy.

Generally considered more linear in approach was that method of combat known as shaolin (often linked to Buddhism and, as we have seen, even to the Zen patriarch Bodhidharma), which called for the use of extremely powerful techniques or methods of delivering blows and kicks. A clear economy of movement—blurred, upon occasion, by the influence of other methods of combat—was said to have characterized the tactics of shaolin fighters who carved a name for themselves in the ancient records of this interesting art. They often appear as leaders of fighting units in Chinese armies, as hired mercenaries protecting the caravans of Chinese merchants, as teachers in certain schools of boxing, and so forth. Shaolin, too, was influenced by "hard" and "soft" methods of employing a man's powers in combat. Ancient manuscripts which contain records of this art refer to these two interpretations which seem to have divided shaolin fighters into two opposing factions, each thoroughly convinced of its own superiority. Perhaps because the "hard" method was more direct and easier to grasp as an approach to the reality of combat, it apparently enjoyed greater popularity, whereas the "soft" school, which required a more comprehensive form of mental concentration and extension, was generally restricted to higher and, therefore, more rarefied strata of Chinese society.

Since they were more popular then, the "hard" styles of these Chinese methods of unarmed combat were those which, in general, were more readily exported to Okinawa and Korea by professional fighters of every type, from the remnants of vanquished armies to the bands of pirates infesting the South China Sea. According to certain students of Asiatic martial arts, this explains why the Okinawan and Korean styles of karate (compared, that is, to the Chinese arts of striking) appear more rugged and linear. According to this school of thought, the popularization of shaolin was the beginning of the art's degeneration in China itself, as emphasis upon muscular strength (always easier to develop than total [that is, mental] coordination) gained ascendancy. This process was further accelerated in such countries as Korea and the Ryukyu Islands, since they were not as advanced, culturally, as China. Both of these countries, however, seem to have contributed to the art of unarmed combat, the former by developing, primarily, the tremendous efficiency of a man's feet, while the latter concentrated upon the fantastic powers of penetration which could be generated by the use of both hands and feet. Korean karate, in fact, is said to rely predominantly, even today, upon foot techniques of percussion. Okinawan karate, on the other hand, is still famous for the apparent ease with which its adherents smash through boards, tiles, bricks, and so forth, using hands or feet. Satow, in his *Notes on Loochoo* (Chinese, Liukiu; Japanese, Ryukyu), read before the Asiatic Society of Japan in 1872, wherein he described Okinawan customs and history, was one of the first Europeans to be particularly impressed by the formidable ability of "a well-trained" Okinawan fighter to "smash a large earthern water jar or kill a man with a single blow of his fists." Chinese methods of unarmed combat seem to have reached the Ryukyu Islands as early as the seventh century and infused, to a certain extent, their dualistic approach into the new culture. In the doctrine of Japanese karate, in fact, we find references to the "two schools" (Namboku *ryu)* of the method of unarmed combat with fists known as kempo: the "soft" (Ju-no-kempo) and the "hard" (Go-no-kempo). These two schools inspired others, such as the famous Okinawan Surite and Nahate—the former embracing the Shorin *ryu,* while the latter was represented by the equally famous Goju *ryu* and Uechi *ryu.* The Goju *ryu* of karate, for example, claims as its founder Kanryu Higaonna, who had studied the art of striking in China and then returned to Okinawa during the middle of the Meiji period. His successor, Miyagi Chojun, named this school Goju ("hard and soft") and exported it to Hawaii in 1933. The esoteric school of karate known as Hakutsuru, or the style of the White Swan (taught by *sensei* Soken in Okinawa), is related to the Shorin *ryu.*

The man who, in modern times, studied most of the methods taught in these schools and then combined the features which impressed him the most from the standpoint of style and efficiency in combat was Funakoshi, the founder of the modern method of karate known as Shotokan. He unquestionably did for the art of striking in Japan what Kano and Uyeshiba have done for judo and aikido, respectively. He

CHART 17

<table>
<tr><td colspan="3">KARATE PROGRAM OF INSTRUCTION
(Shotokan style)</td></tr>
<tr><td rowspan="3">Techniques of attack and counterattack</td><td rowspan="2">with hands and arms</td><td>direct strikes (tsuki-waza)</td></tr>
<tr><td>indirect strikes (uchi-waza)</td></tr>
<tr><td colspan="2">with feet and legs (keri-waza)</td></tr>
<tr><td rowspan="2">Techniques of defense</td><td colspan="2">blocks (uke-waza)</td></tr>
<tr><td colspan="2">evasions (kawashi-waza)</td></tr>
<tr><td colspan="3">Formal exercises (kata)</td></tr>
</table>

publicized his system and taught it openly in Japan, thus setting the basis for the blossoming of styles and schools which is characteristic of Japanese karate today.

The study of modern karate gives us an indirect glimpse into the ancient methods of unarmed combat based on the predominant and specialized use of parts of a man's body as weapons for delivering blows and kicks. In examining the current, specialized literature available on karate, we cannot be other than impressed by the exceptionally large number of techniques of attack, counterattack, and defense in which the arms and legs act as extraordinarily efficient weapons of combat. In attack and counterattack, arms and hands are used to punch *(tsuki)* or strike *(uchi)* with devastating force at a particular target—most often using various parts of the hand which have been hardened by the thorough repetition of certain exercises. The use of legs and feet in kicking *(keri)* is also extremely diversified and powerful. Moreover, these weapons can be used quite effectively as instruments of pure defense—that is, to neutralize a technique of attack or counterattack launched by an opponent, who will thus be unable to even reach his target.

With the development of a modern doctrine of bujutsu that is endeavoring to collect as much information as possible concerning the Oriental arts of striking, it is becoming increasingly clear that Japanese karate is also beginning to reveal within its process of evolution dualistic tendencies in style: the "hard" and "soft" approaches, the "linear" and the "circular," the "external" or muscular and the "internal" or mental emphasis—all of which were omnipresent, like the principles of *yin* and *yang* in the ancient Chinese arts of striking and, in general, in all bujutsu specializations. However, it is difficult to form an entirely clear picture of the Japanese art of striking when faced with such a kaleidoscopic background of practices and influences. The records of the schools which specialized in techniques of percussion are generally fragmented and exclusivistic in approach—each proclaiming, in accordance with the customs of the past, its own original, independent position in the history of man, thus attempting to isolate itself in a sort of cultural limbo of its own creation. With such a lack of continuity and coherence in the sources of information, it becomes difficult, if not impossible, to determine whether the Japanese art of striking and its specializations were all indigenous by-products of Japanese overspecializations of those *atemi-waza* used in armed and unarmed methods of bujutsu or derivations of ancient methods of boxing and kicking popular centuries before on the Asian continent. Perhaps the truth is not to be found exclusively in either interpretation, but in the combination of both. The *bushi,* after all, was often exposed to these methods of hitting and kicking, either directly through supervised training in *atemi-waza* or indirectly when forced to fight against foes who, apparently, often used specialized methods of hitting and kicking unknown to him. Furthermore,

many masters of bujutsu themselves (as the doctrine indicates) reportedly traveled to China and beyond, in order to study various combat methods. In time, these men returned to Yamato, where they blended and adapted the foreign methods they had learned to the firmly rooted traditions of bujutsu, until such methods became indistinguishable from the indigenous facets of the national culture of Japan.

The Art of Kiai

A unique position among the unarmed methods of combat—indeed, among all the specializations of bujutsu—was that occupied by the art of kiai. Even in feudal Japan, with its ready acceptance of mystical interpretations of phenomena, this art was considered esoteric and even miraculous. In this art, unarmed combat reached the zenith of sophistication since there was no visible physical contact between opponents, and techniques or strategies of combat were reduced to the extension of pure, immaterial (in the sense of "not visible to the naked eye") power, sufficient to overwhelm the weaker of the two combatants.

Kiai, like aiki (with which it is often used interchangeably in the doctrine of bujutsu), embraces the now familiar concepts of harmony and spirit, or energy. Harrison wrote that "the word 'Kiai' is a compound of *ki,* meaning mind,' 'will,' 'turn of mind,' 'spirit,' etc....and *ai,* the contraction of the verb *awasu,* signifying 'to unite.' As this combination actually suggests, it denotes a condition in which two minds are united into one in such a manner that the stronger controls the weaker" (Harrison, 129-30). As such, kiai marks the point in bujutsu where the outer factors of these arts (weapons and techniques) were subordinated to factors of an inner nature (control and power), which, according to the leading masters of the warrior arts, made those arts truly effective and relevant in combat.

Unfortunately, very little is known in Japan, and even less elsewhere, about the art of kiai, which, being based upon a concept as broad as *ki,* was understandably characterized by a certain vagueness in theory, while in practice it was often used as a smokescreen to conceal downright fraud. There are many examples in the literature of the martial arts, especially in connection with kenjutsu (see Part 3), of extraordinary powers which were supposedly displayed by self-styled masters of bujutsu who often mastered various arts of misrepresentation (based on hypnosis or exaggerated dexterity) far better than they ever mastered any form of bujutsu. And, of course, as we will see later in greater detail, *ki* was often used in the sense of energy, spirit, character—and, therefore, personality. A magnetic personality has always been able to call upon strong powers of projection and suggestion, and these can often be used to prevent combat, or to win it. There is an episode, for example, said to have involved a samurai who was set upon in the woods by a pack of wolves. According to the story, he merely kept walking straight ahead, his countenance so

stable, aware, and potentially explosive that the animals were frozen in their tracks, while he passed safely through their midst. Other episodes mention men lying in ambush only to confront a victim who, simply by gazing at them, terrorized them so effectively that they were immobilized.

One particular vector of this power—actually a technique used to convey that power to its intended target—was the human voice. Kiai was the name generally given to that specific method of combat based upon the employment of the voice as a weapon. A *bushi* of the higher ranks was expected to master this "technique," and in time certain warriors refined the practice of kiai until it became an art complete in and of itself. Due to the importance of deep, abdominal breathing and mental projection in the channeling of a shout in a coordinated direction, there are indirect indications in the doctrine of bujutsu that Zen masters (usually in monasteries or other isolated retreats) were particularly accomplished teachers of kiai. Zen, in fact, made abundant use of those disciplines which were considered essential in developing and stabilizing that condition of detachment and interior balance without which spiritual enlightenment was generally considered unattainable.

The origins of the art of kiai are closely identified with the image of a man facing a hostile reality. The shout has undoubtedly been one of his first reactions to danger, whether in an effort to summon assistance or in order to warn friends. The fact that the shout, even if passive, could cause a dangerous foe to waver in his aggressive intent, or actually halt his attack (perhaps because in other instances that vocal vibration had indeed brought disaster to the attacker, in the shape of other members of his intended victim's tribe), could very well have been the beginning of the active use of the human voice as part of a strategy of combat which almost all militant societies of the past have used extensively. The shouts of armies, reverberating under leaden skies, often seemed to shake the gods from their slumber and, indeed, had such a quality of invocation that a foe of lesser vocal potency might well shiver involuntarily and look around him fearfully, as if anticipating the arrival of an unseen host.

The Greek and Roman legions were well versed in the paralyzing effect of a sudden clamor erupting from the depths of the usually silent forest, to which they would respond with ferocious answering cries or the din of many instruments. The theory advanced by Gilbey, concerning the origin of the word "panic," is particularly revealing: the hills of Greece were said to have trembled at the sound of Pan's shout, as the god of fertility inexhaustibly expressed his vitality in the joy of seasonal harvests or even his ferociousness through the act of violent insemination. The epic literature of North Africa and the Middle East, from the Phoenicians to the Assyrians, from the Persians to the Hebrews, also resounds with piercing battle cries—sometimes of warriors half-crazed by their own vocal concentration.

The hypnotic effect of such a total shout was not lost upon the knights who jousted during the Middle Ages in continental and eastern Europe. The Muslim and Mongolian hordes, in particular, knew and respected this power. In fact, when European knights faced such Eastern warriors, it often required another type of mental concentration, bordering upon fanaticism, to reduce the crippling effects of this form of sonic onslaught directed against the eardrums and battering the brain with its refined and sensitive receptors. And it required a progression of cymbals, drums, and horns in classic times; drums and trumpets and the piercing, strangely chilling wail of the bagpipes in the Middle Ages and beyond; and finally, the total explosions of modern warfare, to reduce if not entirely eliminate the strategic relevance of a single man's shout in the West.

In the East, from India to China, Tibet, Korea, and Japan, the tactical value of the shout in determining or influencing the outcome of combat had never been underestimated. It would seem that in Tibet and Japan, in particular, this technique had been perfected in ancient times and raised to the level of an art, that is, to the point of making a shout the sole weapon used, even in individual combat, as well as the primary reason for the successful conclusion of a combat enounter—thus differentiating it from the frightening but highly dispersive and indiscriminate shout of the horde.

Indeed, the shout that the Japanese warrior endeavored to develop and control involved much more than a mere exercise in breath control and concentrated expiration. It was (as the name assigned to the art implies) a blending of various factors which comprised the entire personality of the warrior (physical and mental)—all his powers being fused and channeled through the pitch, tone, and vibration of his voice. Moreover, at its highest levels, it did not even depend primarily upon volume—the quality of the sound produced by focusing the entire personality upon a single target being the main feature of kiai. Long years of training were required to produce the exact vocal integration which reportedly could kill an attacker or deflect his attack, and could even be used to cure. Harrison relates a number of episodes which illustrate the skill in kiai displayed by Master Kunishige (a teacher of jujutsu in the Shinden Isshin *ryu),* who once revived a man lying unconscious after a heavy fall by employing a characteristically concentrated shout. But concerning the use of kiai shouts in real combat (other than the cries and grunts of competitors in modern judo and karate tournaments, common to various forms of wrestling the world over), and as to whether there are schools extant where the art is being systematically and efficiently taught and practiced, the records available are regrettably vague.

PART III

INNER FACTORS OF BUJUTSU

The Invisible Range

According to most scholars, sophisticated weapons and complex techniques (the outer factors of bujutsu examined in Part 2), although admittedly impressive, might be compared to the visible part of an iceberg which catches the eye, and often the imagination, but is only a projection of the power hidden below in the depths of the icy waters. Although the possession of a certain weapon and basic training in its functional use often satisfied the individual bujutsu practitioner *(bujin)* of limited ambition and imagination, there were others, many others, who perceived, beyond those outer factors of the various arts, other, more complex factors, less evident perhaps to the naked eye but no less important in determining the practical efficiency of those weapons and their relative techniques. Failure to perceive these inner factors could prove disastrous, as it did for many a complacent *bujin* who had been trained only in the technical ways of handling a spear, a sword, or any other weapon, including his own anatomy. Centuries of experience in the ancient art of combat, in fact, had confronted the *bujin* and his *sensei* with a series of demanding questions, among which the following were of primary importance: When should an opponent be engaged? How was he (as well as oneself) to be controlled? What type of energy was to be used, and how employed to the best advantage? Finally, what was to be the *bujin's* motivation? All these considerations involved factors of a decidedly interior nature which activated the techniques of bujutsu from within, provided them with an effective source of power, and justified their use in a manner calculated to provide the *bujin* with controlled determination, calmness, and clarity of purpose, as well as with a moral justification to sustain him in combat. Bujutsu masters confronted these interrogatives (and others), explored their range and depth, and tried to provide satisfactory answers for themselves and their disciples. Eventually, they provided bujutsu with its own theory, the salient features of which will be explored in the sections which follow.

6
CONTROL AND POWER

The Foundation

Of what use was a sharp, well-balanced *katana,* or an intricate and technically elaborate method of using it in combat, if the *bujin*—and, in particular, the *bushi* who had to be prepared to face death every day—had not also developed a stable, inner platform of mental control from which to act or react according to the circumstances of an encounter? The relationship between this condition of mental stability—which made it possible for the bujutsu expert to assess a situation quickly and coolly, simultaneously deciding upon the proper course of action—and a coherent and powerful execution of that decision had been perceived by almost every martial arts instructor in Japan. The most noted *sensei,* in fact, taught that no method, whatever its apparent merit, had any real value unless it helped to develop a man's character in a manner which would make him master of his weapon and thus truly powerful in its use. These teachers searched continually for ways of inculcating in their pupils a particular mental attitude, always calm and balanced, which would assure that heightened clarity of perception they considered the only proper basis for appropriate decisions. Thus "ways" or disciplines emphasizing the training of the mind were actively sought in an effort to guarantee that necessary control of the inner self which was the prerequisite for any control over an opponent and over the circumstances of combat. To that end, many masters turned increasingly to ancient theories of enlightenment which, in their religious or philosophical interpretations, had endeavored to help man understand his reality better, so that he might cope more effectively with its complexities. In time, many of the disciplines and exercises which adherents of those theories had developed were adapted to the particular requirements of the *bujin.* Eventually, two of these concepts became the lodestone of all training on the highest level of every martial art: the concept of the "Centre" *(hara)* and the concept of "Intrinsic Energy" *(ki),* both of which were contained, in one form or another, in all the major Eastern systems of thought, from the metaphysics of India and Tibet to the cosmogonies of China, Korea, and Japan, and had actually emerged from the earliest animistic formulations of these religious beliefs.

These two concepts (usually abstracted from the various religious, philosophical, or eugenic purposes to which they had been related during their long history) formed the nucleus of a theory of "Centralization" *(haragei),* which the masters of bujutsu astutely adapted for the development and stabilization of that unswerving "courageous" personality which was considered the trademark of a *bushi* (actually regarded as characteristic of every bujutsu expert, whatever his class affiliations). Did they succeed? There is evidence to indicate that, militarily speaking, they did. The fame of the Japanese warrior in the ancient world was apparently well merited. His impassiveness in battle, his absolute dedication and determination in carrying out the orders of a lawful superior, his courage and willingness to sacrifice himself without a moment's hesitation, and, of course, the power, the force of his actions in combat—all these qualities became well known and, in certain quarters on the Asian continent as well as in Japan, greatly feared. Thus the word *samurai* began to identify not only the positive qualities of a military professional when faced with a foe, but others, less admirable, as well: the fanaticism and ultranationalism which, blinding the committed samurai to more diversified dimensions of existence, ofttimes reduced him to the bloody role of a mindless fighting machine.

If we are to understand just how these inner qualities of the *bujin's* personality were developed, we must survey, even if briefly, the two basic concepts upon which that personality was based—that is, the concept of the Centre and that of Intrinsic Energy, as they appear within the cultural dimensions of Asia at large—before we examine the ways in which the masters of bujutsu in Japan interpreted and adapted them to the specific purposes of their individual methods of combat.

The Concept of the Centre

The concept of the Centre *(hara)* is ancient, complex, and, in much of the source material available, exceedingly abstruse. Its main thesis, uniformly consistent from a removed and systematic platform of observation, is scattered throughout all the major doctrines of philosophical and religious thought in Asia, where it is viewed, elaborated upon, and employed from specialized, as well as widely varying, angles and perspectives. Its dimensions range from the cosmic or universal to the particular or individual reality of man—the latter embracing him as a complex and delicate balance of physical, functional, mental, spiritual, and moral components or factors. Consequently, in this section we will attempt to outline its major dimensions, its characteristics, and the system behind it in sufficient detail to explain the influence of the concept upon bujutsu, leaving to another book the task of elaborating upon its complexities.

The theory or idea of a Centre begins with the observation of man's chaotic reality, his confusion, his sorrows. These are attributed to his ignorance, which renders him easy prey to inessential phenomena, to "shadows" which, eventually, turn him against himself, against his fellowman, against his world. In an effort to counteract the effects of man's deadening and enslaving dependency upon the multiple and confusing variety of existential phenomena, the men of wisdom in Asia had sought to perceive the substance or essential Centre of existence—the Centre where the many became one, chaos became order, the particular became universal, death or stillness became life or motion, dazed and pained blindness became calm clarity, the unintelligible became intelligible.

This Centre could be found everywhere and in everything: in the cosmos, in nature, in all forms of life—in man and his creations. It could be qualified as true if it embraced and balanced man's entire reality and harmonized all its aspects and elements, false when it emphasized only some of them to the simultaneous exclusion of the others. According to Asian modes of thought, man's true Centre found its first, physical expression in his lower abdomen. The Japanese word *hara,* in fact, is literally translated as "belly" and, in the Japanese version of the theory which re-echoes throughout all Asia, this area is the Centre of life and death, the Centre of consolidation (immanent) and of development (transcendent) of a man's entire personality. This holds true on all levels of his existence, beginning with the physical, then progressing upward through the functional to the mental and spiritual dimensions. In China the Centre was called *tan t'ien.*

There is a cult of the Centre in Japan (and in Asia at large) and an art *(haragei)* which is its core. Every major doctrine of enlightenment in the Orient refers to this Centre and relies upon it for the achievement of its final aims. In the individual personality, for example, the doctrine of Buddhism refers to centralization in the lower abdomen as a technique of mental integration which can help man to discover himself through introspection and meditation. But the individual *hara* is only the first expression of the Centre. The second expression (without which the former is considered valueless and false) is the social Centre of man's reality: the Centre where he meets and is met by his fellowman. This expanded Centre is located at an extremely elusive point of harmony found only if and when two or more human beings meet and cooperate for their reciprocal welfare. This social aspect of the Centre became the cornerstone of the doctrine of

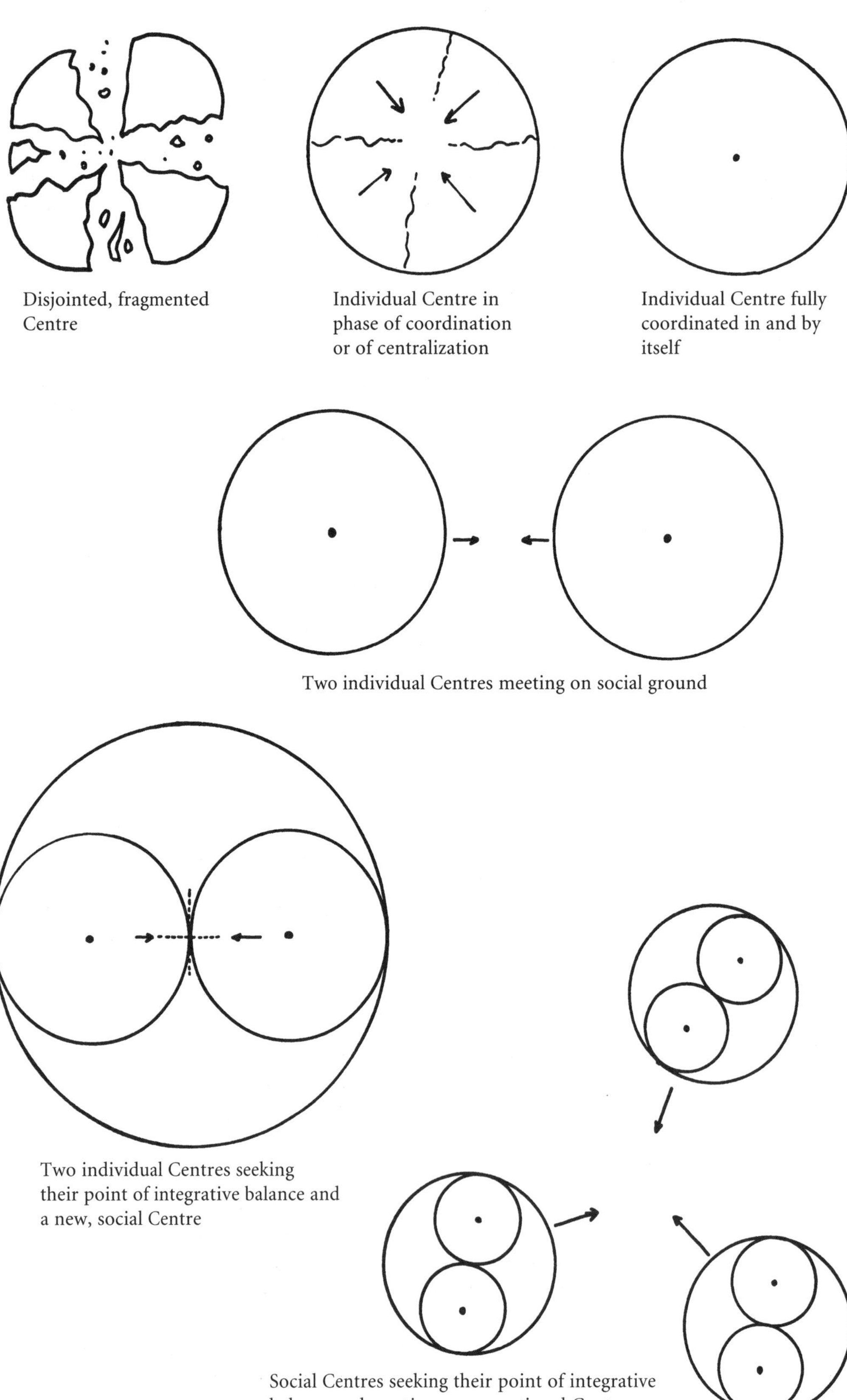

Disjointed, fragmented Centre

Individual Centre in phase of coordination or of centralization

Individual Centre fully coordinated in and by itself

Two individual Centres meeting on social ground

Two individual Centres seeking their point of integrative balance and a new, social Centre

Social Centres seeking their point of integrative balance and creating a new, national Centre

The arrangement of circles and Centres in a painting of the Kasugai School (11th c.), representing Ichijikinrin (Vairochana Buddha)

Confucius. Finally, the *hara,* through centralization at a point of mutual welfare encompassing man and his fellowman (social), reaches the cosmic dimension of centralization at a point of maximum integration, balance, and harmony of mankind with the natural order on earth and the universe at large. This point was the main theorem of ancient Taoism, the basis of its cult of simplicity and natural spontaneity.

The true Centre, as we have said earlier, was the product of a successful fusion of these various Centres which were only apparently different (that is, differing in outer form and manifestation) but which were intrinsically identical in ultimate substance. And the first characteristic of a successful fusion was harmony, peace, fulfillment—with the self, with the other(s), with reality as a whole.

All other, lesser Centres (such as prestige, power, violence, hierarchy, symbols, etc.) were false and painfully limited ones—ofttimes apparently necessary but, in the long run, unsuccessful props which man was forced to invent and employ endlessly in order to survive and continue, however haltingly. For centuries in Asia, a man not properly centralized in the lower abdomen was considered to be (as he still is in Japan) physically unbalanced, functionally uncoordinated, and mentally preoccupied with the tension and the precariousness of existence. Burdened with these handicaps, he was easy prey to any fleeting phenomenon crossing his field of vision or perception, which he might try to use to achieve some sort of stability (even if illusory), or which he might view as only another shadowy nightmare.

Socially speaking, a man who had not discovered his individual Centre of balanced integration and development at a point of inclusion with (not exclusion of) his fellowman was continually at war with his fellow creatures. Both, after all, were substantially of the same essence, actually reflections of one another; both were expressions of life and not mutually alien beings or things, not objects to be used, harmed, or destroyed. Within this context, a man who had not identified himself with the Centre of the natural order, and had not learned to respect and improve upon its laws of composition and functionality, was automatically at war with it. Interestingly enough, by the law of reciprocal exclusion, he would also become the victim of the very disharmony he inflicted upon an order which, one must remember, contained and sustained him.

However easy it might have been for a man to adopt a false Centre due to a natural tendency to be overcome by the phantasmagoria of phenomena, it was just as difficult for him to discover the true Centre and, if he were fortunate enough to find it, still more difficult to develop and maintain it. Consequently, men of wisdom in Asia devised innumerable methods of achieving, developing, and maintaining a position of integrative and harmonious balance between the opposing aspects of human reality.

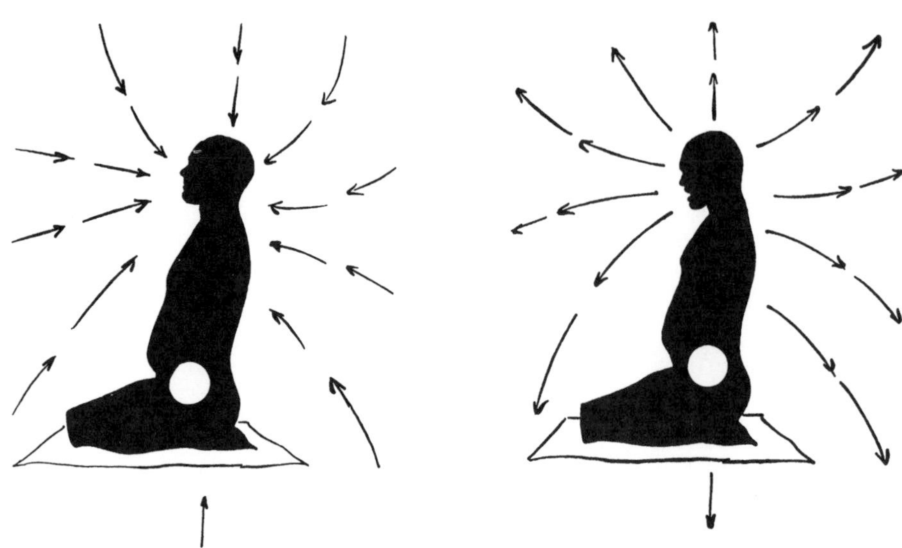

This search for Centralization has been a fundamental preoccupation of all Asiatic cultures, and one finds here (in both content and type or style of discipline) the most diversified collection of methods imaginable for achieving that end, ranging from the specialized disciplines of intellectual development predominant in the Chinese and Tibetan scholastic communities, to the equally (if not more) introspective but markedly more metaphysical or animistic Indian disciplines of mystical and intuitive development. In each method the purpose was the same—that is, liberation from the yoke of existence by developing a position of centralized independence from which to perceive, understand, and improve upon that reality with the utmost clarity and correctness of vision. Among the various exercises devised and practiced for years, those of stillness and of meditation or concentration have predominated, and are still practiced today throughout Asia. In Japan, priests and monks, artists and men of letters, people in the professions and political leaders practice these exercises periodically at home or in appropriate retreats, seeking to redefine and reintegrate themselves in the *hara* in order to be able to live more fully their assigned roles in the society of men.

The Concept of Intrinsic Energy

The element which exerted the most influence upon the doctrine of bujutsu, however, was the discovery that the disciplines of introspection used to achieve centralization in the *hara* seemed to coordinate the various factors of a man's personality in a manner which unlocked the source of a strange form of energy. This energy, moreover, appeared to differ from, or at least be far more encompassing and comprehensive in both substance and intensity than the common type of energy usually associated with the output of man's muscular system alone. It was generally believed that this powerful source of energy could be tapped only if a man had stabilized that position of inner centralization in the *hara,* which would thus be understood not only as an immanent Centre of being, of consolidation, of coordinated independence, but also as a transcendent Centre of becoming, of development, of transformation. The cult of the *hara,* as many men of wisdom in Asia had taught, was not to be viewed purely as an end in itself (although in many doctrines of contemplation, the primary objective was merely to remove the self from the phantasmagoric turbulence of reality). It was to be viewed, primarily, as a means of achieving something beyond detachment, that is, as a method of activating the process of man's evolution and engaging him positively and creatively in that turbulence which he was intended, by his own nature, to comprehend and control—which he would have to comprehend and control if he were to survive and progress.

This active aspect of the *hara* shifts the attention from the natural order (balanced by its cosmic Centre) to the evolution, transformation, and activity of that natural order and, consequently, to its vital force, life. The *hara* as a Centre of vision—independent, coordinated, calm—became the *hara* as the Centre of life—coordinated and powerful, The correlated energy of centralization has been defined in many ways, but all are related to life and its energy, which, like the Centre itself, has innumerable aspects and ranges. In India, for example, it has been known for centuries as *prajna,* in China as *ch'i,* and in Japan as *ki.* It has been referred to as the "essence of life" and as its "breathing."

Harmony and ultimate liberation were achievable, then, through the balanced unification of the individual, the social, and the cosmic Centres. The energy generated by and emanating from these Centres could also be used to attain results of extraordinary proportions by progressively tapping and developing the coordinated energy of the individual Centre and blending its flow with the energy of the social Centres—all finally reaching their apotheosis in the sea of natural, cosmic life considered in the theory as the primary Centre. Down through the centuries, all ancient religious texts, as well as the popular sagas, had spoken of the primeval chaos, the maelstrom of energy characteristic of the dualistic beginning: the dialectical balance of *yin* and *yang* producing endless forms and manifestations of the same energy. The coordinated energy of the *hara,* consequently, had a range of intensity and substance which was directly proportionate to the degree of centralization achieved. The *ki* of individual centralization, for example, resulting from coordination of man's physical, functional, and mental personality in the *hara,* could infuse a man with tremendous vitality and make him extremely powerful in action—much more so than the man who had developed muscular power alone through exercises of coordination based primarily upon purely physical disciplines. But the former although individually coordinated, would be inferior in vitality, character, and power to the man who had advanced his progressive coordination from the individual stage to the social, thus acquiring the attitude, strength, and, in exceptional cases, the charisma associated with the leader who can move men to believe and act in the fulfillment of a collective mission.

In turn, the energy of social centralization, which could link one man to another and move both to act for a common purpose, was still considered inferior to the energy of the universal Centre in the cosmic dimension of existence which (it was said) even men of wisdom (that is, philosophers or mystics) were seldom able to tap. The range of this energy was held to be infinite, flowing from the harmonious Centre of life itself; and it was considered essentially perfect, animating everything and everyone impartially.

The social Centre and its energy could be positive and thus benefit men, but it could also be negative and employed to harm them (in war, for example, or in simple social exploitation). The individual Centre and its coordinated energy could be positive and help man to live and act but it could also be negative and so egotistically self-centered as to foolishly attempt to separate itself from the rest of creation (the only dimension in which and through which that limited self could survive and develop). The cosmic, universal Centre, however, as well as its creative energy, was viewed as ultimately positive because of its impartial munificence and unrestricted dispensation of life in every direction and in every form. Very seldom could a man hope to blend these three Centres and tap their coordinated energies in the fusion of a single stream. For the most part, an individual could perhaps reach one of the lower levels and develop this specialized form of centralization and extension of energy—halting on the threshold of the infinite, often unable or unwilling to take the final, crucial step.

The discovery of coordinated energy (superior to the specialized energy of the muscular system), which could be unleashed through centralization in the lower abdomen, was only the preliminary step to harnessing and utilizing it. Accordingly, Asia produced innumerable schools of development which, from India to China, from Tibet to Japan, proceeded to explore (many of which are still exploring) the range of possibilities of this energy, its degrees of power, its methods of employment, and its techniques of development. As might be expected, the range of these methods is considerable in both variety and depth. And, like its source (the *hara),* this coordinated energy, this *ki,* could be developed and controlled through special exercises of a bewildering variety—each as specialized as the purpose that energy was intended to further. But all of them included, in addition to meditation and concentration, the fundamental exercise of abdominal breathing which had become the prerequisite for the development and control of *ki.* In ancient texts of the doctrine of *ki,* in fact, the word itself is translated as "air," "atmosphere," "breath." The doctrine was a main source of metaphysical and intellectual speculation for Indian, Chinese, Tibetan, and Japanese scholars, philosophers, religious leaders; it was also adopted by the schools of physical welfare, among which the Chinese schools of medicine, eugenic dance, and calisthenics excelled. This energy was also tapped by various arts and crafts so as to channel the vitality of man into his fluid and figurative arts. And, finally, it was used by almost all the important schools of bujutsu.

Applications of Haragei

These two concepts *(hara* as centralization and integration, and *ki* as centralized, extended energy) found their truest expression in that art known in Japan as *haragei;* its theory and practice, in turn, were applied in an effort to surmount the complex problems of existence. The results were often astonishing. Many of the greatest spiritual leaders of Asia displayed, in their lives as well as in their writings, a sublime detachment from the pressure of worldly events and passions, perceiving and assessing reality with unsurpassed calmness and clarity. The main characteristic of this assessment, besides the value it assigned to any aspect of creation, seemed to be a universality of vision which allowed them to embrace the multiple aspects of every phenomenon and explore various dimensions of the human experience from a balanced and centralized position of spiritual independence. This was in stark contrast to the narrow, unilateral, and specialized view of the decentralized man who could see only that which was very close or tangible—his perspective being sadly limited.

The vitality of these "men of wisdom" was reportedly impressive, and *haragei* is repeatedly referred to as one of the main reasons why the oldest among them often remained lucid and actively involved with various aspects of the human experience until the very end of their lives. *Haragei* is also invoked as an explanation of their pursuit of certain ends with a stable, unswerving commitment. As practiced by the famous ascetics and spiritual leaders of monasteries in feudal Japan, *haragei* was also considered responsible for that impassive unconcern in the face of death (whether by fire or sword) which so many monks demonstrated before the warriors of Nobunaga and Hideyoshi. All the *bushi* who witnessed it were quite naturally impressed by such a display of sangfroid, and interpreted that unconcern as contempt for death and thus as unshakable courage. Many ascetics, however, considered both contempt and courage as emotional reactions or responses and thus as forms or expressions of that deep-rooted (and undesirable) involvement with singular aspects of reality which a "man of wisdom" must overcome. The unconcern displayed by such a man was a precise detachment from that reality which seemed to oscillate forever between particular extremes of life and death, light and darkness, joy and sorrow, the moment and eternity. To a true ascetic, reality was substantially uniform, it was one and the same thing; therefore, in the larger scope of things, death by the sword or by fire did not differ substantially from any other form of death, including the peaceful transition from the sleep of old age into eternity. And death was as much a part of life as any of its other facets.

The nucleus of this theory is thus one of balance, of integration, of equanimity and harmony—an ideal which Eastern man had shared with the man of Western culture since time immemorial. Both pursued it, although along different paths, but seldom has either comprehended fully the true meaning of the theory, much less succeeded in living entirely by its tenets. A man would generally take from the theory of *haragei* those concepts he needed to fill immediate, particular needs, leaving to the man of wisdom (a *rara avis* in every age) the task of seeking to understand its complex totality and live by its most comprehensive dictates, which embraced men everywhere on a level of impartial equanimity, as fellow human beings—regardless of their ethnic, cultural, or social specializations and functions. Perhaps man's very constitutional and structural limitations have always made the ideal *of haragei* unattainable except in strongly diluted or modified forms. In Buddhism, for example, *haragei* appears shrouded in metaphysics and in abstruse conceptualism, whether intellectual, as in India, or intuitive, as in Japan. In Taoism it is molded into a pancentrism of cosmic proportions, and in Confucianism it is politically and socially embedded in the inescapable pyramid of the Asiatic concept of hierarchy. Dimly perceived in its integrity by a few ascetics, *haragei* was usually expressed in exotic and abstruse language for intellectuals, in rites and formalism for politicians, and in a body of superstitions for the large masses of people in Asia. Under the most unexpected names and in the most unexpected forms, *haragei* appears again and again in the theories and practices of various doctrines and disciplines invented by man in an effort to cope with the terrors of his existence. As such, it has reached the modern age and is still evident in the Chinese concepts of traditional medicine, longevity, and good health as expressed in the eugenic forms of t'ai ch'i. Such exercises are still practiced extensively in China by young and old alike, at the measured pace typical of those formal exercises which, in Japan, are associated with such disciplines as the tea ceremony *(cha-no-yu)*, theatrical performances of noh drama, kabuki, and traditional dances *(odori)*, as well as with the modern derivations of bujutsu such as aikido, kendo, karate, and judo.

Furthermore, the narrowly specialized application of *haragei*, from an intellectual and rationalistic point of view, has often degenerated into a subjective, egotistical self-centeredness which forced everything and everyone other than the self into a subordinate or dependent position, thus insulating that self from the environment and from the reality surrounding it. The result has been confusion, further insecurity, and often disaster for the isolated part thus detached from the whole. One striking example of such a distorted interpretation of *haragei* in grave matters of political leadership is offered by Premier Suzuki's lack of response to the emperor's wishes during the final phase of World War II. The emperor and his closest advisers (among whom was Baron Kido) desired a quick cessation of hostilities in order to spare their country further hardship and their fellow countrymen further suffering. Their intentions, according to Kido's diary, were communicated "intuitively" to Suzuki—that is, without resorting to specific words or issuing any clearcut instructions, since men versed in the art of *haragei* (as the leaders of the country were expected to be) were not supposedly dependent upon words. Using *haragei*, the "hidden and invisible technique" (Butow, 70), communication was supposed to be direct and immediate, even if nonverbal. Through centralization in the *hara*, different minds were expected to be able to come to an unspoken accord, to see clearly and by themselves the wisdom of adopting a policy more in keeping with the circumstances and flow of events. The result of this attempted application of *haragei*—which thus entered the official records of Japanese history and the Western chronicles of the period—was Japan's prolonged agony, since Suzuki (presumably more skilled in the forms than master of the essence of *haragei)* apparently remained unaware of any need for a change in plans, and so continued Japan's military effort. It is not surprising that Western authorities who studied the records very closely, seeking an explanation for the behavior of Japanese authorities in order to assess responsibility, qualified Kido's reasoning as untenable, and *haragei* as irrational, confusing, deceptive, ambiguous, or an "art of bluff."

To conclude these notes on *haragei,* we must add that the men of wisdom in Asia had realized very early that *ki,* like the *hara,* or any other power which man might acquire in the course of his experience, could be misused, abused, corrupted, and methodically applied not in favor of man (thus identifying with the energy of life), but against him. Almost every respectable school which has contributed to the advancement of Eastern culture has warned its adherents of such a possibility and adopted methodological safeguards intended to prevent abuses. The careful scrutiny of a candidate aspiring to the knowledge imparted by that school, and the stern emphasis placed upon secrecy of transmission, were attempts to prevent such knowledge from falling into the wrong hands. However, while such an aim was not automatically achieved through secrecy (a student always being able to misuse the limited power of *ki* which he had developed), there were many schools which, unfortunately, disappeared—precisely because of this emphasis upon stringent safeguards and restricted transmission of their stores of knowledge and lore.

Haragei in Ancient Specializations of Bujutsu

The concept of centralization *(hara),* in its active form of extension of centralized power *(ki)* embodied in the doctrine of *haragei,* permeated and was absorbed into the mainstream of the ancient schools of bujutsu, whose masters shrewdly divined the powerful possibilities of the application of this doctrine to their various specializations.

The sight of monks, such as those on Mount Hiei, leaping to a fiery death without a moment's hesitation, had impressed the *bushi.* This type of courage and dedication to an ideal appealed to the Japanese warrior, since the violent nature of his profession demanded that he be continually alert to ways in which he could improve his powers of concentration, as well as to methods which would help to insure calm independence of mind, and thus balanced judgment, when engaged in the turbulent reality of combat. In fact, as many martial arts masters pointed out, there was hardly any other form of activity as dramatically charged with life seen as explosive energy, movement, transformation (including the ultimate transformation—death). Nor was there any other form of action which required such complete coordination, such an uninterrupted flow of centralized power *(ki)* to achieve its ends.

The concept of centralized energy emanating from the *hara* thus became a cornerstone of the martial arts. In time, hardly a single reputable school or specialization in the art of combat (that is, among those distinguishing themselves from the "inferior" schools of combat centered upon the concept of brute strength or of technique alone) failed to refer to, or include in its training program, the study *of haragei* and the particular disciplines developed for its practical application in response to the dramatic solicitations of combat. From the rarefied and metaphysical spheres of practical application in the medical, eugenic, and artistic schools of expression, *haragei* was thus finally transposed to help resolve the dramatic problems of reality in the dimension of combat.

Quite naturally, both the theory and its related disciplines underwent alterations in passing from the generic and universal dimensions of *hara* and *ki* to the specialized and highly practical dimension of ancient bujutsu. It was, in fact, the concept of *ki* as the *hara* in action, the Centre at its moment of "becoming," when integration became pure action, which interested the *bushi* and his *sensei.* And their concentration upon this particular application of *haragei* became, in most cases, so absolute, and the results of the train-

ing methods employed for the development and employment of centralized energy so astounding, that *ki* was considered to be "esoteric" in nature and intrinsically "divine." Moreover, this view has persisted in Asia down through the centuries. The Japanese jujutsu master who told Harrison in the early 1900s that "a man who has thoroughly acquired the art of *aiki* verges on the divine" (Harrison, 115) seems to be echoing the Chinese master of shaolin boxing who had qualified *ch'i* as being "truly mysterious and divine" (Smith[2], 35).

A survey of certain texts on Japanese archery (kyujutsu), swordsmanship (kenjutsu), traditional wrestling (sumo), and unarmed combat (jujutsu) will help to clarify those aspects and concepts of *haragei* which the master of bujutsu and the *bujin* of whatever class found particularly suited to the resolution of particular combat problems, as well as those which provided that platform of inner control and power so vital to effective action or reaction in a combat situation.

Kyujutsu

In this traditional specialization of bujutsu, the following qualities were considered of fundamental importance by the teachers of the art: independence of vision, embracing as vast a field as possible; a keen perception of significant detail, without dispersion of attention due to fear or confusion; and power—power to draw back the huge bow, to control the release of the arrow and its trajectory toward the target. Regarding the first two requisites, kyujutsu doctrine made a clear distinction between the idea of aiming at a target *(monomi)* and that of concentrating and stabilizing the sight *(mikomi)*; in the lexicon of this art, concentrating and stabilizing were general and diffused, while aiming was specific. The archer had to be able to enlarge or to narrow his field of vision and attention at will, in order to be aware of and able to control his environment as a whole. At the same time, he had to be capable of perceiving a particular shadow lurking in his vicinity, or even a single small chink in the armor of a galloping foe charging toward his lines on the battlefield. In this context, the art of archery availed itself of doctrines concerning mental control which were already ancient when they reached Japan from India together with the first manuals on Buddhism. The Japanese knew by heart the story of Arjuna the archer, for example. Invited to a tournament in which skill in archery was tested by having the archers aim at the eye of a painted wooden fish set high on a pole, many contestants were asked by a teacher, before they released their arrows, what it was

they saw. With one exception, they all answered, "a fish." Arjuna replied that he saw only the "eye" of the fish, and, as might be expected, he alone hit the target. In order to develop this capacity to see clearly the whole and all its parts, kyujutsu made abundant use of *haragei,* "this art of the belly that runs through all the arts of Japan and whose mastery is a *situ qua non* in every one of them" (Acker, 47).

Exercises of meditation and abdominal concentration, often performed by archers in the same monastic halls where spiritual leaders employed those same exercises for other purposes, such as mystical enlightenment *(satori),* were customary in feudal Japan. Such training was intended to produce a warrior who could calmly and inexorably release all his arrows against selected foes, even in the midst and clamor of battle, or when facing a horde of enemy cavalrymen rapidly converging upon him.

In relation to the power used by the experts of kyujutsu in handling their powerful bows, even the most modern manuals concerned with this art cannot avoid referring to the concept of *ki* (often using the more archaic and authoritative Chinese denomination, *ch'i).* Acker, who wrote a brief introduction to Japanese archery, refers to this "nervous" or "plastic" energy which "runs along our nerves from one part of the body to another like electricity along a wire" (Acker, 44). This energy, for which it is difficult to find an exact definition in the English language, could presumably be developed by appropriate exercises for effective use in kyujutsu. "Systematic breathing," centered upon the *hara,* was naturally considered "the most powerful" exercise of all (Acker, 45) because the relationship between the energy of *ki* and air or breath, that "lord of strength" (Smith[2], 34), was considered to be one of substantial identity. Even today, practitioners of the modern derivation of kyujutsu known as the "way of the bow and arrow" (kyudo) are taught the primary importance of abdominal breathing in the development of power. This exercise, Murakami Hisahi tells us, is called *ikiai,* adding that "every action [in kyudo] should be synchronized with the rhythm of breathing" *(Black Belt,* April, 1967). All kyudo teachers stress this idea of abdominal centralization as the prerequisite for extending the body in full coordination of intention with action, of will with respiration, and of both with every movement in the practice of archery, from the drawing of the bow and the release of the arrow to the mental projection which must accompany the arrow to its target. Thus the physical and mental coordination of archery, today as yesterday, returns full circle to *haragei,* the art of abdominal centralization without which, in Japan, coordination is considered inconceivable in theory and unattainable in practice.

Kenjutsu

As indicated in Part 2, the art of the sword dominated the latter part of Japanese feudal history, and for over three hundred years it was the object of intense study and experimentation. In time, a comprehensive theory of applied coordinated power in swordplay was developed—a theory resulting from a particular adaptation of *haragei.* It is possible, in fact, to follow the evolution of the two basic concepts of abdominal centralization and of coordinated extension of intrinsic or inner energy in the records of this specialization of bujutsu (which made certain men famous all over Japan for their skill with the *katana* and/or their ability as teachers of kenjutsu).

A basic differentiation, unfortunate but unavoidable, had been made by the ancient masters of swordsmanship between the outer and the inner factors of the specialization. Among the former factors, for example, we find weapons, techniques, stances, and all the "practical details such as what you call the five ways of posing the body designated each by one [Chinese] character" (Suzuki, 101). These factors, as indicated in Part 2, were the external characteristics which differentiated the style of one school from those of all other schools of kenjutsu. Among the inner factors of orthodox swordsmanship we find that independence of mind which allowed the techniques to develop and flow freely, without hindrance or paralyzing interruptions—that is, out of the unconscious, in full power. There were evidently schools of kenjutsu which overspecialized by assigning greater importance to one class of factors, thereby either minimizing or neglecting almost entirely the importance of the other class or group of factors. In fact, one of the greatest theorists of kenjutsu, the monk Takuan, perhaps reacting against a common tendency to place undue emphasis upon the outer factors of kenjutsu (that is, upon the weapon and its techniques), warned that "technical knowledge is not enough. One must transcend technique so that the art becomes an artless art, growing out of the unconscious" (Suzuki, 101). But, at the same time, he also repeatedly warned against placing undue emphasis upon the inner factors of kenjutsu. "Training in detailed technique," he wrote, was not to be "neglected," because knowledge of the inner factors of swordsmanship alone "cannot lead one to the mastery of movements of the body and its limbs....The principle of spirituality is to be grasped—this goes without saying—but at the same time one must be trained in the technique of swordplay" (Suzuki, 101). As Takuan's advice to his pupil implies, there were evidently many schools of swordsmanship whose adherents emphasized to an exaggerated degree the inner factors of combat, ranging from the psychic or spiritual to pure mesmerism and prestidigitation. In relation to this last interpretation of the inner factors of the art, we have already encountered ninjutsu in Part 2—an art which was heavily dependent upon the theory and practice of esoteric techniques, many of which would have been considered examples of black magic, witchcraft, or sorcery in medieval Europe.

In his excellent work *The Fighting Spirit of Japan,* Harrison wrote that, according to many of the bu-

jutsu masters with whom he spoke during the early 1900s, warriors who used "hypnotic, mesmeric or odyllic forces" in combat were not unusual. One of these is even said to have "experienced no difficulty" in defeating the celebrated Miyamoto Musashi "with nothing more formidable than an ordinary paper fan" (Harrison, 101). It was (and still is today) extremely difficult to pinpoint the line dividing tricks or sleight of hand from real mental stability and power, sheer suggestion from genuine courage and energy, illusion from stark reality. But it is clear that a *bushi*—however limited in ethical imagination and freedom of choice within the system—was generally expected to abstain from using the former category of tactics, which were considered deceitful and unworthy of any self-respecting warrior. We shall, therefore, leave unanswered the question of those esoteric powers based upon the ability of one man to cloud another man's mind. Our main concern here is to explore the doctrinary evolution of those inner powers which allowed a man to face a skilled and mentally independent swordsman and remain calm, prepared to fight (and, moreover, to fight well) with courage and power equal to that displayed by his opponent.

In the opinion of Takuan (one of the most balanced and integrative among many points of view on the subject), the inner and the outer factors of swordsmanship had to be considered "like two wheels of a cart," and, consequently, training in the art was "never to be one sided" (Suzuki, 101). Nevertheless, it is unquestionably true that virtually every master of kenjutsu recognized the primary importance of mental independence in controlling combat. Moreover, they all emphasized that the mind had to be free of any attachment, whatever its source and nature, if control was to be successfully exercised. Above all, the mind had to be removed from the disturbing influence of the "external" circumstances of combat, such as the weapons employed, because "when the mind is concerned with the sword, you become your own captive. This is all due to your mind being arrested by something external and losing its mastership" (Suzuki, 96). Neither attitudes, gestures, nor techniques were to be allowed to influence or limit the mind's independence. "In the case of swordsmanship, for instance, when the opponent tries to strike you, your eyes at once catch the movement of his sword and you may strive to follow it. But as soon as this takes place, you cease to be master of yourself and you are sure to be beaten. This is called 'stopping'" (Suzuki, 96).

These observations were repeated in chronicles of other martial arts, even the unarmed. The legendary Iso of the Tenjin-Shinyo *ryu* of jujutsu is said to have written in a manual of instruction for that school, "If you happen to wear armour and other military weapons, do not let them influence you—because these 'things' are only but appearances" *(Judo Kodokan,* Spring, 1951). In a more modern study of kenjutsu, another author seems to agree and even quotes a master of the art suggesting a method for putting things in perspective: "Think too much of the sword and you lose sight of the end. Perhaps you might understand this [more easily] if you saw swordplay without a sword, he said" (Gluck, 9). In a kenjutsu classic,

for example, a disciple was firmly rebuked by his teacher for showing anger and thus falling straight into an opponent's trap (Durckheim, 77).

Both this mental independence and its concomitant stability in facing combat, with all its external and internal implications, were considered to be the foundation for the general awareness and clarity of perception which were, in and of themselves, expressions of control over combat because they allowed a man to anticipate a strategic event or deal with it as it was actually developing.

A clear example of the first type of preventive perception (that is, through awareness of an impending attack) is offered by the following episode from the *Gekken Sodai.* A famous teacher of kenjutsu was resting in his garden with one of his students, who was wearing a sword. Seeing his teacher relaxed and immersed in idle contemplation, the boy thought how easy it would be to launch a surprise attack (using a technique of iaijutsu) before his teacher even realized what was happening. At that moment, the master looked up with a frown. Still frowning, he arose and began to search the grounds, looking behind trees and bushes as if expecting to find a foe lurking there. Seeking no one, he grew increasingly uneasy and eventually retreated to his room, where, to his student's anxious inquiries, he replied that, owing to his long training and varied experiences in bujutsu, he could usually sense an impending attack or murderous air before any such attack actually materialized. That day, in the garden, he had "sensed" such an air, but nothing had happened and no one seemed to be in the vicinity except his pupil. It was only when the student explained that it was he who had thought there was an opening for launching an effective attack against his teacher, that the latter relaxed and regained his composure. The master had sensed his pupil's aggressive intention, even though there had been no overt move or sign from the boy.

Episodes illustrating cases of preventive awareness such as the one related above are so numerous in the literature of Japan that they have found their way into the modern *chambara* movies which illustrate those epic ages. In a classic Japanese film which won international acclaim (Kurosawa's *The Seven Samurai),* it is interesting to note that just such a depth and range of awareness and perception was displayed by the leader of the warriors in his efforts to distinguish a true samurai from the many bogus *ronin* thronging the highways in those days. The test he devised was a simple one: a man armed with a club was placed behind the door through which the candidates were to enter. Of the seven masterless warriors invited to cross the threshold, only one (of peasant origins and, therefore, not a rightful member of the military class, nor versed in *haragei)* failed to take those precautionary measures which were customarily and automatically to be taken under such circumstances. He (the peasant) was the only one caught unawares and, of course, hit squarely on the head. In another important film dealing with feudal Japan, shown in the United States under the title *Hara-kiri,* a man bent on avenging his son-in-law's unjust suicide (unjust because forced and brutally executed) waits for his first victim and starts to follow him. Almost automatically, the latter becomes aware of a threat (although no clear indication of hostility has yet been given), and he prepares himself for combat.

An entire theory concerned with this type of awareness has been developed, based upon and derived from inner centralization in the *hara*—the only Centre capable of insuring the necessary clarity and depth of perception. This theory has found its way into the modern age and the Western hemisphere in the invaluable writings of Durckheim, who has authored one of the most perceptive studies extant on the *hara.* He relates, in this connection, the story of a potential aggressor who is "detected" by his victim and, therefore, does not attack—the exchange of information and awareness from one man to the other being automatic and quite precise, although neither looks at the other nor even gives any indication that contact has been made.

> It is not a matter of "feeling," but one of perceiving reality, real facts; it is not a matter of a sudden and fleeting intuition, but of a kind of antenna which remains always available to the one who acquires it. It also happens that, where *haragei* has been developed, there is not only receptivity but also an active force. The adept of *haragei* is not only an ultra-sensitive receiver, but an equally powerful transmitter. (Durckheim, 33)

In relation to perception, *haragei* as a theory uses the famous images of *mizu-no-kokoro* and *tsuki-no-kokoro* to visualize the type of mental attitude which must be developed if one is to face life well in general, and each of its problems (including combat encounters) in particular. *Mizu-no-kokoro* means literally "a spirit like calm water," and it indicates that type of mind as uniformly calm as the unruffled surface of a lake which reflects clearly everything existing or moving in the vicinity, without undue emphasis upon anything in particular. But if the wind sweeps over that surface, those limpid reflections are dispersed into innumerable fragments which distort the original image and confuse the whole. *Tsuki-no-kokoro,* on the other hand, means "a spirit calm as the moon" and represents a dispassionate attitude toward everything, like the moon which shines over everything impartially and is thus "aware" of the entire landscape in general, as well as of its various details. But if a cloud should pass between the moon and the earth, all is obscured; the landscape becomes shadowy, dim, and often frightening. In both images the central idea is: the mind can perceive and evaluate the general and the particular, the farthest and the closest in full independence, only if it is centralized and thus protected from distractions or disturbances of any kind. Therefore, according to the majority of kenjutsu masters, this general awareness of reality expressed through the image of the moon *(tsuki)* would also include a specialized perception of the significant detail, of the important particular elements of combat, just as the individual branches of a tree growing by the side of a lake would be reflected in its calm waters *(mizu).*

As noted earlier, this capacity of the mind to concentrate all its powers of perception upon a single object, while remaining aware of the elements surrounding that object, had been used by ancient doctrines of development and ultimate liberation in India, China, Tibet, and Japan, as a technique for freeing the mind from any dependence upon the multiform and confusing variety of phenomena in man's reality.

The first step, consequently, was that of disciplining and concentrating one's mental powers in order to achieve a first level of independence, peace, and harmony—the necessary prelude to further exploration of the social and cosmic essence of that reality, in a series of progressive expansions of the human personality. This technique of concentration became an art in the Buddhist school of thought which took its name from the method used to achieve and perfect such focusing of consciousness on one spot alone—the schools of meditation being known in India as Dhyana, in China as Ch'an, and in Japan as Zen. Of course, an overwhelming emphasis upon concentration, as noted previously, could become an aberration when interpreted (as it often was) in an absolute sense and as an end in and of itself. In such cases, a man's mind would be captured and become congealed in a condition of total dependence upon the object perceived, to the absolute exclusion of all other elements existing in that reality.

For the masters of bujutsu, however, this intense perception of the single element and significant factor of combat, achieved through the disciplines of concentration and meditation, was considered a basic requirement of the art of kenjutsu. The mind had to be prepared to perceive, for example, an entire tree, to note with blinding clarity a single leaf among the many on its branches, while simultaneously maintaining an awareness of all the others, each clearly and precisely—but without allowing itself to be captured or distracted by any one. These ideas concerning the rapid succession of particular perceptions linked to one another by the *bushi's* general awareness of the whole, his concentration upon the immediate detail at hand, while he simultaneously maintained his awareness of all the others—were the methodological foundations of many schools of kenjutsu, as well as of all the best schools of bujutsu in general. They help to explain the fame of such schools as the Koto-Eiri *ryu,* whose canons of combat against a group of opponents rather than a single swordsman have figured prominently in some of the best Japanese films of the 1960s, including *Yojimbo, Sanjuro,* and *Hara-kiri,* where the hero, with dazzling speed, proceeds to eliminate (or defend himself against) swordsmen and spearmen converging upon him from every side. Centuries ago, Takuan wrote:

> Suppose ten men are opposing you, each in succession ready to strike you with a sword. As soon as one is disposed of, you will move on to another without permitting the mind to "stop" with any. However rapidly one blow may follow another, you leave no time to intervene between the two. Every one of the ten will thus be successively and successfully dealt with. This is possible only when the mind moves from one object to another without being "stopped" or arrested by anything. (Suzuki, 98)

This type of mental independence in the midst of converging foes was even more effective when confronting a single opponent, of course. In this context, Takuan further specified:

> No doubt you see the sword about to strike you, but do not let your mind "stop" there. Have no intention to counterattack him in response to his threatening move, cherish no calculating thoughts whatever. You simply perceive the opponent's move, you do not allow your mind to "stop" with it, you move on just as you are. (Suzuki, 96)

This principle of mental independence reached a particular apex in the theory and practice of kenjutsu with the removal of the most human and also the most paralyzing obstacle to fluidity of action: preoccupation with one's own subjective survival. It had long been known, of course, that a man who, through disciplined training, had relinquished any desire or hope for survival and had only one goal—the destruction of his enemy—could be a redoubtable opponent and a truly formidable fighter who neither asked nor offered any quarter once his weapon had been unsheathed. In this way, a seemingly ordinary man who, by the force of circumstances rather than by profession, had been placed in the position of having to make a desperate choice, could prove dangerous, even to a skilled fencing master. One famous episode, for example, concerns a teacher of swordsmanship who was asked by a superior to surrender a servant guilty of an offense punishable by death. This teacher, wishing to test a theory of his concerning the power of that condition we would call "desperation," challenged the doomed man to a duel. Knowing full well the irrevocability of his sentence, the servant was beyond caring one way or the other, and the ensuing duel proved that even a skilled fencer and teacher of the art could find himself in great difficulty when confronted by a man who, because of his acceptance of imminent death, could go to the limit (and even beyond) in his strategy, without a single hesitation or distracting consideration. The servant, in fact, fought like a man possessed, forcing his master to retreat until his back was almost to the wall. At last the teacher had to cut him down in a final effort, wherein the master's own desperation brought about the fullest coordination of his courage, skill, and determination (Suzuki, 186–88).

Such intense and determined combativity in a swordsman's servant might not be too surprising, since it is conceivable that such a man could have learned how to handle a sword as a result of continuous exposure to his master's teaching. But concentration of this specialized and total type was said to have produced the same fanatical determination and fearless reaction in men of peace who had trained in and been shaped by the various cults of nonviolence, tranquillity, contemplation, and so forth. In this connection, the doctrine of kenjutsu contains the interesting episode of the tea master of Lord Yamanouchi of Tosa province, who had been forced by his lord's insistent requests to leave the quiet of Tosa Castle and follow his master to Edo, where, evidently, Lord Yamanouchi wished to display his retainer's skill in performing the *cha-no-yu*. In Edo one day, the peaceful tea master (who was not of samurai rank, although required, by protocol, to dress like one) had an encounter which he had expected and feared ever since leaving home: he met a *ronin* who challenged him to a duel. The tea master explained his status, but

the *ronin,* hoping to extort money from his victim, continued to threaten him. To pay in order to be left alone would have represented, for the tea master, for his Lord, and for his clan, a dishonorable action. The only alternative was to accept the challenge. Once he had resigned himself to death, the tea master's only wish was to die in a manner befitting a samurai. He therefore asked his opponent's permission to delay the encounter and then rushed off to a school of fencing he had noticed nearby, hoping to receive at least the basic information he required, that is, the rudiments of dying honorably by the sword. Without a letter of introduction, it was usually difficult to secure an audience with the master of a school, but, in this instance, even the gatekeepers could not help but notice how seriously disturbed the tea master was, and they were finally impressed by the desperate urgency with which he entreated that he be allowed to enter. At last he was introduced to the master, who, having listened carefully to the story, requested that the tea master serve him some tea before learning the art of dying. Watching him perform the tea ceremony with total concentration and mental serenity, the story continues that the master swordsman, at a certain point, "struck his own knee, a sign of hearty approval, and exclaimed":

> There you are! No need for you to learn the art of death! The state of mind in which you are now is enough for you to cope with any swordsman. When you see your *ronin* outcast, go on this way: first, think you are going to serve tea for a guest. Courteously salute him, apologizing for the delay, and tell him that you are now ready for the contest. Take off your *haori* (out coat), fold it up carefully, and then put your fan on it just as you do when you are at work. Now bind your head with the *tenugui* (towel), tie your sleeves up with the string, and gather up your *hakama* (divided skirt). Draw your sword, lift it high up over your head, in full readiness to strike down the opponent, and, closing your eyes, collect your thoughts for a combat. When you hear him give a yell, strike him with your sword. It will probably end in mutual slaying. (Suzuki, 191-92)

Thanking the swordsman profusely, the tea master went back to the *ronin,* prepared himself, and waited. The *ronin* saw "an altogether different person" and "asked the Tea Master's pardon for his rude request... leaving the field hurriedly" (Suzuki, 191-92).

Episodes such as the one above and others related frequently by scholars of kenjutsu bring to mind the examples of extraordinary behavior under stressful circumstances which are mentioned in the doctrines of other martial arts. In aikido, for example, there are numerous illustrations of the concept of perfect fusion of the entire personality and all its powers (physical, functional, psychological, etc.) when attempting to resolve any problem. Such total concentration and determination could, in its extreme forms, resemble the fixed intensity of the fanatic or even, as some masters of kenjutsu put it, of the "insane man" (Suzuki, 185-86).

Haragei provided the masters of kenjutsu with the concept of inner centralization in the *hara,* and with the concept of extension of vital or coordinated energy *(ki)* from that Centre which, when properly adapted to the purposes of their art of the sword, could help to develop those qualities of mental independence, general awareness, intensity of perception, and unimpaired, powerful actions upon which combat effectiveness depended. Yamaoka Tesshu, a great teacher of kenjutsu, advised:

> Do not fix your mind on the attitude your rival assumes nor have it riveted on your own attitude or your own sword. Instead, fix your mind on your *saika-tan-den* (that part of the belly situated beneath the navel) and do not think either of dealing a blow at your opponent or of the latter dealing a blow at you. Cast aside all specific designs and rush to the attack the moment you see your enemy in the act of brandishing his sword over his head. (Harrison, 130-31)

An equally clear commitment to the theory and practice of *haragei* as the inner prerequisite of kenjutsu is evident in the writings of Adachi Masahiro, who is considered the founder of the Shimbu *ryu.* This teacher began his *Essentials of Swordsmanship (Hei-jutsu Yokun,* 1790) by recognizing that both "technique" and "psychic training" were essential and that the latter consisted primarily in being "calm and not at all disturbed" when meeting a foe in combat. He specified further that the swordsman "must feel as if nothing critical is happening. When he advances, his steps are securely on the ground, and his eyes are not glaringly fixed on the enemy as those of insane men might be. His behaviour is not in any way different from his everyday behaviour. No change is taking place in his expression" (Suzuki, 185-86). How was one to develop this attitude? *Haragei* supplied the answer. According to Adachi Masahiro, "to be able to act in this fashion, when the swordsman meets his opponent and when his life is at stake with every movement, means that the swordsman must have realized the 'immovable mind.' Physiologically speaking (as we would say today) he must have been thoroughly trained in keeping his *kokoro* way down in the abdominal region" (Suzuki, 185-86).

Many kenjutsu masters, however, realized quite clearly that absolute concentration upon the *hara* (evidently a very common occurrence) could produce a fighting robot but not necessarily even a good, much less excellent, swordsman. Takuan, that great "integrator" of kenjutsu, did not see any difference between exaggerated concentration on external details (against which so many kenjutsu teachers warned) and exaggerated concentration upon the *hara* (which many of those teachers often seem to have favored). Returning in his writings to the ancient sources of *haragei* which were linked to Buddhism in the Japanese version of Zen, he enlarged upon the narrow interpretations of the Japanese scholars, repeating the old truth that "Zen dislikes partialization or localization" and that, consequently, it was a mistake to interpret *haragei* in such a specialized fashion that the mind was kept "imprisoned in the lower region of the abdomen," since such an "imprisonment" would prevent the mind "from operating anywhere else" (Suzuki, 105-8).

For Takuan—and a few other masters who were clearly more removed from that crippling and specialized dimension of kenjutsu intended solely as an art of combat—*haragei* had, of course, a recognizable importance during the initial stages of training because it helped the pupil to discipline himself against the human tendency to fall easy prey to emotions, suggestions, impressions, and so forth. But soon after the "runaway mind" had been stabilized and unified, Takuan instructed that "the thing is not to localize the mind anywhere but to let it fill the whole body, let it flow throughout the totality of your being." The mind (in accordance with its nature) must be free to exercise its functions. "Unhindered and uninhibited," it could "meet the opponent as he moves about trying to strike you down. When your hands are needed, they are there to respond to your order. So with the legs." In synthesis, the mind "must be left to itself, utterly free to move about according to its own nature" (Suzuki, 105-8).

The attainment of this state of mental freedom was, in fact, the "end of spiritual training," over and beyond the narrow confines of specialization, which, in the case of the *bushi,* was professionally and rig-

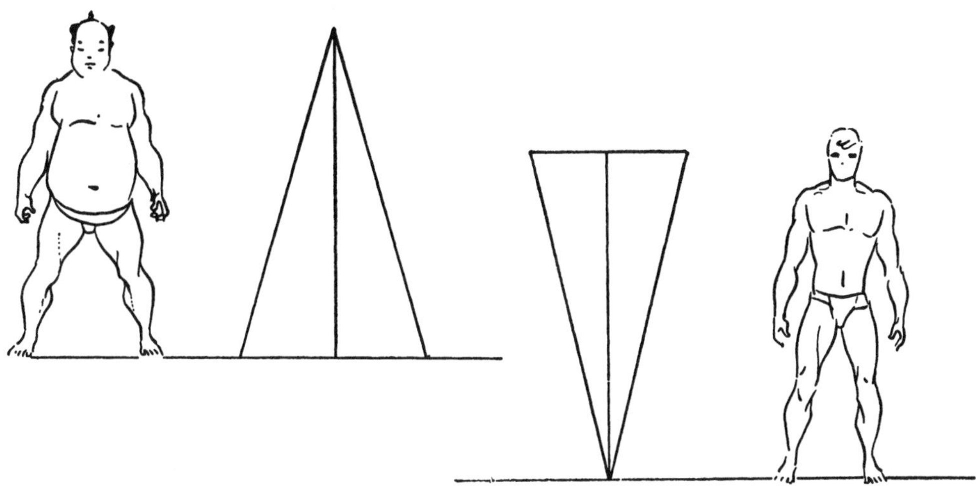

idly military in nature. Apparently, Takuan was visualizing a personality more comprehensive than that of a mere warrior—a personality at ease not only in the military dimension of existence but "anywhere else." Thus Takuan seemed to be in substantial agreement with another great teacher of the Zen school in the sixteenth century, Dokyo Etan (1641-1721), known among the *bushi* as the "Old Gentleman" *(shoju ronin)*. This teacher could skillfully neutralize sword attacks with a fan, regardless of the "technique" used by the swordsman—due, it was felt, to the fact that the "right knowledge" of existence, as taught in Buddhism *(magga*—the first of the Eight-Fold Path) was universal and could be applied to any human art, including kenjutsu. But, at this level, *haragei* emerges from the military dimension of bujutsu and expands into realms of spiritual "centralization," which, due to their complexity, cannot be explored properly in a general study of the martial arts. This universal conception of *haragei* has been dealt with, briefly, in the introductory section to Part 3, and a more detailed examination of its ethical implications will be found in a book on the subject being prepared by the authors of the present study.

As to the particular techniques or training methods developed and adopted by the various schools of kenjutsu in order to help develop this type of inner centralization which could insure a measure of control over the self, we find, in the doctrine of this art of combat, many direct as well as oblique references to techniques of introspection used in monasteries and other centers of spiritual advancement where the aims of Buddhism and Taoism were austerely pursued. The techniques of a particular sect (Zen) seem to have been preferred by the *bushi,* who, as seen earlier, made it the "religion" of his profession. The techniques of meditation and concentration in the still posture known as *zazen* must have been (as they still generally are) predominant; this applies also to the various methods of abdominal breathing—one of which is described by Takuan in his *Kitsu Yoshu,* where he also stresses the close relationship between Zen Buddhism and kenjutsu:

"*Munen mushin* (literally, 'without idea and without mind')—that is the name of Buddha. When you open your mouth wide to expel the air you get *na,* and when you shut your mouth to inhale the air you get *mu.* When you open your mouth you get *a,* and when you close it you get *mi.* When again you open your mouth you get *da,* and when again you shut it you get *butsu.* Thus the thrice repeated exhalation and inhalation is equivalent to the Buddhist invocation '*namu amida butsu*' which is symbolical of the letters *a* and *um.* The sound *a* is produced by opening the mouth and the sound *um* by shutting it. It may therefore be said that in the state of total absence of mind *(munen mushin)* you are always repeating the name of Buddha, even if you do not pronounce it aloud." It will thus be seen that the secret of Buddhism is embodied in this *a, um,* i.e., the art of regulating one's breathing. (Harrison, 132)

In order to be fluidly and powerfully effective in combat, however, the static techniques of meditation, concentration, and abdominal breathing in the *zazen* posture must necessarily have been modified in order to apply centralized power to the dramatic and eventful circumstances of an armed encounter (in this case, with swords). Very few of these dynamic techniques of *haragei* in action survived the feudal era, or if they did reach the modern schools of kenjutsu or kendo they were made public in such a way as to be comprehensible to the layman, even if somewhat obscured by the poetical imagery of the intuitive Japanese approach to instruction. Echoes of advice given by old masters of kenjutsu to their students are faintly discernible in the modern art of aikido, which, more openly than many others, acknowledges its debt to the theory and practice of ancient kenjutsu and, again more than most, recommends that its students act in combat with mind and body thoroughly unified through the *hara,* pouring forth its coordinated power *(ki)* at all times, channeling its force along the circular and spiral patterns of guidance and control devised and used systematically by the best fencing masters of feudal Japan.

Sumo

The art *of haragei,* in the eyes of a connoisseur of traditional wrestling in Japan, is the inspiration for the entire theory and practice of sumo, even today. *Haragei* is visually expressed, to begin with, in the very somatic development of the *sumotori.* Harrison, in the early 1900s, had already noted that, contrary to Western tendencies in the field of athletic training, the Japanese seemed to assign greater importance to a large "base" or "belly" than to a "swelling chest" (Harrison, 103). This observation is equally valid today, when the reasons behind the "barrelly belly" are more widely appreciated. In his book *Zen Combat,* Gluck relates the abdominal development of these Japanese athletes to breathing, "the soul in the stomach idea" (Gluck, 23), which is the primary exercise in *haragei* for developing the tremendous power generated by *sumotori* in action. A demonstration of this power outside the ring was given to Mr. Harrison by Taiho, a former sumo champion, who had invited a young American to kick him in the stomach. He had then set himself "with his legs slightly bent" and his hands on his knees —a posture of powerful defense often seen in Oriental sculpture. As the American leaped at the Japanese and, in the best karate style, sent his right foot smashing into the huge belly of the *sumotori,* the latter "gave his ponderous abdomen a heave forward," hurling the American backward (Harrison, 91-92).

Another author who explored the philosophical content of *haragei,* Durckheim, also used the example of the *sumotori* to describe the kind of power generated by abdominal centralization—a power which allows one athlete to push another over the circle's rope almost without touching him, thus bringing down the house as the discriminating audience explodes in ecstatic recognition of *haragei* in action (Durckheim,

17–18). Brinkley, who was among the first Westerners to elaborate at great length upon Japanese culture as it unfolded before the eyes of the West, described the arena and the elements composing the elevated ring (which was surrounded by sixteen bags of sand), the suspended roof once supported by four pillars, the curtains, and so forth—qualifying all these things as being "allegorical" and based upon "the Chinese philosophy of the *ch'i*" which, as we now know, is the active aspect of *haragei.*

Today, the cult of sumo in Japan is less sophisticated than it was before World War II, although it still remains popular. Many experts are of the opinion that the main reason for a certain decline in the quality of performance at many bouts (as well as in the depth of response on the part of the audience) is lack of appreciation of the inner aspects of sumo—aspects indissolubly linked to the feudal traditions of Japan, as well as to the culture of continental Asia at large. Indirectly, however, the esoteric aspect of the discipline still influences other Japanese methods of combat derived from ancient bujutsu, in which the belt (like the silken band worn by the *sumotori)* is worn very low on the hips by advanced students, and in which an enlarged and fully developed lower abdomen *(koshi)* is still considered to be the most potentially important Centre of stability and of coordinated power an athlete can possess. It is regrettable that, notwithstanding the obvious traditional importance of sumo in bujutsu and its modern derivations, studies concerning the methods of training practiced by ancient and modern masters of sumo schools, as well as the particular applications of *haragei* and the theory behind it, are still few and rather superficial. More complete information about the essence of sumo, in fact, would enable a greater number of people to perceive and appreciate this inner, deeper, and infinitely richer dimension of the art. In addition, it would enable the public at large to differentiate between a bout in which wrestlers collide mindlessly with one another like "mountains of fat and muscle" and a bout in which the contestants skillfully act as centralized masses of energy competing with one another for perfection in coordination and, therefore, in power and total control.

Jujutsu

There is hardly any doubt that almost all major schools of jujutsu, based as they are on the interesting principle of strategic flexibility *(ju),* were influenced by (when not entirely dependent upon) the doctrine of *haragei.* Methods of combat without weapons were often practiced in the same halls and under the direction of the very same masters who taught armed bujutsu (the unarmed methods being considered subsidiary arts), thus allowing the ideas and concepts of inner centralization, of coordinated power activating the latter, to flow freely into and be adopted by the former.

Revelations concerning these inner factors and dimensions of the art began to emerge in the early 1900s, when the temporary decline of the military class after the Meiji Restoration had rendered most methods of combat somewhat irrelevant, thus causing a relaxation of the crippling hold of secrecy which competition among different schools and clans had previously made imperative. It was at that time, in fact, that Mr. Kunishige Nobuyuki, a famous teacher of the Shinden Isshin *ryu,* offered Harrison one of the most systematically clear and impressive presentations of the strategic importance of *haragei* in jujutsu—which Harrison related in his aforementioned *Fighting Spirit of Japan.* This teacher began by stating how fundamental it was to develop the abdominal region of the anatomy *(shita-hara),* subtly distinguishing the active centralization of the man of arms *(bujin)* from the passive centralization of the contemplative man, although both were usually developed initially through the exercise of sitting in meditation *(zazen)* and of abdominal breathing.

> Mr. Kunishige loved to narrate with many appreciative chuckles how many years ago at Kyoto he fell afoul of one of the priests of the Zen sect which inculcates deep breathing as an essential concomitant of its system of mental concentration, the benefits of which, so far as they go, not even Mr. Kunishige

> would have cared to deny....The important point is that meditation is not the be-all and the end-all of mundane existence, and it was in connection with this phase of the subject that Mr. Kunishige and the priestly advocate of Zen came to verbal blows. "Yes," said the former, after listening politely and attentively to a long disquisition from his antagonist on the virtues of the system, "that is all very well as long as you remain squatting upon your three-by-three platform with no one to bother you. There you can develop your *shita-hara* to enormous proportions free from rude and sacrilegious interference; but the moment you descend from your perch and run up against a *bujin* who has developed his *shita-hara,* not by constant squatting but by *constant movement,* where are you?" And Mr. Kunishige showed him as he had showed me how by a simple touch with a single finger he could topple him. Needless to say, the sacerdotal disciple of *zazen* waxed exceeding wrathful over this attack and illustration and departed in high dudgeon. (Harrison, 123)

The aim of the active form of centralization in jujutsu was clearly that of coordinating the fighting powers of the *bushi,* to the extent that all the various terms employed by the doctrine of bujutsu—meaningless when taken individually—would become significant when fused together. Ancient manuscripts of jujutsu had attempted to analyze the inner factors of bujutsu, presenting a list of terms which ranged from the innermost layers of the human personality to its physical or muscular elements. One of these attempts is thus described by Mr. Harrison: "The technical terms *shi, ki* and *chikara* may be broadly defined as idea, spirit and power. A man's intention to pick up something is *shi;* his compliance with the prompting of *shi* is *ki;* and the actual handling of the object is due to *chikara* which obeys the impulse of *ki*" (Harrison, 36). The first fusion seemed to blend the inner force of intention, coordinated determination *(ki),* with the outer force of the muscular system *(chikara)* in almost equal measure—thus making one the complement of the other. But *ki* became undeniably more important than *chikara* in the higher spheres of the jujutsu doctrine, because

> if precedence is given to power *(chikara),* the result is bound to be highly disadvantageous. Power or physical strength should be relegated to a secondary position and efforts should be made to gain experience in the control and employment of spirit or mind *(ki),* for when this is accomplished, the right application of strength will become spontaneous. (Harrison, 36)

Thus, also in jujutsu, the problem of differentiating between muscular power *(chikara)*—which in armed bujutsu was increased by the weapon and technique (the outer factors of the art)—and the intrinsic energy of volition or will, of mental coordination and extension of *ki* (the inner factors), had been acknowledged and overcome by fusing the two spheres. The inner factors *(ki),* however, were usually accorded a position of predominance which became more absolute as each art became increasingly refined by the efforts of advanced students, experts, and teachers of long experience.

It was frequently observed that a young warrior, filled with the natural exuberance of youth but lacking experience, usually relied heavily upon muscular power *(chikara);* but this external power, dependent as it was upon the fullness of youth, tended to wane with the passing of time. On the other hand, the student who based his training and combat strategy upon the coordination of his mental powers, thus activating and controlling his physical powers from within, seemed to grow stronger with the passing years or, at least, to maintain a condition of positive strategic coordination for a longer period of time than was true of the former. As Kunishige put it:

> When . . . precedence is given only to physical strength, the ultimate result is bound to be highly disavantageous inasmuch as the physical strength of an old man must, as a rule, be inferior to that of a young one who is equally assiduous in the pursuit of Bujutsu; whereas the veteran *bujin* (expert of the arts of combat) skilled in the esotericism of Ju-jutsu, can always in the end vanquish his more juvenile antagonist even though in the exoteric wrestling he might be thrown again and again. (Harrison, 104)

By esotericism of jujutsu, the masters of this strategic principle of combat meant the control of coordinated power based on the abdominal Centre of integration. "The student will do well to train his *shita-hara* until he has placed his *ki* at his disposal" (Harrison, 116). This training, as usual, emphasized the practice of abdominal breathing and active exercises of coordination, rather than those exercises of meditation and concentration which Kunishige considered too static for the warrior's purposes.

The question naturally arises: Was the Japanese warrior, trained in the "esoteric factors of jujutsu" (as *haragei* was commonly referred to in the context of this art), as powerful a fighter as the doctrine of this interesting principle of combat would lead us to believe? The only possible answer to this question must be based upon information gleaned from the records and manuscripts of the various jujutsu schools—references which, we must remember, have been qualified even by Japanese scholars as often being "unreliable," "sectarian," "contradictory," and even at times plainly "ridiculous." We can only quote again from Harrison's personal accounts of the demonstrations given by Master Kunishige of the Shinden Isshin *ryu* of jujutsu in the early 1900s, after he had explained that the power he was about to display was not based on that famous power of suggestion employed by so many martial arts masters. This master, heir to an ancient tradition, then proceeded to demonstrate a few practical examples of *haragei* applied to unarmed combat (thus anticipating other demonstrations given by teachers of more modern martial arts), beginning with the exercise of immovable posture which is also found in varying forms in the doctrine of aikido. Kunishige knew, of course, that it was possible to mesmerize an opponent, thus placing him under a form of mental control. Using the power of *ki*, however, the effects were more certain, he felt, and proceeded to prove it by remaining as still and immovable as a rock while Harrison and one of the master's advanced students tried vainly to move him from the position he had assumed on the mat—even using belts tied around his neck to increase the pressure. Mr. Harrison observed with his usual wry humor that Kunishige then proceeded to drag the two of them around the room, despite their resistance—and with hardly any indication of strain or excessive effort on the teacher's part.

It may be surmised that perhaps such feats were possible because an expert *bujin* such as Master Kunishige was extremely well developed muscularly, as might be expected of a man who had spent most of his life on the *tatami* of an ancient school of bujutsu. But, as Harrison noted, the master, notwithstanding his long experience in jujutsu, was well over sixty years old and his weight did not exceed 160 pounds—a weight which he pitted successfully against a *sumotori* in another demonstration of this same power.

Kiaijutsu

The art of kiai, examined in Part 2 in relation to its outer factors (primarily the human voice), is *haragei* at its highest point of strategic specialization. Few details are available about the actual training techniques which were used to develop that preliminary unification of powers in the *hara* which allowed certain *bujin* to paralyze, kill, or, on the other hand, save another warrior's life via a concentrated shout. The art, in fact, seems to be on the verge of extinction; only occasionally is the name of an isolated expert in its techniques mentioned in the circles of modern bujutsu in Japan, accompanied by vague and often unreliable details of his exploits.

It seems indisputable, however, that kiai was vocal *haragei*—that is, abdominal centralization channeling its coordinated power toward a target via a man's vocal cords. Indicating his belief in the fundamental identity of essence of both *aiki* and *kiai,* Mr. Harrison told of his early encounters with Japanese masters of kiaijutsu in the early 1900s, who considered the power of *aiki* as silent, while the *kiai* shout, as a vector of power, was "something in the nature of an auxiliary agent contributing to mental concentration upon one object" (Harrison, 103). In kiaijutsu, too, "the practice of *ki-ai* is supposed to have the effect of strengthening the region of the *saika-tanden* (the part of the abdomen situated about two inches below the navel), and must thus bulk largely as a factor in the development of physical courage and occult power" (Harrison, 103).

The effects of such concentration of vocal power upon a living human being have been noted in Part 2, in specific relation to the Japanese tradition. In the West, those authors who have attempted to arrive at something approaching a scientific explanation of the nature of this power have usually spoken in terms of "subsonics and super-sonics," but, to our knowledge, no analysis *of kiai,* based upon verified experiments and observations, has yet been published. Consequently, we must await further scientific explorations which, hopefully, may shed more light upon this interesting phenomenon.

Haragei in Modern Derivations of Bujutsu

Any study of the inner factors of bujutsu (generally qualified as being esoteric or abstruse) would be incomplete without some reference to their relevance within those disciplines of combat reputedly derived, even if in a modified form, from the ancient arts of combat practiced by the *bujin* of feudal Japan. Among these derivations, the arts of judo, karate, and aikido are currently the most popular (judo even having been included in the 1964 Olympic games in Tokyo and the 1972 games in Munich). *Haragei,* as we will see, was mentioned in the most ancient records of these schools and has influenced (or, in some cases, even determined to a substantial degree) their respective methodologies in both theory and practice, especially at the highest levels of instruction.

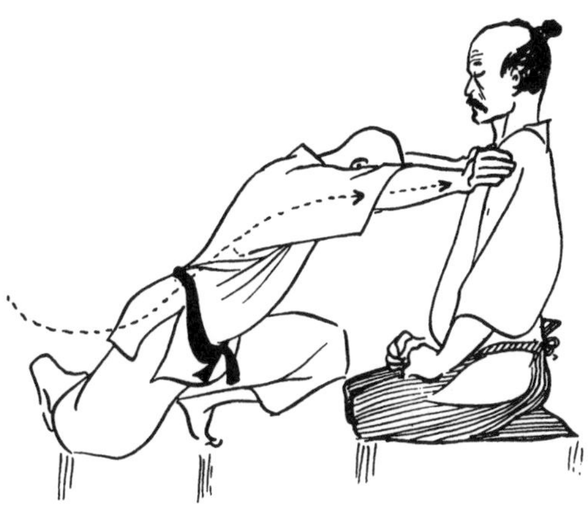

Judo

Most books and treatises on Master Kano's modern discipline do not contain many explicit references to the concept of *hara* (identified in judo more specifically as *seika-tanden, tanden,* or *tan)* or the concept of *ki* (often called *naiki),* as fused in the unified doctrine of *haragei.* Judo, however (at least at its highest levels), is also based upon the doctrine of *haragei* and its system of abdominal centralization and extension, as the main prerequisite for mental stability, control, and power. Master Kano often and openly acknowledged his indebtedness to the ancient schools of jujutsu, many of whose masters were well versed in the practice and practical uses of *haragei.* Among those schools, the ancient Kito *ryu* seems to have been particularly influential—its *koshiki-no-kata,* or "ancient formal exercises," still being required of advanced judo students today. Other exercises cherished by Master Kano and preserved in his system are the fluid *itsutsu-no-kata,* or "forms of five," which he retained, together with the famous *ju-no-kata,* or "exercises of gentleness," "to train what is called *nai-ki* or 'inner energy.'" (Leggett, 13). Such a study of the inner factors of judo was qualified by Master Kano as being essential (Leggett, 120).

In the early part of the 1900s, Harrison outlined the particular value of *haragei* in judo after interviews and practice sessions with several judo teachers of the period. Sumitomo Arima (the "author of a standard work on the subject" of judo, often quoted by Harrison) was quite explicit concerning the cosmic dimension of the *hara* or *tanden.* This teacher (like many of his contemporaries) considered it "the centre of life" and, in judo, the "centre of gravity of the body," further specifying that "it is located in the lower abdomen, approximately two inches below the navel." In unmistakable terms, Sumitomo stated that the *hara* was the fundamental Centre of integration ("concentrate your power in the *tanden!")* and the Centre of coordinated energy ("extend all your force from the abdomen!") which had to be kept active at all times, repeating that "whether sitting, or standing, or moving, you must always take care that your lower abdomen is filled with strength" (Harrison, 105).

The same author also relates the experiences of a Western Black Belt (3rd Dan at the time), Mr. R.E. West, who was introduced to the mysteries *of haragei* by high-ranking judo instructors—all of them giving ample proof of their proficiency in the use of the *hara* as a Centre of power *(ki),* while expressing a certain amused surprise at Mr. West's interest in this "esoteric" aspect of Master Kano's art which, even in Japan, was explored by only a "very few" men. A comparatively simple demonstration of abdominal stability, resembling an exercise of concentrated extension quite common in aikido *(kokyu-dosa),* was offered Mr. West by Nango Jiro, a nephew of Master Kano, who had also been one of the first students of judo. This teacher "expressed surprise" at Mr. West's knowledge of the *hara's* existence.

> He said that it was no part of the regular Judo College teaching but that he would give me a demonstration of its effectiveness. Thereupon we removed our shoes and sat on our knees facing each

> other on the floor. At the time I weighed 175 lbs. and considered myself quite strong. He weighed about 130 lbs. and was old. We placed our right hands on each other's chest. At my option I was to attempt to push him over backwards. I shoved hard, then harder, and finally with all my strength. He didn't move. Then he shoved back and I went over. He then stated that only by the power residing in the *tanden* could this be accomplished. (Harrison, 127-28)

The same instructor, training with Mr. West on the mat at the Kodokan, and purposefully using the *hara* in action as Centre of vertical stability, could neutralize a technique of projection not only by "excellent" evasions but also by simply utilizing the "sinking" power of the abdomen.

Also clearly related to the active dimensions of combat was the demonstration of *haragei* in action given by the late Matsuura, another high-ranking instructor at the Kodokan.

> Sitting on his knees with his back to me and his hands together, he made his mind blank of any conscious thought. The idea was that I was to remain behind him for as long a time as I desired. Then with all the speed and power I could muster I was to grab him by the throat and pull him over backwards. I sweated it out for maybe two or three minutes without making a move. Then I put all the power and speed I could into the effort. My next step was to get up from my back where I landed in front of him. His explanation was that the action was not conscious, but rather sprang from the seat of reflex control, the *tanden*, or second brain. These things are not taught in the Judo College. (Harrison, 127)

The functional effects of inner centralization and extension in judo were related to mental independence, power to act or react, suppleness and stability. Master Kano had clearly recognized the dangers of attachment and its crippling effects upon coordination, and he often used clever psychological tricks to "unblock" his students' minds whenever they seemed unable to perform a technique correctly.

One result of intense training in *haragei* for the purposes of combat, noted by many judo experts, was that a man's vertical stability in combat, especially when confronted with techniques of unbalance and projection, seemed to be more easily maintained. As related by Leggett:

> Balance in most people is extremely poor: they try to align themselves in accordance with supposed vertical and horizontal lines in the objects around them. Experiments have been done in Japan in which a man tries to stand upright while a vertically striped "tent" hangs around him; when the tent is revolved the untrained man invariably loses balance because the visual cues are disturbed, whereas the Judo men with their *inner* sense of balance can stand steadily even on one leg. (Leggett, 8-10)

Suppleness or naturalness of movement and action, another result of correct inner centralization, is often referred to as occurring in a state of relaxation—a term still being debated within the doctrine because it is commonly considered to imply "floppiness" or lack of control. As defined by Leggett, relaxation in judo indicates more Properly an absence of unnecessary tension.

In judo, too, the special exercise of abdominal breathing, practiced in a variety of ways (all centered, however, upon the navel) is considered the best way to develop these inner factors of judo practice. In a classic text, the *Judo Taisen Roku,* considered by many to be the bible of judo, "it is written that 'breathing is to be combined with good position'—both breathing in and breathing out are to be felt as passing [taking place] below the navel" *(Judo Kodokan,* September, 1958). Precise instructions are also given for abdominal breathing in combat. And these instructions, as indicated below, are based upon the methodological heritage of those schools of jujutsu from which judo was derived: "In *Ittoryu Bunsho* ('Observations of the Itto School'), the following advice is written: 'Attack the opponent according to his breathing and watch out for the best relevant opportunity.' It is not specified whether breathing in or breathing out is involved" *(Judo Kodokan,* September, 1958). The controversy over the relevance of each phase of breathing in relation to particular moments of combat continues. Almost every expert seems to agree that abdominal breathing strengthens the body and activates its Centre of coordinated energy. Certain authors also advise against breathing in at the moment an action of attack, counterattack, or defense is being launched, recommending a strong exhalation instead. Such advice, naturally, concerns a fleeting moment in combat during which all the powers of the body (physical, mental, and functional) are unified in a single, dynamic fusion—often expressed in a coordinated shout *(kiai).* Mr. Mifune also seems to have been in general agreement with this view when he wrote that "the attack should be made breathing out the air just breathed in." The predominance of opinion in favor of breathing out at the moment of launching an action seems to link judo (as well as all the other minor martial arts) to the specialized art of kiai, which made that breathing out (when embodied in a shout) a vector of power and a weapon to be used, often by itself, in combat.

Finally, the late Mifune Kyuzo, of the Kodokan school of judo, also based his training program on the hidden pillars of *haragei.* The "essence of Judo," he wrote, "is to keep the centre of gravity" because it "follows the movement of the body; this centre being the most important means of keeping stability, [for] if it is lost, the body will become naturally unbalanced. So keep your mind stable and your body light, move quickly when needed, setting the centre of gravity instantly" (Mifune, 32). He also seemed to view centralization in the *hara* as an evolutionary process, moving from a conscious (hence, necessarily committed and static) condition, to an unconscious, natural, and automatic condition which, once achieved, would allow the mind to roam free "according to its own nature" and thus be able to cope successfully with reality. He added, in fact, that "men evolving in both the spiritual and the physical dimension [must] strive at maintaining their 'centre' to the level of the unconscious through preliminary [conscious] exercise" (Mifune, 29). And he too, eventually, like other instructors who had endeavored to become more than mere specialists of combat and had aimed at educating their students, seemed to emphasize continually the universal dimension of *haragei,* by writing that "the posture in Judo ought to be truly natural, thus avoiding camouflage and affectation. The essence of life is in truth" (Mifune, 32). To the very end of his life, this excellent instructor, whose prowess on the mat amazed his students and the general public alike, was the most convincing proof that, although our present studies in physiology may not have arrived at a satisfactory explanation of the phenomenon, nevertheless, students who perform these exercises regularly appear to generate and display astounding energy, even when quite advanced in age.

Today, only scanty references to the training methods adopted by judo schools for the purpose of developing this fundamental, kinetic condition of centralization are to be found in manuals of judo instruction, but the best treatises never fail to mention their existence and stress their importance.

The various practices of concentration, meditation, and abdominal breathing (not uniformly followed in all judo centers of instruction) are generally left to the discretion of the individual instructor, who may, or may not, find the strategic relevance of the inner factors of judo meaningful. Their cultivation through the static technique of *zazen,* moreover, is still only a preliminary to the more dynamic cultivation of these factors through the thorough practice of judo *kata* that is so firmly recommended by Master Kano himself.

Karate

Very few modern books on the Japanese interpretation of this art refer at great length to the inner factors of the discipline, that is, mental stability for total control and the extension of coordinated power. But those that do seldom fail to link the above factors to their ancient matrices in the theory *of hara* and *ki,* systematized in the art of *haragei.* It should be noted, in fact, that two major exponents of Japanese karate

(Oyama Masutatsu [Mass] and Yamaguchi Gogen) continually emphasize these factors in their teaching and writing. The former, in fact, states quite clearly that "all my attention, all my training, all my thinking is centered on my abdomen" (Gluck, 23). In his eyes, the best representations of an expert in the art of striking are the wooden statues at the doors of many Buddhist temples—especially those unarmed figures which show "an exaggerated abdominal muscular development. No great ripple of muscle, but rows of knots. . . .These are not muscles for hefting weights, they are for speed and power; more akin to the leg development of a track man than the brawn of a weight lifter" (Gluck, 23). Practical examples of the coordinated power of the inner factors of this art, such as the following (demonstrated by Oyama Masutatsu) do not differ, in essence, from those given by masters of other martial arts, such as the late Master Kunishige of jujutsu or Master Uyeshiba of aikido.

> These *nio* statues gripping the ground with their toes, like cats, are still a good basic lesson in Karate, Mass pointed out, striking an identical pose and daring the five of us to budge him. We totaled over three times his weight, but he might as well have been rooted there. When we exerted our maximum against him, he seemed for an instant to give and I found myself seated some distance away, a fifth part of a semi-circle of sprawling bodies around a laughing Karate master. "Give and snap back," he roared. (Gluck, 22)

The special training methods used to develop the inner factors of centralization and extension are strikingly similar in both the school of Oyama Masutatsu and that of Yamaguchi Gogen (the "Cat"), and unmistakably Zen oriented. Abdominal breathing for the development of coordinated power—as is true in all major martial arts—is considered of the utmost importance by these masters. "Fail to master breath control, Mass warned, and you can do nothing in Karate, except possibly a few cute tricks" (Gluck, 26). Becoming more specific, he describes his method and explains its advantages :

> Breathing is with the pit of the stomach. . . .Repeated deep breaths with the chest cause giddiness, an imbalance of oxygen in the blood system that's worse than being short of breath as it takes all the strength away and dulls the senses, leaving you off balance and defenseless. Take a deep breath into your chest, through your nose, mouth tightly closed. Deep, show off your expansion, throw back your shoulders. . . .Force the air down, down . . . force your feet, if you are standing, or your seat, if you are sitting, right through the ground. (Gluck, 25)

In Yamaguchi's system, outlined below, there are two types of breathing. Both, however, are based upon the abdomen and differ only in relation to particular moments of combat and their specific purposes.

> There are two types of breathing practiced [in the Goju brand of Karate of Master Yamaguchi Gogen]: the *in-ibuki* and the *yo-ibuki*. The *in-ibuki* is the soft but firm type of breathing which starts from deep within the abdomen. This is similar to the type of breathing which is practiced in Yoga and Zen meditation, and is usually directed toward spiritual and meditative matters when practiced. Goju adherents never tire of repeating that this is the normal type of breathing that a baby engages in. It is only when we get older that we learn to breathe from our chest. The *yo-ibuki* is the hard style of breathing. The sound effects are menacing. The breathing is loud and heavy and comes from deep within, producing something of the sound of a full-throated lion about to strike. The inhaling is done in quick intakes through the nose while the exhaling is a prolonged process of short breaths through the mouth. In exhaling the whole body is tensed, including the throat and esophagus. This tightens the air passage and the air is forced from the abdomen. This whole process is said to be combative and animal-like. *(Black Belt,* April, 1966)

But if coordinated energy appears to be the primary prerequisite of combat in both these schools of modern karate, the basis for this power is also found in the necessary consolidation of the personality within, in a single Centre of inner stability and control. In fact, the special exercises used in both schools are, like those of meditation, concentration, and isolation in the wilderness, modified adaptations of those of the ancient doctrines of superior coordination which the armed martial arts had also employed in the past. As related in a popular martial arts magazine, "for his summer training, Oyama usually attracts about 125 men and women. In the mountains, they make runs of several miles up and down narrow roads every morning. The days are spent in long sessions of exercises and *kumite,* interspersed with periods of *zazen* meditation" *(Black Belt,* September, 1966). Similarly:

> In Yamaguchi's place, he goes out into the mountains once a month to toughen himself up spiritually and physically. He engages in *sanchin* (breathing exercises) for several hours under an icy waterfall to try to make his mind and spirit impenetrable to adverse conditions. . . .When away from such stimulating environment, Yamaguchi still keeps a rigid schedule at home. He rises early and manages to get an hour or more of meditation and more than an hour of *kata* practice by himself every morning. *(Black Belt,* April, 1966)

Both men obviously consider mental stability through inner centralization to be the only basis for control over combat operations and their effective powers. This view is clearly stated by Oyama and was the basis for an interesting experiment in his school that served to demonstrate the comparative relevance of the inner and outer factors of combat.

> "Brains beats brawn in Karate. . . .We make them [the students of his school] meditate before every work-out and encourage meditation at home or at work...." Some years ago, Mass chose two new students who were as evenly endowed with natural talents as possible. One he trained purely on calisthenics and workouts, taught him all the tricks. The other he gave less physical training, but made him do *zazen* religious meditation every day for half an hour when he awoke and again before his evening work-outs, squatting like a Buddha, forcing all his internal organs into proper alignment, breathing "right down to his toes" and clearing his mind. After six months, both came up for their black belt test and he matched them. The first fellow had beefed up and put on ten pounds, the other had grown wiry. The thinker made mincemeat of the muscle boy. (Gluck, 65-66)

The same point of view was expressed by a high-ranking instructor of another martial art, aikido, when he warned against qualifying as "lazy" those students who devote a greater proportion of their time on the mat to sitting or standing in evident concentration, as compared to those who are busily engaged in techniques, physical exercises, and so forth. This instructor had also realized that the former could often perform better under stress than the latter because they had been working to develop those inner factors of stability, control, and power which are considered to be the necessary foundation for correct outer technique.

The link with continental Asia, in this context, seems well represented by the karate schools in the Ryukyu Islands, thus confirming—even if in a circuitous manner—the derivative dependence of the Japanese form of *haragei* upon its Chinese matrix (a fact most scholars of bujutsu think undeniable). The Hakutsuru *ryu,* for example, is related to the Shorin *ryu,* which, in turn, is linked to the Shurite branch of the Namboku *ryu*—the school of two styles ("hard" *go,* and "soft" *ju*), reflecting the ancient Chinese division of styles into *wai* (hard) and *nei* (soft). The master of this school, Shoken *sensei,* is still active today and, according to a comparatively recent interview given to a Western correspondent, "among the few other characteristics [that he] will reveal of the 'White Swan' technique is the importance of *ch'i* or intrinsic energy—that much-discussed about but seldom achieved abstraction in the mastery of unarmed combat." In the same interview, this master also indicated the method he favors for developing this energy: "Another important element, according to Shoken, is breath control, which he contends should be practiced every day, but not to the point of exhaustion." The importance of this concept of inner energy, as far as Shoken is concerned, is fundamental. He states that "it is the *ch'i* (or *ki* as it is often written) which is the single most emphasized element of this technique and mastery of the *ch'i* is essential and requisite to learning the White Swan" *(Black Belt,* May, 1967).

To conclude: the doctrines of many other methods of combat originating outside Japan but considered to be direct or collateral sources of inspiration (if not of obvious derivation) are even more emphatic about *hara* and *ki* being the conceptual foundations for both the theory and the practice of the art of striking. In some of these methods, karate is actually considered to begin with the centralized, coordinated energy of the lower abdomen. In an interesting manuscript on shaolin, edited by Smith, we read terse passages concerning the essence of the art, its power, and the special exercises used to develop that power. "There are many schools teaching the 'soft' form of the martial arts. All begin and end with the *ch'i* or intrinsic energy" (Smith[2], 31). This energy, centralized in the abdomen, becomes the first prerequisite of any functional coordination. "When the energy is cultivated it is held in balance inside your body. Thus your mind is tranquilized and every movement becomes graceful and harmonious. When this is achieved, you may then talk about how to deal with an enemy" (Smith[2], 31). But even more important than physical suppleness and functional coordination is the mental stability which centralization insures, setting the stage for the control of reality in general and of combat in particular. "To master this energy is to pierce the unknown and to reach the state where life and death lose their qualities of fear. When you achieve this, a threat does not disturb nor a temptation caress. You become true master of yourself" (Smith[1], 31). From such an impervious position of centralized independence, the coordinated energy, the *ch'i* or *ki*, can be controlled with the utmost precision. For example, it can be channeled in the direction of a specific attack or counterattack. More amazingly, this *ch'i* can be directed into the passive channels of pure defense. In fact, it "can be a shield for almost any part of the body. A boxer can direct his *ch'i* to his head, chest, abdomen, etc. . . . and even a blow with an iron bar at that point will not cause pain" (Smith[2], 36). How is this energy developed in shaolin? The answer lies in the primary exercise of abdominal breathing. "The lungs are reservoirs of air, and air is the lord of strength. Whoever speaks of strength must know air—this is a universal truth. Good lungs equal good strength; weak lungs, weak strength. You must learn to breathe properly" (Smith[2], 34).

Such thoughts, so clearly expressed in this particular treatise on shaolin, are repeated in the doctrines of almost all the other variations on the art of striking, and especially in those which have developed the concept of mental projection to an unusual degree—as, for example, in the esoteric and little-known school of hsing-i. In this obscure Chinese method, *ch'i* is also considered to be the essential form of energy, employed under the full command of the mind. Actually, according to certain authors who have delved into the esoterics of this art, this form of energy is even qualified more particularly as being "mental," thus identifying its flow with the commands or volition of the mind itself. The name *hsing-i,* in fact, is often translated as "imaginary intellectual fist," because the role of the mind in developing and projecting the power to be used in the techniques of hsing-i is apparently absolute. The requisite platform for the formation or condensation of this mental energy, however, is still the *tan t'ien,* or *hara.* References to the mental extension of abdominal power in hsing-i often include images and examples such as that of "heavy arms" (when perfoming the techniques) which are also found in other derivations of ancient Japanese bujutsu. In aikido, for example, similar mental representations of various ways of controlling the Centre and extending coordinated energy or *ki* are used so consistently and precisely as to indicate that doctrinary contacts among continental schools of combat and those of Japan (notwithstanding the stern isolation of that country) were not only historically possible, but had obviously been a not uncommon occurrence.

Aikido

Among the modern disciplines of combat derived from the various forms of bujutsu (armed and unarmed) practiced by the *bushi* of feudal Japan, the art of aikido seems to be the one method which, at all levels of its practice, is based upon the doctrine of *haragei*—this doctrine being considered the key to that continuing mental stability and extension of coordinated power upon which (as aikido instructors almost unanimously maintain) the correct solution of strategic problems depends. In the major works published on the subject (see Bibliography), the two basic concepts of the theory are immediately recognized as being the essential, inner foundations of the art. *Hara* (variously defined as *seika-no-itten* or *seika tanden* and translated as the "Centre," "One Point," or "Centrum") and *ki* are considered so vital to the art, in fact, that without them "there is no aikido." Needless to say, the outer factors of the art, the strategies of combat and the techniques of immobilization and projection are important elements of the method, but their correct execution depends upon the proper development and effective utilization of that inner Centre of mental stability and coordinated power. In this context, in fact, a high-ranking aikido instructor is reported to have readily admitted that the physical techniques of the art could be easily learned, but the development of the inner energy necessary to their correct execution took a much longer period of time—becoming a rather extended process as the student moved from the lower to higher levels of interior coordination. The definition of *ki* found in the doctrine of aikido is related to the cosmic dimension of *haragei* which is deeply imbedded in the traditional cosmogony of Japan (particularly as expressed in the forms of Shinto). Beginning with the original state of chaos and the unification of reality in the dynamic flow of life, this doctrine ultimately assigns a spiritual significance to the force of that life and qualifies it as being primarily "mental" or inner. Gluck noted that

> to the *aiki* master, strength is mental. The body is but a tool. If the body only is trained, unbalance results and in old age an athlete suffers, must always "keep in trim" though his internal organs may not be able to support the necessary muscular exertion. But the body only follows the mind, thus the *aiki* man trains the mind, developing his nervous system to the utmost so that the muscles may be more efficiently used. The result is a body strength the *aiki* people call *ki* or "life force," a name we shall have to use until Western physiologists study this phenomenon and give it a more palatable scientific name. (Gluck, 184)

In aikido, therefore, the whole practice is intended to develop this inner centralization and its coordinated extension of vital powers. The art, in fact, employs those ancient disciplines of meditation, concentration, and abdominal breathing which we have already encountered in other martial arts and which explain the superior power of students who pursue interior development, compared to those who concentrate primarily on the outer factors of the art. In aikido the relatively static techniques of meditation, centralization, and abdominal breathing are used as an introduction to the dynamic exercises of extension, as well as to the techniques of combat. All these exercises, however, are viewed as vectors of centralized power, ways of controlling reality (concrete and immediate) and not merely as guides to static contemplation or introspection intended as an end in itself.

> Each *aiki* form is a technique for training us in the control of *ki,* that illusive, elusive, indefinable fluid force. They are graduated in intensity and should be done in fixed order as warm up. When done under direction in the dojo, the entire series takes between 20 minutes and half an hour. More experienced adepts are assumed to have their *ki* in tune, "turned on," most or all of the time, and so do not need much warm up. (Gluck, 194)

The techniques of aikido, as mentioned in Part 2, are functionally based upon those of kenjutsu, an art whose doctrine and literature were both strongly characterized by the contribution of *haragei* to its practice. The founder of aikido, Master Uyeshiba, however, intended to achieve much more than mere inner centralization and coordination of powers as the basis for a new and efficient fighting method. Aikijutsu practitioners, in fact, can achieve this with essentially the same techniques, although applied for the pragmatic and utilitarian purposes of the feudal *bushi* in Japan. Reacting against this martial tradition of "destruction," Master Uyeshiba endeavored to develop a "constructive" method which employed the concepts of *haragei* (the *hara* and its vital energy, *ki)* as intended by the best and most universally minded representatives of Taoism and Buddhism, whose works he undoubtedly had studied and used as terms of reference for his own method of integration.

This spiritual and exquisitely ethical dimension of Master Uyeshiba's aikido and its inner components cannot be examined in depth here. However, it is undeniable that, even without referring aikido to this ultimate aim, the art as it is taught and practiced today in most centers of instruction makes abundant use of *haragei,* of its concepts and special techniques of development.

The Martial Synthesis

The *bujin* of feudal Japan, accordingly, used the concept of *hara* as the main (if not absolute) point of mental concentration—as a way of preventing his attention from attaching itself to anything (emotions, postures, weapons, gestures, surroundings, the number of opponents, etc.) which might distract him from his purpose: defeating his opponent, whatever the cost.

It is interesting to note, in this connection, that many duels in feudal Japan ended (as the fencing master quoted by Dr. Suzuki in the episode of the tea master had confidently expected) "in mutual slaying" (Suzuki, 192) and that the doctrine of *ai-uchi,* or mutual striking down, was an accepted principle of swordsmanship, a principle which enabled many a desperately committed swordsman to dispatch an opponent of greater skill, even if he himself did not survive the encounter. This principle was exemplified in modern times by the famous *kamikaze* pilots who hurled themselves and their planes against warships during World War II, after having completed the traditional formalities and ceremonies of martial dedication to their mission—totally blocking out anything that might have interfered with the accomplishment of that mission, including any concern with the certain self-destruction which was to follow.

The mental attitude of a *bushi* facing combat, for example, was admittedly that of a man who had relinquished any hope of winning but was concentrating upon a single aim—that of rushing to the attack the very moment he confronted an opponent. Such a confrontation, as we have seen in examining the various specializations of bujutsu, was considered so necessary and was so highly valued that it became one of the fundamental norms of the warrior's unwritten code of conduct (Bushido). Some authors, in fact, because of this deadly concentration, called Bushido the "Art of Death which makes our soldiers exult in self-sacrifice" (Okakura[1], 3).

That such an absolute concentration was most effective in combat seems undeniable. We do not have to turn to the highly sectarian manuscripts of the various schools of bujutsu to find examples of the stoic attitude generally adopted by the *bushi* of feudal Japan. Most historical accounts provided by Chinese, as well as Western, sources confirm his total commitment to his mission once an order from the proper authority had been given, as well as his steadfastness and even suicidal determination when carrying out such a command. The order could be issued by his lord or immediate superior, if he was affiliated with a clan (samurai), or it might come from the unwritten code of conduct based upon tradition and custom, if he happened to be masterless *(ronin)*. In either case, he sealed himself within the glacial tower of centralization and acted with that frightening unilaterality of intention and activity which only death could dissipate. It was undoubtedly a highly specialized and narrow interpretation of centralization which the *bushi* adopted. It could be carried to such extremes that, even while expounding and encouraging it, Japanese scholars of the feudal era were forced to admit that it was often, in effect, a kind of madness.

> The *Hagakure* [military classic] emphasizes very much the samurai's readiness to give his life away at any moment, for it states that no great work has ever been accomplished without going mad—that is, when expressed in modern terms, without breaking through the ordinary level of consciousness and letting loose the hidden powers lying further below. These powers may be devilish sometimes, but there is no doubt that they are superhuman and work wonders. (Suzuki, 70)

Thus, *haragei* became a method of attaining a peculiar sort of mental stability centered upon eliminating any inhibitions (whether originating from within or outside the *bushi*'s personality) which might have interfered with his mission or singular purpose. This mission (in accordance with the dictates of his profession) was usually related to combat and to its outcome—the opponent's defeat being his primary goal, regardless of the cost.

As we have noted briefly in dealing with the concept of Intrinsic Energy, the adepts *of haragei*, whether of Buddhist or Taoist persuasion, "realized that during their mental, spiritual and physical training performed in order to obtain the [ultimate] knowledge of and control over their own interior selves, they activated in themselves some strange powers" (translated from Lasserre, 20).

Mental stability, clarity of perception (specific), and crystallized awareness (general) were those qualities of mind which the *bushi* endeavored to achieve and develop through various exercises of abdominal centralization, breathing, immobility, and so forth. But there is no doubt that he was infinitely more interested in active expressions of centralization, that is, in that coordinated power *(ki)* to act which centralization in the *hara* could further. For many adepts of these disciplines of inner centralization—and, in fact, for the military class as a whole—"the original purpose of spiritual realization was cancelled to make room for the cultivation of these physical and mental powers having as their foundation the development, the accumulation, the concentration, and the utilization of the energy" (translated from Lasserre, 20).

In the records of ancient and modern bujutsu, we find the concept of *ki* accepted as being valid in and fundamental to all the major schools of the martial arts, interpreted by each in its own special way, and implemented in combat via the devising of particular exercises for developing *ki*, as well as particular techniques for applying it in combat, which varied from school to school.

In bujutsu, the first distinction was that *ki* differed intrinsically in nature from the extrinsic power of man's muscular system. Of course, the concept of *chikara*, or brute force, whose effectiveness depended almost entirely upon a well-developed set of muscles, was not unknown in Japan. Actually, we may even say that it often tended to predominate in Japanese culture, where purely physical strength was (as it has always been in almost all climes) the easiest form of power to develop and apply. The repeated references to *ki* found in almost all specializations of bujutsu, in fact, should not lead us to believe that this type of energy was so common among the Japanese *bujin* as to be the norm rather than the exception or ideal. Indeed, the contrary was apparently closer to the actual fact. Such terms as esoteric, divine, and mysterious, often used by authors of works on bujutsu when referring to *ki,* are clear indications that knowledge and use of this power were comparatively limited. For example, one author says that "when a man is really in possession of the [centralization in the] *hara,* he does not need muscular force anymore, because he can win by employing a force entirely different" (translated from Durckheim[2], 2). But, as to the nature of this force, the doctrine of bujutsu is often as vague as the concept of *ki* itself, which, in *haragei,* seems to be of such vast proportions that it actually embraces the totality of man's powers from physical to mental, from spiritual to moral, blending finally with that "pervasive vital force that gives life and sustenance to all things under Heaven" (Sze, 61).

In the specific context of bujutsu, therefore, the most immediate level of integration of man's powers was that of blending his mental powers of perception, awareness, and concentration with his physical powers of execution. Very seldom in the doctrine of bujutsu do we find the term *ki* used alone; instead it usually appears in combinations, such as *aiki* or *kiai,* which denote "a compound of *ki* meaning 'mind,' 'will,' 'turn of mind,' 'spirit,' etc. . . .and *ai,* the contraction of the verb *awasu,* signifying 'to unite' " (Harrison, 129). *Aiki* and *kiai,* in fact, seem closely interrelated, although the latter appears specifically associated with the vocal vector of transmission of power from its abdominal source to its target, while in *aiki* "the power which actually accomplishes these seeming miracles, is silent" (Harrison, 103).

The fusion or coordination of mental and physical powers, however, seems to have shifted in emphasis from the former and thus made man's mental capacities to perceive, to be aware, and to concentrate his will in a certain direction the basis of training and, consequently, of combat. The combination of *ki* with *ai,* as Kumashiro Hikotaro explained to Harrison in the early 1900s, meant more precisely that the stronger mind fused with the weaker in order to control it. Thus, in order to be successful in combat, the *bushi* was urged to master *shinki-kitsu,* for example (a method of uniting opposing minds under the control of one).

Apparently this art of integrating and condensing the energy of the whole personality within the abdominal center of that personality gradually evolved into such advanced stages of mental integration that, at a certain level of development in *shinki-kitsu,* it became almost impossible to distinguish real power (intrinsic or extrinstic) from sheer illusion projected by certain peculiarly endowed personalities.

However, turning our attention to the *bujin* at the lower levels of integration, we can follow the attempts of many masters to train him in the development, accumulation, and utilization of a type of energy which, resulting as it did from better coordination of the soma with its inner Centre of mental control, was definitely more integrative and effective than the energy produced by the muscular system acting without the full participation and integrated concentration of the mind. The fusion of *chikara,* or outer, muscular energy, and *ki,* or inner energy, power, and volition, caused them to become, in most schools, "like two wheels of a cart" (Suzuki, 191). This first classification of power as being outer *(chikara)* or inner *(ki)* seems to have originated in the ancient culture of China, which provided military schools with an elaborate system of classification and analysis of the advantages and disadvantages of the outer, extrinsic form of energy *(wai chia),* as compared to those forms of inner or intrinsic energy *(nei chia).* Both of these concepts, in turn, reflect the inexhaustible debate over the nature and function of those primeval opposites or alternates—the *yin* and *yang,* the full *(shih)* and the empty *(hsu),* the "hard" and the "soft"—upon which (especially in the cosmic dimension of Taoism) the entire culture of Asia is largely based, even today.

Volumes have been written about the particular ways of using this coordinated power of the *hara* in combat—each highly specialized in method and technique and all intended to help achieve the primary purposes of combat. Among the innumerable suggestions and instructions concerning the use of *ki* in combat, three major schools of thought seem to have emerged within the doctrine of bujutsu, centered not so much upon the concept itself (which was generally considered unassailable) as upon the directions in which that power could be extended. These three trends are of the utmost importance in bujutsu, for their interplay and reciprocal conditioning has influenced the martial arts of yesterday and continues to affect their modern derivations.

The first trend seems to have involved the extension of coordinated power in a straight line from its source to its objective—that is, the objective being contacted frontally or perpendicularly. This type of extension became known under a variety of names reflected in the terms used to denote basic combat movements, such as *omote* and *irimi,* all identifying a strategy which developed into an intense fusion of energy, movement, action (or technique), and mental concentration, applied against an opponent in a direct, frontal manner. The linear thrust of the *yari,* the frontal blow with the *katana,* the sharp concentration of an ancient *atemi* or of a more modern karate punch, the powerful frontal drive of a sumo charge or of a judo "entering" technique—all were examples of application of this first interpretation of how the coordinated power of the *hara* could be employed.

The second trend (considered equally, if not even more, effective) involved the extension of coordinated power in a circular direction from its source to its target (which, accordingly, would be invested tangentially). This type of extension was reflected in names such as *ura* and *tenkan,* used to identify strategies, movements, actions, or techniques—as well as a form of mental concentration—which developed circularly from their source and acted upon their objective in a centrifugal manner which sent the target whirling orbitally away.

The demarcation line between these two trends seemed to have been quite clear initially—the main point of differentiation being the effect of extension upon the target. Linear, direct extension, by its very nature and functionality, went "through" the target, thus altering its original structure. Circular, tangential extension "invested" the target and removed it completely from a certain position of power, without altering its structure. Linear *ki,* therefore, by "going through," could kill or seriously injure an opponent. Circular *ki,* by "going by," could stun or divert him from his original position of strength, without necessarily doing him any serious or lasting physical injury. This demarcation line seems to have become blurred in the doctrine of bujutsu, however, when the two trends began to merge with each other and the two types of extension were used interchangeably, without necessarily referring to the final effect upon the target of the particular form of extension employed. Expert practitioners of various bujutsu methods, for example, would often evade an attack and begin their counterattack with a circular extension of the coordinated power of *ki* which would then be turned back upon the opponent—often employing a line of extension directly perpendicular to the structure of his anatomy. Was this extension—which, even if circular initially, had ended in a perpendicular line of convergence—circular or linear in nature? The answer, with regard to the final effect of that extension upon the target, was usually clear: linear. True circular extension, in fact, was circular from beginning to end, not only at the beginning of the movement or technique. Its effect upon the target was thus more generalized and diffused than the sharp, penetrating effect of linear extension.

The third form of extension, finally, was diffusive and irradiating—permeating the entire environment and often controlling it psychologically even before combat developed, to the extent of actually changing the conditions for its occurrence. This type of extension, of course, was linked to the very roots of combat and tended to neutralize its dialectic potentialities, thus removing it from the actual military dimension with which those potentialities had been initially developed. This diffusive extension was the type of mental control exercised by the man of peace, the sage, the mystic—examples of humanity the *bujin* could admire in general from afar but imitate in only a very few cases, at the moment when he ceased to be a *bujin.*

The linear and the circular types of extension of centralized energy became, therefore, the two main cornerstones of instruction, training, and strategic application in combat, upon and around which the major

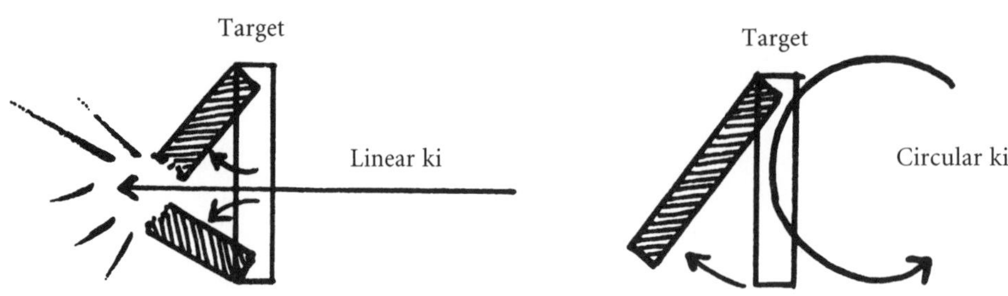

schools of bujutsu built their own methodologies. These two concepts of extension activated such an intense debate among the ancient masters of the martial arts, in relation to their respective strategic advantages and disadvantages, that its echoes are still reverberating today throughout many modern methods and disciplines of combat derived from the ancient specializations of bujutsu. The debate itself, as noted above, was centered upon the adaptation of those two types of extension to the strategies of combat—strategies which were basically three in number: attack, counterattack, and defense. These strategies are examined in the following section, because they involve certain basic premises concerning the role assigned to the opponent's personality in combat and, accordingly, to the effects of extension upon him.

7
STRATEGIC PRINCIPLES OF APPLICATION

The Major Strategies

The integration of mental powers of perception and volition in one direction only, thereby channeling the coordinated energy of the entire personality toward the attainment of a strategic purpose, comprised the inner factors activating and controlling each weapon and the particular techniques devised for its employment (outer factors). The doctrine of *haragei,* abundantly tapped by the masters of bujutsu, was unquestionably instrumental in providing them with the basic ideas and training methods needed to achieve that integration.

Fusion of the interior personality (the mind, its capacity for perception, evaluation, and decision, its power of concentration and volition) and the exterior personality (the soma, the weapons, the specialized functionality of the muscular system) was considered of the utmost importance because it helped to transform a man into a *bujin* (that is, into a fighting unit). It could make him "whole" and thus allow him to react effectively against the dispersive, centrifugal force of existence acting on him in a disintegrative manner (both from within and without), particularly in a combat situation. That fusion, however, was still at the first level of integration; that is, the individual and subjective level of the *bujin's* personality which, however complete and powerful it might have been in and of itself, was pitted against the same basic type of integration and coordination embodied in another personality—that of a worthy and dangerous opponent, also seasoned in the disciplines of integration which were used to prepare all the members of the military class for their profession. This confrontation injected certain additional elements into the nature and role of extension in combat, because the masters of bujutsu had to find satisfactory answers to the following questions: Was this type of subjective integration the only type? Were other types of integration possible, and, if so, which one might be qualified as being strategically superior or as being the most satisfactory method for coping with the problems posed by combat and by its major strategies of attack, counterattack, and defense?

In reality, combat develops according to a certain chronological pattern; that is, it consists of a series of moments or stages, each with its own characteristic problems and set of circumstances, each so complex and ofttimes unexpected that it was not sufficient merely to devise weapons, invent techniques, and develop inner control. It was also necessary to take into account the most appropriate strategy for their effective utilization in combat. Therefore, the basic questions which bujutsu masters and experts had to answer were: When confronted with imminent combat, should a man attack his opponent before the latter could launch his attack; or was it more effective and advantageous, in a strategic sense, to allow an opponent to attack first and then launch a devastating counterattack? Finally, was it better to simply defend oneself by neutralizing an attack effectively, but without necessarily launching a counterattack? In effect, what were the advantages and the disadvantages of these three major strategies of combat?

Experience in the theory and practice of combat demonstrated that attacking was a strategy which made it possible for a person to employ a weapon and technique against an opponent before the latter could launch an attack of his own. It was based, therefore, upon a certain degree of initiative, upon an element of surprise, upon the opponent's lack of preparedness. Counterattack was another primary strategy of combat—one which made it possible for the same subject to employ a weapon and technique against an opponent once the latter had launched his attack. This strategy was based, accordingly, upon a well-timed reaction which actually used the opponent's own attack as a means of defeating him. Defense, finally, was a strategy of combat which allowed the same subject to prevent his opponent's weapon and techniques from reaching their intended objective, thus neutralizing their dangerous potentialities.

The first detectable similarities were those existing between the attack and the counterattack. Both employed the same weapons against the same objective (an opponent) for the same purpose (his subjugation), using relatively the same techniques. The only difference between them (a difference which became a very important factor in the doctrine of bujutsu) was merely chronological and consisted of the fact that an attack took place before a counterattack, while the latter took place after the attack had been launched. We will see later that the counterattack possessed certain additional qualities and advantages which made it a favorite strategy of many bujutsu masters.

The defense had a chronological affinity with the counterattack only because its strategy developed after an attack (or a counterattack) had been launched. It differed from both those strategies, however, in objective and techniques. By definition, in fact, defense was concerned primarily with the neutralization of the potentially dangerous possibilities of either an attack or a counterattack. It was usually directed against a strategy as such—not necessarily against its subject—while the attack and the counterattack, on the other hand, were primarily directed against the man himself. As a strategy, defense was complete and clearly identifiable when its weapons and techniques effectively prevented those factors of the attack or counterattack from reaching their targets. Consequently, it ceased to be defense when, after an action of attack or counterattack had been effectively evaded, it was used as the basis for a counterattack. And it was clearly an attack when, notwithstanding subtle justifications (such as preventive necessity), it involved an attempt to neutralize an attack or a counterattack before either had concretely materialized—before, that is, there was actually anything to neutralize or to defend oneself against.

These strategies were all well known to the practitioners of bujutsu. In the ancient martial arts, they were studied and developed so thoroughly that, either as a whole or in part, they became the cornerstones of many individual schools. The art of iaijutsu, for example, provided a particularly effective demonstration of how irresistible the strategy of attack (and its factors of initiative, speed, and surprise) could be. All the other martial arts also developed and perfected this strategy to a certain degree, leaving behind a tradition of ideas and practices which are reflected even today in armed forms of bujutsu, such as kendo and jodo, and in many unarmed forms of bujutsu, such as sumo, jujutsu, and judo. In all these methods, the notion of the unguarded moment or opening *(suki),* when the opponent's line of defense can be successfully breached before he has a chance to recover, is a basic tenet.

It was, however, the strategy of counterattack which was refined by ancient practitioners of bujutsu to an astonishing degree of strategic sophistication, under the influence of a particular principle of application which, in Asia, has always characterized the art of combat in an unmistakable manner.

Principles of Application

The masters of bujutsu taught that a subjective, totally oriented form of coordination could be applied in combat in accordance with two fundamental principles—the first of which may be qualified as "unilateral" and the second as "bilateral."

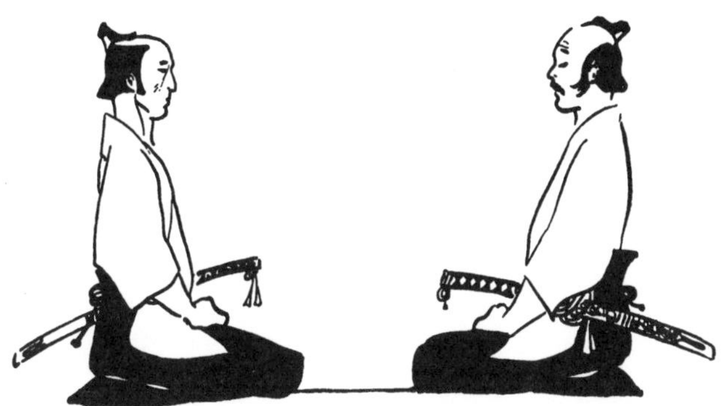

Attack (preventive)

Attack (simultaneous)

Attack, defense, and counterattack

Defense

These two main principles of application are specifically related to the tactical value assigned to the personality of the opponent in combat. According to the unilateral principle of application, the personality of the opponent was considered the primary target of an attack or counterattack, for the purpose of either total or partial subjugation. According to the bilateral principle of application, on the other hand, the opponent's personality was viewed not merely as a target, but also (and by certain bujutsu masters, primarily) as an instrument—that is, as the unwilling but nevertheless useful vector of his own subjugation. In this second, definitely more sophisticated interpretation of the possibilities inherent in combat, the unilaterality and narrowness of the former principle, based as it was upon one man's subjective predominance, was substantially moderated.

These two principles seemed to divide the schools of the martial arts into two broad categories (although a third results from the fusion of both extremes). But it is the principle of bilateral application which seems to represent a tactical differentiation between Japanese bujutsu and the martial arts of the West. Lafcadio Hearn, for example, considered this principle "a uniquely Oriental idea," asking, "What Western brain could have elaborated this strange teaching: never to oppose force to force, but only to direct and utilize the power of attack; to overthrow the enemy solely by his own strength—to vanquish him solely by his own efforts?" (Smith[1], 128). The reader should now be able to recognize that the principle of bilateral application is actually an extension of that famous concept of coordination encountered in the previous section. Subjective coordination of all a man's fighting capacities, inner (perception, evaluation, decision) and outer (the use of various weapons, the performance of certain techniques), produced remarkable fighters who could meet an opponent squarely and under any circumstances give a good account of themselves. But the results were even more impressive when such a warrior was trained to make full use not only of his own but also of his opponent's subjective coordination, when he was taught to exploit it to the fullest by blending with it, by gaining control of its force from within and then achieving the intended purposes of combat through any one of its primary strategies.

In order to make this possible, training in bujutsu included certain exercises and techniques specifically devised to achieve coordination of the warrior's strategy with that of an opponent, that is, to adapt the former to the latter. Through adaptation, control could be established and the chosen strategy carried out fluidly and efficiently to a successful conclusion. This principle was an important factor in almost all the major specializations of bujutsu, especially at their highest levels of instruction. Takuan, writing about the art of swordsmanship in particular, refers to the strategic value of the bilateral principle in the strategy of counterattack against an opponent, when he advised his pupil to "make use of his attack by turning it on to himself. Then, his sword meant to kill you becomes your own and the weapon will fall on the opponent himself. In Zen this is known as 'seizing the enemy's spear and using it as the weapon to kill him'" (Suzuki, 96).

There were certain masters of bujutsu so expert in dealing with opponents of inferior skill that they did not even bother to use their weapons in order to deflect attacks launched by such men. Instead, this type of *sensei* would simply evade a sword or spear cut and send his attacker spinning into a somersault which was usually sufficient to bring the attacker to his senses, even when not followed by a merciless counterattack—in which the would-be attacker's own weapons were often used against him. With an opponent of equal skill and preparation, the principle of bilaterality (i.e., every form of attack being faced with a deadly form of counterattack) often resulted in mutual slaying or a stand-off. The former case, in fact, was quite common, since no *bujin,* however skilled in any specialization of bujutsu, could hope to emerge unscathed from a violent encounter with an opponent equally skilled in the same specialization or in one of a similar nature and functionality. The literature on kenjutsu, for example, contains tales of many encounters in which both combatants lost their lives. In general, however, the masters of bujutsu seemed to prefer to avoid direct confrontations with one another, and only in exceptional cases did they engage in lethal comparisons of styles and techniques.

An episode in the doctrine of kenjutsu, concerning two swordsmen who had evidently delved deeply into the theory and practice of this principle of application, is instructive. When these men met, they both felt an irrepressible urge to test each other's respective skill in swordsmanship. They selected a quiet spot for the encounter, girded themselves for battle, unsheathed their weapons, assumed basic stances and guards, and ...waited. Whenever one or the other would change his posture of readiness to another he felt was better suited to a specific sword attack, the other man would change his posture accordingly. This process of coordinating postures, of adapting to the opponent's strategy and thereby of controlling and neutralizing it from moment to moment, continued until dusk—at which time (or so the story goes) both men burst out laughing, sheathed their swords, and, as peers, went back to town to celebrate a new friendship.

Whether viewed as fact or fantasy, this episode indicates how sophisticated certain methods of combat had obviously become; how effective any technique of reflexive, bilateral reaction could be; and finally, how well bujutsu masters had come to know and recognize a peer by certain attitudes, guards, and postures, however subtle these indications might have been, and however unapparent to the untrained eye.

The Bilateral Principle in Particular

The principle of bilateral application was not a feature of individual combat alone. Its concepts also figured importantly in the collective art of warfare and were quite highly regarded by Japanese generals of the feudal era. In this larger dimension, the principle is often linked to Chinese reference works on the art of war. In particular, the name of the Chinese strategist Hwang Shinkon is frequently mentioned. He is said to have written an interesting treatise on warfare entitled, characteristically, *In Yielding Is Strength,* which dealt with the necessity of adapting to ineluctable circumstances, flowing and blending smoothly with the tide of events which surround and sometimes engulf a man (reflecting, of course, more general concepts present in Oriental culture at large). In fact, although dealing with abstract concepts far above and beyond the narrow and highly specialized confines of bujutsu and the art of war, the great classics of China seem to have provided the master of bujutsu with a practically inexhaustible source of inspiration and direction.

The *Book of Changes* (I *Ching)* is often considered the Oriental apotheosis of adaptation, of flexibility. In this book the recurring theme is one of observing life and blending with its flow in order to survive and develop. In effect, the theme of this work is that everything in existence can be a source of conflict, of danger, and, ultimately, of violence if opposed from the wrong angle or in the wrong manner—that is, if confronted directly at the point of its maximum strength, since this approach renders the encounter potentially devastating. By the same token, any and every occurrence can be dealt with by approaching it from the right angle and in the proper manner—that is, at its source, before it can develop full power, or from the sides (the vulnerable "flanks of a tiger"). If by chance, however, the frontal impact of events should overtake a man, the *I Ching* advises him to avoid any direct opposition and adopt an attitude of "riding along" or "flowing" with the tide of events (a boxer might say "rolling with the punches"), thus keeping slightly ahead of or on top of that massive force which, like any other concentrated force in creation, will inevitably exhaust itself once its concentration has been dissipated. We might point to the modern example of a surfer. When riding a wave, he must strive to stay just slightly ahead of it, since if he moves out too far he will not be "with it"; he will lose contact with the surging power which has been propelling him along and quickly sink below the surface of the water. On the other hand, if he allows the wave to overtake him, he will be overthrown or "wiped out" by the wave's crushing power, since, once again, he will not be "with it."

This line of reasoning—with its emphasis upon the advantages of permitting the play of life (even that which one might consider negative) to blossom and exhaust itself and its innumerable possibilities, without repressing them in the wrong manner, but by shrewdly using their own intrinsic energy to foster life—is considered primarily responsible for the highest achievements of Oriental culture and for the intrinsic quality of peacefulness found in Buddhist, Taoist, and Confucian theories at the highest levels. But it is also considered the motivating force behind the frequent adoption of a perverted attitude of passive resignation and total inactivity in the face of whatever indignity or aberration chance or ignorance, or both, might foist upon man (even though the doctrine itself advises taking measures to evade or circumvent them). It is also considered the key to a number of devastating opportunities for surprising a man or a mass of human beings at their moment of greatest weakness—their reaction(s) to a clever provocation or series of provocations being manipulated in such a way as to destroy or enslave them.

The book of Lao-tzu *(Tao Te Ching)* is a primary source of this theory of flexibility. It enlarges (with its specific concept of nonresistance) upon the theme of cosmic adaptation found in the *I Ching*. The masters of bujutsu used this book with equal assiduousness. The Tao of life (as its inner, central kernel might be considered), however, was held to be an activating factor which man could use in order to live well and to develop in accordance with the positive flow of the cosmic pulse, thus fostering life itself without destroying, perverting, or polluting its stream. This cultural patrimony of Asia filtered into Japan both in a general fashion, through exchanges of scholars, diplomats, and mystics under official patronage; and in particular cases, through the authorized (as well as unauthorized) pilgrimages of masters of bujutsu to the centers of culture in Asia. We have already encountered a number of these masters of arms in Part 2—men who went abroad to study Chinese methods of combat, both armed and unarmed.

The idea of a strategic form of coordination in this more comprehensive sense (i.e., more comprehensive than the subjective, unilateral sense which is typical of any form of attack) seems to have made its first appearance in the records of Japanese bujutsu with the mention of the ancient method of combat known as yawara. The ideogram for *wa* is usually translated as "accord." This method, then, was an art of subtly according or blending one's own strategy of counterattack with the strategy of an opponent, in order to achieve his subjugation. This school and its name, as well as that ideogram, are considered by some authorities to have been one of the earliest indications of this bilateral principle of application and of its existence in the domain of the Japanese art of combat. There is, unfortunately, a disappointing lack of material available concerning this ancient method of combat. Those records which do exist, however, represent "an interesting documentary item which deserves the attention of Ju-jutsu historians" *(Illustrated Kodokan Judo,* 2).

The principle of *wa* (accord) seems to have been the basis for the development of two other major principles: *ju* (suppleness, pliability, adaptability) and *aiki* (harmony, blending, identification, coordination). The former was to become the distinctive characteristic of the art of jujutsu and its schools (from which Master Kano's judo was to emerge), while the latter was to become the essential feature of the art of aikijutsu and its esoteric schools (elements of which were incorporated by Master Uyeshiba Morihei into his method—the martial art of aikido). Certain authors claim, however, that the concept of *ai* (harmony) is as ancient as the concept of *wa*—perhaps even more ancient.

The derivation of the principle of *ju* (intended as suppleness, flexibility, adaptability, and finally as nonresistance) from the principle of *wa* (accord) is repeatedly confirmed by Master Kano's school of judo, the Kodokan, which is still elaborating upon the subject. One of its most noted theorists writes:

> *Wa* or accord is the fundamental principle of the Japanese Martial Arts. Expressed in modern terms and made easy of practice to anyone, it became the principle of gentleness *(ju)*. The principle of gentleness teaches that one should go, not against, but with, the opponent's force and yet maintain one's proper position so as not to lose one's balance. This corresponds to the spirit set forth in Confucius' remark in his Analects: "The superior man is compliant, but not blindly yielding." (Tomiki, 53)

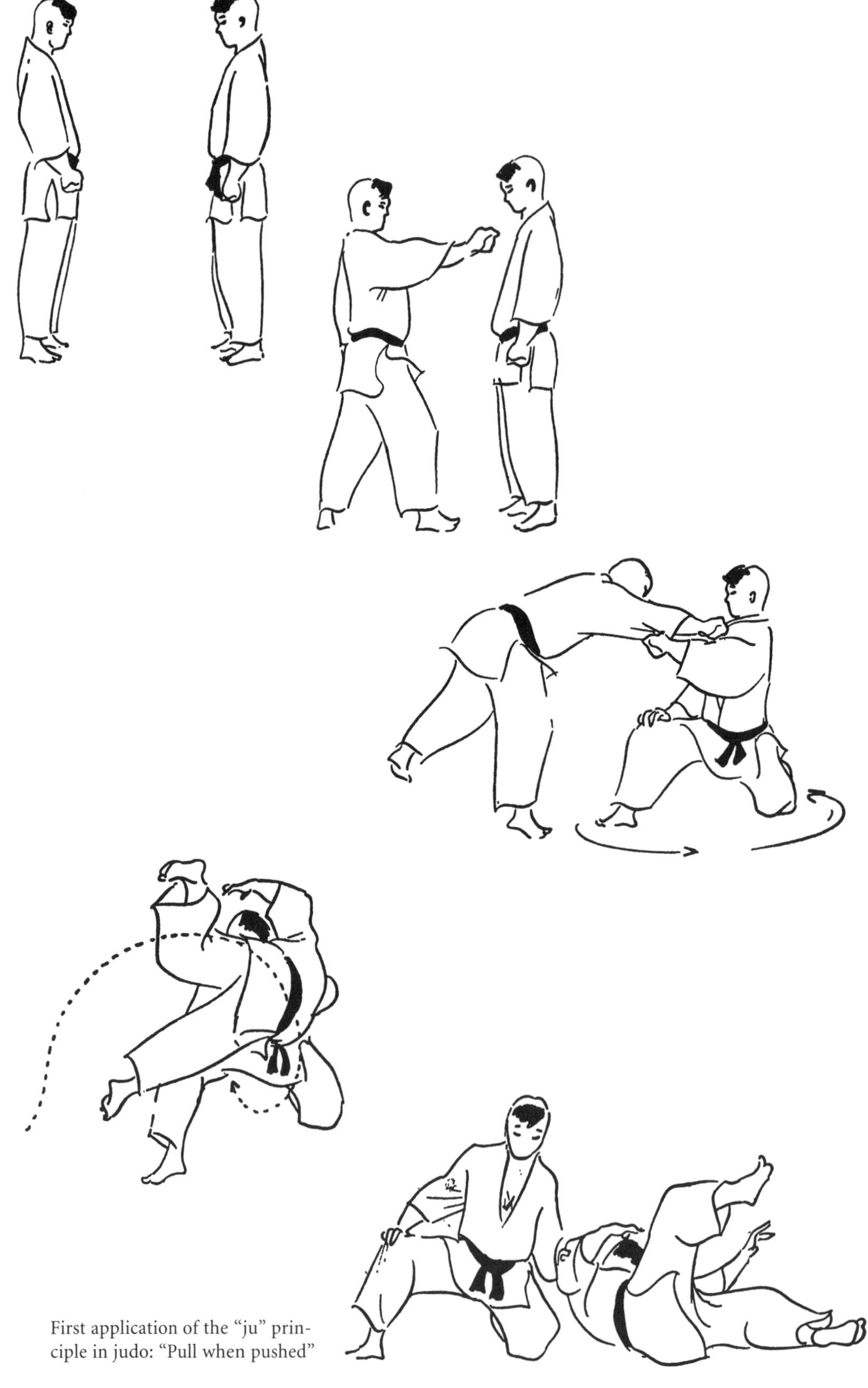

First application of the "ju" principle in judo: "Pull when pushed"

Second application of the "ju" principle in Judo: "Push when pulled"

Other authors find a link between *ju* and *wa* in the ancient names yawara and wajutsu: "The names Ju-Jitsu and Ju-jutsu come from the Chinese characters that represent them, but sometimes the same characters have been pronounced in the Japanese styles—hence the word *yawara* (another name for Ju-jutsu)" *(Kodokan Judo: A Guide to Proficiency,* 2).

To Tomiki, the relationship between *ju* and the more ancient *wa* was one of substantial identity:

> Ju-jutsu (Art of Gentleness) was also formerly called Wa-Jutsu (Art of Accord). This shows that *ju* (gentleness) has also the meaning of *wa* (accord). In the *Ryuko-no-Maki* (literally "Book of Dragon and Tiger") which is regarded as one of the oldest volumes expounding the secrets of the martial arts, there is a passage: "If the enemy turns upon us we meet him; if he leaves we let him leave. Facing the enemy we accord with him. Five and five are ten. Two and eight are ten. One and nine are ten. All this shows accord." (Tomiki, 53)

The concept of *ai* (harmony, fusion, etc.) has also been interpreted by the same author along similar lines: "*Aiki* means making your spirit 'fit in' with your opponent's. In other words, it means bringing your movements into accord with your opponent's. After all, it means the same thing as the 'principle of gentleness' *(ju)* for it is an explanation of the principle from within" (Tomiki, 101). Thus, notwithstanding the rather parochial and often exclusivistic claims to supreme originality and independence put forward by adherents of both concepts, *ju* and *ai* seem to have had much in common.

In practical terms, the principle of *ju* as applied strategically in judo schools was expressed concisely by Professor Kano when he said: "Pull when pushed—and push when pulled." In the first case, the principle of *ju* dictated that when an opponent began an attack by exercising or extending force *toward* a subject, the latter should blend with that force by moving with it, in the same direction, thus dissipating it beyond its maximum limit of expansion, before counterattacking an opponent who would then be virtually powerless, decentralized and unbalanced. In the second case, represented by an opponent exercising force *away* from the subject (i.e., a pull), the same effects of dissipation, decentralization, and unbalance were to be achieved by the subject who would not resist, but would move with that force.

In aikido schools, the principle of *ai* found concrete application in the same strategic principles, which, owing to aikido's characteristic smoothness and circularity, are expressed as follows: "Turn when pushed—and enter when pulled." In the first case, the subject neutralized the force of an attack converging upon him by leading its stream *around* him, thereby establishing a centrifugal rapport between the subject under attack in the center of the action, and his attacker at the orbital periphery.

In the second case, the subject neutralizes the aggressive force flowing away from him by moving in toward its center, introducing a condition of unbalance there so that the force, thus weakened, will become vulnerable to a counterattack. In both judo and aikido, the idea of utilizing the opponent's weapons, his force, his strategy, in order to achieve his subjugation or one's own defense, is fundamental. In both there is this interesting adaptation of one subject of combat to the other, reminiscent of the famous Asiatic expression, "riding the tiger." From Siam came a particularly expressive axiom:

Quand l'elephant tombe, ne te mets pas dessous pour le soutenir; mats quand il est tombé, tu peux pousser pour l'aider à se relever. (Herbert, 223)

When the elephant is falling, do not place yourself under him to hold him up; but after he has fallen, you can push in order to help him get up.

Among the esoteric schools of the martial arts which seem to have based their methodologies almost entirely upon this principle, the doctrine of bujutsu mentions specifically the Daito *ryu* (which is recognized by the modern school of aikido as being one of its links with traditional bujutsu) and the Kito *ryu* (which both the schools of aikido and judo classify as being among their direct and primary

First application of the "ai" principle in aikido: "Turn when pushed"

Second application of the "ai" principle in aikido: Enter when pulled"

foundations). But, unfortunately, very little remains of their methodologies. That which does remain is embodied mainly in the smooth plasticity of those formal exercises *(kata)* still performed in judo and aikido at their highest levels.

The Attack and the Counterattack

How did the relative importance of the strategy of attack compare with the strategy of counterattack in bujutsu? Similarly, how did the principle of unilateral or bilateral application influence those strategies?

By its very nature, the bilateral principle of application was considered particularly suited to the strategy of counterattack, since this would be developed reflexively from the opponent's attack. In the latter, the subjective coordination of the warrior, oblivious to anything but the desired objective and totally committed to its attainment, was the primary expression of the unilateral principle of application. In time, however, notwithstanding its ofttimes powerful and frightening effect in a combat situation, the unilateral

CHART 18

ACTION AND REACTION IN JUDO AND AIKIDO

ACTION	REACTION	
	the judo expert	the aikido expert
When opponent pushes	pulls	turns
When opponent Pulls	pushes	enters

principle of application (that is, employing one's own fully developed, subjective coordination against an opponent) seems to have come to be regarded as inferior to the bilateral principle of application, in all of its various expressions: *wa* (accord), *ju* (suppleness), *ai* (harmony), and so forth. The main reason seemed to be that any direct attack would render the attacker vulnerable at every stage of its development (except, of course, in the case of direct, frontal impact against the target—in which case that subjective coordination would reach its objective and break through it with all the devastating power of unilateral concentration). But from the initial stage of uncoiling at the source of power and during the flight toward its target, there was in every attack an inevitable widening of the defensive perimeter, an extension of force too great to be fully protected or even protectable. This, in turn, made that attack (and the attacker) susceptible to various forms of diversionary infiltration, as well as to abrupt interruptions. Any attack could provide the premises for an equally concentrated and timely action of counterattack or defense. Every attack contained this intrinsic weakness, which intense training in subjective coordination and in the unilateral application of strategies and techniques could help to minimize but never fully eliminate.

The counterattack, on the other hand, seemed to many masters to embody the best strategic characteristics for combat. It could maintain full concentration of power until the very last moment and certainly well after the power of attack had exploded on the way toward its intended target and thus become decentralized. It was, by nature, uncommitted and free to choose from among alternatives, whereas the attack had already been launched on its irreversible course. Consequently, in counterattack, one could choose the appropriate technique for controlling the attack by exploiting its intrinsic weakness. Finally, this strategy left the intended victim free to enter inside the attacker's guard by using the same widening of those defensive perimeters which the attack, now in full dispersion, had inevitably enlarged and exposed. Moreover, he could do so with his own power still centralized and channeled toward the center of the attacker's power—indeed against the very center of the latter's life. This last element, in particular, was the most terrifying characteristic of any counterattack, which could, when closely coordinated with the incredibly swift and fully concentrated determination of an attack, lead the attacker into a trap from which there was seldom any escape (unless, of course, the attacker were quick-witted enough to launch a counterattack of his own).

Those readers who are familiar with that type of Japanese movie qualified as *cham-bara*, or with the Japanese theater *(kabuki)*, in which there is often an inordinate amount of swordplay, will better understand this idea of strategic bilaterality vs. unilaterality (that is, of the predominance of counterattack over attack). The hero, in fact, whether a good man or a villain, usually slays his foes of inferior rank or social status as if butchering sheep, attacking and cutting them down mercilessly in full unilaterality of intent and coordinated, murderous commitment. But when he faces foes of equal status or of advanced skill in

swordplay, he switches strategy automatically to a calculated and timely reaction which allows them to attack, so that it will be possible for him to sink inside or under their lines of convergence, as his sword cleaves or slashes with deadly effect. In almost all these scenes, the attackers seem to seek and find their own destruction by dashing themselves against a cutting edge already there waiting for them, or flashing in or under their attack to join them at a given and apparently irrevocable point.

In the arts of unarmed combat, the bilateral principle of application in counterattack is evident in almost all their techniques of subjugation. Very seldom, when watching a sumo bout, for example, does one see a huge *sumotori* rush toward his opponent, who, by stepping aside or pivoting on the spot, could hurl the attacker out of the circle almost without touching him. These huge wrestlers are usually sophisticated enough not to attack in such an uncontrolled and uncontrollable manner. But if one should, in the rare case where he might be trapped or forced into a negative reaction by a clever opponent, the next stage of the bout will usually feature the unfortunate attacker flying through the air toward certain defeat.

The ancient schools of jujutsu were very emphatic on this subject. A native writer on this art, as quoted by Mr. Harrison, said in relation to the importance of the opponent's personality in devising a strategy of combat that "when the enemy remains motionless you may find it impossible to attack. In that case you must keep strictly on the defensive." But, if he attacks, "do not recklessly resist your opponent's physical strength; imitate the action of a boat adrift upon the surface of the ocean" (Harrison, 37).

Harrison, who did so much in his time for the promotion of judo in the West, gave us one of the best definitions of the bilateral principle of application in his definition of jujutsu, the ancient matrix of judo:

> Ju-jutsu (literally "soft art"), as its name implies, is based upon the principle of opposing softness or elasticity to hardness or stiffness. Its secret lies in keeping one's body full of *ki*, with elasticity in one's limbs, and in being ever on the alert to turn the strength of one's foe to one's own advantage with the minimum employment of one's own muscular force. (Harrison, 131)

Judo, naturally, followed the basic outlines of jujutsu. In his famous lecture on judo methodology, Kano Jigoro elaborated on the concept of *ju* as being bilaterality of strategic application. Actually, Master Kano did not base his entire methodology on this principle, but it is the feature of the art which, more than any other, caught the imagination of the West, with its emphasis upon the intrinsic weakness of an attack as compared to a skilled counterattack: "A main feature of the art is the application of the principles of non-resistance and taking advantage of the opponent's loss of equilibrium; hence the name Ju-jutsu (literally soft or gentle art), or Judo (doctrine of softness or gentleness)" (Smith[1], 29). Through the clever application of this principle to any movement and to any position of an opponent in combat, judo became famous the world over. At its higher levels of performance, in fact, its strategy of counterattack, geared to the techniques of the attack and applied with a fine sense of timing, seems almost effortless.

A doctrinary debate seems to be raging in the school of judo about the relevance of this concept of *ju* in combat, when compared to the collateral principle of unilateral application of an attack executed in full coordinated force *(go)*. More and more, in fact, competitive performance of judo has involved strenuous athletic preparation and the use of any and every possible principle of strategic application when faced with skilled and powerful opponents. Like sumo, this art has also acquired those sport connotations which have inevitably obscured its ancient value as a method of self-defense, based upon the reactive strategy of counterattack. Sport, as we know it, has all the competitive and aggressive connotations of real combat among peers who seek the same object—that is, to defeat or subjugate the opponent. Such a purpose requires intense participation from both subjects in the competition, in an exchange which will transform the encounter into a dramatic and highly fluid series of attacks and counterattacks with high value as a public spectacle. If the principle of bilaterality were to be applied consistently in judo, one athlete would necessarily be asked to attack while the other would be required to counterattack only, thus neutralizing his attacker's strategies by using their own dynamic and technical momentum against the very man who launched them. The dialectical interplay of strategies present in real competition, therefore, would be missing, and we would be witnessing the rather static spectacle of one man vainly attacking another who parries, evades, and/or neutralizes every attack. The principle of bilateral application, therefore, as Ishikawa and Draeger have pointed out in quoting Kano, may not be "applicable in all cases."

Karate may be defined as an art of effective counterattack—an art in which the concept of bilaterality (letting the opponent do most or at least part of the work of self-elimination) predominates. Which one of us is not familiar with this image of an attack being successfully neutralized from the inside in such a way as to leave the attacker open to a number of dangerous counterattacks? The best karate, in fact, according to many ancient as well as modern masters of the art, is often considered to be that performed in counterattack. As in ancient swordsmanship, the attackers rush in to their annihilation, impaling or slashing themselves on hardened edges waiting for them or reaching out to them from inside their guards or near their extended and unprotected flanks.

Aikido, with its predominantly reflexive nature and purpose, is an art closely concerned with the problems of real combat on the immediate, practical level of existence. It can also be an exquisite art of counterattack which emphatically denies the validity of the first, primary strategy of almost any combat encounter, since one often hears it said that there are no attacks in aikido. But the number of possible counterattacks contained in the technical ways of evading an attack, weakening its extended force, and subjugating the attacker via an immobilization, a projection, or a blow are limitless.

The Defense

Exactly what was the position and the value assigned to the strategy of defense within the theory and practice of bujutsu? This strategy, and the idea behind it, are a matter of some controversy because much use (and misuse) has obscured its original significance, and because the word defense is often stretched impossibly thin in an attempt to cover the widest range of meanings and purposes. The controversy seems to stem from the eagerness with which ancient masters of bujutsu have sought (and modern masters seek today) to defend their respective methodologies of combat, and the often morally indefensible and lethal results of their practices, by offering excuses such as "defensive necessity" or "in the interest of self-preservation," which, they obviously feel, justify any evil result, however regrettable—as, for example, in the case of an aggression neutralized by destroying the aggressor. Clearly, defense implies a certain degree of stern necessity springing from the instinct to preserve oneself and, correlatively, the obligation and urge to react against anything that might jeopardize that preservation or that right to live. This necessity and the imperative nature of its principle, however, often tend to obscure the basic fact that any reaction against a threat must obey certain laws in the choice of target and employment of measures and weapons, if it is to be qualified as moral or ethical.

What are these laws? What is the exact meaning, the most precise definition, of defense? In the doctrine of bujutsu we are confronted with certain general interpretations of defense. The first conception (which was predominant) regarded defense as a temporary device, no more than a moment in the strategy of counterattack; that is, it was used as a means of evading or blocking an attack a mere instant before (or even while) launching a counteroffensive. This identification of defense with counterattack has always made it exceedingly difficult to separate the connotations of one from those of the other. As a military man, the *bushi* made full use of this concept. But, even in private encounters, we find defense considered in a purely subjective, self-centered sense—that is, as a device for protecting the self by certain actions of evasion which could produce the same effects as those of a counterattack, even when this strategy was not intentionally being followed.

And, of course, there was always pure attack disguised as defense, for example, when a warrior was advised to "prevent" an attack by profiting from an unguarded moment to neutralize an opponent's line of protection and thus prevent him from "doing any harm." This last case is expressed in the popular axiom: "The best defense is a strong offense."

Finally, we come to a type of defense which fits within an objective framework—that is, pure defense, or defense for the sake of defense and nothing else, wherein the primary aim of any technique is simply that of neutralizing a dangerous action (an attack or a counterattack) without anticipating it (which would make any such defensive reaction actually a preventive form of attack), and without following the defensive movement or technique with a direct counterattack.

The principle of application primarily operative in the strategy of defense in almost all the various conceptions examined above was (and, when used today, is) obviously the bilateral principle. Developing as a reaction to an attack or to a counterattack, the defense was activated by, if, and after such an attack or counterattack had been actually launched. Consequently, the opponent's personality and his strategies were the important activating factors of defense and always had to be taken into serious consideration.

How concretely this principle operated and how effective it was in the strategy of defense we may posit by watching the execution of those techniques of combat in all the armed and unarmed martial arts, at the precise moment an attack or a counterattack is being blocked, evaded, or diverted from its intended target and thus neutralized and deprived of its force and significance.

In judo, for example, repeated attempts made by herculean students to apply a hip throw were neutralized by a great *sensei,* Mifune Kyuzo, via a subtle shifting of weight downward or by a centralized extension of the *hara,* forcing the attacking students to return to their original postures after a number of strenuous, if vain, efforts. A master of karate, Mr. Kubota, is said to have driven his attacking students to a high pitch of frustration by blocking any kind of punch, strike, or kick with his hands and feet, using sophisticated techniques of karate defense to catch them and deflect them at any moment or phase of convergence. Master Uyeshiba of aikido, finally, used to whirl in the midst of several attacking students (bent upon grabbing or hitting him), apparently oblivious to their activities which, however, he skillfully controlled and redirected into dynamic circles and spirals of harmless neutralization.

In most cases, however, defense is (and was) only a device employed in order to achieve an ulterior purpose. Rarely is the neutralization of an attack per se an end in itself (as it would be in pure defense), leaving the opponent comparatively free to resume his efforts after they have been thwarted by an impregnable strategy of evasion. Usually, the instant of defensive action is followed immediately by a counterattack. Defense for the sake of simple neutralization of an aggressive action in attack or counterattack, and for no other purpose than preventing either one from attaining its objective, was extremely rare in ancient bujutsu, which, as we have seen, consisted primarily of methods of earnest combat based on the strategies of attack and counterattack. In the past (and this is true on a large scale, even today), the strategy of defense was viewed as a moment, a temporary combat device which served as the preliminary introduction to an effective counterattack and, therefore, was hardly ever a strategy fully developed and complete in and of itself.

However, there are examples of a few outstanding bujutsu masters who made of defense in a total sense (that is, defense for purposes of defense and nothing more) a refined art. In their interpretations, bujutsu lost much of its martial connotation and became something else, a singular phenomenon which must be examined separately, since it confronted the *bujin* with a set of problems which, by their very nature (ethical), influenced and often determined the means (the arts themselves, as well as those weapons) which were to be used to resolve them.

8
THE MORALITY OF BUJUTSU

The Way of the Warrior

In the doctrine of the martial arts, the practice of bujutsu (that is, the various weapons, techniques, strategies, inner control, and power) is seldom considered to be the sole or even the primary aspect of those arts. In fact, there is hardly a single text, whether of a general nature or concerned strictly with technical instruction (from past eras to the present day) which defines these arts as purely practical, utilitarian methods of combat used in attack, counterattack, and defense to subjugate an opponent. Almost to a man, the most reputable martial arts masters who have written about or taught their specializations have claimed that bujutsu was (and is still considered to be) something more than merely a variety of practical and effective methods of combat. They indicate that these arts are "ways" or disciplines of moral advancement intended to further the formation of a mature, balanced, and integrated personality, of a man at peace with himself and in harmony with his social as well as his natural environment.

They refer, therefore, to a system of ethics, of morality, which motivates and inspires the practice *(jutsu)* from within and leads it toward the achievement of ultimate, remote goals far beyond the immediate and narrow confines of the world of combat between or among men. This system is usually referred to, in the doctrine of bujutsu, as *budo*—a term formed by the combination of the ideogram *bu* (which, as we have seen earlier, denotes the military dimension of Japanese culture) with the ideogram *do,* which is more specifically related to the spiritual domain. *Do,* in fact, is generally translated either as "way" (that is, the way of seeing, of understanding, and of motivating behavior in the philosophical or religious sense) or as "doctrine" (that is, the principles taught and accepted by a body of adherents to a philosophy, a religious sect, a school). As such, *do* denotes belief rather than technique, insight rather than execution, motivation rather than action or its particular instruments.

Budo, accordingly, identifies itself with the ultimate motivations (usually of an ethical nature) which were to regulate the conduct of the Japanese warrior *(bu-shi),* or the Japanese fighting man in general *(bu-jin).* Budo is related, therefore, to the ethics of the military class of Japan, as well as to the disciplines which that class adopted and claimed to follow, in an effort to comply with certain moral dictates and integrate every warrior into the system as a stable, mature, and reliable individual.

The problem we would be faced with in this context (if we truly wished to explore this dimension in depth) would be twofold: first, to ascertain with greater precision the content of this system of ethics adopted by the *bushi* of feudal Japan; and second, to ascertain whether he truly succeeded in living according to its standards—whatever those standards might have been. In brief, we would have to attempt to discover whether his budo was truly of the highest ethical quality and whether his bujutsu really helped him fulfill the high ethical requirements of budo. This problem, naturally, would not arise if by a system of ethics in budo was meant merely a highly specialized code of honor and conduct typical of the military class and based upon particular and highly exclusive concepts of obedience, loyalty, respect, and predominance which did not apply on a universal scale to all human beings, regardless of their social status, but only to the rightful members of the *buke.* In this context, which is clear and specific, bujutsu appears to have served the military class well, since it helped them to carry out forcefully the particular code of ethics which—from the sixteenth century onward— was called *shido* or *bushido.*

We have reviewed this code in Part 1 and discussed its ultimate qualification by the Japanese warriors themselves, who claimed to live by its norms. The concept of absolute loyalty to one's direct superior; the concomitant concept of unquestioning obedience; the requirement that samurai be frugal and spartan in daily living and sternly impervious to either pain or the fear of death; the duty to respect the warriors of other clans and to deal with them according to minute rules of etiquette which regulated the existence and function of all within the social order of the *buke,* and so forth—were all norms applied vertically and recognized as valid or binding for the *bushi* alone, and in relation to his direct superiors only. The other classes of feudal Japan, and therefore the majority of the Japanese population of the feudal era, were not so much subjects of Bushido as forcefully subjected to its dictates. After all, it must be remembered that, even within the *buke,* only minor social significance was assigned to the lower-ranking samurai, who, as retainers, were considered more as instruments of power by their privileged masters than as subjects of a code based on equal standing for all its members. That which gave all retainers a certain social superiority, however, was the attitude of absolute subservience to the members of the military class which the people of all other classes were forced or conditioned to adopt.

If morality is intended in a narrow, specialized sense (that is, as a system of ethics inspired by the political and military predominance of the *buke),* then there is no doubt that Bushido was an excellent and appropriate code. But this judgment does not apply equally when the doctrine of bujutsu attempts to relate the ethics of the warrior to values of the highest quality, valid on a universal scale for everyone, everywhere, and at all times. Significant references contained in the doctrine, in fact, although confused and complex, seem to be oriented toward the moral values propounded by the supreme doctrines of continental Asia, such as the socially inclined Confucianism, the metaphysical and highly humanitarian Buddhism, the serene and cosmically generous Taoism, and so forth. The moral content of these doctrines (regardless of the innumerable interpretations and distortions to which they have been subjected during the troubled history of mankind) seems predominantly inspired by a sovereign respect for human life in general (not only that of a master), by a sublime recognition of the basic identity of all subjects of that life. Interestingly enough, the privileged masters of feudal Japan themselves, in those rare cases in which the essential truths of those doctrines dawned upon them, often relinquished their exalted positions and their weapons and adopted the stark simplicity of the holy man, often entering monasteries or plunging into the heart of the wilderness.

It seems fairly obvious that, generally speaking, the "way" of the fighting man in feudal Japan did not encompass this supremely universal aspect of the major doctrines in Asia. Actually, it is not reasonable to suppose that Japanese society as a whole would be capable of adopting and implementing such a lofty and highly civilized view, any more than Western man, in the aggregate, has ever been able to live in accordance with the dictates of his highest doctrines of inspiration. In this sense, whenever the doctrine of bujutsu attempts to claim the lofty beliefs of the Oriental doctrines of enlightenment as the inspirational motivations underlying the practice of the martial arts, it must be observed that to proclaim one's adherence to those values in theory and to live up to them in practice (as the history of man amply demonstrates) are two entirely different things. To point out in greater detail the major areas of conflict which made it historically difficult, if not impossible, for Confucianism, Buddhism, and Taoism to merge successfully with and influence the Japanese reality of feudal times (i.e., by substantially altering its distinctive character), one need only refer to the stark contrast between the universal character of those doctrines (as originally intended) and the clannish, particularistic, and necessarily sectarian nature of the Japanese culture in feudal Japan with its central notion of a vertical hierarchy which had to be imposed and maintained largely by force of arms. After all, in the West it has always been extremely difficult to attempt to translate the universal character of certain essentially egalitarian and nonviolent doctrines of spiritual development (such as are found in Christ's teachings, for example) into concrete social and political expressions. More often than not, these expressions have been interpreted in a manner guaranteed to reinforce the political structures that, in contemporary parlance, would be defined as the establishment (usually militarily oriented in nature). Only slowly and painfully has the central message of those doctrines shifted from the religious dimension ("all men are equally children of God") to the social and political sphere ("all men are equal before the law"), filtering into Western society under the guise of philosophical concepts whose germination at various levels of Western culture has precipitated much of the relentless struggle and many of the upheavals marking its history.

In Japan, however—due, perhaps at least in part, to that country's isolated position off the continental coast of Asia—the contrast between the universal and egalitarian character of the supreme doctrines of enlightenment and the Japanese conception of human society, of its structures and ultimate destiny, seems to have been even more sharply delineated than in the West, and apparently irreversible without certain powerful and far-reaching modifications.

The doctrines of political government which had evolved in China, for example, were thoroughly examined, laboriously digested, and appropriately adapted to the Japanese conception of a desirable society. This process of adaptation drew primarily upon Confucianism, which was essentially a doctrine of political and social government—equating good government with morality. The Japanese, however, seem to have approached only the first level of the doctrine (the bureaucratic), neglecting to probe below the surface to discover exactly what it was that had justified its various functions in the eyes of Chinese scholars. In China:

> The "scholar-civil servant," the ideal type of this system, attained his position through competitive examination, without regard for social origin. It was this bureaucratic system that the Japanese took over in the seventh century. But it is extremely instructive to observe how they altered it in accordance with the genius of their own system of hereditary aristocracy. They took over the forms of the Chinese bureaucratic system, but instead of opening positions by fair examinations to talent and merit, as was done in China, they assigned them to hereditary groups. Thus, although the Japanese used the titles of the Chinese system, they were in fact hereditary title-holders, not civil servants. (Passim, 46)

As a consequence, they also substantially altered that canon of Confucianism which subjected everyone (even if only in theory) to the notion of social justice and goodness. In fact:

> In the same way, Chinese Confucianism which made absolute obedience to the Emperor contingent on his virtue, so that the removal of an Emperor was quite conceivable and consistent with morality, was in Japan and Korea transformed into the underpinning of the system of hereditary aristocracy. For the Japanese, the position of the Emperor was based upon his birth, it was not contingent on his virtue. (Passim, 46)

Even more deeply affected by this process of adaptation were the more complex, abstruse, and subtly metaphysical doctrines of Buddhism and Taoism, whose ethical message is so deeply embedded in their poetical writings. In their original forms, both these doctrines appear to have been inspired by an intrinsic belief in the perfectability of human nature. In Japan, they were shorn of their essential canons and simplified to such an extent that they finally became little more than expressive forms of a carefully ritualized and externalized aestheticism.

A noticeable characteristic of Japanese culture after the Heian period, in fact, seems to have been this general and pervasive emphasis upon the pragmatic and utilitarian rather than the scholastic and abstract. Japanese scholars, such as Okakura, had become convinced that "ideals in their original homes were ideals no longer in our island home," perhaps because, as Okakura said of his countrymen, "We are, I think, people of the Present and the Tangible, of the broad Daylight and the plainly Visible. The undeniable proclivity of our mind [is] in favour of determination and action, as contrasted with deliberation and calm" (Okakura[1], 104). It is interesting to note that, as if to confirm the opinion of another great Japanese scholar, Nakamura, who found a deep-rooted "anti-intellectualism" in the culture of Japan, Okakura used the term "contrasted" instead of the semantically milder "compared," to express not so much the relationship between two different modes of culture as their irreconcilable natures. The Japanese failed, in fact, to grasp and develop "all the implications of Indian and Chinese thought" (Suzuki, 307), and this deficiency, in Suzuki's estimation, helps to explain why, in general, "the Japanese genius...failed to assert itself on the intellectual and rationalistic plane."

As for Shinto itself, there seems to be general agreement among the scholars who investigated this ancient cult that it did not contain a moral code in the sense of norms of interior judgment and evaluation used to determine exterior conduct. In this context, it is amusing but also extremely illuminating to relate the opinion of "one of the leaders of the modern revivalists of pure Shintoism," Motoori Norinaga (1730-1801), whose stated views give us an indication of the difference between the Japanese idea of morality and the Western concept of morality as a set of universal norms separated from, and at times even antagonistic to, the particular political and social norms. According to this gentleman, "morals were invented by the Chinese because they were an immoral people, but in Japan there was no necessity for any system of morals, as every Japanese acted aright if he only consulted his own heart" (Satow, 135). And exactly what was it that the Japanese in question would find when he searched his heart? Motoori explained that "all the duty of a good Japanese consisted in obeying the command of the Mikado, without questioning whether those commands were right or wrong. It was only immoral people like the Chinese who presumed to discuss the characters of their Sovereigns" (Satow, 135). It should come as no surprise, then, that in the eyes of Satow and many other scholars who analyzed feudal Shinto, this religion became "nothing else than an engine for reducing the people to a condition of mental slavery."

After its militant stage (described in Part 1), during which political ideas had expressed the theocratic tendency prevalent in the culture, Buddhism degenerated into the cultivation of aesthetic forms by members of the leading classes, and animistic superstition indulged in by all. With the rise of the Tokugawa clan, the function of Buddhist schools and temples (once they had ceased warring among themselves) became that of securing their position and prosperity by cooperating with the feudal lords in their maintenance of the feudal social order. According to more than one scholar, the influence of Buddhism

> has been with [the Japanese] more aesthetic than ethical. Japanese feudalism converted the Buddha's doctrine of renunciation into the Stoicism of the warrior. The Japanese Samurai renounced desire, not that he might enter *nirvana,* but that he might acquire the contempt of life which would make him a perfect warrior. (Dickinson, 68)

Considering bujutsu, therefore, as the functional and strategic "how" of combat, while budo would be related more precisely to the ultimate and most humane "why" (that is, to the reasons for engaging in combat), we see that only in a very few cases were certain bujutsu masters successful in harmonizing their *jutsu* with the highest *do* or ethical imperative to the extent of substantially changing or transforming the ancient techniques of selected martial arts (thus removing them from the specialized and narrow dimension of the military experience and transmuting them into disciplines of enlightenment, of social and spiritual fulfillment). These rare instances of success, however, do not justify the assumption that such were the norm or that, from a historical point of *view, jutsu* (or technique), was the same as or identical with the *do* of exalted, ethical intent. Nor should it be assumed that the fighting man of feudal Japan was the prototype of the "good" man merely because he practiced bujutsu. In fact, if he was a *bushi,* his *do* might have been (as it usually seemed to be) a particular and totalitarian system of ethics hardly deserving the qualification of "morally superior" any more than would any other totalitarian and despotic system wherever applied. Or, if he was a *bujin,* belonging to any of the other classes, his *do* might have simply been a utilitarian way of achieving certain practical results by force. In any case, when we speak of a universal *do* (that is, of a system of ethics influenced by the original concepts of Buddhism, Taoism, Confucianism, and so forth, on a truly universal and humanitarian scale which alone deserves the qualification of "morally excellent and superior"), we deem it advisable to keep that *do* separated from bujutsu in the doctrine, just as they were separated in historical applications. Otherwise, we shall be confronted at every turn with the confusing dilemma which still afflicts the doctrine of bujutsu today to a great extent: that is, the contradiction between the technique *(jutsu)* and its ultimate motivation *(do),* easily observable in most martial arts of the past and even in many disciplines derived from them, as they are taught and practiced all over the world today.

The Value of Zen in Bujutsu

Within the context of the ethical motivations of bujutsu, the doctrine of the martial arts contains so many references to the particular sect of Buddhism known in Japan as Zen that a few notes must be added to illustrate, even if only briefly, the nature and extent of the relationship which is emphatically said to have existed between Zen and bujutsu. It is generally claimed, in fact, that Zen was the foundation of the martial arts in feudal Japan, that it provided the doctrine of bujutsu with a theory and a philosophy to explain and justify the practice of the martial arts, and that it provided the *bujin* with appropriate disciplines for developing a strong character and personality. We know, for example, that *bushi* used to join Zen temples and use their halls of meditation where "noble lords and knights retired periodically...to prepare themselves by meditation for their military vocation" (Dumoulin, 188). These halls were called *dojo,* "the name of a place devoted to religious exercise, and its original Sanskrit meaning, *bodhimandala,* is the place of enlightenment" (Suzuki, 128). This name was adopted by the Japanese *bujin* to identify all the halls where he practiced bujutsu, and even today the term is still used to describe the place where a particular derivation of bujutsu, such as judo, karate, aikido, kendo, or kyudo, is taught and practiced. Suzuki tells us that another name also adopted by the *bujin* from the rich nomenclature of Zen was *osko,* which meant "master or teacher, *upadhyana* in Sanskrit, which is commonly the title given to a Buddhist priest" (Suzuki, 127). This title "came to be transferred to all the masters, both of the spear and the sword, irrespective of their Buddhist qualifications."

We also know that Zen priests traveled to various centers or resided in mansions where they instructed the military warlords and their immediate retainers in mental disciplines of control and integration. From the Kamakura period to the end of the Tokugawa period, the relationship between Zen and the warriors had grown until it permeated the entire feudal culture of Japan. As a consequence, it was found in almost all the major arts and crafts of the land, thus justifying the claim that no other school of Buddhism could be considered, even today, "so thoroughly Japanese" as Zen (Suzuki, 346).

This particular school of Buddhism originated, according to some scholars, in reaction against the lofty intellectualism and abstruse metaphysics of the Mahayana doctrine. It constituted, therefore, an attempt to recapture the primitive simplicity of the Hinayana version of Buddhism, and its primary aim was "to restore the experience of original inseparability, which means, in other words, to return to the original state of purity and transparency" (Suzuki, 359)— in order to achieve ultimate knowledge or illumination *(satori)* and, consequently, final liberation *(nirvana)* from the pressures and pains of existence. The ultimate aim of Zen, therefore, was—as it had been for its ancient matrix in the gospel propounded by the Buddha—to gain an insight into the essence of reality in order to distinguish that which was true

from that which was false (that is, the noumena from the phenomena) and the right way from the many wrong paths which continually led man into incoherence and disorder. Originally, Zen, like the primitive versions of Buddhism, shared an intense respect and love for every form of existing life. Zen priests, for example, characteristically carried a whisk for brushing insects away before sitting anywhere in order not to crush life unthinkingly, and a special piece of gauze for filtering water before drinking it in order to save "small creatures" from being inadvertently swallowed. Life, for them, was the same everywhere, regardless of the forms it might assume. According to the basic tenets of Buddhism and its sects, they considered the distinctions we have come to know in written history to be an unsatisfactory means by which man sought to reassure himself against the terrors of existence, only to find himself shackled with terrors of his own construction.

Zen had its own method of reaching the "kernel of reality" or the "truth." In the words of one of the major theorists of Zen, this method "consists in seeing directly into the mystery of our own being which, according to Zen, is reality itself" (Suzuki, 218).

This introspective examination and seeking was one of the major paths toward salvation offered in the ancient teachings of Buddha. It was called *dhyana,* a word which meant meditation. As such, it spread to China, where it became known as *ch'an;* in turn, upon reaching Japan, *dhyana* became *zen.*

Mental concentration on the various aspects of reality and (once the mind had become disciplined and less susceptible to sensorial or psychological diversions) meditation in depth on those aspects in order to comprehend the wholeness of reality became the hallmark of Zen and its primary discipline and technique. Following the example set by so many other Buddhist sects which had sought solitude as the proper enviroment for meditation, Zen priests organized their ranks in monasteries (generally built outside the cities and towns), and their history merged with that of the other militant orders of the age. Unlike other orders of Buddhism, however, their distaste for book-learning and the utter simplicity of their rites was a characteristic which, at least initially, set them apart. Zen leaders of the early periods seem to have been men of scholastic erudition who had become disenchanted with the inefficiency of scholastic knowledge in the search for the truth and who had thus turned to the self and to reality itself in order to "see" and "understand" more clearly. They encouraged their less literate followers to do the same, urging them not to even attempt to pass through the written chronicles evidencing man's struggle to build a social memory. People of all classes and ranks, consequently, found the appeal of this direct and simplified doctrine highly

congenial, especially when the scholastic barriers used by the upper classes and by the literati themselves to maintain their privileged positions had thus been removed. Everyone, regardless of his or her capacity to read, write, or understand the written word, could achieve illumination through meditation under the guidance of an *osho* skilled in assisting the neophyte in maintaining a steady stream of consciousness upon a selected target, in order to eventually identify with it and, through it, with the immense truth which contains and animates all life.

The techniques of meditation and concentration were developed and refined through many exercises of integration, most of which involve the use of the *hara* and its concomitant exercises of abdominal breathing. Both, by increasing the neophyte's vitality and strength, also increased his capacity to concentrate his mental powers upon the introspective search for truth—a truth which, in Zen, is to be found primarily within oneself. The result of such prolonged practices in Zen monasteries were as impressive and astounding as the results of essentially similar practices and disciplines adopted by the adepts of *shugendo*—the *yamabushi* encountered in Part 1.

A man thoroughly versed in the techniques of meditation and concentration could seal himself off so completely from the reality of which he was a part as to become impervious to all sorts of external solicitations, such as physical discomfort, pain, and, eventually, even death. One particularly fierce abbot, Bodhidharma (Japanese Daruma), the first patriarch of the Zen sect, for example, is said to have spent years in silent meditation, facing the same temple wall. He acquired the name of "wall-gazing Brahman." It is also related that when Nobunaga's warriors burned the Erin-ji monastery to the ground in 1582, the Zen abbot Kaisen led his monks into the flames with the famous words: "For a peaceful meditation, we need not go to the mountains and streams; when thoughts are quieted down, fire itself is cool and refreshing" (Suzuki, 79). It is no wonder, then, that the warriors of yore—who were continually and professionally fascinated by the various styles of meeting death with indifference and even contempt—came to believe that Zen masters practically made "sport of death" (Suzuki, 78). This stoic interpretation of Buddhism, quite understandably, was not overly popular in the Japan of pre-Kamakura times (that is, from the early Nara period to the late Heian period), when the court of the emperor in old Kyoto (with his Confucian scholars and metaphysical Buddhist priests) dazzled the country with its splendor. But, as "the rugged virility of the warriors of the Kwanto district [was] proverbial, in contrast to the grace and refinement of the courtiers in Kyoto" (Suzuki, 30), this type of Buddhism soon became very popular with the emerging class of soldiers who had already begun their ascent toward the summit of power in Japan. As explained by Suzuki, "the military mind being—and this is one of the essential qualities of the fighter —comparatively simple and not at all addicted to philosophizing [found] a congenial spirit in Zen. This is probably one of the main reasons for the close relationship between Zen and the Samurai" (Suzuki, 61-62).

The *buke* turned to Zen more than to any other school of Buddhism in order to find ways to steel themselves against the terrors of their profession and, in general, against the terror of existence. Given the nature of the sect, it was obviously not (as has been advanced by certain scholars) the desire to probe the depth of scholarship which inclined them favorably toward Zen. It has been asserted that "book-learning" was "virtually a monopoly of the priesthood" in feudal Japan (Harrison, 141) and that, consequently, the warriors had to turn to priests in order to tap the sources of scholastic knowledge available at the time, which was necessary if their class was to succeed in its efforts to assert and maintain political and military control over the land. There are strong doubts, however, that many Zen priests were able to assist them in this direction. In fact, given the anti-intellectualism prevalent in feudal Japan, how could Zen priests (who were apparently among the strongest advocates of the theory of nonintellectual perception and of the intrinsic worthlessness of book-learning) have helped the warriors in areas of traditional scholastic learning? Warriors, after all, were never known as great philosophers or scholars. Steeped as they were in the violently pragmatic dimension of human reality, and having been constantly engaged for centuries in the exercise of military and political power, they found leisure for "the pursuit of letters" only in a few instances. Even in times of comparative peace (e.g., following the rise of Ieyasu), the literary preparation of the warriors, as Koike Kenji tells us in his *Nisshinkan,* was of superior quality only for a limited number of *bushi* of *kyunin* rank. But the lower ranks of the *koyakunin (kachi),* which comprised the large standing army of foot soldiers and officers, were so generally neglected in matters of learning that one of their number was considered "educated" if he had at least read the Five Classics.

The most important contribution made by Japanese Zen to bujutsu was, naturally, the development of the intuitive powers of the human personality. Intuition, as opposed to intellection and rationalization, had already been a cardinal canon of Zen, since its masters believed that intuition was the more direct way of reaching truth. For a man constantly exposed to danger, intuition was the quality the Japanese fighter of feudal times needed to develop most particularly in order to be able to respond immediately to the promptings of a dangerous reality without hesitating to reflect, much less to weigh any doubts. As we indicated earlier, in discussing the theory of *haragei,* Zen was one of the main sources of inspiration concerning methods of developing and maintaining those mental attitudes of Olympic calmness and of clear perception which were known as *tsuki-no-kokoro* ("a mind as calm as the moon"). Intuition (as understood in Zen *haragei)* became even more finely honed through abdominal centralization, and, as we can see by referring to the classic texts of bujutsu, its development helped to insure mental independence and concentration of volition through the vector of disciplined meditation. It was further developed and strengthened through the practice of abdominal breathing—a technique which soon became characteristic of all the highest manifestations of Japanese culture after the Kamakura period. The culture, it must be remembered, was dominated by the warriors and, through them, by the militant forms of Zen and its disciplines and techniques. Acker wrote that "the idea of the desirability of regular and deep abdominal breathing, effecting a concentration of nervous energy in the *hara* or belly, soon found its way into every art and higher profession" (Acker, 46). This technique was actually as old as Asia itself. In ancient India, the relationship between the "pranic" respiration (i.e., the breathing of that cosmic life of which man is an expression) and man's "physical" respiration was considered to be one of substantial identity (Lasserre, 51). This breathing, in fact (according to Durckheim), reverberated not only throughout the Centre of man, the *hara,* but also throughout his entire spirit and, at large, throughout creation. Seen from another angle, breathing involved man's response to and interexchange with his environment. The more complete the breathing, the more fulfilled and mature the man. It affected not only man's physical condition, his health and general welfare, but also his way of thinking and the general direction of his life. "The entire attitude of man toward life," as Durckheim put it, was "reflected" in the way he breathed. In the ancient texts of Buddhism and Taoism, four types of breathing were mentioned: at the level of the shoulders, then of the chest, then the lower abdomen, and, finally, the toes. As Gluck pointed out, "the warrior is concerned with the first three....Breathing with the toes" was left to the philosophers (Gluck, 24). The Chinese Classics had noted the change in emphasis and significance which took place in their evolution as these concepts of breathing were transplanted from the interior and metaphysical dimensions of Indian culture to the exteriorized and pragmatic Chinese and then Japanese cultures.

> Chwang Tze seems to have noticed that breathing harmony is typical of the calm mind, since he says: "The men of wisdom of old did not dream when they slept. Their breathing came deep and silently. Their breathing comes even from their heels, while men in general breathe only from their chests." At any rate, the counting of breaths is an expedient for calming the mind and elaborate rules were given in the Zen *sutra,* but Chinese and Japanese masters do not lay so much stress on this point as the Indian teachers. *(Judo Kodokan,* January, 1959).

The fighting man of feudal Japan, naturally, was even closer to the surface of his culture, and his interest in abdominal breathing was clearly the most pragmatic and practically centered of all. He required and depended upon stern mental control and instantaneous surges of power in carrying out his professional duties as a *bushi*—or, if he were a *bujin,* he had similar requirements merely in order to be able to fight well. Zen helped him to develop several methods of abdominal breathing which, as has been noted, made it possible for "a real Samurai...to cross the Gojo Bridge in Kyoto in a single breath (Gojo Bridge was 73 yards long)" (Leggett, 64). It allowed him, above all, to explode into full action with devastating force, usually expressed through the concomitant fullness of a *kiai* or "spirit shout."

The techniques of abdominal breathing adopted by the various bujutsu schools from the wealth of methods available in Japanese culture in particular and, at large, in Chinese and Indian cultures were naturally manipulated or drastically altered by the *bushi* in order to make them the perfect vehicle for developing the *hara* as a Centre of that psychological control and power which he would use in combat to control the weapons and the techniques employed to overcome his opponent's resistance and insure his enemy's defeat. Many of the techniques of abdominal breathing used in the schools of bujutsu vanished with the schools themselves, when the policy of secrecy they adopted and strictly enforced caused most of their breathing methods either to degenerate into rituals representative of the pseudomysticism typical of militant ultra-nationalism, or to disappear altogether.

In sum, the main preoccupation in bujutsu was clearly expressed by Master Kuni-shige to Harrison: that is, the development of the active power of the *bujin* within the concrete dimension of his combat reality, which, as that master pointed out, differed in purpose from the contemplative and static dimension of the Zen mystic and would, therefore, differ in technique as well.

From the many references scattered throughout the doctrine of the martial arts, it appears that, in the main, the *bujin* took from the Japanized versions of Zen that which he felt would help him perform more efficiently as a fighting man, so that he might do better that which, by profession, he was expected to do: serve his lord with the utmost concentration, fight well, and die well if necessary. Obligingly, then, the Japanese forms of Zen carefully avoided the intellectual pitfalls of doubt and concern for those universal pronouncements usually found in superior systems of ethics related to human existence at large. Instead, they provided the warrior with appropriate techniques (meditation, concentration, inner centralization, extension of power, breathing, etc.) for improving his professional personality and capabilities. Zen even provided him with theories of combat devised by such masters as Takuan and Dokyo Etan, which combined elements of will power, hidden forces, and that instinctive reactivity usually present in a dispersive condition in the human subconscious (counterbalanced by the conscious, rational faculties) in order to unleash them in a total and explosive manner at the "moment of truth," however immediate and limited that moment might have been in combat.

The instinctive coordination of this simplified interpretation of Zen adopted by the *bushi* (as well as by many of the fighting men of feudal Japan in general) was thus strongly qualified and limited by its very practical specialization. In general, Zen was simply used to improve upon the pragmatic, political, and utilitarian character of the *bushi,* rather than to help him expand his consciousness beyond the narrow confines of sword and spear.

Finally, according to Shioda Gozo, Zen seems to have also influenced the style of recording the techniques of the various *ryu* of bujutsu. The task of writing them down, of preserving them in the documents jealously guarded in each school and transmitted only from father to son, was usually assigned to a Zen priest residing in a nearby monastery, when not performed by the master of the school himself (who was often a militant mystic, well versed in the abstruse and highly allegorical imagery of Zen texts).

The basic aim in employing Zen techniques, naturally, was not to provide the *bushi* with a system of ethics which, if even remotely related to the original gospel of Gautama Buddha, would have been necessarily and intrinsically in opposition to the violent nature of the warrior's profession. The debate concerning whether Zen has any ethical message to impart still rages today. Suzuki, who did so much to explain Japanese Zen to Western readers, for example, seems to have been of the opinion that, in relation to moral conduct, Zen had little or nothing to add to the code of loyalty and obedience which ruled the life of a samurai. In fact, he wrote:

> Zen did not necessarily argue with them about immortality of the soul or righteousness or the divine way or ethical conduct, but it simply urged going ahead with whatever conclusion, rational or irrational, a man has arrived at. Philosophy may be safely left with the intellectual mind; Zen wants to act, and the most effective act, once the mind is made up, is to go on without looking backward. In this respect, Zen is indeed the religion of the Samurai warrior. (Suzuki, 84)

It may seem astounding that a doctrine like Zen, rooted in one of the deepest and most fertile ethical systems in the world, Buddhism, could have been or become so lacking in ethical considerations as to actually encourage its opposite in the form of systematized violence. Suzuki himself faced the dilemma (without resolving it) in the following passage:

> Although [Zen] has never actively incited them to carry on their violent profession, it has passively sustained them when they have, for whatever reason, once entered into it. Zen has sustained them in two ways, morally and philosophically. Morally, because Zen is a religion which teaches us not to look backward once the course is decided upon; and philosophically, because it treats life and death indifferently. (Suzuki, 61)

The same dilemma has been faced by other authors, such as Harrison, for example, who also appears to have strongly doubted the existence of or at least the influence of this "ethical" aspect of Zen in relation to the *bushi:*

> As a method of moral and intellectual culture, Zen has from time immemorial been studied in Japan among the Samurai class, to which latter circumstances, no doubt, may be ascribed the common belief that the secrets of all the branches of the martial arts cannot be acquired without a thorough knowledge of Zen. It is, however, open to question whether Zen has really anything to teach the Samurai under this head. (Harrison, 140)

In synthesis:

> Zen was popular with the samurai because it provided them with a discipline that made fighting endurable, and a few special psychological skills, how to shoot an arrow, how to engage in hand to hand fighting, with the best chance of success. There was a philosophy behind it, but it was the petty, blood-thirsty skill in front of it that was in demand. (Stacton, 30)

Of course, there was another, superior version of Zen—a philosophy of balance and integration, reflecting the high standards of its metaphysical matrix. But we cannot elaborate further upon this version here, within the confining dimension of the martial arts as military disciplines, since it involves the broader ethical dimension of man's reality—of man, that is, as a member of the human race at large and not of man as a specialized, limited "war machine." This dimension will be more appropriately and fully explored in a subsequent volume.

CONCLUSION
The Evolution of Bujutsu

Upon the basis of the doctrinary evidence available, it would seem that, from a historical point of view, the martial arts of feudal Japan have exhibited three major patterns of development and application. Each of these patterns, in turn, has revealed a precise aim which often clashed with the aims of the other two. In brief, they could be applied as methods of combat, as forms of ritualistic representation, or as disciplines of integration.

The first application has always been the most common and commonly impressive. Due to the lethal composition of the instruments used in armed bujutsu and the potentially dangerous ways in which the human body was (and is) used in unarmed bujutsu, it is often exceedingly difficult to qualify bujutsu from other than a strictly utilitarian point of view, closely linked to the ancient dilemma of a man confronted by another in combat: win or lose, defeat or be defeated, subjugate or be subjugated, kill or be killed.

As Japanese history indicates, this utilitarian and practical dimension of bujutsu was the main preoccupation of the *bushi,* since he was, by profession, a fighter, a soldier, a warrior. Whatever his ultimate reasons for resorting to bujutsu—in defense of country on the battlefield or of the self on a lonely road; in the interest of power, riches, prestige —the scope of that conflict was usually limited to strictly utilitarian strategies of combat centered primarily upon achieving an opponent's defeat efficiently and with dispatch.

The dimension itself derived its immense significance from the primeval necessity of insuring one's survival, often within an exceedingly hostile environment. Once survival had been momentarily assured, the next step would logically be an attempt to stabilize and guarantee that survival on a long-term basis. Thus, if combat and its cruel connotations were to be considered initially justifiable, in order to avoid one's own destruction, there was less justification once that destruction had been successfully avoided, but combat continued nevertheless, in the interest of neutralizing future, potential threats to that survival—thus becoming a threat in and of itself to others. From a defensive endeavor in an immediate sense (that is, as a reaction to a definite, tangible threat), it was transformed into a defensive strategy in a remote sense, as a form of prevention directed toward neutralizing an anticipated danger. In this sense, it actually became aggressive and began to explode out of control in the dialectical spiral of defense which actually became aggression, of aggression activating defense, of the latter escalating into new aggression, et cetera, according to a pattern which modern man, in the atomic age, was to come to know only too well.

The practitioners of bujutsu (considering these arts primarily as utilitarian, pragmatic methods of combat) devised and perfected weapons, techniques, and strategies intended to enhance their chance of emerging victorious from combat encounters, for overcoming resistance or neutralizing threats (real or imaginary), for subjugating other men—usually in a lethal manner. In point of fact, the vitality of bujutsu in the feudal era was—and in the modern era still largely is—based upon its value as an art which makes it possible for a man to achieve, efficiently, the utilitarian purposes of combat, any combat, between or among men. Even in times of relative peace, the *bujin* naturally practiced bujutsu as a form of exercise to

Sword dance, KEMBU

"keep himself fit." Even today, the advantages of this practice for euthenic purposes (as is true of so many other sports) are quite apparent.

The second application of bujutsu was once-removed from the stern, brutal dimension of utilitarian combat. It was intended, that is, as a form of social communication, patterned upon the precise sequences of a ritual, with gestures performed and weapons used symbolically to express an idea, evoke a mood, establish and confirm a tradition, erase or ease the fears of man wandering down the corridors of history without a blueprint. In this second sense, bujutsu became a ceremony or a spectacle, part of the pageantry and national lore of a country, thus absorbing that which is noble in its tradition, such as the sense of history, of epic struggle toward a national identity, and so forth—and also that which is less noble, such as superstition, blind ultranationalism, and all the fearsome qualities of the dark, fragmented, and highly exclusivistic feudal ages of man.

The art of archery, for example, was used in this ceremonial sense and still is today (replete with Shinto or religious, occult overtones). The art of swordsmanship has even provided the techniques and the weapons for an animistic dance still performed today, the *kembu,* or sword dance (stemming from the ancient *kagura).* The art of wrestling, in its sumo specialization, was (and still is to a large extent) a part of many religious ceremonies and a celebration in itself of national might. The arts of armed and unarmed bujutsu were also (and still are) displayed before dignitaries in the measured, plastically impressive sequence of formal exercises *(kata)* which, seemingly removed from the dimension of real combat, became a ritualization of otherwise lethal actions. As late as 1930, judo participation in public events took the form of *kata* only, these exercises being performed in costumes reminiscent of ancient periods, and employing gestures and movements typically patterned after those of other arts of representation found in the Japanese theater.

Bujutsu, finally, evolved into something more complex than a mere discipline of calisthenics, as the *bujin* delved deeply into those theories of *hara* and *ki* which transcended the narrow confines of combat and the equally narrow dimensions of individual coordination for limited, individual purposes. Interpreting those theories as devices for social and universal development, certain *bujin* transformed bujutsu into budo and, by employing those concepts on expanded levels and for superior purposes, succeeded in transmuting the specializations of combat from martial arts practiced by a fighter of the feudal era for purposes of military preparation into methods of universal integration which sought the attainment of a balanced position in the Centre of reality and a partaking of its coordinated and boundless energy. Thus, bujutsu could also become a discipline of integration intended to further the development of a man's personality by the adoption of a certain philosophical point of view concerning the meaning of existence and the role of man within its framework. With this purpose in mind, bujutsu was used to help man meet the requirements of that role. The philosophies behind the practice could be of a very broad range and nature: politicoreligious, if strongly Shintoist; religious and metaphysical in the Buddhist interpretation; psychological and existentialist, as in Zen; cosmic or eugenic, as in Taoism; and so forth. Integration, therefore, could be sought on almost every level—it could be personal, social, spiritual; it could be centered upon man in particular, or expanded to embrace his cosmos. It could, in synthesis, be particular or universal. In any case, this interpretation intended bujutsu as an ethical system not strictly related to combat alone or to representations of combat, but to a philosophy—a "way" which the ideogram *do* (as indicated earlier) identifies more specifically within the doctrine.

Almost all the major arts of bujutsu have been applied, at one time or another, in this sense (that is, as religious or philosophical disciplines of integration for the development of the personality). The practice of archery (kyudo), for example, performed according to the ancient rules of *haragei* in a condition of abdominal centralization and extension of power, could help a man to mute the phenomenic turbulence of his inner and outer reality, thus allowing him to achieve a preliminary understanding of himself, of his limits and possibilities, as well as a realistic assessment of the control he could exercise over his own emotional and intellectual responses to reality. Only then could he engage in that reality fruitfully, with another man, so that both could live and prosper in the balanced and centralized harmony of life. At this level, however, the art of the bow and arrow ceases to be a martial art and, like the tea ceremony *(cha-no-ju)*, it enters the realms of those disciplines of introspection wherein the *bujin* and combat become only distant memories of a primitive dimension, ritualized and ultimately transmuted into a philosophy, a particular "way" *(do)* of looking at reality and of living. These realms, because of their range and depth, cannot be examined at length in the present study, but will be discussed in greater detail in a future volume.

The art of the sword (kendo) and the arts of unarmed combat (judo and aikido) have also been and are being used as disciplines of integration which are based upon certain social patterns of communication and reciprocity, as exemplified through the development of physical, functional, and psychological coordination in a particular way. In judo, for example, these patterns are embodied in the concept of mutual welfare and prosperity; in aikido, in the idea of harmony (in the most comprehensive sense of that word).

These major applications of bujutsu: the utilitarian *(waza)*, the formal or ritualistic *(kata)*, and the moral *(do)*, are, of course, never so clearly delineated nor mutually exclusive. They merge and overlap, especially the latter two—the ritualistic merging with and intended to be educational and integrative in a subtle way, and the integrative expanding and blending with the precise performance of the former. Both, furthermore, must acknowledge their indebtedness to the first and significantly dominant application of bujutsu—that is, as a cornucopia of potentially lethal methods of combat. Stylized gesturing and formal exercises *(kata)*, however, may be used to ritualize or sublimate that drive which led to the development of the weapon and to socialize that gesture which could (and often did) terminate a human life.

And it is just this intricate relationship among the various possible applications of bujutsu which has always made it difficult for both the ancient masters and their modern successors to resolve the dilemma posed by the ethical question—by those generally accepted rules, derived from human experience, in accordance with which man has endeavored to regulate his existence and to civilize his life. The experience of bujutsu confronted man in the past—and still confronts him today—with dark reminiscences (clearly present even in the ritualistic or integrative applications of bujutsu) of primeval struggles, of blind forces urging him into a seemingly desperate cycle of destruction and violence—a cycle which even denies the value of bujutsu as an evolutionary form of sublimation.

The basic dilemma was perceived in feudal times by a few masters of bujutsu, who had understood that if man was to survive as an intelligent, civilized species, if he was to find creative rather than destructive outlets for those violent drives and peculiar capabilities which have made him uneasy master of the earth, then he would have to learn precise methods of ritualizing or redirecting those drives. Such masters were thus anticipating contemporary scholars, confronted with methods of combat of infinitely superior annihilating power, who have realized that if man apparently cannot suppress his violent drive without precipitating an internal explosion, then he must find ways to use that drive, rather than allow it to use him. If, however, he continues to express it as he has since emerging from the jungle, he may precipitate that final state of chaos wherein he and all his works will disappear, ironically, in a fireball of his own manufacture.

BIBLIOGRAPHY

Numbers in brackets correspond to the superior numbers appearing in source citations in the text.

Abe, Tadashi, and Zin, Jean. *L'Aikido: L'Arme et l'Esprit du Samourai,* 2 vols. Marseille: private edition, 1958.

Acker, William R. B. *Japanese Archery.* Tokyo: Charles E. Tuttle Co., 1965.

Adams, Brian C. *The Medical Implications of Karate Blows.* South Brunswick & New York: A. S. Barnes & Co. and T. Yoseloff, 1969.

Alcheik, Jim. *Aikido: Méthode du Yoseikan International du Japan.* Paris: private edition, undated.

Anderson, L. J. *Japanese Armour.* Harrisburg, Pa.: Stackpole Books, 1968.

Arai, Hakuseki. *The Armour Book in Honcho Gunkiko.* Edited by H. Russell Robinson. London: Holland Press; Tokyo: Charles E. Tuttle Co., 1964.

Barioli, Cesare. *Manuale Pratico di Karate.* Milano: De Vecchi Editore, 1964.

Beisser, Arnold R. *The Madness in Sport.* New York: Appleton-Century-Crofts, 1967.

Black Belt. Monthly magazine. Los Angeles: Black Belt Inc., since 1961.

Blacker, Carmen. "Kyuhanjo." *Monumenta Nipponka* (translation and comments), vol. 9, nos. 1-2. Tokyo: April, 1953.

Bonar, H. A. C. "On Maritime Enterprise in Japan." *Transactions of the Asiatic Society of Japan,* vol. 15. Yokohama: 1887.

Brinkley, Captain F. [1] *Japan,* 9 vols. Boston: J. B. Millet Co., 1902.

—. [2] Ed. *Japan: Described and Illustrated by the Japanese.* Boston: J. B. Millet Co., 1897.

Brown, William. "Japanese Management." *Monumenta Nipponka,* vol. 21, nos. 1-4. Tokyo: 1966.

Browne, Courtney. *Tojo: The Last Banzai.* New York: Paperback Library, 1967.

Bush, Lewis. *Japanalia.* New York: David McKay Co., 1959.

Butler, William. *The Ring in Meiji.* New York: G. P. Putnam's Sons, 1965.

Butow, J. C. *Japan's Decision to Surrender.* Stanford, California: Stanford University Press, 1967.

Carver, Norman F. *Form and Space of Japanese Architecture.* Tokyo: Shokusha Publishing Co., 1955.

Casal, U. A. "The Lore of the Japanese Fan." *Monumenta Nipponka,* vol. 16, nos. 1–2. Tokyo: April-July, 1960.

Cheng, Man-Ching, and Smith, Robert W. *T'ai-Chi.* Tokyo: Charles E. Tuttle Co., 1967.

Cheng, Yearning K. *T'ai-Chi Chuan: Its Effects and Practical Applications.* Hong Kong: Unicorn Press, 1967.

Cho, Henry Sihak. *Korean Karate: Free Fighting Techniques.* Tokyo: Charles E. Tuttle Co., 1969.

Coggins, Jack. *The Fighting Man.* New York: Doubleday & Co., 1966.

Cole, Wendell. *Kyoto in the Momoyama Period.* Norman, Oklahoma: University of Oklahoma Press, 1967.

Conder, Josiah. "The History of Japanese Costume: II, Armour." *Transactions of the Asiatic Society of Japan,* vol. 9. Yokohama: 1881.

Conze, Edward. *Buddhist Meditation.* London: George Allen & Unwin, 1956.

Cooper, Michael, ed. *They Came to Japan: An Anthology of European Reports on Japan:* 1543-1640. London: Thames & Hudson, 1965.

Dautremer, J. "The Vendetta or Legal Revenge in Japan." *Transactions of the Asiatic Society of Japan,* vol. 13. Yokohama: 1885.

Delsa, Sophia. *Body and Mind in Harmony: T'ai Chi-Chuan.* New York: David McKay Co., 1961.

De Mente, Boye. "Japan's 'Unite to Win' Philosophy." *Worldwide Projects & Installations Planning,* vol. 2, no. 5, September-October, 1968.

Demura, Fumio. *Nunchaku: Karate Weapon of Self-Defense.* Los Angeles: Ohara Publications, 1971.

Dickinson, G. Lowes. *An Essay on the Civilizations of India, China and Japan.* Garden City, N.Y.: Doubleday, Page & Co., 1915.

Diosy, Arthur. [1] "Comments" to Gilbertson's paper on "The Decoration of Sword and Sword Furniture." *Transactions and Proceedings of the Japan Society,* vol. 3. London: 1893-95.

— [2] "Comments" to Salvey's paper "On Japanese Fans." *Transactions and Proceedings of the Japan Society,* vol. 2. London: 1892-93.

Dore, R. P. [1] *City Life in Japan: A Study of a Tokyo Ward.* Berkeley & Los Angeles: University of California Press, 1967.

—. [2] *Education in Tokugawa Japan.* London: Routledge & Kegan Paul, 1965.

Draeger, Donn, and Smith, Robert W. *Asian Fighting Arts.* Tokyo: Kodansha International, 1969.

Dumoulin, Heinrich. *A History of Zen Buddhism.* New York: Pantheon Books, 1963.

Durckheim, Karlfried Graf von. [1] *The Japanese Cult of Tranquillity.* London: Rider & Co., 1960.

—. [2] *Hara: Centre Vital de l'Homme.* Paris: La Colombe, Editions du Vieux Colombier, 1964.

Embree, John F. [1] *The Japanese Nation.* New York: Farrar & Rinehart, 1945.

—. [2] *Suye Mura: A Japanese Village.* Chicago and London: University of Chicago Press, Phoenix Edition, 1964.

Frederic, Louis. *La Vie Quotidienne au Japon a l'Epoque des Samourais:* 1185–1603. Paris: Hachette, 1968.

Fukuzawa, Yuckichi. "Kyuhanjo." *Monumenta Nipponica,* vol. 9, nos. 1-2. Tokyo: April, 1953.

Garbutt, Matt. [1] "Military Works in Old Japan." *Transactions and Proceedings of the Japan Society*, vol. 8. London: 1907-9.

— [2] "Japanese Armour from the Inside." *Transactions and Proceedings of the Japan Society*, vol. 9. London: 1912-13.

Geerts, A. J. C. "The Arima Rebellion and the Conduct of Koeckebacker." *Transactions and Proceedings of the Japan Society*, vol. 11, London: 1883.

Gilbertson, Edward. [1] "Japanese Archery and Archers." *Transactions and Proceedings of the Japan Society*, vol. 4. London: 1895-98.

— [2] "Japanese Blades." *Transactions and Proceedings of the Japan Society*, vol. 4. London: 1895-98.

— [3] "The Decoration of Sword and Sword Furniture." *Transactions and Proceedings of the Japan Society*, vol. 3. London: 1893-95.

Gilbertson, E., and Kowaki, G. "The Genealogy of the Miochin Family: Armourers, Sword-smiths and Artists in Iron, Twelfth to the Eighteenth Century." *Transactions and Proceedings of the Japan Society*, vol. 1. London: 1892.

Gleeson, G. R. *Judo for the West.* New Jersey: A. S. Barnes & Co., 1967.

Gluck, Jay. *Zen Combat.* New York: Ballantine Books, 1962.

Goedertier, Joseph M. *A Dictionary of Japanese History.* Tokyo: Walker-Weatherhill, 1968.

Goodboy, John, ed. *The Japanese Fighting Arts: Karate, Aikido, Kendo, Judo.* New York: A. S. Barnes & Co., 1969.

Gowland, William. "The Dolmens of Japan and Their Builders." *Transactions and Proceedings of the Japan Society*, vol. 4. London: 1895-98.

Greey, Edward. *The Bear-Worshipers of Yedo.* Boston: Lee & Shepard, 1884.

Griffis, W. E. "The Streets and Street-Names of Yedo." *Transactions of the Asiatic Society of Japan*, vol. 1. Yokohama: 1874.

Grinnan, R. B. "Feudal Land Tenure in Tosa." *Transactions of the Asiatic Society of Japan*, vol. 20. Yokohama: 1893.

Gruzanski, Charles V. *Spike and Chain: Japanese Fighting Arts.* Tokyo: Charles E. Tuttle Co., 1968.

Haines, Bruce A. *Karate's History and Tradition.* Tokyo: Charles E. Tuttle Co., 1968.

Haite, George C. "The Chrysanthemum in Japanese Art." *Transactions and Proceedings of the Japan Society*, vol. 3. London: 1893-95.

Hall, J. C. "Japanese Feudal Laws." *Transactions of the Asiatic Society of Japan*, vol. 41, pt. 5. Yokohama: 1913.

Harrison, E. J. *The Fighting Spirit of Japan.* London: W. Foulsham & Co., undated. (Distributed in the U.S.A. by the Sterling Publishing Co., Inc., 419 Park Ave. So., New York).

Hatsumi, Masaaki, and Chambers, Quintin. *Stick Fighting: Techniques of Self-Defense.* Tokyo: Kodansha International, 1971.

Hawley, W. M. "The Swords of Japan." *Black Belt.* Los Angeles: July-August, 1964.

Hayashi, G. "The Fall of the Tokugawa Government." *Transactions and Proceedings of the Japan Society*, vol. 4. London: 1895-98.

Hearn, Lafcadio. *Japan: An Attempt at Interpretation.* Tokyo: Charles E. Tuttle Co., 1959.

Herbert, Jean. *Introduction à l'Asie.* Paris: Editions Albin Michel, 1960.

Herrigel, Eugen. *Zen in the Art of Archery.* New York: Pantheon Books, 1953.

Hibbet, Howard. *The Floating World in Japanese Fiction.* New York: Grove Press, 1960.

Holmberg, Allen. *The Nomads of the Long Bow.* New York: The Museum of Natural History, 1969.

Holtom, D. C. "The Meaning *of Kami: Kami* Considered as *Mana.*" *Monumenta Nipponica*, vol. 4, no. 2. Tokyo: 1941.

Illustrated Kodokan Judo, issued by the Kodokan Institute. Tokyo: Dainippon Yubenkai Kodansha, 1955.

Ishikawa, Takahiko, and Draeger, Donn F. *Judo Training Methods.* Tokyo: Charles E. Tuttle Co., 1962.

Joly, Henry, and Inada, Hogitare. *The Sword and Samé.* London: private edition, 1913.

Jonas, F. M. "The Yatate." *Transactions and Proceedings of the Japan Society*, vols. 28–29. London: 1930-32.

Judo Kodokan. Quarterly Magazine with French and English text. Paris: Judo International A.M.I., since 1950.

Kaigo, Tokiomi. *Japanese Education: Its Past and Present.* Tokyo: Kokusai Bunka Shinkokai, 1968.

Karate Illustrated. Monthly Magazine. Los Angeles, California: Black Belt, Inc.

Kawaishi, Mikonosuke. [1] *Ma Méthode de Judo.* Paris: Judo International, undated.

—. [2] *Standing Judo: The Combinations and Counterattacks.* London: W. Foulsham & Co., 1963.

Kawamura, Teijo. *Judo Combination Techniques.* London: W. Foulsham & Co., undated.

Kennedy, Malcolm. *A Short History of Japan.* New York: A Mentor Book, 1964.

Kenrick, Doug. *The Book of Sumo.* Tokyo: Walker-Weatherhill, 1969.

Kidder, Edward J. *Japan Before Buddhism.* London: Thames & Hudson, 1959.

Kirby, John B. *From Castle to Teahouse: Japanese Architecture of the Momoyama Period.* Tokyo: Charles E. Tuttle Co., 1962.

Kobayashi, Kiyoshi, and Sharp, Harold E. *The Sport of Judo as Practiced in Japan.* Tokyo: Charles E. Tuttle Co., 1956.

Kodokan judo: A Guide to Proficiency, issued by the Kodokan Institute. Tokyo: Kodansha, 1963.

Koike, Kenji. "Nisshinkan: Eine Daimyatschule der Tokugawazeit." *Monumenta Nipponica*, vol. 3, no. 2. Tokyo: July, 1940.

Koizumi, G. *My Study of Judo.* New York: Sterling Publishing Co., 1960.

Kudo, Kazuzo. *Dynamic Judo*, 2 vols. Tokyo: Japan Publications Trading Co., 1967.

Kurzman, Dan. *Kishi and Japan: The Search for the Sun.* New York: Ivan Obolenski, 1960.

Lasserre, Robert. *Éstranges Pouvoirs.* Paris: Editions Judo, 1960.

Lau, D. C. *Lao Tsu: Tao Te Ching.* Baltimore: Penguin Books, 1963.

Leckie, Robert. *Strong Men Armed: The U.S. Marine Against Japan.* New York: Bonanza Books, 1962.

Leggett, T. P. *The Demonstration of Throws: Nage-no-Kata.* London: W. Foulsham & Co., 1963.

Lee, Gordon Ambrose. "Some Notes on Japanese Heraldry." *Transactions and Proceedings of the Japan Society*, vol. 8. London: 1910.

Leonard, Jonathan Norton. *Le Japon Medieval.* Les Grandes Époques de l'Homme: Une Histoire des Civilisations. Amsterdam: Time-Life Collection, 1969 (French edition of *Early Japan*, Great Ages of Man, vol. 20. Time-Life, 1968).

Lidstone, R. A. *An Introduction to Kendo.* Surrey, England: Judo, 1964.
Linden, Millicent. *Tension in Repose.* Greenwich, Connecticut: Fawcett Publications, 1966.
Lorenz, Konrad, *On Aggression.* New York; Harcourt, Brace & World, 1966.
Makiyama, Thomas H. *The Techniques of Aikido.* Honolulu: private edition, 1960.
Maloney, James Clark. *Understanding the Japanese Mind.* New York: N. Y. Philosophical Library, 1954.
Maruyama, Masao. *Thought and Behavior in Modern Japanese Politics.* London: Oxford University Press, 1969.
Matsudaira, Tsuneo. "Sports and Physical Training in Modern Japan." *Transactions and Proceedings of the Japan Society,* vol. 8. London: 1907-9.
Matsushita, Saburo, and Warwick, Stepto. *Contest Judo: Ten Decisive Throws.* London: W. Foulsham & Co., 1961.
McClatchie, Thomas R. H. [1] "The Feudal Mansions in Yedo." *Transactions of the Asiatic Society of Japan,* vol. 7. Yokohama: 1879.
—. [2] "Japanese Heraldry." *Transactions of the Asiatic Society of Japan,* vol. 5, pt 1 Yokohama: 1876-77.
—. [3] "The Sword of Japan: Its History and Tradition." *Transactions of the Asiatic Society of Japan,* vol. 3. Yokohama: 1873-74.
McCullough, Helen Craig. *The Taiheiki.* New York: Columbia University Press, 1959.
Mendel, Douglas H. "Perspectives on Japanese Foreign Policy." *Monumenta Nipponica, vol* 21, nos. 3-4. Tokyo: 1966.
Mere, Gerald. "Japanese Women, Ancient and Modern." *Transactions and Proceedings of the Japan Society,* vols. 18-19. London: 1920-22.
Mifune, Kyuzo. *Canon of Judo.* Tokyo: Seibundo Shinkosha Publishing Co., 1956.
Mitford, A. B. *Tales of Old Japan.* London: Macmillan & Co., 1874.
Mitsui, Takaharu. "The System of Communication at the Time of the Meiji Restoration." *Monumenta Nipponica,* vol. 4. Tokyo: January, 1941.
Moore, Charles, ed. *The Japanese Mind: Essentials of Japanese Philosophy and Culture.* Honolulu: Univeristy of Hawaii Press, 1967.
Morris, Ivan. *The World of the Shining Prince: Court Life in Ancient Japan.* Baltimore: Penguin Books, 1969.
Morton, W. Scott. *Japan: Its History and Culture.* New York: Thomas Y. Crowell Co., 1970.
Mosley, Leonard. *Hirohito: Emperor of Japan.* New Jersey: Prentice-Hall, 1966.
Murdoch, James. *A History of Japan,* 3 vols. London: Kegan Paul, Trench, Trubner & Co 1925-26.
Nakamura, Hajime. *Ways of Thinking of Eastern People—India, China, Tibet, Japan.* Honolulu: East-West Center Press, 1964.
Nakayama, Masatoshi. *Dynamic Karate.* Tokyo: Kodansha International, 1967.
Newman, Joseph. *Goodbye Japan.* New York: L. B. Fischer, 1942.
Nishida, Kazuo. *Storied Cities of Japan.* Tokyo: John Weatherhill, 1963.
Nishiyama, Hidetaka, and Brown, Richard C. *Karate: The Art of Empty-Hand Fighting.* Tokyo: Charles E. Tuttle Co., 1960.
Nitobe, Inazo. [1] *Japan.* London: Ernest Benn, 1931.
—. [2] *Bushido: The Soul of Japan.* Philadelphia: The Leeds & Biddle Co., 1900.
Nobutaka, Ike. *Japanese Politics.* London: Eyre & Spottinswoode, 1958.
Norman, Herbert E. "Ando Shoeki and the Anatomy of Japanese Feudalism." *Transactions of the Asiatic Society of Japan,* vol. 2. Yokohama: December, 1949.
Ohashi, Takumi. *A Guide to Judo Grappling Techniques.* Tokyo: Sankei International, 1958.
Okakura, Kakuzo. [1] "The Japanese Spirit." *Transactions and Proceedings of the Japan Society,* vol. 8. London: 1909.
—. [2] *The Book of Tea.* New York: Dover Publications, 1964.
Okamura, T. Y. "The Progress of the Judicial System of Japan." *Transactions and Proceedings of the Japan Society,* vol. 3. London: 1893-95.
Okudaira, Hideo. *Emaki: Japanese Picture Scrolls.* Tokyo: Charles E. Tuttle Co., 1962.
Okuma, Shigenobu, ed. *Fifty Years of New Japan,* 2 vols. London: Smith, Elder & Co., 1909.
Oyama, Masutatsu. [1] *This Is Karate.* Tokyo: Japan Publications Trading Co., 1965.
—. [2] *What Is Karate?* Tokyo: Japan Publications Trading Co., 1966.
—. [3] *Advanced Karate.* Tokyo: Japan Publications, 1970.
Parker, E. *Secrets of Chinese Karate.* New Jersey: Prentice-Hall, 1963.
Passim, Herbert. "The Paekchong of Korea: A Brief Social History." *Monumenta Nipponica,* nos. 3-4. Tokyo: October, 1956-January, 1957.
Plee, H. D. *Karate: Beginner to Black Belt.* London: W. Foulsham & Co., 1967.
Reischauer, Edwin O. [1] *Japan: Past and Present.* New York: Alfred A. Knopf, 1964.
—. [2] *The United States and Japan.* New York: The Viking Press, 1965.
Renondeau, G. *Le Shugendo: Histoire, Doctrines et Rites des Anachorètes dits Yamabtishi.* Paris: Cahiers de la Societé Asiatique, 1965.
Robinson, B. W. *The Arts of the Japanese Swords.* London: Faber and Faber, 1961.
Robinson, H. Russell. [1] *A Short History of Japanese Armor.* London: H.M. Stationery Office, 1965.
—.. [2] "Kabuto: Japanese Helmets." *Journal of the Arms and Armour Society.* London: 1953.
—. [3] *Japanese Arms and Armor.* New York: Arms and Armour Press, Crown Publishers, 1969.
Rudofsky, Bernard. *The Kimono Mind.* New York: Doubleday & Co., 1965.
Salvey, Charlotte M. "On Japanese Fans." *Transactions and Proceedings of the Japan Society,* vol. 2. London: 1892-93.
Sansom, George. *A History of Japan,* 3 vols. Stanford: Stanford University Press, 1958, 1961, 1963.

Sargeant, J. A. *Sumo: The Sport and the Tradition.* Tokyo: Charles E. Tuttle Co., 1959.
Satow, Ernest M. [1] "Notes on Loochoo." *Transactions of the Asiatic Society of Japan,* vol. 1. Yokohama: October 1872-October 1873.
—. [2] "The Introduction of Tobacco into Japan." *Transactions of the Asiatic Society of Japan,* vol. 6, pt. 1. Yokohama: October 1877-January 1878.
Scalapino, Robert A. *Democracy and the Party Movement in Prewar Japan.* Berkeley & Los Angeles: University of California Press, 1967.
Scidmore, Eliza R. "The Japanese Yano-ne." *Transactions and Proceedings of the Japan Society,* vol. 6. London: 1901-4.
Seligman, C. G. "Japanese Temperament and Character." *Transactions and Proceedings of the Japan Society,* vols. 28-29. London: 1930-32.
Seward, Jack. *Hara-Kiri: Japanese Ritual Suicide.* Tokyo: Charles E. Tuttle Co., 1968.
Shidachi, T. "Ju-jutsu: The Ancient Art of Self-Defense by Sleight of Hand." *Transactions and Proceedings of the Japan Society,* vol. 1. London: 1892.
Shinoda, Minoru. *The Founding of the Kamakura Shogunate:* 1180-1185. New York: Columbia University Press, 1960.
Shioda, Gozo. *Dynamic Aikido.* Tokyo: Kodansha International, 1968.
Simmons and Wigmore. "Notes on Land Tenure and Local Institutions in Old Japan." *Transactions of the Asiatic Society of Japan,* vol. 19. Yokohama: 1890.
Smith, Robert W. [1] *A Complete Guide to Judo.* Tokyo: Charles E. Tuttle Co., 1958.
—. [2] *Secrets of Shaolin Temple Boxing.* Tokyo: Charles E. Tuttle Co., 1964.
—. [3] *Pa-Kua: Chinese Boxing for Fitness and Self-Defense.* Tokyo: Kodansha International, 1967.
Sollier, André, and Gyorbiro, Zsolt. *Japanese Archery: Zen in Action.* Tokyo: Walker-Weather-hill, 1969.
Stacton, David. *Segaki.* New York: Pantheon Books, 1958.
Stone, George Cameron. *A Glossary of the Construction, Decoration and Use of Arms and Armor.* New York: Jack Brussel Publisher, 1961.
Sugimoto, Etsu Inagaki. *A Daughter of the Samurai.* Garden City, N.Y.: Doubleday, Page & Co., 1925.
Suzuki, Daisetz T. *Zen and Japanese Culture.* New York: Pantheon Books, 1960.
Sze, Mai-Mai. *The Way of Chinese Painting.* New York: Random House, Vintage Books, 1959.
Takagaki, Shinzo, and Sharp, Harold E. *The Techniques of Judo.* Tokyo: Charles E. Tuttle Co., 1959.
Thibault, Claude. *Sumo: Sport de Combat Japonais.* Paris: Editions P.L.B., 1960.
Thielemans, Tony. *La Guide Marabout de l'Aikido et du Kendo.* Verviers, Belgium: Gerard & Co., 1967.
Tohei, Koichi. [1] *Aikido: The Arts of Self-Defense.* Tokyo: Rikugei Publishing House, 1961.
—. [2] *What Is Aikido?* Tokyo: Rikugei Publishing House, 1962.
—. [3] *Aikido in Daily Life.* Tokyo: Rikugei Publishing House, 1966.
—. [4] *This Is Aikido.* Tokyo: Japan Publications, 1968.
Tokugawa, Iemasa. "Japanese Wrestling." *Transactions and Proceedings of the Japan Society,* vol. 10. London: 1911-12.
Tolman, Conrad. *Politics in the Tokugawa Bakufu: 1600-1843.* Cambridge, Mass.: Harvard University Press, 1967.
Tomiki, Kenji. *Judo: Appendix, Aikido.* Tokyo: Japan Travel Bureau, 1956.
Tsukahira, Toshio G. *Feudal Control in Tokugawa Japan: The Sankin-Kotai System.* Cambridge, Mass: East Asian Research Center, Harvard University Press, 1966.
Tsunoda, Ryusaku; de Bary, William Theodore; and Keene, Donald; comps. and eds. *Sources of Japanese Tradition.* New York: Columbia University Press, 1959.
Urban, Peter. *The Karate Dojo.* Tokyo: Charles E. Tuttle Co., 1967. Ueshiba, Kisshomaru. *Aikido.* Tokyo: Hozansha Publishing Co., 1963.
Watanabe, Jiichi, and Avakian, Lindy. *The Secrets of Judo.* Tokyo: Charles E. Tuttle Co., 1960.
Webb, Herschel. *The Japanese Imperial Institution in the Tokugawa Period.* New York & London: Columbia University Press, 1968.
Westbrook, A., and Ratti, O. *Aikido and the Dynamic Sphere.* Tokyo: Charles E. Tuttle Co., 1970.
Wilkinson, J. A. W. *Aikido.* Surrey: J. & A. Publications, 1966.
Williams, Harold S. *Shades of the Past: or Indiscreet Tales of Japan.* Tokyo: Charles E. Tuttle Co., 1959.
Wittfogel, Karl A. *Oriental Despotism: A Comparative Study of Total Power.* New Haven, Conn.: Yale University Press. 1957.
Yamada, Senta, and Mclntosh, Alex. *The Principles and Practice of Aikido.* New York: Arco Publishing Co., Inc. 1966.
Yamada, Yoshimitsu. *Aikido Complete.* New York: Lyle Stuart, 1969.
Yamashita, Yoshitaro. "The Influence of Shinto and Buddhism in Japan." *Transactions and Proceedings of the Japan Society,* vol. 4. London: 1895-98.
Yampolski, Philip. *The Platform Sutra of the Sixth Patriarch.* New York: Columbia University Press, 1967.
Yazaki, Takeo. *Social Change and the City in Japan.* Tokyo: Japan Publications, 1968.
Yoshikawa, Eiji. *The Heike Story.* New York: Alfred A. Knopf, 1956.
Yumoto, John. *The Samurai Sword.* Tokyo: Charles E. Tuttle Co., 1968.
Zin, Jean. *Le Tambo.* Marseille: private edition, undated.

INDEX